Frommer's®

P9-CDM-425

Oregon

6th Edition

by Karl Samson

Here's what the critics say about Frommer's:

"Amazingly easy to use. Very portable, very complete."

—*Booklist*

"Detailed, accurate, and easy-to-read information for all price ranges."
—*Glamour Magazine*

"Hotel information is close to encyclopedic."

—*Des Moines Sunday Register*

"Frommer's Guides have a way of giving you a real feel for a place."
—*Knight Ridder Newspapers*

WILEY

Wiley Publishing, Inc.

About the Author

Karl Samson lives in Oregon, where he spends his time juggling his obsessions with traveling, gardening, outdoor sports, and wine. Each winter, to dry out his webbed feet, he flees the soggy Northwest to update *Frommer's Arizona*. However, he always looks forward to his return to the land of good espresso. Karl is also the author of *Frommer's Washington*, *Frommer's Seattle*, and *Frommer's Portable Portland*.

Published by:

Wiley Publishing, Inc.

111 River St.
Hoboken, NJ 07030-5774

ISBN 978-0-470-16414-3
Editor: Jamie Ehrlich
Production Editor: Suzanna R. Thompson
Cartographer: Andrew Dolan
Photo Editor: Richard Fox
Production by Wiley Indianapolis Composition Services

Front cover photo: Mt. Hood National Forest: Scenic reflection of mountain, man rowing in lake
Back cover photo: Tillamook County: Wave Crashing on Rocky Coast

For information on our other products and services or to obtain technical support, please contact our Customer Care Department within the U.S. at 800/762-2974, outside the U.S. at 317/572-3993 or fax 317/572-4002.

Wiley also publishes its books in a variety of electronic formats. Some content that appears in print may not be available in electronic formats.

Manufactured in the United States of America

5 4 3 2 1

Contents

List of Maps

Acknowledgements

Updating a Frommer's guide is always a daunting task, requiring long hours on the road and long hours at the computer. Without good espresso, those hours can turn to tedium. Luckily, I have an office above a remarkable little cafe that is always my first stop before starting work and my last stop before leaving town on a research trip. For providing the pastries and cappuccinos that made the updating of this book not just possible but a pleasure, I would like to thank Lee Thompson: friend, neighbor, *café artiste,* and *pâtissier par excellence. Merci,* Lee.

An Invitation to the Reader

In researching this book, we discovered many wonderful places—hotels, restaurants, shops, and more. We're sure you'll find others. Please tell us about them, so we can share the information with your fellow travelers in upcoming editions. If you were disappointed with a recommendation, we'd love to know that, too. Please write to:

Frommer's Oregon, 6th Edition
Wiley Publishing, Inc. • 111 River St. • Hoboken, NJ 07030-5774

An Additional Note

Please be advised that travel information is subject to change at any time—and this is especially true of prices. We therefore suggest that you write or call ahead for confirmation when making your travel plans. The authors, editors, and publisher cannot be held responsible for the experiences of readers while traveling. Your safety is important to us, however, so we encourage you to stay alert and be aware of your surroundings. Keep a close eye on cameras, purses, and wallets, all favorite targets of thieves and pickpockets.

Other Great Guides for Your Trip:

Frommer's Portable Portland
Frommer's Washington State
Frommer's Seattle

Frommer's Star Ratings, Icons & Abbreviations

Every hotel, restaurant, and attraction listing in this guide has been ranked for quality, value, service, amenities, and special features using a **star-rating system.** In country, state, and regional guides, we also rate towns and regions to help you narrow down your choices and budget your time accordingly. Hotels and restaurants are rated on a scale of zero (recommended) to three stars (exceptional). Attractions, shopping, nightlife, towns, and regions are rated according to the following scale: zero stars (recommended), one star (highly recommended), two stars (very highly recommended), and three stars (must-see).

In addition to the star-rating system, we also use **seven feature icons** that point you to the great deals, in-the-know advice, and unique experiences that separate travelers from tourists. Throughout the book, look for:

Finds	Special finds—those places only insiders know about
Fun Fact	Fun facts—details that make travelers more informed and their trips more fun
Kids	Best bets for kids and advice for the whole family
Moments	Special moments—those experiences that memories are made of
Overrated	Places or experiences not worth your time or money
Tips	Insider tips—great ways to save time and money
Value	Great values—where to get the best deals

The following **abbreviations** are used for credit cards:

AE	American Express	DISC	Discover	V	Visa
DC	Diners Club	MC	MasterCard		

Frommers.com

Now that you have this guidebook to help you plan a great trip, visit our website at **www.frommers.com** for additional travel information on more than 3,600 destinations. We update features regularly to give you instant access to the most current trip-planning information available. At Frommers.com, you'll find scoops on the best airfares, lodging rates, and car rental bargains. You can even book your travel online through our reliable travel booking partners. Other popular features include:

- Online updates of our most popular guidebooks
- Vacation sweepstakes and contest giveaways
- Newsletters highlighting the hottest travel trends
- Online travel message boards with featured travel discussions

What's New in Oregon

The world of travel is always changing. Oregon is no exception, so in this book I've tried to keep tabs on what's new and noteworthy throughout the state. The following are some of the highlights:

PORTLAND **Where to Stay** Hipsters and other creative types on a tight budget will want to make the **Ace Hotel,** 1022 SW Stark St. (© **503/228-2277;** www.acehotel.com), their first choice of accommodations in Portland. The funky retro-dive decor is unique, and you just can't beat the location.

Fans of film noir and Hollywood musicals of yesteryear should opt for downtown's **Hotel Deluxe,** 729 SW 15th Ave. (© **866/895-2094** or 503/219-2094; www.hoteldeluxeportland.com), which is filled with old black-and-white photos of Hollywood stars.

Where to Dine There has been an explosion of great neighborhood restaurants all over Portland in the past few years, so you should be sure to head out from downtown while you're in town. Among my favorites are **Pok Pok,** 3226 SE Division St. (© **503/232-1387;** www.pokpokpdx.com), a very authentic Thai restaurant; **Ken's Artisan Pizza,** 304 SE 28th Ave. (© **503/517-9951;** www.kens artisan.com), which pulls wonderfully creative pizzas from its wood-fired oven; **Lauro Mediterranean Kitchen,** 3377 SE Division St. (© **503/239-7000;** www.laurokitchen.com), where prices are considerably lower than they would be for a comparable meal in the Pearl District;

and **Screen Door,** 2337 E. Burnside St. (© **503/542-0880**), which serves Southern cooking in huge portions.

However, the Pearl District continues to have the greatest concentration of good restaurants in the city. Two that I have added to this edition are **Andina,** 1314 NW Glisan St. (© **503/228-9535;** www.andinarestaurant.com), a Peruvian restaurant serving dishes filled with exotic flavors; and **fenouil,** 900 NW 11th Ave. (© **503/525-2225;** www.fenouilinthe pearl.com), the city's most sophisticated French restaurant.

Seeing the Sights Portland has long been a center for fine crafts, and in 2007, the 70-year-old Contemporary Craft Gallery moved from its location south of town and reopened on the edge of the Pearl District as the **Museum of Contemporary Craft,** 724 NW Davis St. (© **503/223-2654;** www.museumofcontemporarycraft.org). This little museum is well worth a visit.

Portland After Dark Fans of jazz should not miss an opportunity to spend an evening at the new **Jimmy Mak's,** 221 NW Tenth Ave. (© **503/295-6542;** www.jimmymaks.com), Portland's favorite jazz club. If you'd like to sit and sip wine with a view of the Willamette River, head to **Thirst Wine Bar & Bistro,** 0315 SW Montgomery St., Suite 340 (© **503/295-2747;** www.thirstwinebar.com). The Pearl District's **Bridgeport Brewpub & Bakery,** 1313 NW Marshall St. (© **503/241-3612;** www.bridgeportbrew.com), one of

Portland's oldest brewpubs, is now an industrial-chic, bi-level dining and drinking establishment that fits in perfectly with the neighborhood's new upscale aesthetic.

THE WILLAMETTE VALLEY The North Willamette Valley Wine Country With both the popularity and price of Oregon pinot noir continuing to rise, it is no surprise that new inns have been opening up in wine country. My favorites include **Abbey Road Farm,** 10501 NE Abbey Rd., Carlton (© **503/852-6278;** www.abbeyroadfarm.com), created from three converted farm silos; and **Brookside Inn on Abbey Road,** 8243 NE Abbey Rd., Carlton (© **503/852-4433;** www.brooksideinn-oregon.com), a former religious retreat center.

There are also now several good new places to get lunch while you're out wine touring. My favorite is the **South Store Café,** 24485 SW Scholls Ferry Rd. (© **503/628-1920**), between Hillsboro and Newberg. In the little town of Carlton, you can get good quick lunches at **The Filling Station Deli,** 305 W. Main St. (© **503/852-6687;** www.fillingstation deli.com). At **The Horse Radish,** 211 W. Main St. (© **503/852-6616;** www.the horseradish.com), you can get local wines as well as gourmet meats, cheeses, and artisan breads.

Wineries that have opened new tasting rooms include **Dobbes Family Estate,** 240 SE Fifth St., Dundee (© **800/566-8143** or 503/538-1141; www.dobbes familyestate.com); **A to Z,** 990 N. Ore. 99W, Dundee (© **503/538-4881;** www. atozwineworks.com); **The Four Graces,** 9605 NE Fox Farm Rd., Dundee (© **800/ 245-2950;** www.thefourgraces.com); and **Wine Works Oregon,** 475 NE 17th St., McMinnville (© **503/472-3215;** www. walnutcitywineworks.com).

Salem If you're in downtown Salem, be sure to check out the colorful little **Mary**

Lou Zeek Gallery, 335 State St. (© **503/ 581-3229;** www.zeekgallery.com).

Eugene The best new restaurant to open in the Willamette Valley is the **King Estate Restaurant,** 80854 Territorial Rd., Eugene (© **541/685-5189;** www. kingestate.com), which is set on the biggest and prettiest wine estate in the region.

THE OREGON COAST Astoria There are a couple of good new restaurants in Astoria including **Clemente's,** 1335 Marine Dr. (© **503/325-1067**), which serves fresh seafood and great fish and chips; and **BRIDGE***water,* 20 Basin St. (© **503/325-6777;** www.bridgewater bistro.com), with great food and a fabulous view. Also don't miss the historic cannery displays and brewpub at **Pier 39,** 100 39th St. (© **503/325-2502;** www. pier39-astoria.com).

Seaside In this family-oriented beach town, **Yummy Wine Bar & Bistro,** 831 Broadway (© **503/738-3100;** www. yummywinebarbistro.com), now provides adults with a sophisticated place to hang out and sip wine.

Cannon Beach The **Surfsand Resort,** 148 W. Gower St. (© **800/547-6100** or 503/436-2274; www.surfsand.com), is a stylish renovation of what was once an unremarkable family hotel. **Newman's at 988,** 988 S. Hemlock St. (© **503/436-1151;** www.newmansat988.com), owned by the former chef at the luxurious Stephanie Inn, is now the best restaurant in town. For good baked goods, there's **Waves of Grain,** 3116 S. Hemlock St. (© **503/436-9600;** www.wavesofgrain bakery.com).

Tillamook County In the little fishing-port town of Garibaldi, don't miss the interesting little **Garibaldi Museum,** 112 Garibaldi Ave. (© **503/322-8411;** www. garibaldimuseum.com), which chronicles

Captain Robert Gray's discovery of the Columbia River.

Lincoln City The **Starfish Manor Hotel,** 2735 NW Inlet Ave. (© 800/972-6155 or 541/996-9300; www.onthebeachfront.com), and its affiliated inns are good new options for large, comfortable accommodations in a town known mostly for its cheap motels.

Yachats If you spend any time anywhere near the town of Yachats, do not miss an opportunity to dine at the **Yachats River House,** 131 U.S. 101 N. (© 541/547-4100; www.yachatsriverhouse.com), my favorite new Oregon-coast restaurant.

Florence Crave's Wine & Tapas Bar, 294 Laurel St. (© 541/997-3154), is a casual wine bar that's a few blocks removed from most of the Florence tourist restaurants and worth searching out.

Bandon Bandon Inn, 355 U.S. 101 (P.O. Box 1409; © 800/526-0209 or 541/347-4417; www.bandoninn.com), is a recently renovated little hotel high on a hill overlooking old town Bandon. For some of the best food in town or just for a glass of wine, try **Alloro Wine Bar,** 375 Second St. SE (© 541/347-1850; www.allorowinebar.com).

The Southern Oregon Coast For great fish and chips, don't miss Port Orford's **Crazy Norwegian's Fish and Chips,** 259 Sixth St. (© 541/332-8601). In Brookings, you can get good southern Italian fare in an upscale setting at **Bella Italia Ristorante,** 1025 Chetco Ave. (© 866/40-BELLA or 541/469-6647).

THE COLUMBIA GORGE The Hood River area is rapidly becoming another of Oregon's top wine-touring destinations. New wineries to check out

include **Phelps Creek Vineyards,** 1850 Country Club Rd. (© 541/386-2607; www.phelpscreekvineyards.com); **The Pines 1852,** 202 State St. (© 541/993-8301; www.thepinesvineyard.com); and **Quenett Winery,** 111 Oak St. (© 541/386-2229; www.quenett.com). In and near The Dalles, new wineries include **Erin Glenn Wines at The Mint,** 710 E. Second St. (© 877/299-ERIN or 541/296-4707; www.eringlenn.com), which is in downtown The Dalles; and **Syncline,** 111 Balch Rd. (© 509/365-4361; www.synclinewine.com), which is across the river in Washington.

SOUTHERN OREGON Ashland The best new B&B in Oregon is the **Ashland Mountain House,** 1148 Old Highway 99 South (© 866/899-2744 or 541/482-2744; www.ashlandmountainhouse.com), a short drive into the hills south of Ashland. New restaurants worth checking out include **Kobe,** 96 N. Main St. (© 541/488-8058), a modern Japanese restaurant; and **Dragonfly Café and Gardens,** 241 Hargadine St. (© 541/488-4855; www.dragonflyashland.com), an unusual Latino-Asian fusion restaurant.

CENTRAL OREGON Sisters Five-Pine Lodge & Conference Center, 1021 Desperado Trail (© 866/974-5900 or 541/549-5900; www.fivepinelodge.com), a beautiful collection of Craftsman-style cottages set beneath ponderosa pines, is the best new lodge in central Oregon. Also here in Sisters, you'll find one of my favorite restaurants in the state—**Jen's Garden,** 403 E. Hood Ave. (© 541/549-2699; www.intimatecottagecuisine.com).

Bend Check out **deep,** 821 NW Wall St. (© 541/323-9841; www.deepbend.com), downtown Bend's hippest sushi bar.

1

The Best of Oregon

You've probably already heard the jokes: Oregonians have webbed feet and they don't tan, they rust. Even people otherwise unfamiliar with Oregon seem to know that it rains a lot here. There's simply no getting around the fact that few states receive as much rain or cloudy weather as Oregon (except Washington, Oregon's northern neighbor). However, Oregon's rainfall no longer seems to have the effect it once did. Sure, it still keeps the landscape green, but it's no longer keeping people from visiting here.

Once, Oregon was the promised land of 19th-century pioneers, and today, it is an amalgam of American life and landscapes. Within its boundaries, the state reflects a part of almost every region of the country. Take a bit of New England's rural beauty, its covered bridges, and its steepled churches. Temper the climate with that of the upper South to avoid harsh winters. Now bring in some low, rolling mountains such as the Appalachians; glaciated mountains such as the Rockies; and Hawaiian-style volcanoes and lava fields. Add a river nearly as large and important as the Mississippi—complete with paddle wheelers—and a coastline as rugged as California's. You could even throw in the deserts of the Southwest and the wheat fields of the Midwest. A little wine country would be a nice touch, and so would some long, sandy beaches. Finally, you'll need a beautiful city, one whose downtown skyscrapers are framed by high, forested hills and whose gardens are full of roses.

To explore such a diverse state takes planning. I've chosen what I feel are the very best attractions, activities, lodgings, and restaurants. Most are described in more detail elsewhere in this book, but this chapter will give you an overview and get you started.

1 The Best Natural Attractions

- **The Oregon Coast:** Rocky headlands, offshore islands and haystack rocks, natural arches, caves full of sea lions, giant sand dunes, and dozens of state parks make this one of the most spectacular coastlines in the country. The only drawback is that the water is too cold for swimming. See chapter 6.

- **Columbia Gorge National Scenic Area:** Carved by ice-age floodwaters up to 1,200 feet deep, the Columbia Gorge is a unique feature of the Oregon landscape. Waterfalls by the dozen cascade from the basalt cliffs of the gorge, and highways on both the Washington and the Oregon sides of the Columbia River provide countless memorable views. See p. 238.

- **Mount Hood:** As Oregon's tallest mountain and the closest Cascade peak to Portland, Mount Hood is a recreational mecca 12 months a year. Hiking trails, lakes and rivers, and year-round skiing make this one of the most appealing natural attractions in the state. See p. 258.

- **Crater Lake National Park:** At 1,932 feet deep, Crater Lake is the deepest lake in the United States, and its sapphire-blue waters are a bewitchingly beautiful sight when seen from the rim of the volcanic caldera that forms the lake. See p. 271.

- **Central Oregon Lava Lands:** Throughout central Oregon and the central Cascades region, from the lava fields of McKenzie Pass to the obsidian flows of Newberry National Volcanic Monument, you'll find dramatic examples of the volcanic activity that gave rise to the Cascade Range. See chapters 8 and 10.

- **Hells Canyon:** Deeper than the Grand Canyon, this massive gorge along the Oregon–Idaho border is remote and inaccessible, and that is just what makes it fascinating. You can gaze down into it from on high, float its waters, or hike its trails. See p. 346.

2 The Best Outdoor Activities

- **Biking the Oregon Coast:** With U.S. 101 clinging to the edge of the continent for much of its route through Oregon, this road has become one of the most popular cycling routes in the Northwest. The entire coast can be done in about a week, but there are also plenty of short sections that make good day trips. See p. 174.

- **Windsurfing in Hood River:** Summer winds blast through the Columbia Gorge and whip up white-capped standing waves that have turned this area into the windsurfing and kiteboarding capital of the United States. People come from around the world to ride the river here. See p. 242.

- **Fly-Fishing for Steelhead on the North Umpqua River:** Made famous by Zane Grey, the North Umpqua is the quintessential steelhead river, and for part of its length it's open to fly-fishing only. The river and the elusive steelhead offer a legendary fishing experience. See p. 269.

- **Rafting the Rogue River:** Of all the state's white-water-rafting rivers, none is more famous than the Rogue. Meandering through remote wilderness in the southern part of the state, this river has been popular with anglers since early in the 20th century for its beauty and great fishing. Today, you can splash through roaring white water by day and spend your nights in remote lodges that are inaccessible by car. See p. 282 and p. 297.

- **Mountain Biking in Bend:** Outside the town of Bend, in central Oregon, dry ponderosa pine forests are laced with trails that are open to mountain bikes. Routes pass by several lakes, and along the way you'll get great views of the Three Sisters, Broken Top, and Mount Bachelor. See p. 323.

- **Skiing Mount Bachelor:** With ski slopes dropping off the very summit of this extinct volcano, Mount Bachelor ski area, in central Oregon, is the state's premier ski area. Seemingly endless runs of all levels of ability make this a magnet for skiers and snowboarders from around the state, and lots of high-speed quad chairs keep people on the snow instead of standing in line. See p. 322.

3 The Best Beaches

See chapter 6 for details on the beaches listed below.

- **Cannon Beach/Ecola State Park:** With the massive monolith of Haystack Rock rising up from the low-tide line and the secluded beaches of Ecola State Park just north of town, Cannon Beach offers all the best of the Oregon coast. See p. 176.

- **Oswald West State Park:** At this state park south of Cannon Beach, it's a 15-minute walk through the woods to the beach, which keeps the sand from ever getting too crowded. The crescent-shaped beach is on a secluded cove backed by dense forest. This also happens to be a popular surfing spot. See p. 178.

- **Sunset Bay State Park:** Almost completely surrounded by sandstone cliffs, this little beach near Coos Bay is on a shallow cove. The clear waters here get a little bit warmer than unprotected waters elsewhere on the

coast, so it's sometimes possible to actually go swimming. See p. 220.

- **Bandon:** It's difficult to imagine a more picturesque stretch of coastline than the beach in Bandon. Haystack rocks rise up from sand and sea as if strewn there by some giant hand. Motels and houses front this scenic beach, which ensures its popularity no matter what the weather. See p. 223.

- **The Beaches of Samuel H. Boardman State Scenic Corridor:** Some of the prettiest, most secluded, and least visited beaches on the Oregon coast are within this remote south-coast state park. Ringed by rocky headlands, the many little crescents of sand in this park provide an opportunity to find *the* perfect beach. See p. 232.

4 The Best Hikes

- **Cape Lookout Trail:** Leading 2.5 miles through dense forests to the tip of this rugged cape on the north Oregon coast, this trail ends high on a cliff above the waters of the Pacific. Far below, gray whales can often be seen lolling in the waves, and the view to the south takes in miles of coastline. See p. 189.

- **John Dellenback Dunes Trail:** If you've ever dreamed of joining the French Foreign Legion or simply want to play at being Lawrence of Arabia, then the Oregon Dunes National Recreation Area is the place for you. Within this vast expanse of sand dunes, you'll find the highest dunes on the Oregon coast—some 500 feet tall. See p. 214.

- **Eagle Creek Trail:** This trail in the Columbia Gorge follows the tumbling waters of Eagle Creek and passes two spectacular waterfalls in the first 2 miles. Along the way, the trail climbs up the steep gorge walls, and in places it is cut right into the basalt cliffs. See p. 241.

- **Timberline Trail:** As the name implies, this trail starts at the timberline, high on the slopes of Mount Hood. Because the route circles Mount Hood, you can start in either direction and make a day, overnight, or multiday hike of it. Paradise Park, its meadows ablaze with wildflowers in July and August, is a favorite for both day hikes and overnight trips. See p. 259.

- **McKenzie River Trail to Tamolitch Pool:** The McKenzie River Trail stretches for 26 miles along the banks of this aquamarine river, but by far the most rewarding stretch of trail is the 2-mile hike to Tamolitch Pool, an astounding pool of turquoise waters formed as the McKenzie River wells up out of the ground after flowing underground for several miles. The trail leads through rugged, overgrown lava fields. See p. 265.

- **Deschutes River Trail:** The Deschutes River, which flows down from the east side of the Cascades, passes through open ponderosa pine forest to the west of Bend. This easy trail parallels the river and passes tumultuous waterfalls along the way. See p. 323.

5 The Best Scenic Drives

- **Gold Beach to Brookings:** No other stretch of U.S. 101 along the Oregon coast is more breathtaking than the segment between Gold Beach and Brookings. This remote coastline is dotted with offshore islands, natural rock arches, sea caves, bluffs, and beaches. Take your time, stop at the many pull-offs, and make this a leisurely all-day drive. See p. 230.
- **Historic Columbia River Highway:** Built between 1914 and 1926 to allow automobiles access to the wonders of the Columbia Gorge, this narrow, winding highway east of Portland climbs up to the top of the gorge for a scenic vista before diving into forests where waterfalls, including the tallest one in the state, pour off of basalt cliffs. See p. 239.
- **The Santiam and McKenzie Pass Loop:** This loop drive, which crosses the Cascade crest twice, takes in views of half a dozen major Cascade peaks, negotiates a bizarre landscape of lava fields, passes several waterfalls, and skirts aptly named Clear Lake, the source of the McKenzie River. This is one of the best drives in the state for fall color. See p. 263.
- **Crater Lake Rim Drive:** This scenic drive circles the rim of the massive caldera that holds Crater Lake. Along the way are numerous pull-offs where you can admire the sapphire-blue waters and the ever-changing scenery. See p. 272.
- **Cascade Lakes Highway:** This road covers roughly 100 miles as it loops out from Bend along the eastern slope of the Cascades. Views of Broken Top and the Three Sisters are frequent, and along the way are numerous lakes, both large and small. See p. 324.

6 The Best Museums

- **Portland Art Museum:** Although the main focus is on bringing blockbuster, touring shows to town, the Portland Art Museum has an outstanding wing dedicated to contemporary and modern art. The museum also has respectable collections of Native American artifacts and Northwest contemporary art. See p. 96.
- **Evergreen Aviation Museum** (McMinnville): Looking like a cross between a gigantic airplane hangar and a huge barn, this museum is home to Howard Hughes's "Spruce Goose," the largest wooden plane ever built. There are also plenty of smaller planes on display to provide a little perspective for this behemoth of the air. See p. 132.
- **Jensen Arctic Museum** (Monmouth): This museum is not very big, but it contains an amazingly diverse collection of artifacts from the Arctic. Even more surprising than the thoroughness of the collection is the fact that the museum is here in Oregon, not in Alaska. See p. 146.
- **Hallie Ford Museum of Art** (Salem): While this museum's large collection of Native American baskets is a highlight, there are also exhibits of Asian and European art, as well as exhibits of contemporary art. See p. 142.
- **Columbia River Maritime Museum** (Astoria): Located near the mouth of the Columbia River, this large modern museum has fascinating exhibits on the Coast Guard and the dangerous

waters at the mouth of the river. See p. 167.

- **Favell Museum of Western Art and Indian Artifacts** (Klamath Falls): This museum houses an overwhelming assortment of Native American artifacts, including thousands of arrowheads, spear points, and other stone tools. See p. 274.

- **The Museum at Warm Springs** (Warm Springs Reservation): Set in a remote valley in central Oregon, this museum houses an outstanding collection of artifacts from the area's Native American tribes. See p. 311.

- **National Historic Oregon Trail Interpretive Center at Flagstaff Hill** (Baker City): The lives of 19th-century pioneers, who gave up everything to venture overland to the Pacific Northwest, are documented at this evocative museum. Set atop a hill in sagebrush country, the museum overlooks wagon ruts left by pioneers. See p. 336.

7 The Best Family Attractions

- **Oregon Museum of Science and Industry** (Portland): With an OMNIMAX theater, a planetarium, a submarine, and loads of hands-on exhibits, this Portland museum is fun for kids and adults alike. See p. 97.

- **Oregon Coast Aquarium** (Newport): This is the biggest attraction on the Oregon coast, and justly so. Tufted puffins and sea otters are always entertaining, while tide pools, jellyfish tanks, sharks, and a giant octopus also contribute to the appeal of this very realistically designed public aquarium. See p. 201.

- **Sea Lion Caves** (north of Florence): This massive cave, the largest sea cave in the country, is home to hundreds of Steller's sea lions that lounge on the rocks beneath busy U.S. 101. See p. 210.

- **West Coast Game Park Safari** (Bandon): The opportunity to pet baby wild animals, including leopards and bears, doesn't come often, so it's hard to pass up this roadside attraction on the southern Oregon coast. See p. 224.

- **Wildlife Safari** (Winston): Giraffes peer in your window and rhinoceroses thunder past your car doors as you drive the family through this expansive wildlife park. The savannalike setting is reminiscent of the African plains. See p. 305.

- **The High Desert Museum** (Bend): With its popular live-animal exhibits, this is more a zoo than a museum, but exhibits also offer glimpses into the history of the vast and little-known high desert that stretches from the Cascades eastward to the Rocky Mountains. See p. 320.

8 The Best Historical Sites

- **Lewis and Clark National Historical Park** (Astoria): This national park comprises numerous historic sites that explorers Lewis and Clark utilized during the winter of 1805–06. The sites are located around the mouth of the Columbia River. During the summer, costumed interpreters bring the history of the fort to life. See p. 168.

- **Jacksonville:** With more than 80 buildings listed on the National Register of Historic Places, this 19th-century gold-mining town is the best-preserved historic community in Oregon. Here you'll also find two inns housed in buildings constructed in 1861, which makes these some of

Oregon's oldest buildings being used as inns. See p. 290.

- **Oregon Trail Wagon Ruts** (Baker City): It's hard to believe that something as seemingly ephemeral as a wagon rut can last more than 150 years, but the path made by the thousands of pioneers who followed the Oregon Trail cut deep into the land. One place you can see ruts is near Baker City's National Historic Oregon Trail Interpretive Center. See p. 335.

- **Kam Wah Chung & Co. Museum** (John Day): This unusual little museum is way off the beaten path but is well worth a visit if you're anywhere in the vicinity. The museum preserves the home, office, and apothecary of a Chinese doctor who ministered to the local Chinese community in the early part of the 20th century. See p. 341.

9 The Best Hotels for Families

- **Embassy Suites** (Portland; © 800/ EMBASSY or 503/279-9000): Unlike most other Embassy Suites, this is a historic hotel, but it still has those spacious suites that are great for families. Plus, there's a pool and video arcade down in the basement. See p. 72.

- **Hallmark Resort** (Cannon Beach; © 888/448-4449 or 503/436-1566): Set on a bluff with a great view of Cannon Beach's famous Haystack Rock, this is just about the most family-oriented hotel in town. There are two indoor pools. See p. 181.

- **Lake of the Woods** (Klamath Falls; © 866/201-4194 or 541/949-8300): This old-fashioned lakefront lodge in the southern Oregon Cascades is a bit like a summer camp for the whole family. There's great swimming and you can rent boats and mountain bikes. See p. 276.

- **Kah-Nee-Ta High Desert Resort & Casino** (Warm Springs; © 800/554-4786 or 541/553-1112): This remote resort is centered around a huge warm-springs–fed swimming pool that is a major magnet for vacationing families. You can also go rafting and horseback riding. See p. 313.

- **Black Butte Ranch** (Sisters; © 866/901-2961 or 541/595-6211): With stunning views of the Three Sisters peaks, this central Oregon resort has a solid feel of being in the mountains. Five pools, a kayaking lake, horseback riding stables, and bike paths provide plenty of options for keeping the kids entertained. See p. 316.

- **Seventh Mountain Resort** (© 800/452-6810 or 541/382-8711): Although this resort is close to the Mount Bachelor ski area and has an ice-skating rink in the winter, it is most popular with families in the summer, when kids flock to the pools and children's programs give parents some free time. See p. 327.

- **Sunriver Lodge & Resort** (Sunriver; © 800/801-8765 or 541/593-1000): This resort south of Bend in Oregon's high desert is popular with families for its many miles of bike trails that meander through pine forests. There are also riding stables and canoes and kayaks for rent on the gentle waters of the Deschutes River. See p. 327.

10 The Best B&Bs

- **Portland's White House** (Portland; ℂ **800/272-7131** or 503/287-7131): From the circular drive to the portico reminiscent of that other White House to the grand foyer and spacious guest rooms, everything about this inn is impressive. Who needs a presidential suite when you can have the whole house? See p. 75.

- **Springbrook Hazelnut Farm** (Newberg; ℂ **800/793-8528** or 503/538-4606): Set in the midst of the Yamhill County wine country, this working hazelnut farm captures the essence of rural Oregon and distills it into a tranquil and restorative retreat. You can opt to stay in the carriage house or a cottage. See p. 135.

- **Black Walnut Inn** (Dundee; ℂ **866/429-4114** or 503/429-4114): Set high in the hills above Dundee, this inn is designed to resemble a Tuscan villa and is a luxurious retreat amid wine-country vineyards. See p. 134.

- **Abbey Road Farm** (Carlton; ℂ **503/852-6278**): This fantasy farm in the middle of wine country has the most unusual B&B building I've ever seen. The inn is a collection of metal farm silos that have been converted into one of the prettiest and most luxurious inns in the state. See p. 136.

- **The Secret Garden** (Eugene; ℂ **888/484-6755** or 541/484-6755): Housed in what was once a sorority house and before that the home of one of Eugene's founding families, this very elegant inn is utterly tasteful. The garden has some very interesting secrets. See p. 161.

- **Arch Cape House** (Cannon Beach; ℂ **800/436-2848** or 503/436-2800): Patterned after a French château, this mansion-size B&B may seem oddly out of place on the Oregon coast, but no one staying here seems to mind. It could be the huge guest rooms and castlelike ambience, or it could be the abundance of European antiques and original art. See p. 179.

- **Channel House** (Depoe Bay; ℂ **800/447-2140** or 541/765-2140): Situated on the cliff above the narrow channel into tiny Depoe Bay, this B&B offers one of the most striking settings on the Oregon coast. The contemporary design includes guest rooms made for romance—a hot tub on the balcony, a fireplace, and an unsurpassed view out the windows. See p. 199.

- **Heceta Head Lightstation** (Yachats; ℂ **866/547-3696**): Ever dreamed of staying at a lighthouse? Well, on the Oregon coast, your dream can come true at this former lighthouse keeper's home. The Victorian B&B, which claims one of the most spectacular locations on the entire coast, is set high on a hill above the crashing waves. See p. 211.

- **Chetco River Inn & Lavender Farm** (Brookings; ℂ **541/251-0087**): Want to get away from it all without sacrificing luxury and great food? Book a room at this remote B&B on the crystal-clear Chetco River. The setting—in the middle of a national forest—is as tranquil as you could want. See p. 235.

- **Ashland Mountain House B&B** (ℂ **866/899-2744** or 541/482-2744): In a building that was constructed in 1852 and was once a stagecoach stop, this country inn is rich in details and preserves a fascinating piece of southern Oregon history. See p. 283.

11 The Best Small Inns & Lodges

- **Cannery Pier Hotel** (Astoria; ✆ **888/ 325-4996** or 503/325-4996): Located on a pier 600 feet out in the Columbia River, this luxury hotel fits in perfectly on the Astoria waterfront and looks as if it actually could have been a cannery at one time. See p. 170.

- **Stephanie Inn** (Cannon Beach; ✆ **800/633-3466** or 503/436-2221): Combining the look of a mountain lodge with a beachfront setting in Oregon's most artistic town, the Stephanie Inn is a romantic retreat that surrounds its guests with unpretentious luxury. See p. 180.

- **Coast Cabins** (Manzanita; ✆ **800/ 435-1269** or 503/368-7113): Although not actually an inn or a lodge, this collection of five modern cottages is so thoroughly enchanting that I have to include it here. Beautiful perennial gardens surround the cottages. See p. 184.

- **Tu Tu Tun Lodge** (Gold Beach; ✆ **800/864-6357**): Though some might think of this as a fishing lodge, it's far too luxurious for anglers to keep to themselves. A secluded setting on the lower Rogue River guarantees

tranquillity, and choice guest rooms provide the perfect setting for forgetting about your everyday stresses. See p. 233.

- **The Winchester Inn** (Ashland; ✆ **800/972-4991** or 541/488-1113): Located only 2 blocks from the theaters of the Oregon Shakespeare Festival, this place has the feel of a country inn although it's located right in town. Rooms are in three different buildings, including a modern Victorian cottage. See p. 286.

- **FivePine Lodge & Conference Center** (Sisters; ✆ **866/974-5900** or 541/ 549-5900): This collection of modern Craftsman-style cottages is set beneath the shade of ponderosa pines on the edge of Sisters. You'll find a spa, athletic club, movie theater, and restaurant on the grounds. See p. 317.

- **The Lodge at Suttle Lake** (✆ **541/ 595-2628**): There simply is no more luxurious and enjoyable lakeside lodge in the state of Oregon. Grand log beams combine with modern creature comforts to create a modern mountain lodge worth searching out. See p. 317.

12 The Best Historic Hotels & Lodges

- **The Benson** (Portland; ✆ **888/523- 6766** or 503/228-2000): With its crystal chandeliers, walnut paneling, and ornate plasterwork ceiling in the lobby, this 1912 vintage hotel is Portland's most elegant lodging. See p. 72.

- **Hotel Elliott** (Astoria; ✆ **877/378- 1924**): Originally opened in 1924, this hotel retains much of its original character, but now features lots of modern touches and contemporary styling. When it's time to relax, you'll have to choose between the roof-top

garden and the cellar wine bar. See p. 170.

- **Columbia Gorge Hotel** (Hood River; ✆ **800/345-1921** or 541/386- 5566): Opened in 1921 to handle the first automobile traffic up the Columbia Gorge, this Mission-style hotel commands a stunning view across the gorge and is surrounded by colorful gardens. See p. 249.

- **Timberline Lodge** (Mount Hood; ✆ **800/547-1406** or 503/622-7979): Built by the WPA during the Great Depression, this stately mountain lodge with grand stone fireplace, exposed beams, and wide-plank floors showcases the skills of the craftspeople who created it. See p. 262.

- **Crater Lake Lodge** (Crater Lake National Park; ✆ **888/774-2728**): Perched on the rim of the caldera (not crater) that holds the blue waters of Crater Lake, this mountain lodge isn't actually a historic hotel, but it incorporates details from the original lodge that used to stand on this same site. The setting is breathtaking. See p. 273.
- **Ashland Springs Hotel** (Ashland; ✆ **888/795-4545** or 541/488-1700):

This historic high-rise hotel was originally built to cash in on Ashland's mineral springs, but today it is, instead, a superb choice for anyone attending the Oregon Shakespeare Festival. See p. 284.

- **Geiser Grand Hotel** (Baker City; ✆ **888/434-7374** or 541/523-1889): Originally opened in 1889 at the height of the Blue Mountains gold rush, this Baker City grand dame has been completely renovated and succeeds in capturing the feel of a Wild West luxury hotel without sacrificing any modern conveniences. See p. 339.

13 The Best Dining with a View

- **Chart House** (Portland; ✆ **503/246-6963**): Perched high on a hillside, this restaurant boasts the best view of any restaurant in Portland. The Willamette River is directly below and off in the distance stand Mount Hood and Mount St. Helens. See p. 85.
- **Roseanna's Oceanside Café** (Oceanside; ✆ **503/842-7351**): You can expect a long wait to get a table here on a summer weekend, but the view of the haystack rocks just offshore makes this place an absolute legend on the Three Capes Scenic Loop. See p. 190.
- **Pelican Pub & Brewery** (Pacific City; ✆ **503/965-7007**): Cheap pub food and good microbrews are usually enough to keep an Oregon brewpub packed, but this one also has a head-on view of Pacific City's Haystack Rock and is right on the beach. See p. 190.
- **Tidal Raves** (Depoe Bay; ✆ **541/765-2995**): When the surf's up, you can practically forget about getting a table at this oceanfront restaurant. The windows overlook a rugged shoreline

known for putting on some of the coast's best displays of crashing waves. See p. 200.

- **Saffron Salmon** (Newport; ✆ **541/265-8921**): As you dine at this restaurant at the end of a short pier on the Newport bayfront, keep an eye out for sea lions and fishermen unloading their catch. See p. 206.
- **Lord Bennett's Restaurant and Lounge** (Bandon; ✆ **541/347-3663**): The beach in Bandon is strewn with dozens of huge monoliths that make this one of the most impressive stretches of shoreline in the state, and this restaurant has the perfect view for enjoying sunset over the sand, surf, and giant rocks. See p. 227.
- **Multnomah Falls Lodge** (Columbia Gorge; ✆ **503/695-2376**): This historic lodge is at the base of Oregon's tallest waterfall, and although not every table has a view of the waterfall, there are plenty that do, especially in the summer when there is outside seating. See p. 244.

14 The Best Off-the-Beaten-Path Restaurants

- **The Joel Palmer House** (Dayton; © 503/864-2995): Mushrooms are the chef's obsession at this wine-country restaurant, and you'll find them in almost every dish on the menu. The restaurant is quite formal, housed in an immaculately restored old home. See p. 139.
- **Yachats River House** (Yachats; © 541/547-4100): With a highly creative menu and an enviable setting overlooking the mouth of the Yachats River, this restaurant on the central Oregon coast is reason enough to stay in Yachats. All the nearby scenery is just icing on the cake. See p. 210.
- **Cascade Dining Room** (Mount Hood; © 503/622-0700): Located inside the historic Timberline Lodge, the Cascade Dining Room is Oregon's premier mountain-lodge restaurant and has long kept skiers and other hotel guests happy. See p. 262.
- **Jen's Garden** (Sisters; © 541/549-2699): This little cottage in the central Oregon faux cowtown of Sisters is the best thing to happen to this town in years. With superb food and exquisite wines, dinner here is unforgettable. See p. 318.
- **Kokanee Café** (Camp Sherman; © 541/595-6420): Located amid the ponderosa pines on the banks of the Metolius River near the Western theme town of Sisters, this rustic restaurant has the look of an upscale fishing lodge, but its clientele is much broader than just the fly anglers who come to test the waters of the Metolius. The trout is, of course, always a good bet. See p. 318.

15 The Best Wineries Open to the Public

- **Archery Summit** (© 503/864-4300): Big wines with a big reputation are produced from estate-grown pinot noir grapes at this impressive facility in the Dundee Hills. Pinot noir is the only wine they produce here. See p. 125.
- **A to Z** (© 503/538-4881): This winery, which, due to its purchase of Rex Hill Vineyards, is currently the largest winery in Oregon, doesn't produce the best wines in the state, but it does offer the best values. See p. 126.
- **Dobbes Family Estate** (© 800/566-8143): Joe Dobbes perfected his winemaking skills at the large Willamette Valley Vineyards before setting out on his own. Now he makes both high-end and affordable wines under two separate labels. See p. 126.
- **Domaine Drouhin Oregon** (© 503/864-2700): When a French winery starts making pinot noir in Oregon, you know it must be a good climate for wine. Certain vintages of Domaine Drouhin's Laurène pinot noir have been among the best pinots I've ever tasted. See p. 126.
- **Domaine Serene** (© 866/864-6555): Producing pinot noir, chardonnay, and syrah, this winery high in the Red Hills above Dundee is reliably consistent. See p. 126.
- **Panther Creek Cellars** (© 503/274-8080): This winery produces a wide variety of vineyard-designate pinot noirs, so in any given vintage, there are a lot of options here for pinot fans. See p. 128.
- **Penner-Ash Wine Cellars** (© 503/554-5545): Winemaker Lynn Penner-Ash crafts pinot noirs and syrahs of lingering lushness. She also has one of the most beautifully situated wineries in the region. See p. 129.

2

Planning Your Trip to Oregon

Planning your trip ahead of time can make all the difference between enjoying your vacation and wishing you'd stayed home. In fact, for many people, planning a trip is half the fun of going. If you're one of those people, then this chapter should prove useful. When should I go? Can I catch a festival during my visit? Where should I head to pursue my favorite sport? These are some questions I'll answer in this chapter. Additionally, you can contact information sources listed to find out more about Oregon and to take a look at photos (in brochures or on the Web) that will get you excited about your upcoming trip.

1 The Regions in Brief

Geography and climate play important roles in dividing Oregon into its various regions.

The Willamette Valley This is Oregon's most densely populated region and site of the state's largest cities, including Portland, Eugene, and the state capital of Salem. In addition, the valley's fabled farmland grows the greatest variety of crops of any region of the United States. These include berries, hazelnuts, irises, tulips, Christmas trees, hops, mint, grass seed, and an immense variety of landscape plants. The Willamette Valley is also one of the nation's top wine regions, with vineyards up and down the length of the valley.

Summer, when farm stands pop up alongside rural highways, is by far the best time of year to visit the Willamette Valley. If you are interested in wine, though, you might also want to consider October, when vineyards pick and crush their grapes.

The Oregon Coast Stretching for nearly 300 miles, the Oregon coast is one of the most spectacular coastlines in the country. Backed by the densely forested mountains of the Coast Range and alternating sandy beaches with rocky headlands, this rugged shoreline provides breathtaking vistas at almost every turn of the road. Haystack rocks—large monoliths on the beach or just offshore—lend the coast an unforgettable drama and beauty. Along the central coast, huge dunes, some as much as 500 feet tall, have been preserved as the Oregon Dunes National Recreation Area. Small towns, some known as fishing ports and some as artists' communities, dot the coast. Unfortunately, waters are generally too cold for swimming, and a cool breeze often blows even in summer.

Of course, summer is the most popular time of year on the coast, and crowds can be daunting. In Seaside, Cannon Beach, Lincoln City, and Newport, traffic backups try the patience of many vacationers. The north coast, because of its proximity to Portland, is the most visited section of the coast, and it is also one of the most dramatic. The south coast is even more spectacular than the north, and because of its distance from major metropolitan areas it's not nearly as crowded as other stretches of the coast. The central coast, though it boasts the Oregon Dunes National Recreation Area, is less spectacular than the north and south coasts.

The Columbia Gorge Beginning just east of Portland, the Columbia Gorge is a place of immense beauty and natural diversity. Declared a national scenic area, the Gorge is the site of numerous waterfalls, including Multnomah Falls, the fourth highest in the country. As the only sea-level gap in the Cascade Range, the Gorge is also something of a wind tunnel, and the winds that regularly blast through the Gorge attract windsurfing enthusiasts from around the world. Consequently, the town of Hood River is now one of the world's top windsurfing spots. Rising above the waterfalls and basalt cliffs of the Gorge are the snowy slopes of Mount Hood.

Although the Gorge can be explored in a day or two, if you are an avid hiker or windsurfer, you might want to plan a longer visit. Spring is the best time of year to visit. March through May, countless wildflowers, some of which grow nowhere else but in the Columbia Gorge, burst into bloom, and Gorge wildflower hikes are annual rites of spring for many Oregonians.

The Cascade Range Stretching from the Columbia River in the north to the California state line in the south, this mountain range is a natural dividing line between eastern and western Oregon. Dominated by conical peaks of volcanic origin (all currently inactive), the Cascades are almost entirely encompassed by national forests that serve as both sources of timber and year-round recreational playgrounds. Within these mountains there are several designated wilderness areas in which all mechanized travel is prohibited. Among these, the Mount Hood Wilderness, the Mount Jefferson Wilderness, and the Three Sisters Wilderness are the most scenic. In the southern Cascades,

an entire mountain once blew its top, leaving behind a huge caldera that is now filled by the sapphire-blue waters of Crater Lake, Oregon's only national park.

With little private property and few lodges other than rustic (and often run-down) cabin "resorts," the Cascades are primarily a camping destination during the warmer months. In winter, several ski areas and many miles of cross-country ski trails attract skiers and snowboarders.

Southern Oregon Lying roughly midway between San Francisco and Portland, southern Oregon is a jumbled landscape of mountains and valleys through which flow two of the state's most famous rivers. The North Umpqua and the Rogue rivers have been fabled among anglers ever since Zane Grey popularized these waters in his writings. A climate much drier than that of the Willamette Valley to the north gives this region the look of parts of northern California. In fact, several towns in the region are very popular with retired Californians. Among these are Ashland, site of the Oregon Shakespeare Festival, and Jacksonville, a historic gold-mining town that is the site of the Britt Festivals, an annual summer festival of music and modern dance. Also in the region are quite a few wineries that take advantage of the warm climate to produce Oregon's best cabernet sauvignon and merlot.

Although summer is the most popular time of year to visit this region, the Oregon Shakespeare Festival runs through much of the spring and fall, which keeps Ashland busy almost year-round.

Central Oregon When the rain on the west side of the Cascades becomes too much to bear, many of the state's residents flee to central Oregon, the drier and sunnier side of the state. Consisting of the east side of the Cascade Range from the Columbia River to just south of Bend, the region spans the eastern foothills of the Cascades and the western edge of the Great Basin's high desert.

Oregon

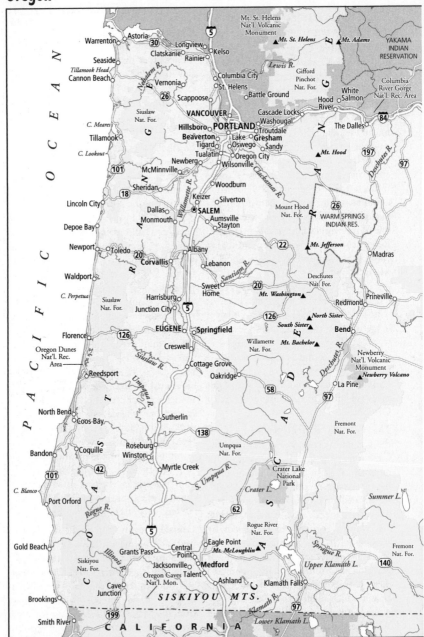

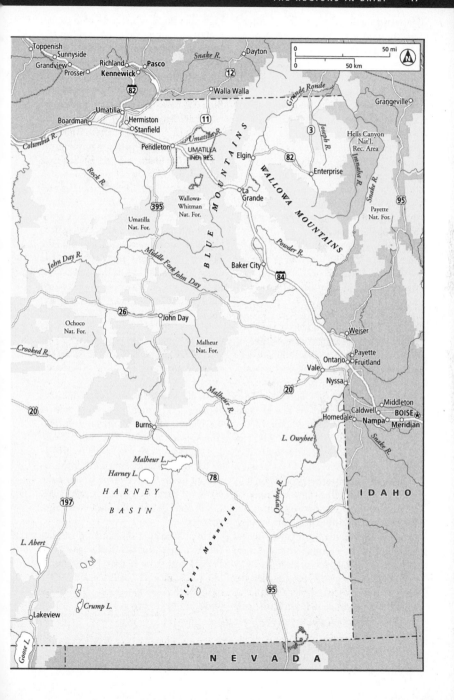

Known primarily for its lack of rain and proximity to the cities of the Willamette Valley, central Oregon is the state's second-most-popular summer vacation destination (after the coast), with resorts clustered around Sisters and Bend. The biggest and most popular resort is Sunriver, an entire community south of Bend. A volcanic legacy has left the region with some of the most fascinating geology in the state, much of which is preserved in Newberry National Volcanic Monument. Also in this region is the High Desert Museum, a combination museum and zoo that is among the state's most popular attractions.

Although summer is the peak season here, central Oregon is also quite popular in winter—Mount Bachelor ski area provides the best skiing in the Northwest.

Eastern Oregon Large and sparsely populated, eastern Oregon is primarily high desert interspersed with small mountain ranges. Despite the desert climate, the region is also the site of several large shallow lakes that serve as magnets for a wide variety of migratory birds. In the northeast corner of the region rise the Blue, Elkhorn, and Wallowa mountains, which are remote, though popular, recreation areas. Carving North America's deepest gorge, and partially forming the border with Idaho, are the Snake River and Hells Canyon. Throughout this region, signs of the Oregon Trail can still be seen.

Because this region is so remote from Portland and the Willamette Valley, it is little visited. However, the breathtaking Wallowa Mountains offer some of the finest backpacking in the state. The towns of Joseph and Enterprise, on the north side of these mountains, are also home to several bronze foundries.

2 Visitor Information

Contact the **Oregon Tourism Commission,** 670 Hawthorne St. SE, Suite 240, Salem, OR 97301 (© **800/547-7842;** www.traveloregon.com), or **Travel Portland,** 1000 SW Broadway, Suite 2300, Portland, OR 97205 (© **877/678-5263** or 503/275-8351; www.travelportland. com).

Most cities and towns in Oregon have either a tourist office or a chamber of commerce that provides information. When approaching cities and towns, watch for signs along the highway directing you to these information centers. See the individual chapters for addresses.

For Oregon regional websites, try the Oregon Tourism Commission's website at **www.traveloregon.com**. Learn about local Oregon news, sports, and entertainment at **www.oregonlive.com**, *The Oregonian* newspaper's website.

To get information on outdoor recreation in Oregon's national forests, contact the **Nature of the Northwest Information Center,** 800 NE Oregon St., Suite 177, Portland, OR 97232 (© **503/872-2750;** www.naturenw.org). For information on Crater Lake, contact **Crater Lake National Park,** P.O. Box 7, Crater Lake, OR 97604 (© **541/594-3000;** www.nps. gov/crla).

For information on camping in Oregon state parks, contact the **Oregon State Park Information Center,** 725 Summers St. NE, Suite C, Salem, OR 97301 (© **800/551-6949** or 503/986-0707; www.oregonstateparks.org).

3 Entry Requirements

PASSPORTS

New regulations issued by the Department of Homeland Security now require virtually every air traveler entering the U.S. to show a passport. As of January 23, 2007, all persons, including U.S. citizens, traveling by air between the United States and Canada, Mexico, Central and South America, the Caribbean, and Bermuda are required to present a valid passport. As of January 31, 2008, U.S. and Canadian citizens entering the U. S. at land and sea ports of entry from within the western hemisphere will need to present government-issued proof of citizenship, such as a birth certificate, along with a government issued photo ID, such as a driver's license. A passport is not required for U.S. or Canadian citizens entering by land or sea, but it is highly encouraged to carry one.

For information on how to obtain a passport, go to "**Passports**" in the "**Fast Facts**" section (p. 44).

VISAS

For specifics on how to get a visa, go to "**Visas**" in the "**Fast Facts**" section of this chapter.

The U.S. State Department has a **Visa Waiver Program (VWP)** allowing citizens of the following countries (at press time) to enter the United States without a visa for stays of up to 90 days: Andorra, Australia, Austria, Belgium, Brunei, Denmark, Finland, France, Germany, Iceland, Ireland, Italy, Japan, Liechtenstein, Luxembourg, Monaco, the Netherlands, New Zealand, Norway, Portugal, San Marino, Singapore, Slovenia, Spain, Sweden, Switzerland, and the United Kingdom. Canadian citizens may enter the United States without visas; they will need to show passports and proof of residence, however. *Note:* Any passport issued on or after October 26, 2006, by a VWP country must be an **e-Passport** for VWP travelers to be eligible to enter the U.S. without a visa. Citizens of these nations also need to present a round-trip air or cruise ticket upon arrival. E-Passports contain computer chips capable of storing biometric information, such as the required digital photograph of the holder. (You can identify an e-Passport by the symbol on the bottom center cover of your passport.) If your passport doesn't have this feature, you can still travel without a visa if it is a valid passport issued before October 26, 2005, and includes a machine-readable zone, or between October 26, 2005, and October 25, 2006, and includes a digital photograph. For more information, go to **www.travel.state. gov/visa**.

Citizens of all other countries must have (1) a valid passport that expires at least 6 months later than the scheduled end of their visit to the United States, and (2) a tourist visa, which may be obtained without charge from any U.S. consulate.

As of January 2004, many international visitors traveling on visas to the United States will be photographed and fingerprinted on arrival at Customs in airports and on cruise ships in a program created by the Department of Homeland Security called **US-VISIT.** Exempt from the extra scrutiny are visitors entering by land or those (mostly in Europe) that don't require a visa for short-term visits. For more information, go to the Homeland Security website at **www.dhs.gov/ dhspublic**.

MEDICAL REQUIREMENTS

Unless you're arriving from an area known to be suffering from an epidemic (particularly cholera or yellow fever), inoculations or vaccinations are not required for entry into the United States. If you have a medical condition that requires **syringe-administered medications,** carry a valid signed prescription from your physician; syringes in carry-on baggage will be inspected. Insulin in any form should have the proper pharmaceutical documentation. If you have a disease that requires treatment with **narcotics,** you should also carry documented proof with you—smuggling narcotics aboard a plane carries severe penalties in the U.S.

For **HIV-positive visitors,** requirements for entering the United States are somewhat vague and change frequently. For up-to-the-minute information, contact **AIDSinfo** (© **800/448-0440** or 301/519-6616 outside the U.S.; www.aidsinfo.nih.gov) or the **Gay Men's Health Crisis** (© **212/367-1000;** www.gmhc.org).

4 When to Go

Summer is the peak season in Oregon, and during these months, hotel and car reservations are almost essential; the rest of the year, they're highly recommended, but not imperative. If you visit in one of the rainier months between October and May, hotel rates are lower. It will also be easier to get reservations, especially on the coast. However, you will have to bring good rain gear. Whenever you go, keep in mind that you usually get better rates by reserving at least 1 or 2 weeks in advance, whether you're booking a plane, hotel, or rental car. Summer holiday weekends are the hardest times of year to get room reservations, especially on the coast. You should book months in advance for Memorial Day, Fourth of July, and Labor Day.

Though Oregon is famous for its gray skies and mild temperatures, the state is actually characterized by a diversity of climates almost unequaled in the United States. For the most part, moist winds off the Pacific Ocean keep temperatures west of the Cascade Range mild year-round. However, summers in the Willamette Valley and southern Oregon can see temperatures over 100°F (38°C), but on the coast you're likely to need a sweater or light jacket at night, even in August. The Oregon rains that are so legendary fall primarily as a light, but almost constant, drizzle between October and early July. Sure, there are windows of sunshine during this period, but they usually last no more than a week or so. There are also, unfortunately, occasional wet summers,

so be prepared for wet weather whenever you visit. Winters usually include one or two blasts of Arctic air that bring snow and freezing weather to the Portland area (usually right around Christmas or New Year's). Expect snow in the Cascades any time during the winter, and even some Coast Range passes can get icy.

If you visit the coast, expect grayer, wetter weather than in the Portland area. It can be quite cool here in the summer and is often foggy or rainy throughout the year. In fact, when the Willamette Valley is at its hottest, in July and August, you can be sure that the coast will be fogged in. The best month for the coast is usually September, with good weather often holding on into October.

In the Cascades and eastern Oregon's Blue, Elkhorn, and Wallowa mountains, snowfall is heavy in the winter and skiing is a popular sport. Summer doesn't come until late in the year here, with snow lingering into July at higher elevations (for instance, the Timberline Lodge area at Mount Hood and the Eagle Cap Wilderness in the Wallowas). At such elevations, late July and on through August are the best times to see wildflowers in alpine meadows.

The region east of the Cascades is characterized by lack of rain and temperature extremes. This high desert area can be very cold in the winter, and at higher elevations it receives considerable amounts of snow. In summer, the weather can be blazingly hot at lower elevations, though nights are often cool enough to require a sweater or light jacket.

If you're planning to go wine touring, avoid January and February, when many wineries are closed. Also keep in mind that many wineries are open daily during the summer months, but in spring and fall are open only on weekends.

Portland's Average Monthly Temperatures & Rainfall

	Jan	Feb	Mar	Apr	May	June	July	Aug	Sept	Oct	Nov	Dec
Temp. (°F)	40	43	46	50	57	63	68	67	63	54	46	41
Temp. (°C)	4	6	8	10	14	17	20	19	17	12	8	5
Days of Rain	18	16	17	14	12	10	4	5	8	13	18	19

OREGON CALENDAR OF EVENTS

February

The Portland International Film Festival, Portland. Although not one of the country's top film festivals, plenty of interesting foreign films and documentaries are shown. Screenings are held at various theaters around the city. 📞 **503/228-7433;** www.nwfilm.org. Last 3 weeks of February.

Oregon Shakespeare Festival, Ashland. This nine-month-long repertory festival features about a dozen plays—some by Shakespeare and others by classical and contemporary playwrights—in four theaters. 📞 **800/219-8161** or 541/482-4331; www.osfashland.org. February through October.

Newport Seafood and Wine Festival, Newport. Taste local seafood dishes and wines while shopping for art. 📞 **800/262-7844** or 541/265-8801; www.newportchamber.org/swf. Last full weekend in February.

March

Tulip Fest, Woodburn. Bold swaths of color paint the landscape at the Wooden Shoe Bulb Company's annual celebration of tulips. 📞 **800/711-2006** or 503/634-2243; www.woodenshoe.com. Late March to late April.

April

Hood River Valley Blossom Festival, Hood River. Celebrates the blossoming of the orchards outside the town of Hood River. 📞 **800/366-3530** or 541/386-2000; www.hoodriver.org. Third weekend in April.

May

Mother's Day Rhododendron Show, Portland. At Crystal Springs Rhododendron Garden, blooming rhododendrons and azaleas transform the tranquil garden into a mass of blazing color. 📞 **503/771-8386.** Mother's Day.

Memorial Day Weekend in the Wine Country, throughout the wine country surrounding Portland. This is one of two weekends celebrated by Willamette Valley wineries with special tastings and events. Many wineries not usually open to the public open on this weekend. 📞 **503/646-2985;** www.willamettewines.com. Memorial Day weekend.

Boatnik, Grants Pass. Jet boats and hydroplanes race on the Rogue River. There's also a parade and carnival. 📞 **800/547-5927;** www.boatnik.com. Memorial Day weekend.

June

Sandcastle Day, Cannon Beach. Artistic sand-sculpted creations are created along the beach. 📞 **503/436-2623;** www.cannonbeach.org. Early June.

Sisters Rodeo and Parade, Sisters. A celebration of the West in this duded-up Western-theme town near Bend. 📞 **800/827-7522** or 541/549-0121;

www.sistersrodeo.com. Second weekend of June.

Portland Rose Festival. From its beginnings back in 1888, the Rose Festival has blossomed into Portland's biggest celebration. The festivities now span nearly a month and include the nation's second-largest all-floral parade, a starlight parade, rose queen contest, music festival, and dragon-boat races. Contact Travel Portland (© **503/227-2681;** www.rosefestival.org) for tickets and information. Most of the events (some of which are free) take place during the middle 2 weeks of June.

Britt Festivals, Jacksonville. Performing arts festival with world-class jazz, pop, classical, folk, and country music, plus dance and musical theater performances in a beautiful natural setting. © **800/882-7488** or 541/773-6077; www.brittfest.org. June through September.

Oregon Bach Festival, Eugene. One of the biggest Bach festivals in the country. Tickets go on sale in mid-January. © **800/457-1486** or 541/682-5000; www.bachfest.uoregon.edu. Late June to mid-July.

July

Fourth of July Fireworks, Vancouver, Washington. Vancouver, which is part of the Portland metropolitan area, hosts the biggest fireworks display west of the Mississippi. © **877/600-0800** or 360/750-1553. July 4.

Waterfront Blues Festival, Portland. This is Portland's biggest summer party and takes place in Tom McCall Waterfront Park. Expect lots of big names in blues. © **503/973-FEST;** www.waterfrontbluesfest.com. Fourth of July weekend.

Oregon Country Fair, Eugene. Counterculture craft fair and festival for Deadheads young and old. © **800/992-8499** or 541/343-4298; www.

oregoncountryfair.org. Second weekend in July.

Sisters Outdoor Quilt Show, Sisters. During this large outdoor quilt show, the entire town gets decked out in colorful handmade quilts. © **541/549-0989;** www.sistersoutdoorquiltshow.org. Second Saturday of July.

Da Vinci Days, Corvallis. Three-day celebration of science and technology with performances, art, interactive exhibits, children's activities, food, and wine. © **541/757-6363;** www.davincidays.org. Third weekend in July.

Salem Arts Festival, Salem. The largest juried art fair in Oregon, under the trees in Bush's Pasture Park, with musical entertainment and food booths. © **503/581-2228;** www.salemart.org. Third weekend in July.

Oregon Brewers Festival, Tom McCall Waterfront Park. One of the country's largest festivals of independent craft brewers features lots of local and international microbrews and music. © **503/778-5917;** www.oregonbrewfest.com. Last weekend in July.

August

Mount Hood Jazz Festival, Gresham (less than 30 min. from Portland). For the jazz fan, this is the most important festival of the summer. © **503/661-2700;** www.mthoodjazz.com. Early August.

Oregon State Fair, Salem. A typical agricultural state fair. © **503/947-3247;** www.oregonstatefair.org. The 12 days before and including Labor Day.

Silverton Fine Arts Festival, Silverton. Arts and fine crafts in a shady park. © **503/873-2480;** www.silvertonarts.org. Third weekend in August.

Cascade Festival of Music, Bend. Classical and world music in a park setting. © **888/545-7435** or 541/

382-8381; www.cascademusic.org. Last week in August.

September

Mt. Angel Oktoberfest, Mount Angel. Biergarten, Bavarian-style oom-pah bands, food booths. © **503/845-9440;** www.mtangel.org. Second weekend after Labor Day.

Shrewsbury Renaissance Faire, Kings Valley (near Corvallis). Go back 500 years to celebrate the age of Elizabeth I and Shakespeare with jousting and period costumes in an Elizabethan village. © **541/929-4897;** www.shrewfaire.com. Second weekend of September.

Pendleton Round-Up and Happy Canyon Pageant, Pendleton. Rodeo, Native American pageant, country-music concert. © **800/457-6336** or 541/276-2553; www.pendletonround up.com. Mid-September.

Bandon Cranberry Festival, Bandon. Cranberry bog tours, arts and crafts. © **541/347-9616.** Mid-September.

Eugene Celebration, Eugene. Street party celebrating the diversity of the community. Festivities include the crowning of the Slug Queen. © **541/681-4108;** www.eugenecelebration.com. Mid- September.

October

Fall Kite Festival, Lincoln City. Kite carnival including a wide and wild variety of kites, from indoor kites to giant kites. © **800/452-2151;** www.oregoncoast.org. Mid-October.

Hood River Valley Harvest Fest, Hood River. At the Hood River Expo Center, enjoy fruit products of the region, crafts, and entertainment; drive the Fruit Loop to visit farm stands and wineries. © **800/366-3530** or 541/386-2000; www.hoodriver.org. Third weekend in October.

November

Stormy Weather Arts Festival, Cannon Beach. Celebration of the rainy season features lots of live music, a gallery walk, and a quick-draw art event in which artists have 1 hour to paint a picture. © **503/436-2623.** www.cannonbeach.org. First weekend in November.

Wine Country Thanksgiving, Willamette Valley. About 30 miles outside of Portland, more than 100 wineries open their doors for tastings of new releases, usually with food and live music. © **503/646-2985;** www.willamettewines.com. Thanksgiving weekend.

Holiday Lights and Open House at Shore Acres State Park, Charleston. Extravagantly decorated gardens near dramatic cliffs at the Oregon coast. © **541/888-4902.** Thanksgiving to early January.

December

Holiday Festival of Light, Ashland. More than a million lights decorate the town. © **541/482-3486;** www.ashland chamber.com. Month of December.

Holiday Parade of Ships, Willamette and Columbia rivers. Boats decked out in fanciful holiday lights parade and circle on the rivers after nightfall. www.christmasships.org. Mid-December.

5 Getting There

Portland is the gateway to Oregon. In addition, driving directions throughout this book often use Portland as a reference point, assuming that the traveler will be flying into Portland and then driving to the destination.

BY PLANE
THE MAJOR AIRLINES

The major carriers to **Portland International Airport** (© 877/739-4636 or 503/460-4040; www.flypdx.com) include the following:

Air Canada Jazz: © 888/247-2262; www.flyjazz.ca

Alaska Airlines: © 800/252-7522; www.alaskaair.com

American Airlines: © 800/433-7300; www.aa.com

Continental: © 800/523-3273; www.continental.com

Delta: © 800/221-1212; www.delta.com

Frontier: © 800/432-1359; www.flyfrontier.com

Horizon Air: © 800/547-9308; www.horizonair.com

JetBlue Airways; © 800/538-2583; www.jetblue.com

Northwest/KLM: © 800/225-2525; www.nwa.com

Southwest: © 800/435-9792; www.southwest.com

United: © 800/864-8331; www.ual.com

US Airways/America West Airlines: © 800/428-4322; www.usairways.com

Lufthansa (© 800/645-3880; www.lufthansa.com) flies direct to Portland from Germany, and Northwest Airlines now flies nonstop from Amsterdam to Portland. International carriers that fly from Europe to Los Angeles and/or San Francisco (from where you can continue to Portland on a domestic carrier) include **Aer Lingus** (© 0818/365-000 in Ireland; www.aerlingus.com) and **British Airways** (© 0870/850-9850; www.british airways.com).

From New Zealand and Australia, there are flights to San Francisco and Los Angeles on **Qantas** (© 13-13-13 in Australia; www.qantas.com.au) and **Air New Zealand** (© 0800/737-000 in New Zealand; www.airnewzealand.co.nz). From Los Angeles, you can continue on to Portland on a regional domestic carrier.

FLYING FOR LESS: TIPS FOR GETTING THE BEST AIRFARE

- Passengers who can book their ticket either **long in advance or at the last minute,** or who **fly midweek** or **at less-trafficked hours** may pay a fraction of the full fare. If your schedule is flexible, say so, and ask if you can secure a cheaper fare by changing your flight plans.

- Search **the Internet** for cheap fares. The most popular online travel agencies are **Travelocity.com** (www.travelocity.co.uk); **Expedia.com** (www.expedia.co.uk and www.expedia.ca); and **Orbitz.com.** In the U.K., go to **Travelsupermarket** (© 0845/345-5708; www.travelsupermarket.com), a flight search engine that offers flight comparisons for the budget airlines whose seats often end up in bucket-shop sales. Other websites for booking airline tickets online include **Cheapflights.com, SmarterTravel. com, Priceline.com,** and **Opodo** (www.opodo.co.uk). Meta search sites (which find and then direct you to airline and hotel websites for booking) include **Sidestep.com** and **Kayak. com**—the latter includes fares for budget carriers like Jet Blue and Spirit as well as the major airlines. In addition, most **airlines** offer online-only fares that even their phone agents know nothing about. British travelers should check **Flights International** (© 0800/0187050; www.flights-international.com) for deals on flights all over the world.

- Watch local newspapers for **promotional specials** or **fare wars,** when airlines lower prices on their most popular routes. Also keep an eye on price fluctuations and deals at websites such as **Airfarewatchdog.com** and **Farecast.com.**

- Try to book a ticket **in its country of origin.** If you're planning a one-way flight from Johannesburg to New York, a South Africa–based travel agent will probably have the lowest fares. For foreign travelers on multi-leg trips, book in the country of the first leg; for example, book New York–Chicago–Montréal–New York in the U.S.
- **Consolidators,** also known as bucket shops, are wholesale brokers in the airline-ticket game. Consolidators buy deeply discounted tickets ("distressed" inventories of unsold seats) from airlines and sell them to online ticket agencies, travel agents, tour operators, corporations, and, to a lesser degree, the general public. Consolidators advertise in Sunday newspaper travel sections (often in small ads with tiny type), both in the U.S. and the U.K. They can be great sources for cheap international tickets. On the down side, bucket shop tickets are often rigged with restrictions, such as stiff cancellation penalties (as high as 50%–75% of the ticket price). And keep in mind that most of what you see advertised is of limited availability. Several reliable consolidators are worldwide and available online. **STA Travel** (www.statravel.com) has been the world's leading consolidator for students since purchasing Council Travel, but their fares are competitive for travelers of all ages. **Flights.com** (© **800/ TRAV-800;** www.flights.com) has excellent fares worldwide, particularly to Europe. They also have "local" websites in 12 countries. **FlyCheap** (© **800/FLY-CHEAP;** www.1800 flycheap.com) has especially good fares to sunny destinations.
- Join **frequent-flier clubs.** Frequent-flier membership doesn't cost a cent, but it does entitle you to free tickets or upgrades when you amass the airline's required number of frequent-flier points. You don't even have to fly to earn points; **frequent-flier credit cards** can earn you thousands of miles for doing your everyday shopping. But keep in mind that award seats are limited, seats on popular routes are hard to snag, and more and more major airlines are cutting their expiration periods for mileage points—so check your airline's frequent-flier program so you don't lose your miles before you use them. *Inside tip:* Award seats are offered almost a year in advance, but seats also open up at the last minute, so if your travel plans are flexible, you may strike gold. To play the frequent-flier game to your best advantage, consult the community bulletin boards on **FlyerTalk** (www.flyertalk.com) or go to Randy Petersen's **Inside Flyer** (www.insideflyer.com). Petersen and friends review all the programs in detail and post regular updates on changes in policies and trends.

ARRIVING AT THE AIRPORT

IMMIGRATION & CUSTOMS CLEARANCE   Foreign visitors arriving by air, no matter what the port of entry, should cultivate patience and resignation before setting foot on U.S. soil. U.S. airports have considerably beefed up security clearances in the years since the terrorist attacks of 9/11, and clearing Customs and Immigration can take as long as 2 hours.

People traveling by air from Canada, Bermuda, and certain Caribbean countries can sometimes clear Customs and Immigration at the point of departure, which is much faster.

BY CAR

The distance to Portland from Seattle is 175 miles; from Spokane, 350 miles;

> ### (Tips Getting Through the Airport
>
> - Arrive at the airport at least 1 hour before a domestic flight and 2 hours before an international flight. You can check the average wait times at your airport by going to the TSA **Security Checkpoint Wait Times** site (waittime/tsa.dhs.gov).
> - Know what you can carry on and what you can't. For the latest updates on items you are prohibited to bring in carry-on luggage, go to **www.tsa.gov/travelers/airtravel**.
> - Beat the ticket-counter lines by using the self-service electronic ticket kiosks at the airport or even printing out your boarding pass at home from the airline website. Using curbside check-in is also a smart way to avoid lines.
> - Bring a current, government-issued photo ID such as a driver's license or passport. Children under 18 do not need government-issued photo IDs for flights within the U.S., but they do need passports for international flights to most countries.
> - Help speed up security before you're screened. Remove jackets, shoes, belt buckles, heavy jewelry, and watches and place them either in your carry-on luggage or the security bins provided. Place keys, coins, cellphones, and pagers in a security bin. If you have metallic body parts, carry a note from your doctor. When possible, pack liquids in checked baggage.
> - Use a TSA-approved lock for your checked luggage. Look for Travel Sentry certified locks at luggage or travel shops and Brookstone stores (or online at www.brookstone.com).

from Vancouver, British Columbia, 285 miles; from San Francisco, 640 miles; and from Los Angeles, 1,015 miles.

If you're driving from California, I-5 runs up through the length of the state and continues north toward the Canadian border; it passes through the heart of Portland. If you're coming from the east, I-84 runs from Idaho and points east into Oregon, eventually ending in Portland.

One of the most important benefits of belonging to the **American Automobile Association** (© **800/222-4357;** www.aaa.com) is that they supply members with emergency road service. In Portland, AAA is located at 600 SW Market St. (© **800/452-1643** or 503/222-6734; www.aaaorid.com).

All the major car-rental companies have offices in Portland at or near Portland International Airport. These include the following:

Alamo: © 800/462-5266 or 503/249-4900; www.goalamo.com
Avis © 800/331-1212 or 503/249-4950; www.avis.com
Budget: © 800/527-0700 or 503/249-6331; www.budget.com
Dollar: (© 800/800-3365 or 503/249-4792; www.dollar.com
Enterprise: © 800/261-7331 or 503/252-1500; www.enterprise.com
Hertz © 800/654-3131 or 503/528-7900; www.hertz.com
National: © 800/227-7368 or 503/249-4900; www.nationalcar.com
Thrifty: © 800/847-4389 or 503/254-6563; www.thrifty.com

There are also many independent and smaller car-rental agencies listed in the Portland Yellow Pages. Currently, weekly rates for an economy car in July (high-season rates) are between $175 and $300 with no discounts. Expect lower rates in the rainy months.

For the best deal on a rental car, make your reservation at least a week in advance. It also pays to shop around and call the same companies a few times over the course of a couple of weeks. If you decide on the spur of the moment to rent a car, check to see whether any weekend or special rates are available. If you're a member of a frequent-flier program, be sure to mention it; you might get mileage credit for renting a car. Always ask about special promotions and try different combinations of where to pick up and drop off your car.

BY TRAIN

Amtrak's (© 800/872-7245; www. amtrak.com) *Coast Starlight* train connects Portland with Seattle, San Francisco, Los Angeles, and San Diego, and stops at historic **Union Station,** 800 NW Sixth Ave. (© 503/273-4860), about 10 blocks from the heart of downtown Portland. Between Portland and Seattle there are both regular trains and modern European-style Talgo trains, which make the trip in 3½ to 4 hours versus 4½ hours for the regular train. On either type of train, one-way fares between Seattle and Portland run $28 to $37. The Talgo train, called *Cascades,* runs between Eugene, Oregon, and Vancouver, British Columbia.

6 Money & Costs

It's always advisable to bring money in a variety of forms on a vacation: a mix of cash, credit cards, and traveler's checks. You should also exchange enough petty cash to cover airport incidentals, tipping, and transportation to your hotel before you leave home, or withdraw money upon arrival at an airport ATM.

ATMs

Nationwide, the easiest and best way to get cash away from home is from an ATM (automated teller machine), sometimes referred to as a "cash machine," or "cashpoint." The **Cirrus** (© 800/424-7787; www.mastercard.com) and **PLUS** (© 800/843-7587; www.visa.com) networks span the country; you can find them even in remote regions. Go to your bank card's website to find ATM locations at your destination. Be sure you know your daily withdrawal limit before you depart.

Note: Many banks impose a fee every time you use a card at another bank's ATM, and that fee is often higher for international transactions (up to $5 or more) than for domestic ones (where they're rarely more than $2). In addition, the bank from which you withdraw cash may charge its own fee. To compare banks' ATM fees within the U.S., use **www.bankrate.com**. Visitors from outside the U.S. should also find out whether their bank assesses a 1% to 3% fee on charges incurred abroad.

CREDIT CARDS & DEBIT CARDS

Credit cards are the most widely used form of payment in the United States: **Visa** (Barclaycard in Britain), **MasterCard** (EuroCard in Europe, Access in Britain, Chargex in Canada), **American Express, Diners Club,** and **Discover.** They also provide a convenient record of all your expenses, and offer relatively good exchange rates. You can withdraw cash advances from your credit cards at banks or ATMs, but high fees make credit card cash advances a pricey way to get cash.

It's highly recommended that you travel with at least one major credit card. You must have a credit card to rent a car, and hotels and airlines usually require a credit card imprint as a deposit against expenses.

ATM cards with major credit card backing, known as **"debit cards,"** are now a commonly acceptable form of payment in most stores and restaurants. Debit cards draw money directly from your checking account. Some stores allow you to receive cash back on your debit-card purchases as well. The same is true at most U.S. post offices.

TRAVELER'S CHECKS

Though credit cards and debit cards are more often used, traveler's checks are still widely accepted in the U.S. Foreign visitors should make sure that traveler's checks are denominated in U.S. dollars; foreign-currency checks are often difficult to exchange.

You can buy traveler's checks at most banks. Most are offered in denominations of $20, $50, $100, $500, and sometimes $1000. Generally, you'll pay a service charge ranging from 1% to 4%.

The most popular traveler's checks are offered by **American Express** (© 800/ 807-6233; © 800/221-7282 for card holders—this number accepts collect calls, offers service in several foreign languages, and exempts Amex gold and platinum cardholders from the 1% fee.); **Visa** (© 800/732-1322)—AAA members can obtain Visa checks for a $9.95 fee (for checks up to $1,500) at most AAA offices or by calling © 866/339-3378; and **MasterCard** (© 800/223-9920).

Be sure to keep a copy of the traveler's check serial numbers separate from your checks in the event that they are stolen or lost. You'll get a refund faster if you know the numbers.

Another option is the new **prepaid traveler's check cards,** reloadable cards that work much like debit cards but aren't linked to your checking account. The **American Express Travelers Cheque Card,** for example, requires a minimum deposit ($300), sets a maximum balance ($2,750), and has a one-time issuance fee of $15. You can withdraw money from an ATM ($2.50 per transaction, not including bank fees), and the funds can be purchased in dollars, euros, or pounds. If you lose the card, your available funds will be refunded within 24 hours.

7 Travel Insurance

The cost of travel insurance varies widely, depending on the cost and length of your trip, your age and health, and the type of trip you're taking, but expect to pay between 5% and 8% of the vacation itself. You can get estimates from various providers through **InsureMyTrip.com.** Enter your trip cost and dates, your age, and other information, for prices from more than a dozen companies.

For **U.K. citizens,** insurance is always advisable when traveling in the States. Travelers or families who make more than one trip abroad per year may find an annual travel insurance policy works out cheaper. Check **www.moneysupermarket. com**, which compares prices across a wide range of providers for single- and multi-trip policies.

Most big travel agents offer their own insurance and will probably try to sell you their package when you book a holiday. Think before you sign. **Britain's Consumers' Association** recommends that you insist on seeing the policy and reading the fine print before buying travel insurance. **The Association of British Insurers** (© 020/7600-3333; www.abi. org.uk) gives advice by phone and publishes *Holiday Insurance*, a free guide to policy provisions and prices. You might also shop around for better deals: Try **Columbus Direct** (© 0870/033-9988; www.columbusdirect.net).

TRIP-CANCELLATION INSURANCE

Trip-cancellation insurance will help retrieve your money if you have to back out of a trip or depart early, or if your travel supplier goes bankrupt. Trip cancellation traditionally covers such events as sickness, natural disasters, and State Department advisories. The latest news in trip-cancellation insurance is the availability of **expanded hurricane coverage** and the **"any-reason"** cancellation coverage—which costs more but covers cancellations made for any reason. You won't get back 100% of your prepaid trip cost, but you'll be refunded a substantial portion. **Travel-Safe** (© **888/885-7233**; www.travel safe.com) offers both types of coverage. Expedia also offers any-reason cancellation coverage for its air–hotel packages.

For details, contact one of the following recommended insurers: **Access America** (© 866/807-3982; www.access america.com); **Travel Guard International** (© 800/826-4919; www.travel guard.com); **Travel Insured International** (© 800/243-3174; www.travel insured.com); and **Travelex Insurance Services** (© 888/457-4602; www.travelex-insurance.com).

MEDICAL INSURANCE

Although it's not required of travelers, health insurance is highly recommended. Most health insurance policies cover you if you get sick away from home—but check your coverage before you leave.

International visitors should note that unlike many European countries, the United States does not usually offer free or low-cost medical care to its citizens or visitors. Doctors and hospitals are expensive, and in most cases will require advance payment or proof of coverage before they render their services. Good policies will cover the costs of an accident, repatriation, or death. Packages such as **Europ Assistance's "Worldwide Healthcare Plan"** are sold by European automobile clubs and travel agencies at attractive rates. **Worldwide Assistance Services, Inc.** (© **800/777-8710;** www. worldwideassistance.com) is the agent for Europ Assistance in the United States.

Though lack of health insurance may prevent you from being admitted to a hospital in nonemergencies, don't worry about being left on a street corner to die: The American way is to fix you now and bill the living daylights out of you later.

If you're ever hospitalized more than 150 miles from home, **MedjetAssist** (© **800/527-7478;** www.medjetassistance. com) will pick you up and fly you to the hospital of your choice in a medically equipped and staffed aircraft 24 hours a day, 7 days a week. Annual memberships are $225 individual, $350 family; you can also purchase short-term memberships.

Canadians should check with their provincial health plan offices or call **Health Canada** (© **866/225-0709;** www. hc-sc.gc.ca) to find out the extent of their coverage and what documentation and receipts they must take home in case they are treated in the United States.

LOST-LUGGAGE INSURANCE

On flights within the U.S., checked baggage is covered up to $2,500 per ticketed passenger. On flights outside the U.S. (and on U.S. portions of international trips), baggage coverage is limited to approximately $9.07 per pound, up to approximately $635 per checked bag. If you plan to check items more valuable than what's covered by the standard liability, see if your homeowner's policy covers your valuables, get baggage insurance as part of your comprehensive travel-insurance package, or buy Travel Guard's "BagTrak" product.

If your luggage is lost, immediately file a lost-luggage claim at the airport, detailing the luggage contents. Most airlines require that you report delayed, damaged, or lost baggage within 4 hours of arrival. The airlines are required to deliver luggage, once found, directly to your house or destination free of charge.

8 Health & Safety

WHAT TO DO IF YOU GET SICK AWAY FROM HOME

If you get sick, consider asking your hotel concierge to recommend a local doctor—even his or her own. You can also try an urgent-care facility or a local hospital, many of which have walk-in clinics for emergency cases that are not life-threatening. You may not get immediate attention, but you won't pay the high price of an emergency room visit.

We list **emergency numbers** under "Fast Facts" (p. 44).

If you suffer from a chronic illness, consult your doctor before your departure. Pack **prescription medications** in your carry-on luggage, and carry them in their original containers, with pharmacy labels—otherwise they won't make it through airport security. Visitors from outside the U.S. should carry generic names of prescription drugs. For U.S.

travelers, most reliable health-care plans provide coverage if you get sick away from home. Foreign visitors may have to pay all medical costs upfront and be reimbursed later. See "Medical Insurance," under "Travel Insurance," above.

SAFETY

Oregon's tourist spots are generally safe. Portland is a relatively safe city, but you should take some precautions. For further information on safety in Portland, see "Safety" in "Fast Facts" in chapter 4.

As a general precaution, avoid deserted areas, especially at night, and don't go into public parks at night. In theaters, restaurants, and other public places, keep your possessions in sight. If you plan to go hiking or participate in outdoor activities, don't leave anything valuable in your car. Park in well-lit, busy areas whenever possible.

9 The Active Vacation Planner

The abundance of outdoor recreational activities is one of the main reasons people choose to live in and visit Oregon. With both mountains and beaches within an hour's drive of the major metropolitan areas, there are numerous choices for the active vacationer.

ACTIVITIES A TO Z

BICYCLING/MOUNTAIN BIKING The Oregon coast is one of the most popular bicycling destinations in the nation, and each summer attracts thousands of dedicated pedalers. Expect to spend about a week pedaling the entire coast if you're in good shape and are traveling at a leisurely pace. During the summer months, it's best to travel from north to south along the coast due to the prevailing winds. Also keep in mind that many

state parks have designated hiker/biker campsites. You can get a free Oregon coast bicycle map, as well as other bicycle maps for the state of Oregon, by contacting the Oregon Department of Transportation's **Oregon Bicycle Map Hot Line** (© 503/986-3556; www.oregon. gov/odot/hwy/bikeped).

Other regions popular with cyclists include the wine country of Yamhill County and other parts of the Willamette Valley. Portland, Salem, Corvallis, Eugene, Cottage Grove, and Central Point all have easy bicycle paths that either are in parks or connect parks. In addition, the region's national forests provide miles of logging roads and single-track trails for mountain biking. Among the most popular mountain-biking areas are the east side

Tips   Serious Reservations

The days of spontaneous summer weekends are a thing of the past in Oregon. If you want to be assured of getting a room or a campsite at some of the busier destinations, you'll need to make your reservations months in advance, especially if you're going on a weekend.

To be sure that you get the state-park campsite, cabin, or houseboat you want, you'll need to make your reservations as much as 9 months in advance (that's the earliest you can reserve) through **ReserveAmerica** (© **800/452-5687**; www.reserveamerica.com).

While National Forest Service campgrounds are generally less developed and less in demand than state park campgrounds, many do stay full throughout the summer months, especially those at the beach. For reservations at forest-service campgrounds, contact **Recreation.gov** (© **877/444-6777** or 518/885-3639; www.recreation.gov). These sites can be reserved up to 6 months in advance.

The same sort of advance planning also applies to just about any lodging on the coast on a summer weekend. Making rooms even more difficult to come by are the many festivals scheduled around the state throughout the summer. Be sure to check whether your schedule might coincide with some popular event.

of Mount Hood, the Oakridge area southeast of Eugene, the Ashland area, and the Bend and Sisters areas of central Oregon.

If you're interested in a guided bike tour in the state, try **Bicycle Adventures,** P.O. Box 11219, Olympia, WA 98508 (© **800/443-6060** or 360/786-0989; www.bicycleadventures.com), which has tours of the Oregon coast, the Columbia Gorge, and Crater Lake National Park. Tour prices range from $1,542 to $2,468 per person including room and meals.

BIRD-WATCHING Oregon offers many excellent bird-watching spots. Malheur National Wildlife Refuge, in central Oregon, is the state's premier bird-watching area and attracts more than 300 bird species. Nearby Summer Lake also offers good bird-watching, with migratory waterfowl and shorebirds most prevalent. There's also good bird-watching on Sauvie Island, outside Portland, where

waterfowl, sandhill cranes, and eagles can be seen, and along the coast, where you can see tufted puffins, pigeon guillemots, and perhaps even a marbled murrelet. The Klamath Lakes region of south-central Oregon is well known for its large population of bald eagles, which are best seen in the winter months.

Throughout the year, the National Audubon Society sponsors expeditions, outings, and field seminars. For more information, contact the **Audubon Society of Portland** (© **503/292-6855**; www.audubonportland.org). For the Rare Bird Report hot line, call © **503/292-0661.**

Birders should also check out Oregon Birding Trails (www.oregonbirdingtrails.org), a website with information on birding trail maps. So far two maps that list birding hotspots have been produced—"Oregon Coast Birding Trail" and "Cascades Birding Trail."

CAMPING   Public and private camp-grounds abound across Oregon. Those along the coast are the most popular, followed by campgrounds on lakes. During the summer, campground reservations are almost a necessity at most state parks, especially those along the coast. For information on making campsite reservations, see "Serious Reservations," above.

Various state parks also offer a variety of camping alternatives. Tops among these are yurts (circular domed tents with electricity, plywood floors, and beds), which make camping in the rain a bit easier. Yurts, which rent for $27 to $66 a night, can be found at 14 coastal parks, as well as at four inland state parks (Champoeg, Valley of the Rogue, Tumalo, and Wallowa Lake).

Cabins are available at a dozen state parks. Nightly rates range from $20 to $80. A couple of state parks also have teepees for rent ($27–$29 per night). On central Oregon's Lake Billy Chinook at The Cove Palisades State Park, you can even rent a houseboat for $1,095 to $7,395 per week. Contact Cove Palisades Marina (© **541/546-3521;** www.cove palisadesmarina.com).

FISHING   The fish of Oregon enjoy near-legendary status, and although there may be few streams in the region of national importance among anglers, there are still plenty of great rivers. Salmon of half a dozen species, steelhead, sturgeon, wild cutthroat, and rainbow trout are all available, as are mackinaw trout and bass. Offshore fishing for salmon, tuna, and bottom fish is also popular.

The most important thing to know about fishing in Oregon is that the rules are complicated and always in flux. It is essential that you know all the regulations for the body of water you are fishing in. To find out what the current regulations are, you'll need to pick up a copy of *Oregon Sport Fishing Regulations*. This publication is free and is available at sporting-goods stores and bait-and-tackle shops. Alternatively, order a copy by contacting the **Oregon Department of Fish and Wildlife,** 3406 Cherry Ave. NE, Salem, OR 97303 (© **800/720-6339** or 503/947-6000; www.dfw.state.or.us).

GOLF   Oregon has hundreds of private and public golf courses, including numerous resort courses, most of which are in the Portland and Bend-Redmond areas. There are also quite a few excellent courses along the coast. However, the courses at the Bandon Dunes Golf Resort, on the central Oregon coast, are the state's most celebrated fairways.

HIKING & BACKPACKING   Oregon is a hiker's paradise. The state has thousands of miles of hiking trails, including the Pacific Crest Trail, which runs along the spine of the Cascades from the Columbia River to the California line (and onward all the way to both Canada and Mexico). The state's hiking trails are concentrated primarily in national forests, especially in wilderness areas, in the Cascade Range. Along the length of the Pacific Crest Trail are such scenic hiking areas as the Mount Hood Wilderness, the Mount Jefferson Wilderness, the Three Sisters Wilderness, the Diamond Peak Wilderness, the Mount Thielsen Wilderness, and the Sky Lakes Wilderness. Many state parks also have extensive hiking-trail systems.

The Oregon Coast Trail is a designated route that runs the length of the Oregon coast. In most places it travels along the beach, but in other places it climbs up and over capes and headlands through dense forests and windswept meadows. The longest stretches of the trail are along the southern coast in Samuel H. Boardman State Park. There's also a long beach stretch in the Oregon Dunes National Recreation Area.

Other coastal parks with popular hiking trails include Saddle Mountain State Park, Ecola State Park, Oswald West State

> **Tips   Travel Tip**
>
> Before heading out to a national forest anywhere in Oregon, be sure to get a Northwest Forest Pass. Most national-forest trail head parking areas in the state now require such a permit, and though they can sometimes be purchased from machines at the most popular trail heads, it's better to have one before heading out. To find out if you need a pass for your particular destination, contact the **Nature of the Northwest Information Center,** 800 NE Oregon St., Room 177, Portland, OR 97232 (© **503/872-2750;** www.naturenw.org). Passes are available at national-forest ranger stations throughout the state and also at many outdoors-supply stores, such as REI. Day passes cost $5 and annual passes are $30. In some cases such passes are required not just for trail heads but for other national forest recreational areas as well.

Park, and Cape Lookout State Park. Silver Falls State Park, east of Salem, is another of my favorite hiking spots. The many trails of the Columbia Gorge National Scenic Area are also well trodden, with Eagle Creek Trail being a long-time favorite. The trails leading out from Timberline Lodge on Mount Hood lead through forests and meadows at the tree line and, unfortunately, can be very crowded on summer weekends. For a quick hiking fix, Portlanders often head for the city's Forest Park.

If you'd like to do your hiking with a guide, contact Joe Whittington at **Oregon Peak Adventures,** P.O. Box 25576, Portland, OR 97298 (© **877/965-5100** or 503/297-5100; www.oregonpeak adventures.com). Whittington leads hikes in the Columbia Gorge, on the Oregon coast, and on Mount St. Helens and Mount Adams. Prices start at around $40 per person for a half-day hike.

KAYAKING & CANOEING   While Puget Sound, up in Washington, is the sea kayaking capital of the Northwest, Oregonians have also taken to this sport. However, sea kayaks in Oregon very rarely make it to the sea, where waters are usually far too rough for kayaks. But there are numerous protected bays along the Oregon coast that are popular paddling spots. Also, the Lewis & Clark National Wildlife Refuge on the Columbia River not far from Astoria offers miles of quiet waterways to explore.

White-water kayaking is popular on many of the rivers that flow down out of the Cascade Range in Oregon, including the Deschutes, the Clackamas, the Molalla, and the Sandy. Down in southern Oregon, the North Umpqua and the Rogue provide plenty of white-water action.

Sundance River Center (© **888/777-7557;** www.sundanceriver.com), which is located near Grants Pass, is one of the premier kayaking schools in the country. They offer a 9-day beginner's program ($1,530) that does a 4-day trip down the wild-and-scenic section of the Rogue River after several days of initial instruction.

Canoeing is popular on many of Oregon's lakes. Some of the best are Hosmer and Sparks lakes west of Bend, Clear Lake south of Santiam Pass, Waldo Lake near Willamette Pass southeast of Eugene, and Upper Klamath Lake (where there's a designated canoe trail).

MOUNTAINEERING   Mount Hood and several other Cascades peaks offer challenging mountain climbing and rock climbing for both the novice and the expert. If you're interested in learning some mountain-climbing skills or want to hone your existing skills, contact

Timberline Mountain Guides, P.O. Box 1167, Bend, OR 97709 (© **541/312-9242;** www.timberlinemtguides.com), a company that offers snow-, ice-, and rock-climbing courses. They also lead summit climbs on Mount Hood. A 2-day Mount Hood mountaineering course with summit climb costs $425.

ROCK CLIMBING   Smith Rock State Park, near Redmond in central Oregon, is a rock-climbing mecca of international renown, and many climbers claim that sport climbing got its American start here. Smith Rock abounds in climbing routes, some of which are among the toughest in the world. If you're a serious climber, pick up a copy of Alan Watts's *Climber's Guide to Smith Rock* (Falcon, 1992), an exhaustive guide to the many climbing routes here. On the Web, check out **www.smithrock.com**.

SKIING   Because the winter weather in Oregon is so unpredictable, the state is not known as a ski destination. Most of the state's ski areas are relatively small and cater primarily to local skiers. Mount Bachelor, in central Oregon outside of Bend, is the one exception. Because of its high elevation and location on the drier east side of the Cascades, it gets a more reliable snowpack and isn't as susceptible to midwinter warming spells, which tend to bring rain to west-side ski slopes with irritating regularity.

Ski areas in Oregon include Mount Hood Meadows, Mount Hood Skibowl, Timberline, Cooper Spur Ski Area, and Summit Ski Area, all of which are on Mount Hood outside Portland. Farther south, there are Hoodoo Ski Area (east of Salem), Willamette Pass Resort (east of Eugene), and Mount Bachelor (outside Bend). In the eastern part of the state, Anthony Lakes and Spout Springs Ski Area provide a bit of powder skiing. Down in the south, Mt. Ashland is the only option.

Many downhill ski areas also offer groomed **cross-country ski trails.** Cross-country skiers will find an abundance of trails up and down the Cascades. Teacup Lake and Mount Hood Meadows, on Mount Hood, offer good groomed trails. Near and at Mount Bachelor, there are also plenty of groomed trails. Crater Lake is another popular spot for cross-country skiing. Backcountry skiing is also popular in the Wallowa Mountains in eastern Oregon.

WHALE-WATCHING   Gray whales, which can reach 45 feet in length and weigh up to 35 tons, migrate annually between Alaska and Baja California, and pass close by the Oregon coast between December and May. However, with more and more whales stopping to spend the summer off the Oregon coast, it is now possible to see them just about any month of the year.

Depoe Bay, north of Newport, is not only the smallest harbor in the world, but also a home port for whale-watching boats that head out throughout the year to look for gray whales. It's also possible to whale watch from shore, with Cape Meares, Cape Lookout, Cape Kiwanda, Devil's Punchbowl, Cape Perpetua, Sea Lion Caves, Shore Acres State Park, Face Rock Wayside (in Bandon), Cape Blanco, Cape Sebastian, and Harris Beach State Park being some of the better places from which to scan the ocean for spouting whales.

WHITE-WATER RAFTING   Plenty of rain and snowmelt and lots of mountains combine to produce dozens of good white-water-rafting rivers in Oregon, depending on the time of year and water levels. Central Oregon's Deschutes River and southern Oregon's Rogue River are the two most popular rafting rivers. Other popular rafting rivers include the Clackamas outside Portland, the McKenzie outside Eugene, and the North

Umpqua outside Roseburg. Out in the southeastern corner, the remote Owyhee River provides adventurers with still more white water. See the respective regional chapters for information on rafting companies operating on these rivers.

WINDSURFING & KITE BOARDING   The Columbia River Gorge is one of the most renowned windsurfing and kite-boarding spots in the world. As the winds whip up the waves, skilled sailors rocket across the water and launch themselves skyward to perform aerial acrobatics.

On calmer days and in spots where the wind isn't blowing so hard, there are also opportunities for novices to learn the basics. Summer is the best sailing season, and the town of Hood River is the center of the boarding scene, with plenty of windsurfing and kite-boarding schools and rental companies. The southern Oregon coast also has some popular spots, including Floras Lake just north of Port Orford and Meyers Creek in Pistol River State Park, south of Gold Beach.

10 Educational & Volunteer Vacations

Want to turn your vacation into an educational experience or give a little back by volunteering? Check out the trips and classes offered by the organizations listed here.

The Nature Conservancy is a nonprofit organization dedicated to the global preservation of natural diversity, and to this end it operates educational field trips and work parties to its own nature preserves. For information about field trips in Oregon, contact **The Nature Conservancy,** 821 SE 14th Ave., Portland, OR 97214 (© **503/802-8100;** www.nature.org).

If your personal interests run to art or the environment, be sure to check the calendar for seminars and classes offered by the **Sitka Center for Art and Ecology,**

P.O. Box 65, Otis, OR 97368 (© **541/ 994-5485;** www.sitkacenter.org), which is located on the northern Oregon coast on the slopes of rugged Cascade Head. The center runs classes and workshops on writing, painting, ecology, ceramics, and other topics.

If you'd like to help keep Oregon beautiful and green, consider spending a day of your vacation volunteering for **SOLV,** 5193 NE Elam Young Pkwy, Hillsboro, OR 97124 (© **800/333-SOLV** or 503/ 844-9571; www.solv.org), which sponsors a variety of tree-planting and litter-removal programs across the state. The beach cleanups, held in both spring and fall, are among this organization's biggest events.

11 Specialized Travel Resources

TRAVELERS WITH DISABILITIES
Most disabilities shouldn't stop anyone from traveling in the U.S. There are more options and resources out there than ever before.

Most hotels now provide wheelchair-accessible rooms, and some of the larger and more expensive hotels also have TDD telephones and other amenities for the hearing- and sight-impaired.

The **America the Beautiful–National Park and Federal Recreational Lands Pass–Access Pass** (formerly the **Golden Access Passport**) gives people (regardless of age) who are visually impaired or have permanent disabilities free lifetime entrance to federal recreation sites administered by the National Park Service, including the Fish and Wildlife Service, the Forest Service, the Bureau of Land

Management, and the Bureau of Reclamation. This may include national parks, monuments, historic sites, recreation areas, and national wildlife refuges.

The America the Beautiful Access Pass can only be obtained in person at any NPS facility that charges an entrance fee. You need to show proof of medically determined disability. Besides free entry, the pass also offers a 50% discount on some federal-use fees charged for such facilities as camping, swimming, parking, boat launching, and tours. For more information, go to www.nps.gov/fees_passes.htm or call © 888/467-2757.

Organizations that offer a vast range of resources and assistance to travelers with disabilities include **MossRehab** (© 800/CALL-MOSS;** www.mossresourcenet. org); the **American Foundation for the Blind** (AFB; © 800/232-5463; www. afb.org); and **SATH (Society for Accessible Travel & Hospitality;** © 212/447-7284; www.sath.org). **AirAmbulance-Card.com** is now partnered with SATH and allows you to preselect top-notch hospitals in case of an emergency.

Access-Able Travel Source (© 303/232-2979; www.access-able.com) offers a comprehensive database on travel agents from around the world with experience in accessible travel; destination-specific access information; and links to such resources as service animals, equipment rentals, and access guides.

Many travel agencies offer customized tours and itineraries for travelers with disabilities. Among them are **Flying Wheels Travel** (© 507/451-5005; www.flying wheelstravel.com) and **Accessible Journeys** (© 800/846-4537 or 610/521-0339; www.disabilitytravel.com).

Flying with Disability (www.flying-with-disability.org) is a comprehensive information source on airplane travel. **Avis Rent a Car** (© 888/879-4273) has an "Avis Access" program that offers services for customers with special travel needs. These include specially outfitted vehicles with swivel seats, spinner knobs, and hand controls; mobility scooter rentals; and accessible bus service. Be sure to reserve well in advance.

Also check out the quarterly magazine ***Emerging Horizons*** (www.emerging horizons.com), available by subscription ($16.95 year in U.S.; $21.95 outside U.S).

The "Accessible Travel" link at **Mobility-Advisor.com** (www.mobility-advisor. com) offers a variety of travel resources to persons with disabilities.

British travelers should contact **Holiday Care** (© 0845-124-9971 in U.K. only; www.holidaycare.org.uk) to access a wide range of travel information and resources for elderly travelers and those with disabilities.

GAY & LESBIAN TRAVELERS

Gay and lesbian travelers visiting Portland should be sure to pick up a free copy of ***Just Out*** (© 503/236-1252; www.just out.com), a bimonthly newspaper for the gay community. You can usually find copies at **Powell's Books,** 1005 W. Burnside St. Another publication to look for is ***Portland's Gay & Lesbian Community Yellow Pages*** (© 503/230-7701; www. pdxgayyellowpages.com), which is also usually available at Powell's.

For a list of gay-friendly accommodations in the Portland area, go to the **Purple Roofs** website (www.purpleroofs.com).

Many agencies offer tours and travel itineraries specifically for gay and lesbian travelers. **Above and Beyond Tours** (© 800/397-2681; www.abovebeyond tours.com) specialize in gay Australia tours. San Francisco–based **Now, Voyager** (© 800/255-6951; www.nowvoyager. com) offers worldwide trips and cruises. **Olivia** (© 800/631-6277; www.olivia. com) offers lesbian cruises and resort vacations.

Gay.com Travel (© 800/929-2268 or 415/644-8044; www.gay.com/travel or www.outandabout.com), is an excellent online successor to the popular *Out & About* print magazine. It provides regularly updated information about gay-owned, gay-oriented, and gay-friendly lodging, dining, sightseeing, nightlife, and shopping establishments in every important destination worldwide. British travelers should click on the "Travel" link at **www.uk.gay.com** for advice and gay-friendly trip ideas.

The Canadian website **GayTraveler** (**www.gaytraveler.ca**) offers ideas and advice for gay travel all over the world.

The following travel guides are available at many bookstores, or you can order them from any online bookseller: *Spartacus International Gay Guide, 35th Edition* (Bruno Gmünder Verlag; www.spartacusworld.com/gayguide); *Odysseus: The International Gay Travel Planner, 17th Edition;* and the *Damron* guides (www.damron.com), with separate, annual books for gay men and lesbians.

SENIOR TRAVEL

Don't be shy about asking for discounts, but always carry some kind of identification, such as a driver's license, that shows your date of birth—especially if you've kept your youthful glow. In Portland most attractions, theaters, and tour companies offer senior discounts. These can add up to substantial savings, but you have to remember to ask.

Members of **AARP,** 601 E St. NW, Washington, DC 20049 (*C* **888/687-2277;** www.aarp.org), get discounts on hotels, airfares, and car rentals. AARP offers members a wide range of benefits, including *AARP: The Magazine* and a monthly newsletter. Anyone over 50 can join.

The U.S. National Park Service offers an **America the Beautiful–National Park and Federal Recreational Lands Pass–Senior Pass** (formerly the **Golden Age Passport**), which gives seniors 62 years or older lifetime entrance to all properties administered by the National Park Service—national parks, monuments, historic sites, recreation areas, and national wildlife refuges—for a one-time processing fee of $10. The pass must be purchased in person at any NPS facility that charges an entrance fee. Besides free entry, the America the Beautiful Senior Pass also offers a 50% discount on some federal-use fees charged for such facilities as camping, swimming, parking, boat launching, and tours. For more information, go to www.nps.gov/fees_passes.htm or call *C* **888/467-2757.**

Many reliable agencies and organizations target the 50-plus market. **Elderhostel** (*C* **800/454-5768;** www.elderhostel.org) arranges worldwide study programs for those aged 55 and over. **ElderTreks** (*C* **800/741-7956** or 416/558-5000 outside North America; www.eldertreks.com) offers small-group tours to off-the-beaten-path or adventure-travel locations, restricted to travelers 50 and older.

Recommended publications offering travel resources and discounts for seniors include: the quarterly magazine *Travel 50 & Beyond* (www.travel50andbeyond.com) and the bestselling paperback *Unbelievably Good Deals and Great Adventures That You Absolutely Can't Get Unless You're Over 50 2005–2006, 16th Edition* (McGraw-Hill), by Joann Rattner Heilman.

FAMILY TRAVEL

If you have enough trouble simply getting your kids out of the house in the morning, dragging them thousands of miles away may seem like an insurmountable challenge. But family travel can be immensely rewarding, giving you new ways of seeing the world through smaller pairs of eyes.

To locate accommodations, restaurants, and attractions that are particularly kid-friendly, refer to the "Kids" icon throughout this guide.

Frommers.com: The Complete Travel Resource

It should go without saying, but we highly recommend **Frommers.com,** voted Best Travel Site by *PC Magazine.* We think you'll find our expert advice and tips; independent reviews of hotels, restaurants, attractions, and preferred shopping and nightlife venues; vacation giveaways; and online booking tool indispensable before, during, and after your travels. We publish the complete contents of over 128 travel guides in our **Destinations** section covering nearly 3,800 places worldwide to help you plan your trip. Each weekday, we publish original articles reporting on **Deals and News** via our free **Frommers.com Newsletter** to help you save time and money and travel smarter. We're betting you'll find our new **Events** listings (http://events.frommers.com) an invaluable resource; it's an up-to-the-minute roster of what's happening in cities everywhere—including concerts, festivals, lectures, and more. We've also added weekly **Podcasts, interactive maps,** and hundreds of new images across the site. Check out our **Travel Talk** area featuring **Message Boards** where you can join in conversations with thousands of fellow Frommer's travelers and post your trip report once you return.

Families traveling in Oregon should be sure to take note of family admission fees at many museums and other attractions. These admission prices are often less than what it would cost for individual tickets for the whole family. At hotels and motels, children usually stay free if they share their parent's room and no extra bed or crib is required, and sometimes they also get to eat for free in the hotel dining room. Be sure to ask.

Recommended family travel websites include **Family Travel Forum** (www.familytravelforum.com), a comprehensive site that offers customized trip planning; **Family Travel Network** (www.familytravelnetwork.com), an online magazine providing travel tips; **TravelWithYourKids.com** (www.travelwithyourkids.com), a comprehensive site written by parents for parents offering sound advice for long-distance and international travel with children.

12 Staying Connected

TELEPHONES

Generally, hotel surcharges on long-distance and local calls are astronomical, so you're better off using your **cellphone** or a **public pay telephone.** Many convenience groceries and packaging services sell **prepaid calling cards** in denominations up to $50; for international visitors these can be the least expensive way to call home. Many public pay phones at airports now accept American Express, MasterCard, and Visa credit cards. **Local calls** made from pay phones in most locales cost either 35¢ or 50¢ (no pennies, please).

Most long-distance and international calls can be dialed directly from any phone. **For calls within the United States and to Canada,** dial 1 followed by the area code and the seven-digit number. **For other international calls,** dial 011 followed by the country code, city code, and the number you are calling.

Calls to area codes **800, 888, 877,** and **866** are toll-free. However, calls to area codes **700** and **900** (chat lines, bulletin boards, "dating" services, and so on) can be very expensive—usually a charge of 95¢ to $3 or more per minute, and they sometimes have minimum charges that can run as high as $15 or more.

For **reversed-charge or collect calls,** and for person-to-person calls, dial the number 0 then the area code and number; an operator will come on the line, and you should specify whether you are calling collect, person-to-person, or both. If your operator-assisted call is international, ask for the overseas operator.

For **local directory assistance** ("information"), dial 411; for long-distance information, dial 1, then the appropriate area code and 555-1212.

CELLPHONES

Just because your cellphone works at home doesn't mean it'll work everywhere in the U.S. (thanks to our nation's fragmented cellphone system). It's a good bet that your phone will work in major cities, but take a look at your wireless company's coverage map on its website before heading out; T-Mobile, Sprint, and Nextel are particularly weak in rural areas. If you need to stay in touch at a destination where you know your phone won't work, **rent** a phone that does from **InTouch USA** (© **800/872-7626;** www.intouch global.com) or a rental car location, but beware that you'll pay $1 a minute or more for airtime.

If you're not from the U.S., you'll be appalled at the poor reach of our **GSM (Global System for Mobile Communications) wireless network,** which is used by much of the rest of the world. Your phone will probably work in most major U.S. cities; it definitely won't work in many rural areas. To see where GSM phones work in the U.S., check out www. t-mobile.com/coverage/national_popup. asp. And you may or may not be able to send SMS (text messaging) home.

VOICE-OVER INTERNET PROTOCOL (VOIP)

If you have Web access while traveling, you might consider a broadband-based telephone service (in technical terms, **Voice over Internet Protocol,** or **VoIP**) such as Skype (www.skype.com) or Vonage (www.vonage.com), which allows you to make free international calls if you use their services from your laptop or in a cybercafe. The people you're calling must

---

Online Traveler's Toolbox

Veteran travelers usually carry some essential items to make their trips easier. Following is a selection of handy online tools to bookmark and use.

- **Airplane Food** (www.airlinemeals.net)
- **Airplane Seating** (www.seatguru.com and www.airlinequality.com)
- **Foreign Languages for Travelers** (www.travlang.com)
- **Maps** (www.mapquest.com)
- **Time and Date** (www.timeanddate.com)
- **Travel Warnings** (http://travel.state.gov, www.fco.gov.uk/travel, www.voyage.gc.ca, and www.dfat.gov.au/consular/advice)
- **Universal Currency Converter** (www.xe.com/ucc)
- **Visa ATM Locator** (www.visa.com); **MasterCard ATM Locator** (www.mastercard.com)
- **Weather** (www.intellicast.com and www.weather.com)

also use the service for it to work; check the sites for details.

INTERNET/E-MAIL
WITHOUT YOUR OWN COMPUTER

To find cybercafes in your destination check **www.cybercaptive.com** and **www.cybercafe.com**.

Most major airports have **Internet kiosks** that provide basic Web access for a per-minute fee that's usually higher than cybercafe prices. Check out copy shops like **Kinko's** (FedEx Kinkos), which offers computer stations with fully loaded software (as well as Wi-Fi).

WITH YOUR OWN COMPUTER

More and more hotels, resorts, airports, cafes, and retailers are going Wi-Fi (wireless fidelity), becoming "hotspots" that offer free high-speed Wi-Fi access or charge a small fee for usage. Wi-Fi is even found in campgrounds, RV parks, and even entire towns. Most laptops sold today have built-in wireless capability. To find public Wi-Fi hotspots at your destination, go to **www.jiwire.com**; its Hotspot Finder holds the world's largest directory of public wireless hotspots.

For dial-up access, most business-class hotels in the U.S. offer dataports for laptop modems, and a few thousand hotels in the U.S. and Europe now offer free high-speed Internet access.

Wherever you go, bring a **connection kit** of the right power and phone adapters, a spare phone cord, and a spare Ethernet network cable—or find out whether your hotel supplies them to guests.

13 Packages for the Independent Traveler

Package tours are simply a way to buy the airfare, accommodations, and other elements of your trip (such as car rentals, airport transfers, and sometimes even activities) at the same time and often at discounted prices.

One good source of package deals is the airlines themselves. Most major airlines offer air/land packages, including **American Airlines Vacations** (© 800/321-2121; www.aavacations.com), **Delta Vacations** (© 800/654-6559; www.deltavacations.com), **Continental Airlines Vacations** (© 800/301-3800; www.covacations.com), and **United Vacations** (© 888/854-3899; www.unitedvacations.com). Several big **online travel agencies**—Expedia, Travelocity, Orbitz, and Lastminute.com—also do a brisk business in packages.

Travel packages are also listed in the travel section of your local Sunday newspaper. Or check ads in the national travel magazines such as *Arthur Frommer's Budget Travel Magazine, Travel + Leisure, National Geographic Traveler,* and *Condé Nast Traveler.*

14 Getting Around Oregon

BY CAR

A car is by far the best way to see Oregon. There just isn't any other way to get to the more remote natural spectacles or to fully appreciate such regions as the Oregon coast or eastern Oregon. See "By Car" in the "Getting There" section of this chapter for information on car rentals in Portland.

GASOLINE   Oregon is an anachronism when it comes to gas stations; there are no self-service gas stations in the state. So, when you pull into a gas station, just sit back and let the attendant fill your tank. Also, keep in mind that Oregon is a big state, so keep your gas tank as full as possible when traveling in the mountains

Before you invest in a package deal or an escorted tour:

- Always ask about the **cancellation policy.** Can you get your money back? Is there a deposit required?
- Ask about the **accommodations choices and prices** for each. Then look up the hotels' reviews in a Frommer's guide and check their rates online for your specific dates of travel. Also find out what types of rooms are offered.
- Request a complete **schedule.** (Escorted tours only.)
- Ask about the **size** and demographics of the group. (Escorted tours only.)
- Discuss what is included in the **price** (transportation, meals, tips, airport transfers, and such). (Escorted tours only.)
- Finally, look for **hidden expenses.** Ask whether airport departure fees and taxes, for example, are included in the total cost—they rarely are.

or on the sparsely populated east side of the Cascades.

MAPS Maps are available at most highway tourist information centers, at the tourist information offices listed earlier in this chapter and throughout this book, and at gas stations throughout the region. For a map of Oregon, contact the **Oregon Tourism Commission** (© **800/ 547-7842**). Members of AAA can get detailed road maps of Oregon by calling their local AAA office.

SPECIAL DRIVING RULES You may turn right on a red light after a full stop, and if you are in the far-left lane of a one-way street, you may turn left into the adjacent left lane of a one-way street at a red light after a full stop. Everyone in a moving vehicle is required to wear a seat belt.

BREAKDOWNS In the event of a breakdown, stay with your car, lift the hood, turn on your emergency flashers, and wait for a police patrol car. *Do not leave your vehicle.*

DRIVING TIMES It takes about 1½ hours to drive from Portland to Canon

Beach on the Oregon coast; from Portland to Mount Hood, about 1 hour; and from Portland to Bend, about 3 hours. Portland to Seattle is about a 3½-hour trip, depending on traffic.

BY PLANE

Overseas visitors can take advantage of the APEX (Advance Purchase Excursion) reductions offered by all major U.S. and European carriers. In addition, some large airlines offer transatlantic or transpacific passengers special discount tickets under the name **Visit USA,** which allows mostly one-way travel from one U.S. destination to another at very low prices. Unavailable in the U.S., these discount tickets must be purchased abroad in conjunction with your international fare.

Although there are airports with regular commercial service in Redmond, Eugene, and Medford, flying isn't usually a very appropriate way to get around Oregon. However, if you are heading to the central or southern Oregon coast, you might consider flying into either the Eugene or the Medford Airport. If you are headed to Bend or Sunriver, flying into Redmond might work for you. If you are headed to Ashland for some Shakespeare, you could consider the Medford airport.

BY RECREATIONAL VEHICLE (RV)

An economical way to tour Oregon is with a recreational vehicle. If you're considering renting an RV, look under "Recreational Vehicles—Rent and Lease"

in the Yellow Pages of your local phone book. They can be rented for a weekend, a week, or longer. In Portland, you might try **Cruise America,** 8400 SE 82nd Ave. (℃ **800/671-8042** or 503/777-9833; www.cruiseamerica.com). If you're going to be traveling in the peak season of summer, it's important to make reservations for your RV at least 2 months ahead of time. The rest of the year, a couple of weeks' lead time is usually sufficient.

15 Tips on Accommodations

It's always a good idea to make hotel reservations as soon as you know your trip dates. Portland and the Oregon coast are particularly busy during summer months, and hotels book up in advance—especially on holiday and festival weekends. If you do not have reservations, it is best to look for a room in the midafternoon because hotels may be filled by evening. Major downtown hotels, which cater primarily to business travelers, commonly offer weekend discounts of as much as 50% to entice vacationers to fill up the empty rooms. However, resorts and hotels near tourist attractions tend to have higher rates on weekends.

For information on B&Bs in Oregon, contact the **Oregon Bed and Breakfast Guild,** P.O. Box 12702, Salem, OR 97309 (℃ **800/944-6196;** www.obbg.org).

SURFING FOR HOTELS

In addition to the online travel booking sites **Travelocity, Expedia, Orbitz, Priceline,** and **Hotwire,** you can book

hotels through **Hotels.com; Quikbook** (www.quikbook.com); and **Travelaxe** (www.travelaxe.net).

HotelChatter.com is a daily webzine offering smart coverage and critiques of hotels worldwide. Go to **TripAdvisor. com** or **HotelShark.com** for helpful independent consumer reviews of hotels and resort properties.

It's a good idea to **get a confirmation number** and **make a printout** of any online booking transaction.

SAVING ON YOUR HOTEL ROOM

The **rack rate** is the maximum rate that a hotel charges for a room. Hardly anybody pays this price, however, except in high season or on holidays. To lower the cost of your room:

- **Ask about special rates or other discounts.** You may qualify for corporate, student, military, senior, frequent flier, trade union, or other discounts.

- **Dial direct.** When booking a room in a chain hotel, you'll often get a better deal by calling the individual hotel's reservation desk rather than the chain's main number.
- **Book online.** Many hotels offer Internet-only discounts, or supply rooms to Priceline, Hotwire, or Expedia at rates much lower than the ones you can get through the hotel itself.
- **Remember the law of supply and demand.** Resort hotels are most crowded and therefore most expensive on weekends, so discounts are usually available for midweek stays. Business hotels in downtown locations are busiest during the week, so you can expect big discounts over the weekend.
- **Look into group or long-stay discounts.** If you come as part of a large group, you should be able to negotiate a bargain rate. Likewise, if you're planning a long stay (at least 5 days), you might qualify for a discount. As a general rule, expect 1 night free after a 7-night stay.
- **Sidestep excess surcharges and hidden costs.** Many hotels have the unpleasant practice of nickel-and-diming their guests with opaque surcharges. When you book a room, ask what is included in the room rate, and what is extra. Avoid dialing direct from hotel phones, which can have exorbitant rates. And don't be tempted by the room's minibar offerings: Most hotels charge through the nose for water, soda, and snacks. Finally, ask about local taxes and service charges, which can increase the cost of a room by 15% or more.
- **Book an efficiency.** A room with a kitchenette allows you to shop for groceries and cook your own meals. This is a big money saver, especially for families on long stays.
- **Consider enrolling in hotel "frequent-stay" programs,** which are upping the ante lately to win the loyalty of repeat customers. Frequent guests can now accumulate points or credits to earn free hotel nights, airline miles, in-room amenities, merchandise, tickets to concerts and events, discounts on sporting facilities—and even credit toward stock in the participating hotel, in the case of

Finds Cruising the Columbia River

Paddle-wheel steamboats played a crucial role in the settling of Oregon, shuttling people and goods up and down the Columbia River before railroads came to the region. Today, the *Queen of the West* and the *Empress of the North,* two paddle-wheel cruise ships operated by the **Majestic America Line,** 2101 Fourth Ave., Suite 1150, Seattle, WA 98121 (© **800/434-1232;** www.majesticamericaline.com), cruise the Columbia offering a luxury never before known in Columbia River paddle wheelers. Fares for the 7-night cruise start at $2,170 per person.

If you'd rather cruise aboard a smaller vessel, consider a trip with **Cruise West** (© **888/851-8133;** www.cruisewest.com), which offers an 8-day cruise from Portland on the Columbia and Snake rivers. Fares start at $2,949 per person. Similar trips, though with naturalists and historians on board, are offered by **Lindblad Expeditions** (© **800/397-3348;** www.expeditions.com), starting at $1,820.

the Jameson Inn hotel group. Perks are awarded not only by many chain hotels and motels (Hilton HHonors, Marriott Rewards, Wyndham ByRequest, to name a few), but individual inns and B&Bs. Many chain hotels partner with other hotel chains, car-rental firms, airlines, and credit card companies to give consumers additional incentive to do repeat business.

FAST FACTS: Oregon

American Express **Azumano Travel,** 400 SW Stark St. ((C) **800/777-2018** or 503/294-2000), is an **American Express Travel Services Representative.** For card member services, call (C) **800/528-4800.** For other locations or general information, call (C) **800/AXP-TRIP** or go to www.americanexpress.com.

Area Codes Currently, Oregon has three area codes. In the Portland area, where 10-digit dialing is required for local calls, 503 is the main area code. However, you may occasionally encounter the 971 area code. Outside of the northwest corner of the state (roughly Mount Hood and Portland to the coast and south to Salem), the area code is 541.

ATM Networks See "Money & Costs," p. 27.

Business Hours The following are general guidelines; specific establishments' hours may vary. Banks are open Monday through Friday from 9am to 5pm (some also on Sat 9am–noon). Stores are open Monday through Saturday from 10am to 6pm and Sunday from noon to 5pm (malls usually stay open until 9pm Mon–Sat). Bars can stay open until 1am.

Car Rentals See "Getting There, By Car," earlier in this chapter.

Currency The most common bills are the $1 (a "buck"), $5, $10, and $20 denominations. There are also $2 bills (seldom encountered), $50 bills, and $100 bills (the last two are usually not welcome as payment for small purchases).

Coins come in seven denominations: 1¢ (1 cent, or a penny); 5¢ (5 cents, or a nickel); 10¢ (10 cents, or a dime); 25¢ (25 cents, or a quarter); 50¢ (50 cents, or a half dollar); the gold-colored Sacagawea coin, worth $1; and the rare silver dollar.

For additional information see "Money & Costs," p. 27.

Customs **What You Can Bring into the United States:** Every visitor more than 21 years of age may bring in, free of duty, the following: (1) 1 liter of wine or hard liquor; (2) 200 cigarettes, 100 cigars (but not from Cuba), or 3 pounds of smoking tobacco; and (3) $100 worth of gifts. These exemptions are offered to travelers who spend at least 72 hours in the United States and who have not claimed them within the preceding 6 months. It is altogether forbidden to bring into the country foodstuffs (particularly fruit, cooked meats, and canned goods) and plants (vegetables, seeds, tropical plants, and the like). Foreign tourists may carry in or out up to $10,000 in U.S. or foreign currency with no formalities; larger sums must be declared to U.S. Customs on entering or leaving, which includes filing form CM 4790. For details regarding U.S. Customs and Border Protection, consult your nearest U.S. embassy or consulate, or **U.S. Customs** ((C) **202/927-1770;** www.customs.ustreas.gov).

What You Can Take Home from the United States:

Canadian Citizens: For a clear summary of Canadian rules, write for the booklet *I Declare,* issued by the **Canada Border Services Agency** (✆ **800/461-9999** in Canada, or 204/983-3500; www.cbsa-asfc.gc.ca).

U.K. Citizens: For information, contact **HM Customs & Excise** at ✆ **0845/010-9000** (from outside the U.K., 020/8929-0152), or consult their website at www.hmce.gov.uk.

Australian Citizens: A helpful brochure available from Australian consulates or Customs offices is *Know Before You Go.* For more information, call the **Australian Customs Service** at ✆ **1300/363-263,** or log on to www.customs.gov.au.

New Zealand Citizens: Most questions are answered in a free pamphlet available at New Zealand consulates and Customs offices: *New Zealand Customs Guide for Travellers, Notice no. 4.* For more information, contact **New Zealand Customs,** The Customhouse, 17–21 Whitmore St., Box 2218, Wellington (✆ **04/473-6099** or 0800/428-786; www.customs.govt.nz).

Drinking Laws The legal minimum drinking age in Oregon is 21. Aside from on-premises sales of cocktails in bars and restaurants, hard liquor can only be purchased in liquor stores. Beer and wine are available in convenience stores and grocery stores. Brewpubs tend to sell only beer and wine, but some also have licenses to sell hard liquor.

Driving Rules See "Getting Around Oregon," earlier in this chapter.

Embassies & Consulates All embassies are located in the nation's capital, Washington, D.C. Some consulates are located in major U.S. cities, and most nations have a mission to the United Nations in New York City. If your country isn't listed below, call for directory information in Washington, D.C. (✆ **202/555-1212**) or log on to www.embassy.org/embassies.

The embassy of **Australia** is at 1601 Massachusetts Ave. NW, Washington, DC 20036 (✆ **202/797-3000;** www.austemb.org). There are consulates in New York, Honolulu, Houston, Los Angeles, and San Francisco.

The embassy of **Canada** is at 501 Pennsylvania Ave. NW, Washington, DC 20001 (✆ **202/682-1740;** www.canadianembassy.org). Other Canadian consulates are in Buffalo (New York), Detroit, Los Angeles, New York, and Seattle.

The embassy of **Ireland** is at 2234 Massachusetts Ave. NW, Washington, DC 20008 (✆ **202/462-3939;** www.irelandemb.org). Irish consulates are in Boston, Chicago, New York, San Francisco, and other cities. See website for complete listing.

The embassy of **New Zealand** is at 37 Observatory Circle NW, Washington, DC 20008 (✆ **202/328-4800;** www.nzemb.org). New Zealand consulates are in Los Angeles, Salt Lake City, San Francisco, and Seattle.

The embassy of the **United Kingdom** is at 3100 Massachusetts Ave. NW, Washington, DC 20008 (✆ **202/588-7800;** www.britainusa.com). Other British consulates are in Atlanta, Boston, Chicago, Cleveland, Houston, Los Angeles, New York, San Francisco, and Seattle.

Emergencies Call ✆ **911** for fire, police, and ambulance.

Gasoline (Petrol) At press time, in the Portland area, the cost of gasoline (also known as gas, but never petrol) was around $3.10 per gallon. However, the price of gas has been subject to much fluctuation. Taxes are already included in the printed price. One U.S. gallon equals 3.8 liters or .85 imperial gallons. Fill-up locations are known as gas or service stations.

Holidays Banks, government offices, post offices, and many stores, restaurants, and museums are closed on the following legal national holidays: January 1 (New Year's Day), the third Monday in January (Martin Luther King, Jr., Day), the third Monday in February (Presidents' Day), the last Monday in May (Memorial Day), July 4 (Independence Day), the first Monday in September (Labor Day), the second Monday in October (Columbus Day), November 11 (Veterans' Day/Armistice Day), the fourth Thursday in November (Thanksgiving Day), and December 25 (Christmas). The Tuesday after the first Monday in November is Election Day, a federal government holiday in presidential-election years (2008 is an election year).

See "Oregon Calendar of Events," earlier in this chapter.

Information See "Visitor Information," earlier in this chapter.

Liquor Laws The legal minimum drinking age in Oregon is 21. Bars can legally stay open until 2am. Beer and wine can often be purchased in supermarkets, but liquor can be purchased only in state-licensed liquor stores, of which there are very few, and a handful of grocery stores.

Lost & Found Be sure to tell all of your credit card companies the minute you discover your wallet has been lost or stolen and file a report at the nearest police precinct. Your credit card company or insurer may require a police report number or record of the loss. Most credit card companies have an emergency toll-free number to call if your card is lost or stolen; they may be able to wire you a cash advance immediately or deliver an emergency credit card in a day or two. Visa's U.S. emergency number is © 800/847-2911 or 410/581-9994. American Express cardholders and traveler's check holders should call © 800/221-7282. MasterCard holders should call © 800/307-7309 or 636/722-7111. For other credit cards, call the toll-free number directory at © 800/555-1212.

If you need emergency cash over the weekend when all banks and American Express offices are closed, you can have money wired to you via **Western Union** (© 800/325-6000; www.westernunion.com).

Mail At press time, domestic postage rates were 26¢ for a postcard and 41¢ for a letter. For international mail, a first-class letter of up to 1 ounce costs 90¢ (69¢ to Canada and Mexico); a first-class postcard costs 90¢ (69¢ to Canada and Mexico). For more information go to www.usps.com and click on "Calculate Postage."

If you aren't sure what your address will be in the United States, mail can be sent to you, in your name, c/o General Delivery at the main post office of the city or region where you expect to be. (Call © 800/275-8777 for information on the nearest post office.) The addressee must pick up mail in person and must produce proof of identity (driver's license, passport, and such). Most post offices will hold your mail for up to 1 month, and are open Monday to Friday from 8am to 6pm, and Saturday from 9am to 3pm.

Always include zip codes when mailing items in the U.S. If you don't know your zip code, visit www.usps.com/zip4.

Maps See "Getting Around Oregon," earlier in this chapter.

Newspapers & Magazines The *Oregonian* is the Portland daily paper and is available throughout most of the state. *Portland Monthly* is a good lifestyle monthly that offers plenty of coverage of what's hot in Portland. *Oregon Coast* magazine is another publication worth picking up.

Pets Some hotels and motels in Oregon accept small, well-behaved pets. However, a small fee often is charged to allow them into guest rooms. Many places, in particular bed-and-breakfasts, don't allow pets at all. (Policies can change frequently, so always be sure to confirm.) On the other hand, many bed-and-breakfasts have their own pets, so if you have a dog or cat allergy, be sure to mention it when making a B&B reservation. Pets are usually restricted in national parks for their own safety, so check before setting out.

Passports **For Residents of Australia:** You can pick up an application from your local post office or any branch of Passports Australia, but you must schedule an interview at the passport office to present your application materials. Call the **Australian Passport Information Service** at ✆ **131-232,** or visit the government website at www.passports.gov.au.

For Residents of Canada: Passport applications are available at travel agencies throughout Canada or from the central **Passport Office,** Department of Foreign Affairs and International Trade, Ottawa, ON K1A 0G3 (✆ **800/567-6868;** www.ppt.gc.ca). *Note:* Canadian children who travel must have their own passport. However, if you hold a valid Canadian passport issued before December 11, 2001, that bears the name of your child, the passport remains valid for you and your child until it expires.

For Residents of Ireland: You can apply for a 10-year passport at the **Passport Office,** Setanta Centre, Molesworth Street, Dublin 2 (✆ **01/671-1633;** www.irlgov.ie/iveagh). Those under age 18 and over 65 must apply for a 3-year passport. You can also apply at 1A South Mall, Cork (✆ **021/272-525**) or at most main post offices.

For Residents of New Zealand: You can pick up a passport application at any New Zealand Passports Office or download it from their website. Contact the **Passports Office** at ✆ **0800/225-050** in New Zealand or 04/474-8100, or log on to www.passports.govt.nz.

For Residents of the United Kingdom: To pick up an application for a standard 10-year passport (5-year passport for children under 16), visit your nearest passport office, major post office, or travel agency or contact the **United Kingdom Passport Service** at ✆ **0870/521-0410** or search its website at www.ukpa.gov.uk.

Police To reach the police, dial ✆ **911.**

Safety See "Health & Safety," earlier in this chapter.

Smoking Many restaurants in Oregon are nonsmoking establishments, and in 2009, a statewide indoor-smoking ban will go into effect.

Taxes Oregon is a shopper's paradise—there's no sales tax. However, you may have to pay taxes on a rental car or hotel room (even some campgrounds charge a "bed tax").

Telegraph, Telex & Fax **Telegraph and telex services** are provided primarily by Western Union. You can telegraph money, or have it telegraphed to you, very quickly over the Western Union system, but this service can cost as much as 15 to 20 percent of the amount sent.

Most hotels have **fax machines** available for guest use (be sure to ask about the charge to use it). Many hotel rooms are even wired for guests' fax machines. A less expensive way to send and receive faxes may be at stores such as **The UPS Store** (formerly Mail Boxes Etc.),

Time The continental United States is divided into **four time zones:** Eastern Standard Time (EST), Central Standard Time (CST), Mountain Standard Time (MST), and Pacific Standard Time (PST). Alaska and Hawaii have their own zones. For example, when it's 9am in Los Angeles (PST), it's 7am in Honolulu (HST),10am in Denver (MST), 11am in Chicago (CST), noon in New York City (EST), 5pm in London (GMT), and 2am the next day in Sydney. With the exception of far-eastern Oregon near Ontario, the state is on Pacific Standard Time (PST), making it 3 hours behind the East Coast.

Daylight saving time is in effect from 1am on the second Sunday in March to 1am on the first Sunday in November, except in Arizona, Hawaii, the U.S. Virgin Islands, and Puerto Rico. Daylight saving time moves the clock 1 hour ahead of standard time.

Tipping Tips are a very important part of certain workers' income, and gratuities are the standard way of showing appreciation for services provided. (Tipping is certainly not compulsory if the service is poor!) In hotels, tip **bellhops** at least $1 per bag ($2–$3 if you have a lot of luggage) and tip the **chamber staff** $1 to $2 per day (more if you've left a disaster area for him or her to clean up). Tip the **doorman** or **concierge** only if he or she has provided you with some specific service (for example, calling a cab for you or obtaining difficult-to-get theater tickets). Tip the **valet-parking attendant** $1 every time you get your car.

In restaurants, bars, and nightclubs, tip **service staff** 15% to 20% of the check, tip **bartenders** 10% to 15%, tip **checkroom attendants** $1 per garment, and tip **valet-parking attendants** $1 per vehicle.

As for other service personnel, tip **cab drivers** 15% of the fare; tip **skycaps** at airports at least $1 per bag ($2–$3 if you have a lot of luggage); and tip **hairdressers** and **barbers** 15% to 20%.

Toilets You won't find public toilets or "restrooms" on the streets in most U.S. cities, but they can be found in hotel lobbies, bars, restaurants, museums, department stores, railway and bus stations, and service stations. Large hotels and fast-food restaurants are often the best bet for clean facilities. If possible, avoid the toilets at parks and beaches, which tend to be dirty; some may be unsafe. Restaurants and bars in resorts or heavily visited areas may reserve their restrooms for patrons.

Visas For information about U.S. Visas go to **http://travel.state.gov** and click on "Visas." Or go to one of the following websites:

Australian citizens can obtain up-to-date visa information from the **U.S. Embassy Canberra**, Moonah Place, Yarralumla, ACT 2600 (*(*02/6214-5600*) or by checking the U.S. Diplomatic Mission's website at http://usembassy-australia.state.gov/consular.

British subjects can obtain up-to-date visa information by calling the **U.S. Embassy Visa Information Line** (© **0891/200-290**) or by visiting the "Visas to the U.S." section of the American Embassy London's website at www.us embassy.org.uk.

Irish citizens can obtain up-to-date visa information through the **Embassy of the USA Dublin,** 42 Elgin Rd., Dublin 4, Ireland (© **353/1-668-8777;** or by checking the "Consular Services" section of the website at http://dublin.us embassy.gov.

Citizens of **New Zealand** can obtain up-to-date visa information by contacting the **U.S. Embassy New Zealand,** 29 Fitzherbert Terrace, Thorndon, Wellington (© **644/472-2068**), or get the information directly from the website at http://wellington.usembassy.gov.

3

Suggested Oregon Itineraries

Where should I go? What should I see? What's the best route? How do I make the most of my limited vacation time? I know all these questions well. This chapter should help you answer them. I'm not going to get down to the nitty-gritty details, but I do mention the occasional not-to-be-missed or out-of-the-way restaurant or lodge.

If you read through all these itineraries, you'll notice a bit of overlap. Indeed, there are some destinations and attractions that just should not be missed on any visit to the state. For example, a trip to Oregon should include at least a day in Portland, and, to really get a feel for the state, you have to explore both the mountains and the coast.

1 Oregon in 1 Week

Oregon is a big state, so don't expect to see it all in a week's vacation. However, if your vision of Oregon includes everything from forests of towering trees to snow-capped volcanic peaks and waves crashing on rugged shores, you're in luck: You can take in all of these, plus plenty of the state's famous wineries and brewpubs, during a 7-day visit—if you're willing to drive quite a bit. The following 1-week itinerary will allow you to experience many of the state's highlights.

Day ❶: Portland ✸✸

Start your visit in Portland, Oregon's largest city and a model of livability. Head to Washington Park to visit the **Japanese Garden** (p. 100) and the **International Rose Test Garden** (p. 100). Hang out in a cafe, wine bar, or brewpub to find out how Portland relaxes. Ride the MAX or the Portland Streetcar (they're both free downtown) to visit some outlying neighborhoods. Wander around the Pearl District and stop by the **Saturday Market** (p. 97) if it happens to be the weekend. Stroll through **Tom McCall Waterfront Park** (p. 96) on the banks of the Willamette River, and then be sure to take a quick ride on the **Portland Aerial Tram.**

Day ❷: The Mount Hood Loop ✸✸✸

On your second day, head east from Portland through the Columbia River Gorge

and around Mount Hood. In the Gorge, drive the **Historic Columbia River Highway** (p. 239) and try to avoid straining your neck while gazing up at **Multnomah Falls** (p. 239) and the gorge's many other falls. Take a short hike on the Eagle Creek Trail. Have lunch in Hood River, a town that has become one of the world's premier windsurfing and kiteboarding spots. As you loop around snow-capped Mount Hood, Oregon's tallest peak, stop at the historic **Timberline Lodge** (p. 262). Go for a short hike through the wildflower meadows.

Day ❸: Astoria ✸✸

Next head west to the Oregon coast. Starting at the mouth of the Columbia River, you can explore **Astoria** (p. 166), a historic river port and home to the **Lewis and Clark National Historical Park**

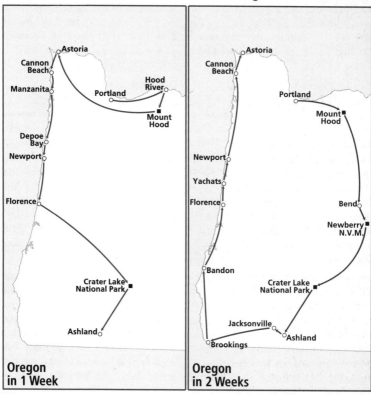

Oregon
in 1 Week

Oregon
in 2 Weeks

(p. 168). This town is still an active shipping and fishing port and has loads of character. Astoria's **Columbia River Maritime Museum** (p. 167) is one of the state's best museums. Don't miss it.

Day ❹: Cannon Beach to the Three Capes Scenic Loop ★★★

The next day, head south from Astoria to **Cannon Beach** (p. 176), the most charming town on the coast and home to the impressive **Haystack Rock.** Just north of town, visit the rugged beaches of **Ecola State Park** (p. 178) and south of town, stop at **Hug Point** and **Arcadia waysides** (p. 178) as well as **Oswald West State Park** (p. 178). At this latter park, a short trail leads to one of the prettiest beaches in the state. Longer trails lead up onto rugged headlands. South of here,

mellow out in **Manzanita** (p. 184) before continuing south to the **Three Capes Scenic Loop** (p. 188), which takes in Cape Meares, Cape Lookout, and Cape Kiwanda.

Day ❺: Newport ★★

Continue driving south, through miles of traffic congestion in Lincoln City, to **Depoe Bay** (p. 197), where you'll find not only the smallest natural harbor on the coast but also, south of town, the **Otter Crest Scenic Loop** (p. 198) and **Devil's Punchbowl State Natural Area** (p. 199). Continuing south you'll come to **Newport** (p. 200), my personal favorite of the coast's family-vacation destinations. The big attraction here is the **Oregon Coast Aquarium** (p. 201). On the **Newport Bayfront** (p. 203), you'll find both fish-packing plants and sou-venir shops. Here in Newport, you can also visit the **Yaquina Bay Lighthouse** (p. 202) and the **Yaquina Head Light-house** (p. 202).

Day ❻: Crater Lake National Park ⋆⋆⋆

Today is your longest drive, so get an early start and spend some time at **Cape Perpetua Scenic Area** (p. 208), **Heceta Head Lighthouse State Scenic View-point** (p. 210), and **Sea Lion Caves** (p. 210). Head inland at the historic river town of **Florence** (p. 212), perhaps after grabbing some lunch on that town's his-toric waterfront. Follow the beautiful

blue waters of the North Umpqua River from Roseburg to **Crater Lake National Park** (p. 271). If you reach the national park early enough, drive the scenic road that circles the lake.

Day ❼: Ashland ⋆⋆

This morning, take a **boat tour** (p. 272) on Crater Lake, and then head down out of the mountains to the town of **Ashland** (p. 278), which is the home of the **Ore-gon Shakespeare Festival** (p. 280). It runs from February to October and is the state's premier performing arts festival. Ashland has loads of great shops and restaurants. The next day either drive back to Portland or fly out of Medford.

2 Oregon in 2 Weeks

Plan on spending 2 weeks in Oregon and you'll get a much better sense of this state's diverse landscapes. You'll also get to spend more time exploring the great outdoors and taking interesting tours.

Days ❶ & ❷: Portland ⋆⋆

Start your Oregon vacation in Portland, where parks and gardens are the main attractions. Downtown, stroll through **Tom McCall Waterfront Park** (p. 96), ride the **Portland Aerial Tram** (p. 65), and visit the **Portland Classical Chinese Garden** (p. 97). In Washington Park, visit the **Japanese Garden** (p. 100) and the **International Rose Test Garden** (p. 100). If you're the outdoorsy type, go for a hike in **Forest Park** (p. 99) or pad-dle the Willamette River in a sea kayak (p. 106). Alternatively, do a jet-boat tour with **Willamette Jetboat Excursions** (p. 104). Go shopping in the Pearl Dis-trict or on Nob Hill, and check out the **Portland Art Museum** (p. 96). Spend some time in a brewpub, wine bar, or cafe.

Days ❸ & ❹: The Mount Hood Loop ⋆⋆⋆

Spend the next 2 days circling snow-cov-ered Mount Hood by way of the Colum-bia River Gorge. Drive the **Historic Columbia River Highway** (p. 239) and

stop at **Multnomah Falls** (p. 239) and other waterfalls. Hike the **Eagle Creek Trail** (p. 241), and then relax on a river cruise aboard the **Sternwheeler *Colum-bia Gorge*** (p. 242). As you loop around snow-capped Mount Hood, Oregon's tallest peak, stop in Hood River or at the historic **Timberline Lodge** (p. 262) for the night. Go for a hike, perhaps at **Cooper Spur** (p. 259), on the northwest side of Mount Hood.

Days ❺ & ❻: Bend ⋆⋆

From Mount Hood, head south into cen-tral Oregon's high desert and ponderosa-pine landscapes. This region gets more sunshine than the west side of the Cas-cades and consequently has several golf resorts. Near the town of Bend, you can explore the lava fields, cinder cones, and volcanic crater of **Newberry National Volcanic Monument** (p. 321); go **white-water rafting** (p. 324); and hike beneath the jagged peaks of the **Three Sisters** (p. 314). In winter, go skiing or snow-boarding at **Mount Bachelor** (p. 322).

Day ❼: Crater Lake National Park ⭐⭐⭐

Continue south from the Bend area to **Crater Lake National Park** (p. 271), which preserves the deepest lake in the United States. Drive the scenic road around the lake and take a **boat tour** (p. 272). Do one or two short hikes to high points along the rim of the caldera that forms this gorgeous blue lake. Stay at **Crater Lake Lodge** (p. 273).

Days ❽ & ❾: Ashland & Jacksonville ⭐⭐

If you're a fan of Shakespeare or the theater in general, you'll want to spend a couple of days in the hip retirement town of Ashland, where the **Oregon Shakespeare Festival** (p. 280) stages the Bard's works from February to October. Plenty of other playwrights also get equal time. When you aren't at the theater, shop the great boutiques, do a little wine touring, and eat out at the best restaurants in southern Oregon. Drive over to the historic town of Jacksonville, which is also home to the **Britt Festivals** (p. 291), a summer-long series that brings in great musicians and dance troupes.

Days ❿ & ⓫: The Southern Oregon Coast ⭐⭐⭐

From Ashland, head to the southern Oregon coast (the highway will take you briefly into the redwood country of northern California). The most scenic stretch of the coast is between Brookings and Gold Beach. Most of this area is preserved as the **Samuel H. Boardman State Scenic Corridor** (p. 232), which has lots of overlooks and also includes many stretches of the **Oregon Coast Trail** (p. 232). In Gold Beach, take a **jet-boat tour** (p. 231) up the Rogue River. Spend a night in **Bandon** (p. 223), where the beach is littered with monolithic haystack rocks.

Day ⓬: The Central Coast ⭐⭐⭐

North of Bandon, there is a trio of state parks—**Cape Arago, Sunset Bay,** and **Shore Acres** (p. 220)—that should not be missed. North of Coos Bay, you drive through the **Oregon Dunes National Recreation Area** (p. 213), where some sand dunes are 500 feet tall. There are lots of hiking trails through the Sahara-like landscape. Stop for lunch in the historic river town of **Florence** (p. 212). North of Florence, the mountains once again meet the sea. Stop at **Sea Lion Caves** (p. 210) and the picturesque **Heceta Head Lighthouse** (p. 210) before exploring the rugged shoreline of **Cape Perpetua Scenic Area** (p. 208). Stay in **Yachats** (p. 207).

Day ⓭: The Three Capes Loop ⭐⭐⭐

From Yachats, drive north to Newport and visit the **Oregon Coast Aquarium** (p. 201). Then work your way through the traffic congestion and sprawl of Lincoln City to reach the little fishing town of Pacific City and the start of the Three Capes Scenic Loop. Climb the giant sand dune at **Cape Kiwanda State Park** (p. 189), then drive north to **Cape Lookout State Park** (p. 189), and, if you have time, hike out to the end of the cape. The last stop on this loop is **Cape Meares State Park** (p. 188).

Day ⓮: Astoria ⭐⭐

Continue north, stopping in **Manzanita** (p. 184) and artsy **Cannon Beach** (p. 176) to see two of my favorite Oregon-coast towns. Also be sure to take the short hike to the beach at **Oswald West State Park** (p. 178). Finish your tour in **Astoria** (p. 166), a working port town with lots of grand old Victorian homes. Just outside of town, you'll find **Lewis and Clark National Historical Park** (p. 168), which commemorates the explorers who spent the winter of 1805–06 here at the mouth of the Columbia River. The next day, head back to Portland.

3 Oregon for Families

While Oregon doesn't have a major amusement park to attract families, it does have lots of great child-oriented museums in Portland, and there are several other children's attractions in nearby Salem. Plus, the state has loads of the great outdoors, including wild ocean beaches, a dormant volcano with snow-skiing all summer, and an extinct volcano that really blew its top.

Days ❶ & ❷: Portland 👧👧

Start your Oregon family vacation in Portland, where you and the kids have lots of options for fun activities. For example, you can spend a whole day in Washington Park. Here you'll find the **Oregon Zoo** (p. 100), the **World Forestry Center Discovery Museum** (p. 101), and the **Portland Children's Museum** (p. 103). The next day, head to the **Oregon Museum of Science and Industry** (p. 97), where you can watch an OMNIMAX movie, see a planetarium show, and explore a submarine. Afterwards, you can head out on the Willamette River on a high-speed **jetboat ride** (p. 104). If you've got young kids, don't miss a chance to eat at **Peanut Butter & Ellie's** (p. 85).

Days ❸, ❹ & ❺: The Northern Oregon Coast 👧👧

From Portland, head west to the coast. Although the waters on the Oregon coast are too cold for most adults, children don't seem to mind the chilly temperatures at all. However, you'll be better off buying some kites and spending your time on the beach rather than in the water. **Seaside** is the north coast's premier family beach town and is full of arcades, saltwater-taffy stores, and places where you can rent unusual cycles (beach trikes, four-wheel surreys, tandems). However, I recommend staying in Cannon Beach, a much prettier town. In Cannon Beach, you can explore the tide pools at the base of Haystack Rock, fly kites, and, as in Seaside, rent beach bikes. There are also several nearby state parks.

Day ❻: Salem 👧

After you've built enough sand castles, head back inland to the state capital of Salem, which has a great waterfront park that's home to **Salem's Riverfront Carousel** (p. 143), the fun **A. C. Gilbert Discovery Village** (p. 144), and the *Willamette Queen* (p. 142) paddle wheeler. A few miles south of town, you'll find **Enchanted Forest** and **Thrill-Ville USA** (p. 144), two more great children's attractions.

Day ❼: Crater Lake National Park 👧👧👧

Although it's a long drive from Salem to **Crater Lake National Park** (p. 271), you shouldn't miss the opportunity to visit this amazing natural attraction that was created when a large volcano blew its top. If your kids can hike a mile downhill (and back up), or if you don't mind carrying the little ones, be sure to take the boat ride around the lake.

Days ❽ & ❾: Bend & Sunriver 👧👧

Next, head north to central Oregon, which is the state's favorite sunshine destination. Here, near Bend and Sunriver, you'll find several resorts that are geared toward keeping families entertained. There are big swimming pools, bikes, and lots of scheduled activities for kids of all ages. The short **white-water rafting trips** (p. 311) on the Deschutes River just outside Bend are always a big hit with kids. The other must-visit attraction in the area is the **High Desert Museum** (p. 320), which is as much a zoo as it is a museum. You can also stop at **Newberry**

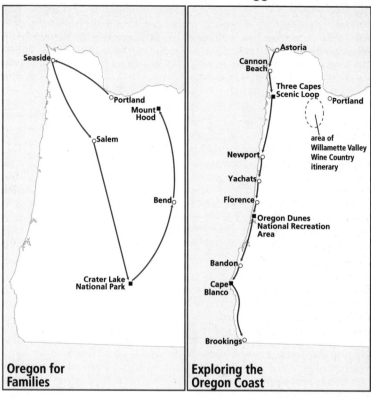

Oregon for Families

Exploring the Oregon Coast

National Volcanic Monument (p. 321) and the **Lava Lands Visitor Center** (p. 321).

Day ⑩: Mount Hood ★★★

Finally, head up to Mount Hood and try to stay at the historic **Timberline Lodge** (p. 262), where you just might bump into the lodge's St. Bernard mascot. In the winter, this is a popular family ski area; in summer, you can do a little summer skiing or snowboarding at **Timberline Ski Area** (p. 260), or check out all the fun rides and activities at the **Adventure Park at SkiBowl** (p. 260) in Government Camp. The trail to Mirror Lake is an easy hike that's popular with families.

4 A Week in the Willamette Valley Wine Country

Here's an itinerary for serious oenophiles. If the sleeper hit movie *Sideways* got you curious about pinot noir, then you definitely need to spend a week in wine country. Because there are so many wineries in Oregon's Willamette Valley, a week of wine tasting here can easily lead to your having a fabulous cellar full of Oregon wines.

Day ❶: Portland

Start your wine tour in Portland. Here you should spend some time at **Oregon Wines on Broadway** (p. 113), a combination wine bar and wine shop specializing in Oregon wines. On any given day, you can sample 30 different Oregon pinot noirs and get an idea of which wineries you might want to visit. If you plan your trip just right, you can also attend a wine-blending class at **Urban Wineworks** (p. 118).

Day ❷: Dundee & the Red Hills

From Portland, it is less than 45 minutes to the start of wine country. **August Cellars** (p. 126) and **Rex Hill Vineyards** (p. 127), just east of Newberg, are the first wineries you'll come to. A few miles farther on Ore. 99W, you'll come to Dundee, which is the heart of the wine country. The Red Hills north of town are covered with vineyards and there are numerous wineries within a few miles of town. **Dobbes Family Estate/Wine by Joe** (p. 126), **Lange Estate Winery & Vineyards** (p. 127) and **Torii Mor** (p. 127) are a couple of my favorite area wineries. Have dinner at one of Dundee's great restaurants.

Day ❸: West of Dundee

Today, explore the hills west of Dundee, where you'll find some of the most highly regarded pinot noir producers in the state. **Archery Summit** (p. 125), **Domaine Drouhin Oregon** (p. 126), and **Domaine Serene** (p. 126) should not be missed. Also in this area, you'll find **Sokol Blosser Winery** (p. 127). Don't pass up the opportunity to stop at some of the area's fruit stands. In the morning, you might want to do some

antiques shopping in Lafayette, stroll around downtown McMinnville, or visit the **Evergreen Aviation Museum** (p. 132), which is home to Howard Hughes's "Spruce Goose."

Days ❹ & ❺: Carlton 👉👉

The little town of Carlton is home to some of Oregon's best wineries and deserves a couple of days of wine tasting. You won't want to miss the **Carlton Winemakers Studio** (p. 128), **Cana's Feast Winery** (p. 128), **Penner-Ash Wine Cellars** (p. 129), **Soléna** (p. 129), **Tyrus Evan** (p. 129), and **Willakenzie Estate** (p. 129). Plan to have dinner at **Cuvée** (p. 139), Carlton's delightful little French restaurant; the next night, head to McMinnville for dinner.

Days ❻ & ❼: The Eola Hills & the West Valley 👉👉

South of McMinnville lie the Eola Hills and lots of good wineries. Be sure to visit **Amity Vineyards** (p. 131), one of the state's oldest wineries. Other wineries worth searching out include **Bethel Heights Vineyards** (p. 131), **St. Innocent Winery** (p. 132), **Kristin Hill Winery** (p. 131), **Cristom Vineyards** (p. 131), **Mystic** (p. 131), **Stangeland Vineyards** (p. 131), and **Witness Tree Vineyard** (p. 132). One morning, visit the interesting little **Jensen Arctic Museum** (p. 146) or drive in to Salem to the **Hallie Ford Museum of Art** (p. 142). The next morning, start out at the **Lawrence Gallery** (p. 134), which is next door to the **Oregon Wine Tasting Room** (p. 128). If you like chocolate, be sure to visit the **Brigittine Monastery** (p. 134) to buy some fudge.

5 Exploring the Oregon Coast

While inland Oregon has loads to offer visitors, it is the coast that is the state's crown jewel. To be sure, Oregon's beaches are not the lounge-chair and margarita beaches of Mexico and the Caribbean, but this coast is one of the most dramatic shorelines in America. Hiking, kite flying, and exploring tide pools are the top recreational activities on the Oregon coast, so come prepared for an active vacation.

Day ❶: Astoria ⪫⪫

Start your Oregon coast vacation by flying into Portland and driving down the Columbia River to Astoria. You will be following the route of explorers Lewis and Clark, who spent the winter of 1805–06 near present-day Astoria. Visit the **Lewis and Clark National Historical Park** (p. 168), then head to **Fort Stevens State Park** (p. 169) at the mouth of the Columbia River. Also visit the **Columbia River Maritime Museum** (p. 167).

Day ❷: Cannon Beach ⪫⪫

Head south down the coast to the arts community of **Cannon Beach** (p. 176), which lies on the south side of Tillamook Head. Check out all the art galleries, and marvel at the massive **Haystack Rock,** which rises up from the beach in the middle of town. Just north of Cannon Beach, you can hike the trails of **Ecola State Park** (p. 178). To escape the crowds, head south of town to **Arcadia** or **Hug Point wayside** (p. 178) or the larger **Oswald West State Park** (p. 178).

Day ❸: The Three Capes Scenic Loop ⪫⪫⪫

Drive around Tillamook Bay to the **Three Capes Scenic Loop.** The first cape you'll come to on this drive is **Cape Meares State Scenic Viewpoint** (p. 188), which is a good place from which to spot gray whales. Further south is **Cape Lookout State Park** (p. 189), where there is a trail through the forest to the end of the cape. The southernmost of the three capes is **Cape Kiwanda State Natural Area** (p. 189), where a giant sand dune rises up from the beach and the huge Haystack Rock (yes, it has the same name as the one in Cannon Beach) rises just offshore. Here at Cape Kiwanda you'll find a great hotel and brewpub.

Days ❹ & ❺: Newport & Yachats ⪫⪫⪫

Continue south through the sprawl and congestion of Lincoln City to Newport. En route, be sure to drive the **Otter Crest Scenic Loop** (p. 198), just north of Depoe Bay, and stop to marvel at the **Devil's Punchbowl** (p. 199). Newport's main attraction is the not-to-be-missed **Oregon Coast Aquarium** (p. 201). Outside of town, you can also visit **Yaquina Bay Lighthouse** (p. 202) and the **Yaquina Head Lighthouse** (p. 202). South of Newport 24 miles is Yachats, one of the prettiest stretches of the central coast. Hike the rocky shoreline here, and visit **Cape Perpetua Scenic Area** (p. 208), **Heceta Head Lighthouse** (p. 210), and **Sea Lion Caves** (p. 210).

Days ❻ & ❼: Oregon Dunes National Recreation Area to Bandon ⪫⪫⪫

South of Cape Perpetua, you leave the mountains behind and drive through 50 miles of forests, lakes, and giant sand dunes that have been preserved as the **Oregon Dunes National Recreation Area** (p. 213). Stop for lunch in historic **Florence** (p. 212), then continue on to visit **Sunset Bay, Shore Acres,** and **Cape Arago state parks** (p. 220) outside Coos Bay. Finish the day amid the dramatic boulders and haystack rocks that litter the beach at **Bandon** (p. 223).

Days ❽ & ❾: The Southern Oregon Coast ✹✹✹

This is the most remote and least developed section of the coast, and it has numerous state parks and waysides. Wander the headlands at **Cape Blanco** (p. 229) and **Cape Sebastian** (p. 232). Explore the beach and Battle Rock in **Port Orford** (p. 229). In Gold Beach, take a **jet-boat tour** (p. 231) up the wild Rogue River. South of Gold Beach, stop to marvel at the monoliths at **Pistol River State Scenic Viewpoint** (p. 232) and hike segments of the Oregon Coast Trail within the **Samuel H. Boardman State Scenic Corridor** (p. 232). From Brookings, drive back north and then west to reach I-5, which is the fastest route back to Portland.

4

Portland

Situated at the confluence of the Willamette and Columbia rivers, Portland, Oregon, with a metropolitan population of roughly two million, is a city of discreet charms. That it claims a rose garden as one of its biggest attractions should give you an idea of just how laid-back this city is. Sure, Portlanders are just as attached to their cellphones and laptops as residents of other urban areas, but this is the City of Roses, and people still take time to stop and smell the flowers. Spend much time here, and you, too, will likely feel the leisurely pace seeping into your bones.

While nearby Seattle, Washington, has zoomed into the national consciousness, Portland has, until recently, managed to dodge the limelight and the problems that come with skyrocketing popularity. For many years now Portland has looked upon itself as a small, accessible city, vaguely European in character. *Clean* and *friendly* are the two most common descriptors of the city. However, as word has spread about overcrowding in Seattle, people looking for the good life and affordable housing have turned to Portland, which is now experiencing the same sort of rapid growth that Seattle began going through more than a decade ago.

Portland does not have any major tourist sights. Instead, it is a city of quiet charms that must be searched for and savored—the shade of the stately elms in the South Park Blocks, the tranquillity of the Japanese Garden, the view from the

grounds of Pittock Mansion, the miles of hiking trails in Forest Park. Sure, there's a good art museum and a world-class science museum, but these are not nearly as important to the locals as the many parks and public gardens. Not only does Portland claim beautiful rose gardens, the most authentic Japanese Garden in North America, and the largest classical Chinese garden in the country, but it also has the world's smallest city park and one of the largest forested urban parks in the country.

The city is also the nation's microbrew capital. Espresso may be the beverage that gets this town going in the morning, but it is microbrewed beer that helps the city maintain its mellow character. There are so many brewpubs here in Portland that the city has been nicknamed Munich on the Willamette. Wine bars are also popular hangouts, which shouldn't come as a surprise, considering how close the city is to the Willamette Valley wine country.

Portland itself may be short on things for visitors to do, but the city's surroundings certainly are not. Within a 1½- to 2-hour drive from Portland, you can be strolling a Pacific Ocean beach, walking beside a waterfall in the Columbia Gorge, hiking on Mount Hood (a dormant volcano as picture perfect as Mt. Fuji), driving through the Mount St. Helens blast zone, or sampling world-class pinot noirs in the Oregon wine country. It is this proximity to the outdoors that makes Portland a great city to use as a base for exploring some of the best of the Northwest.

1 Orientation

ARRIVING

BY PLANE

Portland International Airport (**PDX;** *C* **877/739-4636** or 503/460-4234; www. flypdx.com) is located 10 miles northeast of downtown Portland, adjacent to the Columbia River. There's an information booth by the baggage-claim area where you can pick up maps and brochures and find out about transportation into the city. Many hotels near the airport provide courtesy shuttle service to and from the airport; be sure to ask when you make a reservation.

GETTING INTO THE CITY BY CAR   If you've rented a car at the airport and want to reach central Portland, follow signs for downtown. These signs will point you first to I-205 and then I-84 west, which brings you to the Willamette River. Take the Morrison Bridge exit to cross the river. The trip takes about 20 minutes and is entirely on interstates. For more information on renting a car, see section 2 of this chapter, "Getting Around," below.

GETTING INTO THE CITY BY TAXI, SHUTTLE, BUS, OR LIGHT RAIL   If you haven't rented a car at the airport, the best way to get into town is to take the **Airport MAX (Red Line)** light-rail line. The MAX operates daily roughly every 15 minutes between 5am and midnight and the trip from the airport to Pioneer Courthouse Square in downtown Portland takes approximately 35 minutes. (All but one or two of the downtown hotels lie within 4 or 5 blocks of the square; plan on walking since taxis in Portland don't generally cruise for fares. Folks arriving with a lot of luggage will be better off taking a cab or shuttle van from the airport.) The adult fare is $2.05. For information on this service, contact **TriMet** (*C* **503/238-7433;** www.trimet.org).

A taxi to downtown generally costs between $30 and $35.

BY TRAIN OR BUS

Amtrak trains stop at the historic **Union Station,** 800 NW Sixth Ave. (*C* **800/872-7245** or 503/273-4860; www.amtrak.com), about 10 blocks from the heart of downtown Portland. Taxis are usually waiting to meet trains and can take you to your hotel. Alternatively, you might be able to get your hotel to send a van to pick you up, or, if you are renting a car from a downtown car-rental office, the agency will usually pick you up at the station. Until the new MAX line begins running past Union Station some time in 2009, you can catch a public bus a block south of the station (toward downtown). Buses are free within the downtown area.

The **Greyhound Bus Lines** station is at 550 NW Sixth Ave. (*C* **800/231-2222** or 503/243-2310; www.greyhound.com), on the north side of downtown near Union Station. As with getting into downtown from the train station, there is no charge to ride any public city bus if you catch it outside the Greyhound terminal, which is within Portland's Fareless Square area (see below). Sometime in 2009, you'll be able to hop on the MAX light rail outside the bus station.

Although you could easily walk from the station into the heart of downtown, you have to pass through a somewhat rough neighborhood for a few blocks. Although this area is currently undergoing a renaissance and is not nearly as bad as it once was, I don't recommend walking, especially after dark.

VISITOR INFORMATION

Travel Portland, 701 SW Sixth Ave. (© **877/678-5263** or 503/275-8355; www.travel portland.com), is in Pioneer Courthouse Square in downtown Portland. There's also an information booth by the baggage-claim area at the Portland Airport.

CITY LAYOUT

Portland is in northwestern Oregon at the confluence of the Columbia and Willamette rivers. To the west are the West Hills, which rise to more than 1,000 feet. Some 90 miles west of the city are the spectacular Oregon coast and the Pacific Ocean. To the east are rolling hills that extend to the Cascade Range, about 50 miles away. The most prominent peak in this section of the Cascades is Mount Hood (11,235 ft.), a dormant volcanic peak that looms over the city on clear days. From many parts of Portland it's also possible to see Mount St. Helens, a volcano that erupted violently in 1980.

With about two million people in the entire metropolitan area, Portland remains a relatively small city. This is especially evident when you begin to explore the compact downtown area. Nearly everything is accessible on foot, and the city does everything it can to encourage walking and using public transit.

MAIN ARTERIES & STREETS   I-84 (**Banfield Fwy.** or **Expwy.**) enters Portland from the east. East of the city is **I-205,** which bypasses downtown Portland and runs past the airport. **I-5** runs through on a north–south axis, passing along the east bank of the Willamette River directly across from downtown. **I-405** circles around the west and south sides of downtown. **U.S. 26 (Sunset Hwy.)** leaves downtown heading west toward Beaverton and the coast. **Oregon Highway 217** runs south from U.S. 26 in Beaverton.

The most important artery within Portland is **Burnside Street.** This is the dividing line between north and south Portland. Dividing the city from east to west is the **Willamette River,** which is crossed by eight bridges in the downtown area. From north to south these bridges are the Fremont, Broadway, Steel, Burnside, Morrison, Hawthorne, Marquam, and Ross Island. Additional bridges beyond the downtown area include the Sellwood Bridge, located between downtown and Lake Oswego, and the St. John's Bridge, which connects Northwest Portland with north Portland.

For the sake of convenience, we have defined downtown Portland as the 300-block area within the **Fareless Square.** This is the area (shaded in on the maps on p. 69 and p. 93) in which you can ride for free on the city's public buses, the MAX light-rail system, and the Portland Streetcar. In downtown, the Fareless Square is bounded by I-405 on the west and south, by Irving Street on the north, and by the Willamette River on the east. A Fareless Square extension also allows transit riders to travel free between downtown Portland and both the Oregon Convention Center and Lloyd Center Mall. There is no charge to ride either the MAX light-rail trolleys or any of the buses that connect downtown with the Rose Quarter and Lloyd District across the Willamette River in northeast Portland.

FINDING AN ADDRESS   Finding an address in Portland can be easy. Almost all addresses in Portland, and for miles beyond, include a map quadrant—NE (northeast), SW (southwest), and so forth. The dividing line between east and west is the Willamette River; between north and south it's Burnside Street. Any downtown address will be labeled either SW (southwest) or NW (northwest). An exception to this rule is the area known as North Portland, which is the area across the Willamette River from downtown going toward the Columbia River and Vancouver, Washington.

Fun Fact **Did You Know?**

- The flasher in the famous "Expose Yourself to Art" poster is none other than Bud Clark, the former mayor of Portland.
- Portland is the only city in the United States with an extinct volcano within the city limits (Mount Tabor).
- Matt Groening, creator of *The Simpsons,* got his start in Portland.
- More Asian elephants have been born in Portland (at the Oregon Zoo) than in any other city in North America.
- Twenty downtown water fountains were a gift to the city from teetotaling early-20th-century timber baron Simon Benson, who wanted his mill workers to have something other than alcohol to drink during the day.

Streets here have a plain "North" designation. Also, Burnside Street is designated either "East" or "West."

Avenues run north–south and streets run east–west. Street names are the same on both sides of the Willamette River. Consequently, there is a SW Yamhill Street and a SE Yamhill Street. In Northwest Portland, street names are alphabetical going north from Burnside to Wilson. Naito Parkway is the street nearest the Willamette River on the west side, and Water Avenue is the nearest on the east side. Beyond these are numbered avenues. On the west side you'll also find Broadway and Park Avenue between Sixth Avenue and Ninth Avenue. With each block, the addresses increase by 100, beginning at the Willamette River for avenues and at Burnside Street for streets. Odd numbers are generally on the west and north sides of the street, and even numbers on the east and south sides.

Here's an example: You want to go to 1327 SW Ninth Ave. Because it's in the 1300 block, you'll find it 13 blocks south of Burnside and, because it's an odd number, on the west side of the street.

STREET MAPS   Stop by **Travel Portland,** 701 SW Sixth Ave., Suite 1 (© **877/ 678-5263** or 503/275-8355; www.travelportland.com), in Pioneer Courthouse Square in downtown Portland for a free map of the city.

Powell's City of Books, 1005 W. Burnside St. (© **800/878-7323** or 503/228-4651), has an excellent free map of downtown that includes a walking-tour route and information on many of the sights you'll pass along the way.

Members of the **American Automobile Association (AAA)** can get a free map of the city at the AAA offices at 600 SW Market St. (© **503/222-6734;** www. aaaorid.com).

THE NEIGHBORHOODS IN BRIEF

Portland's neighborhoods are mostly dictated by geography. The Willamette River forms a natural dividing line between the eastern and western portions of the city, while the Columbia River forms a boundary with the state of Washington on the north. The West Hills, comprising Portland's prime residential neighborhoods, are a beautiful backdrop for this attractive city. Covered in evergreens, the hills rise to a height of 1,000 feet at the edge of downtown. Within these hills are the Oregon Zoo, the International Rose Test Garden, the Japanese Garden, and several other attractions.

For a map of Portland neighborhoods, turn to the "Portland Attractions" map on p. 93.

Downtown This term usually refers to the business and shopping district south of Burnside and north of Jackson Street between the Willamette River and 13th Avenue. Here you'll find a dozen or more high-end hotels, dozens of restaurants of all types, and loads of shopping. Within downtown's **Cultural District** (along Broadway and the South Park blocks), are most of the city's performing arts venues and a couple of museums.

Skidmore Historic District Also known as Old Town, this is Portland's original commercial core and centers around SW Ankeny Street and SW First Avenue. Many of the restored buildings have become retail stores, but despite the presence of the **Saturday Market,** the neighborhood has never become a popular shopping district, mostly because of its welfare hotels, missions, street people, and drug dealing. However, with its many clubs and bars, it is the city's main nightlife district. The neighborhood is safe during the day, but visitors should exercise caution at night.

Chinatown Portland has had a Chinatown almost since its earliest days. This small area, with its numerous Chinese groceries and restaurants, is wedged between the Pearl District and the Skidmore Historic District and is entered through the colorful Chinatown Gate at West Burnside Street and Fourth Avenue. The neighborhood's main attraction is the impressive **Portland Classical Chinese Garden.** Because of its proximity to bars on West Burnside Street and the homeless missions and welfare hotels in Old Town, this is not a good neighborhood to explore late at night. However, it has been undergoing something of a renaissance in recent years.

The Pearl District This neighborhood of galleries, residential and business

lofts, cafes, breweries, and shops is bounded by the North Park blocks, Overton Street, I-405, and Burnside Street. Crowds of people come here on **First Thursday** (the first Thurs of every month) when art galleries and other businesses are open late. This is Portland's hip urban loft scene and one of the city's main upscale-restaurant neighborhoods.

Northwest/Nob Hill Located along NW 23rd and NW 21st avenues, this is one of Portland's two most fashionable neighborhoods. Here you'll find many of the city's best restaurants (mostly along NW 21st Ave.), as well as lots of cafes, boutiques, and national chain stores. Surrounding the two main business streets of the neighborhood are blocks of restored Victorian homes on shady tree-lined streets.

South Waterfront This is the newest neighborhood in Portland and is a collection of high-rise offices and condominiums a half mile south of Tom McCall Waterfront Park. The South Waterfront is where you'll find the lower terminal for the Portland Aerial Tram.

Irvington Though neither as attractive nor as large as the Northwest/Nob Hill neighborhood, Irvington, centered around Broadway in northeast Portland, is almost as hip. For several blocks along Broadway (around NE 15th Ave.) you'll find interesting boutiques and numerous good, inexpensive restaurants.

Hawthorne District This enclave of southeast Portland is full of eclectic boutiques, moderately priced restaurants, and hip college students from nearby **Reed College.** Just south of Hawthorne Boulevard, beginning at SE 12th Avenue, you'll find the interesting **Ladd's Addition** neighborhood, which has five rose gardens and a great pastry shop. Belmont Street, just north of Hawthorne Boulevard, and Division Street, to the south, are two of the city's up-and-coming hip neighborhoods, and both areas are well worth exploring.

Sellwood/Westmoreland Situated in southeast Portland, this is the city's antiques district and contains many restored Victorian houses. Just north of the Sellwood antiques district, surrounding the intersection of SE Milwaukie Avenue and SE Bybee Boulevard, you'll find the heart of the Eastmoreland neighborhood, home to numerous good restaurants.

2 Getting Around

BY PUBLIC TRANSPORTATION

FREE RIDES Portland is committed to keeping its downtown uncongested, and to this end has invested heavily in its public transportation system. The single greatest innovation—as well as the best reason to ride the TriMet public buses, the MAX light-rail system, and the Portland Streetcar—is that they're free within an area known as the **Fareless Square.** That's right, free!

There are 300 blocks of downtown included in the Fareless Square, and as long as you stay within the boundaries, you don't pay a cent. The Fareless Square covers the area between I-405 on the south and west, Hoyt Street on the north, and the Willamette River on the east. The Fareless Square extension also makes it possible to take public transit (either the bus or the MAX light-rail trolley) between downtown Portland and both the Rose Quarter (site of the Oregon Convention Center) and the Lloyd District (site of the Lloyd Center Mall), which are both across the Willamette River in northeast Portland.

BY BUS TriMet buses operate daily over an extensive network. You can pick up the *TriMet Schedule Book,* which lists all the bus routes with times, or individual route maps and time schedules, at the **TriMet Ticket Office,** behind and beneath the waterfall fountain at Pioneer Courthouse Square (© 503/238-7433; www.trimet.org). The office is open Monday through Friday from 8:30am to 5:30pm. Bus and MAX passes and transit information are also available at area Fred Meyer, Safeway, and most Albertsons grocery stores. Due to construction of new light rail lines on the Portland Mall (Transit Mall) along Fifth and Sixth avenues, buses now stop on Third and Fourth avenues and will continue to do so through at least spring 2009.

Outside the Fareless Square, adult fares on TriMet buses, MAX light-rail trains, and Portland Streetcars are $1.75 or $2.05, depending on how far you travel. Seniors 65 years and older pay 85¢ with valid proof of age; children 7 through 17 pay $1.40. You can also make free transfers between the bus and both the MAX light-rail system and the Portland Streetcar. All-day tickets costing $4.25 are good for travel to all zones and are valid on buses, MAX, and streetcars. These tickets can be purchased from any bus driver, at MAX stops, and on board Portland Streetcars.

BY LIGHT RAIL The **Metropolitan Area Express (MAX)** is Portland's aboveground light-rail system that connects downtown Portland with the airport, the eastern suburb of Gresham, the western suburbs of Beaverton and Hillsboro, and North Portland. MAX is basically a modern trolley, but there are also replicas of vintage trolley cars (© 503/323-7363). Between March and December these operate between downtown Portland and the Lloyd Center on Sundays from noon to 6:30pm. One of the most convenient places to catch the MAX is at Pioneer Courthouse Square. The MAX light-rail system crosses the Transit Mall on SW Morrison Street and SW Yamhill Street. Transfers to the bus are free.

As with the bus, MAX is free within the Fareless Square, which includes all the downtown area. A Fareless Square extension also makes it possible to ride the MAX between downtown Portland and both the Rose Quarter (site of the Oregon Convention Center) and the Lloyd District (site of the Lloyd Center Mall). Both are across the Willamette River in northeast Portland. If you are traveling outside of the Fareless Square, be sure to buy your ticket and stamp it in the time-punch machine on the platform before you board MAX. There are ticket-vending machines at all MAX stops that tell you how much to pay for your destination; these machines also give change. The MAX driver cannot sell tickets. Fares are the same as on buses. There are ticket inspectors who randomly check to make sure passengers have stamped tickets.

The **Portland Streetcar** (© 503/238-RIDE; www.portlandstreetcar.org) operates from the new South Waterfront District (site of the Portland Aerial Tram) south of downtown, through Portland State University, downtown, and the Pearl District to Northwest Portland. The route takes in not only the attractions of the Cultural District but also all the restaurants and great shopping in the Pearl District and along NW 21st and 23rd avenues, which makes this streetcar a great way for visitors to get from downtown (where most of the hotels are located) to the neighborhoods with the greatest concentrations of restaurants. Streetcar fares for trips outside the Fareless Square are $1.75 for adults, $1.40 for youths, and 85¢ for seniors. Note that these fares are valid all day, so once you've paid your fare, you won't have to buy another ticket all day.

Hospitals aren't usually considered tourist destinations, but in Portland's case, one medical center, the Oregon Health & Sciences University Hospital has become something of an accidental destination. The hillside hospital is connected to the newly developed South Waterfront District by the **Portland Aerial Tram** (www.portland tram.org), and this tram has become a popular Portland excursion. There may not be much to do once you get to the hospital, but the ride up and back sure is fun and provides great views over the city. The tram's silvery, egg-shaped gondolas operate Monday through Friday from 6am to 1pm and Saturday from 9am to 5pm, with departures every 5 minutes. The round-trip fare is $4 and children under 6 ride free. You'll find the lower terminal on SW Bond Street, ½ mile south of downtown. The Portland Streetcar stops at the tram station.

BY CAR

CAR RENTALS Portland is a compact city, and public transit will get you to most attractions within its limits. However, if you are planning to explore outside the city—and Portland's greatest attractions, such as Mount Hood and the Columbia River Gorge, lie not in the city itself but in the countryside within an hour's drive—you'll definitely need a car.

The major car-rental companies are all represented in Portland and have desks at Portland International Airport, which is the most convenient place to pick up a car. There are also many independent and small car-rental agencies listed in the Portland Yellow Pages. Weekly rates for an economy car in July (high-season rates) can run from $175 to $300 (with no discounts), so it really pays to shop around. Expect lower rates in the rainy months.

On the ground floor of the airport parking deck, across the street from the baggage-claim area, you'll find the following companies: **Avis** (© 800/331-1212 or 503/249-4950; www.avis.com), **Budget** (© 800/527-0700 or 503/249-6331; www.budget.com), **Dollar** (© 800/800-3365 or 503/249-4792; www.dollar.com), **Enterprise** (© 800/261-7331 or 503/252-1500; www.enterprise.com); and **Hertz** (© 800/654-3131 or 503/528-7900; www.hertz.com). Outside the airport, but with desks adjacent to the other car-rental desks, are **Alamo** (© 800/462-5266 or 503/249-4900; www.goalamo.com), **National** (© 800/227-7368 or 503/249-4900; www.nationalcar.com), and **Thrifty** (© 800/847-4389 or 503/254-6563; www.thrifty.com).

PARKING   Throughout most of downtown Portland and the Pearl District, you won't find any parking meters on the streets. However, in the middle of every block, you will find an electronic parking meter that takes coins, credit cards, and debit cards. These machines issue little parking receipts that you then have to tape in the curbside window of your car. Although a bit inconvenient, this system allows you to buy time while parked in one space and still use your remaining time if you move your car to another space. In most parts of town, you don't have to feed the meters after 7pm or on Sunday.

The best parking deal in town is at the **Smart Park** garages, where the cost is $1.25 per hour for the first 4 hours (but after that the hourly rate jumps to $3, so you'd be well advised to move your car), $2 to $6 for the entire evening after 6pm, or $4 to $5 all day on the weekends. Look for the red, white, and black signs featuring the image of a smart parking attendant. You'll find Smart Park garages at First Avenue and Jefferson Street, Fourth Avenue and Yamhill Street, 10th Avenue and Yamhill Street, Third Avenue and Alder Street, O'Bryant Square, Naito Parkway and Davis Street, and Station Place (in the Pearl District near Union Station). Hundreds of downtown merchants validate Smart Park tickets for 2 hours if you spend at least $25, so don't forget to take your ticket along with you.

SPECIAL DRIVING RULES   You may turn right on a red light after a full stop, and if you are in the far left lane of a one-way street, you may turn left into the adjacent left lane of a one-way street at a red light after a full stop. Everyone in a moving vehicle is required to wear a seat belt.

BY TAXI

Because most everything in Portland is fairly close, getting around by taxi can be economical. Although there are almost always taxis waiting in line at major hotels, you won't find them cruising the streets—you'll have to phone for one. **Broadway Cab** (© **503/227-1234;** www.broadwaycab.com) and **Radio Cab** (© **503/227-1212;** www.radiocab.net) charge $2.50 for the first mile, $2.20 for each additional mile, and $1 for additional passengers.

ON FOOT

City blocks in Portland are about half the size of most city blocks elsewhere, and the entire downtown area covers only about 13 blocks by 26 blocks. This makes Portland a very easy place to explore on foot. The city has been very active in encouraging people to get out of their cars and onto the sidewalks downtown. The sidewalks are wide and there are many fountains, works of art, and small parks with benches.

FAST FACTS: Portland

AAA The **American Automobile Association** (℡ 800/452-1643; www.aaaorid. com) has a Portland office at 600 SW Market St. (℡ 503/222-6734), which offers free city maps to members.

Airport See "Getting There" in chapter 2, and "Arriving," earlier in this chapter.

Area Codes The Portland metro area has two area codes—503 and 971—and it is necessary to dial all 10 digits of a telephone number, even when making local calls.

Babysitters If your hotel doesn't offer babysitting services, call **Northwest Nannies** (℡ 503/245-5288; www.nwnanny.com).

Car Rentals See "Getting Around," earlier in this chapter.

Climate See "When to Go," in chapter 2.

Dentist Contact the **Multnomah Dental Society** (℡ 503/513-5010; www. multnomahdental.org) for a referral.

Doctor If you need a physician referral while in Portland, contact the **Legacy Referral Service** (℡ 503/335-3500; www.legacyhealth.org).

Emergencies For police, fire, or medical emergencies, phone ℡ 911.

Eyeglass Repair Check out **Binyon's,** 803 SW Morrison St. (℡ 503/226-6688).

Hospitals Three conveniently located area hospitals are **Legacy Good Samaritan,** 1015 NW 22nd Ave. (℡ 503/413-7711; www.legacyhealth.org); **Providence Portland Medical Center,** 4805 NE Glisan St. (℡ 503/215-1111; www.providence. org); and the **Oregon Health & Sciences University Hospital,** 3181 SW Sam Jackson Park Rd. (℡ 503/494-8311; www.ohsu.edu), which is just southwest of the city center and has a walk-in clinic.

Information See "Visitor Information," earlier in this chapter.

Internet Access If you need to check e-mail while you're in Portland, first check with your hotel, or, if you have your own laptop with a wireless card, find a cafe with Wi-Fi access. Otherwise, visit a **FedEx Kinko's.** There's one downtown at 221 SW Alder St. (℡ 503/224-6550; fedex.kinkos.com), and northwest at 950 NW 23rd Ave. (℡ 503/222-4133). You can also try the **Multnomah County Library,** 801 SW 10th Ave. (℡ 503/988-5123), which is Portland's main library and offers online services.

Maps See "City Layout," earlier in this chapter.

Newspapers & Magazines Portland's morning daily newspaper is *The Oregonian.* For arts and entertainment information and listings, consult the "A&E" section of the Friday *Oregonian* or pick up a free copy of *Willamette Week* at Powell's Books and other bookstores, convenience stores, cafes, and sidewalk newspaper boxes.

Pharmacies Convenient to most downtown hotels, **Central Drug,** 538 SW Fourth Ave. (℡ 503/226-2222; www.centraldrugportland.com), is open Monday through Friday from 9am to 6pm, Saturday from 10am to 4pm.

Photographic Needs **Camera World,** 400 SW Sixth Ave. (℡ 503/205-5900), is the largest camera and video store in the city.

Police To reach the police, call ℂ **911.**

Post Offices The most convenient downtown post office is University Station, 1505 SW Sixth Ave. (ℂ **800/ASK-USPS** or 503/274-1362; www.usps.com), open Monday through Friday from 7am to 6pm, Saturday from 10am to 3pm.

Restrooms There are public restrooms underneath Starbucks coffee shop in Pioneer Courthouse Square, in downtown shopping malls, and in hotel lobbies.

Safety Because of its small size and progressive emphasis on keeping the downtown alive and growing, Portland is still a relatively safe city. Take extra precautions, however, if you venture into the entertainment district along West Burnside Street and in Chinatown at night. If you plan to go hiking in Forest Park, don't leave anything valuable in your car. This holds true in the Skidmore Historic District (Old Town) as well.

Smoking Although many of the restaurants listed in this book are smoke-free, many Portland restaurants still allow smoking. That is all scheduled to change in 2009 when an indoor smoking ban goes into effect. Until then, at most high-end restaurants that do allow smoking, the smoking area is usually in the bar/lounge. There are a few nonsmoking bars in Portland; you can find a list on www.barflymag.com.

Taxes Portland is a shopper's paradise—there's no sales tax. However, there is a 12.5% tax on hotel rooms within the city and a 12.5% tax on car rentals (plus an additional airport-use fee if you pick up your rental car at the airport; this additional fee is anywhere from around 10% to around 16%). Outside the city, the room tax varies.

Taxis See "Getting Around," earlier in this chapter.

Time Zone Portland is on Pacific time, 3 hours behind the East Coast. In the summer, daylight saving time is observed and clocks are set forward 1 hour.

Transit Info For bus, MAX, and Portland Streetcar information, call the **TriMet Customer Assistance Office** (ℂ **503/238-7433**).

Weather If it's summer, it's sunny; otherwise, there's a chance of rain. This rule of thumb almost always suffices, but for specifics, call the Portland Oregon Visitor Association's **weather information hot line** (ℂ **503/275-9792**). If you want to know how to pack before you arrive, check **www.cnn.com/weather** or **www.weather.com**.

3 Where to Stay

Whether you're looking for a downtown corporate high-rise, a restored historic hotel, a hip boutique hotel, a romantic B&B, or just something relatively inexpensive, you'll find it in Portland. You even have a couple of good choices for riverfront hotels.

If your budget won't allow for a first-class downtown business hotel, try near the airport or elsewhere on the outskirts of the city (Troutdale and Gresham on the east side; Beaverton and Hillsboro on the west; Wilsonville and Lake Oswego in the south; and Vancouver, Washington, in the north), where you're more likely to find inexpensive to moderately priced motels.

Portland Accommodations

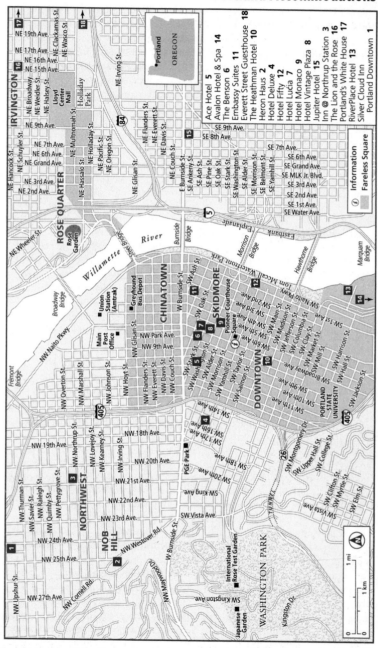

Ace Hotel **5**
Avalon Hotel & Spa **14**
The Benson **6**
Embassy Suites **11**
Everett Street Guesthouse **18**
The Heathman Hotel **10**
Heron Haus **2**
Hotel Deluxe **4**
Hotel Lucia **7**
Hotel Fifty **12**
Hotel Monaco **9**
Hotel Vintage Plaza **8**
Jupiter Hotel **15**
Inn @ Northrup Station **3**
The Lion and the Rose **16**
Portland's White House **17**
RiverPlace Hotel **13**
Silver Cloud Inn **13**
Portland Downtown **1**

ⓘ Information

Fareless Square

You'll find the greatest concentration of bed-and-breakfasts in the Irvington neighborhood of northeast Portland. This area is close to downtown and is generally quite convenient even if you are here on business.

In the following listings, price categories are based on the rate for a double room in high season. (Most hotels charge the same for a single or double room.) Keep in mind that the rates listed do not include local room taxes, which vary between 7% and 12.5%.

For comparison purposes, we list what hotels call "rack rates," or walk-in rates—but you should never have to pay these highly inflated prices. Various discounts (AAA, senior, corporate, and Entertainment Book) often reduce these rates, so be sure to ask (and check each hotel's website for Internet specials). In fact, you can often get a discounted corporate rate simply by flashing a business card (your own, that is). At inexpensive chain motels, there are almost always discounted rates for AAA members and seniors.

You'll also find that room rates are almost always considerably lower October through April (the rainy season), and large downtown hotels often offer weekend discounts of up to 50% throughout the year. Some of the large, upscale hotel chains have now gone to an airline-type rate system based on occupancy, so if you call early enough, before a hotel books up, you might get a really good rate. On the other hand, call at the last minute and you might catch a cancellation and still be offered a low rate. However, it's always advisable to make reservations as far in advance as possible if you're planning to visit during the busy summer months. Also be sure to ask about special packages (romance, golf, or theater), which most of the more expensive hotels usually offer.

Most hotels offer nonsmoking rooms, and most bed-and-breakfasts are exclusively nonsmoking. The majority of hotels also offer wheelchair-accessible rooms.

HELPING HANDS

If you're having trouble booking a room, try **Travel Portland,** 701 SW Sixth Ave., Portland, OR 97205 (② **877/678-5263** or 503/275-8355; www.travelportland.com), which offers a reservation service for the Portland metro area.

For information on **bed-and-breakfasts** in the Portland area, call the POVA or contact the **Oregon Bed and Breakfast Guild** (② **800/944-6196;** www.obbg.org).

DOWNTOWN
EXPENSIVE

Avalon Hotel & Spa ⭐⭐⭐   This hotel sits right on the banks of the Willamette River a mile south of downtown and half a mile south of the new South Waterfront District. Although this location is a bit inconvenient for exploring the city on foot, there is a riverside bike path right in front of the hotel, making this a good bet if you're a jogger or like to take leisurely walks. The Avalon's contemporary decor makes it one of the most stylish hotels in the city, and the riverfront rooms, most of which have balconies, provide good views and a chance to breathe in some fresh air. The hotel's stylish restaurant boasts the same great river views and walls of glass to make the most of the setting. A full-service spa gives this luxurious boutique hotel the feel of a much larger resort.

0455 SW Hamilton Court, Portland, OR 97239. ② **888/556-4402** or 503/802-5800. Fax 503/802-5820. www.avalon hotelandspa.com. 99 units. $160–$215 double; $285–$650 suite. Rates include continental breakfast. Children under 18 stay free in parent's room. AE, DISC, MC, V. Valet parking $15. **Amenities:** Restaurant (Italian); lounge; health club; day spa; concierge; courtesy car; business center; room service; massage; laundry service; dry cleaning. *In room:* A/C, TV, dataport, coffeemaker, hair dryer, iron, safe, free local calls, high-speed Internet access, Wi-Fi.

The Heathman Hotel 🎔🎔 The Heathman has long been considered one of Portland's top hotels, but in many ways this hotel suffers from an identity crisis. An incongruous beefeater doorman ushers guests into a minimalist lobby that is adjacent to an utterly traditional "tea court," which itself is adjacent to the hotel's French restaurant, which is owned by the McCormick and Schmick's restaurant chain and is decorated with Andy Warhol prints. Most standard guest rooms are done in a vaguely Art Deco motif that feels quite cluttered. The over-decorated rooms tend to feel even smaller than they actually are, and the basic rooms are definitely small (upgrade to a suite if you can).

1001 SW Broadway, Portland, OR 97205. **(C) 800/551-0011** or 503/241-4100. Fax 503/790-7110. www.heathman hotel.com. 150 units. $199–$249 double; $249–$1,000 suite. Children under 13 stay free in parent's room. AE, DC, DISC, MC, V. Parking $29. Pets accepted ($35). **Amenities:** Restaurant (French/Northwest); lounge; exercise room and access to nearby health club; concierge; 24-hr. room service; laundry service; dry cleaning. *In room:* A/C, TV, dataport, minibar, coffeemaker, hair dryer, iron, high-speed Internet access.

Hotel Deluxe 🎔🎔 If you're a fan of 1930s to 1950s Hollywood movies, then this glamorous hotel should be your first choice in Portland. Not only are there old photos of movie stars throughout the hotel, but the lobby, with its potted palms, gilded plasterwork ceiling, and crystal chandeliers is prime for an entrance by Fred and Ginger. Guest rooms are equally classic, though with a hip aesthetic geared toward younger travelers. There are iPod docks and flat-panel HDTVs, plus pillow-top mattresses and pillow menus. Sure, the basic rooms are small, but they're so pretty, it's easy to overlook the tight quarters. It's all delightfully playful, which is a welcome change from downtown's many sterile corporate business hotels. In summer, outdoor movies are shown on top of the hotel's parking garage.

729 SW 15th Ave., Portland, OR 97205. **(C) 866/895-2094** or 503/219-2094. Fax 503/219-2095. www.hoteldeluxe portland.com. 130 units. $149–$299 double; $219–$399 suite. AE, DC, DISC, MC, V. Parking $16. Pets accepted ($45 fee). **Amenities:** Restaurant (American); lounge; exercise room; business center; 24-hour room service; dry cleaning. *In room:* A/C, HDTV, coffeemaker, hair dryer, iron, safe, high-speed Internet access, Wi-Fi.

Hotel Lućia 🎔🎔 Portland may not have a W Hotel, but it does have the Lućia, which is just as hip. Located across from the prestigious and very traditional Benson hotel, the Lućia is the Portland address of choice for young business travelers with a taste for contemporary style. There's a big emphasis on the visual arts here, with paintings by Northwest artists on the lobby walls, and black-and-white photos by famed White House photographer David Hume Kennerly throughout the hotel. Guest rooms are some of the prettiest in the city, with great beds and bathrooms that have lots of chrome and frosted-glass counters. The hotel's restaurant, **Typhoon!**, is one of Portland's best Thai restaurants.

400 SW Broadway, Portland, OR 97205. **(C) 877/225-1717** or 503/225-1717. Fax 503/225-1919. www.hotel lucia.com. 127 units. $159–$289 double; $339–$759 suite. Children under 13 stay free in parent's room. AE, DC, DISC, MC, V. Parking $29. Pets accepted ($45 fee). **Amenities:** 2 restaurants (Thai, Asian fusion); 2 lounges; exercise room; concierge; business center; 24-hr. room service; massage; dry cleaning. *In room:* A/C, TV, dataport, minibar, coffeemaker, hair dryer, iron, safe, Wi-Fi.

Hotel Monaco 🎔🎔 Located a block from Pioneer Courthouse Square and within a few blocks of the best downtown shopping, this unpretentious yet sophisticated hotel is housed in what was originally a department store. Artwork by Northwest artists fills the lobby, and in the afternoon there are complimentary tastings of Oregon and other wines. Guest rooms, most of which are suites, are done in a whimsical decor—striped wallpaper, big padded headboards on the beds, red couches. In other

words, colors and patterns everywhere, but it all comes together in a pleasantly theatrical fashion that makes these some of my favorite rooms in Portland. Plus, bathrooms have lots of counter space. In the suites, sliding French doors with curtains
divide the living room from the bedrooms.

506 SW Washington St., Portland, OR 97204. ✆ **888/207-2201** or 503/222-0001. Fax 503/222-0004. www.monaco-
portland.com. 221 units. $149–$289 double; $159–$459 suite. Children under 18 stay free in parent's room. AE, DC, DISC,
MC, V. Valet parking $29. Pets accepted. **Amenities:** Restaurant (American); lounge; exercise room; access to nearby health
club; bike rentals; children's programs; concierge; business center; room service; massage; laundry service; dry cleaning. *In
room:* A/C, TV/DVD, dataport, minibar, fridge, coffeemaker, hair dryer, iron, safe, high-speed Internet access, Wi-Fi.

RiverPlace Hotel 🏨🏨🏨   With the Willamette River at its back doorstep and the
sloping lawns of Waterfront Park to one side, the RiverPlace is Portland's only downtown waterfront hotel. This alone would be enough to recommend the hotel, but its
quiet boutique-hotel atmosphere would make it an excellent choice even if it weren't
on the water. Understated contemporary furnishings and plush beds make this a very
comfortable choice, and more than half the rooms are suites, some of which have
wood-burning fireplaces and whirlpool baths. However, the riverview standard king
rooms are the best deal. The hotel's restaurant overlooks the river, and there's also a
bar with a patio overlooking the river. All in all, what you're paying for here is primarily the waterfront locale.

1510 SW Harbor Way, Portland, OR 97201. ✆ **800/227-1333** or 503/228-3233. Fax 503/295-6190. www.riverplace
hotel.com. 84 units. $189–$239 double; $219–$269 junior suite; $219 and up suite. AE, DC, DISC, MC, V. Valet park-
ing $25. Pets accepted ($45 fee). **Amenities:** Restaurant (Northwest); lounge; access to nearby health club; day spa;
Jacuzzi; sauna; concierge; business center; room service; dry cleaning. *In room:* A/C, TV/DVD, dataport, fridge, coffeemaker, hair dryer, iron, high-speed Internet access, Wi-Fi.

MODERATE
The Benson 🏨🏨🏨   Built in 1912, The Benson exudes old-world sophistication and
elegance. In the French baroque lobby, walnut paneling frames a marble fireplace,
Austrian crystal chandeliers hang from the ornate plasterwork ceiling, and a marble
staircase allows for grand entrances. These are the poshest digs in Portland, and guest
rooms are luxuriously furnished in a plush Euro-luxe styling. Rooms vary considerably
in size, and most of the deluxe kings are particularly spacious. However, the corner
junior suites, which are large and have lots of windows, are the hotel's best deal. All
the guest rooms have Tempur-Pedic mattresses. Bathrooms, unfortunately, are small
and have little shelf space. The hotel's **London Grill** is well known for its Sunday
brunch, and El Gaucho, just off the lobby, serves some of the best steaks in Portland.
In the lobby, the elegant Palm Court lounge has live jazz in the evenings.

309 SW Broadway, Portland, OR 97205. ✆ **888/523-6766** or 503/228-2000. Fax 503/471-3920. www.benson
hotel.com. 287 units. $139–$229 double; $209–$299 junior suite; $450–$1,100 suite. AE, DC, DISC, MC, V. Valet parking $28. Pets accepted ($75). Children under 18 stay free in parent's room. **Amenities:** 3 restaurants (Northwest/Con-
tinental, steaks); lounge; exercise room; access to nearby health club; concierge; business center; 24-hr. room service;
massage; babysitting; laundry service; dry cleaning. *In room:* A/C, TV, dataport, minibar, hair dryer, iron, high-speed
Internet access, Wi-Fi.

Embassy Suites 🏨 *Kids* *Value*   Located in the restored former Multnomah Hotel,
which originally opened in 1912, the Embassy Suites has a beautiful large lobby that
is a masterpiece of gilded plasterwork. The accommodations here are primarily two-
room suites, with the exception of a handful of studio suites. In keeping with the historic nature of the hotel, the suites have classically styled furnishings. What's much
more important, though, is that they give you lots of room to spread out, a rarity in

downtown hotels. The hotel's Portland Steak and Chophouse has a classic dark and woody steakhouse decor as well as a large bar.

319 SW Pine St., Portland, OR 97204. © 800/EMBASSY or 503/279-9000. Fax 503/497-9051. www.embassyportland. com. 276 units. $139–$209 double. Rates include full breakfast and nightly manager's reception. Children 18 and under stay free in parent's room. AE, DC, DISC, MC, V. Valet parking $23; self-parking $15. **Amenities:** Restaurant (steak); lounge; indoor pool; exercise room; access to nearby health club; day spa; Jacuzzi; sauna; concierge; car-rental desk; courtesy van; business center; room service; massage; laundry service; dry cleaning. *In room:* A/C, TV, dataport, fridge, coffeemaker, hair dryer, iron, Wi-Fi.

Hotel Vintage Plaza 🏨🏨   This hotel, which was built in 1894 and is on the National Register of Historic Places, is *the* place to stay in Portland if you are a wine lover. A wine theme predominates in the hotel's decor, and there are complimentary evening tastings of Northwest wines. There are a wide variety of room types here, and though the standard rooms are worth recommending, the starlight rooms and bi-level suites are the real scene stealers. The starlight rooms in particular are truly extraordinary. Though small, they have solarium-style windows that provide very romantic views at night and let in floods of light during the day. The bi-level suites, some with Japanese soaking tubs, are equally attractive spaces. **Pazzo Ristorante** is a sort of contemporary trattoria.

422 SW Broadway, Portland, OR 97205. © 800/243-0555 or 503/228-1212. Fax 503/228-3598. www.vintageplaza. com. 107 units. $139–$259 double; $165–$399 suite. Children under 18 stay free in parent's room. AE, DC, DISC, MC, V. Valet parking $29. Pets accepted. **Amenities:** Restaurant (Italian); lounge; exercise room; access to nearby health club; concierge; business center; 24-hr. room service; massage; dry cleaning. *In room:* A/C, TV, dataport, minibar, coffeemaker, hair dryer, iron, Wi-Fi.

INEXPENSIVE

Ace Hotel 🏨   Bauhaus meets industrial salvage center at this über-hip hotel a block away from Powell's City of Books. Young creative types will adore this fun and funky place that conjures up cheap European hotels of the past. In the lobby, a large, old industrial door serves as a giant coffee table, while over in the corner, there's a vintage photo booth. Every guest room is different, with very unusual murals on the walls. There are Pendleton blankets on the platform beds, and, in rooms with private bathrooms, you might find an old wooden apple crate serving as a step up into the clawfoot tub. Book one of the larger rooms and you can play old vinyl records on a genuine turntable. How cool is that? A hip espresso bar and eclectic restaurant are off the lobby. Ask for a room in back if you're a light sleeper.

1022 SW Stark St., Portland, OR 97205. © 503/228-2277. Fax 503/228-2297. www.acehotel.com. 79 units (10 with shared bath). $95 double with shared bath; $140 double with private bath; $250 suite. AE, DC, DISC, MC, V. Parking $20. Pets accepted. **Amenities:** 3 restaurants (New American, deli, espresso bar); lounge; bike rentals; concierge; business center; room service; coin-op laundry; laundry service; dry cleaning. *In room:* A/C, TV, dataport, minibar, free local calls, high-speed Internet access, Wi-Fi.

Hotel Fifty 🏨 ⟨Value⟩   Overlooking Waterfront Park and located on the MAX light-rail line, this 1960s vintage hotel is nondescript from the outside, but the inside has a contemporary look that makes it surprisingly stylish for an economically priced hotel. You are only steps from the Willamette River (although not actually on the water), and are also close to businesses, fine restaurants, and shopping. Guest rooms are comfortable and have a modern styling.

50 SW Morrison St., Portland, OR 97204-3390. © 877/505-7220 or 503/221-0711. Fax 503/484-1417. www.hotel fifty.com. 140 units. $119–$229 double; $259–$289 suite. AE, DC, DISC, MC, V. Parking $15. Pets accepted. **Amenities:** Restaurant (American/International); lounge; exercise room; access to nearby health club; business center; room service; laundry service; dry cleaning. *In room:* A/C, TV, dataport, coffeemaker, hair dryer, iron, high-speed Internet access, Wi-Fi.

Kids Family-Friendly Hotels

Embassy Suites (p. 72) Located in the center of the city, this renovated historic hotel offers spacious rooms (mostly two-room suites). You and the kids will have room to spread out and can hang out by the indoor pool when you tire of exploring Portland.

Homewood Suites by Hilton Vancouver/Portland (p. 77) This hotel is on the north side of the Columbia River, in Vancouver, Washington. A paved riverside trail, a fun family restaurant, and a brewpub—not to mention its location right across the street from the river—all add up to convenience for families. That you'll get a one- or two-bedroom apartment with a full kitchen just makes life on vacation that much easier.

The Lakeshore Inn (p. 77) This reasonably priced inn is right on the shore of the lake, and it also has a pool. The big rooms with kitchenettes are great for families; for more space, opt for a one- or two-bedroom suite.

NOB HILL & NORTHWEST PORTLAND
EXPENSIVE

Heron Haus 🐦 A short walk from the bustling Nob Hill shopping and dining district of Northwest Portland, the Heron Haus B&B offers outstanding accommodations, spectacular views, and tranquil surroundings. Surprisingly, the house still features some of the original plumbing. In most places this would be a liability, but not here, since the same man who plumbed Portland's famous Pittock Mansion (p. 101) did the plumbing here. Many of that building's unusual bathroom features are also found at the Heron Haus—one shower has *seven* showerheads. In another room there's a modern whirlpool spa with excellent views of the city. All the rooms have fireplaces.

2545 NW Westover Rd., Portland, OR 97210. ✆ 503/274-1846. Fax 503/248-4055. www.heronhaus.com. 6 units. $135–$350 double. Rates include continental breakfast. MC, V. Free parking. *In room:* A/C, TV, dataport, hair dryer, iron, high-speed Internet access.

MODERATE

Inn @ Northrup Station 🐦 *Finds* Colorful, hip, retro. That about sums up this hotel in the trendy Nob Hill neighborhood. On top of this high style, the hotel has large rooms with kitchens or kitchenettes, and the Portland Streetcar stops right outside, which makes this a convenient hotel for exploring the city's most interesting neighborhoods. The colorful retro decor really sets this all-suite hotel apart from more cookie-cutter corporate hotels around town, and if you appreciate bright colors and contemporary styling, this should be your first choice in town. Lots of the rooms here have balconies, and there's a roof-top terrace. The hotel's location in a quiet residential neighborhood is another plus, and some of Portland's top restaurants are within a short walk.

2025 NW Northrup St., Portland, OR 97209. ✆ 800/224-1180 or 503/224-0543. Fax 503/273-2102. www.northrup station.com. 70 units. $129–$199 double. Rates include continental breakfast. Children under 12 stay free in parent's room. AE, DC, DISC, MC, V. Free parking. **Amenities:** Laundry service; dry cleaning. *In room:* A/C, TV, dataport, fridge, coffeemaker, hair dryer, Wi-Fi.

Silver Cloud Inn Portland Downtown ✦   This hotel is on the edge of Portland's trendy Nob Hill neighborhood, and though it's also near an industrial area, it is still a very attractive and comfortable place (ask for a room away from Vaughn St.). Reasonable rates are the main draw here, but the rooms are also well designed. The minisuites have microwave ovens and separate seating areas, but the king minisuites with whirlpool tubs are my favorites. The best thing about the hotel is its location within a 5-minute drive (or 15-min. walk) of a half-dozen of the city's best restaurants. To find the hotel, take I-405 to Ore. 30 west and get off at the Vaughn Street exit.

2426 NW Vaughn St., Portland, OR 97210. ✆ 800/205-6939 or 503/242-2400. Fax 503/242-1770. www.silvercloud. com. 82 units. $139–$189 double. Rates include continental breakfast. Children under 18 stay free in parent's room. AE, DISC, MC, V. Free parking. **Amenities:** Exercise room; courtesy shopping shuttle; business center; guest laundry; dry cleaning. *In room:* A/C, TV, fridge, microwave, coffeemaker, hair dryer, iron, free local calls, high-speed Internet access, Wi-Fi.

THE ROSE QUARTER, IRVINGTON & SOUTHEAST PORTLAND
EXPENSIVE
Lion and the Rose Victorian Bed & Breakfast Inn ✦   This imposing Queen Anne–style Victorian inn, located in the historic Irvington District a block off Northeast Broadway, is a real gem. In the Lavonna Room, there's a turret sitting area and a Sleep Number bed, while in the Starina Room you'll find an imposing Edwardian bed and armoire. The Garden Room has a claw-foot tub; other bathrooms are small but attractive. If you have problems climbing stairs, ask for the ground floor's Rose Room, which has a whirlpool tub. Breakfasts are sumptuous affairs, great for lingering. Restaurants, cafes, eclectic boutiques, and a huge shopping mall are all within 4 blocks.

1810 NE 15th Ave., Portland, OR 97212. ✆ 800/955-1647 or 503/287-9245. Fax 503/287-9247. www.lionrose.com. 7 units. $134–$224 double. No children under 10. AE, DISC, MC, V. Rates include full breakfast. 2-night minimum on holiday weekends. **Amenities:** Concierge. *In room:* A/C, TV, dataport, hair dryer, iron, free local calls, Wi-Fi.

Portland's White House ✦✦   With massive columns framing the portico, a circular driveway, and, in the front garden, a bubbling fountain, this imposing Greek-revival mansion bears a more than passing resemblance to its namesake in Washington, D.C. Behind the mahogany front doors, a grand foyer with original hand-painted wall murals is flanked by a parlor and the formal dining room, where the large breakfast is served beneath sparkling crystal chandeliers. A double staircase leads past a large stained-glass window to the second-floor accommodations. Canopy beds, four-poster beds, antique furnishings, and bathrooms with claw-foot or whirlpool tubs further the feeling of luxury here. Request the balcony room, and you can gaze out past the Greek columns and imagine you're in the Oval Office. There are also three rooms in the restored carriage house.

1914 NE 22nd Ave., Portland, OR 97212. ✆ 800/272-7131 or 503/287-7131. Fax 503/249-1641. www.portlands whitehouse.com. 8 units. $150–$225 double. Rates include full breakfast. AE, DISC, MC, V. *In room:* A/C, TV, dataport, free local calls, high-speed Internet access, Wi-Fi.

INEXPENSIVE
Everett Street Guesthouse *Finds*   No teddy bears, no frilly curtains, no potpourri—that's the mantra at this gorgeous little hideaway on a quiet residential street in northeast Portland. Innkeeper Terry Rusinow, who once owned a craft gallery in the California wine country, has an impeccable eye for interior decor, so public spaces and guest rooms here are beautifully decorated. This little homestay-style inn has only two rooms, and, at press time, was adding a small sleeping cottage with a kitchenette.

When you stay in the main house, you almost feel as though you've rented the entire place. Note that this is a no-smoking and perfume-free house, and there is a resident cat. The neighborhood has loads of great restaurants within walking distance.

2306 NE Everett St., Portland, OR 97232. © **503/230-0211** or 503/830-0650. http://tmr.rusin.googlepages.com. 3 units. $75–$95 double. Rates include continental breakfast. No credit cards. No children. 2-night minimum. **Amenities:** Concierge; bike rentals; art-studio tours. *In room:* Wi-Fi, no phone.

Jupiter Hotel *(Finds* Although this place calls itself a boutique hotel, it's actually a boutique motel. The Jupiter has had an extreme makeover and is now an überhip address for the Portland arts crowd and those in town to participate in the city's hip scene. With its glowing blue wall panels, piped in music in the courtyard, and log-cabin swank Doug Fir Lounge, the Jupiter has enough going on to keep the party going all night long, so don't plan on getting much sleep if you stay here. Platform beds, fuzzy pillows, photo-murals on the walls, retro accents, and dim lighting (or is it supposed to be romantic lighting?) provide guest rooms with plenty of retro-hip styling for young travelers on a tight budget.

800 E. Burnside St., Portland, OR 97214. © **877/800-0004** or 503/230-9200. www.jupiterhotel.com. 80 units. $99–$149 double; $350–$400 suite. AE, DISC, MC, V. **Amenities:** Restaurant (New American); lounge; massage. *In room:* A/C, TV, dataport, hair dryer, Wi-Fi.

McMenamins Kennedy School *(Finds* The Kennedy School, which was an elementary school from 1915 to 1975, is owned by the same folks who turned Portland's old poor farm into the most entertaining and unusual lodge in the state (see the listing for McMenamins Edgefield on p. 243). In the guest rooms you'll still find the original blackboards and great big school clocks (you know, like the one you used to watch so expectantly). However, the classroom/guest rooms here now have their own bathrooms, so you won't have to raise your hand or walk down the hall. On the premises you'll also find a restaurant, a movie theater pub, a cigar bar, and a big hot soaking pool. The Kennedy School is located well north of stylish Irvington neighborhood in an up-and-coming part of the city that dates from the early years of the 20th century.

5736 NE 33rd Ave., Portland, OR 97211. © **888/249-3983** or 503/249-3983. www.mcmenamins.com. 35 units. $99–$125 double. Children 6 and under stay free. AE, DC, DISC, MC, V. **Amenities:** Restaurant (American); 4 lounges; soaking pool. *In room:* A/C, Wi-Fi.

VANCOUVER, WASHINGTON

Located just across the Columbia River from Portland, Vancouver, Washington, is an economical and convenient area from which to explore Portland.

MODERATE

The Heathman Lodge *(Value* Mountain lodge meets urban chic at this suburban Vancouver hotel adjacent to the Vancouver Mall. Just 20 minutes by car from downtown Portland, the hotel is well placed for exploring both the Columbia Gorge and Mount St. Helens. With its log, stone, and cedar-shingle construction, this hotel conjures up the Northwest's historic mountain lodges. As at Timberline Lodge on Oregon's Mount Hood, the Heathman Lodge is filled with artwork and embellished with rugged Northwest-inspired craftwork, including totem poles, Eskimo kayak frames, and Pendleton blankets. Guest rooms feature a mix of rustic pine and peeled-hickory furniture, as well as rawhide lampshades and Pendleton-inspired bedspreads. Most rooms also have Tempur-Pedic mattresses.

7801 NE Greenwood Dr., Vancouver, WA 98662. © **888/475-3100** or 360/254-3100. Fax 360/254-6100. www.heathmanlodge.com. 142 units. $79–$149 double; $159–$350 suite. AE, DC, DISC, MC, V. **Amenities:** Restaurant

(Northwest); lounge; indoor pool; exercise room; Jacuzzi; sauna; concierge; business center; room service; guest laundry; laundry service; dry cleaning. *In room:* A/C, TV, dataport, fridge, microwave, coffeemaker, hair dryer, iron, Wi-Fi.

Homewood Suites by Hilton Vancouver/Portland ℛ *Kids*   Located across the street from the Columbia River, this modern all-suite hotel is a great choice for families. The hotel charges surprisingly reasonable rates for large apartmentlike accommodations that include full kitchens. Rates include not only a large breakfast, but afternoon snacks as well (Mon–Thurs). These snacks are substantial enough to pass for dinner if you aren't too hungry. The hotel is right across the street from both a beach-theme restaurant and a brewpub. Across the street, you'll also find a paved riverside path that's great for walking or jogging. The only drawback is that it's a 15- to 20-minute drive to downtown Portland.

701 SE Columbia Shores Blvd., Vancouver, WA 98661. ℭ **800/CALL-HOME** or 360/750-1100. Fax 360/750-4899. www.homewoodsuites.com. 104 units. $139–$259 double. Rates include full breakfast. AE, DC, DISC, MC, V. Free parking. Pets accepted ($25 1st day, $10 subsequent days). **Amenities:** Outdoor pool; sports court; exercise room; Jacuzzi; business center; coin-op laundry; laundry service; dry cleaning. *In room:* A/C, TV, dataport, kitchen, fridge, coffeemaker, hair dryer, iron, free local calls, high-speed Internet access.

THE AIRPORT AREA & TROUTDALE

Moderately priced hotels abound in the airport area, which makes this a good place to look for a room if you arrive with no reservation.

INEXPENSIVE

Clarion Hotel *Value*   Conveniently located right outside the airport, this hotel has one of the best backyards of any hotel in the Portland area. A lake, lawns, and trees create a tranquil setting despite the proximity of both the airport and a busy nearby road. Rooms are designed primarily for business travelers, but even if you aren't here on an expense account, the rooms here are a good value, especially those with whirlpool tubs or gas fireplaces. Best of all, almost every room has a view of the lake. An indoor pool is another big plus. To find this hotel, take the complimentary airport shuttle or head straight out of the airport, drive under the I-205 overpass, and watch for the hotel sign ahead on the left.

11518 NE Glenn Widing Dr., Portland, OR 97220. ℭ **800/424-6423** or 503/252-2222. Fax 503/257-7008. www. choicehotels.com. 101 units. $75–$135 double. Rates include full breakfast. Children under 19 stay free in parent's room. AE, DC, DISC, MC, V. Free parking. **Amenities:** Indoor pool; exercise room; Jacuzzi; courtesy airport shuttle; business center; guest laundry. *In room:* A/C, TV, dataport, fridge, microwave, coffeemaker, hair dryer, iron, free local calls, high-speed Internet access, Wi-Fi.

LAKE OSWEGO
INEXPENSIVE

The Lakeshore Inn *Finds Kids*   Considering that the town of Lake Oswego is Portland's most affluent bedroom community, this motel is quite reasonably priced. It's right on the shore of the lake, and there's a pool on a deck built on the water's edge, making it a great place to stay in summer. Rooms have standard motel furnishings but are large and have kitchenettes. There are also one- and two-bedroom suites. The 7-mile drive into downtown Portland follows the Willamette River and is quite pleasant. There are several restaurants and cafes within walking distance.

210 N. State St., Lake Oswego, OR 97034. ℭ **800/215-6431** or 503/636-9679. Fax 503/636-6959. www.thelakeshore inn.com. 33 units. $84–$109 double; $99–$179 suite. Rates include continental breakfast. Children under 12 stay free in parent's room. AE, DC, DISC, MC, V. **Amenities:** Outdoor pool; access to nearby health club. *In room:* A/C, TV/DVD, kitchen, fridge, coffeemaker, hair dryer, iron, free local calls, Wi-Fi.

4 Where to Dine

The Portland restaurant scene is hot and it's not just because of all the wood ovens that have been brought in to new restaurants in the past couple of years. The city has recently developed a reputation to rival Seattle's when it comes to great restaurants. What's driving this restaurant renaissance are lots of creative young chefs and their affinity for local produce and wines from Willamette Valley wineries. Bounteous ingredients can be sourced locally, including organic fruits and vegetables, hazelnuts and walnuts, wild mushrooms, even Oregon truffles. Pinot noir, pinot gris, pinot blanc. The list goes on and on. All I can say is, cheers!

The only catch to the Portland dining scene is that it is spread out, and some of the most talked-about restaurants are basically neighborhood spots in up-and-coming residential districts away from the city center. Even more inconvenient is that these great neighborhood restaurants often don't take reservations. For this reason, I'm still partial to the less hyped but more reliable restaurants downtown and in the Pearl District and the Nob Hill/Northwest neighborhoods. Call me old-fashioned, but I'm just not interested in waiting three hours for a table when I'm going to spend $50 or $60 on dinner.

DOWNTOWN (INCLUDING THE SKIDMORE HISTORIC DISTRICT & CHINATOWN)
EXPENSIVE

The Heathman Restaurant and Bar ⭐⭐⭐ NORTHWEST/FRENCH   Serving Northwest cuisine with a French accent, the Heathman Restaurant is Portland's grande dame nouvelle/regional restaurant. Philippe Boulot, a James Beard Foundation Award winner, changes his menu daily, but one thing remains constant: The ingredients used are the freshest of Oregon and Northwest seafood, meat, wild game, and produce. The interior is Art Deco inspired, the atmosphere bistrolike. An extensive wine list spotlights Oregon wines. The Heathman Hotel has an extensive collection of classic and contemporary art, and on the restaurant walls you'll find Andy Warhol's *Endangered Species* series.

In the Heathman Hotel, 1001 SW Broadway. ⓒ 503/790-7752. www.heathmanrestaurantandbar.com. Reservations highly recommended. Main courses $9–$22 lunch, $18–$35 dinner. AE, DC, DISC, MC, V. Mon–Thurs 6:30–11am, 11:30am–3pm, and 5:30–10pm; Fri 6:30–11am, 11:30am–3pm, and 5:30–11pm; Sat 6:30am–3pm and 5:30–11pm; Sun 6:30am–3pm and 5:30–10pm.

Higgins ⭐⭐⭐ NORTHWEST/MEDITERRANEAN   Higgins strikes a perfect balance between contemporary and classic in both decor and cuisine. The menu, which changes frequently, explores contemporary culinary horizons, while the decor in the tri-level dining room opts for wood paneling and elegant place settings. Despite all this, the restaurant remains unpretentious, and portions can be surprisingly generous for a high-end restaurant. Flavors change with the season, but are often both subtle and earthy. Such dishes as a risotto of chanterelle mushrooms, pumpkin, and chilis highlight the restaurant's emphasis on seasonal ingredients. Be sure to leave room for dessert, and if you happen to be a beer lover, you'll be glad to know that Higgins has one of the most interesting beer selections in town (and plenty of good wine, too).

1239 SW Broadway. ⓒ 503/222-9070. Reservations recommended. Main courses $8.50–$17 lunch, $20–$32 dinner. AE, DC, DISC, MC, V. Mon–Fri 11:30am–2pm and 5–10:30pm; Sat–Sun 5–10:30pm; bistro menu served in the bar daily until between 11pm and midnight.

Downtown Portland Dining

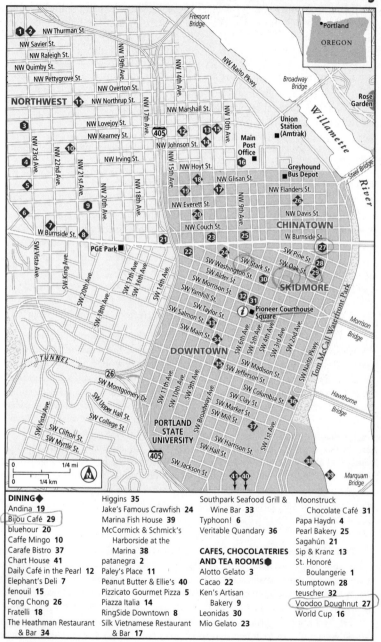

Veritable Quandary 🦀🦀 NEW AMERICAN   With the prettiest garden patio in downtown Portland, the VQ, as it's known to locals, is a little historic gem of a restaurant and should not be missed on a summer visit. The restaurant is conveniently located in an old brick building just a block off Tom McCall Waterfront Park, and windows and the patio look out on a small tree-shaded pocket park. The menu changes daily, but keep an eye out for the grilled prawns, and don't pass up the *osso buco*. The chef here pulls in all kinds of influences, so don't be surprised if you find bacon-wrapped dates stuffed with goat cheese or duck-confit spring rolls served with wasabi-ginger sauce.

1220 SW First Ave. 🕐 **503/227-7342**. www.veritablequandary.com. Reservations recommended. Main courses $10–$15 lunch, $19–$28 dinner. AE, DC, DISC, MC, V. Mon–Fri 11:30am–3pm and 5–10pm; Sat–Sun 9:30am–3pm and 5–10pm.

MODERATE

There's an outpost of **Typhoon!** at 410 SW Broadway (🕐 **503/224-8285**), in the Hotel Lucía. See the complete review on p. 84.

Carafe Bistro 🦀🦀 FRENCH   With its small zinc bar, wicker patio chairs, and warm interior hues, Carafe feels just the way you'd expect a neighborhood bistro in Paris to feel. The menu is simple bistro fare (everything from baked escargot to *croque monsieur*), and there are economical nightly three-course prix-fixe dinners for $20. With many appetizers, salads, and side dishes, you can easily assemble a thoroughly Gallic meal. On top of all this, Carafe is right across the street from Keller Auditorium.

200 SW Market St. 🕐 **503/248-0004**. www.carafebistro.com. Main courses $8–$21. AE, DC, DISC, MC, V. Mon–Thurs 11:30am–9pm; Fri 11:30am–10pm; Sat 5–10pm.

Jake's Famous Crawfish 🦀🦀 SEAFOOD   Jake's has been a Portland institution since 1909 and boasts a back bar that came all the way around Cape Horn in 1880. Much of the rest of the decor looks just as old and well worn as the bar and therein lies this restaurant's charm. However, it's the great seafood at reasonable prices that makes this place a real winner. There's a daily menu listing a dozen or more specials, but there's really no question about what to eat at Jake's: crawfish, which is always on the menu and served several different ways. Monday through Friday from 3 to 6pm and Monday through Saturday from 10pm to close, bar appetizers are only $1.95. The noise level after work, when local businesspeople pack the bar, can be high, and the wait for a table can be long if you don't make a reservation, but don't let these obstacles put you off.

401 SW 12th Ave. 🕐 **503/226-1419**. www.jakesfamouscrawfish.com. Reservations recommended. Main courses $7–$18 lunch, $14–$39 dinner. AE, DC, DISC, MC, V. Mon–Thurs 11am–11pm; Fri 11am–midnight; Sat noon–midnight; Sun 3–11pm.

Marina Fish House 🅺🅸🅳🆂 SEAFOOD   This restaurant, affiliated with Newport Bay restaurants in the Portland area, has by far the best location of any restaurant in town—floating on the Willamette River. Located in the marina at Portland's River-Place shopping-and-dining complex, the Marina Fish House provides excellent views of the river and the city skyline, especially from the deck. Popular with young couples, families, and boaters, this place exudes a cheery atmosphere, and service is efficient. Nearly everything on the menu has some sort of seafood in it, even the sandwiches, salads, and pastas. Entrees are straightforward and well prepared—nothing too fancy.

0425 SW Montgomery St. 🕐 **503/227-3474**. www.newportbay.com. Reservations recommended. Main courses $9–$35; Sun brunch $11–$19. AE, DC, DISC, MC, V. Sun–Thurs 11am–10pm; Fri–Sat 11am–11pm.

McCormick and Schmick's Harborside at the Marina ★★ SEAFOOD
Anchoring the opposite end of RiverPlace Esplanade from the RiverPlace hotel, this
large, glitzy restaurant, part of a national chain, serves up reliable seafood and a great
view of the Willamette River. With four dining levels, you can be assured that you'll
have a view of the river and marina below, and, in summer, you can head out to tables
on the sidewalk. Because it's so popular, this place tends to be noisy and the help can
sometimes be a bit harried; this doesn't detract from the fine food, though. Seafood
dishes (such as sturgeon with mustard, peppercorns, and basil-butter sauce or salmon
sautéed with mushrooms and hazelnuts) are the main attraction here, but the menu is
quite extensive. Customers tend to be well heeled and well dressed, especially at lunch
and during after-work hours.

0309 SW Montgomery St. ② 503/220-1865. www.mccormickandschmicks.com. Reservations recommended. Main
courses $7–$14 lunch, $15–$40. AE, DC, DISC, MC, V. Sun–Thurs 11am–10pm; Fri–Sat 11am–11pm.

Southpark Seafood Grill & Wine Bar ★★ *Value* MEDITERRANEAN/ SEAFOOD
With its high ceiling, long heavy drapes, and interesting wall mural, the wine bar here
is a contemporary interpretation of late-19th-century Paris, and the main dining room
is both comfortable and classy. For a starter, don't pass up the fried calamari and vegetables served with spicy aioli. Equally delicious is the butternut squash and ricotta-
filled ravioli with toasted hazelnuts, which comes in a rich Marsala wine sauce that
begs to be sopped up with the crusty bread. An extensive wine list presents some compelling choices, and the desserts are consistently excellent.

901 SW Salmon St. ② 503/326-1300. Reservations recommended. Main courses $8.50–$16 lunch, $18–$28 dinner. AE, DISC, MC, V. Mon–Thurs 11:30am–midnight; Fri 11:30am–1am; Sat 11am–1am; Sun 11am–11pm.

INEXPENSIVE
Bijou Café ★ *Kids* NATURAL FOODS   Although the Bijou is ostensibly just a
breakfast joint, the folks who run the restaurant take food very seriously. The fresh
oyster hash is an absolutely unforgettable way to start the day, as is the brioche French
toast. Other big hits include the sautéed potatoes and the muffins, which come with
full breakfasts; don't leave without trying them. Local and organic products are used
as often as possible at this comfortably old-fashioned, yet thoroughly modern cafe.

132 SW Third Ave. ② 503/222-3187. Breakfast and lunch $6–$13. MC, V. Mon–Fri 7am–2pm; Sat–Sun 8am–2pm.

Fong Chong CHINESE   This place may not look like much from the outside (or
from the inside, for that matter), but the throngs of people crowding the tables in the
middle of the day should give you an idea that this place does good dim sum. This
traditional Chinese midday meal of small plates is ordered off of carts that are wheeled
around the dining room and is served throughout the day. With lots of steamed
dumplings, pot stickers, and shrimp balls, it's easy to order more than you can eat.
Pace yourself. Located 2 blocks from the Portland Classical Chinese Garden, this is a
great place to stick with the Chinese theme after a visit to the gardens.

301 NW Fourth Ave. ② 503/228-6868. Main courses $6.50–$13; dim sum $3.50–$6.50. MC, V. Mon–Thurs
10am–9pm; Fri–Sun 10am–9:30pm.

NORTHWEST PORTLAND (INCLUDING THE PEARL DISTRICT & NOB HILL)
EXPENSIVE
Andina ★★ PERUVIAN   If you've never tried Peruvian food before, don't miss
an opportunity to eat at Andina. If you have had Peruvian food before, don't miss an

opportunity to eat at Andina. It's that simple. I've been known to eat here several times in the same week, because I just couldn't get enough of the spicy bread-dipping sauces, the grilled octopus, and the beautifully presented *causa* (mashed purple potatoes flavored with lime and layered with savory fillings; I like the smoked trout best). Because there is so much on the menu to try, I suggest sticking with the small plates and trying lots of them. Also, be sure to have a glass of the unusual *chicha morada,* a juice made from purple corn.

1314 NW Glisan St. © 503/228-9535. www.andinarestaurant.com. Reservations recommended. Small plates $6.50–$15; main courses $16–$29. AE, DISC, MC, V. Mon–Thurs 11:30am–2:30pm and 5–9:30pm (tapas until 11pm); Fri–Sat 11:30am–2:30pm and 5–10:30pm (tapas until midnight); Sun 5–9:30pm (tapas until 11pm).

bluehour ★ MEDITERRANEAN   Restaurateur Bruce Carey has long dominated the Portland restaurant scene, and at this high-style restaurant, he perennially wows local trendsetters. Located in a converted warehouse that serves as headquarters for Portland advertising giant Wieden+Kennedy, bluehour has a very theatrical atmosphere. With superb service and sophisticated menu items such as American sturgeon caviar and seared foie gras, it's obvious that bluehour is Portland's most haute restaurant—though this is also the sort of place where being seen by the right people is as important as the food.

250 NW 13th Ave. © 503/226-3394. www.bluehouronline.com. Reservations highly recommended. Main dishes $10–$26 lunch, $24–$43 dinner. AE, MC, V. Mon–Thurs 11:30am–2:30pm and 5–10pm; Fri 11:30am–2:30pm and 5–10:30pm; Sat 5–10:30pm; Sun 5–9pm.

fenouil ★★★ FRENCH   Rarely do I feel so good about spending so much on dinner as I do when I eat here at the Pearl District's poshest restaurant. With two-story walls of glass that look out to the pretty little Jamison Square park and with a large patio that puts you right in the park in the summer, fenouil couldn't possibly be better placed. Throw in a gorgeous interior decor, and you have the perfect special-occasion restaurant. Be sure to start with the onion soup, which is the best my wife and I have ever had. Also, no matter what you order for an entree, get a side of truffle-oil french fries. The menu includes plenty of classic dishes, but it also holds plenty of unexpected surprises. You can save money by coming for lunch or eating a light meal in the bar.

900 NW 11th Ave. © 503/525-2225. www.fenouilinthepearl.com. Reservations highly recommended. Main courses $19–$30. AE, DISC, MC, V. Mon–Wed 11am–2pm and 5–9pm; Thurs–Sat 11am–2pm and 5–10pm; Sun 9am–2pm and 5–9pm.

Paley's Place ★★ NORTHWEST/FRENCH   Located in a Victorian-era house, Paley's is another favorite of Portland foodies. Chef Vitaly Paley continues to receive accolades year after year, and back in 2005 he won a James Beard Foundation Award. The menu relies extensively on the freshest local organic ingredients and ranges from traditional bistro fare to dishes with complex flavors and a hint of Northwest inspiration. Whether you're in the mood for spit-roasted suckling lamb, braised elk shoulder, or corn-and-chanterelle ravioli, you'll certainly find something that appeals to you. If you've never tried sweetbreads, this is the place to do so, and the signature *frites,* with a mustard aioli, are not to be missed. Big on wines, Paley's offers wine tastings on Wednesdays. For dessert, I can't pass up the warm chocolate soufflé cake with outrageously rich house-made ice cream. Inside, the restaurant is small and stylishly comfortable but can be quite noisy.

1204 NW 21st Ave. © 503/243-2403. www.paleysplace.net. Reservations highly recommended. Main courses $22–$35. AE, MC, V. Mon–Thurs 5:30–10pm; Fri–Sat 5:30–11pm; Sun 5–10pm.

RingSide Downtown ⭐ STEAK   Despite the location on a rather unattractive stretch of West Burnside Street, RingSide has been a favorite Portland steakhouse for more than 60 years. Boxing may be the main theme of the restaurant, but the name is a two-fisted pun that also refers to the incomparable onion rings that are an essential part of any meal here. Have your rings with a side order of one of their perfectly cooked steaks for a real knockout meal. The three-course prix-fixe dinners are only $25 if you order before 5:45pm or after 9pm.

2165 W. Burnside St. ✆ 503/223-1513. www.ringsidesteakhouse.com. Reservations highly recommended. Steaks $28–$65; other main courses $21–$59. AE, DC, DISC, MC, V. Mon–Sat 5pm–midnight; Sun 4–11:30pm.

MODERATE
Caffe Mingo ⭐⭐ *Finds* ITALIAN   This intimate little neighborhood restaurant has terrific food and relatively reasonable prices. If there's any problem with this immensely popular place it's that you almost always have to wait for a table, and they only take reservations for large parties. The solution? Get here as early as possible. The menu is short and focuses on painstakingly prepared Italian comfort food. Just about all the items on the menu are winners, from the antipasto platter, which might include roasted fennel, fresh mozzarella, and roasted red pepper, to an unusual penne pasta dish with tender beef braised in chianti and espresso. The *panna cotta* dessert ("cooked cream" with fruit) is reason enough to come back here again and again, even if you have to wait in the rain to get a seat.

807 NW 21st Ave. ✆ 503/226-4646. Reservations accepted only for parties of 6 or more. Main courses $11–$21. AE, DC, DISC, MC, V. Mon–Sat 5–10pm; Sun 4:30–9:30pm.

Fratelli ⭐⭐ REGIONAL ITALIAN   In this rustic-yet-chic restaurant, cement walls provide a striking contrast to dramatic draperies and softly glowing candles. Dishes are consistently good, with surprisingly moderate prices for the Pearl District. Be sure to start with the mix-and-match antipasto plate that might include chicken-liver mousse on crostini; roasted Meyer lemon stuffed with buffalo mozzarella; frittata with seasonal vegetables; and a salad of roasted fennel, blood orange, and chicken confit. The polenta with wild mushrooms and the seared chicken wrapped in prosciutto are longtime favorites here. This restaurant's aesthetic and menu are similar to Caffe Mingo's (see above), but at Fratelli you can make reservations.

1230 NW Hoyt St. ✆ 503/241-8800. www.fratellicucina.com. Reservations recommended. Main courses $13–$21. AE, DC, MC, V. Sun–Thurs 5–9pm; Fri–Sat 5–10pm.

patanegra ⭐ *Finds* SPANISH   Located next door to one of my favorite bakeries, this Spanish restaurant specializes in Spanish-style tapas (small plates) but also serves a few different types of paella. Still, I can't ever get past all the flavor-packed little tapas dishes. The best way to approach this rather exotic menu is to just start ordering whatever sounds most interesting and then order more if your first round doesn't fill you up. You can also opt for large orders of all the tapas on the menu. Let me warn you, though, that the tapas menu is heavy on proteins and starches and a bit light on veggies. Oh well, you can always have a salad tomorrow.

1818 NW 23rd Place. ✆ 503/227-7282. www.patanegra-restaurant.com. Main courses $16–$22; tapas $5.75–$25. AE, DISC, MC, V. Mon–Thurs 5–10pm; Fri–Sat 5–11pm.

Piazza Italia ⭐⭐ ITALIAN   Portland has more than its fair share of good Italian restaurants, but none feels as much like a trip to Italy as this one. The staff speaks Italian most of the time and the TV over the bar is usually tuned to Italian soap operas and soccer matches. Just inside the front door is a glass case full of the imported meats, cheeses, and olives that go into the antipasto plate. This place is small and has a very limited menu, but it's always bustling. Try the simple linguine *squarciarella*, made with eggs, prosciutto, onions, and Parmesan cheese. During the summer, the tables on the sidewalk are the in-demand seats.

1129 NW Johnson St. © 503/478-0619. www.piazzaportland.com. Main courses $11–$16. Reservations recommended. AE, DISC, MC, V. Mon–Sat noon–10pm; Sun noon–8pm.

Silk Vietnamese Restaurant & Bar ⋆ VIETNAMESE   If you think of Formica tables and fluorescent lights when you think of Vietnamese restaurants, think again. This is one of the most stylish restaurants in town, with rippling walls of back-lit glass and decor drawing on a modern Asian aesthetic. The prices, however, are quite reasonable, especially for the Pearl District. You can get flavorful *pho* soup (a Vietnamese staple), but I prefer the more substantial entrees, as well as such unusual dishes as banana-flower salad and the clay-pot catfish.

1012 NW Glisan St. © 503/248-2172. Reservations recommended. Main courses $8–$16 lunch, $8.75–$24 dinner. AE, DISC, MC, V. Mon–Sat 11am–3pm and 5–10pm.

Typhoon! ⋆ THAI   Located just off NW 23rd Avenue, this Thai restaurant is one of my favorites in town for its many unusual menu offerings that generally aren't available at other Portland Thai restaurants. Be sure to start a meal with the *miang kum*, which consists of dried shrimp, tiny chilies, ginger, lime, peanuts, shallots, and toasted coconut drizzled with a sweet-and-sour sauce and wrapped up in a spinach leaf. The burst of flavors on your taste buds is absolutely astounding. (I first had this in Thailand and waited years to get it in the United States.) The whole front wall of the restaurant slides away for Thai-style open-air dining in the summer. There is an extensive tea list.

There's another **Typhoon!** at 410 SW Broadway (© **503/224-8285**), in the Hotel Lućia.

2310 NW Everett St. © 503/243-7557. www.typhoonrestaurants.com. Reservations recommended. Main courses $9–$18. AE, DISC, MC, V. Mon–Thurs 11:30am–2pm and 4:30–9pm; Fri 11:30am–2pm and 4:30–10pm; Sat noon–3pm and 4:30–10pm; Sun noon–3pm and 4:30–9pm.

INEXPENSIVE

Daily Café in the Pearl AMERICAN/SANDWICHES   Healthy, flavorful breakfasts and creative sandwiches are the mainstays of this hip-yet-casual urban cafe in the heart of the Pearl District. On sunny days, take your meal out onto the converted loading dock and ogle all the buff people coming and going from the area's gym. In the morning you can get a grilled baguette with Nutella, while at lunch, you might opt for a saltimbocca or fajita panini. This is primarily a lunch spot, but dinners are also served. Other Daily Cafés can be found in southeast Portland inside Rejuvenation House Parts, 1100 SE Grand Ave. (© **503/234-8189**); and in the south waterfront district in the OHSU Center for Health and Healing, 3335 SW Bond Ave. (© **503/224-9691**).

902 NW 13th Ave. © 503/242-1916. Main courses $4.75–$6.75 lunch, $15–$18 dinner. AE, MC, V. Mon–Tues 7am–5pm; Wed–Sat 7am–9pm; Sun 9am–2pm.

Elephant's Deli DELI   This is definitely not your corner deli and it pushes the boundaries of what can even be considered a deli. Elephant's is a behemoth, which of course makes the name appropriate, and it's mouthwateringly diverse in its food offerings. Whether you want some pastrami to go or a full gourmet meal, you can get it here, and this is the best place in town to put together a picnic before heading up to Washington Park. Want a cocktail? Elephant's has a full bar and plenty of good appetizers to accompany the drinks. Now, don't you wish you had one of these pachyderms in your town?

115 NW 22nd Ave. © **503/299-6304**. www.elephantsdeli.com. Reservations not accepted. Main courses $6–$15. AE, MC, V. Mon–Sat 7am–8:30pm; Sun 9:30am–6:30pm.

SOUTHWEST PORTLAND
EXPENSIVE
Chart House ★★ SEAFOOD   Although this place is part of a chain with lots of outposts all over California and the rest of the West, it also happens to boast the best view of any restaurant in Portland. On top of that, it serves the best New England clam chowder in the state. While you savor your chowder, you can marvel at the views of the Willamette River, Mount Hood, and Mount St. Helens. Fresh fish—either grilled, baked, or blackened—is the house specialty. You'll also find a selection of excellent steaks. No dinner here is complete without the hot chocolate lava cake, which has to be ordered at the start of your meal. I recommend coming here for lunch or the early-bird dinner specials, which cost $15 to $18 and are available Sunday through Thursday between 5 and 6:30pm. Because the Chart House is in a 10-minute drive from downtown Portland, you should be sure to call ahead and get driving directions.

5700 SW Terwilliger Blvd. © **503/246-6963**. www.chart-house.com. Reservations recommended. Main courses $9–$22 lunch, $18–$43 dinner. AE, DC, DISC, MC, V. Mon–Thurs 11:30am–2pm and 5–9:30pm; Fri 11:30am–2pm and 5–10pm; Sat 5–10pm; Sun 5–9pm.

INEXPENSIVE
Peanut Butter & Ellie's ★ *Finds* *Kids* AMERICAN   This cozy, colorful spot in an upscale southwest Portland neighborhood takes the term "kid-friendly" to the extreme. This place is exclusively for children, though their parents are welcome if they are well behaved. The menu features—you guessed it—peanut-butter-and-jelly sandwiches (which can be topped with grapes, raisins, shredded carrots, or many other toppings). Okay, so there are soups, salads, chicken sandwiches, grilled-cheese sandwiches, and even some adult-oriented dinner entrees, but the peanut butter-constructions are the real highlights. Oh, and by the way, the peanut butter is organic and made right here.

4405 SW Vermont St. © **503/282-1783**. www.peanutbutterellies.com. Main courses $5.50–$22. MC, V. Mon 10am–2pm; Tues–Sat 10am–8pm; Sun 10am–7pm.

NORTH AND NORTHEAST PORTLAND
MODERATE
Pambiche ★ *Finds* CUBAN   Driving past this tiny hole-in-the-wall neighborhood eatery, you'd never guess that it's one of Portland's most popular restaurants. But you can't pass by the old building, which is painted garish tropical colors, without giving it a glance. Don't just gawk—get in there! The food is straight out of Havana, with taro-root fritters, codfish-and-potato croquettes, fried yucca root, and fried bananas. And that's just on the appetizer list. Don't fill up on all those tasty little tropical treats, though; the main dishes, such as shrimp Creole, Cuban-style beef hash, and oxtail braised in red wine, are all served in huge portions.

2811 NE Glisan St. © **503/233-0511**. www.pambiche.com. Main courses $7–$10 lunch, $8.50–$18 dinner. MC, V. Mon–Thurs 11am–10pm; Fri 11am–midnight; Sat 7am–midnight; Sun 7am–10pm.

(Kids) Family-Friendly Restaurants

Bijou Cafe (p. 81)   Parents who care about the food their children eat will want to bring the family to this cozy old-fashioned diner that serves great breakfasts made with organic ingredients.

Marina Fish House (p. 80)   A cheery atmosphere, straightforward meals, and a great location on the Willamette River make this a good family pick.

Peanut Butter & Ellie's (p. 85)   This place isn't just family friendly, it's designed exclusively for kids, and, of course, the various peanut-butter-and-jelly sandwiches are big hits with the little ones.

Screen Door ⚶ SOUTHERN   Shrimp and grits, boudin, Carolina pulled-pork barbecue, po-boys. I don't think we're in Oregon anymore, Toto. This casual restaurant just a few blocks from the restaurant-heavy crossroads of E. Burnside Street and 28th Avenue serves down-home Southern comfort food in huge portions, and the northwesterners who eat here seem to love it. Since this is Portland, though, you can get a side of organic vegetables from a weekly list of nearly a dozen different sides/starters. Be sure to order cornbread and the sweet-potato fries.

2337 E. Burnside St. ✆ **503/542-0880.** Reservation not accepted. Main courses $9.75–$15. AE, DISC, MC, V. Tues–Fri 5:30–10pm; Sat 9:30am–2:30pm and 5:30–10pm; Sun 9:30am–2:30pm and 5:30–9pm.

Toro Bravo ⚶⚶⚶ SPANISH   I don't usually applaud for a meal, but the first time I ate at this neighborhood restaurant, my dinner companions and I just couldn't help ourselves. A meal here is so filled with seductive flavors that the smile that lights up your face after your first bite (perhaps buttery chanterelle mushrooms or bacon-wrapped, almond-stuffed dates) remains there right through dessert (olive oil cake with wild huckleberries or maybe a crepe filled with lemon curd). In between, every plate is a revelation—whole fresh anchovies with fried lemon slices, rabbit terrine, creamy duck rillette, seared romanesco cauliflower with chopped olives. Just be sure to order the house-smoked coppa steak—phenomenal. Tapas prices are low, but you'll likely eat enough that the tab will add up.

120 NE Russell St. ✆ **503/281-4464.** www.torobravopdx.com. Reservations not accepted. Tapas $1–$14. AE, DISC, MC, V. Sun–Thurs 5–10pm; Fri–Sat 5–11pm.

SOUTHEAST PORTLAND
EXPENSIVE

Caprial's Bistro & Wine ⚶⚶ NORTHWEST   If you're a foodie, you're probably already familiar with celebrity chef Caprial Pence, who helped put the Northwest on the national restaurant map and has since gone on to write several cookbooks and host TV and radio food shows. That her eponymous restaurant is a fairly casual place tucked away in a quiet residential neighborhood in southeast Portland may come as a surprise. The menu changes monthly and is limited to six or seven main dishes and 10 or so appetizers. Entrees combine perfectly cooked meat and seasonal seafood dishes with vibrant sauces. Desserts are usually rich without being overly sweet. There is also a wine bar offering a superb selection of wines at reasonable prices.

East of Downtown Dining

DINING◆
Castagna **4**
Esparza's **10**
Genoa **12**
Ken's Artisan Pizza **11**
Lauro **15**
Nicholas's **2**
Pambiche **7**
Pok Pok **14**
Screen Door **6**
Toro Bravo **1**

**CAFES, CHOCO-
LATERIES AND
TEA ROOMS■**
Alma Chocolate **9**
Palio Dessert House **5**
Pix Patisserie **16**
Rimsky-Korsakoffee
House **3**
Staccato Gelato **8**
Tao of Tea **13**

7015 SE Milwaukie Ave. ℂ **503/236-6457**. www.caprialandjohnskitchen.com. Reservations highly recommended. Main courses $9.50–$12 lunch, $17–$29 dinner. AE, DISC, MC, V. Tues–Thurs 11:30am–2:30pm and 5–9pm; Fri–Sat 11:30am–2:30pm and 5–9:30pm.

Castagna ⊛⊛ FRENCH/ITALIAN Located on a rather nondescript stretch of Hawthorne Boulevard and much removed from the bustle of this boulevard's central commercial area, Castagna is a magnet for Portland foodies. Considering the less-than-stylish location and minimalist (though thoroughly designed) interior, it's obvious that the food's the thing here. Dishes tend toward simple preparations that allow the freshness of the ingredients to express themselves. Entrees such as sautéed black cod with celery root purée, coriander beurre blanc, and fried celery leaves sum up the dominant culinary aesthetic at this restaurant. In addition to the main dining room, there is an adjacent cafe serving much simpler and less expensive fare.

1752 SE Hawthorne Blvd. ℂ **503/231-7373**. www.castagnarestaurant.com. Reservations highly recommended. Main dishes $23–$30, 3-course dinner $30; cafe main courses $11–$21. AE, DISC, MC, V. Main restaurant Wed–Thurs 5:30–9:30pm, Fri–Sat 5:30–10:30pm; cafe Tues–Thurs 11:30am–2pm and 5–10pm, Fri–Sat 11:30am–2pm and 5–11pm, Sun 5–9:30pm.

Genoa ⊛⊛⊛ REGIONAL ITALIAN This has long been the best Italian restaurant in Portland, and with fewer than a dozen tables, it's also one of the smallest. Everything, from the breads to the luscious desserts, is made fresh in the kitchen with the best local seasonal ingredients. This is an ideal setting for a romantic dinner, and service is attentive—the waiter explains dishes in detail as they are served, and dishes are magically whisked away as they're finished. The fixed-price menu changes frequently, but a typical dinner might start with an heirloom tomato tart, followed by pumpkin soup with chorizo and squash blossoms. Next might be wild-mushroom agnolotti pasta with grilled pork belly and then seared scallops with hearts of palm, purple carrots, and watermelon. For a main course, you might opt for guinea-hen roulade with ratatouille or suckling pig with candied olives, pickled jalapeños, and bacon broth. Then, of course, there's dessert, which is followed up with petit fours.

2832 SE Belmont St. (C) 503/238-1464. www.genoarestaurant.com. Reservations required. Fixed-price a la carte 4-course menu $65; 7-course chef's tasting menu $80. AE, DC, DISC, MC, V. Tues–Sun 5:30–9:30pm.

MODERATE

Ken's Artisan Pizza ✸ PIZZA   The aroma hits you as soon as you walk in the front door of this causal neighborhood restaurant just a few blocks south of E. Burnside Street. Heavenly aromas mingle with the tang of wood smoke from the oven in which the pizzas here are baked. Start your meal with the wood-oven roasted vegetable plate, which comes with a trio of seasonal veggies that are wonderfully sauced. You could make a meal on this platter alone, but since this is a pizza place, you have to have a pie. My wife and I always get the one with fennel sausage and roasted onion, but the *amatriciana,* with house-cured pancetta, is good too.

304 SE 28th Ave. (at Pine St.). (C) 503/517-9951. www.kensartisan.com. Reservations not accepted. Main courses $11–$14. MC, V. Tues–Sat 5–10pm.

Lauro Mediterranean Kitchen ✸✸ MEDITERRANEAN   Dark, romantic, and stylish, this sleek southeast Portland restaurant, in one of the city's burgeoning restaurant districts, is well worth the drive out from downtown. I like to start with the Egyptian flatbread with *dukka* (spicy toasted sesame seeds) and honey. The paella is a good bet, but also keep an eye out for lamb shanks, perhaps served with caramelized pears and shallots. Prices here are considerably lower than they would be for comparable food in the Pearl District, so Lauro represents a pretty good value.

3377 SE Division St. (C) 503/239-7000. www.laurokitchen.com. Reservations not accepted. Main courses $11–$21. AE, DISC, MC, V. Sun–Thurs 5–9pm; Fri–Sat 5–10pm.

Pok Pok ✸ THAI   I spent part of my childhood in Thailand and have returned many times as an adult, so trust me when I say that Pok Pok is the most authentic Thai restaurant I've ever eaten at outside of Thailand. Not only are the flavors of the dishes here some of the most vibrant and exotic you'll ever taste, but the whole atmosphere succeeds in conjuring up casual restaurants on the beaches of Thailand. Get the *kai yang* (grilled chicken) and *khao man som tam* (green papaya salad) for an absolute classic straight off the streets of Bangkok. Some people fault this place for serving skimpy portions, but it's the same way in Thailand. Just order another dish; you'll be glad you did.

3226 SE Division St. (C) 503/232-1387. http://pokpokpdx.com. Reservations accepted for parties of 5 or more. Main courses $7.50–$14. AE, MC, V. Mon–Fri 11:30am–10:30pm; Sat 5–10:30pm.

INEXPENSIVE

Esparza's Tex-Mex Café (Kids) TEX-MEX   With red-eyed cow skulls on the walls and marionettes, model planes, and stuffed iguanas and armadillos hanging from the ceiling, the decor here can only be described as Tex-eclectic, a description that is just as appropriately applied to the menu. Sure there are enchiladas and tamales and tacos, but they might be filled with ostrich or buffalo. Rest assured Esparza's also serves standard ingredients such as chicken and beef. Main courses come with some pretty good rice and beans, and if you want your meal hotter, they'll toss you a couple of jalapeño peppers. The *nopalitos* (fried cactus) are worth a try, and the margaritas are some of the best in Portland. While you're waiting for a seat (there's almost always a wait), check out the vintage tunes on the jukebox.

2725 SE Ankeny St. ☏ 503/234-7909. Reservations not accepted. Main courses $8.50–$18. AE, DC, DISC, MC, V. Mon–Sat 11:30am–10pm (in summer Fri–Sat until 10:30pm).

Nicholas's *(Finds)* MIDDLE EASTERN   This little hole-in-the-wall on an unattractive stretch of Grand Avenue is usually packed at mealtimes, and it's not the decor or ambience that pulls people in. The big draw is the great food and cheap prices. In spite of the heat from the pizza oven and the crowded conditions, the customers and waitstaff still manage to be friendly. My favorite dish is the *Manakish,* Mediterranean pizza with thyme, oregano, sesame seeds, olive oil, and lemony-flavored sumac. Also available are a creamy hummus, baba ghanouj, kabobs, falafel, and gyros.

318 SE Grand Ave. (between Pine and Oak sts.). ☏ 503/235-5123. www.nicholasrestaurant.com. Reservations not accepted. Main courses $4.75–$13. No credit cards. Mon–Sat 10am–9pm; Sun noon–9pm.

COFFEE, TEA, BAKERIES, PASTRY SHOPS & CHOCOLATIERS
CAFES
If you're in search of Portland's cafe culture or just need a good cup of coffee, I recommend the following places:

With an upscale Starbucks-style interior decor, a social conscience, and a Pearl District location, **World Cup,** 721 NW Ninth Ave. (☏ **503/546-7377;** www.worldcup coffee.com), is a coffee haven for the politically correct. It's even located in an unusual environmentally friendly "green" building that has a rooftop terrace. Other World Cups are located inside Powell's City of Books, 1005 W. Burnside St. (☏ **503/228-4651,** ext. 234), and in the Nob Hill neighborhood at 1740 NW Glisan St. (☏ **503/228-4152**).

Many a Portlander swears by the coffee at **Stumptown Coffee Roasters,** 128 SW Third Ave. (☏ **503/295-6144;** www.stumptowncoffee.com), a big, trendy cafe with an art-school aesthetic. Whether you go for the French press or a double shot of espresso, you're sure to be satisfied. There's another Stumptown in the lobby of the Ace Hotel, 1026 SW Stark St. (☏ **503/224-9060**). Over on the east side of the Willamette River are Stumptown's two original cafes: 4525 SE Division St. (☏ **503/230-7702**) and 3356 SE Belmont St. (☏ **503/232-8889**), which both tend to attract a young, hip clientele.

If you've got the kids with you but desperately need a place to sit down for a latte, head to **Sip & Kranz,** 901 NW Tenth Ave. (☏ **503/336-1335;** www.sipandkranz. com), a Pearl District coffee lounge that has a playroom for toddlers and young children. Right outside the front door is the immensely popular Jamison Square, where all summer long, kids splash in the wading pool fountain.

Not a coffee drinker? Try the funky **Tao of Tea,** 3430 SE Belmont St. (☏ **503/736-0119;** www.taooftea.com), which feels like it could be in some Kathmandu back alley and specializes in traditional Chinese tea service. There's a second tea room, called the Tower of Cosmic Reflection, inside the Portland Classical Chinese Garden, 239 NW Everett St. (☏ **503/224-8455**).

All you chocoholics out there will be relieved to know that Portland is a fabulous town for chocolate addicts. Whether you're looking for a hand-made truffle, a fair-trade chocolate bar, or a cup of drinking chocolate, there's a chocolatier in town for you. If hot chocolate, not coffee, is your cup of choice, then be sure to stop by **Moonstruck Chocolate Café**, 608 SW Alder St. (© **503/241-0955;** www.moonstruck chocolate.com), where you can choose from a wide variety of hot chocolate drinks. There's another Moonstruck in the Nob Hill neighborhood at 526 NW 23rd Ave. (© **503/542-3400**). **Cacao,** 414 SW 13th Ave. (© **503/241-0656;** www.cacaodrink chocolate.com), just off W. Burnside Street, offers a variety of chocolate confections from some of the Northwest's most noteworthy purveyors. **Alma Chocolate,** 140 NE 28th Ave. (© **503/517-0262;** www.almachocolate.com), uses fair-trade and organic ingredients in its chocolates. For hand-dipped truffles, head to **Sahagún,** 10 NW 16th Ave. (© **503/274-7065;** www.sahagunchocolates.com). Even big European chocolatiers have shops here in town. From Belgium come the pralines, buttercreams, and ganaches of **Leonidas,** 607 SW Washington St. (© **503/224-9247;** www.leonidas portland.com); and from Switzerland come the truffles of **teuscher,** 531 SW Broadway (© **503/827-0587;** www.teuscherportland.com).

BAKERIES & PASTRY SHOPS

Pearl Bakery ★★, 102 NW Ninth Ave. (© **503/827-0910**), in the heart of the Pearl District, is famous in Portland for its breads and European-style pastries. The gleaming bakery cafe is also good for sandwiches, such as a roasted eggplant and tomato pesto on crusty bread.

Say the words "Papa Haydn" to a Portlander, and you'll see a blissful smile appear. What is it about this little bistro that makes locals start gushing superlatives? The desserts. The lemon chiffon torte, raspberry gâteau, black velvet, and tiramisu at **Papa Haydn West** ★★, 701 NW 23rd Ave. (© **503/228-7317;** www.papahaydn.com), are legendary. There's another location at 5829 SE Milwaukie Ave. (© **503/232-9440**) in the Westmoreland neighborhood.

Also in the Nob Hill neighborhood, you'll find **Ken's Artisan Bakery,** 338 NW 21st Ave. (© **503/248-2202;** www.kensartisan.com). Ken's doesn't do a wide variety of pastries, but what it does do, it does very well. Yum! Try the fruit tarts. My current favorite bakery in the neighborhood is the utterly Gallic **St. Honoré Boulangerie,** 2335 NW Thurman St. (© **503/445-4342;** www.sainthonorebakery.com); not only does this place turn out awesome pastries and breads, but you can read *Le Monde* while eating your croissant.

Located in Ladd's Addition, an old neighborhood full of big trees and Craftsman-style bungalows, **Palio Dessert & Espresso House** ★, 1996 SE Ladd Ave. (© **503/232-9412;** www.palio-in-ladds.com), is a very relaxed place with a timeless European quality. To get there, take Hawthorne Boulevard east to the corner of 12th and Hawthorne, and then go diagonally down Ladd Avenue.

The **Rimsky-Korsakoffee House** ★, 707 SE 12th Ave. (© **503/232-2640**), a classic old-style coffeehouse, has been Portland's favorite dessert hangout for more than 25 years. Live classical music and great desserts keep patrons loyal. It's open from 7pm to midnight on Sunday through Thursday and 7pm until 1am on Friday and Saturday.

We've saved the best for last: **Pix Patisserie,** 3402 SE Division St. (© **503/232-4407;** www.pixpatisserie.com), makes by far the most decadent pastries in Portland. Every sweet little jewel here is a work of art, and it can sometimes be a real challenge to desecrate these creations with a fork. Go ahead, take a bite—you won't soon forget the experience. There are also two other Pix Patisserie locations: 3731 SE Hawthorne Blvd. (© **503/236-4760**); and 3901 N. Williams Ave. (© **503/282-6539**).

If doughnuts are your guilty pleasure of choice, then do not miss Portland's **Voodoo Doughnut,** 22 SW Third Ave. (© **503/241-4704;** http://voodoodoughnut.com). Open 24 hours a day and boasting that "the magic is in the hole," this downtown nightlife-district hole in the wall is not your usual doughnut shop. There are voodoo-doll doughnuts, bacon-topped maple bars, vegan doughnuts, and even x-rated doughnuts.

If it's hot out and nothing will do but something cold and creamy, check out one of Portland's gelaterias. These Italian-style frozen-dessert parlors have taken Portland by storm. In the Nob Hill neighborhood, there's **Alotto Gelato,** 931 NW 23rd Ave. (© **503/228-1709;** http://alottogelato.biz); in the Pearl District, there's **Mio Gelato,** 25 NW 11th Ave. (© **503/226-8002**); and in northeast Portland, just off East Burnside Street, there's **Staccato Gelato,** 232 NE 28th Ave. (© **503/231-7100;** www.staccato gelato.com).

QUICK BITES & CHEAP EATS

If you're just looking for something quick, cheap, and good to eat, there are lots of great options around the city. Among my personal favorite choices are the many ethnic food carts that set up in parking lots around downtown. Two places to check out include the corner of SW Stark Street and SW Fifth Avenue and the corner of SW Alder Street and SW Ninth Avenue.

Designer pizzas topped with anything from roasted eggplant to wild mushrooms to Thai peanut sauce can be had at **Pizzicato Gourmet Pizza** (www.pizzicatopizza. com). Find them downtown at 705 SW Alder St. (© **503/226-1007**); in Northwest Portland at 505 NW 23rd Ave. (© **503/242-0023**); and in southeast Portland at 2811 E. Burnside (© **503/236-6045**). However, if you find yourself near a **Hot Lips Pizza** (www.hotlipspizza.com), give it a try. They're located at SE Hawthorne Blvd. and SE 22nd Ave. (© **503/234-9999**), NW 10th Ave. at NW Irving St. (© **503/ 595-2342**), and SW Sixth Ave. at SW Hall St. (© **503/224-0311**). For inexpensive sushi, stop by one of Portland's many outposts of **Mio Sushi** (www.miosushi.com). Locations include 2271 NW Johnson St. (© **503/221-1469**), 3962 SE Hawthorne Blvd. (© **503/230-6981**), and 4204 NE Halsey St. (© **503/288-4778**). For fast organic and mostly vegetarian food, search out a **Laughing Planet** (www.laughing planetcafe.com). You'll find them at 922 NW 21st Ave. (© **503/445-1319**), 3320 SE Belmont St. (© **503/235-6472**), and 3765 N Mississippi St. (© **503/467-4146**).

5 Seeing the Sights

Most American cities boast about their museums and historic buildings, shopping, and restaurants; Portland, as always, is different. Ask a Portlander about the city's must-see attractions, and you'll probably be directed to the Japanese Garden, the International Rose Test Garden, the Portland Classical Chinese Garden, and the Portland Saturday Market.

This isn't to say that the Portland Art Museum, which often hosts blockbuster exhibits, isn't worth visiting or that there are no historic buildings around. It's just that Portland's gardens, thanks to the weather here, are some of the finest in the country. What's more, all the rain seems to keep artists indoors creating beautiful art and crafts for much of the year, work that many artists sell at the Portland Saturday Market.

Moments **Keep Portland Weird**

"Keep Portland weird," an often-seen bumper sticker here in Stumptown, has become something of a mantra for many Portlanders. This town attracts a lot of independent thinkers, counterculturalists, and artistic types of all sorts. Not surprisingly, some of these people have chosen to share their personal passions through small, private museums. Here are some of my favorites.

- **The Hat Museum** (✆ **503/232-0433**; www.thehatmuseum.com): Hundreds of hats and lots more. Tours by costumed museum owner. Open daily 10am to 6pm; admission is $10.
- **Mike's Movie Memorabilia Collection**, 4320 SE Belmont St. (✆ **503/234-4363**; www.moviemadnessvideo.com): Costumes and props from Hollywood movies inside a video-rental store. Open Sunday to Thursday 10am to 11pm, Friday to Saturday 10am to midnight; admission is free.
- **Stark's Vacuum Museum**, 107 NE Grand Ave. (✆ **503/232-4101**; www.starks.com): A vacuum-cleaner store with vacuums dating from the 1880s to the 1960s. This place really sucks. Open Monday to Friday 8am to 7pm, Saturday 9am to 5pm, Sunday 11am to 4pm; admission is free.
- **3D Center of Art & Photography**, 1928 NW Lovejoy St. (✆ **503/227-6667**; www.3dcenter.us): Contemporary and vintage 3-D photos and art. Open Thursday to Saturday 11am to 5pm, Sunday 1 to 5pm; on first Thursday of the month, it's also open 6 to 9pm. Admission is $4.
- **Velveteria**, 2448 E. Burnside St. (✆ **503/233-5100**; www.velveteria.com): A museum of velvet paintings. 'Nuff said? Open Friday to Sunday noon to 5pm; admission is $3.
- **Wells Fargo History Museum**, 1300 SW Fifth Ave. (✆ **503/886-1102**; www.wellsfargohistory.com): Stagecoaches in the soggy Northwest? Yee-haw. Open Monday to Friday 9am to 6pm; admission is free.

Gardening is a Portland obsession, and there are numerous world-class public gardens and parks within the city. Visiting all the city's gardens alone can take up 2 or 3 days of touring, so leave plenty of time in your schedule if you have a green thumb.

Once you've seen the big attractions, it's time to start learning why everyone loves living here so much. Portlanders for the most part are active types, who enjoy skiing on Mount Hood and hiking in the Columbia Gorge just as much as they enjoy going to art museums, so no visit to Portland would be complete without venturing out into the Oregon countryside. Within 1½ hours you can be skiing on Mount Hood, walking beside the chilly waters of the Pacific, sampling pinot noir in wine country, or hiking beside a waterfall in the Columbia Gorge. But for those who prefer urban activities, the museums and parks listed below should satisfy.

DOWNTOWN PORTLAND'S CULTURAL DISTRICT

Any visit to Portland should start at the corner of Southwest Broadway and Yamhill Street on **Pioneer Courthouse Square.** The brick-paved square is an outdoor stage for everything from flower displays to concerts to protest rallies, but not too many

Portland Attractions

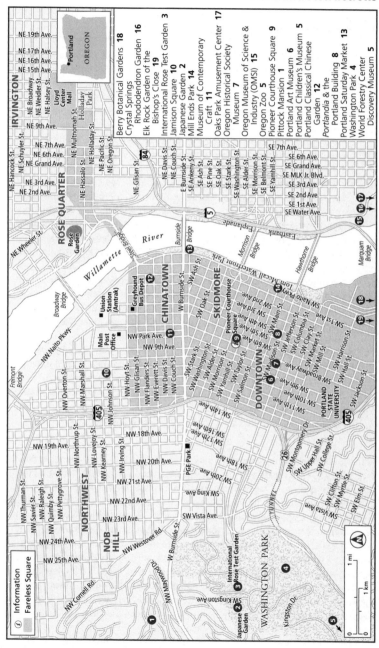

Berry Botanical Gardens **18**
Crystal Springs
Rhododendron Garden **16**
Elk Rock Garden of the
Bishop's Close **19**
International Rose Test Garden **3**
Jamison Square **10**
Japanese Garden **2**
Mill Ends Park **14**
Museum of Contemporary
Craft **11**
Oaks Park Amusement Center **17**
Oregon Historical Society
Museum **7**
Oregon Museum of Science &
Industry (OMSI) **15**
Oregon Zoo **5**
Pioneer Courthouse Square **9**
Pittock Mansion **1**
Portland Art Museum **6**
Portland Children's Museum **5**
Portland Classical Chinese
Garden **12**
Portlandia & the
Portland Building **8**
Portland Saturday Market **13**
Washington Park **4**
World Forestry Center
Discovery Museum **5**

Frommer's Favorite Portland Experiences

- **Strolling the Grounds at the Japanese Garden.** This is the best Japanese garden in the United States, perhaps the best anywhere outside of Japan. My favorite time to visit is in June when the Japanese irises are in bloom. There's no better stress reducer in the city.
- **Beer Sampling at Brewpubs.** They may not have invented beer here in Portland, but they've certainly turned it into an art form. Whether you're looking for a cozy corner pub or an upscale taproom, you'll find a brewpub where you can feel comfortable sampling what local brewmeisters are concocting.
- **Kayaking around Ross Island.** Seattle may be the sea-kayaking capital of the Northwest, but Portland's not a bad spot for pursuing this sport either. You can paddle on the Columbia or Willamette rivers, but our favorite easy kayak is around Ross Island in the Willamette River, about a quarter mile from the downtown high-rises. You can even paddle past the submarine at the Oregon Museum of Science and Industry and pull out at Tom McCall Waterfront Park.
- **Mountain Biking the Leif Erickson Road.** Forest Park is one of the largest forested city parks in the country, and running its length is unpaved Leif Erickson Road. The road is closed to cars and extends for 12 miles. Along the way, there are occasional views of the Columbia River. This is a long but relatively easy ride, without any strenuous climbs.
- **Hanging Out at Powell's.** They don't call Powell's the City of Books for nothing. This bookstore, which sells both new and used books, is so big you have to get a map at the front door. No matter how much time I spend here, it's never enough. A large cafe makes it all that much easier to while away the hours.

years ago this beautiful area was nothing but a parking lot. The parking lot had been created in 1951 (in the days before historic preservation) when the Portland Hotel, an architectural gem of a Queen Anne–style château, was torn down.

Today the square, with its waterfall fountain and freestanding columns, is Portland's favorite gathering spot, especially at noon, when the **Weather Machine** 𝕬, a mechanical sculpture, forecasts the weather for the next 24 hours. Amid a fanfare of music and flashing lights, the Weather Machine sends up clouds of mist and then either a sun (clear weather), a dragon (stormy weather), or a blue heron (clouds and drizzle) appears.

Keep your eyes on the square's brick pavement, too. Every brick contains a name (or names) or statement, and some are rather curious. Also on the square, you'll find the **Travel Portland** visitor's information center and a Starbucks. Unfortunately, you'll also find plenty of street kids hanging out here all hours of the day and night, so don't be surprised if they ask you for spare change.

Also not to be missed in this neighborhood are *Portlandia* 𝕬𝕬 and the **Portland Building,** 1120 SW Fifth Ave. The symbol of the city, *Portlandia* is the second-largest hammered bronze statue in the country (the largest is the Statue of Liberty). The massive kneeling figure holds a trident in one hand and reaches toward the street with the

- **Free Rides on the Vintage Trolleys.** TriMet buses, MAX light-rail trolleys, and Portland Streetcars are all free within a large downtown area known as the Fareless Square. That alone should be enough to get you on some form of public transit while you're in town, but if you're really lucky, you might catch one of the vintage trolley cars that operate on the MAX line on Sundays from March through December. There aren't any San Francisco–style hills, but the old streetcars are still fun to ride.
- **An Afternoon at the Portland Saturday Market.** This large arts-and-crafts market is an outdoor showcase for hundreds of the Northwest's creative artisans. You'll find one-of-a-kind clothes, jewelry, kitchenwares, musical instruments, and much, much more. The food stalls serve up some great fast food, too.
- **Summertime Concerts at the Washington Park Zoo.** Summertime in Portland means partying with the pachyderms. Throughout the summer you can catch live music at the zoo's amphitheater. Musical styles include blues, rock, bluegrass, folk, Celtic, and jazz. Sometimes for nothing more than the regular zoo admission, you can catch the concert and tour the zoo (if you arrive early enough). Picnics are encouraged, and beer and wine are for sale during concerts.
- **First Thursday Art Walk.** On the first Thursday of every month, Portland goes on an art binge. People get dressed up and go gallery hopping from art opening to art opening. There are usually hors d'oeuvres and wine available, and sometimes there's even live music. The galleries stay open until 9pm.

other. This classically designed figure perches incongruously above the entrance to architect Michael Graves' controversial Portland Building, considered to be the first postmodern structure in the United States. Today, anyone familiar with the bizarre constructions of Los Angeles architect Frank Gehry would find it difficult to understand how such an innocuous and attractive building could have ever raised such a fuss, but it did just that in the early 1980s.

Shopping for produce may not be on your usual vacation itinerary, but the **Portland Farmers Market** (© **503/241-0032;** www.portlandfarmersmarket.org), which can be found in this neighborhood's South Park Blocks between SW Harrison and SW Montgomery streets, is such a quintessentially Portland experience that you will not be able to say you have gained a sense of what this city is about unless you visit. Portland is a city obsessed with food, and nowhere is this more apparent than at this weekly market. Fresh berries, wild mushrooms and other foraged produce, salmon, oysters, pastries, artisan breads, hazelnuts, local wines. You'll find all of this and more here at the market. Live music and cooking demonstrations by local chefs add to the market's appeal. The market is held on Saturdays from 8:30am to 2pm between early April and late December.

Oregon Historical Society Museum ⚲   In the middle of the 19th century, the Oregon Territory was a land of promise and plenty. Thousands of hardy individuals set out along the Oregon Trail, crossing a vast and rugged country to reach the fertile valleys of this region. Others came by ship around Cape Horn. If you'd like to learn about the people who discovered Oregon before you, visit this well-designed museum. Fascinating exhibits chronicle Oregon's history from before the arrival of the first Europeans to well into the 20th century. Museum docents, with roots stretching back to the days of the Oregon Trail, are often on hand to answer questions. You can't miss this museum—look for the eight-story-high trompe l'oeil mural stretching across the front.

1200 SW Park Ave. 𝄢 **503/222-1741.** www.ohs.org. Admission $10 adults, $8 students and seniors, $5 children 6–18, free for children under 6. Tues–Sat 10am–5pm; Sun noon–5pm. Bus: 6 or 8. MAX: Library Station. Portland Streetcar: Art Museum (northbound); 11th Ave. and Jefferson St. (southbound).

Portland Art Museum ⚲⚲   This is the oldest art museum in the Northwest, and it has an excellent collection of modern and contemporary art. This collection begins with European Impressionists and moves right up to the present. However, the best reason to visit is to see the extensive collection of Native American art and artifacts. There's also a good collection of Northwest contemporary art that includes a fascinating two-story wall of "artifacts" by glass artist William Morris. Other collections include European, Asian, and American art, and there's a small sculpture court. The Portland Art Museum is frequently the Northwest stop for touring blockbuster exhibits.

1219 SW Park Ave. 𝄢 **503/226-2811.** www.portlandartmuseum.org. Admission $10 adults, $9 seniors and college students, $6 children 5–18, free for children under 5. Tues–Wed and Sat 10am–5pm; Thurs–Fri 10am–8pm; Sun noon–5pm. Closed Christmas. Bus: 6. MAX: Library Station. Portland Streetcar: Art Museum (northbound); 11th Ave. and Jefferson St. (southbound).

SKIDMORE HISTORIC DISTRICT, CHINATOWN, THE PEARL DISTRICT & THE WILLAMETTE RIVER WATERFRONT

If Pioneer Courthouse Square is the city's living room, **Tom McCall Waterfront Park** ⚲, along the Willamette River, is the city's front-yard play area. There are acres of lawns, shade trees, sculptures, and fountains, and the paved path through the park is popular with in-line skaters and joggers. This park also serves as the site of numerous festivals each summer. Also in the park is the Japanese-American Historical Plaza, dedicated to Japanese Americans who were sent to internment camps during World War II.

Just north of this plaza, a pedestrian walkway crosses the Steel Bridge to the east side of the Willamette River and the **Vera Katz Eastbank Esplanade,** which stretches for about 1½ miles along the east bank of the river. Although this paved multiuse path gets a lot of traffic noise from the adjacent freeway, it offers great views of the Portland skyline. Along the route there are small parks and gardens, interesting sculptures, and benches for sitting and soaking up the view. The highlight of this path is a section that floats right on the river and is attached to pilings in much the same way that a floating dock is constructed. You can access the Eastbank Esplanade by way of the pedestrian pathway on the Steel Bridge. This bridge is at the north end of Waterfront Park.

Museum of Contemporary Craft ⚲⚲   Founded in 1937, this is one of the country's finest museums of contemporary craft, and in 2007, the museum moved to this new location on the tree-shaded North Park Blocks. Throughout the year, works from the permanent collection share space with changing exhibits that might focus on an individual artist or a single theme. Cutting-edge ceramics and jewelry are always highlights of exhibits here, but you might catch a show focusing on crafts incorporating bamboo or an exhibition of artist-made books. From here it is just a few blocks to the art galleries in the Pearl District.

724 NW Davis St. (②) 503/223-2654. http://museumofcontemporarycraft.org. Free admission. Tues–Wed and Fri–Sun 11am–6pm; Thurs 11am–8pm. Closed New Year's Day, July 4, Thanksgiving, Christmas.

Oregon Museum of Science and Industry (OMSI) 🦅 *Kids*

Located on the east bank of the Willamette River across from the south end of Waterfront Park, this modern science museum has six huge halls, and both kids and adults find the exhibits fun and fascinating. This is a hands-on museum, and everyone is urged to get involved with displays, from a science playground for young children to physics and chemistry labs for older children. Simulated earthquakes and tornadoes are perennial favorites. There's plenty of pure entertainment at an **OMNIMAX theater** and the **Kendall Planetarium,** which features laser-light shows and astronomy presentations. The USS *Blueback* submarine (used in the film *The Hunt for Red October*) is docked here, and tours are given daily.

A paved pathway runs beside OMSI and heads north to the Vera Katz Eastbank Esplanade and south 3 miles to Oaks Bottom amusement park. Along the pathway beside the museum, there are several interesting informational plaques about the history of Portland and its relationship to the Willamette River. OMSI is also the departure point for several different boat cruises up and down the Willamette River.

1945 SE Water Ave. (②) 800/955-6674 or 503/797-6674. www.omsi.edu. Museum $9 adults, $7 seniors and children 3–13; OMNIMAX shows $8.50 adults, $6.50 seniors and children 3–13; $5.50 submarine tours, planetarium shows, and matinee laser-light shows; $7.50 evening laser shows; discounted combination tickets available. Thurs 2pm until closing all tickets are 2 for 1. Mid-June to Aug daily 9:30am–7pm; Sept to mid-June Tues–Sun 9:30am–5:30pm. Closed Thanksgiving and Christmas. Bus: 4, 14, or 33.

Portland Classical Chinese Garden 🦅🦅

This classically styled Chinese garden takes up an entire city block and is the largest of its type outside of China. The walls surrounding these gardens in Portland's Chinatown separate the urban 21st century from the timeless Chinese landscape within. The landscape is designed to evoke the wild mountains of China and to create a tranquil oasis within an urban setting. The gardens are centered around a small pond, which, at one end, has a rock wall meant to conjure up the sort of images often seen in Chinese scroll paintings. Numerous pavilions, a small bridge, and a winding pathway provide ever-changing views of the gardens. With its many paved paths and small viewing pavilions, this garden has a completely different feel from the Japanese Garden. Try to visit as soon as the gardens open in the morning; when the crowds descend and the guided tours start circulating—well, so much for tranquillity. On the other hand, if you want to learn more about the garden, you can join a guided tour at noon or 1pm. Be sure to stop and have a cup of tea and maybe a snack in the garden's tearoom.

NW Everett St. and NW Third Ave. (②) 503/228-8131. www.portlandchinesegarden.org. Admission $7 adults, $6 seniors, $5.50 students and children 6–18, free for children 5 and under. Apr–Oct daily 9am–6pm; Nov–Mar daily 10am–5pm. Bus: 1, 4, 5, 8, 10, 16, 33, 40, or 77. MAX: Old Town/Chinatown Station.

Portland Saturday Market 🦅

The Portland Saturday Market (actually held on both Sat and Sun) is arguably the city's best-loved event. For years the Northwest has attracted artists and craftspeople, and every Saturday and Sunday nearly 300 of them can be found selling their creations here. In addition to the dozens of crafts stalls, you'll find ethnic and unusual foods and lots of free entertainment. This is one of the

Pearls in the Pearl District

The Pearl District is Portland's hottest neighborhood, and in addition to all the restaurants, wine bars, and boutiques, there are some fun works of public art, a beautiful little park that looks like a small park in Paris, and an innovative park that is something of a quiet natural area within an urban setting.

Stroll through the tree-shaded parks of the North Park blocks, which form the eastern edge of the Pearl District, and, at the Burnside Street end of these parks, you'll see a huge Chinese bronze elephant that was a gift from one of Portland's sister cities. A couple of blocks north of this elephant, watch for a bronze dog-bowl water fountain set in a checkerboard floor of stone. This odd sculpture was created by William Wegman, famous for his humorous photos of his dogs.

Right in the heart of the Pearl District, at the corner of NW Johnson Street and NW 10th Avenue, you'll find Jamison Square, a park with an unusual wall-like cascading waterfall that fills a shallow pool. Around the graveled areas of the park, you'll find bistro chairs where you can sit and enjoy a latte from a nearby espresso bar. Be sure to notice the totem-pole–inspired sculptures along the western edge of the park. Two blocks north of Jamison Square, at the corner of NW 10th Avenue and NW Marshall Street, you'll find Tanner Springs Park, an unusual little natural area that revives the springs that once flowed here while at the same time commemorating the railroad yards that predate the Pearl District's many new developments.

best places in Portland to shop for one-of-a-kind gifts. The atmosphere is always cheerful and the crowds colorful. Located at the heart of the Skidmore District, Portland Saturday Market makes an excellent starting or finishing point for a walk around Portland's downtown historic neighborhood. On Sunday, on-street parking is free.

Underneath the west end of the Burnside Bridge between SW First Ave. and SW Naito Pkwy. © 503/222-6072. www.portlandsaturdaymarket.com. Free admission. 1st weekend in Mar to Christmas Eve Sat 10am–5pm and Sun 11am–4:30pm. Bus: 12, 19, or 20. MAX: Skidmore Fountain Station.

WASHINGTON PARK & PORTLAND'S WEST HILLS

Portland is justly proud of its green spaces, and foremost among them are **Washington Park** and **Forest Park.**

Within Washington Park, you'll find the **Japanese Garden** and **International Rose Test Garden,** which are adjacent to one another on the more developed east side of the park (see the listings below). On the west side of the park (farther from the city center), you'll find not only the Hoyt Arboretum but also the Oregon Zoo, World Forestry Center Discovery Museum, and the Portland Children's Museum.

The 185-acre **Hoyt Arboretum** ✦ (© **503/865-8733;** www.hoytarboretum.org) includes over 1,000 species of trees and shrubs from temperate regions around the world and has several miles of hiking trails. Between April and October, there are free 1-hour guided tours of the arboretum on the first Saturday of the month at 10am. At the south end of the arboretum, adjacent to the World Forestry Center Discovery Museum and the Oregon Zoo, is the **Vietnam Veterans Living Memorial.** At the arboretum's Visitor Center, 4000 SW Fairview Blvd. (Mon–Fri 9am–4pm and Sat 9am–3pm), you can pick up maps and guides to the arboretum. The arboretum can be reached either from the Oregon Zoo/World Forestry Center Discovery Museum/Portland Children's Museum area or by following the arboretum signs from West Burnside Street.

To the north of Hoyt Arboretum is **Forest Park** ★★ (© 503/823-PLAY), which, with more than 5,000 acres of forest, is one of the largest forested city parks in the United States. Within the park, there are more than 74 miles of trails and old fire roads for hiking, jogging, and mountain biking. More than 100 species of birds call this forest home, making it a great spot for urban bird-watching. Along the forest trails, you can see huge old trees and find quiet picnic spots tucked away in the woods. One of the most convenient park access points is at the top of NW Thurman Street (just keep heading uphill until the road dead-ends). You can also park at the Hoyt Arboretum Visitor Center (see above) or the Audubon Society (see below), pick up a map of Forest Park, and head out from either of these locations.

Adjacent to Forest Park, you'll also find the **Portland Audubon Society,** 5151 NW Cornell Rd. (© **503/292-6855;** www.audubonportland.org), which has a couple of miles of hiking trails on its forested property. In keeping with its mission to promote enjoyment, understanding, and protection of the natural world, these nature trails are open to the public. You can also visit the Nature Store or Wildlife Care Center here. To find this facility from downtown Portland, first drive to NW 23rd Avenue, and then head uphill on NW Lovejoy Street, which becomes NW Cornell Road. (*Warning:* Car break-ins are commonplace at the parking area just down the road from the Audubon Society, so don't leave anything of value in your car.)

By car, the easiest route to the Washington Park attractions from downtown Portland is to take SW Jefferson Street west, turn right onto SW 18th Avenue, left on SW

Great Photo Ops

If you've seen a photo of Portland with conical snow-covered Mount Hood looming in the background and you want to snap a similar photo while you're in town, there are several places to try. Most popular are probably the terraces of the International Rose Test Garden and from behind the pavilion at the Japanese Garden. Another great view can be glimpsed from the grounds of the Pittock Mansion. All three of these places are described in detail elsewhere in this chapter.

One other not-to-be-missed vista is located atop Council Crest, a hilltop park in Portland's West Hills. To reach this park, take the Sylvan exit off U.S. 26 west of downtown Portland, turn south and then east (left) on Humphrey Boulevard, and then follow the signs. Alternatively, you can follow SW Broadway south out of downtown Portland and follow the signs. This road winds through attractive hillside neighborhoods for a ways before reaching Council Crest.

Salmon Street, right on SW King Street, and then left onto SW Park Place. Although this sounds confusing, you'll find most of the route well marked with "Scenic Drive" signs. Alternatively, you can drive west on West Burnside Street and watch for signs to the arboretum, or take the zoo exit off U.S. 26. All of these attractions can also be reached via Bus 63. You can also take the MAX line to the Washington Park Station, which is adjacent to the Oregon Zoo, World Forestry Center Discovery Museum, Portland Children's Museum, and Hoyt Arboretum. From here, it is possible (in the summer months) to take a bus shuttle to the Japanese Garden and International Rose Test Garden. There's also a miniature train that runs from the zoo to a station near the two public gardens. However, to ride this train, you must first pay zoo admission.

International Rose Test Garden ★★   Covering more than 5 acres of hillside in the West Hills above downtown Portland, these are among the largest and oldest rose test gardens in the United States and are the only city-maintained test gardens to bestow awards on each year's best roses. The gardens were established in 1917 by the American Rose Society and are used as a testing ground for new varieties of roses. Though you will probably see some familiar roses in the Gold Medal Garden, most of the 400 varieties on display are new hybrids being tested before marketing. Among the various gardens here, which have blooms from late spring through early winter, you'll find a separate garden of miniature roses and a Shakespeare Garden that includes flowers mentioned in the bard's works. After seeing these acres of roses, you'll understand why Portland is known as the City of Roses and why the Rose Festival in June is the city's biggest annual celebration. The small Rose Garden Store, 850 SW Rose Garden Way (© 503/227-7033; www.rosegardenstore.com) is packed with rose-inspired products.

400 SW Kingston Ave., Washington Park. © 503/823-3636. Free admission (donations accepted). Daily dawn–dusk. Bus: 63.

The Japanese Garden ★★★   Considered the finest example of a Japanese garden in North America, this exquisitely manicured green space should not be missed. Not only are there five different styles of Japanese gardens scattered over 5½ acres, but there's also a view of volcanic Mount Hood, which bears a strong resemblance to Mount Fuji.

Although Japanese gardens are traditionally not designed with colorful floral displays, this garden definitely has its seasonal highlights. In early spring there are the cherry trees, in mid-spring there are the azaleas, in late spring a huge wisteria bursts into bloom, and in early summer, large Japanese irises color the banks of a pond. Among the gardens, there's a beautiful and very realistic waterfall.

This is a very tranquil spot and is even more peaceful on rainy days, when the crowds stay away, so don't pass up a visit just because of inclement weather. Also, May through October, on the third Saturday of each month, there's a demonstration of the Japanese tea ceremony in the garden's teahouse.

611 SW Kingston Ave. (in Washington Park). © 503/223-1321. www.japanesegarden.com. Admission $8 adults, $6.25 seniors and college students, $5.25 youths 6–17, free for children under 6. Apr–Sept Mon noon–7pm and Tues–Sun 10am–7pm; Oct–Mar Mon noon–4pm and Tues–Sun 10am–4pm. Closed New Year's Day, Thanksgiving, Christmas. Bus: 63. MAX: Washington Park Station (then, in summer months, take the shuttle bus or the zoo train).

Oregon Zoo ★ Kids   The Oregon Zoo is perhaps best known for its elephants and has the most successful breeding herd of elephants in captivity. However, in recent years, the zoo has been adding new exhibits and branching out beyond the world of

All Aboard!

The **Washington Park and Zoo Railway** travels between the zoo and the International Rose Test Garden and Japanese Garden. Tickets for the miniature railway are $3.50 for adults, $2.75 for seniors and children 3 to 11, and free for children under 3. There's also a shorter route that just loops around the zoo.

pachyderms. The Africa exhibit, which includes a very lifelike rainforest and a savanna populated by zebras, rhinos, giraffes, hippos, and other animals, is one of the most realistic habitats you'll ever see at a zoo. Equally impressive is the Alaskan tundra exhibit, with grizzly bears, wolves, and musk oxen. The Cascade Crest exhibit includes mountain goat habitat, and in the Steller Cove exhibit, you can watch the antics of Steller's sea lions and sea otters. Don't miss the bat house or the Amazon Flooded Forest exhibit.

The zoo's SimEx-Iwerks Simulation Theatre, a 3-D thrill ride, is a big hit with kids. In the summer, there are **outdoor concerts** in the zoo's amphitheater; admission prices vary.

4001 SW Canyon Rd., Washington Park. ✆ 503/226-1561. www.oregonzoo.org. Admission $9.75 adults, $8.25 seniors, $6.75 children 3–11, free under age 3; $2 admission for all 2nd Tues of each month. Apr 15–Sept 15 daily 9am–6pm; Sept 16–Apr 14 daily 9am–4pm. Closed Christmas. Bus: 63. MAX: Washington Park Station.

Pittock Mansion ✿   At nearly the highest point in the West Hills, 1,000 feet above sea level, stands the most impressive mansion in Portland. Once slated to be torn down to make way for new housing, this grand château, built by the founder of Portland's *Oregonian* newspaper, is fully restored and open to the public. Built in 1914 in a French Renaissance style, the mansion featured many innovations, including a built-in vacuum system and amazing multiple showerheads in the baths. Today it's furnished with 18th- and 19th-century antiques, much as it might have been at the time the Pittocks lived here. With an expansive view over the city to the Cascade Range, the lawns surrounding the mansion are great for picnics. You can also access Forest Park's Wildwood Trail from here.

3229 NW Pittock Dr. ✆ 503/823-3623. www.pittockmansion.org. Admission $7 adults, $6 seniors, $4 children 6–18. June daily 11am–4pm; July–Aug daily 10am–4pm; Sept–Dec and Feb–May daily noon–4pm. Closed Christmas and the month of Jan.

World Forestry Center Discovery Museum ✿   Although Oregon depends less and less on the timber industry with each passing year, this museum is still busy educating visitors about the importance of forest resources around the world. Step inside the huge wooden main hall, and you come face to bark with several large and very lifelike trees. Press a button at its base and you can pilot a video camera around the tree's branches. Pay an extra $4, and you can climb into a chairlift that lets you explore these same trees. In another exhibit, you can practice being a smoke jumper (firefighter), while in another area, you can go on a video raft ride. There are also interesting temporary exhibits staged here throughout the year, from photographic exhibits to displays of the woodworker's art.

4033 SW Canyon Rd. ✆ 503/228-1367. www.worldforestry.org. Admission $7 adults, $6 seniors, $5 children 3–18, free for children under 3. Daily 10am–5pm. Closed Thanksgiving, Christmas Eve, and Christmas. Bus: 63. MAX: Washington Park Station.

The World's Smallest Park

Don't blink as you cross the median strip on Naito Parkway at the corner of SW Taylor Street, or you might just walk right past **Mill Ends Park,** the smallest public park in the world.

Covering a whopping 452 square *inches* of land, this park was the whimsical creation of local journalist Dick Fagen. After a telephone pole was removed from the middle of Naito Parkway (then known as Front Ave.), Fagen dubbed the phone pole hole Mill Ends Park (Mill Ends, a lumber mill term, was the name of Fagen's newspaper column). The columnist, whose office looked down on the hole in the middle of Front Avenue, peopled the imaginary park with leprechauns and would often write of the park's goings-on in his column. On St. Patrick's Day 1976, it was officially designated a Portland city park. Rumor has it that despite its diminutive size, the park has been the site of several weddings (although the parks department has never issued a wedding permit for it).

PORTLAND'S OTHER PUBLIC GARDENS

For Portland's two best-loved public gardens, the **International Rose Test Garden** and the **Japanese Garden,** see "Washington Park & Portland's West Hills," above.

If roses are your passion, you'll also want to check out the **Peninsula Park Rose Garden** at the corner of North Portland Boulevard and North Albina Avenue (take the Portland Blvd. exit off I-5 and go 2 blocks east), which has even more rose bushes than the International Rose Test Garden.

The Berry Botanic Garden 🦋   Originally founded as a private garden, the Berry Botanic Garden is now one of Portland's favorite public gardens. Among the highlights is a large, forestlike collection of mature rhododendron shrubs. There are also rock gardens with unusual plants, a native plant trail, and a fern garden. The garden is open by reservation only.

11505 SW Summerville Ave. ⓒ **503/636-4112.** www.berrybot.org. Adults $5. Open daylight hours by appointment. Bus: 35.

Crystal Springs Rhododendron Garden 🦋   Nowhere do rhododendrons do better than in the cool, rainy Northwest, and nowhere in Portland is there a more impressive planting of rhodies than at Crystal Springs. Eight months out of the year, this is a tranquil garden, with a waterfall, a lake, and ducks to feed. But when the rhododendrons and azaleas bloom from March to June, it becomes a spectacular mass of blazing color. The Rhododendron Show and Plant Sale is held here on Mother's Day weekend.

SE 28th Ave. (1 block north of SE Woodstock Blvd.). ⓒ **503/771-8366.** Admission $3 Mar 1 to Labor Day Thurs–Mon 10am–6pm; free at other times. Open year-round daily dawn to dusk. Bus: 19.

Elk Rock Garden of the Bishop's Close 🦋   Set on a steep hillside above the Willamette River between Portland and Lake Oswego, this was once a private garden but was donated to the local Episcopal bishop of Oregon on the condition that it be opened to the public. The mature gardens are at their best through the spring and early summer. There's also an excellent view of Mount Hood from the grounds.

11800 SW Military Lane. ✆ 800/452-2562 or 503/636-5613. www.diocese-oregon.org/theclose. Free admission. Daily 8am–5pm. Bus: 35.

6 Especially for Kids

In addition to the attractions listed below, the kids will especially enjoy the **Oregon Museum of Science and Industry** (p. 97), which has lots of hands-on exhibits, and the **Oregon Zoo** (p. 100). From inside the zoo, it's possible to take a small train through Washington Park to the International Rose Test Garden, below which there is the **Rose Garden Children's Park,** a colorful play area for younger children. The **Salmon Street Springs fountain,** in downtown's Tom McCall Waterfront Park (at SW Naito Pkwy. and SW Salmon St.), is another fun place to take the kids. During hot summer months, there are always lots of happy kids playing in the jets of water that erupt from the pavement here. There are also big lawns in **Waterfront Park,** so the kids can run off plenty of excess energy. There's also a splashy play-pond at **Jamison Square** in the Pearl District.

Oaks Park Amusement Center *Kids*   What would summer be without the screams of happy thrill seekers risking life and limb on a roller coaster? Covering more than 44 acres, this amusement park first opened in 1905 to coincide with the Lewis and Clark Exposition. Beneath the shady oaks for which the park is named, you'll find waterfront picnic sites, miniature golf, music, and plenty of thrilling rides. Check out the largest wood-floored roller-skating rink in the West, where an organist still plays the Wurlitzer for the skaters.

7805 SE Oaks Park Way (east end of the Sellwood Bridge). ✆ 503/233-5777. www.oakspark.com. Free admission; individual-ride tickets $2.25, limited-ride bracelet $11.25, deluxe-ride bracelet $14. Rides open Apr–Sept; skating rink open year-round. Hours vary seasonally; call for details. Bus: 70.

Portland Children's Museum ⭑ *Kids*   Located across the parking lot from the Oregon Zoo, this large, modern children's museum includes exhibits for children ages 6 months to 13 years. Kids can play in a magical forest, go shopping in a kid-size grocery store, or help build a house. However, it is the Water Works exhibit that is likely to make the biggest splash with your kids. There are also six studios with changing exhibits and opportunities for exploring the visual, literary, and performing arts. Combined with the nearby zoo, this museum makes for an easy all-day kid-oriented outing.

4015 SW Canyon Rd. ✆ 503/223-6500. www.portlandcm.org. Admission $7 adults and children, $6 seniors, free for children under 1. Tues–Sun 9am–5pm. Closed some national holidays. Bus: 63. MAX: Washington Park Station.

7 Organized Tours
CRUISES
With two large rivers winding through the city, Portland is a town that needs to be seen from the water. Try the *Portland Spirit* (✆ 800/224-3901 or 503/224-3900; www.portlandspirit.com), a 150-foot yacht that specializes in meal cruises. Lunch, brunch, and dinner cruises feature Northwest cuisine with views of the city skyline. There are also basic sightseeing cruises, and on Friday nights July through September, there are also Friday afternoon cocktail cruises with a live band. Call for reservations and schedule. Prices range from $18 to $64 for adults and $15 to $59 for children.

This company also operates jet-boat tours that go up the Columbia River to the Bonneville Dam and down the Columbia to Astoria.

For high-speed tours up the Willamette River, book a tour with **Willamette Jetboat Excursions** (✆ **888/538-2628** or 503/231-1532; www.willamettejet.com). These high-powered open-air boats blast their way from downtown Portland to the impressive Willamette Falls at Oregon City. The 2-hour tours, which start at OMSI, are $31 for adults and $19 for children 4 to 11, and free for children under 4. Tours are offered from late April to late September. There are also less expensive 1-hour tours, but these do not go upriver to the falls.

BUS TOURS

If you want to get a general overview of Portland, **Gray Line** (✆ **888/684-3322** or 503/243-6789; www.grayline.com) offers several half-day and full-day tours. Itineraries take in the International Rose Test Garden, the Japanese Garden, Pittock Mansion, the Pearl District, and other city sights. There are also tours to see the waterfalls in the Columbia Gorge, wine country, to Mount Hood, and to the Oregon coast. Tour prices range from $38 to $80 for adults, and from $19 to $38 for children.

RAIL EXCURSIONS

While Portland is busy reviving trolleys and streetcars as a viable mass transit option, the **Willamette Shore Trolley** (✆ **503/697-7436;** www.trainweb.org/oerhs/wst. htm) offers scenic excursions along the Willamette River in historic trolley cars (including a double-decker) from the early part of the 20th century. The old wooden trolleys rumble over trestles and through a tunnel as they cover the 7 miles between Portland and the upscale suburb of Lake Oswego (a 40-min. trip). Along the way, you pass through shady corridors with lots of views of the river and glimpses into the yards of posh riverfront homes. In Lake Oswego, the trolley station is on State Street, between A Avenue and Foothills Road. In Portland, the station is about 1 mile south of downtown (and ¼ mile south of the Portland Aerial Tram) in the South Waterfront District off Macadam Avenue at the corner of SW Moody Avenue and SW Bancroft Street. The round-trip fare is $10 for adults, $9 for seniors, and $6 for children 3 to 12. The trolleys usually run between May and October and then again during the Christmas season; call for a schedule.

WALKING TOURS

Peter's Walking Tours of Portland (✆ 503/665-2558; www.walkportland.com), led by Peter Chausse, are a great way to learn more about Portland. The walking tours of downtown last 3 hours and take in the city's fountains, parks, historic places, art, and architecture. Tours are by reservation and cost $10 for adults and $5 for teens (free for children under 8 with a paying adult).

Two to three times a year, Sharon Wood Wortman, author of *The Portland Bridge Book,* offers a **Bridge Tour** that explores several Portland bridges. These tours are offered through the Outdoor Recreation Program of **Portland Parks and Recreation** (✆ 503/823-2525; www.portlandparks.org). Many other walking tours are also available through Portland Parks and Recreation.

The seamy underbelly of history is laid bare on **Portland Underground Tours** (✆ 503/622-4798; www.members.tripod.com/cgs-mthood), which are operated by the Cascade Geographic Society and head down below street level in the historic Old Town neighborhood. On these unusual tours, which are only for those who are steady on their feet and able to duck under pipes and joists and such, you'll hear tales of the days when Portland was known as one of the most dangerous ports on the Pacific Rim. Sailors were regularly shanghaied (kidnapped) from bars and brothels in this area and a vast network of tunnels and underground rooms was developed to support the shanghaiing business. Tours cost $12 for adults and $7 for children under 12 and are offered by reservation only.

8 Outdoor Pursuits

If you're planning ahead for a visit to Portland, contact **Metro,** 600 NE Grand Ave., Portland, OR 97232-2736 (© **503/797-1850;** www.metro-region.org/parks), for its *Metro GreenScene* publication that lists tours, hikes, classes, and other outdoor activities and events being held in the Portland metro area.

BIKING

Portland is a very bicycle-friendly city, and you'll notice plenty of cyclists on the streets. There are also miles of paved bike paths around the city, and some good mountain biking areas as well. For mountain-bike rentals, head to **Fat Tire Farm,** 2714 NW Thurman St. (© **503/222-3276;** www.fattirefarm.com), where bikes go for $40 to $75 for a 24-hour rental. Straight up Thurman Street from this bike shop, you'll find the trail head for **Leif Erickson Drive,** an old gravel road that is Forest Park's favorite route for cyclists and runners (the road is closed to motor vehicles); the trail is 12 miles long.

If you'd like to explore Portland's riverfront bike paths, stop in at **Waterfront Bicycle Rentals,** 0315 SW Montgomery St., Suite 360 (© **503/227-1719;** www.waterfront bikes.net), where you can rent a bike for $8.50 to $13 per hour or $28 to $40 per half-day. From here head through Tom McCall Waterfront Park, cross the Steel Bridge, and ride down the Vera Katz Eastbank Esplanade path. This trail leads 4 miles south to the upscale Sellwood neighborhood.

GOLF

If you're a golfer, don't forget to bring your clubs along on a trip to Portland. There are plenty of public courses around the area, and greens fees at municipal courses range from $23 to $40 for 18 holes. Municipal golf courses operated by the Portland Bureau of Parks and Recreation include **Redtail Golf Course,** 8200 SW Scholls Ferry Rd. (© **503/646-5166**); **Eastmoreland Golf Course,** 2425 SE Bybee Blvd. (© **503/775-2900**), which is the second-oldest golf course in the state (this one gets my vote for best municipal course); **Heron Lakes Golf Course,** 3500 N. Victory Blvd. (© **503/289-1818**), which has two courses designed by Robert Trent Jones; and **Rose City Golf Course,** 2200 NE 71st Ave. (© **503/253-4744**), on the site of a former country club. For more information, log on to **www.portlandonline.com/parks**.

If you want to tee off where the pros play, head west from Portland 20 miles to **Pumpkin Ridge Golf Club** ★★, 12930 NW Old Pumpkin Ridge Rd., North Plains (© **503/647-4747;** www.pumpkinridge.com), a 36-hole course that has hosted the U.S. Women's Open. Green fees range from $30 to $150 on the one course that is open to the public.

Also west of the city, on the south side of Hillsboro, you'll find **The Reserve Vineyards and Golf Club** ★★, 4805 SW 229th Ave., Aloha (© **503/649-8191;** www. reservegolf.com). Green fees range from $45 to $85 depending on time of year and day of the week.

HIKING

Hiking opportunities abound in the Portland area. For shorter hikes, you don't even have to leave the city, just head to **Forest Park.** Bordered by West Burnside Street on the south, Newberry Road on the north, St. Helens Road on the east, and Skyline Road on the west, this is one of the largest forested city parks in the country. Within this urban wilderness, you'll find more than 70 miles of trails. One of my favorite access points is at the top of NW Thurman Street in Northwest Portland. (After a hike, you can stop for a post-exercise payoff at a neighborhood brewpub, an espresso bar, or a bakery along NW 23rd Ave. or NW 21st Ave.) The 30-mile Wildwood Trail is the longest trail in the park and along its length offers lots of options for loop hikes. For a roughly 2.5-mile hike, head up Leif Erickson Drive to a left onto the Wild Cherry Trail to a right onto the Wildwood Trail to a right onto the Dogwood Trail, and then a right on Leif Erickson Drive to get you back to the trail head. There are also good sections of trail to hike in the vicinity of the Hoyt Arboretum. To reach the arboretum's **visitor center,** 4000 SW Fairview Blvd. (Mon–Fri 9am–4pm and Sat 9am–3pm), drive west on West Burnside Street from downtown Portland and follow signs to the arboretum. You can get a trail map here at the visitor center.

About 5 miles south of downtown, you'll find **Tryon Creek State Park** off Terwilliger Boulevard. This park is similar to Forest Park and is best known for its displays of trillium flowers in the spring. There are several miles of walking trails within the park, and a bike path to downtown Portland starts here.

You can buy or rent camping equipment from **REI Co-Op,** 1405 NW Johnson St. (✆ **503/221-1938;** www.rei.com). This huge outdoor recreation supply store also sells books on hiking in the area.

SEA KAYAKING

If you want to check out the Portland skyline from water level, arrange for a sea kayak tour through the **Portland River Company** 🐾🐾, 0315 SW Montgomery St., Suite 330 (✆ **888/238-2059** or 503/229-0551; www.portlandrivercompany.com), which operates out of the RiverPlace Marina at the south end of Tom McCall Waterfront Park. A 2½-hour tour that circles nearby Ross Island costs $43 to $47 per person. This company also rents sea kayaks (to experienced paddlers) for $10 to $20 per hour.

9 Spectator Sports

Tickets to events at the Rose Garden arena and Memorial Coliseum are sold through the **Rose Quarter** box office (✆ **503/797-9619;** www.rosequarter.com). The Rose Garden arena is home to the Portland Trail Blazers and is the main focal point of Portland's **Rose Quarter.** This sports and entertainment neighborhood includes the Rose Garden, Memorial Coliseum, and several restaurants and bars. To reach the Rose Garden or adjacent Memorial Coliseum, take the Rose Quarter exit off I-5. Parking is expensive, so you might want to consider taking the MAX light-rail line from downtown Portland (the Rose Quarter stop is in the Fareless Square).

AUTO RACING   Portland International Raceway, West Delta Park, 1940 N. Victory Blvd. (✆ **503/823-RACE;** www.portlandraceway.com), hosts road races, drag races, motocross and other motorcycle races, go-kart races, and even vintage-car races. February through October are the busiest months here.

BASEBALL   The Portland Beavers (✆ **503/553-5400** or 503/224-4400 for tickets; www.portlandbeavers.com), the AAA affiliate of the San Diego Padres, play minor-league ball at PGE Park, SW 20th Avenue and Morrison Street. Tickets are $8 to $13.

BASKETBALL   The NBA's **Portland Trail Blazers** (℃ **503/231-8000** or 503/797-9600; www.nba.com/blazers) do well enough each year to have earned them a very loyal following. Unfortunately, they have a habit of not quite making it all the way to the top. The Blazers pound the boards at the Rose Garden arena. Call for current schedule and ticket information. Tickets are $10 to $139. If the Blazers are doing well, you can bet that tickets will be hard to come by.

10 Day Spas

If you prefer massages and facials to hikes in the woods, consider spending a few hours at a day spa. These facilities typically offer massages, facials, body wraps, and the like. Portland day spas include the **Avalon Hotel & Spa,** 0455 SW Hamilton Ct. (℃ **503/564-4663;** www.avalonhotelandspa.com); and **Salon Nyla—The Day Spa,** 327 SW Pine St. (℃ **503/228-0389;** www.salonnyla.com), which is adjacent to the Embassy Suites hotel. However, the most unusual day spas in town are in the Pearl District. **Nirvana Apothecary & Day Spa,** 736 NW 11th Ave. (℃ **503/546-8155;** www.nirvanadayspa.com), is done up sort of like a Moroccan palace, while **Aequis,** 419 SW 11th Ave. (℃ **503/223-7847;** www.aequisspa.com), is an Asian-inspired retreat. Expect to pay about $85 or $130 for a 1-hour massage and $200 to more than $1,000 for a multi-treatment spa package.

11 Shopping

Portland has no sales tax, making it a popular shopping destination for Washingtonians, who cross the Columbia River to avoid paying their state's substantial sales tax.

THE SHOPPING SCENE

The **blocks around Pioneer Courthouse Square** are the heartland of upscale shopping in Portland. It's here that you'll find Nordstrom, Macy's, NIKETOWN, Saks Fifth Avenue, Tiffany, Pioneer Place shopping mall, and numerous upscale boutiques and shops.

However, Portland's hippest shopping districts are the **Pearl District** and **Nob Hill/Northwest,** both of which are in Northwest Portland. Most of the Pearl District's best shopping is along NW 10th and 11th avenues going north from West Burnside Street. Here you'll find all kinds of trendy boutiques, art galleries, and home-furnishing stores. The best Nob Hill shopping is along NW 23rd Avenue going north from West Burnside Street. Both neighborhoods have block after block of interesting, hip boutiques, and, along NW 23rd Avenue, a few national chains such as Gap, Urban Outfitters, and Pottery Barn.

For shops with a more down-to-earth, funky flavor, head out to the **Hawthorne District,** which is the city's counterculture shopping area (lots of tie-dye and imports).

Most small stores in Portland are open Monday through Saturday from 9 or 10am to 5 or 6pm. Shopping malls are usually open Monday through Friday from 9 or 10am to 9pm, Saturday from 9 or 10am to between 6 and 9pm, and Sunday from 11am until 6pm. Many department stores stay open past 6pm. Most art galleries and antiques stores are closed on Monday.

SHOPPING A TO Z
ANTIQUES

The **Sellwood/Westmoreland** neighborhood (south of downtown at the east end of the Sellwood Bridge) is Portland's main antiques-shopping district, with about a dozen antiques shops and antiques malls along SE 13th Avenue and SE Milwaukie Avenue. With its old Victorian homes and 19th-century architecture, Sellwood and Westmoreland are the ideal setting for these shops. There are plenty of good restaurants in the area in case it turns into an all-day outing.

You'll also find three more large antiques malls (all under the same ownership) nearby on Milwaukie Avenue: **Stars,** at 6717 SE Milwaukie Ave. (⟨ **503/235-9142;** www.starsantique.com), and at 7027 SE Milwaukie Ave. (⟨ **503/239-0346**); and **Stars & Splendid,** 7030 SE Milwaukie Ave. (⟨ **503/235-5990**).

ART GALLERIES

On the **first Thursday of the month,** galleries in downtown Portland schedule coordinated openings in the evening. Stroll from one gallery to the next, meeting artists and perhaps buying an original work of art. On the last Thursday of each month, galleries in the NE Alberta Street neighborhood stage a similar event. This latter event tends to attract a very culturally diverse crowd. To find NE Alberta Street, drive north from downtown Portland on I-5 and watch for the NE Alberta Street exit.

Augen Gallery   When it opened nearly 20 years ago, the Augen Gallery focused on internationally recognized artists such as Jim Dine, Andy Warhol, and David Hockney. Today, the gallery has expanded its repertoire to regional contemporary painters and printmakers as well. There's a second gallery at 817 SW Second Ave. (⟨ **503/ 224-8182**). 716 NW Davis St. ⟨ **503/546-5056.** www.augengallery.com.

Blackfish Gallery   Artist-owned since 1979, the Blackfish is a large space featuring contemporary images. Since this gallery is a cooperative, it doesn't have the same constraints as a commercial art gallery and thus can present more cutting-edge and thought-provoking work. 420 NW Ninth Ave. ⟨ **503/224-2634.** www.blackfish.com.

The Bullseye Connection Gallery   Located in the Pearl District, the Bullseye Gallery is Portland's premier art-glass gallery and shows the art work of internationally acclaimed glass artists. 300 NW 13th Ave. ⟨ **503/227-0222.** www.bullseyegallery.com.

The Laura Russo Gallery   The focus here is on Northwest contemporary artists, showcasing talented emerging artists as well as the estates of well-known regional artists. Laura Russo has been on the Portland art scene for a long time and is highly respected. 805 NW 21st Ave. ⟨ **503/226-2754.** www.laurarusso.com.

Metalurges   This attractive little light-filled gallery in southeast Portland showcases the work of metal-worker Susan Levine. You'll find colorful metal clocks, mirrors, outdoor sculptures, and other works. Hours are limited, so call first. 3601 SE Division St. ⟨ **503/230-0588.** www.metalurges.com.

Portland Art Museum Rental Sales Gallery   This downtown gallery has a wide selection of works by 250 Northwest artists. Sales here help support the Portland Art Museum. 1237 SW Tenth Ave. ⟨ **503/224-0674.** www.portlandartmuseum.org.

Pulliam Deffenbaugh Gallery   This gallery represents a long list of both talented newcomers and masters from the Northwest. Solo shows and salon-style group shows are held here. 929 NW Flanders St. ⟨ **503/228-6665.** www.pulliamdeffenbaugh.com.

The City of Books

Portland's own **Powell's City of Books**, 1005 W. Burnside St. (© **800/878-7323** or 503/228-4651; www.powells.com), is the bookstore to end all bookstores. Powell's, which covers an entire city block three floors deep, claims to be the world's largest bookstore. At any given time, the store has roughly three-quarters of a million books on the shelves. Both new and used books are shelved side by side, which is why browsing is what Powell's is all about.

Once inside the store, be sure to pick up a store map, which will direct you to the color-coded rooms. Serious book collectors won't want to miss a visit to the Rare Book Room.

One warning: If you haven't got at least an hour of free time, enter at your own risk. It's so easy to lose track of time at Powell's that many customers miss meals and end up in the store's in-house cafe.

Believe it or not, City of Books is even bigger than what you see here; it has several satellite stores, including **Powell's Technical Books,** 33 NW Park Ave.; **Powell's Books for Home and Garden,** 3747 SE Hawthorne Blvd.; **Powell's Books on Hawthorne,** 3723 SE Hawthorne Blvd.; and **Powell's Books at PDX,** Portland International Airport, 7000 NE Airport Way, Suite 2250.

Quintana Galleries   This large, bright space is a virtual museum of Native American art, selling everything from Northwest Coast Indian masks to Navajo rugs to contemporary paintings and sculptures by Native American artists. They also carry a smattering of Native American artifacts from both the Northwest and the Southwest. The jewelry selection is outstanding. Prices, however, are not cheap. 120 NW Ninth Ave. © **800/321-1729** or 503/223-1729. www.quintanagalleries.com.

BOOKS

Major chain bookstores in Portland include **Barnes & Noble,** 1720 Jantzen Beach Center (© **503/283-2800;** www.barnesandnoble.com), and **Borders,** 708 SW Third Ave. (© **503/220-5911;** www.borders.com). For information on Portland's massive Powell's City of Books, see the box below.

CRAFTS

For the largest selection of local crafts, visit the **Portland Saturday Market** (see "Markets," below), which is a showcase for local crafts.

City Arts   Sort of a smaller, indoor version of the Portland Saturday Market, this downtown gallery showcases the work of dozens of local artists and craftspeople. You'll find everything from fine art to fashions. 902 SW Morrison St. © **503/224-4777.** www.cityartsoregon.com.

Hoffman Gallery   The Hoffman Gallery is on the campus of the Oregon College of Art and Craft, one of the nation's foremost crafts education centers since 1906. The gallery hosts installations and group shows by local, national, and international artists. The adjacent gift shop has a good selection of handcrafted items. 8245 SW Barnes Rd. © **503/297-5544.** www.ocac.edu.

Museum of Contemporary Craft Gallery   In business since 1937, and located on the North Park Blocks, which are on the edge of the Pearl District, this is the nation's oldest not-for-profit art gallery. It shows only works of clay, glass, fiber, metal, and wood. The bulk of the large gallery is filled with glass and ceramic pieces. There are also several cabinets of jewelry. 724 NW Davis St. Ⓒ **503/223-2654**. www.contemporary crafts.org.

The Real Mother Goose   This is Portland's premier fine crafts shop and one of the top such shops in the United States. It showcases only the very best contemporary American crafts, including imaginative ceramics, colorful art glass, intricate jewelry, exquisite wooden furniture, and sculptural works. Hundreds of craftspeople and artists from all over the United States are represented here. 901 SW Yamhill St. Ⓒ **503/223-9510**. www.therealmothergoose.com. Also at Portland International Airport, Main Terminal (Ⓒ **503/284-9929**).

Twist   This large store has quite a massive selection of wildly colorful and imaginative furniture, crockery, glassware, and lamps, and also a limited but impressive selection of handmade jewelry by artists from around the United States. 30 NW 23rd Place Ⓒ **503/224-0334**. www.twistonline.com. Also at Pioneer Place, 700 SW Fifth Ave. (Ⓒ **503/222-3137**).

DEPARTMENT STORES

Macy's   Completely renovated and remodeled in 2007, this department store is in a historic building overlooking Pioneer Courthouse Square. If you didn't find it at Nordstrom, across the square, maybe you'll find it here. 621 SW Fifth Ave. Ⓒ **503/223-0512**. www.macys.com.

Nordstrom   Directly across the street from Pioneer Courthouse Square, Nordstrom is a top-of-the-line department store that originated in Seattle and takes great pride in its personal service and friendliness. 701 SW Broadway. Ⓒ **503/224-6666**. www.nordstrom.com. Also at 1001 Lloyd Center (Ⓒ **503/287-2444**) and 9700 SW Washington Square Rd., Tigard (Ⓒ **503/620-0555**).

FASHION
Sportswear

Columbia Sportswear Company   This flagship store is surprisingly low-key, given that the nearby Nike flagship store and REI in Seattle are designed to knock your socks off. Displays showing Columbia Sportswear's well-made outdoor clothing and sportswear are rustic, with lots of natural wood. The most dramatic architectural feature of the store is the entryway—a very wide tree trunk seems to support the roof. 911 SW Broadway. Ⓒ **503/226-6800**. www.columbia.com.

Columbia Sportswear Company Factory Outlet Store 𝒱alue   This outlet store in the Sellwood neighborhood south of downtown and across the river sells remainders and past-season styles from the above-mentioned sportswear company, which is one of the Northwest's premiere outdoor clothing manufacturers. You'll pay 30% to 50% less here than you will at the downtown flagship store. 1323 SE Tacoma St. Ⓒ **503/238-0118**. www.columbia.com.

Nike Factory Company Store 𝒱alue   The Nike outlet is one season behind the current season at NIKETOWN (see below), selling swoosh-brand running, aerobic, tennis, golf, basketball, kids, and you-name-it shoes, sports clothing, and accessories at discounted prices. 2650 NE Martin Luther King Jr. Blvd. Ⓒ **503/281-5901**. www.nike.com.

NIKETOWN Portland   Sure, you may have a NIKETOWN back home, but this one is the closest to Nike's headquarters in nearby Beaverton, which somehow makes it just a little bit special. A true shopping experience. 930 SW Sixth Ave. ℭ **503/221-6453.** www.nike.com.

Men's & Women's

Langlitz Leathers   This family-run shop produces the Rolls Royce of leather jackets. Even though there may be a wait (the shop turns out only six handmade jackets a day), motorcyclists ride their Harleys all the way from the East Coast to be fitted. 2443-A SE Division St. ℭ **503/235-0959.** www.langlitz.com.

Portland Outdoor Store   In business since 1919, this westernwear store is a Portland institution that feels little changed from decades ago. The big neon sign out front and the old general store atmosphere is enough to pull in even people who aren't into playing cowboy or cowgirl. 304 SW Third Ave. ℭ **800/222-1051** or 503/222-1051.

The Portland Pendleton Shop   Pendleton wool is as much a part of life in the Northwest as forests and salmon. This company's fine wool fashions for men and women define the country-club look in the Northwest and in many other parts of the United States. Pleated skirts and tweed jackets are de rigueur here, as are the colorful blankets that have warmed generations of Northwesterners through long chilly winters. 900 SW Fifth Ave. (entrance is actually on Fourth Ave. between Salmon and Taylor). ℭ **800/241-9665** or 503/242-0037.

Women's Clothing

CHANGES/Designs to Wear   This shop specializes in handmade clothing, including handwoven scarves, jackets, shawls, handpainted silks, and other wearable art. 927 SW Yamhill St. ℭ **503/223-3737.** www.therealmothergoose.com.

Desperado   Let your inner cowgirl run wild at this fun shop in the Pearl District. While the custom boots are among the most popular items here, you can put together an entire wardrobe of westernwear here. Men and kids are welcome, too. 428 NW 11th Ave. ℭ **503/294-2952.** www.godesperado.com.

Imelda's   Ooooh! Look at those, and those, and those! That's the usual response when women first gaze through the window of Imelda's. If you live for shoes (don't deny it; you know you do), do not miss Imelda's. There's a second shop at 3426 SE Hawthorne Blvd. (ℭ **503/233-7476**). 935 NW Everett St. ℭ **503/595-4970.** imeldas andlouies.com.

Kathleen's of Dublin   The classic styles here, imported from Ireland, Scotland, and the Celtic isles are meant to last a lifetime, not just a season, and many are made from Irish linen and wool. 737 SW Salmon St. ℭ **503/224-4869.** www.kathleensofdublin.com.

Paloma Clothing   In business for 30 years, this store specializes in comfortable and artistic clothes for travel, work, and play, and has long been one of my wife's favorite places to shop. The store is a short drive from downtown, so call for directions. Hillsdale Shopping Center, 6316 SW Capitol Hwy. ℭ **503/246-3417.** www.palomaclothing.com.

Seaplane   Portland's most celebrated boutique, featured in numerous national fashion magazines, is a collective of cutting edge fashion designers. The styles here are definitely for the young fashionistas, but even if you aren't about to wear any of these outfits, you should stop by to see what local designers are up to. 827 NW 23rd Ave. ℭ **503/234-2409.** www.e-seaplane.com.

Children's Clothing

hanna anderson   If you've ever seen the hanna anderson catalog, you know about the classic kids' clothes that they sell here. Moms and grandmas should not miss an opportunity to visit one of this company's limited number of brick-and-mortar stores. 327 NW Tenth Ave. *℗* 503/321-5275. www.hannaanderson.com.

FOOD

The **Made in Oregon** shops offer the best selection of local food products. See "Gifts & Souvenirs," below, for details.

GIFTS & SOUVENIRS

For unique locally made souvenirs, your best bet is the **Portland Saturday Market** (see "Markets," below, for details).

Made in Oregon   This is your one-stop shop for all manner of made-in-Oregon gifts, food products, and clothing. Every product sold is either grown, caught, or made in Oregon. You'll find smoked salmon, filberts, jams and jellies, Pendleton woolens, and Oregon wines. All branches are open daily, but hours vary from store to store. 600 SW Tenth Ave., Suite 101 (in the Galleria). *℗* **866/257-0938** or 503/241-3630. www.madeinoregon.com. Also at Portland International Airport (*℗* **503/282-7827**); and in Lloyd Center mall, SE Multnomah St. and SE Broadway (*℗* **503/282-7636**).

JEWELRY

For some of the most creative jewelry in Portland, visit **Twist,** the **Hoffman Gallery,** the **Contemporary Crafts Gallery,** and the **Real Mother Goose.** See "Crafts," above.

MALLS & SHOPPING CENTERS

Pioneer Place   Just a block from Pioneer Courthouse Square, this is Portland's most upscale shopping center. Anchored by a Saks Fifth Avenue, Pioneer Place is filled with stores selling designer fashions and expensive gifts. 700 SW Fifth Ave. (between Third and Fifth aves.). *℗* **503/228-5800**. www.pioneerplace.com.

MARKETS

Portland Saturday Market   The Portland Saturday Market (held on both Sat and Sun) is a Portland tradition. Every weekend, nearly 300 artists and craftspeople can be found selling their creations at this open-air market. In addition to the dozens of crafts stalls, you'll find ethnic and unusual foods, and lots of free entertainment. This is one of the best places in Portland to shop for one-of-a-kind gifts that are small enough to fit into your suitcase. On Sunday, on-street parking is free. The market is open from the first weekend in March to Christmas Eve Saturdays 10am to 5pm and Sundays 11am to 4:30pm. Under the west end of the Burnside Bridge (between SW First Ave. and SW Naito Pkwy.). *℗* **503/222-6072**. www.portlandsaturdaymarket.com.

TOYS

Finnegan's Toys and Gifts   This is the largest toy store in downtown Portland and appeals to the kid in all of us. It'll have your inner child kicking and screaming if you don't buy that silly little toy you never got when you were young. 922 SW Yamhill St. *℗* 503/221-0306. www.finneganstoys.com.

WINE & SPIRITS

Clear Creek Distillery   The Portland area is not known just for microbrews and pinot noir, it also produces some outstanding liquors. This distillery in northwest

Portland produces astonishingly fragrant and flavorful fruit spirits in a variety of European styles. There are apple and pear brandies (with fruit in the bottles), grappas, eau de vies, and fruit liqueurs. You can sample them all at this tasting room. 2389 NW Wilson St. (℃) 503/248-9470. www.clearcreekdistillery.com.

Oregon Wines on Broadway   This cozy wine bar/shop is located diagonally across from the Hotel Vintage Plaza in downtown Portland. Here you can taste some of Oregon's fine wines, including 30 different pinot noirs, as well as chardonnays, Gewürztraminers and Washington State cabernet sauvignons, merlots, and Syrahs. 515 SW Broadway. (℃) 800/943-8858 or 503/228-4655. www.oregonwinesonbroadway.com.

12 Portland After Dark

Portland is the Northwest's number-two cultural center (after Seattle, of course). The city's symphony orchestra, ballet, and opera are all well regarded, and the many theater companies offer classic and contemporary plays. In summer, festivals move the city's cultural activities outdoors.

To find out what's going on during your visit, pick up a copy of *Willamette Week,* Portland's free weekly arts-and-entertainment newspaper. The *Oregonian,* the city's daily newspaper, also publishes lots of entertainment-related information in its Friday "A&E" section and also in the Sunday edition of the paper.

THE PERFORMING ARTS

For the most part, the Portland performing-arts scene revolves around the **Portland Center for the Performing Arts (PCPA),** 1111 SW Broadway (℃) **503/248-4335;** www.pcpa.com), which comprises five performance spaces in three buildings. The **Arlene Schnitzer Concert Hall,** 1037 SW Broadway, known locally as the Schnitz, is an immaculately restored 1920s movie palace that still displays the original Portland theater sign and marquee out front and is home to the Oregon Symphony. This hall also hosts popular music performances, lectures, and many other special events. Directly across Main Street from the Schnitz, at 1111 SW Broadway, is the glass jewel box known as **Antoinette Hatfield Hall.** This building houses the **Newmark** and **Dolores Winningstad theaters** and **Brunish Hall.** The two theaters host stage productions by local and visiting companies. Free tours of all three of these theaters are held Wednesdays at 11am, Saturdays every half-hour between 11am and 1pm, and the first Thursday of every month at 6pm.

A few blocks away from this concentration of venues is the 3,000-seat **Keller Auditorium,** 222 SW Clay Street, the largest of the four halls and the home of the Portland Opera and the Oregon Ballet Theatre. The auditorium was constructed shortly after World War I and completely remodeled in the 1960s. In addition to the resident companies mentioned above, these halls host numerous visiting companies each year, including touring Broadway shows.

The PCPA's box office is open for ticket sales Monday through Saturday from 10am to 5pm. Tickets to PCPA performances, and also performances at many other venues around the city, are also sold through either **Ticketmaster** (℃) **503/224-4400;** www.ticketmaster.com), which has outlets at area Joe's Sports, Outdoors & More, and Fred Meyer stores, or **Tickets West** (℃) **800/992-8499** or 503/224-8499; www.ticketswest.com), which has outlets at area Safeway stores. The PCPA also has a **Half-Price Ticket Hotline** (℃) **503/275-8358**) that sells day-of-show, half-price tickets.

One other performing arts venue worth checking out is **The Old Church,** 1422 SW 11th Ave. (© **503/222-2031;** www.oldchurch.org). Built in 1883, this wooden Carpenter Gothic church is a Portland landmark. It incorporates a grand traditional design, but was constructed with spare ornamentation. Today the building serves as a community facility, and every Wednesday at noon it hosts free lunchtime concerts. There are also many other performances held here throughout the year.

OPERA & CLASSICAL MUSIC

Founded in 1896, the **Oregon Symphony** (© **800/228-7343** or 503/228-1353; www.orsymphony.org), which performs at the Arlene Schnitzer Concert Hall, 1037 SW Broadway (see above), is the oldest symphony orchestra on the West Coast, and is currently under the baton of conductor Carlos Kalmar. Each year between September and May, the symphony stages several series, including classical, pops, Sunday matinees, and children's concerts. Ticket prices range from $15 to $102 (seniors and students may purchase half-price tickets 1 hr. before classical and pops concerts).

Each season, the **Portland Opera** (© **866/739-6737** or 503/241-1802; www.portlandopera.org), which performs at Keller Auditorium, SW Third Avenue and SW Clay Street (see above) and at the Hampton Opera Center, 211 SE Caruthers St., offers five different productions that include both grand opera and light opera. The season runs September through March. Ticket prices range from $42 to $148.

Summer is the time for Portland's annual chamber music binge. **Chamber Music Northwest** (© **503/294-6400;** www.cmnw.org) is a month-long series that starts in late June and attracts the world's finest chamber musicians. Performances are held at Reed College and St. Mary's Cathedral (tickets $22–$43).

THEATER

Portland Center Stage (© **503/445-3700;** www.pcs.org), which holds performances in the Pearl District's converted Portland Armory building, which now goes by the name Gerding Theater at the Armory, 128 NW Eleventh Ave., is Portland's largest professional theater company. They stage a combination of eight to nine classic and contemporary plays during their September-to-June season (tickets $22–$62).

Portland's other main theater company, **Artists Repertory Theatre,** 1516 SW Alder St.(© **503/241-1278;** www.artistsrep.org), often stages more daring plays. They can be hit or miss, but they're frequently very thought-provoking. The season often includes a world premiere. Tickets run $25 to $47.

If it's musicals you want, you've got a couple of options in Portland. At the Keller Auditorium, you can catch the **Broadway in Portland** series (© **503/241-1802;** www.broadwayacrossamerica.com). Tickets mostly range from around $25 to $70, but some shows are more expensive.

DANCE

The **Oregon Ballet Theatre** (© **888/922-5538** or 503/222-5538; www.obt.org), which performs at the Keller Auditorium and the Newmark Theatre (see above), is best loved for its performances each December of *The Nutcracker.* The rest of each season includes performances of classic and contemporary ballets (tickets $14–$130).

Fans of modern dance should be sure to check to see what's being staged by **White Bird** (© **503/245-1600;** www.whitebird.org). This organization brings in such celebrated companies as Twyla Tharp Dance, the Merce Cunningham Dance Company, the Paul Taylor Dance Company, and the Alvin Ailey American Dance Theater.

Also keep an eye out for performances by **Imago Theatre,** 17 SE Eighth Ave. (© 503/ 231-9581; www.imagotheatre.com), which, though it is also a live theater company, is best known for its wildly creative productions of *Frogz* and *Big Little Things,* both of which are fanciful dance performances that appeal to both adults and children. **Do Jump** (© 503/231-1232; www.dojump.org), is another highly creative dance company worth watching for. Their performances incorporate dance, acrobatics, aerial work, and plenty of humor.

PERFORMING ARTS SERIES

When summer hits, Portlanders like to head outdoors to hear music. The city's top outdoor music series is held at **Washington Park Zoo,** 4001 SW Canyon Rd. (© 503/ 226-1561; www.oregonzoo.org), which brings in the likes of the Keb' Mo', Gipsy Kings, Pink Martini, and Los Lobos. Ticket prices range from $9.75 to $24.

THE CLUB & MUSIC SCENE
ROCK, BLUES & FOLK

Aladdin Theater This former movie theater now serves as one of Portland's main venues for touring performers such as Richard Thompson, Bruce Cockburn, Judy Collins, and Greg Brown. The very diverse musical spectrum represented includes blues, rock, ethnic, country, folk, and jazz. 3017 SE Milwaukie Ave. © 503/233-1994. www.aladdin-theater.com. Tickets $10–$35.

Berbati's Pan Located in Old Town, this has long been one of Portland's best and most popular rock clubs. A wide variety of acts play here, primarily the best of the local rock scene and bands on the verge of breaking into the national limelight. Be sure to check out the back bar, which is 150 years old. 10 SW Third Ave. © 503/226-2122. www.berbati.com. Cover $6–$20.

Crystal Ballroom The Crystal Ballroom first opened before 1920, and since then has seen performers ranging from early jazz musicians to James Brown, Marvin Gaye, and the Grateful Dead. The McMenamin Brothers (of local brewing fame) renovated the Crystal Ballroom and refurbished its dance floor, which, due to its mechanics, feels as if it's floating. The ballroom now hosts a variety of performances and special events nearly every night of the week. **Lola's Room,** a smaller version of the Ballroom, is on the second floor and also has a floating dance floor. You'll find **Ringlers Pub** (a colorful brewpub) on the ground floor. 1332 W. Burnside St. © 503/225-0047. www.danceonair.com. Cover $5–$30.

Doug Fir Lounge North woods log-cabin styling meets Scandinavian modern at this eclectic underground alt-rock club in the burgeoning lower Burnside neighborhood of southeast Portland. The club is associated with the über-hip Jupiter Hotel. 830 E. Burnside St. © 503/231-9663. www.dougfirlounge.com. Cover $6–$22.

Roseland Theater & Grill The Roseland Theater, though it isn't all that large, is currently one of Portland's two or three main venues for performances by touring national rock acts. Be sure to check the schedule; you never know who might be playing. 8 NW Sixth Ave. © 503/224-2038. Cover $15–$70.

JAZZ

Jimmy Mak's This Pearl District club is the best place in Portland to catch some live jazz and is considered one of the best jazz clubs in the country. With great resident groups performing on weeknights and guest performers on weekends, Jimmy

Mak's showcases some of Portland's best jazz musicians. 221 NW Tenth Ave. ☏ **503/295-6542.** www.jimmymaks.com. Cover free to $15.

The Palm Court   Hands down the most elegant old-world bar in Portland, the Palm Court is in the city's most luxurious hotel. The Circassian walnut paneling and crystal chandeliers will definitely put you in the mood for a martini or single malt. Tuesday through Saturday, there's live jazz in the evening. In the Benson Hotel, 309 SW Broadway. ☏ **503/228-2000.** www.bensonhotel.com. No cover.

CABARET
Darcelle's XV   In business since 1967 and run by Portland's best-loved cross-dresser, this cabaret is a campy Portland institution with a female-impersonator show that has been a huge hit for years. There are shows Wednesday through Saturday. 208 NW Third Ave. ☏ **503/222-5338.** www.darcellexv.com. Cover $10. Reservations recommended.

DANCE CLUBS
See also the listing for **Saucebox,** below, under "Bars"; this restaurant and bar becomes a dance club most nights, when DJs begin spinning tunes.

Andrea's Cha-Cha Club   Located in the basement of the Grand Cafe and open Wednesday through Saturday nights, this is Portland's premier dance spot for fans of Latin dancing. Whether it's cha-cha, salsa, or the latest dance craze from south of the border, they'll be doing it here. Lessons are available Wednesday and Friday nights at 9pm ($12 with a drink included). 832 SE Grand Ave. ☏ **503/230-1166.** Cover $3–$6.

THE BAR & PUB SCENE
BARS
Bartini   Located just off NW 21st Avenue, this dark little bar specializes in, you guessed it, martinis. In fact, they've got a list of more than 100 martinis on offer. Good happy hour, too. 2108 NW Glisan St. ☏ **503/224-7919.**

The Brazen Bean   This hip cocktail and cigar bar in an old Victorian home in Northwest Portland has a cool *fin de siècle* European elegance that makes it a very classy place to sip a martini. There's a pretty little front porch and discounted martinis at happy hour. 2075 NW Glisan St. ☏ **503/294-0636.**

Huber's   No night out on the town in Portland is complete until you've stopped in at Huber's for a Spanish coffee. These potent pick-me-ups are made with rum, Kahlúa, Triple Sec, coffee, and cream, and the preparation of each drink is an impressive show. 411 SW 3rd Ave. ☏ **503/228-5686.** www.hubers.com.

Jake's Famous Crawfish   In business since 1892, Jake's is a Portland institution and should not be missed (see the full review on p. 80). The bar is one of the busiest in town when the downtown offices let out. 401 SW 12th Ave. ☏ **503/226-1419.** www.jakesfamous crawfish.com.

McCormick and Schmick's Harborside Pilsner Room   Located at the south end of Tom McCall Waterfront Park overlooking the Willamette River and RiverPlace Marina, this restaurant/bar is affiliated with Hood River's Full Sail brewery and keeps plenty of Full Sail brews on tap (plus other area beers as well). The crowd is upscale, the view one of the best in town. (See p. 81 for a review of the restaurant.) 0309 SW Montgomery St. ☏ **503/220-1865.** www.mccormickandschmicks.com.

Mint/820   Mixologist Lucy Brennan, owner of this swanky place, has single-handedly turned Portland into a town full of cocktail connoisseurs. Using fresh fruit juices, purées, and unusual ingredients, Brennan has reinvented the cocktail. How about a beet-infused martini or a creamy avocado cocktail? 816/820 N. Russell St. ℂ **503/284-5518.** www.mintand820.com.

¡Oba!   One of the trendiest bars in Portland, this big Pearl District bar/nuevo Latino restaurant has a very tropical feel despite the warehouse district locale. After work, the bar is always packed with the stylish and the upwardly mobile taking advantage of great happy hour deals. Don't miss the tropical-fruit margaritas! 555 NW 12th Ave. ℂ **503/228-6161.** www.obarestaurant.com.

Portland City Grill   Located way up on the 30th floor, this restaurant/bar has the best view in downtown Portland. Come for the great happy hour so you can catch the sunset, or stop by later in the night to catch some live jazz and check out the upscale singles scene. Unico/U.S. Bank Tower, 111 SW Fifth Ave. ℂ **503/450-0030.** www.portlandcitygrill.com.

Saucebox   Popular with the city's dressed-in-black scene makers, this downtown restaurant/bar is a large, dramatically lit dark box that can be very noisy. DJs spin music most nights, transforming this downtown bar into a dance club. Great cocktails. 214 SW Broadway. ℂ **503/241-3393.** www.saucebox.com.

Vault Martini   No need for a combination or secret code to get into this Vault, but it does help to dress the part when drinking at this trendy Pearl District bar. The decor is sleek and stylish, and the cocktail menu is lengthy. This is one of the Pearl District's busiest singles' bars. 226 NW 12th Ave. ℂ **503/224-4909.** www.vault-martini.com.

WINE BARS

Noble Rot   With a garage door for a front wall, this stylish little wine bar opens up to the fresh air whenever the weather is conducive. You can get various wine flights (selections of 2-oz. tastings), and there are plenty of Oregon wines available. The wine bar also serves excellent food. By the way, *noble rot* is a type of grape fungus that is utilized in the production of sweet dessert wines. 2724 SE Ankeny St. ℂ **503/233-1999.** www.noblerotpdx.com.

Oregon Wines on Broadway   With just a handful of stools at the bar and a couple of cozy tables, this tiny place is the best spot in Portland to learn about Oregon wines. On any given night there will be 30 Oregon pinot noirs available by the glass, and plenty of white wines as well. 515 SW Broadway. ℂ **800/943-8858** or 503/228-4655. www.oregonwinesonbroadway.com.

Southpark Seafood Grill & Wine Bar   With its high ceiling, long heavy drapes, halogen lights, and lively wall mural, the wine bar at Southpark (see the full dining review on p. 81) is a contemporary interpretation of a Parisian cafe from the turn of the last century. Very romantic. 901 SW Salmon St. ℂ **503/326-1300.**

Thirst Wine Bar & Bistro   This may not be the most stylish wine bar in town, but it has by far the best view of any wine bar in the city. Thirst looks out over the RiverPlace Marina and the Willamette River, and, when the weather is good, you can sit at an outdoor table on the esplanade. 0315 SW Montgomery St., Suite 340. ℂ **503/295-2747.** www.thirstwinebar.com.

Vino Paradiso   Located in the heart of the Pearl District, this is Portland's swankiest wine bar and has live music as well as lots of good wines. There are also some tasty menu items to go with your wine. 417 NW 10th Ave. ℂ **503/295-9536.** www.vinoparadiso.com.

Blend Your Own Wine

Tired of wines that just don't do it for you? Why not bottle up your own personal *cuvée*? At **Urban Wineworks,** 407 NW 16th Ave. (© **503/226-9797;** www.urbanwineworks.com), at the corner of NW Flanders Street, that's exactly what you get to do on Tuesday evenings between 6:30 and 7:30pm and Saturday afternoons between 1 and 2pm. You don't get to ferment the wine or manage the vineyard, but blending your own wine is both fun and educational. This winery also has a tasting room and wine bar, and on the first Thursday of every month between 5:30 and 8:30pm, artists paint an original work of art on the end of a wine barrel.

BREWPUBS

Although brewpubs have now become commonplace throughout much of the country, here in Portland, they're still brewing beers the likes of which you won't taste in too many other places this side of the Atlantic. This is the heart of the Northwest craft-brewing explosion, and if you're a beer connoisseur, you owe it to yourself to go directly to the source.

Brewpubs have become big business in Portland, and there are now glitzy upscale pubs as well as warehouse-district locals. No matter what vision you have of the ideal brewpub, you're likely to find it. Whether you're wearing bike shorts or a three-piece suit, there's a pub in Portland where you can enjoy a handcrafted beer, a light meal, and a convivial atmosphere.

With almost three dozen brewpubs in the Portland metropolitan area, the McMenamins chain is Portland's biggest brewpub empire. The owners think of themselves as court jesters, mixing brewing fanaticism with a Deadhead aesthetic. Throw in historic preservation and a strong belief in family-friendly neighborhood pubs and you'll understand why these joints are so popular.

Downtown

Ringlers Pub   With mosaic pillars framing the bar, Indonesian antiques, and big old signs all around, this cavernous place is about as eclectic a brewpub as you'll ever find. A block away are the two associated pubs of **Ringlers Annex,** 1223 SW Stark St. (© **503/525-0520**), which is in a flat-iron building. One of these pubs is below street level with a beer-cellar feel, and the other has walls of multipaned glass. These three pubs get my vote for most atmospheric alehouses in town. 1332 W. Burnside St. © 503/225-0627. www.mcmenamins.com.

Northwest Portland

Bridgeport Brewpub & Bakery   This stylish brewpub, bakery, and restaurant is the latest incarnation of one of Portland's oldest brewpubs. On any given day, you'll find eight or more Bridgeport beers on tap. This place is loud, but the beers (and the food) are good. Don't miss the upstairs bar area. 1313 NW Marshall St. © 503/241-3612. www.bridgeportbrew.com.

Lucky Labrador Beer Hall   Housed in a former trucking warehouse and with a five-ton crane still hanging in the beer hall, this is a haven of beer-driven funkiness in the trendy Northwest neighborhood. You'll find all the great beers from Southeast Portland's original Lucky Lab, but a limited food menu. 1945 NW Quimby St. ℂ **503/517-4352.** www.luckylab.com.

MacTarnahan's Tap Room   With huge copper fermenting vats proudly displayed and polished to a high sheen, this is by far the city's most ostentatious, though certainly not its largest, brewpub. This pub's flagship brew, MacTarnahan's Amber Ale, has some very loyal local fans. 2730 NW 31st Ave. ℂ **503/228-5269.** www.macsbeer.com.

Rogue Ales Public House   This Pearl District pub is an outpost of a popular microbrewery headquartered in the Oregon coast community of Newport. Rogue produces just about the widest variety of beers in the state, and, best of all, keeps lots of them on tap at this pub. If you're a fan of barley-wine ale, don't miss their Old Crustacean. 1339 NW Flanders St. ℂ **503/222-5910.** www.rogue.com.

Southeast

The Lucky Labrador Brew Pub   With a warehouse-size room, industrial feel, and picnic tables on the loading dock out back, this brewpub is a classic of southeast Portland. The crowd is young, and dogs are welcome. (They don't even have to be Labs.) 915 SE Hawthorne Blvd. ℂ **503/236-3555.** www.luckylab.com.

Roots Organic Brewing Company   Leave it to Portland, craft-brewing capital of the country, to have an all-organic brewpub. But wait, Roots is more than just an organic brewery, it crafts some of the most distinctive beers in town, including a unique ale made with heather flowers instead of hops. 1520 SE Seventh Ave. ℂ **503/235-7668.** www.rootsorganicbrewing.com.

Northeast & North Portland Pubs

Alameda Brewhouse   With its industrial chic interior, this high-ceilinged neighborhood pub brews up some of the most reliably flavorful beers in Portland. It's worth searching out this pub for a chance to wander the Beaumont neighborhood's few blocks of interesting shops. 4765 NE Fremont St. ℂ **503/460-9025.** www.alamedabrewhouse.com.

Amnesia Brewing Company   With the look of an old warehouse and a "beer garden" in the parking lot, this little north Portland brewpub is another of Portland's old-school brewpubs, which means laid back in the extreme. The beers are good, but the food is pretty limited. 832 N. Beech St. ℂ **503/281-7708.**

McMenamins Kennedy School   Never thought they'd ever start serving beer in elementary school, did you? However, in the hands of the local McMenamins brewpub empire, an old northeast Portland school is now a sprawling complex complete with brewpub, beer garden, movie-theater pub, and even a bed-and-breakfast inn. Order up a pint and wander the halls checking out all the cool artwork. 5736 NE 33rd Ave. ℂ **503/249-3983.** www.mcmenamins.com.

Widmer Brewing and Gasthaus   Located on the edge of a rapidly reviving industrial area just north of the Rose Garden arena, this place has the feel of a classic blue-collar pub. This pub is part of Portland's largest craft brewing company, which is best known for its hefeweizen. German and American food is served. On the MAX Yellow Line. 929 N. Russell St. ℂ **503/281-3333.** www.widmer.com.

THE GAY & LESBIAN NIGHTLIFE SCENE
DANCE CLUBS

Boxxes/Redcap Garage   Billing itself as Portland's original gay dance club, Boxxes and the connected Redcap Garage, together provide a dynamic duo of dance floors. You can work up an appetite from all that dancing, and then head to the club's Fish Grotto Seafood Restaurant for a meal. 1035 SW Stark St. © **503/226-4171.** www.boxxes.com. Cover free–$3.

C.C. Slaughters   Popular with a young crowd, this big Old Town nightclub spins disco sounds most nights, with a night of country music each week. 219 NW Davis St. © **503/248-9135.** www.ccslaughterspdx.com. Cover free–$5.

The Egyptian Club   Portland is well known for its large lesbian community, and this bar has long been a favorite with young, partying women. The club is really three clubs in one, with a pool room, karaoke bar, and dance bar. Lots of special events, too. 3701 SE Division St. © **503/236-8689.** www.eroompdx.com. Cover free–$5.

The Embers Avenue   Though primarily a gay disco, Embers is also popular with straights. There are always lots of flashing lights and sweaty bodies until the early morning. Currently Wednesday is goth night and Sunday is Latino night. Look for drag shows several nights a week. 110 NW Broadway. © **503/222-3082.** www.emberspdx.net. Cover free–$6.

BARS

The area around the intersection of **SW Stark Street and West Burnside Street** has the largest concentration of gay bars in Portland.

Crush Bar   This big, hip bar is over in southeast Portland and attracts a very diverse crowd that includes not only gay men but lesbians and straights as well. There are three distinct settings here, including a comfortable lounge, a room for dining and dancing, and a room where smoking is allowed. DJs spin dance tunes most nights. 1400 SE Morrison St. © **503/235-8150.** www.crushbar.com.

Eagle Bar   If leather and Levi's are your uniform, then you'll feel right at home at this bar. Loud rock and DJ dance music plays most nights, and Sundays are currently leather night. 1300 W. Burnside St. © **503/241-0105.** www.portlandeagle.com.

Scandal's   In business for more 25 years, this bar/restaurant is both literally and figuratively at the center of the Portland gay-bar scene. Try to get a window seat so you can keep an eye on passersby on the sidewalk. 1125 SW Stark St. © **503/227-5887.**

13 A Side Trip to Oregon City & The Aurora Colony
OREGON CITY

When the first white settlers began crossing the Oregon Trail in the early 1840s, their destination was Oregon City and the fertile Willamette Valley. At the time, Portland had yet to be founded, and Oregon City, set beside powerful Willamette Falls, was the largest town in Oregon. However, with the development of Portland and the shifting of the capital to Salem, Oregon City began to lose its importance. Today it is primarily an industrial town, though one steeped in Oregon history and worth a visit. To get here from downtown Portland, drive south on SW First Avenue and continue on SW Macadam Avenue, which is Ore. 43. Follow this road for roughly 12 miles to reach Oregon City. (It should take 30–45 min.) You can also take I-5 south to I-205 east.

CLOSED
due to
accidental demolition

WEGEN BISSIGEN
EICHHÖRNCHEN GESCHLOSSEN

CERRADO
CABRAS

Κλειστό
Μετεωρίτες

プール も
POOL CLOSED
閉鎖中
ELECTRIC EELS

Hotel
closed for
facelifting

FERMÉ POUR
RAISON
DE GRÈVE
DES BONNES

FECHADO!
POR CAUSA DE
ATAQUES DOS CROCODILOS

— I don't speak
sign language.

A hotel can close for all kinds of reasons.
Our Guarantee ensures that if your hotel's undergoing construction, we'll
let you know in advance. In fact, we cover your entire travel experience.
See www.travelocity.com/guarantee for details.

travelocity
You'll never roam alone.

Once in Oregon City, your first stop should be just south of town at the **Willamette Falls overlook** ⚓ on Ore. 99E. Though the falls have been much changed by industry over the years, they are still an impressive sight.

End of the Oregon Trail Interpretive Center ⚓

With its three Paul Bunyan–size wagons parked in the middle of Abernethy Green (the official end of the Oregon Trail), this interpretive center is impossible to miss. Inside the first of the giant wagons you'll find an exhibit hall, hands-on area, and gift shop. After looking around this first wagon, you'll then be led through the next one by costumed interpreters who explain the difficulties of provisioning for the overland trek. The third wagon houses a multimedia presentation based on three Oregon Trail diaries.

1726 Washington St., Oregon City. ⓒ 503/657-9336. www.endoftheoregontrail.org. Admission $7 adults, $5 children 5–12, free for children under 5. Memorial Day to Labor Day Mon–Sat 9:30am–5:30pm, Sun 10:30am–5:30pm; Nov–Feb Tues–Sat 11am–4pm, Sun noon–4pm; Mar–May and Sept–Oct Mon–Sat 9:30am–5pm, Sun 10:30am–5pm. Tour hours vary by day and season. Closed New Year's Day, Thanksgiving, Christmas Eve, Christmas.

McLoughlin House

Oregon City's most famous citizen, retired Hudson's Bay Company chief factor John McLoughlin, helped found this mill town on the banks of the Willamette River in 1829. By the 1840s, immigrants were pouring into Oregon, and McLoughlin provided food, seeds, and tools to many of them. Upon retirement in 1846, McLoughlin moved to Oregon City, where he built what was at that time the most luxurious home in Oregon. Today McLoughlin's house is a National Historic Site and is furnished as it would have been when McLoughlin lived there. Many of the pieces on display are original to the house.

713 Center St., Oregon City. ⓒ **503/656-5146.** www.mcloughlinhouse.org. Free admission. Wed–Sat 10am–4pm; Sun 1–4pm. Closed Dec 22–Jan 31 and major holidays.

THE AURORA COLONY

An interesting chapter in Oregon pioneer history is preserved 13 miles south of Oregon City in the town of Aurora, which was founded in 1855 as a Christian communal society. Similar to such better-known communal experiments as the Amana Colony and the Shaker communities, the Aurora Colony lasted slightly more than 20 years. Today Aurora is a National Historic District and the large old homes of the community's founders have been restored. Many of the old commercial buildings now house antiques stores. You can learn the history of Aurora at the **Old Aurora Colony Museum,** Second and Liberty streets (ⓒ **503/678-5754;** www.auroracolonymuseum.com). February through December, the museum is open Tuesday through Saturday from 11am to 4pm and on Sunday from noon to 4pm. The museum is closed in January. Admission is $6 for adults, $5 for seniors, and $2 for students (free for children 5 and under).

5

The Willamette Valley: The Bread (& Wine) Basket of Oregon

For more than 150 miles, from south of Eugene to the Columbia River at Portland, the Willamette River (pronounced "wih-*lam*-it") flows between Oregon's two major mountain ranges. Tempered by cool moist air from the Pacific Ocean, yet protected from winter winds by the Cascade Range to the east, the Willamette Valley enjoys a mild climate that belies its northerly latitudes. It was because of this relatively benign climate and the valley's rich soils that the region's first settlers chose to put down roots here. Today, the valley is home to Oregon's largest cities, its most productive farmlands, the state capital, and the state's two major universities.

Despite the many hardships, families were willing to walk 2,000 miles across the continent for a chance at starting a new life in the Willamette Valley. The valley very quickly became the breadbasket of the Oregon country, and today, it still produces an agricultural bounty unequaled in its diversity. Throughout the year, you can sample the produce of this region at farms, produce stands, and wineries. In spring, commercial fields of tulips and irises paint the landscape with bold swaths of color. In summer, there are farm stands near almost every town, and many farms will let you pick your own strawberries, raspberries, blackberries, peaches, apples, cherries, and plums. In autumn, you can sample the filbert and walnut harvest, and at any time of year, you can do a bit of wine tasting at dozens of wineries.

1 The North Willamette Valley Wine Country

McMinnville: 38 miles SW of Portland, 26 miles NW of Salem

Were it not for Prohibition, wine connoisseurs might be comparing California wines to those of Oregon rather than vice versa. Oregon wines had already gained a national reputation back in the days when Oregon became one of the earliest states to vote in Prohibition. It would be a few years before more liberal California would outlaw alcohol, and, in the interim, the Golden State got the upper hand. When Prohibition was rescinded, California quickly went back to wine production, but no one bothered to revive Oregon's wine-producing potential until the 1970s. By then, Napa Valley had popped the cork on its wine dominance. Perhaps one day Willamette Valley wineries will be as well known as those in California, and for fans of pinot noir, those days have already arrived. Oregon's pinot noirs have gained such international attention that even some French wineries have planted vineyards here and begun producing their own Oregon wines.

The north Willamette Valley wine country begins in the town of Newberg and extends south to the Salem area. The majority of the region's wineries flank Ore. 99W, and a drive down this rural highway will turn up dozens of blue signs pointing to wineries within a few miles of the road. To the south of Salem, there are more wineries in the Corvallis and Eugene areas, which are dealt with in the appropriate sections of this chapter. To the north of Ore. 99W, there are still more wineries in Washington County, which is actually in the drainage of the Tualatin River, a tributary of the Willamette. These latter wineries are included in this section.

The most important wine-growing areas within this region, and the areas that produce the best wines, are the Red Hills above the town of Dundee, the slopes outside the town of Carlton, and the Eola Hills northwest of Salem. In Dundee, you'll find the greatest concentration of good restaurants, while in McMinnville, the largest town in the area, you'll find plenty of hotel rooms and more good restaurants.

ESSENTIALS

GETTING THERE   You'll find the heart of wine country between Newberg and McMinnville along Ore. 99W, which heads southwest out of Portland.

VISITOR INFORMATION   Contact the **McMinnville Area Chamber of Commerce,** 417 NW Adams St., McMinnville, OR 97128 (© **503/472-6196;** www.mcminnville.org), or the **Chehalem Valley Chamber of Commerce,** 415 E. Sheridan St., Newberg, OR 97132 (© **503/538-2014;** www.chehalemvalley.org). The **Willamette Valley Visitors Association,** 553 NW Harrison Blvd., Corvallis, OR 97330 (© **866/548-5018;** www.oregonwinecountry.org), is another good source of information on this area.

FESTIVALS   The most prestigious festival of the year is the **International Pinot Noir Celebration,** P.O. Box 1310, McMinnville, OR 97128 (© **800/775-4762** or 503/472-8964; www.ipnc.org), held each year on the last weekend in July or first weekend in August. The 3-day event includes tastings, food, music, and seminars. Registration forms are mailed out in February each year and tickets are currently $795 per person. Passport to Pinot, a separate event held during the celebration, is only $125.

TOURING THE WINERIES

Forget pretentiousness, grand villas, celebrity wineries, snobbish waiters, or high prices for tastings—this is not Napa Valley. Oregon wineries are, for the most part, still small establishments. Even the new wineries that have been opening up right on Ore. 99W (and that seem calculated to provide beach-bound vacationers with a bit of distraction and some less-than-impressive wine for the weekend) are still small affairs compared to the wineries of Napa Valley. Although in recent years more and more "corporate" wineries have been opening with the sole purpose of producing high-priced pinot noir, many of the region's wineries are still family-owned and -operated and produce moderately priced wines.

Forget about cabernet sauvignon, merlot, and zinfandel while you're here. The Willamette Valley just isn't hot enough to produce these varietals. With the exception of southern Oregon wineries and a few Willamette Valley wineries that buy their grapes from warmer regions (the Columbia Gorge, southern Oregon, California, and Washington's Yakima Valley), Oregon wineries have, thankfully, given up on trying to produce cabs and zins to compete with those of California. The wines of the

---

Tips Taster's Tip

Although few Oregon wineries have regularly scheduled winery tours, if you're interested and there is someone on hand to show you around, you're usually welcome to tour the facilities.

Willamette Valley are primarily the cooler climate varietals traditionally produced in Burgundy, Alsace, and Germany. Pinot noir is the uncontested leader of the pack, with pinot gris running a close second. However, Gewürztraminer and Riesling are also produced, and, with the introduction of early ripening Dijon-clone chardonnay grapes, the region is finally beginning to produce chardonnays that can almost compete with those of California. Other wines you'll likely encounter in this area include Müller-Thurgaus (usually off-dry white wines), muscats (dessert wines), and sparkling wines (often made from pinot noir and chardonnay grapes).

Wine country begins only a few miles west and southwest of Portland. Approaching the town of Newberg on Ore. 99W, you leave the urban sprawl behind and enter the rolling farm country of Yamhill County. These hills form the western edge of the Willamette Valley and provide almost ideal conditions for growing wine grapes. The views from these hills take in the Willamette Valley's fertile farmlands as well as the snowcapped peaks of the Cascades.

Between Newberg and Rickreall, you'll find dozens of wineries and tasting rooms that are open on a regular basis. There are concentrations of wineries in Dundee's Red Hills and in the Eola Hills northwest of Salem, and if you head north from Ore. 99W, you'll find another dozen or so wineries near Carlton, Yamhill, Hillsboro, and Forest Grove. Each of these groupings of wineries makes a good day's tasting route, and they have been organized here so that you can easily link them together as such.

Most, but not all, wineries maintain tasting rooms that are usually open between 11am or noon and 5pm. During the summer, most tasting rooms are open daily, but in other months they may be open only on weekends or by appointment. Wineries located right on Ore. 99W are usually open throughout the year. Many wineries also have a few picnic tables, so if you bring some goodies with you and then pick up a bottle of wine, you'll be set for a great picnic.

For anyone simply interested in tasting a little Oregon wine, the wineries along the highway are a good introduction. If you have more than a passing interest in wine, you'll want to explore the wineries that are located up in the hills a few miles off Ore. 99W.

Many of the best wineries, however, are only open by appointment or on Memorial Day and Thanksgiving weekends. If you're serious about your wine, you might want to make appointments to visit some of these smaller wineries or plan a visit to coincide with Thanksgiving or Memorial Day weekend. Oenophiles, especially pinot noir fans, are likely to uncover some rare gems and discover a few new favorite wineries this way.

At most wineries, you'll be asked to pay a tasting fee, usually $5, but this fee is often waived if you buy some wine. In the past few years, as pinot noir prices have risen into the $40 to $60 range, tasting room fees have also been creeping up. At some of the more prestigious wineries, you may have to pay a tasting fee between $10 and $20. Many wineries have celebrations, festivals, music performances, and picnics throughout the

The Twice-a-Year Wineries

Harvest season aside, Memorial Day weekend and Thanksgiving weekend are the two most important times of the year in wine country. On these weekends, wineries often introduce their new releases and sometimes offer barrel tastings of wines that haven't yet been bottled. Many wineries offer live music, and most offer some sort of food, often exotic cheeses, to accompany the wines they are tasting.

Many of the area's best boutique wineries are open to the public *only* on these two weekends. So, if you're serious about wine, you won't want to pass up a Willamette Valley wine tour on one or the other of these holidays.

For information on what wineries will be open, contact **Willamette Valley Wineries,** P.O. Box 25162, Portland, OR 97298 (© 503/646-2985; www. willamettewines.com) or the **Washington County Visitors Association,** 11000 SW Stratus St., Suite 170, Beaverton, OR 97008 (© 503/644-5555; www.come playyourway.com).

summer, and during these celebrations there is often a fee to cover the cost of the appetizers and wine that are served. The Memorial Day and Thanksgiving weekend tastings usually carry a fee of between $5 and $20.

For more information about the Oregon wine scene, including a calendar of winery events, pick up a copy of *Oregon Wine Press,* a monthly newspaper (available at area wine shops and wineries), or contact **Oregon Wine Press,** P.O. Box 727, McMinnville, OR 97128 (© **503/883-6266;** www.oregonwinepress.com). **Willamette Valley Wineries,** P.O. Box 25162, Portland, OR 97298 (© **503/646-2985;** www. willamettewines.com), a regional wineries association, publishes a free map and guide to the local wineries. You can pick up a copy at almost any area winery.

THE NEWBERG & DUNDEE AREA

You can get more information on area wineries from the **Dundee Hills Winegrowers Association** (© 503/864-2700; www.dundeehills.org).

Adelsheim Vineyard ⊕ If you're from out of state and you're at all familiar with Oregon pinot noir, you've probably had some Adelsheim wine. This winery has been around since the 1970s and consistently produces well-regarded pinots. The single-vineyard wines here are the standouts. If you'd like to tour a winery, this is a good choice; call ahead to arrange your tour ($20).

16800 NE Calkins Lane, Newberg. © 503/538-3652. www.adelsheim.com. Tasting fee $10. Wed–Sun 11am–4pm.

Archery Summit ⊕⊕⊕ With big wines, a big winery, and a big reputation, Archery Summit is one of Oregon's premier producers of pinot noir. Only pinot noir is produced, and the grapes all come from Archery Summit's own vineyards. Wines are aged almost exclusively in new-oak barrels and spend time in some of the only barrel-aging caves in the state. Prices are in the $45 to $85 range. Tours are available ($25).

18599 NE Archery Summit Rd., Dayton. © 503/864-4300. www.archerysummit.com. Daily 10am–4:30pm. Tasting fee $15. West of Dundee on Ore. 99W, turn right on Archery Summit Rd.

Argyle Winery   Located right on the highway in Dundee, this winery specializes in sparkling wines and chardonnay. Most wines here are in the $20 to $30 range, with pinot noirs in the $35 to $50 range. If you're in the state for a special occasion, be sure to pick up a bottle of bubbly here. Due to traffic congestion in Dundee, this winery is best visited when heading east on Ore. 99W.

691 Ore. 99W, Dundee. ℭ 888/4-ARGYLE or 503/538-8520. www.argylewinery.com. Daily 11am–5pm.

A to Z ℱ   Producing what they call "aristocratic wines at democratic prices," A to Z, which also owns Rex Hill Vineyards, is Oregon's largest producer of wine. Not only that, they produce some of the best-value wines in the state. If you're looking for deals, be sure to stop by this tasting room in Dundee.

990 N. Ore. 99W, Dundee. ℭ 503/538-4881. www.atozwineworks.com. Sun–Thurs 10am–4pm; Fri–Sat 10am–5pm.

August Cellars   This is the first winery you'll come to along Ore. 99W as you reach the Yamhill County wine country. The big winemaking facility here is just off the highway and is actually home to several small wineries. Stop by on a weekend to taste wines by some of the tenants here.

14000 NE Quarry Rd., Newberg. ℭ 503/554-6766. www.augustcellars.com. May–Sept daily 11am–5pm; Oct–Apr Fri–Sun 11am–5pm. Just off Ore. 99W east of Newberg.

Dobbes Family Estate ℱℱ   This tasting room right in Dundee pours the wines of both Dobbes Family Estate and the affiliated Wine by Joe. These are both labels of winemaker Joe Dobbes, one of Oregon's top winemakers. The Dobbes Family label offers some superb, highly extracted pinot noirs and Syrahs, while the "Wine by Joe" label is all about good values.

240 SE Fifth St., Dundee. ℭ 800/566-8143 or 503/538-1141. www.dobbesfamilyestate.com. Daily 11am–6pm. Just south of Ore. 99W in Dundee.

Domaine Drouhin Oregon ℱℱℱ   Years ago, when France first heard that Oregon wineries were making pinot noir, most French winemakers scoffed. Not Maison Joseph Drouhin of Burgundy; the family bought land in the Red Hills of Dundee and planted vines. Today, the Burgundian-style wines of Domaine Drouhin Oregon are superb examples of old-world winemaking—silky, seductive, and well balanced. Tours of the winery are available ($20).

6750 Breyman Orchards Rd., Dayton. ℭ 503/864-2700. www.domainedrouhin.com. Tasting fee $10. Wed–Sun 11am–4pm. West of Dundee on Ore. 99W, turn right on McDougall Rd. and right again onto Breyman Orchards Rd.

Domaine Serene ℱℱ   Located across the road from Domaine Drouhin Oregon, this is another of Oregon's top wineries, with an impressive winemaking facility and impressive prices ($40–$75) to prove it. Great ratings from *Wine Spectator* have made these wines some of the most sought after in the state. Pinot noir, chardonnay, and Syrah are produced here.

6555 Hilltop Lane, Dayton. ℭ 866/864-6555 or 503/864-4600. www.domaineserene.com. Tasting fee $15. Wed–Sun 11am–4pm. West of Dundee on Ore. 99W, turn right on McDougall Rd. and right again onto Breyman Orchards Rd.

Erath Vineyards ℱ   In business since 1972, Erath Vineyards, set high in the Red Hills of Dundee, was founded by Dick Erath, one of the pioneers of modern Oregon winemaking. A wide variety of wines is produced here and you can usually sample 10 or more during your visit to the tasting room. Be sure to pay for a tasting of the single-vineyard pinot noirs, which usually sell for around $40. Today, this winery is owned by Washington state's Chateau Ste. Michelle Winery.

9409 NE Worden Hill Rd., Dundee. ✆ 800/539-9463 or 503/538-3318. www.erath.com. Daily 11am–5pm. Tasting fee: free–$10. In Dundee, go north on Ninth St., which becomes Worden Hill Rd.

The Four Graces ✿   With vineyards that stretch up the hill from the highway and a tasting room in a little cottage, this winery is conveniently located and does an excellent job with pinot gris, pinot blanc, and pinot noir. White wines are under $20, while pinot noirs are in the $30 to $40 range.

9605 NE Fox Farm Rd., Dundee. ✆ 800/245-2950. www.thefourgraces.com. Daily 10am–5pm. Tasting fee $10. Just off Ore. 99W northeast of Dundee.

Lange Estate Winery & Vineyards ✿   Superb pinot noirs are the hallmark of this small winery. The estate wines produced here are among the best pinot noirs in the state and tend to be priced from $40 to $60. Lange also produces a few wines (mostly pinot gris and chardonnay) in the $16 to $20 range.

18380 NE Buena Vista Rd., Dundee. ✆ 503/538-6476. www.langewinery.com. Daily 11am–5pm. Tasting fee $10. In Dundee, go north on Ninth St. and follow signs.

Ponzi Vineyards/Ponzi Wine Bar ✿   Ponzi Vineyards was one of the Oregon wine pioneers, and though it has its winery north of here near Beaverton, this tasting room/wine bar is a more convenient place to sample Ponzi wines. Expect excellent pinot gris and chardonnay and be sure to sample the Arneis, an Italian varietal dry white wine that is aged in oak and is rarely planted in this area. Also don't miss the Vino Gelato, a dessert wine made from frozen grapes.

100 SW Seventh St., Dundee. ✆ 503/554-1500. www.ponziwinebar.com. Daily 11am–5pm.

Rex Hill Vineyards   One of the oldest wineries in Oregon, Rex Hill was purchased by A to Z winery in 2007, so you can expect some changes here in the future. However, A to Z usually does a very good job producing reasonably priced pinot noir and pinot gris, so Rex Hill should be worth a visit. This winery is set amid mature vineyards.

30835 N. Hwy. 99W., Newberg. ✆ 800/739-4455. www.rexhill.com. Tasting fee $10. Dec to late May daily 11am–5pm; Memorial Day weekend to Thanksgiving weekend daily 10am–5pm.

Sokol Blosser Winery   Another of the big Oregon wineries, Sokol Blosser sits high on the slopes above the west end of Dundee. Off-dry whites are a strong point here, and the Evolution No. 9, a blend of 10 different grapes, shouldn't be missed. Pinot noirs, on the other hand, tend to be overpriced and overrated in my opinion. A walk-through showcase vineyard provides an opportunity to learn about the growing process, and tours of the winery are offered ($10).

5000 Sokol Blosser Lane, Dundee. ✆ 800/582-6668 or 503/864-2282. www.sokolblosser.com. Tasting fee $5–$15. Daily 10am–4pm. Southwest of Dundee off Ore. 99W.

Torii Mor Winery ✿   With the Japanese-inspired name (*torii* means "gate" in Japanese) and Japanese gardens outside the tasting room, you might expect this winery to produce sake, but Torii Mor actually produces some of the region's best pinot noirs. Expect to pay between $45 and $75 for one of this winery's single-vineyard pinot noirs.

18325 NE Fairview Dr., Dundee. ✆ 503/538-2279. www.toriimorwinery.com. Tasting fee $10. Daily 11am–5pm. In Dundee, go north on Ninth St. (which becomes Worden Hill Rd.), and turn right on Fairview Rd.

THE MCMINNVILLE AREA

For a selection of area wines (several of which can be tasted on any given day), visit **Noah's–A Wine Bar,** 525 NE Third St., McMinnville (© **503/434-2787**). West of McMinnville on Ore. 18, at the **Oregon Wine Tasting Room & Bellevue Market,** 19690 SW Ore. 18, McMinnville (© **503/843-3787**), you can sample wines from numerous area wineries. This tasting room is open daily from 11am to 5:45pm. There's also a gourmet market here that is a great place to get picnic supplies.

The Eyrie Vineyards   This winery is the oldest producer of pinot noir in Oregon and was responsible for putting Oregon on the international wine map when its 1975 pinot noir won major competitions in France in 1979 and 1980. Pinot noirs here are done in a Burgundian style and are often held back for years before they're released, making this a good place to sample old vintages.

935 NE 10th Ave. © 888/440-4970. www.eyrievineyards.com. Tasting fee $5. Wed–Sun noon–5pm.

Panther Creek Cellars 🍷🍷   To find out just how different pinot noirs from different vineyards can be, stop in at Panther Creek's facility in downtown McMinnville. In any given year, this winery produces four or more vineyard-designate pinot noirs, and some of these wines have been rated among the best in the world.

455 N. Irvine St., McMinnville. © 503/472-8080. www.panthercreekcellars.com. Tasting fee $5. Daily noon–5pm.

Wine Works Oregon 🍷🍷   This little wine-making facility near downtown McMinnville houses four separate wineries, and in the little tasting room, you can sample wines from all of these wineries. The best part of a stop here is that you'll be able to taste the different wine-making styles of the various winemakers here. The Z'Ivo wines are always my favorites.

475 NE 17th St. (at Evans St.), McMinnville. © 503/472-3215. www.walnutcitywineworks.com. Thurs–Sun 11am–4:30pm. From Ore. 99W in McMinnville, drive south on Evans St.

THE YAMHILL & CARLTON AREA

In the town of Carlton, you'll find **The Tasting Room,** 105 W. Main St. (© **503/852-6733;** www.pinot-noir.com), which specializes in wines from wineries that are not usually open to the public; indeed, this is an absolute must if you can't be around on Memorial Day or Thanksgiving weekend. Most wines featured here are from wineries in the immediate vicinity of Carlton. Also here in Carlton, you'll find the **Carlton Winemakers Studio,** 801 N. Scott St. (© **503/852-6100;** www.winemakers studio.com), which represents numerous wineries, including Andrew Rich Wines, Hamacher Wines, and Domaine Meriwether. This tasting room is open daily from 11am to 5pm.

Anne Amie Vineyards   Set amid nearly 100 acres of vines and located high on a hill with one of the best views in the area, this winery has a large tasting room and does a few respectable white wines, which usually sell for less than $20. The winery also produces several vineyard-designate pinot noirs.

6580 NE Mineral Springs Rd., Carlton. © 800/248-4835. www.anneamie.com. Daily 10am–5pm. Tasting fee $5–$7. Take Ore. 99W to Lafayette and go north on Mineral Springs Rd.

Cana's Feast Winery 🍷   Big reds are the specialty of this winery. Cabernet sauvignon, sangiovese, and Syrah all show up here, making this a distinctly different stop in this region of pinot noirs. If you like assertive red wines, don't miss this small winery.

750 W. Lincoln St., Carlton. ✆ **503/852-0002**. www.canasfeastwinery.com. Daily 11am–5pm. Tasting fee $5. Located just off Ore. 47 on the north side of town.

Penner-Ash Wine Cellars ⚐⚐   Winemaker Lynn Penner-Ash has been on the Oregon wine scene for years, and her winery between Newberg and Yamhill is one of the more impressive wineries in the area. Set high on a hill with a stupendous view, it would be worth a visit even if Penner-Ash didn't produce excellent wines. The pinot noirs and Syrahs here are some of the best in the state.

15771 NE Ribbon Ridge Rd., Newberg. ✆ **503/554-5545**. www.pennerash.com. Thurs–Sun 11am–5pm. Closed Jan. From Ore. 240 between Newberg and Yamhill, drive north on NE Ribbon Ridge Rd.

Soléna Cellars ⚐   Can you say inky? I knew you could. Highly extracted pinot noirs that look more like Syrah than pinot are the hallmark of this husband-and-wife winery. Along with that deep, dark color comes plenty of tannin, which means these are wines for your cellar. In addition to the usual Willamette Valley varietals, this winery also produces merlot, zinfandel, and Syrah from southern Oregon grapes and cabernet sauvignon from Washington grapes.

213 S. Pine St., Carlton. ✆ **503/852-0082**. www.solenacellars.com. Thurs–Sun noon–5pm.

Tyrus Evan/The Depot ⚐   Located in Carlton's old railroad depot and operated by the celebrated Ken Wright Cellars winery, Tyrus Evan specializes in bordeaux blends (here referred to as clarets) and Syrahs. These wines tend to be big and juicy and the winery is a must for anyone who is not a fan of pinot noir.

120 N. Pine St., Carlton. ✆ **503/852-7010**. Tasting fee $10. Sun–Thurs 11am–5pm; Fri–Sat 11am–6pm (shorter hours in winter).

Willakenzie Estate ⚐   Situated on a 400-acre estate above the Chehalem Valley, this winery produces primarily pinot noir, pinot gris, pinot blanc, and pinot meunier, plus a bit of chardonnay in its gravity-fed facility. There's a nice picnic area with good views. This is one of the prettiest spots in all of wine country, and the wines are excellent.

19143 NE Laughlin Rd., Yamhill. ✆ **888/953-9463** or 503/662-3280. www.willakenzie.com. May–Oct daily noon–5pm; Nov–Apr Fri–Sun noon–5pm. From Ore. 240 just east of Yamhill, drive north on NE Laughlin Rd.

THE HILLSBORO & BEAVERTON AREA

Cooper Mountain Vineyards   Now nearly surrounded by upscale suburbs, this mountaintop winery is one of the few in the state that uses only organic grapes. The pinot gris is moderately priced and can be decent. Chardonnays, which go light on the oak, can also be good. Pinot noirs are decent and for those who like dessert wines, there is a delicious pinot blanc.

9480 SW Grabhorn Rd., Beaverton. ✆ **503/649-0027**. www.coopermountainwine.com. Daily noon–5pm. From Ore. 217 on the west side of Portland, take Ore. 210 (Scholls Ferry Rd.) west approximately 5 miles, turn right on Tile Flat Rd. and right again on Grabhorn Rd.

Oak Knoll Winery   Although the only grape they actually grow here is a Niagara, from which they make a fruity but very drinkable wine, Oak Knoll also purchases grapes from area vineyards. Many of the wines here sell for under $10, so if you're wine touring on a tight budget, be sure to stop here. Oak Knoll's Frambrosia is an ambrosial raspberry dessert wine.

29700 SW Burkhalter Rd., Hillsboro. ✆ **800/625-5665** or 503/648-8198. www.oakknollwinery.com. May–Sept daily Mon–Fri 11am–6pm, Sat–Sun 11am–5pm; Oct–Apr daily 11am–5pm. From Hillsboro, go south on Ore. 219 and turn left on Burkhalter Rd.

(Finds) Saké It to Me, Baby

When you've had it with fruit-forward pinot noir, crisp pinot gris, and oaky chardonnay, why not try a little sake? In Forest Grove you'll find **Saké One,** 820 Elm St. off Ore. 47 ((© **800/550-SAKE** or 503/357-7056; www.sakeone.com), which is the world's only American-owned sake brewery and produces premium sakes that are meant to be served cold. Saké One also bottles fruit-flavored sakes that are made with, among other flavorings, Asian pear and raspberry. The tasting room is open daily from 11am to 5pm, excluding major holidays.

Ponzi Vineyards   Although Ponzi's tasting room/wine bar on Ore. 99W in Dundee is more convenient for most people touring wine country, it is also possible to taste wines here at the winery. Although there are no views, the quiet setting and old shade trees make this a good spot for a picnic. See the listing above for information on wines produced by this pioneering Oregon winery.

14665 SW Winery Lane, Beaverton. (© **503/628-1227.** www.ponziwines.com. Reserve wines tasting fee $10. Daily 11am–5pm. From Ore. 217 on the west side of Portland, take Ore. 210 (Scholls Ferry Rd.) west 4½ miles to a left on Vandermost Rd.

THE GASTON & FOREST GROVE AREA

David Hill Winery   This winery, up a gravel road, overlooks the forested foothills of the Coast Range and has its tasting room in a picturesque farmhouse. Here you'll usually find more than a dozen wines available for tasting. The sparkling wine and dessert wines (including a port) are particularly noteworthy. For the most part, wines here are very reasonably priced ($10–$15 range).

46350 David Hill Rd., Forest Grove. (© **877/992-8545** or 503/992-8545. www.davidhillwinery.com. Daily noon–5pm. West of Forest Grove off Ore. 8.

Elk Cove Vineyards &   In business since 1974 and located in an idyllic setting in the hills above the community of Gaston, this is another of the state's larger wineries. Pinot noir and pinot gris make up the bulk of the wine produced here, and the Roosevelt pinot noir, although expensive, can be very good. The Ultima dessert wine is delicious.

27751 NW Olson Rd., Gaston. (© **877/ELK-COVE** or 503/985-7760. www.elkcove.com. Daily 10am–5pm. From Ore. 47 in Gaston, go west on Olson Rd.

Montinore Vineyards &   This is another of Oregon's big wineries, and as several other of the state's large wineries, the wines are often somewhat lacking. White wines are the specialty and prices are quite reasonable. The vineyard setting, with an old farmhouse that seems straight out of the antebellum South, is quite picturesque.

3663 SW Dilley Rd., Forest Grove. (© **888/359-5012** or 503/359-5012. www.montinore.com. Mon–Fri 11am– 4:30pm; Sat–Sun 11am–5pm. South of Forest Grove off Ore. 47 at Dilley.

Shafer Vineyard Cellars &   Small enough that the owners still work the tasting room but large enough to have a dozen or more wines available for tasting on any given day, this winery is strong on white wines, which it sells at very reasonable prices. Expect good Müller-Thurgaus and Gewürztraminers, and the Rieslings are also very consistent.

6200 NW Gales Creek Rd., Forest Grove. (© **503/357-6604.** www.shafervineyardcellars.com. Daily 11am–5pm. From Forest Grove, go 4½ miles west on Ore. 8.

THE EOLA HILLS AREA

Some people claim the best pinot noirs in Oregon come from the Eola Hills north-west of Salem. Why not decide for yourself?

Amity Vineyards 🎯   Founded in 1974, this was one of the earliest wineries in Oregon and helped set the stage for the Willamette Valley becoming one of the world's top pinot noir–producing regions. Amity Vineyards is now one of the few wineries in the state producing gamay noir, and it also produces unsulfited pinot noir from organically grown grapes. Pinot noirs are usually in the $40 range and are often excellent. Its late-harvest and dessert wines are delicious.

18150 Amity Vineyards Rd., Amity. ✆ **888/264-8966** or 503/835-2362. www.amityvineyards.com. Reserve wines tasting fee $5–$10. June–Sept daily 11am–5pm; Oct–May noon–5pm. In Amity, go east on Rice Lane.

Bethel Heights Vineyards 🎯   Set high on a hill and surrounded by more than 50 acres of grapes, Bethel Heights primarily produces chardonnays and pinot noirs. Even their least expensive pinot noirs usually start around $25, and while their best chardonnays are also around $25, they can be very good.

6060 Bethel Heights Rd. NW., Salem. ✆ **503/581-2262**. www.bethelheights.com. June–Aug Tues–Sun 11am–5pm; Mar–May and Sept–Nov Sat–Sun 11am–5pm. Closed Dec–Feb. From Ore. 221 in Lincoln, take Zena Rd. west and turn right on Bethel Heights Rd.

Cristom Vineyards 🎯   With a beautiful setting high in the Eola Hills, this winery is an ideal place for a picnic. Each vintage, a wide range of pinot noirs, in a variety of styles and price ranges, is produced here. The estate chardonnay can be quite good and is usually priced around $25. Cristom is also one of the few wineries in the region producing Viognier from estate-grown grapes and has planted some Syrah grapes as well.

6905 Spring Valley Rd. NW, Salem. ✆ **503/375-3068**. www.cristomwines.com. Mid-Apr to Memorial Day and Labor Day to Thanksgiving Sat–Sun 11am–5pm; Memorial Day to Labor Day Wed–Sun 11am–5pm. Closed Dec to mid-Apr. From Ore. 221 in Lincoln, take Zena Rd. west and turn right on Spring Valley Rd., or take Spring Valley Rd. west from Ore. 221 north of Lincoln.

Kristin Hill Winery   "Méthode champenoise" sparkling wines are a specialty here and make this small family-run winery well worth a visit. The Fizzy Lizzy, a cherry-infused dry sparkling wine, is one of Kristin Hill's most popular wines.

3330 SE Amity-Dayton Hwy., Amity. ✆ **503/835-0850**. Mar–Dec daily noon–5pm; Jan–Feb Sat–Sun noon–5pm. Just north of Amity at the junction with Ore. 233.

Mystic Wines 🎯🎯   This little winery on the north side of the Eola Hills bucks the Oregon pinot noir trend by producing excellent Syrah, zinfandel, cabernet sauvignon, and merlot with grapes that come from near the Oregon town of The Dalles, as well as from Washington state. Prices are mostly in the $20 to $30 range.

11931 Hood View Rd. NW, Amity. ✆ **503/581-2769**. www.mysticwine.com. May–Nov Sat–Sun noon–5pm. Closed Dec to Memorial Day. Off Ore. 221 about 1 mile north of Hopewell.

Stangeland Vineyards 🎯   With an attractive stone-walled tasting room, this small family-owned winery north of Salem is a good place to start a wine tour of the Eola Hills. Stangeland produces some excellent fruit-forward pinot noirs in a variety of price ranges and has won numerous national and international awards.

8500 Hopewell Rd. NW, Salem. ✆ **800/301-9482** or 503/581-0355. www.stangelandwinery.com. Mar–Dec Sat–Sun noon–5pm; other months by appointment. From West Salem, go north on Ore. 221 for 9 miles and turn left on Hopewell Rd.

Tips Leave the Driving to Us

If you're interested in learning more about Oregon wines, contact **Grape Escape** (© **503/283-3380**; www.grapeescapetours.com), which offers in-depth winery tours of the Willamette Valley. All-day tours include stops at several wineries, appetizers, lunch, and dessert, and pickup and drop-off at your hotel ($95–$155 per person). For people with less time, there are half-day afternoon trips that take in two or three wineries ($75–$95 per person). **Oregon Wine Tours** (© **503/681-WINE**; www.orwinetours.com) offers similar all-day tours that stop at four or five wineries. These tours cost $160 each if there are just two of you.

St. Innocent Winery ⓐ This winery produces very drinkable white wines as well as some excellent pinot noirs. It is also one of the few wineries in the state to produce sparkling wines. The tasting room is in a new Eola Hills facility that opened in 2007.

5657 Zena Rd. NW, Salem. © **503/378-1526**. www.stinnocentwine.com. Daily noon–5pm. From Ore. 221 in Lincoln, take Zena Rd. west.

Witness Tree Vineyard ⓐ Named for a tree used by surveyors in the 19th century, this unpretentious winery produces estate-grown chardonnays and pinot noirs. In a region of high-priced pinots, Witness Tree is noteworthy for offering very drinkable bottles at around $25 (though they also produce pricier vintage select pinots that are often very good). Witness Tree is also one of the only wineries in the region producing Dolcetto and Vognier.

7111 Spring Valley Rd. NW, Salem. © **888/GR8T-PNO** or 503/585-7874. www.witnesstreevineyard.com. June–Aug Tues–Sun 11am–5pm; Mar–May and Sept–Dec Sat–Sun 11am–5pm; Jan–Feb limited hours and dates. From Ore. 221 in Lincoln, take Zena Rd. west and turn right on Spring Valley Rd. or take Spring Valley Rd. west from Ore. 221 north of Lincoln.

OTHER WINE COUNTRY ACTIVITIES
THE SPRUCE GOOSE

Evergreen Aviation Museum ⓐⓐ The middle of wine country may seem an odd landing place for Howard Hughes's famous "Spruce Goose" flying boat, but that's exactly what you'll find in this massive, barnlike museum. Although designed during World War II as a flying troop transport that wouldn't have to worry about attacks from German U-boats, the "Spruce Goose" wasn't completed until 1947, at which point it was no longer needed. The plane flew only one time, with Howard Hughes at the controls. The massive wooden plane rests in the company of many smaller planes. Among these are an SR-71 Blackbird spy plane, a Ford Trimotor, a P-51D Mustang, a Spitfire, and a replica of the Wright Brothers' 1903 plane. By the way, the term "Spruce Goose" is actually a misnomer; most of the plane is made of birch. The museum also has an IMAX theater.

500 NE Capt. Michael King Smith Way, McMinnville. © **503/434-4180**. www.sprucegoose.org. Admission $13 adults, $12 seniors, $11 children 3–17, free for children under 3. Daily 9am–5pm. Closed New Year's Day, Easter, Thanksgiving, Christmas. On Ore. 18 (the McMinnville bypass).

GETTING OUTDOORS IN WINE COUNTRY

You can see wine country from the air on a hot-air balloon ride with **Vista Balloon Adventures** (© **800/622-2309** or 503/625-7385; www.vistaballoon.com), which charges $189 per person for a 1-hour flight (that includes brunch at the end of the flight). Alternatively, between March and early November, you can opt for a flight over the region in a glider. Contact **Cascade Soaring,** McMinnville Airport (© **503/472-8805** or 503/864-3735; www.cascadesoaring.com), which offers a variety of flights ranging in duration from 15 to 45 minutes and in price from $50 to $160. Gliders carrying one or two passengers are used.

Seven miles south of Newberg off Ore. 219, on the banks of the Willamette River, is **Champoeg State Park** (pronounced "sham-*poo*-ee"; © **503/678-1251;** www.oregon stateparks.org). The park includes a campground, a bike path, disk-golf course, a picnic area, a historic home, a log cabin, and a visitor center that traces Champoeg's history from its days as a Native American village up through its pioneer farming days. Park admission is $3.

SHOPPING IN THE AREA

The Willamette Valley wine country is not just about wine. It also produces quite a few other crops, and a tour of this region can include stops at a variety of interesting roadside stands and farms.

South of Hillsboro there is a wonderful grouping of farms in the community of Scholls. To reach this area, which is on the northern edge of wine country, take U.S. 26 west from Portland, go south on Ore. 217 and then take the Scholls Ferry Road (Ore. 210) exit and drive southwest for about 8 miles. Here you'll find the **Hoffman Farms Store,** 18407 SW Scholls Ferry Rd. (© **503/628-1436;** www.hoffmanfarms store.com), where in the summer, you can buy fresh berries. A little farther out, you'll come to **Oregon Heritage Farms,** 22801 SW Scholls Ferry Rd. (© **503/628-2775;** www.oregonheritagefarms.com), which sells apples and cider in the autumn months. During the summer—peak season is the month of July—you can pick your own berries at **Rowell Brothers U-Pick,** 24000 SW Scholls Ferry Rd. (© **503/628-0431**). This farm also sells pre-picked berries. More berries, plus gourmet foods and lots more, can be found at **Smith Berry Barn Farm and Garden Market,** 24500 SW Scholls Ferry Rd. (© **503/628-2172;** www.smithberrybarn.com). Across the street from this big red barn, you'll find the South Store Café (see below), my favorite area lunch spot. Scholls Ferry Road becomes Hillsboro Highway (Ore. 219) at this point and leads over Chehalem Mountain to the heart of the wine country. A little ways up this road, you'll come to **Mountainside Lavender Farm,** 17805 SW Hillsboro Hwy. (© **503/936-6744;** www.mountainsidelavender.com), where you can pick your own lavender during the summer. The little shop here sells lots of lavender products. In early July, this farm participates in the Oregon Lavender Festival.

Between Dundee and McMinnville, there are several other good places to stop. **Firestone Farms,** 18400 N. Hwy. 99W, Dayton (© **503/864-2672**), just west of Dundee, sells a wide selection of local produce, wines, and gourmet foods. For fresh local fruit, don't miss **Sweet Oregon Berry Farm** (© **503/864-2897**), which is at the junction of Ore. 18 and Ore. 99W, between Dundee and Lafayette. Dried flowers, herbs, soaps, and other garden-related gifts can also be found at the beautiful **Red Ridge Farms,** 5510 NE Breyman Orchards Rd., Dayton (© **503/864-8502;** www. redridgefarms.com), a nursery and gift shop high in the hills west of Dundee and near Domaine Drouhin Oregon and Domain Serene. Call for directions and hours.

If you enjoy shopping for antiques and collectibles, check out the **Lafayette Schoolhouse Antique Mall,** 784 Ore. 99W, Lafayette (© **503/864-2720**), housed in a 1910 schoolhouse and filled with more than 100 dealers. Lafayette is 6 miles east of McMinnville on Ore. 99W.

Southwest of McMinnville, off Ore. 18, you can buy fresh produce spring through fall at **Farmer John's Produce & Nursery,** 15000 SW Oldsville Rd., McMinnville (© **503/474-3514;** www.farmerjohnsproduce.com). If you like chocolate, head to nearby Amity and stop in at the **Brigittine Monastery,** 23300 Walker Lane (© **503/ 835-8080;** www.brigittine.org), which is known for its heavenly fudge. The fudge and truffles are for sale at the guest reception area, which is open Monday through Saturday from 9am to 5:30pm and Sunday from 1 to 5:30pm.

On the western edge of wine country, 7 miles west of McMinnville near Sheridan, you can shop for art at the **Lawrence Gallery,** Ore. 18 (© **800/894-4278** or 503/ 843-3633; www.lawrencegallery.net). This large art gallery features regional artists and has a sculpture garden and a water garden.

WHERE TO STAY
THE NEWBERG & DUNDEE AREA

Avellan Inn   The Avellan Inn is a small country inn that has just two guest rooms. From the outside, the inn resembles an old barn, complete with weathered cedar board-and-batten siding. Inside, however, it is nothing like a barn. Big walls of glass illuminate the breakfast area and a wood stove keeps the room nice and cozy in cooler months. Emily's Room, my personal favorite here, has a private entrance and a huge covered deck that, when the weather is clear, has a view of Mount Hood. When you stay here, you'll be within a 5- to 10-minute drive of several good wineries.

16900 NE Ore. 240, Newberg, OR 97132. © 503/537-9161. www.avellaninn.com. 2 units. $125–$155 double. Rates include full breakfast. Children under 2 stay free in parent's room. DISC, MC, V. Pets accepted. *In room:* A/C, fridge, hair dryer, free local calls.

Black Walnut Inn ✿✿✿   Perched high in the Red Hills of Dundee with a view that seems to take in all of Oregon wine country, this inn looks for all the world as though it had been transported here from Tuscany. Guest rooms are luxuriously homey and gorgeously decorated, and some are absolutely huge. Some have antique furnishings and some are more contemporary, so there's a room that's just right for nearly anyone. Some rooms have a soaking tub, and all have a balcony or patio. The gardens and patios here are the perfect place to sip a glass of wine at sunset.

9600 NE Worden Hill Rd., Dundee, OR 97115. © 866/429-4114 or 503/429-4114. Fax 503/538-4194. www.black walnut-inn.com. 9 units. $295–$525 suite. Rates include full breakfast. Children 12 and older accepted. AE, MC, V. **Amenities:** Concierge; business center; massage. *In room:* A/C, TV, hair dryer, iron, free local calls, high-speed Internet access, Wi-Fi.

The Lion's Gate Inn ✿   The town of Newberg is slowly beginning to see itself as a wine-country town, and this pretty B&B in one of the oldest homes in town is your best bet for a place to stay right in town. With its wide veranda and attractive gardens, it is one of prettiest old homes in town. Inside, this Craftsman bungalow has lots of beautiful woodwork. Guest rooms, which take their themes from the four seasons, are not all that large, but they have plush beds and a contemporary elegance. Bathrooms are gorgeous, and three of the rooms have gas fireplaces. Restaurants, a wine bar, and a winery tasting room are all within walking distance. The inn also rents a fairy-tale house out in the middle of wine country.

401 N. Howard St. (P.O. Box 92), Newberg, OR 97132. © 503/476-2211. www.distinctivedestination.net. 4 units. $150–$200 double. MC, V. Children over 12 accepted. **Amenities:** Concierge; massage. *In room:* A/C, TV, hair dryer, Wi-Fi.

Red Ridge Farm Suite ★★   There's only one huge suite available at this luxurious little place, and it is such a quintessential wine-country retreat that you should make this your first choice if you're looking for a romantic hideaway in the hills. The suite takes up the entire second floor of a gorgeous building that has a garden-oriented gift shop on the ground floor. Access is via a spiral staircase up the building's turret (in which lavender hangs to dry in summer). The modern styling, big windows, and wine-country views make this the sort of place you'd see in *Sunset* magazine.

5510 NE Breyman Orchards Rd., Dayton, OR 97114. *C* **503/864-8502.** Fax 503/864-8391. www.redridgefarms.com. 1 unit. $200 double. MC, V. *In room:* A/C, TV/VCR/DVD, kitchen, fridge, microwave, coffeemaker, hair dryer, iron, free local calls.

Springbrook Hazelnut Farm ★★   Located only 20 miles from Portland, this 70-acre working farm is a convenient rural getaway for anyone who craves a slow-paced vacation. The four Craftsman-style buildings are listed on the National Register of Historic Places and include the main house, a carriage house, and a cottage. Original artwork abounds in the boldly decorated, colorful main house. Both of the main buildings overlook the farm's pond and lovely back garden, and there are also tennis courts and a swimming pool. Through the hazelnut orchard is Rex Hill Vineyards, and there's also a small winery operating here on the farm. The little white cottage, with its antique fireplace mantle, fir floors, and tiled bathroom, overlooks the farm's pond and a meadow that's filled with daffodils in the spring.

30295 N. Ore. 99W, Newberg, OR 97132. *C* **800/793-8528** or 503/538-4606. www.nutfarm.com. 2 units. $225 cottage or carriage house. Rates include full breakfast. AE, DC, MC, V. **Amenities:** Outdoor pool; tennis court. *In room:* A/C, kitchen, fridge, microwave, coffeemaker, hair dryer, iron, no phone.

Wine Country Farm   Located on 13 acres high in the hills between Dundee and Lafayette and surrounded by vineyards, this B&B has one of the best views in the area. The inn also has a winery and tasting room and offers massages and horseback and horse-and-buggy rides through the vineyards. With so much to offer, it's easy to spend all your time here and never venture out to out to other wineries. The inn looks like an old French farmhouse, and inside you'll find attractively appointed rooms, many of which have decks, views, and fireplaces. If you happen to stay in a room without a view, you can soak up the views from the deck that runs the length of the house. You can also hang out in the gazebo or play croquet, bocce ball, or horseshoes. The inn also has two suites on 12 acres nearby.

6855 Breyman Orchards Rd., Dayton, OR 97114. *C* **800/261-3446** or 503/864-3446. Fax 503/864-3109. www. winecountryfarm.com. 9 units. $130–$205 double; $300–$500 suite. Rates include full breakfast. Children 12 and older accepted. MC, V. **Amenities:** Jacuzzi; sauna; massage; laundry service; horseback riding. *In room:* A/C.

THE MCMINNVILLE AREA

Mattey House   This restored 1892 Queen Anne Victorian farmhouse sits on 10 acres of farmland behind 1½ acres of grapevines. This is a grand old house, and up on the second floor, you'll find a tiny balcony overlooking the vineyard. It's the perfect spot for a glass of wine in the afternoon. Guest rooms are decorated in country Victorian style, with antique beds. The Riesling Room, with its claw-foot bathtub, is my favorite. Innkeepers Jack and Denise Seed are always glad to help you plan your day's explorations.

10221 NE Mattey Lane, McMinnville, OR 97128. *C* **503/434-5058.** Fax 503/434-6667. www.matteyhouse.com. 4 units. $130–$150 double. Rates include full breakfast. Children 10 and older welcome. AE, MC, V. *In room:* A/C, hair dryer, no phone.

McMenamins Hotel Oregon ✦   This restored historic hotel in downtown McMinnville is operated by a Portland-based chain of brewpubs, nightclubs, and unusual hotels that are all filled with interesting artwork. Guest rooms here are done in a simple, classic style, with antique and reproduction furniture. The corner kings with private baths and big windows on two sides are the nicest rooms; most rooms here have shared bathrooms. Offsetting this inconvenience is the hotel's genuinely historic feel. The ground-floor brewpub/dining room, cellar bar, and rooftop bar and deck overlooking McMinnville and the Yamhill Valley all help make the Hotel Oregon eminently recommendable. There are also a couple of good restaurants within a few blocks.

310 NE Evans St., McMinnville, OR 97128. ℂ **888/472-8427** or 503/472-8427. www.mcmenamins.com. 42 units (6 with private bathroom). $50–$115 double with shared bathroom; $80–$133 double with private bath. Children 6 and under stay free in parent's room. AE, DC, DISC, MC, V. **Amenities:** 2 restaurants (American); 3 lounges. *In room:* A/C.

Youngberg Hill Inn ✦✦   Set on a 50-acre farm that includes pinot noir vineyards, this is the quintessential wine-country inn. A mile-long gravel driveway leads to the inn, which sits atop a hill with commanding views of the Willamette Valley, snow-capped Cascades peaks, and the Coast Range. Large decks wrap around both floors of the inn, and some of the rooms have their own fireplaces. Big breakfasts get visitors off to a good start each morning. Pull up a chair on the porch, pour a glass of the inn's own pinot noir, and gaze out over the rolling hills, and you'll probably start thinking about cashing in the mutual funds to start a vineyard of your own.

10660 SW Youngberg Hill Rd., McMinnville, OR 97128. ℂ **888/657-8668** or 503/472-2727. Fax 503/472-1313. www.youngberghill.com. 7 units. $169–$199 double; $219–$269 suite. Rates include full breakfast. Children over 4 are welcome. MC, V. **Amenities:** Concierge; massage. *In room:* A/C, hair dryer, iron, high-speed Internet access, Wi-Fi.

THE YAMHILL & CARLTON AREA

Abbey Road Farm ✦✦   This is one of the most unusual bed-and-breakfast inns in Oregon and should be your first choice for a wine-country getaway. The large and luxurious guest rooms are located in a building that was constructed from three large metal silos. Now, lest you think you'll be sleeping in a barn, let me assure you that the silos have been transformed into an architectural gem of a building, a testament to the imagination of owners John and Judi Stuart. The large guest rooms have whirlpool tubs, memory-foam beds, and bucolic views. When you're not out wine touring, you can visit with the goats, sheep, llamas, chickens, and other farm animals that live here.

10501 NE Abbey Rd., Carlton, OR 97111. ℂ **503/852-6278.** www.abbeyroadfarm.com. 5 units. $195–$225 double. Rates include full breakfast. AE, MC, V. 2-night minimum on weekends. No children. **Amenities:** Concierge. *In room:* A/C, hair dryer, iron. Closed Dec–Feb.

Brookside Inn on Abbey Road ✦   With 22 acres of woods, park-like grounds, fields, and a pretty pond complete with weeping willows growing along the shore, this inn, formerly a religious retreat, is wonderfully tranquil. In the main lodge, there's a pretty great room with lots of windows and a stone fireplace. Various decks provide plenty of outdoor gathering spaces. The inn has rooms both in the lodge-like main house and in a separate carriage house. My favorite room is the Kyoto, which has several windows overlooking the garden. Rooms are not as large as at some area inns, but they have beautiful hardwood furnishings

8243 NE Abbey Rd., Carlton, OR 97111. ℂ **503/852-4433.** www.brooksideinn-oregon.com. 9 units. $185–$325 double; $350 suite. Rates include full breakfast. AE, DISC, MC, V. Children over 12 accepted. Pets accepted ($100 fee). **Amenities:** Access to nearby health club; bike rentals; concierge; massage. *In room:* A/C, hair dryer, high-speed Internet access, Wi-Fi.

THE GASTON & FOREST GROVE AREA

McMenamins Grand Lodge ✿ Housed in a former Masonic retirement home, this sprawling lodge is part of a local microbrewery chain and has a decidedly countercultural feel. Although only five of the rooms here have private baths, there are plenty of well-appointed bathrooms, and most rooms do have sinks. There's also lots of colorful artwork incorporated into the design of the building. However, the principal attractions here are the brewpub, beer garden, and numerous small lounges scattered around the main building. The lodge is surrounded by huge lawns and has its own disc golf course, wine bar, and movie theater.

3505 Pacific Ave., Forest Grove, OR 97116. ✆ **877/922-9533** or 503/992-9533. www.mcmenamins.com. 77 units (5 with private bathroom). $45–$105 double with shared bathroom; $115–$215 double with private bathroom. Children 6 and under stay free in parent's room. AE, DC, DISC, MC, V. **Amenities:** 2 restaurants (American); 4 lounges; soaking pool; day spa; massage. *In room:* Wi-Fi, no phone.

WHERE TO DINE
THE NEWBERG & DUNDEE AREA

If wine tasting has made you sleepy and you need a good latte, head to the **Coffee Cottage,** 808 E. Hemlock St., Newberg (✆ **503/538-5126**). For wine and light meals, check out **Crush Wine Lounge & Bistro,** 115 N. Washington St. (✆ **503/538-5113;** www.crushwinelounge.com), in a beautiful old Victorian house at the west end of Newberg.

The Dundee Bistro ✿ NORTHWEST   Located in the same building as the Ponzi Wine Bar and the Your Northwest gift shop, this chic eatery would be right at home in Portland's trendy Pearl District. The bistro's hip, urban style, however, also epitomizes a modern wine-country aesthetic, which makes this place quite popular with people touring the area wineries. The menu is relatively short and changes on a regular basis to reflect the region's best seasonal ingredients, which translates into the likes of wild mushroom pizza with spinach, roasted onions, and basil pesto; pork loin with mashed sweet potatoes, grilled pear, and currant sauce; and roasted mushroom pasta with spinach and truffle butter. The wine list focuses on area wines.

100-A SW Seventh St., Dundee. ✆ 503/554-1650. www.dundeebistro.com. Reservations recommended. Main courses $10–$13 lunch, $11–$24 dinner. AE, MC, V. Sun–Thurs 11:30am–8:30pm; Fri–Sat 11:30am–9pm.

The Painted Lady ✿✿ FRENCH/NORTHWEST   Located just off Ore. 99W in a restored Victorian home in downtown Newberg, the Painted Lady brings sophistication and creativity to a town that has long thought of Chinese and Mexican as exotic foods. Chef/owner Allen Routt, whose credentials include study at the prestigious Culinary Institute of America, serves three-course prix fixe dinners that nonetheless offer plenty of choices. The menu changes with the seasons, but a recent night featured, among many other offerings, corn bisque with goat-cheese crème; chanterelle-mushroom ragout served over gnocchi; herb-crusted Oregon albacore; roast duck breast with wild mushrooms and fig *jus;* and for dessert, chevre cheesecake with Oregon cherries.

201 S. College St., Newberg. ✆ **503/538-3850.** www.thepaintedladyrestaurant.com. Reservations highly recommended. Prix fixe menus $45–$60. AE, DISC, MC, V. Wed–Sun 5–10pm.

Red Hills Provincial Dining ✿ FRENCH/CONTINENTAL/NORTHWEST   Housed in a 1920s Craftsman bungalow, this restaurant sums up the Oregon wine-country appeal with both its setting and its food. The dinner menu changes regularly, and you can be sure it will always include plenty of fresh local produce, as well as Northwest meats and seafoods. The menu draws on a variety of European influences and can be counted upon to feature the likes of chicken breast with figs, walnuts, and pastis; grape vine-smoked duck breast, filet mignon with pinot noir demi-glace, or wild mushroom pasta with dark rum and sherry cream. There's a very good selection of wines available (local wines are featured), and dishes are calculated to pair well with the wines of the region.

276 Ore. 99W, Dundee. ℭ **503/538-8224.** Reservations recommended. Main courses $24–$32. AE, DISC, MC, V. Tues–Sat 5–9; Sun 5–8pm.

Tina's 🏵🏵 CONTINENTAL/NORTHWEST   Despite its rather small and non-descript building right on the highway in Dundee, Tina's has long been one of the Yamhill County wine country's premier restaurants, and with its contemporary menu and decor, it's my favorite place to eat in the area. The menu changes regularly and usually has only six to eight entrees and as many appetizers. However, a balance between the traditional (braised short ribs) and the less familiar (pan-roasted duck breast with rice pancake and green-peppercorn sauce), keeps diners content. There are usually almost as many desserts available as there are entrees, and the wine selection, of course, emphasizes local wines.

760 Ore. 99W. ℭ **503/538-8880.** www.tinasdundee.com. Reservations recommended. Main courses $8–$10 lunch, $22–$30 dinner. AE, DISC, MC, V. Tues–Fri 11:30am–2pm and 5–9pm; Sat–Sun 5–9pm.

THE MCMINNVILLE AREA

For casual and inexpensive meals, try the **McMenamins Pub,** Hotel Oregon, 310 NE Evans St. (ℭ **503/472-8427;** www.mcmenamins.com), which serves decent pub fare, plus good microbrews and regional wines. More pub fare, microbrews, and local wines can be had at the **Golden Valley Brewery & Pub,** 980 E. Fourth St. (ℭ **503/472-2739;** www.goldenvalleybrewery.com). For espresso, drop by **Union Block Coffee,** 403 NE Third St. (ℭ **503/472-0645**).

Bistro Maison 🏵 FRENCH   This cozy little spot in an old house in downtown McMinnville is a casual French restaurant with great food. The husband-and-wife owners bring loads of experience to the restaurant, including time spent at famed New York restaurants the Russian Tea Room and Tavern on the Green. The menu offers such French standards as escargot and coq au vin, but whatever you order for an entree, be sure to start with the mussels or the very authentic fondue. There are daily *plats du jour,* with Sundays featuring a good cassoulet. In summer, ask for a table on the tree-shaded patio.

729 NE Third St. ℭ **503/474-1888.** www.bistromaison.com. Reservations recommended. Main courses $9–$17 lunch, $18–$27 dinner. DISC, MC, V. Wed–Thurs 11:30am–2pm and 6–9pm; Fri 11:30am–2pm and 5–9pm; Sat 5–9pm; Sun noon–8pm.

The Fresh Palate Cafe SEAFOOD/NORTHWEST   This casual spot is popular both with people touring the wine country and those headed to or from the coast. The crab cakes here are a must-have, and are best accompanied by a local pinot gris. Other good choices include a sandwich made with hazelnut-crusted salmon and wild-mushroom ravioli. There are usually a half-dozen or so daily specials. Because this is the best place for miles around, there is usually a wait for a table on summer weekends. If the weather is nice, try to get a table on the deck.

19706 SW Ore. 18 (between McMinnville and Sheridan). ℭ **503/843-4400.** Reservations recommended on weekends. Main courses $11–$20 lunch, $23–$30 dinner. AE, MC, V. Sun–Thurs 11am–3pm; Fri–Sat 11am–3pm and 5–7:30pm.

The Joel Palmer House ✹✹✹ FRENCH/NORTHWEST If you love mushrooms in all their earthy guises, then you'll find culinary nirvana in this downtown Dayton restaurant, east of McMinnville. Chef/owner Jack Czarnecki is a man obsessed with mushrooms, and nearly every dish has mushrooms in it. Start your meal with the extraordinary wild-mushroom soup made with suillis mushrooms, then move on to the filet mignon with porcini sauce or the beef Stroganoff with wild mushrooms. The rack of lamb with a hazelnut-pepper sauce, though it lacks mushrooms, is a quintessential wine-country entree. Mushroom lovers will be in good hands if they opt for the "Jack's Mushroom Madness" prix-fixe dinner. The extensive wine list features Oregon wines. The restaurant is in a house built in the 1850s and is quite formal.

600 Ferry St., Dayton. ✆ 503/864-2995. www.joelpalmerhouse.com. Reservations highly recommended. Main courses $29–$37; prix fixe menu $75. AE, DC, DISC, MC, V. Tues–Sat 5–9pm. Closed Jan to early Feb.

Nick's Italian Café ✹ NORTHERN ITALIAN Nick's is a McMinnville institution with a loyal following, especially among the older winemakers in the region. Each evening, there's a fixed-price five-course dinner that might start with prosciutto-wrapped melon and pears, followed by minestrone soup and a salad of mixed greens with pancetta. From there you'll move on to a pasta dish (perhaps lasagna with Dungeness crab and pine nuts) and then the entree, which might be grilled salmon; rabbit braised in pinot gris with Gorgonzola polenta; or lamb chops marinated in garlic and sage. If you still have room after all that, be sure to try the chocolate-hazelnut brandy torte.

521 NE Third St., McMinnville. ✆ 503/434-4471. www.nicksitaliancafe.com. Reservations recommended. 5-course fixed-price dinner $45. AE, MC, V. Tues–Thurs 5:30–9pm; Fri–Sat 5:30–10pm; Sun 5–8pm.

THE YAMHILL & CARLTON AREA

If you want to have a picnic at one of the Carlton-area wineries, be sure to stop first at **The Horse Radish,** 211 W. Main St. (✆ 503/852-6616; www.thehorseradish. com), a combination wine bar and gourmet deli that sells wonderful cheeses, cured meats, and artisan breads. There are also small plates to go with the wine they serve here. The Horse Radish is open Monday through Thursday from 11am to 7pm, Friday and Saturday from 11am to 9pm, and Sunday from noon to 7pm. Alternatively, you can get good sandwiches at **The Filling Station Deli,** 305 W. Main St. (✆ 503/852-6687; www.fillingstationdeli.com), which is open daily from 7am to 3:30pm (closed Mon in winter).

Cuvée ✹✹ FRENCH Chef/owner Gilbert Henry had long established himself as one of the top toques in Portland before moving to the small town of Carlton in the heart of the wine country. Here Henry's classic French cuisine is the perfect foil for fine wines from Carlton-area wineries. The menu leans toward seafood dishes, which go well with local pinot gris, but there's also usually a lamb dish (perhaps Moroccan lamb tagine) on the menu. Be sure to start your meal with some oysters or sautéed wild mushrooms and local pinot gris or chardonnay.

214 W. Main St., Carlton. ✆ 866/421-1347 or 503/852-6555. www.cuveedining.com. Reservations highly recommended. Main courses $10–$13 lunch, $19–$23 dinner. AE, DISC, MC, V. Wed–Fri 5:30–9:30pm; Sat noon–3pm and 5:30–9:30pm; Sun noon–3pm and 5–8pm.

THE HILLSBORO & BEAVERTON AREA

The South Store Café ꜰɪɴᴅs COMFORT FOOD I have a weakness for old general stores, and this century-old clapboard building, at a rural crossroads on the northern edge of wine country, holds a special place in my heart. I always start my wine tours here. If it's early, I come for cappuccino and owner Lee Thompson's incomparable pastries. If it's lunchtime, I always get a big bowl of the soup of the day, which might be a nostalgia-inducing ham-and-white-bean, or perhaps a spicy and warming tortilla soup. When I'm particularly hungry, I'll add a sandwich or a half-sandwich, perhaps a comforting meatloaf or a panini with pesto. And after an afternoon of wine tasting, this is always my end-of-the-day coffee stop.

24485 SW Scholls Ferry Rd., Hillsboro. © 503/628-1920. www.southstorecafe.com. Soups, salads & sandwiches $4.50–$6.75. MC, V. Tues–Fri 6:30am–5pm, Sat 9am–5pm, Sun 9am–3pm (closes 1 hr. earlier in winter).

THE GASTON & FOREST GROVE AREA

You can get decent pub food at the **Ironwork Grill,** McMenamins Grand Lodge, 3505 Pacific Ave. (© **503/992-9533;** www.mcmenamins.com), in Forest Grove. This hotel also has a beer garden in the summer.

EN ROUTE TO THE BEACH

It used to be almost impossible to get beach-bound traffic on Ore. 18 to stop for anything, but that was before the **Spirit Mountain Casino,** 27100 SW Salmon River Hwy. (© **800/760-7977;** www.spiritmountain.com), opened in the town of Grand Ronde and became the most popular casino in Oregon. These days a lot of the traffic on this highway isn't even going to the beach; it's headed straight to this large, glitzy temple of luck.

2 Salem & the Mid-Willamette Valley

47 miles S of Portland, 40 miles N of Corvallis, 131 miles W of Bend, 57 miles E of Lincoln City

Although it's the state capital, the third largest city in the state, and home to Willamette University, Salem feels more like a small Midwestern college town than a Pacific Rim capital. Founded by a Methodist missionary, the city still wears its air of conservatism like a minister's collar. No one has ever accused Salem of being too raucous or rowdy. Even when both the school and the legislature are in session, the city barely seems charged with energy. The quiet conservatism does, however, give the city a certain charm that's not found in the other cities of the Willamette Valley. Although there are some interesting museums and the state capitol building to be visited here, it is the countryside surrounding Salem that is the real attraction. Within 20 to 25 miles of Salem, you'll find the Oregon Garden, Silver Falls State Park (one of the most beautiful state parks in Oregon), wineries, commercial flower fields, and several quaint small towns (Silverton, Mt. Angel, Independence, and Monmouth) that conjure up the Willamette Valley's pioneer past.

Salem's roots date from 1834, when Methodist missionary Jason Lee, who had traveled west to convert the local Indians, founded Salem, making it the first American settlement in the Willamette Valley. In 1842, 1 year before the first settlers crossed the continent on the Oregon Trail, Lee founded the Oregon Institute, the first school of higher learning west of the Rockies. In 1857, the first textile mill west of the Mississippi opened here, giving Salem a firm industrial base. However, despite all these historic firsts, Oregon City and Portland grew much faster and quickly became the region's population centers. Salem seemed doomed to backwater status until the year 1859, when Oregon became a state and Salem was chosen as its capital.

Salem

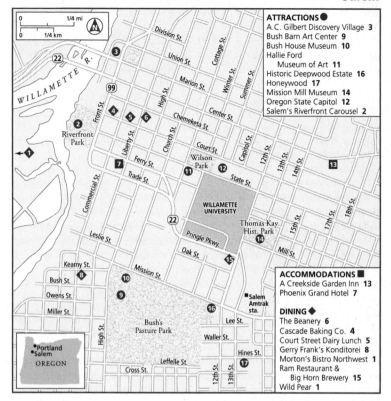

ATTRACTIONS ●
A.C. Gilbert Discovery Village **3**
Bush Barn Art Center **9**
Bush House Museum **10**
Hallie Ford
    Museum of Art **11**
Historic Deepwood Estate **16**
Honeywood **17**
Mission Mill Museum **14**
Oregon State Capitol **12**
Salem's Riverfront Carousel **2**

ACCOMMODATIONS ■
A Creekside Garden Inn **13**
Phoenix Grand Hotel **7**

DINING ◆
The Beanery **6**
Cascade Baking Co. **4**
Court Street Dairy Lunch **5**
Gerry Frank's Konditorei **8**
Morton's Bistro Northwest **1**
Ram Restaurant &
    Big Horn Brewery **15**
Wild Pear **1**

ESSENTIALS

GETTING THERE   Salem is on I-5 at the junction of Ore. 22, which heads west
to connect with Ore. 18 from Lincoln City and southeast to connect with U.S. 20
from Bend.

   Amtrak has passenger rail service to Salem. The station is at 500 13th St. SE
between Leslie and Bellevue streets.

VISITOR INFORMATION   Contact the **Salem Convention & Visitors Association,** 1313 Mill St. SE, Salem, OR 97301 (℗ **800/874-7012** or 503/581-4325;
www.travelsalem.com). For more information on the Silverton area, contact the **Silverton Chamber of Commerce,** P.O. Box 257, Silverton, OR 97381 (℗ **503/873-
5615;** www.silvertonor.com).

FESTIVALS   Two of the biggest events of the year in Salem are the **Oregon State
Fair** (℗ **503/947-3247;** www.oregonstatefair.org), which is held from late August to
Labor Day, and the **Salem Arts Festival** (℗ **503/581-2228;** www.salemart.org),
which is the largest juried art fair in Oregon and is held the third weekend in July.

   Each year on the second weekend after Labor Day, the town of Mt. Angel is the site
of the huge **Mt. Angel Oktoberfest** ✦ (℗ **503/845-9440;** www.mtangel.org). With
polka bands from around the world, beer and wine gardens, German food, and dancing in the streets, this is just about the biggest party in the state.

SALEM
SEEING THE SIGHTS

Though it is sometimes easy to forget, Salem is a river town. On the western edge of downtown, you'll find Salem's Riverfront Park, which features a state-of-the-art playground, amphitheater, carousel, and meandering pathways. It is also home to the A.C. Gilbert Discovery Village (see below). Here in the park, you'll also find the dock for the *Willamette Queen* (© 503/371-1103; www.willamettequeen.com), a paddle wheeler that cruises the Willamette River. Cruises range from basic 1-hour outings to lunch, brunch, and dinner cruises. Prices range from $12 ($6 for children 4–10) for a 1-hour cruise to $48 for a 2-hour dinner or brunch cruise ($28 for children 4–10). Seniors receive a 10% discount. Reservations are required.

From the carousel, a stroll up State Street will take you past some of Salem's most interesting shops and boutiques. To see the work of local artists, stop in at **Mary Lou Zeek Gallery,** 335 State St. (© 503/581-3229; www.zeekgallery.com).

Bush Barn Art Center ⭑ The Salem Art Association's Bush Barn Art Center includes a sales gallery as well as exhibition spaces that feature changing art exhibits. The focus is on local and regional artists, and the quality is quite high. Each year on the third weekend in July, Bush's Pasture Park is the site of the Salem Art Fair and Festival, one of the most popular art festivals in the Northwest.

Bush and High sts. © 503/581-2228. www.salemart.org. Free admission. Tues–Fri 10am–5pm; Sat–Sun noon–5pm. Closed major holidays.

Bush House Museum ⭑ Set at the top of a shady hill in the 100-acre Bush's Pasture Park, this imposing Italianate Victorian home dates back to 1878. Inside, you can see the original furnishings, including 10 fireplaces and the original wallpaper. At the time it was built, this home had all the modern conveniences—indoor plumbing, gas lights, and central heating. Also on the grounds is Oregon's oldest greenhouse conservatory.

600 Mission St. SE. © 503/363-4714. www.salemart.org. Admission $4 adults, $3 students and seniors, $2 children 6–12. May–Sept Tues–Sun noon–5pm; Oct–Dec and Mar–Apr Tues–Sun 1–4pm; Jan–Feb call for hours. Closed major holidays.

Hallie Ford Museum of Art ⭑⭑ This is one of the three top art museums in Oregon and features collections of Native American baskets and Northwest, European, and Asian art. The first-floor galleries are devoted to contemporary art and feature changing exhibitions. Upstairs, you'll find one gallery filled with more than 70 Native American baskets, the finest collection of such baskets in the state. Other galleries contain artifacts ranging from an ancient Egyptian coffin mask to 19th-century Chinese porcelain.

700 State St. © 503/370-6855. www.willamette.edu/museum_of_art. Admission $3 adults, $2 seniors and students; free admission Tues. Tues–Sat 10am–5pm; Sun noon–5pm. Closed Easter, July 4, Thanksgiving, day after Thanksgiving, and Dec 24–Jan 1.

Historic Deepwood Estate ⭑ Set on 5½ acres of English-style gardens and woodlands, this Queen Anne Victorian home is a delicate jewel box of a house. The house, with its many stained-glass windows, golden-oak moldings, and numerous lightning rod–topped peaked roofs and gables, was built in 1894, and the gardens, designed by the Northwest's first women-owned landscape architecture firm, were added in the 1930s.

1116 Mission St. SE. © 503/363-1825. www.oregonlink.com/deepwood. Admission $4 adults, $3 seniors and students, $2 children 6–12. Grounds daily dawn–dusk; guided house tours May–Sept Sun–Fri noon–5pm, Oct–Apr Tues–Sat noon–5pm.

Mission Mill Museum ✪   The sprawling red Thomas Kay Woolen Mill, a water-powered mill built in 1889, is one of the most fascinating attractions in Salem. (The Salem Visitors Information Center on site also makes this the best place to start a tour of the state capital.) The restored buildings house exhibits on every stage of the wool-making process, and in the main mill building, the water-driven turbine is still in operation, producing electricity for the buildings. Also on these neatly manicured grounds are a cafe, a collection of interesting shops, and several other old structures, including the Jason Lee House, which was built by Salem's founder in 1841 and is the oldest frame house in the Northwest. The Marion County Historical Society Museum (✆ **503/364-2128**; www.oregonlink.com/historical_society/index.html), also on the grounds, houses exhibits on the history of the area with a particularly interesting section on the local Kalapuya Indians. This museum is open Tuesday through Saturday from 9:30am to 4:30pm.

1313 Mill St. SE. ✆ **503/585-7012**. www.missionmill.org. Admission $8 adults, $7 seniors, $4 children 6–18. Mon–Sat 10am–5pm. Closed major holidays.

Oregon State Capitol   Where's the dome? That's the first thing that strikes most visitors to the Oregon State Capitol, which looks as if construction was never completed (perhaps due to a lack of funds in the state budget). However, it was actually designed without a dome, and, consequently, the building, which opened in 1938, has a stark appearance (not unlike that of a mausoleum). If you look closer, though, you'll recognize the pared down lines of Art Deco design aesthetics in this building. *The Oregon Pioneer,* a 23-foot-tall gilded statue, tops the building, which is faced with white Italian marble. Outside the building, there are numerous sculptures and attractive gardens; inside, there are murals of historic Oregon scenes. Tours of the capitol are available during the summer. There are also changing art exhibits and videos about the history of the building and the state.

900 Court St. NE. ✆ **503/986-1388**. www.leg.state.or.us. Free admission. Building Mon–Fri 7:30am–5:30pm, Sat 9am–4pm; tours offered Memorial Day to Labor Day Mon–Sat 9am–3pm. Closed national holidays.

A NEARBY STATE PARK & TWO WILDLIFE REFUGES

North of Salem 8 miles you'll find **Willamette Mission State Park** (✆ **503/393-1172**; www.oregonstateparks.org), which preserves the site of the first settlement in the Willamette Valley. It was here that Methodist missionary Jason Lee and four assistants established their first mission in 1834. Today, there are 8 miles of walking, biking, and horseback-riding paths through the park, which is also home to the largest black cottonwood tree in the country.

If it's bird-watching that interests you, there are two national wildlife refuges in the area that are excellent places to observe ducks, geese, swans, and raptors. Ankeny National Wildlife Refuge is 12 miles south of Salem off I-5 at exit 243. Basket Slough National Wildlife Refuge is northwest of the town of Rickreall on Ore. 22, which passes through the north end of downtown Salem. Fall through spring is the best time of year for birding here. For more information, contact the **Willamette Valley National Wildlife Refuge Complex** (✆ **541/757-7236**; www.fws.gov/willamettevalley).

ESPECIALLY FOR KIDS

In addition to the two attractions listed below, the younger ones will likely enjoy a ride on **Salem's Riverfront Carousel** ✪, 101 Front St. NE (✆ **503/540-0374;** www.salemcarousel.org), which is a modern carousel with 42 hand-carved horses. The carousel has its own building in Riverfront Park and is within walking distance of A.C. Gilbert Discovery Village.

June through September, the carousel operates Monday through Thursday from 10am to 7pm, Friday and Saturday from 10am to 9pm, and Sunday from 11am to 6pm; other months the carousel closes 1 to 2 hours earlier. Rides are $1.25.

A.C. Gilbert Discovery Village 🐿 *Kids* Known as the "man who saved Christmas," Salem's A. C. Gilbert may not be familiar to most people, but the toy he invented, the Erector Set, certainly is. Erector Sets have inspired generations of budding engineers, and it was during World War I that Gilbert saved Christmas. It seems Congress wanted to turn his toy factory into a munitions factory, but after taking Erector Sets to Congress, he convinced the legislators that America needed to prime its next generation of inventors just as much as it needed to prime its war machine. Here, in two Queen Anne Victorian homes, a few other small historic buildings, and a half-acre outdoor play/recreation center, the 21st century's inventors can let loose their own creative energies. Among the many interactive exhibits here, there are plenty of Erector Set constructions and a bubble room.

116 Marion St. NE. ✆ 503/371-3631. www.acgilbert.org. Admission $5.50 adults and children over 3, $4 seniors, $2.50 children 1–2 years old; free for children under 1. Mon–Sat 10am–5pm; Sun noon–5pm. Closed New Year's Day, Easter, Thanksgiving, Christmas.

Enchanted Forest *Kids* Classic children's stories come to life at this amusement park for kids. In addition to Storybook Lane, English Village, and Western Town, there's a haunted house, a bobsled run, a log-flume ride, and a comedy theater. Rides cost extra. Adjacent to Enchanted Village is **Thrill-Ville USA** (✆ **503/363-9376;** www.thrillville usa.homestead.com), a small amusement park with the world's biggest slide, plus a roller coaster, water slides, and other rides and activities. It's open in summer daily from 11am to 6pm; rides cost $2 to $3, and an all-day waterslide pass is $12.

8462 Enchanted Way SE, Turner. ✆ 503/363-3060. www.enchantedforest.com. Admission $8.50 adults, $8 seniors, $7.50 children 3–12, free for children under 3. Mar 15–31 Mon–Fri 9:30am–5 or 6pm; Apr and Sept Sat–Sun 9:30am–6pm; May Mon–Fri 9:30am–5pm, Sat–Sun 9:30am–6pm; June daily 9:30am–6pm; July to Labor Day Mon–Fri 9:30am–6pm, Sat–Sun 9:30am–7pm. Closed Oct–Mar 14. Take I-5 7 miles south of Salem to Exit 248.

SILVERTON

Set in the foothills of the Cascade Range, Silverton is a quaint community on the banks of Silver Creek. The creek-side setting gives the town something of the feel of an old New England mill town, and although the area's major attractions—Silver Falls State Park and The Oregon Garden—are both outside of town, the downtown, where a pedestrian-covered bridge leads to a pleasant, shady park, is also worth a stroll.

WATERFALLS & DISPLAY GARDENS

The Oregon Garden 🐿🐿 The Oregon Garden is one of the largest public display gardens in the Northwest, and was created to showcase the state's horticultural heritage and the wide variety of plants grown in Oregon's commercial plant nurseries. In addition to an incredible array of plantings, the numerous display gardens include several water features and ponds, terraced gardens, a sensory garden, a children's garden, and a native oak grove. During the summer months, concerts are held in the garden's amphitheater. The Oregon Garden is also home to the **Gordon House** (✆ **503/ 874-6006;** www.thegordonhouse.org), a small Frank Lloyd Wright home that was moved to this site and is open for tours.

879 W. Main St., Silverton. ℂ 877/674-2733 or 503/874-8100. www.oregongarden.org. Admission: May–Sept $10 adults, $9 seniors, $8 students 8–17; Oct & Apr $8 adults, $7 seniors, $6 students 8–17; Nov–Mar $5 adults, $4 senior and students 8–17; Gordon House admission: $5 guided tour. May–Sept Mon–Tues, Thurs–Fri, and Sun 10am–6pm, Wed and Sat 7am–6pm; Oct–Apr daily 10am–4pm. Closed New Year's Day, Thanksgiving, Christmas Eve, Christmas.

Silver Falls State Park 🐸🐸   Located 26 miles east of Salem on Ore. 214, this is the largest state park in Oregon and one of the most popular. Hidden in the lush canyons and dark old-growth forests of the park are 10 silvery waterfalls ranging in height from 27 to 177 feet. The trails are some of the most enjoyable in the state and can usually be hiked any time of year. Although the best hike is the 7-mile loop trail that links all the falls, shorter hikes are also possible. You can even walk behind the South, Lower South, and North falls. You can spend an afternoon or several days exploring the park. Camping (for reservations, contact **ReserveAmerica** ℂ **800/452-5687;** www.reserveamerica.com), swimming, picnicking, and bicycling are all popular activities.

15 miles southeast of Silverton on Ore. 214. ℂ 503/873-8681. www.oregonstateparks.org. Admission $3 per car. Daily dawn–dusk.

OTHER AREA ATTRACTIONS & ACTIVITIES

While in Silverton, be sure to wander around town and admire the many murals. Local artists who display their work at the **Lunaria Gallery,** 113 N. Water St. (ℂ **503/873-7734;** www.lunariagallery.com), painted some of these. Between mid-May and mid-September, you should be sure to stop at **Havenhill Lavender Farm,** 582 Drift Creek Rd. SE (ℂ **866/430-8396** or 503/873-0396; www.havenhilllavender.com), which is about 7 miles outside Silverton (call for directions). The farm is open Friday through Sunday from 10am to 6pm.

WHERE TO STAY

Water Street Inn 🐸   Located in downtown Silverton in an 1890 vintage Victorian home, this inn is the ideal place to stay if you want to take extra time for exploring the Oregon Gardens and nearby Silver Falls State Park. This old house has some of the most attractive B&B rooms in the Willamette Valley. Most of the rooms are quite spacious and two have double whirlpool tubs. Rooms 1 and 5 are my favorites.

421 N. Water St., Silverton, OR 97381. ℂ 866/873-3344 or 503/873-3344. www.thewaterstreetinn.com. 5 units. $115–$165 double. Children over 12 are accepted. AE, MC, V. **Amenities:** Massage; guest laundry. *In room:* A/C, TV/VCR, dataport, hair dryer, free local calls, Wi-Fi.

WHERE TO DINE

For a quick pick-me-up, try the **Silver Creek Coffee House,** 111 N. Water St. (ℂ **503/874-9600**), which has a deck overlooking Silver Creek and also serves wine. Alternatively, try **Not Your Mama's Coffee,** 201 E. Main St. (ℂ **503/873-4215**), which is in the historic Wolf Building and is a combination bookstore and espresso bar.

Silver Grille Cafe & Wines 🐸 NORTHWEST   This classy little restaurant in an old storefront is a welcome outpost of urban culinary aesthetics in this small town. The menu, which changes frequently, emphasizes fresh local produce and hormone-free meats, but you might find a house-made pâté or a curried carrot soup with mint foam. Among the entrees, there are always good pastas, such as penne pasta with snow peas, snap peas, and Oregon blue cheese.

206 E Main St. ℂ 503/873-4035. www.silvergrille.com. Main courses $17–$22. DISC, MC, V. Wed–Sun 5–9:30pm.

MT. ANGEL

Mt. Angel is best known as the site of Oregon's most popular Oktoberfest celebration, but should you be here any other time of year besides the second weekend after Labor Day, you might want to visit the **Mount Angel Abbey** (© 503/845-3303; www.mtangel.edu), which stands atop a 300-foot bluff on the edge of town and has peaceful gardens, an architecturally interesting library designed by famous Finnish architect Alvar Aalto, and a collection of rare books. Established by Benedictine monks in 1882, the abbey has a gift shop and offers tours by appointment. The abbey is also the site of the annual **Abbey Bach Festival** (© 800/845-8272 or 503/845-3066), which takes place each year on the last Wednesday, Thursday, and Friday in July, and usually sells out shortly after tickets go on sale in March. However, last-minute tickets are sometimes available.

MONMOUTH

Jensen Arctic Museum ★★ *Finds*   Although Monmouth may seem an unlikely location for a museum dedicated to the natural and cultural history of the Arctic, it is here that the museum's founder lived while working with Alaskan Eskimo peoples. The core of the museum's exhibits is Dr. Jensen's personal collection, but over the years, the museum has become a repository for more than 60 other collections. Though small, this museum has fascinating displays, including a parka made from cormorant feathers, salmon-skin mukluks, a waterproof seal-intestine jacket, and woven-baleen baskets.

590 W. Church St., Monmouth. © 503/838-8468. www.wou.edu/president/advancement/jensen/index.php. Admission by suggested donation: $2 adults, $1 children. Wed–Sat 10am–4pm.

BROOKS

Antique Powerland Museum   Dedicated to the preservation of old farm equipment and related items, this sprawling open-air museum is home to lots of old tractors and steam-driven mills. For the kids, there's a miniature railroad. This museum is best known as the site of the annual Great Oregon Steamup, held each year on the last weekend in July and the first weekend in August. Also on the grounds is the **Pacific Northwest Truck Museum** (© 503/463-8701; www.pacificnwtruckmuseum.org), open on weekends April through September.

3995 Brooklake Rd. NE, Brooks. © 503/393-2424. www.antiquepowerland.com. Admission $2. Mar–Oct Wed–Sun 9am–5pm. Closed Nov–Feb.

WINE TOURING

For information on the many wineries in the Eola Hills northwest of Salem, see "The North Willamette Valley Wine Country" section earlier in this chapter.

Ankeny Vineyard   Located south of Salem not far from Willamette Valley Vineyards, this small family-run winery overlooks a national wildlife area and is surrounded by neighboring vineyards. Pinot noir and pinot gris are the specialties here, but they also produce Marechal Foch. Prices are generally quite reasonable.

2565 Riverside Dr. S., Salem. © 503/378-1498. www.ankenyvineyard.com. Daily 11am–5pm. From Salem, drive south on I-5, take exit 243 and continue 5 miles west.

Eola Hills Wine Cellars   Well known in the area for its Sunday brunches, this winery on the outskirts of Rickreall offers everything from cabernet sauvignon to zinfandel—almost all at reasonable prices. While many of the wines here seem to be crafted for the grocery-store market, there are the occasional gems.

Blossom Time

Each year between mid-May and early June, the countryside around Salem bursts into color as commercial iris fields come into bloom. During blossom time, the two biggest growers open up their farms to the public. **Cooley's Gardens,** 11553 Silverton Rd. NE, Silverton (*(C)* **503/873-5463;** www.cooleys gardens.com), with millions of irises in bloom each spring, is the world's largest bearded-iris grower. This farm is open daily from 8am to 7pm between mid-May and early June. To reach the gardens, take the Market Street exit and drive east to Lancaster Drive; at Lancaster, turn left and drive north to Silverton Road, where you make a right turn. It's less than 10 miles on Silverton Road. **Schreiner's Iris Gardens,** 3625 Quinaby Rd. NE, Salem (*(C)* **800/525-2367;** www.schreinersgardens.com), has 200 acres of irises and is an equally impressive sight. To reach Schreiner's, take the Chemawa exit (exit 260) off I-5 north of Salem, drive west on Chemawa Road, turn right once you're west of the freeway and follow signs to Volcano Stadium. Continue north past the stadium and turn right on Quinaby Road. Also in the area are **Adelman Peony Gardens,** 5690 Brooklake Rd. NE (*(C)* **503/393-6185;** www.peonyparadise.com), which has 8 acres of fields and sells more than 160 varieties of peonies. Bloom season is from May to mid-June, and during this time, the farm is open daily from 9am to 7pm. From the Brooks exit, go east on Brooklake Road.

From late March to late April, you can see more than 90 acres of tulips in bloom at **Wooden Shoe Bulb Company,** 33814 S. Meridian Rd., Woodburn (*(C)* **800/711-2006** or 503/634-2243; www.woodenshoe.com). Throughout the blossom season, there are wooden shoe–making seminars, steam-tractor demonstrations, live music, and lots of other activities.

501 S. Pacific Hwy., Rickreall. *(C)* **800/291-6730** or 503/623-2405. www.eolahillswinery.com. Daily 10am–5pm. Closed Thanksgiving and Christmas. On Ore. 99W between Rickreall and Monmouth.

Honeywood   This winery, which dates back to 1933, is the oldest in Oregon. The winery specializes in sweet fruit-wines, which they do very well. The raspberry, boysenberry, and marionberry wines are all great accompaniments to chocolate desserts.

1350 Hines St. SE, Salem. *(C)* **800/726-4101** or 503/362-4111. www.honeywoodwinery.com. Mon–Fri 9am–5pm; Sat 10am–5pm; Sun 1–5pm. Between Mission and 13th sts. in southeast Salem.

Left Coast Cellars   This winery, set amid large vineyards 13 miles northwest of Salem, is conveniently located right on Ore. 99W north of Rickreall. While they do produce pinot gris and chardonnay here, it is the pinot noirs, including the Latitude 45 and the Suzanne's Reserve, that are the real reason to visit. The 2004 vintages of these two wines were both excellent.

4225 N. Pacific Hwy, Rickreall. *(C)* **888/831-4916** or 503/831-1044. www.leftcoastcellars.com. Feb–Nov daily noon–5pm. Tasting fee $5. Take Ore. 22 west from Salem, then go north on Ore. 99W for 4 miles.

Van Duzer Vineyards *(R)*   Producing primarily pinot noir, pinot gris, and chardonnay in the Burgundian style, this winery is built on the side of an oak-shaded knoll with a commanding view across the valley to the Eola Hills. The tasting room is small and only a few wines are available at any given time.

11975 Smithfield Rd., Dallas. ⓒ 503/623-6420. www.vanduzer.com. Mar–Dec daily 11am–5pm. North of Rickreall off Ore. 99W; take graveled Smithfield Rd. 3 miles west.

Willamette Valley Vineyards ⟮ꞗ⟯ Willamette Valley Vineyards, one of the largest wine producers in the state, sits high on a hill overlooking the Willamette Valley, and with its large facility and fabulous views, it's about as close to a Napa Valley wine-tasting experience as you'll find in Oregon. With nearly 20 wines usually available for tasting and several separate labels available, Willamette Valley manages to produce wines to please almost every palate and pocketbook. Be sure to try the reserve wines, for which there is a $6 tasting fee.

8800 Enchanted Way SE, Turner. ⓒ **800/344-9463** or 503/588-9463. www.wvv.com. Daily 11am–6pm. Take exit 248 or 244 off I-5.

WHERE TO STAY

A Creekside Garden Inn ⟮ꞗ⟯ ⟮Value⟯ This B&B is located on a narrow lane in a quiet residential neighborhood and has Mill Creek running through the backyard. The gardens here are a highlight of a stay, and the guest rooms take their themes from the flowers and greenery that surround the inn. Among the rooms are the Greenhouse, Picket Fences, and the Arbor, all of which are decorated with plenty of floral motifs.

333 Wyatt Ct. NE, Salem, OR 97301. ⓒ **503/391-0837.** Fax 503/391-1713. www.salembandb.com. 5 units (4 with private bathroom). $75 double with shared bathroom; $85–$110 double with private bathroom. Rates include full breakfast. Children over 14 welcome. MC, V. *In room:* A/C.

Phoenix Grand Hotel ⟮ꞗꞗ⟯ From the moment you drive into the slate-walled portico at this large downtown conference hotel, it's obvious that this is by far the best hotel in Salem. Although the Phoenix Grand is primarily a place for conference attendees to stay, the rooms here are just too nice to be left to business travelers. With beautiful leather couches and chairs in the large guest rooms and suites, this place is not your standard corporate hotel. Although the huge lobby might make you wonder when the crowds are going to descend, the Phoenix Grand is often a very laid-back and relaxed place.

201 Liberty St. SE, Salem, OR 97301. ⓒ **877/540-7800** or 503/540-7800. Fax 503/540-7830. www.phoenixgrand hotel.com. 193 units. $129–$139 double; $149–$399 suite. Rates include continental breakfast. Children under 16 stay free in parent's room. AE, DC, DISC, MC, V. **Amenities:** Restaurant (New American); lounge; indoor pool; exercise room; access to nearby health club; Jacuzzi; business center; room service; coin-op laundry; dry cleaning. *In room:* A/C, TV, dataport, fridge, coffeemaker, hair dryer, iron, high-speed Internet access, Wi-Fi.

WHERE TO DINE
SALEM

If you have a sweet tooth, you won't want to miss **Gerry Frank's Konditorei,** 310 Kearney St. SE (ⓒ **503/585-7070;** www.gerryfrankskonditorei.com), which has an amazing selection of extravagant cakes and pastries. For artisan breads and simpler pastries, try downtown's **Cascade Baking Co.,** 229 State St. (ⓒ **503/589-0491;** www.cascadebaking.com). For a good cup of espresso (or a sandwich), head to **The Beanery,** 220 Liberty St. NE (ⓒ **503/399-7220**). If you're looking for a microbrew and a burger, try **Ram Restaurant & Big Horn Brewery,** 515 12th St. SE (ⓒ **503/ 363-1904;** www.theram.com). For Sunday brunch, consider **Eola Hills Wine Cellars,**

501 S. Pacific Hwy., Rickreall (© **800/291-6730** or 503/623-2405; www.eolahills winery.com), which serves gourmet omelets, pan-fried oysters, pasta, Belgian waffles, sparkling wine, and more for $25. Reservations recommended.

Court Street Dairy Lunch *(Finds* BURGERS   In business since the 1920s, the Court Street Dairy Lunch is the quintessential small-town diner and a Salem institution. Burgers and sandwiches "just like Mom used to make" are the attraction. The specialties of the house are the ranch burger and ranch dog, marionberry pie, and chocolate malts.

347 Court St. NE. © 503/363-6433. Meals $3–$8.25. AE, DISC, MC, V. Mon–Fri 6am–3pm.

Morton's Bistro Northwest ✦✦ AMERICAN REGIONAL   This romantic little bistro, across the river from downtown Salem, serves up the most imaginative meals in town. The menu changes regularly, depending on the whim of the chef, the availability of ingredients, and even the weather, but flavors might range from the subtle scents of prawns with saffron, clams, Spanish chorizo sausage, and couscous to the fiery flavors of penne diablo made with Dungeness crab and andouille sausage. Be sure to order the superb Caesar salad for two (if it's not on the menu, just ask). Instead of a wine list, Morton's has a wine wall for diners to peruse.

1128 Edgewater St. NW. © 503/585-1113. www.mortonsbistronw.com. Reservations recommended. Main courses $17–$27. MC, V. Tues–Sat 5–9 or 10pm.

Wild Pear ✦ NEW AMERICAN   Although this is really just a downtown lunch spot, it serves some of the most creative food in town. For a satisfying lunch, try the coconut curry-butternut squash soup and the wild pear salad (made with chicken, candied pecans, pears, and bleu cheese). If you're in the mood for something more substantial, there's a lobster-and-seafood melt on focaccia as well as a shepherd's pie topped with whipped parsnips and potatoes.

372 State St. © 503/378-7515. www.wildpearcatering.com. Main courses $6–$11. AE, MC, V. Mon–Sat 10am–5pm.

SALEM AFTER DARK

There are regularly scheduled performances by touring companies at the historic **Elsinore Theater,** 170 High St. SE (© **503/375-3574;** www.elsinoretheatre.com). Since 1954, **Pentacle Theatre,** 324 52nd Ave. NW (© **503/364-7200;** www.pentacle theatre.org), located in the West Salem hills, has been bringing live theater to the state capital.

3 Corvallis & Albany

40 miles S of Salem, 45 miles N of Eugene, 55 miles E of Newport

In Latin, Corvallis means "heart of the valley," and that is exactly where this college town is located. Set in the middle of the Willamette Valley and surrounded by farmlands, Corvallis is home to Oregon State University (OSU), a noted center for agricultural research. Life in this town revolves around the university, but the lively downtown, with its riverfront setting, makes this a pleasant base for exploring nearby wine country and the historic town of Albany. Numerous walking and bicycling paths add to the appeal of a stay here.

In addition to being home to OSU, Corvallis is at the center of the Willamette Valley's grass-seed fields. Area farms produce much of the nation's grass-seed crop. Visitors should note that in late summer, after the seed has been harvested, the remaining stubble has traditionally been burned off. The field burnings can blanket the valley with dense black smoke, making driving quite difficult along certain roads. So, don't be too alarmed if you encounter smoky skies in the area in August.

Nearby Albany, 13 miles northeast, was a prosperous town in territorial days. Located on the banks of the Willamette River, the town made its fortune as a shipping point in the days when the river was the main transportation route for the region. More than 500 historic homes make Albany the best-preserved historic town in the state, but, owing to the large and unpleasant-smelling wood-pulp mill on the outskirts of town, the city has never really been able to cash in on its historic character.

ESSENTIALS

GETTING THERE   Albany is on I-5 at the junction with U.S. 20, which heads east to Bend and west to Newport. Corvallis is 12 miles west of I-5 at the junction of U.S. 20, Ore. 99W, and Ore. 34.

VISITOR INFORMATION   Contact **Corvallis Tourism,** 553 NW Harrison St., Corvallis, OR 97330 (© **800/334-8118** or 541/757-1544; www.visitcorvallis.com), or the **Albany Visitors Association,** 250 Broadalbin St. SW, Suite 110 (P.O. Box 965), Albany, OR 97321 (© **800/526-2256** or 541/928-0911; www.albanyvisitors.com).

GETTING AROUND   Public bus service around the Corvallis area is provided by the **Corvallis Transit System** (© **541/766-6916;** www.ci.corvallis.or.us/pw/cts). Adult fare is 75¢.

FESTIVALS   DaVinci Days (© **541/757-6363;** www.davinci-days.org), held each year in mid-July, is Corvallis's most fascinating festival. The highlight of this celebration of art, science, and technology is the **Kinetic Sculpture Race** in which competitors race homemade, people-powered vehicles along city streets, through mud and sand, and down the Willamette River. Prizes are given for engineering and artistry. Another offbeat celebration, the **Shrewsbury Renaissance Faire** (© **541/929-4897;** www.shrewfaire.com), is held each year in the community of Kings Valley (north of nearby Philomath) in early September.

EXPLORING OFF-CAMPUS CORVALLIS

The tree-shaded streets of downtown Corvallis are well worth a wander. Here you'll find lots of interesting shops, as well as the stately **Benton County Courthouse,** 120 NW Fourth Street, built in 1888 and still in use today. A few blocks away, you'll find the **Corvallis Arts Center,** 700 SW Madison Ave. (© **541/754-1551;** www.artcentric. org), which is housed in an old church and schedules rotating exhibits of works by regional artists. The gift shop has a good selection of crafts. The center is open Tuesday through Sunday from noon to 5pm; admission is free.

Corvallis's pretty Riverfront Commemorative Park stretches for 10 blocks along the Willamette River in downtown Corvallis, and includes walkways and lawns,

---

(*Tips*   **Beaver Believers**

If you're a "Beaver Believer"—in other words, a fan of Oregon State University's NCAA football team—you can find out about getting game tickets by contacting the **OSU Beaver Ticket Office** (© **800/GO-BEAVS** or 541/737-4455; www. osubeavers.com).

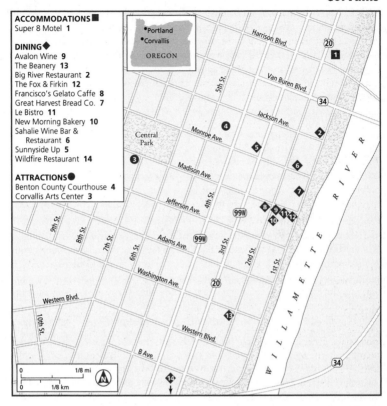

ACCOMMODATIONS ■
Super 8 Motel **1**

DINING ◆
Avalon Wine **9**
The Beanery **13**
Big River Restaurant **2**
The Fox & Firkin **12**
Francisco's Gelato Caffe **8**
Great Harvest Bread Co. **7**
Le Bistro **11**
New Morning Bakery **10**
Sahalie Wine Bar &
     Restaurant **6**
Sunnyside Up **5**
Wildfire Restaurant **14**

ATTRACTIONS ●
Benton County Courthouse **4**
Corvallis Arts Center **3**

river-viewing decks and plazas, sculptures, and a fountain that doubles as a map of the region's rivers. On Saturday mornings from spring through fall, the park is also the site of the Corvallis Saturday Farmers Market. The park's pathways connect to Corvallis's extensive network of biking paths, one of which crosses a covered bridge.

EXPLORING HISTORIC ALBANY

Albany is a hidden jewel right on I-5 that is often overlooked because the only thing visible from the interstate is a smoke-belching wood-pulp mill. Behind this industrial screen lies a quiet town that evokes days of starched crinolines and straw boaters. Throughout the mid- to late 19th century, Albany prospered, shipping agricultural and wood products down river to Oregon City and Portland. Though every style of architecture popular during that period is represented in downtown Albany's historic districts, it is the town's many elegant Victorian homes that are the most compelling. Each year, on the last Saturday of July, many of the historic homes are opened to the public for a **Historic Interior Homes Tour,** and on the third Sunday in December, homes are opened for a **Christmas Parlour Tour.** For a guide to the historic buildings, and information on the tours, contact the **Albany Visitors Association.**

Among the town's more noteworthy buildings are two sparkling white 1890s churches—the **Whitespires Church** and **St. Mary's Church**—both built in the Gothic revival style. The **Monteith House,** 518 Second Ave. SW (© **541/928-0911**), built in 1849, is the town's oldest frame building. The house is open from mid-June to mid-September Wednesday through Sunday from noon to 4pm; admission is free. To learn more about Albany's past, stop in at the **Albany Regional Museum,** 136 Lyon St. SW (© **541/967-7122;** www.armuseum.com). It's open Monday through Saturday from noon to 4pm. Admission is by donation. While touring the historic districts, you can stop in at nearly a dozen antiques stores, most of which are on First and Second avenues downtown.

WINE TOURING

In downtown Corvallis, across the street from Riverfront Commemorative Park, check out **Sahalie Wine Bar & Restaurant,** 151 NW Monroe St., Suite 101 (© **541/754-7457;** www.sahaliewine.com), a big basement wine bar and restaurant with cozy couches and live music. You can taste Sahalie Wine Cellars wines as well as wines from other Corvallis-area wineries. The wine bar is open Tuesday through Saturday from noon to 10:30pm. Also, be sure to stop in at **Avalon Wine,** 201 SW Second St. (© **541/752-7418;** www.avalonwine.com), which is one of the best wine shops in Oregon and has a fabulously informative website focusing on Northwest wines.

Airlie Winery   This winery is quite a distance from the main wine-touring routes, but its setting in a narrow valley surrounded by forested hills is idyllic. There's a large pond and a covered picnic area, making it a good place to stop for a picnic lunch. They produce a wide variety of wines, but their Müller-Thurgaus and Gewürztraminers, which are usually very good values, are highlights.

15305 Dunn Forest Rd., Monmouth. © 503/838-6013. www.airliewinery.com. Mar–Dec Sat–Sun noon–5pm. Closed Jan–Feb. From Ore. 99W between Corvallis and Monmouth, go 7 miles west on Airlie Rd., turn left on Maxfield Creek Rd. and continue another 3 miles.

Emerson Vineyards   This little family winery is only open one day a week and production is limited, but if you happen to be in the area on a Saturday, be sure to stop by. Prices for pinot gris, chardonnay, and even pinot noir are very reasonable. This winery is quite close to Airlie Winery.

11665 Airlie Rd., Monmouth. © 503/838-0944. www.emersonvineyards.com. Memorial Day to Christmas Sat noon–5pm. Drive north on Ore. 99W for 13 miles, turn left on Airlie Road, and continue 2.2 miles.

Springhill Cellars 🌟   This small family-run winery a few miles outside Albany produces excellent pinot noir and pinot gris, for around $20, as well as reserve pinot noirs in the $40 range. This is one of my favorite small wineries in the state.

2920 NW Scenic View Dr., Albany. © 541/928-1009. www.springhillcellars.com. Memorial Day to Thanksgiving Sat–Sun 1–5pm. Take Ore. 20 east 8 miles, turn left on Scenic Dr. and continue just over 2 miles north.

Tyee Wine Cellars 🌟   The Tyee Wine Cellars tasting room is in an old milking barn from the days when this was a dairy farm. Although Tyee usually does a decent pinot noir, their real strength lies in the consistency of their whites—pinot gris, pinot blanc, chardonnay, and Gewürztraminer all tend to be dry and light. Be sure to walk the 1½-mile trail through farm and forest.

26335 Greenberry Rd., Corvallis. © 541/753-8754. www.tyeewine.com. Apr to mid-June and early Sept to Dec Sat–Sun noon–5pm; mid-June to Labor Day daily noon–5pm. Closed Jan–Mar. From Corvallis, go 7 miles south on Ore. 99W and then 2⅓ miles west on Greenberry Rd.

A COVERED BRIDGE TOUR

If you're a fan of covered bridges, you won't want to pass up an opportunity to drive the back roads east of Albany. Here you'll find nine wooden covered bridges dating mostly from the 1930s. For a map to these covered bridges, contact the **Albany Convention & Visitors Association.** A 10th covered bridge, the Irish Bend Bridge, can be found in Corvallis on a pedestrian/bicycle path on the west side of the university campus.

OUTDOOR ACTIVITIES

If you're a bird-watcher, the **William L. Finley National Wildlife Refuge** (© 541/757-7236; www.fws.gov/willamettevalley/finley/index.html), 12 miles south of Corvallis on Ore. 99W, is a good place to add a few more to your list. This refuge has three short, easy hiking trails that provide the region's best glimpse of what the Willamette Valley looked like before the first settlers arrived.

For superb views of the valley and a moderately strenuous hike, head west 16 miles from Corvallis on Ore. 34 to 4,097-foot **Mary's Peak,** the highest peak in the Coast Range. A road leads to the top of the mountain, but there is also a trail that leads from the campground up through a forest of old-growth noble firs to the meadows at the summit. For more information, contact the **Siuslaw National Forest,** 4077 SW Research Way (P.O. Box 1148) Corvallis, OR 97339 (© **541/750-7000;** www.fs.fed. us/r6/siuslaw).

WHERE TO STAY
IN CORVALLIS

Hanson Country Inn ⚑   Situated atop a knoll on the western edge of town and surrounded by fields and forests, this B&B feels as if it's out in the country, yet is within walking distance of the university. The Dutch colonial-style farmhouse was built in 1928 and features loads of built-in cabinets, interesting woodwork, and lots of windows. Plenty of antiques fill the rooms and lend the inn a feeling appropriate to its age. Two of the rooms have large balconies. The two-bedroom cottage, ideal for families, sits behind the main house and is tucked back in the trees.

795 SW Hanson St., Corvallis, OR 97333. © **541/752-2919.** www.hcinn.com. 4 units (including a cottage). $145–$165 double. Rates include full breakfast. AE, DC, DISC, MC, V. Pets accepted ($10 per night). Take Western Blvd. to West Hills Rd.; Hanson St. is on the right just past the fork onto West Hills Rd. **Amenities:** Guest laundry. *In room:* A/C, TV/VCR/DVD, dataport, free local calls, high-speed Internet access, Wi-Fi.

Super 8 Motel   It may seem hard to believe that a Super 8 Motel could be one of the best accommodations in town, but Corvallis just doesn't have too many places to stay. This budget motel has a great location on the bank of the Willamette River only a few blocks from downtown.

407 NW Second St., Corvallis, OR 97330. © **800/800-8000** or 541/758-8088. Fax 541/758-8267. 101 units. $79–$95 double. Rates include continental breakfast. Children under 18 stay free in parent's room. AE, DC, DISC, MC, V. **Amenities:** Indoor pool; Jacuzzi; coin-op laundry. *In room:* A/C, TV, dataport, free local calls.

WHERE TO DINE
IN CORVALLIS

When you just have to have a jolt of java and a pastry, drop by **The Beanery,** 500 SW Second St. (© 541/753-7442), or **New Morning Bakery,** 219 SW Second St. (© 541/754-0181). For great breakfasts, head to **Sunnyside Up,** 116 NW Third St. (© 541/758-3353; sunnyside-up-cafe.com). If you're looking for some picnic fare, stop by **Great Harvest Bread Co.,** 134 SW First St. (© 541/754-9960; www.great harvest.com). On hot summer days, head to **Francesco's Gelato Caffe,** 208 SW Second St. (© 541/752-1326), for creamy gelato. For microbrews and pub fare, try **The**

Fox & Firkin, 202 SW First St. (© 541/753-8533), which serves an astonishing number of good beers on tap.

Big River Restaurant 🌾 INTERNATIONAL   Housed in a renovated warehouse-like space across the street from the Willamette River, this big, lively place serves everything from designer brick-oven pizzas to Asian-inspired pastas to Cuban pork loin to various smoked chicken dishes. The owners of the restaurant have a commitment to fresh local produce (often organic), local wines, Oregon-caught seafood (when possible), and organic meats. Though Big River is a big place, you probably won't be able to miss the case full of tempting desserts. Be forewarned that this restaurant is very noisy.

101 NW Jackson St. © **541/757-0694.** www.bigriverrest.com. Call-ahead wait list. Main courses $15–$23. AE, DC, MC, V. Mon–Thurs 11am–2pm and 5–9:30pm; Fri 11am–2pm and 5–10:30pm; Sat 5pm–10:30pm.

Le Bistro 🌾🌾 *(Finds* FRENCH   This minimally decorated restaurant focuses on country French preparations, and is popular with professors and local high-tech employees. Although there are daily specials, the main menu offers no surprises, just well-prepared steaks (with a variety of French sauces) and down-home French country cooking. Among other dishes, you'll find lobster bisque, coq au vin, and lamb chops with a pinot noir demi glace. The restaurant is only half a block from the river and the Riverfront Commemorative Park.

150 SW Madison Ave. © **541/754-6680.** www.lebistrocorvallis.com. Reservations recommended. Main courses $22–$30. AE, DISC, MC, V. Daily 5–9:30pm.

Wildfire Restaurant 🌾🌾 *(Finds* INTERNATIONAL   This place is just so Oregon it should not be missed. The menu is eclectic, the ingredients are usually organic, and the wood-fired oven and patio are made of mud! Actually, the owners of the restaurant like to call it earth, not mud. If you're intrigued, come by for a meal and order something from the earth oven, which, by the way, is named Maya. Offerings include lots of creative pizzas, fire-grilled salmon with the sauce of the moment, and fire-grilled prawn shish kebabs.

1115 SE Third St. © **541/754-6958.** www.intabas.com. Reservations recommended. Main courses $13–$27. MC, V. Tues–Sat 11:30am–2:30pm and 5–9:30pm; Sun 10am–2pm and 5–9:30pm.

IN ALBANY

For a good cup of coffee, try **Boccherini's Coffee & Tea House,** 208 First Ave. (© **541/ 926-6703;** www.boccherinis.com). If it's a good pint of ale and some pub food you crave, check out **Wyatt's Eatery & Brewhouse,** 211 First Ave. (© **541/917-3727;** www.wyattseatery.com).

4 Eugene & Springfield

40 miles S of Salem, 71 miles N of Roseburg, 61 miles E of Florence

Although Eugene, with more than 100,000 residents, is the third-largest city in Oregon, tie-dyed T-shirts are more common than silk ties on downtown streets. This laid-back character is due in large part to the presence of the University of Oregon, the state's liberal arts university. Life in Eugene tends to revolve around the university and not around the somewhat run down and surprisingly lifeless downtown. Consequently, you'll want to spend time on the school's tree-shaded 250-acre campus, where you'll find both an excellent art museum and a small natural-history museum.

Eugene

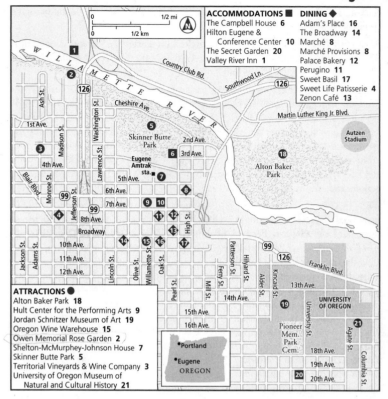

ACCOMMODATIONS ■
The Campbell House **6**
Hilton Eugene &
    Conference Center **10**
The Secret Garden **20**
Valley River Inn **1**

DINING ◆
Adam's Place **16**
The Broadway **14**
Marché **8**
Marché Provisions **8**
Palace Bakery **12**
Perugino **11**
Sweet Basil **17**
Sweet Life Patisserie **4**
Zenon Café **13**

ATTRACTIONS ●
Alton Baker Park **18**
Hult Center for the Performing Arts **9**
Jordan Schnitzer Museum of Art **19**
Oregon Wine Warehouse **15**
Owen Memorial Rose Garden **2**
Shelton-McMurphey-Johnson House **7**
Skinner Butte Park **5**
Territorial Vineyards & Wine Company **3**
University of Oregon Museum of
    Natural and Cultural History **21**

Eugene has for years been home to liberal-minded folks who have adopted alternative lifestyles. At the **Saturday Market,** a weekly outdoor craft market, you can see the works of many of these colorful and creative spirits. Adding to the city's diverse cultural scene is the grandiose, glass-gabled **Hult Center for the Performing Arts,** which schedules a wide range of performances throughout the year. Throw in a couple of beautiful riverfront parks with miles of bike paths, several excellent restaurants, brewpubs, nearby wineries, and proximity to both mountains and coast, and you have a decent base for exploring a good chunk of the state.

ESSENTIALS

GETTING THERE   Eugene is located just off I-5 at the junction with I-105, which connects Eugene and Springfield, and Ore. 126, which leads east to Bend and west to Florence. Ore. 58 leads southeast from Eugene to connect with U.S. 97 between Klamath Falls and Bend. Ore. 99W is an alternative to I-5.

The **Eugene Airport,** 28855 Lockheed Dr. (© **541/682-5430;** www.eugeneairport. com), is 9 miles northwest of downtown off Ore. 99W. Delta Air Lines, Horizon Air, United, and US Airways fly here. There's nonstop service to Portland, Seattle, San Francisco, Los Angeles, Las Vegas, Denver, Salt Lake City, Phoenix, and Redmond, Oregon.

Amtrak (© **800/USA-RAIL**) passenger trains stop in Eugene. The station is at 433 Willamette Street.

VISITOR INFORMATION   Contact the **Convention & Visitors Association of Lane County Oregon,** 754 Olive St., Eugene, OR 97401 (© **800/547-5445** or 541/484-5307; www.visitlanecounty.org).

GETTING AROUND   Car rentals are available at the Eugene airport from **Avis, Budget, Enterprise,** and **Hertz.** If you need a taxi, contact **Oregon Taxi** (© **541/434-8294**). **Lane Transit District (LTD;** © **541/687-5555;** www.ltd.org) provides public transit throughout the metropolitan area and out to a number of nearby towns including McKenzie Bridge; some routes do not run on Sunday. You can pick up bus-route maps and other information at the **LTD Customer Service Center** at the corner of 11th Avenue and Willamette Street. LTD fares are $1.25 for adults, 60¢ for seniors and youths 6 to 18.

FESTIVALS   Eugene's two biggest and most important music festivals are the **Oregon Bach Festival** (© **800/457-1486** or 541/682-5000; www.oregonbachfestival. com) and the **Oregon Festival of American Music** (© **541/687-6526** or 541/434-7000 for tickets; www.ofam.org). The former is just what its name implies and is held the last week in June and the first week in July. The latter is a celebration of everything from blues to gospel to jazz and is held in early August. The **Eugene Celebration** (© **541/681-4108;** www.eugenecelebration.com), held in mid-September, is a 3-day celebration that includes a wacky parade and the crowning of the annual Slug Queen. In mid-July, all the region's hippies, both young and old, show up in nearby Veneta for the **Oregon Country Fair** ✸✸ (© **541/343-4298;** www.oregoncountry fair.org), a showcase for alternative music and unusual crafts. Also of note is **Junction City's Scandinavian Festival** (© **541/998-9372;** www.scandinavianfestival.com), which celebrates the region's Scandinavian heritage and is held each year on the second weekend in August. Junction City is 14 miles northwest of Eugene.

SEEING THE SIGHTS
MUSEUMS, HISTORIC BUILDINGS & SUCH
Cascades Raptor Center   Whether you're an avid birder or not, this raptor-rehabilitation center in the hills on the south side of town is a fascinating place to visit. There are more than 30 species of raptors on display here, ranging from diminutive pygmy owls to bald and golden eagles. For one reason or another, whether due to injuries or human imprinting, none of the birds here can be released into the wild. The large outdoor aviaries are set under a dense canopy of shady trees.

32275 Fox Hollow Rd. © 541/485-1320. www.eraptors.org. Admission $5 adults, $4 seniors and teens; $3 children under 12. Apr–Oct Tues–Sun 10am–6pm; Nov–Mar Tues–Sun noon–5pm (also open holiday Mon).

Jordan Schnitzer Museum of Art ✸✸   An extensive Asian arts collection and exhibits of contemporary art are the main focus of this large art museum on the campus of the University of Oregon. Among the highlights of the Asian arts collection are a small jade pagoda, silk Chinese imperial robes, a suit of 18th-century Japanese armor, and a 19th-century Japanese palanquin. Keep an eye out for the exhibit on foot-binding in China. You'll also find a small exhibit of paintings by Northwest artist Morris Graves.

1430 Johnson Lane. © 541/346-3027. http://uoma.uoregon.edu. Admission $5 adults, $3 seniors and students, free for children 13 and under (free for all on 1st Fri of each month). Thurs–Sun 11am–5pm; Wed 11am–8pm. Closed major holidays. East of 14th Ave. and Kincaid St. on the U of O campus.

The Bridges of Lane County

There are more than 50 covered bridges in Oregon. Built of wood and covered to protect them from the rain and extend their life, the covered bridges of Oregon are found primarily in the Willamette Valley, where early farmers needed safe river and stream crossings to get their crops to market. The highest concentration of covered bridges is found in Lane County, which stretches from the crest of the Cascade Range all the way to the Pacific Ocean and is home to 20 covered bridges.

You can get a map and guide to Lane County's covered bridges from the **Convention & Visitors Association of Lane County Oregon,** 754 Olive St., Eugene, OR 97401 (© **800/547-5445** or 541/484-5307; www.visitlanecounty. org).

Shelton-McMurphey-Johnson House ⚷   Built in 1888, this ornate Queen Anne Victorian home stands on the south slope of Skinner Butte on the north edge of downtown Eugene and was long referred to as the Castle on the Hill. Tours of the beautiful old home focus on the families that lived here over the century that it was a private residence.

303 Willamette St. © **541/484-0808.** www.smjhouse.org. Admission $5 adults, $2 children under 12. Tues–Fri 10am–1pm; Sat–Sun 1–4pm.

University of Oregon Museum of Natural and Cultural History ⚷   This small museum is housed in a building designed to vaguely resemble a traditional Northwest Coast Indian longhouse. The ancient peoples and even more ancient animals that once roamed the Northwest are the main focus of the museum's exhibits. Geology, botany, and archaeology topics also get plenty of display space here.

1680 E. 15th Ave. © **541/346-3024.** http://natural-history.uoregon.edu. Admission $3 adults, $2 seniors and youths 3–18. Wed–Sun 11am–5pm.

PARKS & GARDENS

Alton Baker Park, on the north bank of the Willamette River, is Eugene's most popular park and offers jogging and biking trails. Across the river, **Skinner Butte Park,** on the north side of downtown Eugene, has more paved paths. Nearby is the **Owen Rose Garden.** At the **Mount Pisgah Arboretum,** 34901 Frank Parrish Rd. (© **541/ 747-3817;** www.efn.org/~mtpisgah), south of town, you can hike 7 miles of trails through meadows and forests. There are good views along the way, but watch out for poison oak. Set beneath towering fir trees high on a hill overlooking the city, **Hendricks Park and Rhododendron Garden,** 2200 Summit Ave. (© **541/682-5324**), is one of the prettiest parks in the city, especially in the spring when the rhododendrons bloom. There are free public tours of the garden between early April and late May. You'll find this park in southeast Eugene off Franklin Boulevard (U.S. 99). Take Walnut Street to Fairmount Boulevard and then turn east on Summit Avenue. If you're crazy about rhododendrons (as so many Northwesterners are), be sure to schedule a visit to **Greer Gardens,** 1280 Goodpasture Island Rd. (© **800/548-0111** or 541/ 686-8266; www.greergardens.com), one of the Northwest's most celebrated nurseries.

WINE TOURING

Eugene is at the southern limit of the Willamette Valley wine region, and there are half a dozen wineries within 30 miles of the city. For a good introduction to the wines of the region, stop in at the **Oregon Wine Warehouse,** 943 Olive St. (© **541/ 342-8598;** www.oregonww.com), which is open Wednesday and Thursday from noon to 8pm and Friday and Saturday from noon to 10pm.

Benton-Lane Winery   This winery has a big reputation in Oregon, and it is well worth searching out the off-the-beaten-path winery and tasting room. Benton-Lane focuses primarily on pinot noir and does a superb job. The wide range of prices means there's a pinot for every budget. The valley views from the tasting room are great.

23924 Territorial Hwy. © 541/847-5792. www.benton-lane.com. Apr–Nov Mon–Fri noon–4:30pm, Sat–Sun noon–5pm; Dec–Apr Mon–Fri noon–4:30pm. Take Ore. 126 west to Ore. 99E, head north; turn onto Ore. 99W and drive north to Monroe and turn left Territorial Hwy.

Chateau Lorane 🍷   Chateau Lorane produces a greater variety of wines than just about any other winery in the state, and many of these you won't find at other Oregon wineries. Several are also made from organic grapes. Some of the more unusual wines include huxelrebe, baco noir, and several meads.

27415 Siuslaw River Rd., Lorane. © 541/942-8028. www.chateaulorane.com. June–Sept daily noon–5pm; Oct–May Sat–Sun noon–5pm. Take Ore. 126 west to Veneta and go south through Crow to Lorane.

High Pass Winery   This small winery was founded in 1984 by Dieter Boehm, who produces several different vineyard-designate pinot noirs. However, the winery is most noteworthy for its unusual huxelrebe and scheurebe white wines, which are made from grapes that were developed in Germany. These wines are intensely floral and are often used in dessert wines.

24757 Lavell Rd., Junction City. © 541/998-1447. www.highpasswinery.com. Sat–Sun noon–5pm. Take Ore. 126 west to Veneta and then go north on Territorial Hwy., west on High Pass Rd., and north again on Lavell Rd.

King Estate Winery 🍷   Set in an idyllic valley southwest of Eugene, this is one of the largest and most impressive wineries in the state. The winery, part of a 1,000-acre estate, is surrounded by hundreds of acres of certified-organic vineyards and features a huge, châteaulike facility. If you want to tour a winery, this is one of the best to visit. The winery also has a restaurant, so if you're out this way wine tasting, plan to stay for lunch or dinner.

80854 Territorial Rd. © 800/884-4441 or 541/942-9874. www.kingestate.com. Daily 11am–8pm. Take Ore. 126 west to Veneta and go south through Crow almost to Lorane.

LaVelle Vineyards 🍷   Consistently good white wines (fruit forward but not too much residual sugar) are the hallmark here. The pinot gris and Riesling are usually quite good. LaVelle also has a tasting room/wine bar/bistro in downtown Eugene at the Fifth Street Public Market, 296 E. Fifth Ave. (© **541/338-9875**). This latter facility is a good place to start a wine tour of the area.

89697 Sheffler Rd., Elmira. © 541/935-9406. www.lavelle-vineyards.com. Vineyard: daily noon–5pm. Eugene Tasting Room: Sun noon–6pm; Mon–Thurs noon–8pm; Fri–Sat noon–9pm. Closed Thanksgiving, Christmas, and New Year's Day. Off Ore. 126 west of Eugene.

Pfeiffer Vineyards 🍷   For many years, this winery has sold grapes to King Estate Winery, which even bottles some of their pinot noir under a Pfeiffer Vineyards designation. Here at this pretty little family-run winery, you can sample what the Pfeiffers do with their own grapes. Expect to pay between $40 and $60 for a bottle of pinot noir.

25040 Jaeg Rd., Junction City. ⓒ **541/998-2828.** www.pfeiffervineyards.com. Memorial Day weekend to Thanksgiving weekend Sat–Sun noon–5pm. Take Ore. 126 west to Veneta and then go north on Territorial Hwy., west on High Pass Rd., and north again on Jaeg Rd.

Silvan Ridge ⓐ If you happen to enjoy sweet wines, you'll definitely want to drop by this winery. The semi-sparkling muscat here is outstanding, the perfect summer sipper. There are also respectable merlots and cabernet sauvignons with grapes from southern Oregon, and the pinot gris can be quite good. All in all, one of the most reliable wineries in the state. You'll usually find a few wines for under $20.

27012 Briggs Hill Rd., Eugene. ⓒ **866/5-SILVAN** or 541/345-1945. www.silvanridge.com. Daily noon–5pm. Closed major holidays. Take Ore. 126 west to Bertelsen Rd. and go south to Spencer Creek Rd.; turn right and continue for 2 miles; turn left on Briggs Hill Rd. and continue 3½ miles.

Sweet Cheeks Winery Set high on a hill across Crow Valley from Silvan Ridge winery and with an impressive, big tasting room, Sweet Cheeks is one of the area's newest wineries. Visit for award-winning white wines and reasonable prices. The twilight tastings are a very pleasant way to spend a summer evening.

27007 Briggs Hill Rd., Eugene. ⓒ **877/309-9463** or 541/349-9463. www.sweetcheekswinery.com. Sat–Thurs noon–6pm; Fri noon–9pm. Take Ore. 126 west to Bertelsen Rd. and go south to Spencer Creek Rd.; turn right and continue for 2 miles; turn left on Briggs Hill Rd. and continue 3½ miles.

Territorial Vineyards & Wine Company This is another of Eugene's in-town wineries and has a swanky tasting room that's open 2 days a week. The winery produces pinot gris, Riesling, chardonnay, and several pinot noirs.

907 W. Third Ave. ⓒ **541/684-9463.** www.territorialvineyards.com. Fri–Sat 3–8pm.

OUTDOOR ACTIVITIES

Eugene has long been known as Tracktown, USA, and if you want to follow in the footsteps of Steve Prefontaine, there are plenty of routes around town for doing some running. At the Convention & Visitors Association of Lane County Oregon (see above), you can pick up a map of area running trails. These jogging routes include the popular **Pre's Trail,** a 3.87-mile system of loops in Alton Baker Park, which is just across the Willamette River from downtown Eugene. You'll find Hayward Field off Agate Street in the southeast corner of the campus. Runners may also want to drop by the **Nike Store,** 5th Street Public Market, 296 E. Fifth Ave. (ⓒ **541/342-5155;** www. nike.com), which has an interesting exhibit about Steve Prefontaine, Bill Bowerman, and Phil Knight, who together laid the foundation for Nike's success.

With two rivers, the McKenzie and the Willamette, flowing through the area, it isn't surprising that Eugene has quite a few water-oriented activities. You can rent canoes and kayaks at **Oregon River Sports,** 3400 Franklin Blvd. (ⓒ **888/790-PADL** or 541/334-0696; www.oregonriversports.com), which has its canoe-rental facility in Alton Baker Park. Canoes and kayaks rent for $10 per hour. See the "The Santiam

---

Go Ducks!

Fans of the University of Oregon's Ducks football team can try to buy tickets by contacting the **UO Athletic Ticket Office** (ⓒ **800/WEB-FOOT** or 541/346-4461; www.goducks.com).

Pass, McKenzie Pass & McKenzie River" section of chapter 9 for information on rafting the nearby McKenzie River.

SHOPPING

You can shop for one-of-a-kind crafts at Eugene's **Saturday Market** (© 541/686-8885; www.eugenesaturdaymarket.org), which covers more than 2 downtown blocks beginning at the corner of Eighth Avenue and Oak Street. The bustling market was founded in 1970 and is something of a bastion of hippie crafts. There are also food vendors, fresh produce, and live music. The market, held April through mid-November, takes place on Saturdays between 10am to 5pm.

Other days of the week, you can explore the **Market District,** a 6-block area of restored buildings that houses unusual shops, galleries, restaurants, and nightclubs. The **5th Street Public Market,** 296 E. Fifth Ave. (© 541/484-0383; www.5stmarket. com), at the corner of Fifth Avenue and High Street, is the centerpiece of the area. In this shopping center, you'll find **New Twist** (© 541/342-8686), selling fine crafts and wildly artistic jewelry; **French Quarter Linens** (© 541/343-8904; www.french quarterlinens.com), selling fine linens; **Destinations . . . The Travel Store** (© 541/302-0787; www.destinations-thetravelstore.com), a travel store; and **The Nike Store** (© 541/342-5155). Also nearby is **Down to Earth,** 532 Olive St. (© 541/342-6820; www.down-to-earth.com), a fascinating garden and housewares shop housed in an old granary building.

If you're interested in art, there is a monthly **First Friday Artwalk** during which downtown art galleries have openings and stay open late. For information, contact the **Lane Arts Council** (© **541/485-2278;** www.lanearts.org). Other times of the month, stop by **Opus6ix,** 22 W. Seventh Ave. (© **541/393-0743;** www.opus6ix.com), a downtown gallery featuring works by regional artists.

WHERE TO STAY

The Campbell House 👫👫   Located only 2 blocks from the Market District and set at the base of Skinner's Butte overlooking the city, this large Victorian home was built in 1892 and now offers luxury, convenience, and comfort. The guest rooms here vary considerably in size and price, but you're sure to find something you like in your price range. Several of the guest rooms on the first floor have high ceilings, and on the lower level there's a pine-paneled room with a fishing theme and another with a golf theme. The upstairs rooms have plenty of windows, and in the largest room you'll find wood floors and a double whirlpool tub. A separate carriage house contains some of the inn's most luxurious and most thoughtfully designed rooms. Breakfasts are served in a room with a curving wall of glass.

252 Pearl St., Eugene, OR 97401. © **800/264-2519** or 541/343-1119. Fax 541/343-2258. www.campbellhouse.com. 20 units. $129–$349 double. AE, DC, DISC, MC, V. Rates include full breakfast. Pets accepted ($50). **Amenities:** Restaurant (Northwest); access to nearby health club; concierge; business center; room service; massage; babysitting; laundry service; dry cleaning. *In room:* A/C, TV, dataport, minibar, hair dryer, iron, free local calls, high-speed Internet access, Wi-Fi.

Hilton Eugene & Conference Center   This is Eugene's only downtown corporate high-rise convention hotel, and it caters primarily to business travelers and conventioneers. However, with the Hult Center for the Performing Arts next door and dozens of restaurants and cafes within a few blocks, it's also a good choice if you want to take in a show or explore downtown Eugene on foot. Try to get a room on an upper floor so you can enjoy the views. The restaurant just off the lobby features a North-west fishing theme and serves moderately priced meals.

66 E. Sixth Ave., Eugene, OR 97401. (C) 800/HILTONS or 541/342-2000. Fax 541/342-6661. www.eugene.hilton.com. 274 units. $134–$179 double; $149–$548 suite. Children under 18 stay free in parent's room. AE, DC, DISC, MC, V. Self parking $7; valet parking $12. Pets accepted ($25). **Amenities:** Restaurant (Northwest); lounge; indoor pool; exercise room; Jacuzzi; bike rentals; concierge; courtesy airport shuttle; business center; room service; laundry service; dry cleaning; executive-level rooms. *In room:* A/C, TV, dataport, coffeemaker, hair dryer, iron, high-speed Internet access, Wi-Fi.

The Secret Garden *Finds* This B&B is housed in a former sorority house, which had previously been the home of Eugene pioneer Alton Baker. Today, the large inn features European and Asian art and antiques, and guest rooms that are beautifully and tastefully decorated. One of our favorites is the Scented Garden, which has floor lamps made from Tibetan horns and a gorgeous sitar on display. And yes, there is a secret garden, a unique outdoor room with living walls concealing a whirlpool tub.

1910 University St., Eugene, OR 97403. (C) 888/484-6755 or 541/484-6755. Fax 541/431-1699. www.secretgarden bbinn.com. 10 units. May–Nov & holidays $125–$245 double; Dec–Apr $115–$225 double. Rates include full breakfast. AE, MC, V. **Amenities:** Access to nearby health club; Jacuzzi. *In room:* A/C, TV/VCR, fridge, hair dryer, iron.

Valley River Inn Although this lushly landscaped low-rise hotel boasts an enviable location on the bank of the Willamette River, the rates are aimed at those with expense accounts, not at vacationers. However, if you can get any sort of substantial discount, this might be a good choice. The hotel is only a few minutes' drive from downtown and the university, and is adjacent to Eugene's largest shopping mall. All the rooms are large and have a balcony or patio, but the riverside rooms have the best views. Sweetwater's Restaurant has a long wall of glass overlooking the river and serves primarily Northwest cuisine.

1000 Valley River Way, Eugene, OR 97401. (C) 800/543-8266 or 541/743-1000. Fax 541/683-5121. www.valley riverinn.com. 257 units. $149–$225 double; $200–$350 suite. Children under 18 stay free in parent's room. AE, DC, DISC, MC, V. Pets accepted. **Amenities:** Restaurant (Northwest); lounge; outdoor pool; exercise room; access to nearby health club; Jacuzzi; sauna; bike rentals; concierge; courtesy airport and shopping shuttle; business center; room service; dry cleaning; concierge-level rooms. *In room:* A/C, TV, dataport, coffeemaker, hair dryer, iron, high-speed Internet access, Wi-Fi.

WHERE TO DINE

For artisan breads and cheeses, pastries, pizza, and picnic supplies, I always go to **Marché Provisions,** 296 E. Fifth Ave. ((C) **541/743-0660;** www.marcheprovisions. com), which is inside the 5th Street Public Market and is affiliated with Marché, my favorite Eugene restaurant. For gourmet food to go, perhaps for a picnic at a winery, there is also **The Broadway,** 200 W. Broadway ((C) **541/685-0790;** www.oregonwine andmore.com), which is a sort of gourmet deli, grocery store, wine shop, and cafe all rolled into one. For rustic breads, breakfast pastries, and desserts, you can also try the **Palace Bakery,** 844 Pearl St. ((C) **541/484-2435**), which is an offshoot of the popular Zenon Café. If you've got a sweet tooth, don't miss out on **Sweet Life Patisserie,** 755 Monroe St. ((C) **541/683-5676**), which bakes the best pastries in Eugene. For good espresso, pastries, and gelato, stop by downtown's **Perugino,** 767 Willamette St. ((C) **541/687-9102**).

EXPENSIVE

Adam's Place NORTHWEST Located downtown on the pedestrian mall, Adam's Place's interior conjures up an old English inn and is one of the most elegant dining establishments in the city. The menu is short, changes frequently, and relies heavily on fresh local produce. On a recent evening the appetizer menu included creamy cambozola fondue as well as a plate of assorted Northwest artisanal cheeses. Entree flavors tend to be simple yet creative. Filet mignon might have a black-pepper crust and come with Boursin-cheese sauce, and cedar-planked salmon might be topped by horseradish crust. In the summer, you can dine under the stars out on the patio. Several nights each week there is live music in the adjacent Luna nightclub.

30 E. Broadway. ⓒ 541/344-6948. www.adamsplacerestaurant.com. Reservations recommended. Main courses $23–$36. AE, MC, V. Tues–Thurs 4:30–10pm; Fri–Sat 4:30–midnight.

King Estate Restaurant ⓐⓐ NORTHWEST   King Estate is the biggest and most beautiful wine estate in the Willamette Valley, and its restaurant, inside the winery tasting room, is the quintessential wine-country restaurant. People drive from miles around to eat here, and I have to say it is well worth it. Creative Northwest cuisine is prepared using organic produce grown here on the estate, and wines served are from grapes that grow only a few feet from your table. The menu changes with the seasons, but I recently started with a wonderfully subtle dish of Pacific cod atop creamy potatoes accompanied by saffron aioli. I then moved on to a smoked and roasted chicken with chanterelle mushrooms that was one of the best chicken dishes I've ever had. Service is excellent and the views from the patio are just gorgeous.

80854 Territorial Rd., Eugene. ⓒ 541/685-5189. www.kingestate.com. Reservations highly recommended. Main courses $8–$12 lunch, $19–$32 dinner. AE, DISC, MC, V. Daily 11am–8pm. See winery listing above for directions.

Marché ⓐⓐ MEDITERRANEAN   Marché, located in the 5th Street Public Market, is the quintessential urban American bistro, and, with its hip decor, tiny (but popular) bar, patio, and display kitchen with a few settings for solo diners, the restaurant pulls in a wide range of customers, from couples on dates to pretheater parties and even families. The menu is as creative as you'll find in Eugene, and preparations are fairly reliable. As often as possible, ingredients are organic and non-GMO (genetically modified). There's an extensive list of reasonably priced wines, plus plenty of wines by the glass. This restaurant also has a more casual cafe in the same building.

296 E. Fifth Ave. ⓒ 541/342-3612. www.marcherestaurant.com. Reservations recommended. Main courses $10–$15 lunch, $20–$34 dinner. AE, DC, DISC, MC, V. Sun–Thurs 11:30am–11pm; Fri–Sat 11:30am–midnight.

MODERATE

Zenon Café ⓐ INTERNATIONAL   Zenon has long been the city's top outpost for cutting-edge cookery. If you've read about it in the latest issue of *Gourmet* or *Bon Appétit*, you'll probably find it on the menu here. The setting is fairly stark, though with some raw wood for warmth. The menu, which changes daily, is long and includes plenty of small plates as well as full-size entrees. You're almost assured of finding something you've never tried before. Their dessert case usually flaunts about 20 irresistible cakes, pies, tortes, and other pastries.

898 Pearl St. ⓒ 541/343-3005. Main courses $9–$16 lunch, $16–$26 dinner. AE, DISC, MC, V. Sun–Mon and Wed–Thurs 8am–11pm; Fri–Sat 8am–midnight.

INEXPENSIVE

Sweet Basil ⓥⓐⓛⓤⓔ THAI   With its chic urban decor, zesty flavors, artful presentation, and reasonable prices, this upscale Thai restaurant serves some of the best Thai food I've had in Oregon. The *pad phet gai* (chicken and vegetables with homemade curry sauce) is a riot of vibrant flavors. They even do a good job with the *pad thai*, a dish that can often be rather insipid at some Thai restaurants. On sunny days, try to get a sidewalk table. Lunches are one of the best deals in Eugene.

941 Pearl St. © 541/284-2944. www.sweetbasileug.com. Reservations recommended. Main courses $6.25–$9.25 lunch, $9.25–$21 dinner. AE, DISC, MC, V. Mon–Thurs 11:30am–3pm and 5–9pm; Fri 11:30am–3pm and 5–10pm; Sat noon–3pm and 5–10pm; Sun noon–3pm and 5–9pm.

EUGENE AFTER DARK

With its two theaters and nonstop schedule, the **Hult Center for the Performing Arts,** One Eugene Center, Seventh Avenue and Willamette Street (© 541/682-5746 or 541/682-5000 for tickets; www.hultcenter.org), is the heart and soul of this city's performing arts scene. The center's huge glass gables are unmistakable, and each year this sparkling temple of the arts puts together a first-rate schedule of performances by the Eugene Symphony, the Eugene Ballet Company, the Eugene Opera, and other local and regional companies, as well as visiting companies and performers. During the summer, the center hosts the Oregon Bach Festival. Also be sure to see what the **Shedd Institute for the Arts,** East Broadway and High Street (© 541/687-6526 or 541/434-7000 for tickets; www.theshedd.org), has scheduled at its Jaqua Concert Hall. Summer concerts with the likes of Jackson Browne and Crosby, Stills, and Nash are also held at the **Cuthbert Amphitheater** (© 541/762-8099; www.thecuthbert.com)in Alton Baker Park.

To find out what's happening, pick up a copy of the free *Eugene Weekly,* which is available at restaurants and shops around town.

BREWPUBS

You'll find plenty of microbreweries in Eugene. These include the **High Street Brewery & Cafe,** 1243 High St. (© 541/345-4905; www.mcmenamins.com), in an old house near downtown; the **East 19th Street Cafe,** 1485 E. 19th St. (© 541/342-4025; www.mcmenamins.com), adjacent to the university campus; **Steelhead Brewing Co.,** 199 E. Fifth Ave. (© 541/686-2739; www.steelheadbrewery.com); and **Eugene City Brewery,** 844 Olive St. (© 541/345-4155; www.rogue.com), the most conveniently located pub if you're staying downtown. This latter pub is operated by Rogue Brewing in Newport and offers Eugene's widest selection of house brews.

Eugene's top two rock concert venues are **WOW Hall,** 291 W. Eighth Ave. (© 541/687-2746; www.wowhall.org), the former Woodmen of the World Hall, and **McDonald Theatre,** 1010 Willamette St. (© 541/345-4442; www.mcdonaldtheatre.com), a historic downtown theater owned by the family of the late Ken Kesey, a long-time resident of the area.

NIGHTCLUBS & BARS

Luna 🎜 This downtown restaurant and bar books an eclectic range of live music from Brazilian samba to Middle Eastern (complete with belly dancers). There's also plenty of jazz, blues, and rock. This is Eugene's top spot for a martini. 30 E. Broadway. © 541/434-LUNA. www.lunajazz.com. Cover varies (free–$12).

Oregon Electric Station 🎜🎜 This building dates from 1912, and with a wine cellar in an old railroad car, lots of oak, and a back bar that requires a ladder to access all the bottles of premium spirits, it's the poshest bar in town. There's occasional live jazz, too. 27 E. Fifth Ave. © 541/485-4444. www.oesrestaurant.com. No cover.

The Oregon Coast

Extending from the mouth of the Columbia River in the north to California's redwood country in the south, the Oregon coast is a shoreline of jaw-dropping natural beauty. Yes, it's often rainy or foggy, and, yes, the water is too cold and rough for swimming, but the coastline more than makes up for these shortcomings with its drama and grandeur. Wave-pounded rocky shores; dense, dark forests; lonely lighthouses; rugged headlands—these all set this shoreline apart.

In places, the mountains of the Coast Range rise straight from the ocean's waves to form rugged, windswept headlands that still bear the colorful names given them by early explorers—Cape Foulweather, Cape Blanco, and Cape Perpetua. With roads and trails that scale these heights, these capes provide ideal vantage points for surveying the wave-washed coast. Between these rocky headlands stretch miles of sandy beaches. In fact, on the central coast there's so much sand that dunes rise as high as 500 feet.

Wildlife-viewing opportunities along the Oregon coast are outstanding. From the beaches and the waters just offshore rise countless haystack rocks, rocky islets, monoliths, and other rock formations that serve as homes to birds, sea lions, and seals. Harbor seals loll on isolated sand spits, and large colonies of California sea lions lounge on rocks and docks, barking incessantly and entertaining people with their constant bickering. The best places to observe sea lions are on the Newport waterfront, at Sea Lion Caves north of Florence and at Cape Arago State Park

outside of Coos Bay. Hundreds of gray whales also call these waters home, and each year thousands more can be seen during their annual migrations. Twice a year, in late winter and early spring, gray whales migrate between the Arctic and the waters off Baja California. They pass close by the coast and can be easily spotted from headlands such as Tillamook Head, Cape Meares, Cape Lookout, and Cape Blanco. In coastal meadows, majestic elk graze contentedly, and near the town of Reedsport, the Dean Creek meadows have been set aside as an elk preserve. It's often possible to spot 100 or more elk grazing here. The single best introduction to the aquatic flora and fauna of the Oregon coast is Newport's Oregon Coast Aquarium, where you can learn about the animals and plants that inhabit the diverse aquatic environments of the Oregon coast.

Rivers, bays, and offshore waters are also home to some of the best **fishing** in the country. The rivers, though depleted by a century of overfishing, are still home to salmon, steelhead, and trout, most of which are now hatchery raised. Several charter-boat marinas up and down the coast offer saltwater-fishing for salmon and bottom fish. Few anglers return from these trips without a good catch. **Crabbing** and **clamming** are two other productive coastal pursuits that can turn a trip to the beach into a time for feasting.

To allow visitors to enjoy all the beauties of the Oregon coast, the state has created nearly 80 state parks, waysides, recreation areas, and scenic viewpoints

The Northern Oregon Coast

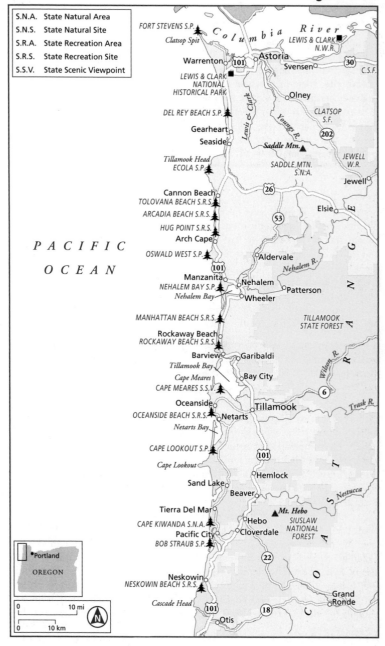

S.N.A.   State Natural Area
S.N.S.   State Natural Site
S.R.A.   State Recreation Area
S.R.S.   State Recreation Site
S.S.V.   State Scenic Viewpoint

FORT STEVENS S.P.
Clatsop Spit
Warrenton
Astoria
Svensen
LEWIS & CLARK N.W.R.
C.S.F.
Columbia River
101
30

LEWIS & CLARK NATIONAL HISTORICAL PARK
Lewis & Clark
Olney
CLATSOP S.F.

DEL REY BEACH S.P.
Gearheart
Seaside
Young's R.
202
Saddle Mtn.
JEWELL W.R.
Jewell

Tillamook Head
ECOLA S.P.
SADDLE MTN. S.N.A.
26

Cannon Beach
TOLOVANA BEACH S.R.S.
ARCADIA BEACH S.R.S.
HUG POINT S.R.S.
Arch Cape
OSWALD WEST S.P.
Elsie
53

Aldervale
Nehalem R.
101

Manzanita
NEHALEM BAY S.P.
Nehalem Bay
Nehalem
Wheeler
Patterson

MANHATTAN BEACH S.R.S.
Rockaway Beach
ROCKAWAY BEACH S.R.S.
TILLAMOOK STATE FOREST

Barview
Garibaldi
Tillamook Bay
Cape Meares
CAPE MEARES S.S.V.
Bay City
Wilson R.
6

Oceanside
OCEANSIDE BEACH S.R.S.
Netarts
Netarts Bay
Tillamook
Trask R.

CAPE LOOKOUT S.P.
Cape Lookout
101
Hemlock

Sand Lake
Beaver
Nestucca

Tierra Del Mar
CAPE KIWANDA S.N.A.
Pacific City
BOB STRAUB S.P.
Hebo
Cloverdale
Mt. Hebo
SIUSLAW NATIONAL FOREST
22

PACIFIC OCEAN

COAST RANGE

Neskowin
NESKOWIN BEACH S.R.S.
Cascade Head
101
18
Otis
Grand Ronde

Portland
OREGON

0   10 mi
0   10 km
N

Value The Cost of the Coast

State parks, county parks, national-forest recreation areas, outstanding natural areas—along the Oregon coast, there are numerous state and federal access areas that now charge day-use fees. You can either pay these fees as you encounter them or purchase an Oregon Pacific Coast Passport for $10. These passes are good for 5 days, and get you into all state and federal parks and recreation areas along the coast. (However, you'll still have to pay campsite fees.) A $35 annual pass is also available. Passports are available at most state parks that charge a day-use fee. For more information contact **Oregon State Parks Information Center** (© **800/551-6949**).

between Fort Stevens State Park in the north and McVay Rock State Recreation Site in the south. Among the more popular activities at these parks are kite flying and beachcombing (but not swimming; the water is too cold).

As I've already mentioned, it rains a lot here. Bring a raincoat, and don't let a little moisture prevent you from enjoying one of the most beautiful coastlines in the world. In fact, the mists and fogs add an aura of mystery to the coast's dark, forested mountain slopes. Contrary to what you might think, the hot days of July and August are not always the best time to visit. When it's baking inland, the coast is often shrouded in fog. The best months to visit tend to be September and early October, when the weather is often fine and the crowds are gone.

1 Astoria

95 miles NW of Portland; 20 miles S of Long Beach, WA; 17 miles N of Seaside

Astoria, situated on the banks of the Columbia River just inland from the river's mouth, is the oldest American community west of the Mississippi. More a river port than a beach town, Astoria's greatest attraction lies in its hillsides of restored Victorian homes and the scenic views across the Columbia to the hills of southwestern Washington. The combination of historical character, scenic vistas, a lively arts community, and some interesting museums make this one of the most intriguing towns on the Oregon coast. Although it still has seamy sections of waterfront, the town has been busy over the past few years developing something of a tourist-oriented waterfront character.

Astoria's Euro-American history got its start in the winter of 1805 to 1806 when Lewis and Clark built a fort near here and established an American claim. Five years later, in 1811, fur traders working for John Jacob Astor arrived at the mouth of the Columbia River to set up a fur-trading fort that was named Fort Astoria. During the War of 1812, the fort was turned over to the British, but by 1818 it reverted to American hands. When the salmon-canning boom hit in the 1880s, Astoria became a bustling little city—the second largest in Oregon—and wealthy merchants began building the ornate, Victorian-style homes that today give Astoria its historic character.

ESSENTIALS

GETTING THERE   From Portland, take U.S. 30W. From the north or south, take U.S. 101.

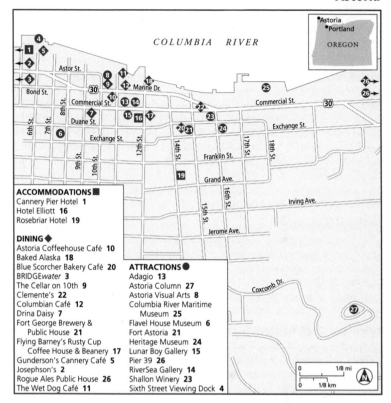

COLUMBIA RIVER

Astoria
Portland

OREGON

Astor St.

Bond St.

Marine Dr.

Commercial St.

Commercial St.

Duane St.

6th St. 7th St. 8th St.

Exchange St.

Exchange St.

9th St. 10th St. 12th St. 14th St. 15th St. 16th St. 17th St. 18th St.

Franklin St.

Irving Ave.

Grand Ave.

Jerome Ave.

Coxcomb Dr.

0   1/8 mi
0   1/8 km

ACCOMMODATIONS ■
Cannery Pier Hotel **1**
Hotel Elliott **16**
Rosebriar Hotel **19**

DINING ◆
Astoria Coffeehouse Café **10**
Baked Alaska **18**
Blue Scorcher Bakery Café **20**
BRIDGE*water* **3**
The Cellar on 10th **9**
Clemente's **22**
Columbian Café **12**
Drina Daisy **7**
Fort George Brewery &
  Public House **21**
Flying Barney's Rusty Cup
  Coffee House & Beanery **17**
Gunderson's Cannery Café **5**
Josephson's **2**
Rogue Ales Public House **26**
The Wet Dog Café **11**

ATTRACTIONS ●
Adagio **13**
Astoria Column **27**
Astoria Visual Arts **8**
Columbia River Maritime
  Museum **25**
Flavel House Museum **6**
Fort Astoria **21**
Heritage Museum **24**
Lunar Boy Gallery **15**
Pier 39 **26**
RiverSea Gallery **14**
Shallon Winery **23**
Sixth Street Viewing Dock **4**

VISITOR INFORMATION Contact the **Astoria-Warrenton Area Chamber of Commerce,** 111 W. Marine Dr. (P.O. Box 176), Astoria, OR 97103 (© **800/875-6807** or 503/325-6311; www.oldoregon.com).

FESTIVALS The **Astoria Regatta** (www.astoriaregatta.org), held each year in early August, is the city's biggest festival and includes lots of sailboat races. You've probably heard of cowboy poetry, but have you heard of fisher poetry? Astoria's annual **Fisher Poets Gathering** (www.clatsopcc.edu/fisherpoets), held in late February, celebrates the poetry of commercial fishermen and women.

DELVING INTO ASTORIA HISTORY

Columbia River Maritime Museum ⊛⊛   The Columbia River, the second-largest river in the United States, was the object of centuries of exploration in the Northwest, and, since its discovery in 1792, it has been essential to the region. This boldly designed museum, built to resemble waves on the ocean, tells the story of the river's maritime history. High seas and constantly shifting sands make this one of the world's most difficult rivers to enter; displays of shipwrecks, lighthouses, and historical lifesaving missions testify to the danger. The Coast Guard, fishing, navigation, and naval history are also subjects of museum exhibits, with a dramatic Coast Guard motor lifeboat display a highlight of the museum. Docked beside the museum and open to visitors is the lightship *Columbia,* the last seagoing lighthouse ship to serve on the West Coast. This is one of the best museums in the state.

1792 Marine Dr. ✆ **503/325-2323.** www.crmm.org. Admission $8 adults, $7 seniors, $4 children 6–17. Daily 9:30am–5pm. Closed Thanksgiving and Christmas.

Flavel House Museum ✦   The Flavel House, owned and operated by the Clatsop County Historical Society, is the grandest and most ornate of Astoria's many Victorian homes. This Queen Anne–style Victorian mansion was built in 1885 by Capt. George Flavel, who made his fortune operating the first pilot service over the Columbia River Bar and was Astoria's first millionaire. When constructed, this house was the envy of every Astoria resident. The high-ceilinged rooms are filled with period furnishings that accent the home's superb construction, and throughout the house there is much ornate woodwork.

441 Eighth St. ✆ **503/325-2203.** www.cumtux.org. Admission $5 adults, $4 seniors and students, $2 children 6–17. May–Sept daily 10am–5pm; Oct–Apr daily 11am–4pm.

Heritage Museum   Housed in Astoria's former city hall, this small museum chronicles the history of Astoria and surrounding Clatsop County. The main exhibits consist of Native American and pioneer artifacts, as well as historic photos, and there are also exhibits on Lewis and Clark and the movie *The Goonies,* which was filmed here in Astoria.

1618 Exchange St. ✆ **503/325-2203.** www.cumtux.org. Admission $4 adults, $3 seniors, $2 children 6–17. May–Sept daily 10am–5pm; Oct–Apr Tues–Sat 11am–4pm.

Lewis and Clark National Historical Park ✦✦   During the winter of 1805–06, Meriwether Lewis, William Clark, and the other members of the Corps of Discovery camped at a spot near the mouth of the Columbia River. They built a log stockade and named their encampment Fort Clatsop after the local Clatsop Indians who had befriended them. In the 1950s, a reproduction of that fort was constructed, but in the fall of 2005, as the fort's big bicentennial celebration approached, the fort burned down. The fort has since been reconstructed and once again provides an insightful glimpse into what life was like that dreary, wet winter more than 200 years ago. This historical park includes not only the fort, but also the 6-mile Fort to Sea Trail, and several sites in Washington state. Over on the Washington side of the Columbia, there are new sculptures, including two installations by celebrated artist Maya Lin. From late spring to Labor Day, park rangers clad in period clothing give demonstrations of historical activities including flintlock use, buckskin preparation, and candle making.

Off U.S. 101, 5 miles southwest of Astoria. ✆ **503/861-2471.** www.nps.gov/lewi. Admission $3–$5 adults; free–$2 children 4–15. Labor Day to mid-June daily 9am–5pm; mid-June to Labor Day daily 9am–6pm. Closed Christmas.

OTHER ASTORIA ACTIVITIES & ATTRACTIONS

Atop Coxcomb Hill, which is reached by driving up 16th Street and following the signs, you'll find the **Astoria Column.** Built in 1926, the column was patterned after Trajan's Column in Rome and stands 125 feet tall. On the exterior wall, a mural depicts the history of the area. There are 164 steps up to the top of the column, and on a clear day the view makes the climb well worth the effort. The column is open daily from dawn to dusk and admission is free. On the way to the Astoria Column, stop by **Fort Astoria,** on the corner of 15th and Exchange streets. A log blockhouse and historical marker commemorate the site of the trading post established by John Jacob Astor's fur traders.

There are several places in downtown where you can linger by the riverside atop the docks that once made up much of the city's waterfront. Stop by the **Sixth Street Viewing Dock,** where there is a raised viewing platform as well as a fishing dock. From here you can gaze out at the massive Astoria-Megler Bridge, stretching for more than 4 miles across the mouth of the river. Also keep an eye out for sea lions. The best way to see the waterfront is aboard the restored 1913 streetcar operated by **Astoria Riverfront Trolley** (© 503/325-8790). This trolley operates daily from Memorial Day to Labor Day and on a limited schedule other months. Rides are $1.

The Astoria waterfront is rapidly turning into a shoreline of waterfront condos and hotels, but you can still catch a glimpse of the old days on the waterfront on the east end of town at **Pier 39,** 100 39th St. (© 503/325-2502; www.pier39-astoria.com). Originally built in 1875, this cannery was home to Bumble Bee Seafoods, which was founded here in Astoria. Today the old cannery is the largest and oldest building on the waterfront, and inside you'll find displays on the cannery's history. The pier is also home to a brewpub and a coffeehouse. On the breakwater adjacent to Pier 39, sea lions can often be seen and heard.

Right in downtown Astoria, you'll find one of the most unusual wineries in the state. **Shallon Winery,** 1598 Duane St. (© 503/325-5978; www.shallon.com), specializes in fruit wines, but it is the unique whey wines that are winemaker Paul van der Veldt's greatest achievement. The Cran du Lait, made with local cranberries and whey from the Tillamook cheese factory, is surprisingly smooth and drinkable. Also look for the amazing chocolate-orange wine, a thick nectar that will make a chocoholic of anyone.

If you'd like to see what local artists are up to, stop by the gallery of **Astoria Visual Arts,** 433-A 11th St. (© 503/325-4589; www.astoriaarts.com), a not-for-profit arts organization. For more regional art, visit the **RiverSea Gallery,** 1160 Commercial St. (© 503/325-1270; www.riverseagalleryastoria.com). At **Lunar Boy Gallery,** 1133 Commercial St. (© 503/325-1566; www.lunarboygallery.com), you'll find a truly bizarre selection of art derived from the worlds of graphic design, cartoons, and animated films. **Adagio,** 1174 Commercial St. (© 503/338-4825), an unusual high-end import store with a very eclectic selection, is also well worth a stop.

OUTDOOR ACTIVITIES

Fort Stevens State Park (© 503/861-1671; www.oregonstateparks.org), 8 miles from Astoria at the mouth of the Columbia, preserves a fort that was built during the Civil War to protect the Columbia River and its important port cities. Though Fort Stevens had the distinction of being the only mainland military reservation to be fired on by the Japanese, the fort was deactivated after World War II. Today the fort's extensive grounds include historic buildings and gun emplacements, and the **Fort Stevens State Park Military Museum** (© 503/861-2000). Throughout the summer, the museum operates tours of the fort in a military surplus truck. There are also miles of bicycle paths, beaches, a campground, and a picnic area. Admission is $3. At the north end of the park, you can climb to the top of a viewing tower and get a good look at the South Jetty, which was built to make navigating the mouth of the Columbia easier. Also within the park you can see the wreck of the *Peter Iredale,* one ship that did not make it safely over the sandbars at the river's mouth. Each year over Labor Day weekend, there is a Civil War reenactment here at the park.

A few miles south of Fort Stevens on U.S. 101, you'll find **Sunset Beach State Recreation Area;** it provides beach access and is the western end of the 6-mile-long

Fort to Sea Trail, which stretches from here to Fort Clatsop in Lewis and Clark National Historical Park.

Several charter-fishing boats operate out of nearby Warrenton. Arrange trips through **Tiki Charters** (© **503/325-7818;** www.ifish.net/tiki.html) and **Charlton Deep Sea Charters** (© **503/861-2429;** www.charltoncharters.com). Expect to pay $90 to $185 per person.

A few miles east of town on Ore. 30, bird-watchers will find a roadside viewing platform overlooking the marshes of the **Twilight Creek Eagle Sanctuary.** Take Burnside Road off Ore. 30 between the John Day River and Svenson.

WHERE TO STAY

Cannery Pier Hotel ★★ This hotel is one of my favorite lodgings on the Oregon coast, although it is actually on the Columbia River and not the Pacific Ocean. In fact, this hotel isn't just on the waterfront, it's *in* the river. Built 600 feet out in the river on an old cannery pier, this modern hotel fits in perfectly with old wooden waterfront buildings around Astoria. Guest rooms are exceedingly comfortable, with window seats, little balconies, gas fireplaces, and super-plush beds. In the bathrooms, you'll find a claw-foot tub, from which you can gaze out at the river while you soak. Your view will take in not only the waters of the mighty Columbia River, but also the Astoria-Megler Bridge looming high overhead and tankers and cruise ships rumbling up and down the river.

10 Basin St., Astoria, OR 97103. © **888/325-4996** or 503/325-4996. Fax 503/325-8350. www.cannerypierhotel. com. 46 units. Summer $299 double; $325–$550 suite; other months $159–$209 double, $325–$550 suite. Rates include continental breakfast. Children under 18 stay free in parent's room. AE, DISC, MC, V. Pets accepted ($40 fee). **Amenities:** Exercise room; full-service spa; Jacuzzi; sauna; bike rentals; business center; massage; coin-op laundry. *In room:* TV, dataport, fridge, microwave, coffeemaker, hair dryer, iron, free local calls, high-speed Internet access, Wi-Fi.

Hotel Elliott ★★ Historic hotels are few and far between on the Oregon coast, but even if they were a dime a dozen, this beautiful hotel would be the best. The Elliott blends a vintage feel with a thoroughly modern interior decor. Rooms have lots of nice touches, including heated tile floors in the bathrooms, handblown glass globes on reading lights, regional artwork, furniture with comfortable contemporary styling, plush feather-top beds, and, in suites, granite-topped wet bars. Down in the cellar, there's a cigar-and-wine bar, and up on the roof, there's a roof-top garden with fire pits and grand views.

357 12th St., Astoria, OR 97103. © **877/EST-1924** or 503/325-2222. www.hotelelliott.com. 32 units. $109–$169 double; $165–$650 suite. Rates include continental breakfast and evening wine reception. AE, DISC, MC, V. Pets accepted ($25). **Amenities:** Access to nearby health club; room service; babysitting; laundry service; dry cleaning. *In room:* TV, dataport, minibar, coffeemaker, hair dryer, iron, high-speed Internet access.

Rosebriar Inn Bed & Breakfast ★ Originally built as a private home in 1902, the Rosebriar became a convent in the 1950s, then was renovated and turned into a small 1920s-style hotel in the 1990s. Ornate wainscoting, scrollwork ceilings, and lots of wood trim show the quality of workmanship that went into this home. The grand old Georgian mansion sits high above the river and the street, with commanding views from the two front rooms. The carriage-house cottage has its own fireplace, whirlpool tub, and private patio.

636 14th St., Astoria, OR 97103. © **800/487-0224** or 503/325-7427. www.rosebriar.net. 12 units. June–Sept $90–$175 double, $190–$275 suite; Oct–May $75–$148 double, $160–$230 suite. Rates include full breakfast. 2-night minimum on weekends. Children over 12 accepted and stay free in parent's room. AE, DISC, MC, V. Pets accepted. *In room:* TV/DVD, free local calls, Wi-Fi.

> **(Tips** Plan Ahead—Campground Reservations
>
> For information on **camping** in area state parks, call the state parks information line at © **800/551-6949.** To make a camping reservation, contact **ReserveAmerica** (© **800/452-5687;** www.reserveamerica.com).

CAMPGROUNDS

Fort Stevens State Park, on the beach at the mouth of the Columbia River, is one of the largest and most popular state park campgrounds on the Oregon coast. For reservations, contact **ReserveAmerica** (© **800/452-5687;** www.reserveamerica.com).

WHERE TO DINE

In addition to the restaurants listed below, you should be sure to stop by **Josephson's,** 106 Marine Dr. (© **800/772-3474** or 503/325-2190; www.josephsons.com), a local seafood-smoking company that sells smoked salmon by the pound and has a take-out deli counter with clam chowder, smoked seafood on rolls, and more. If you're looking for some local ale, you've got several excellent choices in Astoria. Downtown on the waterfront, there's **The Wet Dog Cafe,** 144 11th St. (© **503/325-6975**), and at the east end of town, there's the **Rogue Ales Public House,** Pier 39, 100 39th St. (© **503/ 325-5964;** www.rogue.com), where you can usually watch sea lions just outside the window. Some of the most unusual brews in town are on tap at the **Fort George Brewery & Public House,** 1483 Duane St. (© **503/325-PINT;** www.fortgeorge brewery.com). This latter pub is right next door to the **Blue Scorcher Bakery Café,** 1493 Duane St. (© **503/338-RISE**), Astoria's best bakery. You can also get good espresso at the hip **Astoria Coffeehouse Cafe,** 243 11th St. (© **503/325-1787**), or the funky little **Flying Barney's Rusty Cup Coffee House & Beanery,** 1213 Commercial St. (© **503/325-8265**). If it's wine you're after, stop by **The Cellar on 10th,** 1004 Marine Dr. (© **503/325-6600;** www.thecellaron10th.com), a well-stocked wine shop that has weekly tastings and occasional winemaker dinners.

Baked Alaska NORTHWEST   Built on a pier in downtown Astoria, this restaurant isn't just on the waterfront, it's over the waves. Not only are there great views (keep an eye out for sea lions), but the menu includes both comfort food and creative dishes. This place started out as a mobile soup trailer in Alaska, and when the chef/owner and his wife decided to settle down, they picked Astoria. Begin with the soup in a sourdough bread bowl—it's what got this place started. Beyond soup, try the campfire salmon, blackened New York steak, or the unusual thundermuck tuna (seared tuna dusted with ground coffee).

1 12th St. © **503/325-7414.** www.bakedak.com. Reservations recommended. Main courses $8–$14 lunch, $18–$21 dinner. AE, DISC, MC, V. Daily 11am–10pm.

BRIDGE Water Bistro NORTHWEST   Located inside a restored red cannery building with the Astoria-Megler Bridge looming overhead and the Cannery Pier Hotel just across the water, this restaurant sums up the new Astoria. Melding a historic cannery building with a contemporary design aesthetic, the BRIDGE*water* offers casual sophistication and creative cuisine. The menu here is long, with lots of small plates, and a variety of both traditional fare and more creative regional dishes. There's something for everyone, from pickled herring, to steak on a stick, to smoked-sturgeon mousse, to spice-encrusted duck with wild blackberries and truffle demi-glace. The BRIDGE*water* is affiliated with Long Beach, Washington's, celebrated Shoalwater Restaurant and shares space with the Flying Dutchman Winery tasting room.

20 Basin St. 🕿 **503/325-6777.** www.bridgewaterbistro.com. Reservations recommended. Main courses $13–$30. AE, DISC, MC, V. Tues–Sun 11am–9pm.

Clemente's 🏨🏨 MEDITERRANEAN/SEAFOOD   This casual little place may ostensibly be a Mediterranean restaurant specializing in seafood, but lots of people know it for its great fish and chips, which are available with a variety of seafoods, including salmon, albacore tuna, shrimp, and oysters. However, they also do a good cioppino. At dinner, try the pesto halibut or the sole piccata. The glass case full of fish lets you see what's fresh that day.

1335 Marine Dr. 🕿 **503/325-1067.** Reservations recommended. Main courses $8–$17. AE, DISC, MC, V. Tues 11am–6pm; Wed–Sun 11am–4pm and 6–10pm.

Columbian Café *Finds* VEGETARIAN/SEAFOOD   With offbeat and eclectic decor, this tiny place looks a bit like a cross between a college hangout and a seaport diner, and, indeed, the clientele reflects this atmosphere. There are only a handful of booths and a lunch counter, and the cafe's reputation for good vegetarian fare keeps the seats full. Crepes are the house specialty and come with a variety of fillings, including avocado, tomato, and cheese, or curried bananas. Dinner offers a bit more variety, with an emphasis on seafood, and there are always lots of specials. Even the condiments here, including pepper jelly and garlic jelly, are homemade. Next door, and affiliated with the cafe, are the Voodoo Room nightclub and the Columbian Theater movie theater.

1114 Marine Dr. 🕿 **503/325-2233.** www.columbianvoodoo.com. $6–$13 breakfast or lunch, $13–$22 dinner. No credit cards. Mon–Tues 8am–2pm; Wed–Fri 8am–2pm and 5–8pm; Sat 10am–2pm and 5–8pm; Sun 10am–2pm.

Drina Daisy BOSNIAN   Ever had Bosnian food? Probably not, but here in Astoria, you can give it a try. The specialty here is whole spit-roasted lamb, but since it is not always available, you should be sure to call in advance to see if it will be on the menu the night you plan to dine here. Even if there's no lamb roasting on the spit when you're in town, there are plenty of other tasty dishes to try, including beef in phyllo dough, stuffed cabbage with beef or vegetables, and Bosnian goulash flavored with paprika. Be sure to finish your meal with a little cup of thick, Sarajevo-style coffee or Bosnian espresso, which is topped with whipped cream

915 Commercial St. 🕿 **503/338-2912.** www.drinadaisy.com. Main courses $8.50–$16 lunch, $11–$22 dinner. AE, DISC, MC, V. Wed–Sun 11am–9:30pm.

Gunderson's Cannery Cafe 🏨 SEAFOOD/NORTHWEST   Housed in a former salmon cannery, this casual restaurant offers creative food and great views. You might even spot sea lions while you're dining. For nightly specials, the chef draws upon world cuisines for inspiration; and on the main menu, you'll also find international influences in such dishes as pan-Asian salmon and Mediterranean halibut. The crab and shrimp cakes are perennial favorites. Lunches are mostly sandwiches (the panini are my favorite), salads, and good chowder.

1 Sixth St. (on the Columbia River). 🕿 **503/325-8642.** www.cannerycafe.com. Reservations recommended. Main courses $7–$14 lunch, $15–$26 dinner. AE, DISC, MC, V. Daily 8am–9pm.

ASTORIA AFTER DARK

If you're here in the summer, try to catch a performance of *Shanghaied in Astoria,* a musical melodrama that is staged each year by the **Astor Street Opry Company,** 279 W. Marine Dr. (© **503/325-6104;** www.shanghaiedinastoria.com). Performances are usually held from mid-July to mid-September. Also be sure to check the schedule of the **Liberty Theater,** 12th and Commercial streets (© **503/325-5922;** www.liberty-theater.org), a beautifully restored 1920s movie palace.

2 Seaside

17 miles S of Astoria, 79 miles W of Portland, 7 miles N of Cannon Beach

Seaside is the northern Oregon coast's top family vacation destination. The town is one of the oldest beach resorts on the coast (dating from 1899) and is filled with quaint historic cottages and tree-lined streets. However, it is better known for its miniature golf courses, bumper boats, video arcades, and souvenir shops.

This is not the sort of place most people imagine when they dream about the Oregon coast, and if you're looking for a quiet, romantic weekend getaway, Seaside is *not* the place. As one of the closest beaches to Portland, crowds and traffic are a way of life on summer weekends. The town is also a very popular conference site, and several of the town's largest hotels cater primarily to this market (and have the outrageous rates to prove it). However, the nearby community of Gearhart, which has long been a retreat for wealthy Portlanders, is as quiet as any town you'll find on this coast.

ESSENTIALS

GETTING THERE   Seaside is on U.S. 101 just north of the junction with U.S. 26, which connects to Portland.

VISITOR INFORMATION   Contact the **Seaside Chamber of Commerce,** 7 N. Roosevelt St., Seaside, OR 97138 (© **888/306-2326** or 503/738-3097; www.seaside or.com).

FESTIVALS   The weekend before Labor Day weekend, the **Hood to Coast Run** celebration is held in Seaside.

ENJOYING THE BEACH & SEASIDE'S OTHER ATTRACTIONS

Seaside's centerpiece is its 2-mile-long beachfront **Promenade** (or Prom), built in 1921. At the west end of Broadway, the Turnaround divides the walkway into the North Prom and the South Prom. Here a bronze statue marks the official end of the trail for the Lewis and Clark expedition. South of this statue on Lewis & Clark Way between the Promenade and Beach Drive, 8 blocks south of Broadway, you'll find the **Lewis and Clark Salt Works,** a reconstruction of a fire pit used by members of the famous expedition. During the winter of 1805–06, while the expedition was camped at Fort Clatsop, near present-day Astoria, Lewis and Clark sent several men southwest 15 miles to a good spot for making salt from seawater. It took three men nearly 2 months to produce 4 bushels of salt for the return trip east. Five kettles were used for boiling seawater, and the fires were kept stoked 24 hours a day.

History is not what attracts most people to Seaside, though. Rather, it's the miles of **white-sand beach** that begin just south of Seaside at the foot of the imposing Tillamook Head and stretch north to the mouth of the Columbia River. Though the waters here are quite cold and only a few people venture in farther than knee-deep, there are

Biking the Oregon Coast

The Oregon coast is one of the nation's best-known bicycle tour routes, ranking right up there with the back roads of Vermont, the Napa Valley, and the San Juan Islands. Cyclists will find breathtaking scenery, interesting towns, parks and beaches to explore, wide shoulders, and well-spaced places to stay. You can stay in campgrounds (all state-park campgrounds have hiker/biker campsites) or in hotels. If you can afford it, an inn-to-inn pedal down this coast is the way to go; as you slowly grind your way up hill after hill, you'll appreciate not having to carry camping gear.

The entire route, from Astoria to California, covers between 368 and 378 miles (depending on your route) and includes a daunting 16,000 total feet of climbing. Although most of the route is on U.S. 101, which is a 55-mph highway for most of its length, the designated coast route leaves the highway for less crowded and more scenic roads whenever possible.

During the summer, when winds are generally out of the northwest, you'll have the wind at your back if you ride from north to south. In the winter (when you'll likely get very wet), you're better off riding from south to north to take advantage of winds out of the southwest. Planning a trip along the coast in winter is not advisable; even though there is less traffic, winter storms frequently blow in with winds of up to 100 mph.

For a map and guide to bicycling the Oregon coast, contact the **Oregon Department of Transportation** (© 503/986-3556; www.oregon.gov/odot/hwy/bikeped). You might also want to get a copy of the *Umbrella Guide to Bicycling the Oregon Coast* (Umbrella Books, 1990), by Robin Cody.

lifeguards on duty all summer, which is one reason Seaside is popular with families. At the south end of Seaside beach is one of the best surf breaks on the north coast. You can rent a board and wetsuit at **Cleanline Surf,** 725 First Ave. (© 503/738-7888; www.cleanlinesurf.com). A complete rental package runs $35 a day.

Because of the cold water, kite flying, beach cycling, and other nonaquatic activities prove far more popular than swimming or surfing. All over town there are places that rent four-wheeled bicycles, called surreys, and three-wheeled cycles (funcycles) for pedaling on the beach. The latter are the most popular and the most fun, but can really be used only when the tide is out and the beach is firm enough to pedal on. Cycles go for between $10 and $15 an hour, and multipassenger surreys rent for between $20 and $30 an hour. Try **Wheel Fun Rentals,** 407 S. Holladay Dr. (© 503/738-8447; www.wheelfunrentals.com), which has a second location at 153 Ave. A (© 503/738-7212).

If you prefer hiking to cycling, head south of town to the end of Sunset Boulevard, where you'll find the start of the **Tillamook Head Trail,** which leads 6 miles over the headland to Indian Beach in **Ecola State Park.** This trail goes through shady forests of firs and red cedars with a few glimpses of the Pacific along the way.

Golfers can play a round at the 9-hole **Seaside Golf Club,** 451 Ave. U (© 503/738-5261; www.seasidegolf.us), which charges $15 to $16 for 9 holes; another 9-hole course, **The Highlands at Gearhart,** 1 Highlands Rd. (© 503/738-5248), also charges $14 for 9 holes. However, the area's best course is the **Gearhart Golf Links,** 1157 N. Marion St., Gearhart (© 800/547-0115 or 503/738-3538; www.gearhart golflinks.com), where you'll pay $30 to $60 for 18 holes. This course was established in 1892, which makes it the oldest golf course in Oregon.

The **Seaside Aquarium,** 200 N. Promenade (© 503/738-6211; www.seaside aquarium.com), where you can feed seals, is popular. Admission is $7 for adults, $5.75 for seniors, and $3.50 for children ages 6 to 13. In a big case visible from outside the aquarium, there is a 36-foot-long gray whale skeleton. Kids will also enjoy the gaudily painted **carousel** at the Seaside Town Center Mall at 300 Broadway.

WHERE TO STAY
IN SEASIDE
The Gilbert Inn ⚘   One block from the beach and 1 block south of Broadway, on the edge of both the shopping district and one of Seaside's old residential neighborhoods, the Gilbert Inn is a big yellow Queen Anne–style Victorian house with a pretty little yard. Alexander Gilbert, who had this house built in 1892, was once the mayor of Seaside, and he built a stately home worthy of someone in such a high position. Gilbert made good use of the area's plentiful fir trees; the interior walls and ceilings are constructed of tongue-and-groove fir planks. The inn is decorated in country French decor that enhances the Victorian ambience.

341 Beach Dr., Seaside, OR 97138. © 800/410-9770 or 503/738-9770. Fax 503/717-1070. www.gilbertinn.com. 10 units. $89–$130 double; $105–$140 suite. 2-night minimum on weekends; 3-night on minimum on holiday weekends. Rates include full breakfast. AE, DISC, MC, V. *In room:* TV/DVD, hair dryer, iron, free local calls, Wi-Fi.

Inn of the Four Winds ⚘   You'll find this little oceanfront hotel up at the north end of the Promenade, away from all the activity in the center of town but still only a short walk from good restaurants. Most guest rooms have balconies, ocean views, and gas fireplaces. There are also large suites. All the rooms have a vaguely Italianate style, though it's obvious the decorator was on a tight budget. Some suites have kitchens. Keep in mind that although this hotel is right on the beach, it's a very wide beach.

820 N. Promenade, Seaside, OR 97138. © 800/818-9524 or 503/738-9524. www.innofthefourwinds.com. 14 units. $99–$189 double; $139–$229 suite. AE, DC, DISC, MC, V. **Amenities:** Massage. *In room:* TV/DVD, fridge, coffeemaker, hair dryer.

IN GEARHART
Gearhart Ocean Inn *(Value)*   This old motor-court-style motel offers modest and economical accommodations that have been renovated with the sort of care usually reserved for historic homes. A taupe exterior with blue-and-white trim gives the two rows of wooden buildings a touch of sophistication, and roses, Adirondack chairs, and little pocket gardens add character to the grounds. The rooms all have lots of character and have been decorated in a mix of country cute and casual contemporary. Some rooms have kitchens and/or fireplaces.

67 N. Cottage St. (P.O. Box 2161), Gearhart, OR 97138. © 800/352-8034 or 503/738-7373. Fax 503/717-8008. www.gearhartoceaninn.com. 12 units. $90–$160 double. Children under 2 stay free in parent's room. AE, MC, V. Pets accepted ($15 fee). **Amenities:** Access to nearby health club; bike rentals; guest laundry. *In room:* TV/DVD, fridge, coffeemaker, free local calls.

WHERE TO DINE
IN SEASIDE

If you're looking for a quick meal, some picnic food, or something to take back and cook in your room, drop by the old-timey **Bell Buoy Crab Co.,** 1800 S. Roosevelt St. (© **800/529-2722** or 503/738-6354; www.bellbuoyofseaside.com), which sells not only cooked Dungeness crabs, but award-winning chowder, smoked salmon, fresh seafood, and shrimp or crab melts.

Goose Hollow at the Cove *Finds* AMERICAN   The neon sign in the front window proclaims "the best Reuben in the universe," and if you've ever had the Reuben at the original Goose Hollow in Portland, you know enough not to argue with this claim. This casual south Seaside restaurant is hands-down my favorite lunch spot in the area. In fact, I would drive miles to have one of those awesome Reubens.

220 Ave. U. © **503/717-1940.** www.goosehollowinn.com. Main courses $6.25–$13. AE, DISC, MC, V. Sun–Thurs 11:30am–10pm; Fri–Sat 11:30am–11pm.

Yummy Wine Bar & Bistro *Finds* NEW AMERICAN   "I'm moving in, and I'm not leaving," exclaimed a customer recently at this stylish wine bar in downtown Seaside. That sums up how well appreciated this place is in a town very short on good places to eat. With its hip, retro decor, casual attitude, and long wine list, Yummy is a fun place not only for a glass of wine and a snack but for a full meal as well. The menu changes seasonally and there are always interesting specials, but you might start with a white-bean-and-linguisa-sausage soup and then move on to venison meatloaf, oysters steamed in a red-pepper sauce, or monkfish wrapped in serrano ham. If you're just here for wine and something light, try to grab one of the couches by the fireplace.

831 Broadway. © **503/738-3100.** www.yummywinebarbistro.com. Reservations only for 8 or more. Main courses $9–$16. AE, MC, V. Sun–Mon and Thurs 3–10pm; Fri–Sat 3pm–midnight.

IN GEARHART
Pacific Way Cafe and Bakery *Finds* SANDWICHES/NORTHWEST   This former mom-and-pop grocery store is in the center of Gearhart and has such a classic old-fashioned Cape Cod–style beach feel that it's well worth searching out. The vintage interior of the restaurant harkens to the 1930s. At lunch, there are appetizing sandwiches and salads. In the evening, try the wild mushroom macaroni and cheese or the prosciutto-wrapped scallops, if either is on the menu. There's an adjacent bakery open Saturday and Sunday from 7am to 1pm.

601 Pacific Way. © **503/738-0245.** Main dishes $8.50–$12 lunch, $18–$29 dinner. MC, V. Thurs–Mon 11am–3:30pm and 5–9pm.

3 Cannon Beach

7 miles S of Seaside, 112 miles N of Newport, 79 miles W of Portland

When most people dream of a vacation on the Oregon coast, chances are they're thinking of a place such as **Cannon Beach:** weathered cedar-shingle buildings, picket fences behind drifts of nasturtiums, quiet gravel lanes, interesting little art galleries, and massive rock monoliths rising from the surf just off the wide sandy beach. If it weren't for all the other people who think Cannon Beach is a wonderful place, this town would be perfect. However, Cannon Beach is suffering from its own quaintness and the inevitable upscaling that ensues when a place begins to gain national recognition. Once the Oregon coast's most renowned artists' community, Cannon Beach is

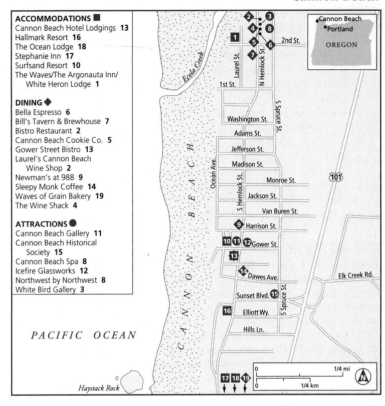

ACCOMMODATIONS ■
Cannon Beach Hotel Lodgings **13**
Hallmark Resort **16**
The Ocean Lodge **18**
Stephanie Inn **17**
Surfsand Resort **10**
The Waves/The Argonauta Inn/
  White Heron Lodge **1**

DINING ◆
Bella Espresso **6**
Bill's Tavern & Brewhouse **7**
Bistro Restaurant **2**
Cannon Beach Cookie Co. **5**
Gower Street Bistro **13**
Laurel's Cannon Beach
  Wine Shop **2**
Newman's at 988 **9**
Sleepy Monk Coffee **14**
Waves of Grain Bakery **19**
The Wine Shack **4**

ATTRACTIONS ●
Cannon Beach Gallery **11**
Cannon Beach Historical
  Society **15**
Cannon Beach Spa **8**
Icefire Glassworks **12**
Northwest by Northwest **8**
White Bird Gallery **3**

PACIFIC OCEAN

Haystack Rock

now going the way of California's Carmel—lots of upscale shopping tucked away in utterly tasteful little plazas along a neatly manicured main street. Despite the crowds, it still has a village atmosphere, and summer throngs and traffic jams can do nothing to assault the fortresslike beauty of the rocks that lie just offshore.

ESSENTIALS

GETTING THERE   Cannon Beach is on U.S. 101 just south of the junction with U.S. 26.

VISITOR INFORMATION   Contact the **Cannon Beach Chamber of Commerce,** 207 N. Spruce St. (P.O. Box 64), Cannon Beach, OR 97110 (© **503/436-2623;** www.cannonbeach.org).

GETTING AROUND   The **Cannon Beach Shuttle,** which provides free van service up and down the length of town, operates daily with seasonal hours. Watch for signed shuttle stops. Donations for the ride are accepted.

FESTIVALS   Each year in late April, the **Puffin Kite Festival** fills the skies over Cannon Beach with colorful kites and features stunt-kite exhibitions. In early June, the **Sand Castle Day** contest turns the beach into one vast canvas for sand sculptors from all over the region, and in early November, the **Stormy Weather Arts Festival** celebrates the arrival of winter storms.

> ⌐Fun Fact **Cannon Beach Trivia**
> _____
>
> - Cannon Beach was named for a cannon that washed ashore after the U.S. Navy schooner *Shark* wrecked on the coast north of here in 1846.
> - Cannon Beach's Haystack Rock, which rises 235 feet above the water, is the most photographed monolith on the Oregon coast.
> - The offshore rocks are protected nesting grounds for sea birds. Watch for tufted puffins, something of a Cannon Beach mascot.
> - Tillamook Rock is the site of the **Tillamook Rock Lighthouse** (aka "Terrible Tilly"), which was subject to huge storm waves that occasionally sent large rocks crashing through the light, 133 feet above sea level. The lighthouse was decommissioned in 1957 and is now used as a columbarium (a vault for the interment of the ashes of people who have been cremated).

HITTING THE BEACH

Ecola State Park ⍟⍟ (© **800/551-6949** or 503/436-2844; www.oregonstateparks. org), just north of the town of Cannon Beach, marks the southernmost point that Lewis and Clark explored on the Oregon coast. The park offers the most breathtaking vantage point from which to soak up the view of Cannon Beach, Haystack Rock, and the Tillamook Rock Lighthouse. The park also has several picnic areas perched on bluffs high above the crashing waves and a trail that leads 6 miles over Tillamook Head to Seaside. The 1-mile stretch of trail between the main bluff-top picnic area and Indian beach is particularly rewarding, passing through old-growth forests and offering good views of the ocean and beaches far below. There's also the 2.5-mile Clatsop Loop Trail, which leads through dense forest to a viewpoint high on Tillamook Head. The day-use fee is $3 per vehicle.

Kite flying and beachcombing are the most popular Cannon Beach pastimes. But you can also enjoy the beach in a variety of other ways, too. Between mid-May and Labor Day, guided horseback rides to Cove Beach and Haystack Rock are offered by **Sea Ranch Stables,** 415 Fir St. (© **503/436-2815;** www.cannon-beach.net/searanch), which is at the north entrance to Cannon Beach. Rides cost $50 to $90, and you must drop by the stables and make a reservation.

Another great way to see the beach is from a funcycle, a three-wheeled beach cycle. These cycles enable you to ride up and down the beach at low tide. Funcycles can be rented from **Mike's Bike Shop,** 248 N. Spruce St. (© **800/492-1266** or 503/436-1266; www.mikesbike.com) for $12 for an hour and a half. Mountain bikes and road bikes are also available for rent from Mike's.

Three miles south of town is **Arcadia Beach Wayside** ⍟, one of the prettiest little beaches on the north coast; and another mile farther south you'll find **Hug Point State Recreation Site** ⍟, which has picnic tables, a sheltered beach, and the remains of an old road that was cut into the rock face of this headland. **Oswald West State Park** ⍟⍟, 10 miles south of Cannon Beach, is one of my favorites of all the parks on the Oregon coast. A short paved trail leads to a driftwood-strewn cobblestone beach on a small cove. Headlands on either side of the cove can be reached by hiking trails that offer splendid views. The waves here are popular with surfers, and there's a walk-in campground.

If you want to try riding the wild (and very cold) surf, you can rent a surfboard and wetsuit from **Cannon Beach Surf,** 1088 S. Hemlock St. (℗ **503/436-0475;** www. cannonbeachsurf.com). Don't know how to surf? You can take lessons from **Oregon Surf Adventures,** 1235 S. Hemlock St. (℗ **503/436-1481;** www.oregonsurfadventures. com).

EXPLORING THE TOWN

For many Cannon Beach visitors, **shopping** is the town's greatest attraction. In the heart of town, along Hemlock Street, you'll find dozens of densely packed small shops and galleries offering original art, fine crafts, unusual gifts, and casual fashions. Galleries worth seeking out include **Northwest by Northwest,** 232 N. Spruce St. (℗ **800/ 494-0741** or 503/436-0741; www.nwbynwgallery.com), which features works by established Northwest artists; **White Bird Gallery,** 251 N. Hemlock St. (℗ **503/436- 2681;** www.whitebirdgallery.com), a good gallery for colorful contemporary art and fine crafts. **Icefire Glassworks,** 116 E. Gower St. (℗ **503/436-2359**), a glassblowing studio south of downtown; and **Cannon Beach Gallery,** 1064 S. Hemlock St. (℗ **503/ 436-0744;** www.cannonbeacharts.org), which is operated by a local arts organization and mounts shows in a wide variety of styles not usually seen in other Cannon Beach galleries (which tend to be heavy on beach landscapes). On the surface, Cannon Beach may not look as though it has much history, but from Lewis and Clark's visit to the cannon that washed up on shore and gave the town its name, there is a bit to learn about this town's past. Visit the **Cannon Beach Historical Society,** 1387 S. Spruce St. (℗ **503/436-9301;** www.cbhistory.org), where modern, well-designed exhibits tell the story of the town's past, including the history of tourism here.

Want to turn a Cannon Beach getaway into a truly relaxing escape? Book a massage or a skin or hydrotherapy treatment at the **Cannon Beach Spa,** 232 N. Spruce St. (℗ **888/577-8772** or 503/436-8772; www.cannonbeachspa.com). Prices run between $65 and $85 for an hour massage.

WHERE TO STAY

If you're heading here with the whole family or plan to stay a while, consider renting a house, a cottage, or an apartment. Offerings range from studio apartments to large luxurious oceanfront houses, and prices span an equally wide range. Contact **Cannon Beach Property Management,** 3188 S. Hemlock St. (P.O. Box 231), Cannon Beach, OR 97110 (℗ **877/386-3402;** www.cbpm.com) for more information.

EXPENSIVE

Arch Cape House 🐾🐾 *Finds*   If you can't find time in your schedule for that trip to France this year, a stay at Arch Cape House will provide a reasonable facsimile. Although the setting, just off U.S. 101 between Cannon Beach and Manzanita, won't convince you that you're in Provence, the building itself is as grand a manor house as any in France. Incorporating elements from castles and châteaux, it's straight out of a fairy tale. European antiques, original art, and an abundance of tapestry-cloth furnishings fill the house. Each of the rooms fulfills a different fantasy of the perfect romantic escape. There is the circular Tower Room, with its own soaking tub; the Gauguin, filled with reproductions of paintings by you-know-who; and the Tapestry Room, with a stained-glass ceiling and a soaking tub. Lavish, three-course breakfasts are served in the conservatory. So luxurious is this place that the fact that you aren't right on the beach doesn't even seem to matter.

31970 E. Ocean Lane, Arch Cape, OR 97102. © **800/436-2848** or 503/436-2800. Fax 866/595-8340. www.arch capehouse.com. 8 units. $129–$239 double. Rates include full breakfast and evening wine social hour. No children under 12. AE, DISC, MC, V. Pets accepted ($35 fee). **Amenities:** Sauna; concierge. In room: TV/VCR, fridge, free local calls, Wi-Fi.

The Ocean Lodge 🐸🐸🐸   Located right next door to the Stephanie Inn, this lodge is every bit as deluxe, but boasts a more laid-back, vintage Northwest feel. The lobby has huge rough-cut timber beams and warm wood tones. All rooms are spacious suites with fireplaces and decks, most have in-room Jacuzzis, and some boast good views of Haystack Rock—if you can afford the premium, the views are well worth requesting. Ground-floor oceanfront rooms also have direct access to the beach. The lodge's beach bungalows are across the street and some are up two flights of stairs.

2864 S. Pacific St. (P.O. Box 1037), Cannon Beach, OR 97110. © **888/777-4047** or 503/436-2241. www.theocean lodge.com. 45 units. Late June to mid-Oct $249–$349 double, $299–$329 suite; mid-Oct to late June $179–$299 double, $239–$289 suite. Rates include continental breakfast. AE, DC, DISC, MC, V. Pets accepted ($15). **Amenities:** Access to nearby health club. In room: TV/DVD, dataport, fridge, microwave, coffeemaker, hair dryer, iron, Wi-Fi.

Stephanie Inn 🐸🐸🐸   The Stephanie Inn is the most classically romantic inn on the Oregon coast—the perfect place for an anniversary or other special weekend away. With flower boxes beneath the windows and neatly manicured gardens by the entry, the inn is reminiscent of New England's country inns, but the beach out the back door is definitely of Pacific Northwest origin. Inside, the lobby feels warm and cozy with its river-rock fireplace, huge wood columns, and beamed ceiling. The guest rooms, all individually decorated, are equally cozy, and most have double whirlpool tubs and gas fireplaces. The higher you go in the three-story inn, the better the views and the more spacious the outdoor spaces (patios, balconies, and decks). A bounteous breakfast buffet is served each morning, and complimentary afternoon wine and evening nightcaps are also served. Creative four-course prix-fixe dinners ($49) are served in the evening (reservations are required).

2740 S. Pacific St. (P.O. Box 219), Cannon Beach, OR 97110. © **800/633-3466** or 503/436-2221. www.stephanie-inn.com. 50 units. $229–$459 double; $479–$509 suite. Rates include full breakfast. Children over 12 are welcome. AE, DC, DISC, MC, V. **Amenities:** Restaurant (Northwest); access to nearby health club; courtesy shopping shuttle; room service; massage. In room: A/C, TV/DVD, fridge, coffeemaker, hair dryer, iron, safe, free local calls, Wi-Fi.

Surfsand Resort 🐸🐸   This sprawling resort, under the same ownership as the Stephanie Inn, underwent a major transformation in 2007 and is now a beautiful blend of Northwest-lodge styling on the exterior and bold, contemporary interior design in the guest rooms. There are wall-hung flat-screen TVs, separate tubs and showers, gas fireplaces, and lots of other welcome details that make these rooms great for romantic getaways. However, with an indoor pool and many room types, it is also a good choice for families. Best of all, the resort is almost right in front of Haystack Rock.

148 W. Gower St. (P.O. Box 219), Cannon Beach, OR 97110. © **800/547-6100** or 503/436-2274. Fax 503/436-9116. www.surfsand.com. 123 units. $159–$359 double; $259–$439 suite. Children under 18 stay free in parent's room. AE, DC, DISC, MC, V. Pets accepted ($12 per day). **Amenities:** Restaurant (Northwest); lounge; indoor pool; access to nearby health club; Jacuzzi; sauna; children's programs; concierge; room service; massage. In room: TV/DVD, fridge, microwave, coffeemaker, hair dryer, iron, safe, free local calls, high-speed Internet access, Wi-Fi.

MODERATE

Cannon Beach Hotel Lodgings   Although not in the town's best location (there are parking lots all around), this hotel, in a cute little historic building, manages to capture Cannon Beach's spirit economically. A white fence, black shutters, and cedar-shingle siding give the hotel plenty of character, while inside you'll find attractively furnished rooms that vary in size and price. The best rooms are those with fireplaces and whirlpool tubs, and two of these have partial ocean views. Rooms are also available in three nearby buildings, with some of these rooms being more luxurious than those in the main hotel.

1116 S. Hemlock St. (P.O. Box 943), Cannon Beach, OR 97110. (℃) **800/238-4107** or 503/436-1392. Fax 503/436-1396. www.cannonbeachhotel.com. 37 units. Mid-June to Sept $120–$220 double; Oct–Nov and Mar to mid-June $85–$175 double; Dec–Feb $70–$165 double. Rates include continental breakfast (for rooms in hotel only). Children 10 and under stay free in parent's room. AE, DC, DISC, MC, V. Pets accepted in 1 building ($15 per night). **Amenities:** Restaurant (Northwest); room service. *In room:* TV, free local calls.

Hallmark Resort ⚡ *(Kids)*   Situated on a bluff with a head-on view of Haystack Rock, the Hallmark appeals primarily to families, and a wide range of rates reflects the variety of rooms available. The lowest rates are for nonview standard rooms, and the highest rates are for oceanfront two-bedroom suites. Between these extremes are all manner of rooms, studios, and suites. The best values are the limited-view rooms, many of which have fireplaces and comfortable chairs set up to take in what little view there might be. Some rooms also have kitchens.

1400 S. Hemlock St. (P.O. Box 547), Cannon Beach, OR 97110. (℃) **888/448-4449** or 503/436-1566. Fax 503/436-0324. www.hallmarkinns.com. 142 units. Summer $139–$299 double, $199–$359 suite; other months $99–$279 double, $159–$329 suite. AE, DC, DISC, MC, V. Pets accepted ($20). **Amenities:** 2 indoor pools; exercise room; 3 Jacuzzis; concierge; massage; coin-op laundry. *In room:* TV/VCR, fridge, coffeemaker, hair dryer, iron, free local calls, high-speed Internet access.

The Waves/The Argonauta Inn/White Heron Lodge ⚡⚡   Variety is the name of the game in eclectic Cannon Beach, and The Waves plays the game better than any other accommodations in town. This lodge, only a block from the heart of Cannon Beach, consists of more than four dozen rooms, suites, cottages, and beach houses. The Garden Court rooms (with no ocean views) are the least expensive. My favorites, however, are the cottages of The Argonauta Inn. Surrounded by beautiful flower gardens in the summer, these old oceanfront cottages capture the spirit of Cannon Beach. For sybarites and romantics, there are fireplaces in some rooms and whirlpool spas overlooking the ocean. If you want to get away from the crowds, ask for a suite at the White Heron Lodge. The Waves itself offers contemporary accommodations, some of which are right on the beach and have great views.

188 W. Second St. (P.O. Box 3), Cannon Beach, OR 97110. (℃) **800/822-2468** or 503/436-2205. Fax 503/436-1490. www.thewavesmotel.com. 55 units. The Waves $84–$225 double $189–$429 suite; White Heron Lodge $199–$299; Argonauta: $89–$429 suite. 3-night minimum July–Aug; 2-night minimum on weekends Sept–June. Children under 6 stay free in parent's room. DISC, MC, V. **Amenities:** Jacuzzi; coin-op laundry. *In room:* TV/VCR/DVD, dataport, kitchen, fridge, microwave, coffeemaker, hair dryer, iron, free local calls, Wi-Fi.

CAMPGROUNDS

Despite the fact that **Oswald West State Park,** which is south of Cannon Beach, is the only area state park campground with walk-in campsites, the sites are closer together than those at most car campgrounds. Don't say I didn't warn you if the guy in the next campsite keeps you up all night with his snoring. At the north end of town, the **Sea Ranch R.V. Park & Stables,** 415 Fir St. (P.O. Box 214), Cannon Beach, OR 97110 (℃ **503/436-2815;** www.cannon-beach.net/searanch), offers sites for RVs and tents. The campground is green and shady and is right across the street from the road to Ecola State Park. Rates range from $24 to $28 per night. There are also some small cabins for rent for $75 to $85 per night. You can also try **Wright's for Camping,** P.O. Box 213, Cannon Beach, OR 97110 (℃ **503/436-2347;** www.wrightsforcamping.com), which is set back in the trees on the inland side of the road at the second Cannon Beach exit off U.S. 101 and charges $24 for campsites. At either of these, you'll need to make reservations at least a month in advance for summer weekends.

WHERE TO DINE

For pastries, cookies, and wraps, head south of downtown Cannon Beach to the Tolovana Park neighborhood, where you'll find the cozy little **Waves of Grain Bakery,** 3116 S. Hemlock St. (© 503/436-9600; www.wavesofgrainbakery.com). For good locally brewed beer, visit **Bill's Tavern & Brewhouse,** 188 N. Hemlock St. (© 503/436-2202). For good espresso, try **Bella Espresso,** 231 Hemlock St. (© 503/436-2595; www.bella-espresso.com), or **Sleepy Monk Coffee,** 1235 S. Hemlock St. (© 503/436-2796; www.sleepymonkcoffee.com), which specializes in organic coffee. For cookies, head to the **Cannon Beach Cookie Co.,** 239 Hemlock St. (© 503/436-1129). If you're looking for some wine for your romantic weekend, stop in at **The Wine Shack,** 124 Hemlock St. (© 800/787-1765 or 503/436-1100; www.beachwine.com), or **Laurel's Cannon Beach Wine Shop,** 263 N. Hemlock St. (© 503/436-1666). Also, foodies should consider booking a cooking class at **EVOO Cannon Beach Cooking School,** 188 S. Hemlock St. (© 877/436-3866; www.evoo.biz).

Bistro Restaurant 🎀 NORTHWEST If you're looking for atmosphere and good food, this is the place. Bistro Restaurant is set back a bit from the street behind a small garden and down a brick walkway. Step through the door and you'll think you've just walked into a French country inn. Stucco walls, old prints of flowers, and fresh flowers on the tables are the only decor this tiny place can afford without growing cramped. Dining choices here include well prepared seafood dishes such as seared scallops, grilled wild salmon with wasabi and soy-citrus sauce, and seafood stew.

263 N. Hemlock St. © **503/436-2661.** Reservations highly recommended. Main courses $9.50–$23. MC, V. Daily 5–9:30pm or 10pm; closed Wed in off season.

Gower Street Bistro 🎀 NEW AMERICAN This little restaurant is positively adorable. The white-tile floors, wicker chairs, white wainscoting, pressed-tin ceiling, and display case full of imported meats and cheese all set the scene for superb food. The quiches (served at brunch and dinner) are big, fat works of art that should not be missed, although I can never pass up the pulled-pork sandwich, which is the best I've had outside of North Carolina. At dinner, start with a charcuterie or cheese plate and then go for the chicken with calvados or the down-home meatloaf.

1116 S. Hemlock St. © **503/436-2729.** www.gowerstreetbistro.com. Reservations recommended. Main courses $7.50–$14 brunch, $14–$22 dinner. AE, MC, V. Summer daily 8am–3pm and 5–10pm; other months Thurs–Mon 9am–3pm and 5–9pm, Tues–Wed 5–9pm.

Newman's at 988 🎀 FRENCH/ITALIAN Chef/owner John Newman was for many years the executive chef at Cannon Beach's Stephanie Inn, and here, in his own restaurant, he continues to wow both new and long-time customers. The restaurant, inside a cottage, is small, dark, and very romantic, the perfect place for a special night out. The menu is short, but you can expect such delicacies as foie gras pasta with shaved black truffles, wild mushroom polenta, fresh fish with caviar butter, and lobster ravioli with hazelnuts and marsala-cream sauce.

988 S. Hemlock St. © **503/436-1151.** www.newmansat988.com. Reservations highly recommended. Main courses $19–$26. MC, V. Daily 5:30–9pm (closed Mon in winter).

EN ROUTE TO OR FROM PORTLAND

If you'd like to see a large herd of **Roosevelt elk,** watch for the Jewell turnoff about 37 miles before reaching Cannon Beach on U.S. 26. From the turnoff, continue 10 miles north following the wildlife-viewing signs to the **Jewell Meadows Wildlife Area** 🌟🌟 (🕐 **503/755-2264;** www.dfw.state.or.us/wildlifearea/jewellmeodows.htm), where there's a large pasture frequented in the cooler months by up to 300 elk. Although November through March are the best months to see the elk, September and October are rutting season and, at this time, big bulls can often be heard bugling and seen locking antlers. Summer is not usually a reliable time for seeing the elk, but in June, you may see elk cows with calves. During the winter, the elk are provided with supplemental hay to keep the herd healthy, and it is possible to assist in the daily feeding. Participants are taken out into the meadows on a flatbed trailer loaded with hay, which is then tossed out to the expectant elk. To participate, however, you'll need to call on the morning of December 1 to make your reservation. (Weekends fill up the fastest.)

Twelve miles past the U.S. 26 turnoff for Jewell, you'll find **Saddle Mountain State Natural Area** 🌟🌟, which is a favorite day hike in the area. A strenuous 2.5-mile trail leads to the top of Saddle Mountain, from which there are breathtaking views up and down the coast. In the spring, rare wildflowers are abundant along this trail. The trail is steep and rocky, so wear sturdy shoes or boots and carry water.

WHERE TO DINE

Camp 18 Restaurant AMERICAN   There is no better place than this combination restaurant and logging museum to learn how logging was done in the days before clear-cutting. The restaurant is in a huge log lodge with lots of chain-saw art, axes for door handles, and a hollowed-out stump for a hostess desk. The restaurant's 85-foot-long ridge pole (the log beam that runs along the inside of the peak of the roof) is the largest of its kind in the country, and weighs 25 tons. There are also stone fireplaces and lots of old logging photos. After tucking into logger-size meals (don't miss the marionberry cobbler), you can wander the grounds studying old steam logging equipment. Oh, and the food? Basic steak and seafood, mostly fried, with a few pasta and chicken dishes thrown in.

42362 U.S. 26 (Milepost 18, 22 miles east of Seaside). 🕐 800/874-1810 or 503/755-1818. Main courses $5.25–$13 lunch, $14–$23 dinner. AE, DISC, MC, V. Daily 7am–8pm.

4 Tillamook County

75 miles W of Portland, 51 miles S of Seaside, 44 miles N of Lincoln City

Although this is one of the closest stretches of coast to Portland, it is not a major destination because there are no large beachfront towns in the area. The town of Tillamook, which lies inland from the Pacific at the south end of Tillamook Bay, is the area's commercial center, but it is the surrounding farmland that has made Tillamook County famous in Oregon. Ever since the first settlers arrived in Tillamook in 1851, dairy farming has been the mainstay of the economy, and today large herds of contented cows graze in the area's odiferous fields. With no beaches to attract visitors, the town of Tillamook has managed to turn its dairy industry into a tourist attraction. No, this isn't the cow-watching capital of Oregon, but the town's cheese factory is now one of the most popular stops along the Oregon coast. Most of the milk produced by area cows goes to the Tillamook County Creamery Association's cheese factory, which turns out a substantial share of the cheese consumed in Oregon.

Although the town of Tillamook has no beaches, there are a few beachside hamlets in the area that offer a variety of accommodations, activities, and dining options. Tillamook is also the starting point for the scenic Three Capes Loop, which links three state parks and plenty of great coastal scenery. By the way, Tillamook is a mispronunciation of the word *Killamook,* which was the name of the Native American tribe that once lived in this area. The name is now applied to a county, a town, and a bay.

ESSENTIALS

GETTING THERE   Tillamook is on U.S. 101 at the junction with Ore. 6, which leads to Portland.

VISITOR INFORMATION   For more information on the area, contact the **Tillamook Area Chamber of Commerce,** 3705 U.S. 101 N., Tillamook, OR 97141 (© 503/842-7525; www.tillamookchamber.org); or the **Nehalem Bay Area Chamber of Commerce,** P.O. Box 601, Wheeler, OR 97147 (© 877/368-5100; www.nehalembay chamber.com).

MANZANITA

As the crowds have descended on Cannon Beach, people seeking peace and quiet and a slower pace have migrated south to the community of Manzanita. Located south of Neahkanie Mountain, Manzanita enjoys a setting similar to Cannon Beach but without the many haystack rocks. There isn't much to do except walk on the beach and relax, which is exactly why most people come here.

The beach at Manzanita stretches for 5 miles from the base of Neahkanie Mountain to the mouth of the Nehalem River and is a favorite of both surfers and windsurfers. The latter have the option of sailing either in the oceanfront waves or in the quieter waters of Nehalem Bay, which is just across Nehalem Spit from the ocean. Access to both the bay and the beach is provided at **Nehalem Bay State Park** (© 503/368-5154; www.oregonstateparks.org), which is just south of Manzanita and encompasses all of Nehalem Spit. The park, which includes a campground (and an airstrip), has a 2-mile paved bike path, a horse camp, and horse trails. The day-use fee is $3. During the summer, horseback rides are usually available here in the park. Out at the south end of the spit, more than 50 harbor seals can often be seen basking on the beach. To reach the seal area requires a 5-mile round-trip hike. Alternatively, you can take a brief seal-watching boat excursion through **Jetty Fishery** (see below).

If you absolutely must do something while you're here, you could play a round of golf on the meandering fairways of the 9-hole **Manzanita Golf Course,** Lake View Drive (© 503/368-5744), which charges $18 for 9 holes.

WHERE TO STAY

If you want to rent a vacation house in Manzanita, contact **Manzanita Rental Company,** 686 Manzanita Ave. (P.O. Box 162), Manzanita, OR 97130 (© 800/579-9801 or 503/368-6797; www.manzanitarentals.com).

Coast Cabins ★★ *(Finds)*   These five modern cabins are set back a ways from the beach but are the most impressive cabins on the entire coast. Done in a sort of modern interpretation of Scandinavian cabins, these accommodations are designed as romantic getaways for couples. Two of the cabins are tall, two-story structures, and the second-floor bedrooms have walls of windows. The cabin interiors are well designed and artfully decorated, with such touches as Tibetan carpets, original art, and unusual lighting fixtures. Now imagine the burnished glow of the cabins' cedar exteriors accented by lovely terraced perennial gardens, and you'll have an idea of just how the perfect getaway on the Oregon coast should look.

635 Laneda Ave., Manzanita, OR 97130. © 503/368-7113. www.coastcabins.com. 5 units. $155–$395 double. 2-night minimum on weekends and throughout the summer. AE, MC, V. Pets accepted ($30 deposit plus $25 per night). **Amenities:** Sauna. *In room:* TV/VCR/DVD, kitchen, fridge, microwave, coffeemaker, hair dryer, iron, free local calls, high-speed Internet access, Wi-Fi.

The Inn at Manzanita ⟨*⟩ Searching for an unforgettably romantic spot for a weekend getaway? This is it. Right in the heart of Manzanita, the Inn at Manzanita is a great place to celebrate a special event. All the rooms have double whirlpool tubs and fireplaces, and most rooms have balconies. The weathered cedar-shingle siding blends unobtrusively with the natural vegetation, and the grounds are planted with beautiful flowers for much of the year.

67 Laneda Ave. (P.O. Box 243), Manzanita, OR 97130. © 503/368-6754. Fax 503/368-5941. www.innatmanzanita.com. 14 units. $150–$180 double (Oct–May $120–$135 midweek); $385 penthouse suite (Oct–May $295 midweek). 2-night minimum on weekends and July 1 to Labor Day; 3 nights on holidays. AE, DISC, MC, V. **Amenities:** Bike rentals; concierge. *In room:* TV/VCR/DVD, fridge, coffeemaker, hair dryer, free local calls, Wi-Fi.

WHERE TO DINE

Do not visit Manzanita without buying some bread, pastries, or a sandwich from **Bread and Ocean,** 154 Laneda Ave. (© 503/368-5823; www.breadandocean.com). This little hole-in-the-wall is deservedly Manzanita's most popular lunch spot. For lattes and the latest news, head to **Manzanita News & Espresso,** 500 Laneda Ave. (© 503/368-7450). For fresh and smoked seafood to go, or for a light meal, stop in at **Manzanita Seafood & Chowder House,** 519 Laneda Ave. (© 503/368-CRAB). At the end of the day, wind down at **Vino Manzanita,** 387-D Laneda Ave. (© 503/368-VINO), a hip little wine bar.

WHEELER

Located on Nehalem Bay, this wide spot in the road has long been popular for crabbing and fishing. However, in recent years it has also become a favorite for sea-kayaking. The marshes of the bay provide plenty of meandering waterways to explore, and several miles of the Nehalem River can also be easily paddled if the tides are in your favor. You can rent a sea kayak at **Wheeler Marina,** 278 Marine Dr. (© 503/368-5780; www. neahkahnie.net/wheelermarina), right on the waterfront in Wheeler or at adjacent **Wheeler on the Bay Lodge & Marina,** 580 Marine Dr. (© 800/469-3204 or 503/368-5858; www.wheeleronthebay.com). Rates range from around $22 to $28 per hour and from $44 to $50 per day; higher rates are for double kayaks.

If you're interested in trying your hand at crabbing, contact **Jetty Fishery** (© 503/368-5746; www.jettyfishery.com), located just south of Wheeler at the mouth of the Nehalem River. They rent boats and crab rings and offer dock crabbing. The folks here also offer a ferry service ($10 per person) across the river to Nehalem Bay State Park, where you can often see dozens of harbor seals lying on the beach. You can also sometimes see seals close up if you sit on the jetty rocks at nearby Neadonna, which is just south of Jetty Fishery.

You can also arrange to go out fishing for salmon or sturgeon with **Nehalem Bay Charters** (© 503/368-5858 or 503/812-6833; www.wheeleronthebay.com), which charges $80 per person for a half day of fishing or $140 for a full day.

WHERE TO STAY

The Nehalem River Inn *(Finds)*   The Oregon coast is not just about beaches and rocky headlands; it's also about meandering tidal rivers, and this country inn is set on just such a river. Situated a couple of miles off U.S. 101 between Nehalem and Wheeler, the inn is a hideaway par excellence. You can choose among rooms, suites, or a cottage, and all of the accommodations have been recently remodeled and updated with a stylish contemporary look. The inn has an excellent restaurant that uses organic ingredients as much as possible. One caveat: This valley has dairy farms and, to be polite, the air can be somewhat fragrant at times.

34910 Ore. 53, Nehalem, OR 97131. © **503/368-7708.** www.nehalemriverinn.com. 5 units. Summer $99–$175 double; other months $79–$150 double. MC, V. **Amenities:** Restaurant (Northwest); access to nearby health club; bike rentals. *In room:* TV/VCR, coffeemaker, hair dryer, high-speed Internet access, Wi-Fi.

Wheeler on the Bay Lodge & Marina   Located right on the shore of Nehalem Bay, this is one of the north coast's most economical waterfront lodges. It's not fancy, but the bayfront location is great. The Honeymoon Room, the best room here, has walls of glass looking onto the bay, a private deck, a fireplace, and, best of all, a whirlpool tub with great views. Six of the rooms have spas, and most of these have water views. All the rooms sport distinctive decor. Kayak rentals and fishing charters make this an ideal spot for active vacationers.

580 Marine Dr. (P.O. Box 580), Wheeler, OR 97147. © **800/469-3204** or 503/368-5858. www.wheeleronthebay.com. 10 units. $80–$155 double. Children 15 and under stay free in parent's room. MC, V. Pets accepted ($10 per night). **Amenities:** Kayak rentals; massage. *In room:* TV/VCR/DVD, dataport, fridge, microwave, coffeemaker, hair dryer, free local calls.

CAMPGROUNDS

At **Nehalem Bay State Park,** there are yurts as well as plenty of campsites. To make reservations, contact **ReserveAmerica** (© **800/452-5687;** www.reserveamerica.com).

WHERE TO DINE

If you like smoked salmon, don't miss **Karla's Smokehouse** ✪, 2010 U.S. 101 N. (© **503/355-2362**), which is at the north end of nearby Rockaway Beach and sells some of the best smoked fish and oysters on the coast. For the best breakfasts in Tillamook County, head to **Wanda's Café & Bakery** (© **503/368-8100**), which is right on U.S. 101 in Nehalem (watch for it on the left as you come down the hill from Manzanita).

Nehalem River Inn ✪ *(Finds)* FRENCH/NORTHWEST   Set on the banks of the Nehalem River, this restaurant, part of a secluded little country inn, serves some of the best food on the Oregon coast. The menu is contemporary, and although it changes with the seasons, you might start your meal with roasted garlic and butternut squash soup with nutmeg crème fraiche or house-cured Gravlax salmon with orange, goat cheese, fennel, and red onion. For an entree, try the succulent filet mignon, which might be accompanied by truffled gnocchi and a balsamic reduction. The hidden-away location and high caliber of the meals make this restaurant a real find.

34910 Ore. 53 (less than 3 miles off U.S. 101). © **503/368-7708.** www.nehalemriverinn.com. Reservations highly recommended. Main courses $27–$33. MC, V. Thurs–Mon 5:30–8 or 8:30pm. No children under 12.

GARIBALDI

Named (by the local postmaster) in 1879 for Italian patriot Giuseppi Garibaldi, this little town is at the north end of Tillamook Bay and is the region's main sportfishing and crabbing port. If you've got an urge to do some salmon or bottom fishing, this is the place to book a trip. Try **Garibaldi Charters** (© **800/900-HOOK** or 503/322-0007; www.garibaldicharters.com), which charges between $75 and $95 for a full day of salmon fishing. Deep-sea halibut fishing will run you about $165 per day. **Whale-watching** and **bird-watching** trips are also offered. At the **Garibaldi Marina,** 302 Mooring Basin Rd. (© **800/383-3828** or 503/322-3312; www.garibaldimarina. com), you can rent boats, tackle, and crab rings, if you want to do some fishing or crabbing on your own.

Garibaldi is also where you'll find the depot for the **Oregon Coast Scenic Railroad** (© **503/842-7972;** www.ocsr.net), an excursion train that runs along some of the most scenic portions of this section of coast. The train usually runs weekends during the summer. Call to see if it's operating when you visit. The round-trip fare is $13 to $16 for adults and $7 to $10 for children ages 3 to 10.

Also here in Garibaldi, you'll find the fascinating little **Garibaldi Museum,** 112 Garibaldi Ave. (U.S. 101; © **503/322-8411;** www.garibaldimuseum.com), a small, privately owned maritime museum that focuses on the history of Tillamook Bay and Captain Robert Gray, the American ship's captain who discovered the Columbia River. The museum is open May through October Thursday through Monday from noon to 4pm. Admission is $3 for adults and $2.50 for seniors and children 5 to 18.

TILLAMOOK

Tillamook has long been known as one of Oregon's foremost dairy regions, and Tillamook cheese is ubiquitous in the state. So it's no surprise that the **Tillamook Cheese Factory,** 4175 Hwy. 101 N. (© **800/542-7290** or 503/815-1300; www. tillamookcheese.com), located just north of Tillamook, is the most popular tourist attraction in town. Visitors can observe the cheese-making process (cheddars are the specialty), and there's also a large store where all manner of cheeses and other edible gifts are available. From mid-June to Labor Day, the factory is open daily from 8am to 8pm, and from Labor Day to mid-June, it's open 8am to 6pm.

If the Tillamook Cheese Factory seems too crowded for you, head back toward town a mile and you'll see the **Blue Heron Cheese & Wine Company,** 2001 Blue Heron Dr. (© **800/275-0639** or 503/842-8281; www.blueheronoregon.com), which is on the same side of U.S. 101 as the Tillamook Cheese Factory. Located in a big old dairy barn with a flagstone floor, this store stocks the same sort of comestibles as the Tillamook Cheese Factory, though the emphasis here is on brie (which, however, is not made locally). Farm animals make this a good stop for kids. Blue Heron is open daily from 8am to 8pm in summer and 9am to 6pm in winter.

Quilters and other fiber-arts aficionados will want to visit the **Latimer Quilt & Textile Center,** 2105 Wilson River Loop (© **503/842-8622;** www.latimerquiltand textile.com), which is housed in a 1930s schoolhouse. The center has a large collection of textiles and mounts a variety of exhibits throughout the year. May through September, the center is open daily from 10am to 5pm; October through April, it's open Tuesday through Saturday from 10am to 4pm and Sunday from noon to 4pm (Nov–Feb also closed Sun). Admission is $2.50 for adults, $2 for seniors, and $1 for children age 12 to 17. The **Tillamook County Pioneer Museum,** 2106 Second St. (© **503/842-4553;** www.tcpm.org), is also worth a visit for its reproduction tree-stump house and interesting natural-history exhibit. The museum is open Tuesday through Saturday from 9am to 5pm and Sunday from 11am to 5pm. Admission is $3 for adults, $2.50 for seniors.

To learn more about the forests and 20th-century forest fires in the nearby Coast Range, visit the fascinating **Tillamook Forest Center,** 45500 Wilson River Hwy. (© **503/815-6800;** www.tillamookforestcenter.org). This modern interpretive center tells the story of massive forest fires that devastated this area four times in the middle of the 20th century. After the fires, it took decades of intensive replanting to bring these forests back to the lush woodlands you see today. At the center, there is a reproduction of a fire lookout tower and access to the Wilson River Trail. In summer, the center is open daily from 10am to 5pm (other months it's open Wed–Sun 10am–4pm).

A hangar built during World War II for a fleet of navy blimps is 2 miles south of town off U.S. 101 and lays claim to being the largest freestanding wooden building in the world. Statistics bear this out: It's 296 feet wide, 1,072 feet long, and 192 feet high. The blimp hangar now houses the **Tillamook Air Museum,** 6030 Hangar Rd. (© **503/842-1130;** www.tillamookair.com), which contains more than 30 restored vintage planes, including a P-51 Mustang, an F4U-7 Corsair, and an F-14A Tomcat. The museum is open daily from 9am to 5pm. Admission is $11 for adults, $10 for seniors, and $6.50 for youths 6 to 17.

Between April and September, you can go up in a small plane to see this section of the coast, and you may even see whales. Contact **Tillamook Scenic Air Tours** (© **503/ 842-1942;** www.tillamookairtours.com), which offers tours in a restored 1942 Stinson Reliant V-77 plane and a 1928 Travel Air open cockpit two-passenger biplane. Flights start at $63 per person if you have four people in your group.

Anglers interested in going after salmon or steelhead in Tillamook Bay or area rivers should contact **Fishing Oregon** (© **503/842-5171;** www.fish-oregon.com).

WHERE TO DINE

If you need to stock up your larder for the beach house or are on your way back from a weekend at the beach, don't miss an opportunity to stop in at **Bear Creek Artichokes** (© **503/398-5411**), which is located 11 miles south of Tillamook on U.S. 101. This is one of the few commercial artichoke farms in Oregon and usually has fresh artichokes throughout the summer and fall. The farm stand has lots of other great produce, as well as jams, mustards, and salsas.

THE THREE CAPES SCENIC LOOP

The **Three Capes Scenic Loop** begins just west of downtown Tillamook and leads past Cape Meares, Cape Lookout, and Cape Kiwanda. Together these capes offer some of the most spectacular views on the northern Oregon coast. All three capes are state parks, and all make great whale-watching spots in the spring or storm-watching spots in the winter. To start the loop, follow Third Street out of town and watch for the right turn for Cape Meares State Scenic Viewpoint. This road will take you along the shore of Tillamook Bay and around the north side of Cape Meares, where the resort town of Bayocean once stood. Built early in the 20th century by developers with a dream to create the Atlantic City of the West, Bayocean was constructed at the end of a sand spit that often felt the full force of winter storms. When Bayocean homes began falling into the ocean, folks realized that this wasn't going to be the next Atlantic City. Today there's no sign of the town, but the long sandy beach along the spit is a great place for a walk and a bit of bird-watching.

Just around the tip of the cape, you'll come to **Cape Meares State Scenic Viewpoint,** which is the site of the **Cape Meares Lighthouse** (www.capemeareslighthouse. org). April through October, the lighthouse is open daily from 11am to 4pm. The views from atop this rocky headland are superb. Continuing around the cape, you come to the residential community of **Oceanside,** from where you have an excellent view of the **Three Arch Rocks** just offshore. The beach at Oceanside is a popular spot and is often protected from the wind in the summer. At the north end of the beach, a pedestrian tunnel leads under a headland to a secluded beach.

Three miles south of Oceanside, you'll come to tiny **Netarts Bay,** which is known for its excellent clamming and crabbing. Continuing south, you come to **Cape Lookout State Park** *(★★ (𝒞 503/842-4981;* www.oregonstateparks.org), which has a campground, picnic areas, beaches, and several miles of hiking trails. The most breathtaking trail leads 2.5 miles out to the end of Cape Lookout, where, from several hundred feet above the ocean, you can often spot gray whales in the spring and fall. There is a $3 day-use fee here.

Cape Kiwanda *(★★,* which lies just outside the town of Pacific City, is the last of the three capes and is preserved as Cape Kiwanda State Natural Area. At the foot of the cape's sandstone cliffs, you'll find sand dunes and tide pools, and it's possible to scramble up a huge sand dune to the top of the cape for dramatic views of this rugged piece of shoreline. At the base of the cape is the staging area for Pacific City's beach-launched dory fleet. These flat-bottomed commercial fishing boats are launched from the beach and plow through crashing breakers to get out to calmer waters beyond. When the day's fishing is done, the dories roar into shore at full throttle and come to a grinding stop as high up on the beach as they can. This is Oregon's only such fishing fleet and is celebrated each year during the annual Dory Derby on the third weekend in July. If you'd like to go out in one of theses dories and fish for salmon or albacore tuna, contact **Haystack Fishing** (𝒞 **866/965-7555** or 503/965-7555; www. haystackfishing.com), which charges anywhere from $105 to $190 for a day of fishing. Trips are offered June through September.

WHERE TO STAY
In Pacific City
Inn at Cape Kiwanda *(★★ (Finds*   Although it's across the street from the beach (and Cape Kiwanda State Natural Area), this modern cedar-shingled three-story hotel has one of the best views on the Oregon coast: Directly offshore rises Haystack Rock, a huge jug-handled monolith. Since a great view isn't quite enough, the hotel was designed with contemporary rooms, all of which have balconies and fireplaces. A few have whirlpool tubs, and there is also a very luxurious suite. The corner rooms are my favorites. The inn also rents out modern timeshare cottages that are right on the beach. The inn is affiliated with the Pelican Pub & Brewery, which is right across the street, and on the inn's ground floor there is an art gallery and an espresso bar.

33105 Cape Kiwanda Dr., Pacific City, OR 97135. 𝒞 888/965-7001 or 503/965-7001. Fax 503/965-7002. www. innatcapekiwanda.com. 35 units. $129–$279 double; $209–$329 suite. 2-night minimum on holidays, and on weekends July–Aug. Children under 18 stay free in parent's room. AE, DC, DISC, MC, V. Pets accepted ($20). **Amenities:** Restaurant (brewpub); lounge; exercise room; bike rentals; concierge; business center; room service; coin-op laundry. *In room:* TV/DVD, fridge, coffeemaker, hair dryer, free local calls, high-speed Internet access, Wi-Fi.

CAMPGROUNDS
Cape Lookout State Park is the largest campground along the Three Capes Loop. For reservations, contact **ReserveAmerica** (𝒞 **800/452-5687;** www.reserveamerica.com). **Whalen Island County Park,** on the south side of Sand Lake just off Sand Lake Road, is a smaller and less crowded alternative (though it's not right on the ocean).

WHERE TO DINE
In Oceanside
Roseanna's Oceanside Café SEAFOOD/INTERNATIONAL Roseanna's is such a Scenic Loop legend that people come from miles around to eat here and don't seem to mind the dated decor or the long waits to get a table. What lure them are the views of the beach and offshore rocks, and the selection of big desserts. Appetizers and entrees often seem to be just an afterthought. Lunch prices are reasonable, with such offerings as cioppino and oyster sandwiches. At dinner, entrees include a choice of shellfish or fish with a choice of sauces (apricot-ginger glaze, aioli, or spicy garlic-chile, for example). The wait for a table can be long, so if you just want dessert or a quick snack, grab a stool at the counter.

1490 Pacific Ave. (C) **503/842-7351.** Main courses $7.25–$13 lunch, $15–$18 dinner. MC, V. Daily 10am–9pm (may close 1 hr. earlier in winter).

In Pacific City
For tasty baked goods and lunches, stop in at **The Grateful Bread Bakery & Restaurant,** 34805 Brooten Rd. ((C) **503/965-7337**), with tables both inside and out on a deck. If you enjoy good books and good coffee you'll appreciate **Migrations,** 33105 Cape Kiwanda Dr. ((C) **503/965-4661**), which is located on the ground floor of the Inn at Cape Kiwanda.

Pelican Pub & Brewery ⚘ PUB FOOD With massive Haystack Rock looming just offshore and the huge dune of Cape Kiwanda just up the beach, this oceanfront brewpub claims the best view of any pub in Oregon. There's a good selection of brews, including Tsunami Stout and my personal favorite, the Doryman's Dark Ale. Sandwiches, burgers, great fish and chips, and pizzas are the menu mainstays here. Kids are welcome, and the beach location makes this a great spot for lunch or dinner if you're hanging out on the beach all day.

33180 Cape Kiwanda Dr. (C) **503/965-7007.** www.pelicanbrewery.com. Main courses $9–$26. AE, DISC, MC, V. Sun–Thurs 8am–10pm; Fri–Sat 8am–11pm.

The Riverhouse AMERICAN This tiny place is built on the banks of the Nestucca River and has great river views out its many windows. With its casual, friendly atmosphere, The Riverhouse has the feel of a place that time and contemporary fads have passed by. Although burgers and sandwiches are the order of the day at lunch, the dinner menu features prawns in a creamy wine sauce; fresh fish amandine; halibut basted with butter, lemon pepper, and dill; filet mignon, and crepes Florentine. Be sure to check out the photos of the 1999 flood that caused this restaurant to be raised up to the second floor.

34450 Brooten Rd. (C) **503/965-6722.** Main courses $7.50–$27. MC, V. Daily 11am–9pm (in winter, closes at 8pm Sun–Thurs).

NESKOWIN
The quaint little community of Neskowin is nestled at the northern foot of Cascade Head, 12 miles north of Lincoln City. Inland families have spent their summers in these tiny cottages and tree-lined lanes for decades. Quiet vacations are the norm in Neskowin, where you'll find only condominiums and rental houses. The beach is accessible at **Neskowin Beach State Recreation Site,** which faces Proposal Rock, a tree-covered haystack rock bordered by Neskowin Creek. On the beach, keep an eye out for the stumps of trees that died hundreds of years ago when an earthquake lowered the shoreline in this area.

If you're interested in art, check out the **Hawk Creek Gallery,** 48460 U.S. 101 S. (*©* **503/392-3879;** www.hawkcreekgallery.com), which features the paintings of Michael Schlicting, a master watercolorist.

Just to the south of Neskowin is rugged, unspoiled **Cascade Head.** Rising 1,770 feet above sea level, this is one of the highest headlands on the coast. Lush forests of Sitka spruce and windswept cliff-top meadows thrive here and are home to such diverse flora and fauna that the Nature Conservancy purchased much of the headland. Trails onto Cascade Head start about 2 miles south of Neskowin. The Nature Conservancy's preserve has been set aside primarily to protect the habitat of the rare Oregon silverspot butterfly; the upper trail is closed from January 1 to July 15 due to the timing of the butterflies' life cycle. However, a lower trail, reached from Three Rocks Road (park at Knight Park and walk up Savage Rd. to the trail head), is open year-round.

On the south side of Cascade Head, you'll find the **Sitka Center for Art and Ecology,** P.O. Box 65, Otis, OR 97368 (*©* **541/994-5485;** www.sitkacenter.org), which runs classes and workshops on writing, painting, ecology, ceramics, and other topics.

WHERE TO STAY

There are numerous vacation cottages and beach houses for rent in Neskowin. Contact **Sea View Vacation Rentals,** 6340 Pacific Ave. (P.O. Box 1049), Pacific City, OR 97135 (*©* **888/701-1023** or 503/965-7888; www.seaview4u.com), or **Grey Fox Vacation Rentals,** P.O. Box 364, Neskowin, OR 97149 (*©* **888/720-2154** or 503/392-4355; www.oregoncoast.com/greyfox).

5 Lincoln City/Gleneden Beach

88 miles SW of Portland, 44 miles S of Tillamook, 25 miles N of Newport

Lincoln City is the Oregon coast's number-one family destination, and, despite the name, it is not really a city at all. It's a collection of five small towns that grew together over the years and that now stretch for miles along the coast. Today there's no specific downtown, and though there may be more motel rooms here than anywhere else on the Oregon coast, there's little to distinguish most of the thousands of rooms. However, families looking for a long beach and steady winds for flying kites will likely enjoy Lincoln City. Motel rates here, though often high for what you get, are generally better than those in beach towns that are longer on charm, and you'll find an abundance of vacation homes for rent, too. Likewise, restaurants catering to big families and small pocketbooks are the norm. Such restaurants purvey hot meals rather than haute cuisine, and you can eat your fill of seafood without going broke.

Once referred to as "20 miracle miles," Lincoln City is no longer the miracle it once was. Miracle miles have become congested sprawl, and a summer weekend in Lincoln City can mean coping with bumper-to-bumper traffic. Not surprisingly, many have come to think of this as "20 miserable miles." If at all possible, come during the week or during the off season to avoid the crowds.

Once you get off U.S. 101, though, Lincoln City has neighborhoods as charming as any on the coast, and at the south end of town, in the Taft District, the city has been working hard to bring back a historical character and provide an attractive, pedestrian-friendly area. In Gleneden Beach just south of Lincoln City, you'll find the coast's most prestigious resort. Also in the Lincoln City area are some of Oregon's best art galleries and some interesting artists' studios.

ESSENTIALS

GETTING THERE   Ore. 22 from Salem merges with Ore. 18 before reaching the junction with U.S. 101. From Portland, take Ore. 99W to McMinnville and then head west on Ore. 18.

VISITOR INFORMATION   For more information on the area, contact the **Lincoln City Visitor and Convention Bureau,** 801 SW U.S. 101, Suite 1, Lincoln City, OR 97367 (© **800/452-2151** or 541/996-1274; www.oregoncoast.org).

FESTIVALS   Annual **kite festivals** include the Summer Kite Festival in late June and the Fall Kite Festival in mid-October. In addition, Lincoln City hosts the annual **Cascade Head Music Festival** (www.cascadeheadmusic.org) in mid- to late June, and in August there's the annual **Sandcastle Building Contest.** On the nearby Siletz Indian Reservation, the **Nesika Illahee,** the annual Siletz Pow Wow, takes place on the second weekend in August.

ENJOYING THE BEACH & THE OUTDOORS

Lincoln City's 7½-mile-long **beach** is its main attraction. However, cold waters and constant breezes conspire to make swimming a pursuit for Polar Bear Club members only. The winds, on the other hand, make this beach the best kite-flying spot on the Oregon coast. If you didn't bring your own kite, you can buy one at **Catch the Wind,** 240 SE U.S. 101 (© **800/227-7878** or 541/994-9500; www.catchthewind.com). Among the better beach-access points are the D River State Wayside, on the south side of the river, and the Road's End State Wayside, up at the north end of Lincoln City. Road's End is also a good place to explore some tide pools. You'll find more tide pools on the beach at Northwest 15th Street and at Southwest 32nd Street.

Adding to the appeal of Lincoln City's beach is **Devil's Lake,** which drains across the beach by way of the D River, the world's shortest river. Formerly called Devil's River, the D River is only 120 feet long, flowing from the outlet of Devil's Lake, under U.S. 101, and across the beach to the Pacific Ocean. Boating, sailing, water-skiing, windsurfing, swimming, fishing, and camping are all popular Devil's Lake activities. Access points on the west side of the lake include **Devil's Lake State Recreation Area (West),** NE Sixth Street (© **541/994-2002;** www.oregonstateparks.org), which has a campground, and **Regatta Grounds Park,** which is off West Devil's Lake Road and has a boat ramp and picnic tables. On the east side you'll find **Devil's Lake State Park (East)** 2 miles east on East Devil's Lake Road, and **Sand Point Park** on View Point Lane near the north end of East Devil's Lake Road. Both of these parks have picnic tables and swimming areas. If you don't have your own boat, you can rent canoes, kayaks, paddleboats, aquabikes, and various motorboats at **Blue Heron Landing,** 4008 W. Devil's Lake Rd. (© **541/994-4708**). Rates range from $10 an hour for a kayak up to $90 for a 2-hour personal watercraft rental. You'll also find bumper boats here at Blue Heron Landing.

If you're a gardener or enjoy visiting public gardens, schedule time to visit the **Connie Hansen Garden,** 1931 NW 33rd St. (© **541/994-6338;** www.conniehansengarden.com). This cottage garden was created over a 20-year period and abounds in primroses, irises, and rhododendrons, making it a great place to visit in the spring. The gardens are open daily from dawn to dusk. Call for directions.

Golfers have two options. The top choice is the Scottish-inspired (though solidly Northwestern in character) **Salishan Spa & Golf Resort** *✦*, 7760 U.S. 101, Gleneden Beach (© **541/764-3632;** www.salishan.com), which charges $79 to $119 for 18

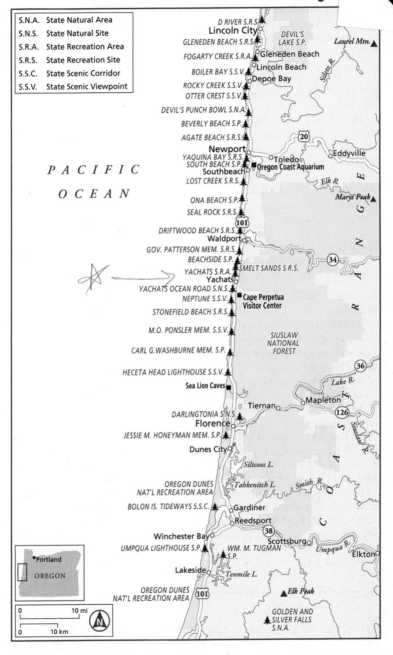

S.N.A.   State Natural Area
S.N.S.   State Natural Site
S.R.A.   State Recreation Area
S.R.S.   State Recreation Site
S.S.C.   State Scenic Corridor
S.S.V.   State Scenic Viewpoint

D RIVER S.R.S.
Lincoln City
GLENEDEN BEACH S.R.S.
FOGARTY CREEK S.R.A.
BOILER BAY S.S.V.
ROCKY CREEK S.S.V.
OTTER CREST S.S.V.
DEVIL'S PUNCH BOWL S.N.A.
BEVERLY BEACH S.P.
AGATE BEACH S.R.S.
Newport
YAQUINA BAY S.R.S.
SOUTH BEACH S.P.
Southbeach
LOST CREEK S.R.S.
ONA BEACH S.P.
SEAL ROCK S.R.S.
DRIFTWOOD BEACH S.R.S.
Waldport
GOV. PATTERSON MEM. S.R.S.
BEACHSIDE S.P.
YACHATS S.R.A.
Yachats
YACHATS OCEAN ROAD S.N.S.
NEPTUNE S.S.V.
STONEFIELD BEACH S.R.S.
M.O. PONSLER MEM. S.S.V.
CARL G. WASHBURNE MEM. S.P.
HECETA HEAD LIGHTHOUSE S.S.V.
Sea Lion Caves
DARLINGTONIA S.N.S.
Florence
JESSIE M. HONEYMAN MEM. S.P.
Dunes City
OREGON DUNES
NAT'L RECREATION AREA
BOLON IS. TIDEWAYS S.S.C.
Winchester Bay
UMPQUA LIGHTHOUSE S.P.
Lakeside
OREGON DUNES
NAT'L RECREATION AREA

DEVIL'S
LAKE S.P.
Gleneden Beach
Lincoln Beach
Depoe Bay

Laurel Mtn.

Silver R.

20
Eddyville

Toledo
Oregon Coast Aquarium

Elk R.
Marys Peak

101

SMELT SANDS S.R.S.
Cape Perpetua
Visitor Center

34

SIUSLAW
NATIONAL
FOREST

36
Lake R.

Tiernan
Mapleton
126

Siuslaw R.

Siltcoos L.
Tahkenitch L.   Smith R.

Gardiner
Reedsport
38   Scottsburg
WM. M. TUGMAN   Umpqua R.   Elkton
S.P.

Tenmile L.

Elk Peak

GOLDEN AND
SILVER FALLS
S.N.A.

PACIFIC

OCEAN

Portland

OREGON

0   10 mi

0   10 km

N

holes. This resort course is a longtime Oregon coast favorite. The town's other main course is the **Chinook Winds Golf Resort,** 3245 NE 50th St. (© **541/994-8442;** www.chinookwindscasino.com), which is affiliated with Chinook Winds Casino. This course charges $35 to $50 for 18 holes.

If you want to challenge the waves, you can rent a wetsuit, surfboard, or body board down at the south end of town at the **Lincoln City Surf Shop,** 4792 SE U.S. 101 (© **541/996-7433;** www.lcsurfshop.com); or the **Oregon Surf Shop,** 4933 SW U.S. 101 (© **541/996-3957;** www.oregonsurfshop.com).

Hikers should head inland approximately 10 miles to **Drift Creek Falls Trail** *,* which leads through coastal forest to a 240-foot-long suspension bridge above a 75-foot-tall waterfall. From the bridge you have a bird's-eye view not only of the falls but of the treetops as well. It's a 1.3-mile hike to the bridge, and the route is moderately difficult. To find the trail head (Northwest Forest Pass is required), head east from U.S. 101 on Drift Creek Road, which is just north of Salishan lodge at the south end of Lincoln City. Turn right onto South Drift Creek Road and then left onto Forest Road 17 (not Anderson Creek Rd.) and continue 10 miles on this single-lane road.

Sharing a name with this hiking trail is a historic covered bridge—the **Drift Creek Bridge.** Completely restored a few years back, this covered bridge was built in 1933 and is 66 feet long. To find the bridge, drive east from Lincoln City on Ore. 18; at milepost 4.9, turn south onto Bear Creek Road, and continue 1 mile to the bridge.

INDOOR PURSUITS

These days the hottest thing in town is the **Chinook Winds Casino,** 1777 NW 45th St. (© **888/CHINOOK** or 541/996-5825; www.chinookwindscasino.com), a massive casino run by the Confederated Tribes of Siletz Indians and located right on the beach at the north end of town. The casino offers blackjack, poker, slot machines, keno, and bingo. There's plenty of cheap food, as well as a video-game room for the kids. Big-name entertainers help attract folks who might not otherwise consider visiting a casino.

You can catch live jazz at **Eden Hall,** 6645 Gleneden Beach Loop Rd., Gleneden (© **541/764-3826;** www.edenhall.com), a big club and restaurant just south of the Salishan Lodge.

The casino may actually be second in popularity to the **Tanger Outlet Center,** 1500 SE East Devils Lake Rd. (© **541/996-5000;** www.tangeroutlet.com), which is on the corner of U.S. 101. Among the many expected name-brand shops here, you'll also find the Chateau Benoit winery tasting room.

Lincoln City has a surprising number of interesting art galleries and artists' studios. At the north end of town, the first gallery you'll come to is the **Ryan Gallery,** 4270 N. U.S. 101 (© **541/994-5391;** www.ryanartgallery.com). Right in the heart of Lincoln City's main business strip, watch for the **Earthworks Gallery,** 620 NE U.S. 101 (© **541/557-4148**), which emphasizes ceramic and glass art, but also carries a variety of other fine crafts.

Fun Fact Finders Keepers

Each year between mid-October and Memorial Day, Lincoln City hides more than 2,000 art-glass balls, similar to the much-prized Japanese handblown glass fishing floats that sometimes drift ashore on this coast. Look above the high-tide line for the colorful globes of glass. Some are hidden each week.

South of Lincoln City proper, you'll find the impressive **Freed Gallery,** 6119 SW U.S. 101 (© **541/994-5600;** www.freedgallery.com), which has an excellent selection of art glass and ceramic work, as well as sculptures and paintings in a wide variety of styles. Just off U.S. 101, north of Salishan Resort, you'll find **Alder House III,** 611 Immonen Rd. (no phone; www.alderhouse.com), the oldest glassblowing studio in Oregon. The shop and studio are open daily from 10am to 5pm between mid-March and Thanksgiving weekend. Nearby, you'll also find **Mossy Creek Pottery,** 483 Immonen Rd. (© **541/996-2415;** www.mossycreekpottery.com), with an eclectic selection of porcelain and stoneware by Oregon potters.

WHERE TO STAY

In addition to the town's many hotels and motels, Lincoln City has plenty of vacation rental houses and apartments offering good deals, especially for families. For information, contact **Horizon Rentals** (© **800/995-2411** or 541/994-2226; www.horizon rentals.com) or **Pacific Retreats** (© **800/473-4833** or 541/994-4833; www.pacific retreats.com). Rates generally range from around $100 up to $400 nightly for houses for anywhere from 4 to 12 people.

EXPENSIVE

The O'dysius Hotel 🏵🏵 Although it seems a bit out of place, this hotel offers the sort of luxury you would expect from a downtown Portland historic hotel but with a beach right across the street. Traditional European styling dominates, and the lobby, with its antique furniture, has the feel of a very classy living room. It's here that the hotel serves its complimentary afternoon wine. Guest rooms have lots of nice touches, including slate entries, down comforters, Art Nouveau lamps, gas fireplaces, and VCRs. All the rooms have ocean views, and some have balconies. If you enjoy luxury but aren't into the golf-resort scene, this is definitely the place for you. For the best view, ask for a room on the fifth floor.

120 NW Inlet Court, Lincoln City, OR 97367. © **800/869-8069** or 541/994-4121. Fax 541/994-8160. www.odysius. com. 30 units. $159–$195 double; $225–$365 suite. Rates include continental breakfast. AE, DISC, MC, V. Children 12 and older welcome. Pets accepted ($10 per night). **Amenities:** Concierge; massage. *In room:* TV/DVD, dataport, minibar, coffeemaker, hair dryer, iron.

Salishan Spa & Golf Resort 🏵🏵🏵 *(Kids)* The largest resort on the coast, Salishan is nestled amid towering evergreens on a hillside at the south end of Siletz Bay. However, because the resort is almost half a mile from the beach and on the inland side of U.S. 101, it's more of a golf resort than a beach resort. An extensive network of walking paths meanders through the 760-acre grounds, and there are plenty of activities for kids. Guest rooms come in three sizes. Whichever size you opt for, try to get a second-floor room. Most of these have cathedral ceilings and stone fireplaces. For breathtaking views, you'll have to shell out top dollar for a deluxe or premier room. The Salishan Dining Room is one of the most upscale restaurants on the entire coast and has a superb wine collection.

7760 U.S. 101 N., Gleneden Beach, OR 97388. © **800/452-2300** or 541/764-3600. www.salishan.com. 205 units. $160–$230 double. AE, DC, DISC, MC, V. Pets accepted ($25). **Amenities:** 3 restaurants (Northwest, American); lounge; indoor pool; 18-hole golf course; 1 outdoor and 3 indoor tennis courts; exercise room; full-service spa; Jacuzzi; sauna; children's programs; game room; room service; massage; babysitting; laundry service; dry cleaning. *In room:* TV, dataport, fridge, coffeemaker, hair dryer, iron, high-speed Internet access.

The Starfish Manor Hotel 🏵🏵 This modern inn is located in a quiet neighborhood at the north end of Lincoln City away from the crowds and traffic, which gives it one of the best locations in town as far as I'm concerned. Large suites with gas fireplaces, two-person oceanview whirlpool tubs, and double-headed showers are perfect for romantic getaways. My favorite suites have their whirlpool tubs out on the balcony where you can listen to the crashing waves. This hotel is also affiliated with the nearby Nelscott Manor, Nantucket Inn, and the Beachfront Manor Hotel, all of which are equally good options.

2735 NW Inlet Ave., Lincoln City, OR 97367. © **800/972-6155** or 541/996-9300. www.onthebeachfront.com. 17 units. $159–$425 suite. AE, DISC, MC, V. No children under 12. **Amenities:** Coin-op laundry. In room: TV/DVD/VCR, kitchen, fridge, microwave, coffeemaker, hair dryer, iron, free local calls, Wi-Fi.

MODERATE

Looking Glass Inn ⊛   While most hotels that claim to be pet-friendly simply tolerate dogs, this hotel welcomes dogs with open arms. Bring your pooch with you, and your canine companion will get a basket with a water bowl and doggy treats at check in. But you too will be welcomed and you will likely enjoy this hotel even more than Fido does. Located in the historic Taft District across the street from Siletz Bay, the Looking Glass, with its cedar shingles and white trim, has a classic Cape Cod feel. Rooms are available with whirlpool tubs, balconies, or gas fireplaces.

861 SW 51st St., Lincoln City, OR 97367. © **800/843-4940** or 541/996-3996. www.lookingglass-inn.com. 30 units. July to Labor Day $129–$149 double, $139–$229 suite; Labor Day to June $89–$129 double, $129–$189 suite. Rates include continental breakfast. Children under 5 stay free in parent's room. AE, DISC, MC, V. Pets accepted ($10). In room: TV/VCR, dataport, fridge, coffeemaker, hair dryer, Wi-Fi.

Siletz Bay Lodge   Located at the south end of Lincoln City right on Siletz Bay, this modern motel is a particularly good choice for families but is also a good option for couples. Although the motel isn't on the ocean, it is on a driftwood-strewn beach that has quiet waters that are perfect for kids, and across the bay you can often see harbor seals lounging on the beach. About half of the standard rooms have balconies. Spa rooms and spa suites are also available if you happen to be in town for a romantic getaway.

1012 SW 51st St. (P.O. Box 952), Lincoln City, OR 97367. © **888/430-2100** or 541/996-6111. Fax 541/996-3992. www.siletzbaylodge.com. 44 units. Summer $138–$185 double, $155 suite; off season $79–$140 double, $130 suite. Rates include continental breakfast. Children under 13 stay free in parent's room. AE, DC, DISC, MC, V. **Amenities:** Jacuzzi; coin-op laundry. In room: TV/DVD, dataport, fridge, microwave, coffeemaker, hair dryer.

CAMPGROUNDS

There's a campground at **Devil's Lake State Recreation Area,** just off U.S. 101 north of the D River. To make reservations, contact **ReserveAmerica** (© **800/452-5687;** www.reserveamerica.com).

WHERE TO DINE

If you're looking for some good smoked salmon or smoked oysters, stop by **Mr. Bill's Village Smokehouse,** 2981 SW U.S. 101 (© **888/MR-BILLS;** www.mrbillsvillage smokehouse.com).

EXPENSIVE

Bay House ⊛⊛ NORTHWEST   With a big wall of glass overlooking Siletz Bay and Salishan Spit, the Bay House, between Lincoln City and Gleneden Beach, provides fine dining and dramatic sunsets (and good bird-watching if you're interested). There are snowy linens on the tables, and service is gracious. The menu here is the most creative on the central coast and changes seasonally to take advantage of fresh ingredients. A recent autumn menu included Oregon wild huckleberries in several dishes, including rack of lamb with huckleberry demi glace and parsnip gnocchi with huckleberry-braised duck.

5911 SW Hwy. 101. ⓒ 541/996-3222. www.bayhouserestaurant.com. Reservations recommended. Main courses $12–$15 lunch, $34–$53 dinner. AE, DISC, MC, V. Tues–Sat 11:30am–2pm and 5:30–9pm; Sun–Mon 5:30–9pm.

MODERATE

Blackfish Café ⓖ SEAFOOD   Located near the north end of Lincoln City, this restaurant has a big reputation for such a casual and unpretentious spot. The grilled prawn "martini" and Dungeness crab "margarita" (basically just seafood cocktails) make great starters. The menu includes everything from fish and chips to citrus-marinated breast of duck and sea bass with kalamata olive-pepper butter. Keep an eye out for any dish served with the Asian slaw, which is probably the most unusual slaw you'll ever taste. Lunches just might be the best on the entire coast.

2733 NW U.S. 101. ⓒ 541/996-1007. www.blackfishcafe.com. Reservations recommended. Main courses $9.50–$18. AE, MC, V. Wed–Thurs and Sun–Mon 11:30am–9pm; Fri–Sat noon–10pm.

Kyllo's Seafood Grill SEAFOOD   Providing a lively "beach party" atmosphere on a family-oriented beach, Kyllo's is housed in an architecturally unusual contemporary building with curved walls that make the restaurant impossible to miss. Inside, you'll find a big copper fireplace, plenty of deck space, and a facade of glass to take in the view of the D River and the ocean. If all this sounds like you're going to be paying for the atmosphere, think again. Prices are reasonable, and while none of the food is all that memorable, this is still the best oceanfront dining in town. Expect to wait for a table if you come here on a summer evening.

1110 NW First Court. ⓒ 541/994-3179. Main courses $8.50–$17 lunch, $14–$28 dinner. AE, DISC, MC, V. Sun–Thurs 11:30am–9pm; Fri–Sat 11am–10pm (closes 1 hr. earlier in winter).

INEXPENSIVE

Otis Café ⓕinds AMERICAN   If you've ever seen the determination with which urbanites flock to the beach on summer weekends, you can understand what a feat it is to get cars to stop before they have sand in the treads of their tires. This tiny roadside diner, 5 miles north of Lincoln City and 4 miles shy of the beach, manages to do just that with its black bread, cinnamon rolls, and fried red potatoes. The homemade mustard and salsa are also favorites. Pies—marionberry, strawberry/rhubarb, or walnut—have crusts to be savored only by people unconcerned with cholesterol and are memorable even in a region of numerous perfect pies. Expect a line out the screen door, even in the rainy season.

1259 Salmon River Hwy. (Ore. 18), Otis. ⓒ 541/994-2813. Breakfast, lunch, and dinner $5–$13. AE, DISC, MC, V. Sun–Thurs 7am–8pm; Fri–Sat 7am–9pm.

6 Depoe Bay

13 miles S of Lincoln City, 13 miles N of Newport, 70 miles W of Salem

Depoe Bay calls itself the smallest harbor in the world, and though the tiny harbor covers only 6 acres, it's home to more than 100 fishing boats. These boats must all enter the harbor through a narrow rock-walled channel, little more than a crack in the coastline's solid rock wall. During stormy seas, it's almost impossible to get in or out of the harbor safely.

Shell mounds and kitchen middens around the bay indicate that Native Americans long ago called this area home. In 1894, the U.S. government deeded the land surrounding the bay to a Siletz Indian known as Old Charlie Depot, who had taken his name from an army depot at which he had worked. Old Charlie later changed his name to DePoe, and when a town was founded here in 1927, it took the name Depoe Bay. Though most of the town is a bit off the highway, you'll find a row of garish souvenir shops right on U.S. 101, which sadly mar the beauty of this rocky section of coast. Among these shops are several family restaurants and charter-fishing and whale-watching companies.

ESSENTIALS

GETTING THERE   From the north, the most direct route is Ore. 99W/18 to Lincoln City, and then south on U.S. 101. From the south take U.S. 20 from Corvallis to Newport, and then go north on U.S. 101.

VISITOR INFORMATION   Contact the **Depoe Bay Chamber of Commerce,** 223 SW U.S. 101, Suite B (P.O. Box 21), Depoe Bay, OR 97341 (© **877/485-8348** or 541/765-2889; www.depoebaychamber.org).

FESTIVALS   Memorial Day is time for the **Fleet of Flowers,** during which local boats carry flower wreaths out to sea in memory of loved ones. In mid-September, the town holds its annual **Salmon Bake,** which is a great opportunity to enjoy some traditionally prepared salmon. Contact the chamber of commerce for details.

DEPOE BAY ACTIVITIES & ATTRACTIONS

Aside from standing on the highway bridge watching the boat traffic passing in and out of the world's smallest harbor, the most popular activity here, especially when the seas are high, is watching the **spouting horns** across U.S. 101 from Depoe Bay's souvenir shops. Spouting horns, which are similar to blowholes, can be seen all along the coast, but nowhere are they more spectacular than here. These geyserlike plumes occur in places where water is forced through narrow channels in basalt rock. As the channels become more restricted, the water shoots skyward under great pressure and can spray 60 feet into the air. If the surf is really up, the water can carry quite a ways, and more than a few unwary visitors have been soaked.

Be sure to stop in at Depoe Bay's **Whale Watching Center,** 119 U.S. 101 (© **541/765-3304;** www.oregonstateparks.org), which is perched on the cliff above the entrance to the harbor. There are displays about whales, and rangers and volunteers are on hand to point out gray whales if they happen to be visible. Memorial Day to Labor Day, the center is open daily from 9am to 5pm; call for hours in other months.

At **Fogarty Creek State Recreation Area,** a couple of miles north of Depoe Bay, you'll find a beautiful little cove with basalt cliffs at one end and a creek flowing across the beach. The parking area is on the east side of U.S. 101. **Boiler Bay State Scenic Viewpoint,** a mile north of Depoe Bay, is a good picnic spot from which to look for gray whales. There are also tide pools among the rocks in some small coves here. Although the beach itself is not accessible from the state park pull-off, about midway between Boiler Bay and Fogarty Creek, a mile north of here, there's a trail that leads down to the beach.

South of Depoe Bay, U.S. 101 winds through scenes of rugged splendor, passing several small, picturesque coves. Just south of town, **Rocky Creek State Scenic Viewpoint,** with windswept lawns, picnic tables, and great views of buff-colored cliffs and spouting horns, is a good picnic spot. In a few more miles you'll come to the Otter Crest Scenic Loop, which leads to Cape Foulweather and the **Otter Crest State Scenic Viewpoint.** Named by Capt. James Cook in 1778, the cape was his first glimpse of land after leaving the Sandwich Islands (Hawaii). The cape frequently lives up to its name, with winds often gusting to more than 100 miles per hour. However, the views are quite stupendous. Keep an eye out for the sea lions that sun themselves on offshore rocks near Cape Foulweather. A historic building now used as a gift shop provides a protected glimpse of the sea from atop Cape Foulweather.

At the south end of the Otter Crest Scenic Loop, you'll find an overlook at **Devil's Punchbowl State Natural Area** ★★. The overlook provides a glimpse into a collapsed sea cave that during high tides or stormy seas becomes a churning cauldron of foam. Adjacent to Devil's Punchbowl, in a small cove, you'll find numerous tide pools that can be explored at low tide. From this cove, you can also explore inside the Devil's Punchbowl. South of Devil's Punchbowl State Natural Area lies **Beverly Beach State Park** (© 541/265-9278), which has a large campground and is a popular surfing spot. Here at the Devil's Punchbowl, you'll also find **Mo's Chowder House** (© 541/765-2442) and the **Flying Dutchman Winery** (© 541/765-2553; www.dutchman winery.com).

If you're interested in **sportfishing** or **whale-watching** ★★, contact **Tradewinds Charters** (© 800/445-8730 or 541/765-2345; www.tradewindscharters.com), at the north end of the bridge or **Dockside Charters** (© 800/733-8915 or 541/765-2545; www.docksidedepoebay.com), down by the marina. Whale-watching trips run $18 to $45, depending on the type of boat you go out on and how long you stay out. Fishing trips run from $65 for 5 hours to $175 or $180 for a day of halibut or tuna fishing.

WHERE TO STAY

Channel House ★★   Perched above the narrow, cliff-bordered channel into tiny Depoe Bay is the Channel House, one of the coast's most luxurious and strikingly situated small inns. A contemporary building with lots of angles and windows, the Channel House has large rooms, and the gas fireplaces and private decks with whirlpool tubs make it one of the most romantic inns on the coast. You can sit and soak as fishing boats navigate their way through the channel below you.

35 Ellingson St. (P.O. Box 56), Depoe Bay, OR 97341. © 800/447-2140 or 541/765-2140. Fax 541/765-2191. www.channelhouse.com. 12 units. Apr–Oct $100–$260 double, $295–$330 suite; Nov–Mar (Sun–Thurs) $100–$199 double, $222–$250 suite. Rates include continental breakfast. AE, DISC, MC, V. Children 16 and over accepted. **Amenities:** Concierge. *In room:* TV/DVD, fridge, microwave, coffeemaker, hair dryer, free local calls, high-speed Internet access, Wi-Fi.

Inn at Arch Rock *Finds*   You just won't find a better view from any hotel on the Oregon coast. This collection of renovated Cape Cod–style buildings sits above the cliffs on the north side of Depoe Bay, and you can sit in your room and watch the waves crashing against the rocks. When you want to get your feet wet in the summer, follow the flight of stairs that leads down to a tiny beach. Guest rooms have a simple cottage decor, and some have kitchens or fireplaces. Out on the lawns overlooking the ocean you'll find white Adirondack chairs and a fire pit. The inn also rents out an adjacent condominium and is just around the corner from the Tidal Raves restaurant.

70 NW Sunset St. (P.O. Box 1516), Depoe Bay, OR 97341. © 800/767-1835 or 541/765-2560. www.innatarchrock. com. 13 units. $79–$229 double (lower rates in winter). Rates include continental breakfast. Children 6 and under stay free in parent's room. AE, DISC, MC, V. Pets accepted ($10 per night). *In room:* TV/DVD, fridge, microwave, coffeemaker, free local calls.

The Surfrider ★   Though it has been around for many years and is nothing fancy, this low-rise motel, just north of Depoe Bay, claims an enviable location and view, and has long been a family favorite. It's hidden from the highway, which gives it a secluded feel, and there are great views from the open bluff-top setting. You can choose between basic motel rooms and rooms with fireplaces, kitchens, or whirlpool tubs. At the foot of a long staircase is the wide beach of Fogarty Creek State Recreation Area, which is on a pretty little cove. The dining room and lounge have great views of this cove.

3115 NW U.S. 101 (P.O. Box 219), Depoe Bay, OR 97341. © 800/662-2378 or 541/764-2311. Fax 541/764-4634. www.surfriderresort.com. 55 units. July–Aug $114–$159 double, $139–$199 suite; Mar–June and Sept–Oct $79–$129 double, $99–$179 suite; Nov–Feb $69–$129 double, $79–$179 suite. Children under 13 stay free in parent's room. AE, DC, DISC, MC, V. **Amenities:** Restaurant (American); lounge; indoor pool; Jacuzzi; sauna; massage; coin-op laundry. *In room:* TV/VCR, dataport, fridge, coffeemaker, hair dryer, Wi-Fi.

WHERE TO DINE

Tidal Raves *(Finds)* SEAFOOD   With bright, uncluttered decor and big windows for taking in the wave-carved sandstone cliffs outside, Tidal Raves, located at the north end of Depoe Bay's strip of tourist shops, is the most dramatically situated restaurant on the Oregon coast. This place has had folks raving for years now, and on days when the surf is up, it's hard to take your eyes off the wave-pounded cliffs outside the window and concentrate on your food. The menu offers plenty of straightforward seafood, but it also includes some creative preparations such as green curry with halibut, linguine puttanesca with oysters, and Thai grilled tiger shrimp. For light eaters, there are small portions of many menu favorites.

279 NW U.S. 101. © 541/765-2995. Reservations highly recommended. Main courses $8–$22. AE, MC, V. Daily 11am–9pm.

7 Newport

23 miles S of Lincoln City, 58 miles W of Corvallis, 24 miles N of Yachats

As Oregon coast towns go, Newport has a split personality. Dockworkers unloading fresh fish mingle with vacationers licking ice-cream cones, and both fishing boats and pleasure craft ply the waters of the bay. The air smells of fish and shrimp, and freeloading sea lions doze on the docks while they wait for their next meal from the processing plants along the waterfront. Directly across the street, art galleries and souvenir shops stand side by side. Across Yaquina Bay from the waterfront, you'll find the Oregon Coast Aquarium (the coast's top tourist attraction) and the Hatfield Marine Science Center. If you're looking for a balance of the old and the new on the Oregon coast, Newport is the place.

Newport got its start in the late 1800s as both an oystering community and one of the earliest Oregon beach resorts, and many of the old cottages and historic buildings can still be seen in the town's Nye Beach neighborhood. Although Nye Beach has the feel of a 19th-century resort, the downtown bayfront is, despite its souvenir shops, galleries, and restaurants, still a working port and home to the largest commercial fishing fleet on the Oregon coast. Oysters are also still important to the local economy and are raised in oyster beds along Yaquina Bay Road, east of town.

Though in recent years it has come close to matching the overdevelopment of Lincoln City, this fishing port on the shore of Yaquina Bay still manages to offer a balance of industry, history, culture, beaches, and family attractions.

ESSENTIALS

GETTING THERE   Newport is on U.S. 101 at the junction with U.S. 20, which leads to Corvallis.

Newport

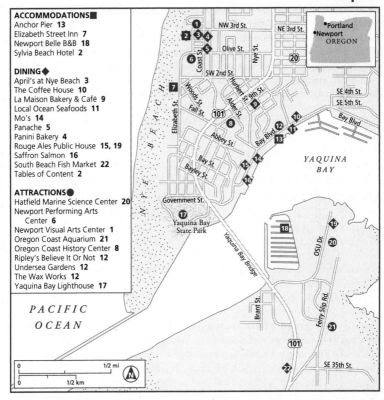

VISITOR INFORMATION   Contact the **Greater Newport Chamber of Commerce,** 555 SW Coast Hwy., Newport, OR 97365 (© **800/262-7844** or 541/265-8801; www.newportchamber.org).

FESTIVALS   In February, there's the **Seafood and Wine Fest;** contact the Newport Chamber of Commerce for information.

FINS & FLIPPERS

Hatfield Marine Science Center ✦ *(Kids*   This facility, though primarily a university research center, also contains displays that are open to the public. Exhibits are not as impressive as those at the Oregon Coast Aquarium, but they do highlight current topics in marine research and include an octopus aquarium and a "touch" tank. Interpretive exhibits explain life in the sea. A worthwhile adjunct to a visit to the Oregon Coast Aquarium.

2030 SE Marine Science Dr. © **541/867-0100.** http://hmsc.oregonstate.edu. Admission by donation. Memorial Day to Labor Day daily 10am–5pm; Labor Day to Memorial Day Thurs–Mon 10am–4pm. Closed Thanksgiving, Christmas, New Year's Day.

Oregon Coast Aquarium ✦✦✦ *(Kids*   Considered one of the top aquariums in the country, the Oregon Coast Aquarium focuses primarily on sea life native to the Oregon coast. There are so many fascinating displays that it's easy to spend the better part of a day here. The stars are the playful sea otters, but the clown-faced tufted puffins, which are kept in a walk-through aviary, are big favorites as well. The sea lions sometimes rouse from their naps to put on impromptu shows, and the lucky visitor even gets a glimpse of a giant octopus with an arm span of nearly 20 feet. Artificial waves surge in a tank that reproduces, on a speeded-up scale, life in a rocky intertidal zone. And so far, you haven't even made it to the indoor displays. One of the most fascinating exhibits here is a walk-through deep-sea shark tank featuring a 200-foot-long acrylic walkway. There are examples of sandy beaches, rocky shores, salt marshes, kelp forests, and the open ocean. Because this is the most popular attraction on the Oregon coast, lines to get in can be very long. Arrive early if you're visiting on a summer weekend.

2820 SE Ferry Slip Rd. © 541/867-3474. www.aquarium.org. Admission $13 adults, $11 seniors, $7.75 children 3–12. Memorial Day to Labor Day daily 9am–6pm; Labor Day to Memorial Day daily 10am–5pm. Closed Christmas.

SEEING THE LIGHTS

Newport is home to two historic lighthouses, which are just 3 miles apart. The **Yaquina Bay Lighthouse** began operation in 1871 but in 1874 was replaced by the **Yaquina Head Lighthouse.** The latter was supposed to be built on Cape Foulweather, farther to the north, but heavy seas made it impossible to land there. Instead, the light was built on Yaquina Head, and so powerful was the light that it supplanted the one at Yaquina Bay.

At 93 feet tall, the **Yaquina Head Lighthouse,** 3 miles north of Newport, is the tallest lighthouse on the Oregon coast and is still a functioning light. The lighthouse lies within the **Yaquina Head Outstanding Natural Area** (© 541/574-3100), and adjacent to the lighthouse, you'll find the **Yaquina Head Interpretive Center,** which houses displays covering everything from the life of lighthouse keepers and their families to the sea life of tide pools. Cormorants and pigeon guillemots can be seen roosting on the steep slopes, and harbor seals lounge on the rocks. In early winter and spring, you may spot gray whales migrating along the coast. On the cobblestone beach below the lighthouse, you can explore tide pools at low tide, and there is even a wheelchair-accessible tide-pool trail in a cove that once was the site of a rock quarry. In summer, the interpretive center is open daily from 10am to 5pm and the lighthouse is open daily from 10am to 4pm; in other months, the interpretive center is open from 10am to 4pm and the lighthouse is open from noon to 4pm. Admission to Yaquina Head is $5 per car.

The older of the two lighthouses, **Yaquina Bay Lighthouse,** is now part of Yaquina Bay State Park, 846 SW Government St. (© **800/551-6949** or 541/265-5679; www. oregonstateparks.org), which can be found just north and west of the Yaquina Bay Bridge. This 1871 lighthouse is the oldest building in Newport, and it is unusual in that the light is in a tower atop a two-story wood-frame house. The building served as both home and lighthouse, and supposedly is haunted. The lighthouse is open from Memorial Day weekend to the end of September daily from 11am to 5pm; from October to Memorial Day weekend, it's open daily from noon to 4pm. Entrance is free.

BEACHES

Beaches in the Newport area range from tiny rocky coves to long, wide stretches of sand perfect for kite flying. Right in town, north and west of the Yaquina Bay Bridge, you'll find **Yaquina Bay State Recreation Site,** which borders on both the ocean and the bay. North of Newport is **Agate Beach,** which was once known for the beautiful agates that could be found there. However, sand now covers the formerly rocky beach, hiding the stones from rock hunters. This beach has a stunning view of Yaquina Head. Two miles south of Newport, you'll find **South Beach State Park** (© 541/867-4715; www.oregonstateparks.org), a wide sandy beach with picnic areas and a large campground (that also rents yurts).

Six miles south of Newport, you'll find **Ona Beach State Park,** a sandy beach with a picnic area under the trees. Beaver Creek, a fairly large stream, flows through the park and across the beach to the ocean. The state park offers guided kayak tours on Beaver Creek. For information or reservations, call © **541/867-6590.** Another 2 miles south will bring you to **Seal Rock State Recreation Site,** where a long wall of rock rises from the waves and sand and creates numerous tide pools and fascinating nooks and crannies to explore.

For an unusual way to experience Newport area beaches, contact Guy DiTorrice, the **Oregon Fossil Guy** (© **541/961-1762;** www.oregonfossilguy.com), who leads tours to coastal fossil sites and explains Oregon's fascinating coastal geology. Tours start at $29 per person.

THE BAYFRONT

The Bayfront is tourist central for Newport. Here you'll find ice-cream parlors, saltwater-taffy stores, chowder houses, and souvenir shops. The Bayfront is also home to commercial fishermen, seafood processing plants, and art galleries, and in its waters are numerous sea lions, which love to sleep on the floating docks adjacent to Undersea Gardens. From the adjacent pier, you can observe the sea lions at close range. Their bickering and barking makes for great free entertainment.

As one of the coast's most popular family vacation spots, Newport has all the tourist traps one would expect. Billboards up and down the coast advertise the sorts of places that kids have to visit. Tops on this list are **Ripley's Believe It or Not!** and **The Wax Works.** Across the street from these you'll find **Undersea Gardens,** where a scuba diver feeds fish in a large tank beneath a boat moored on the Bayfront. All three attractions are on the Bayfront and share the same address and phone number: Mariner Square, 250 SW Bay Blvd. (© **541/265-2206;** www.marinersquare.com). Admission for each is $9.95 for adults, $5.95 for children 5 to 12; or $22 for adults and $13 for children to visit all three attractions.

The Bayfront is also the place to arrange **whale-watching tours** and **fishing trips.** Two-hour whale-watching tours are offered throughout the year by **Marine Discovery Tours,** 345 SW Bay Blvd. (© **800/903-BOAT** or 541/265-6200; www.marine discovery.com), which charges $32 for adults, $30 for seniors, and $16 for kids ages 4 to 13. You can charter a fishing boat on the Bayfront at **Newport Tradewinds,** 653 SW Bay Blvd. (© **800/676-7819** or 541/265-2101; www.newporttradewinds.com). Salmon, tuna, halibut, and bottom fish can all be caught off the coast here depending on the season. Fishing trips cost anywhere from $65 to $175.

Newport claims to be the Dungeness crab capital of the world, and if you'd like to find out if this claim is true, you can rent crab rings and boats at **Sawyer's Landing,** 4098 Yaquina Bay Rd. (© **541/265-3907;** www.sawyerslandingnewport.com), for $55 for 3 hours or $75 for the whole day.

NYE BEACH

Newport was one of the earliest beach vacation destinations in Oregon, and it was in Nye Beach that the first hotels and vacation cottages were built. Today this neighborhood, north of the Yaquina Bay Bridge along the beach, is slowly being renovated and has both historic and hip hotels, good restaurants, some interesting shops, and, of course, miles of sandy beach. There's public parking at the turnaround on Beach Drive.

The works of local and regional artists are showcased at the **Newport Visual Arts Center,** 777 NW Beach Dr. (© **541/265-6540;** www.coastarts.org). The center is open Tuesday through Sunday from 11am to 5pm. Just a few blocks away, the **Newport Performing Arts Center,** 777 W. Olive St. (© **541/265-ARTS;** www.coastarts.org), hosts local and nationally recognized performers.

OTHER NEWPORT ACTIVITIES & ATTRACTIONS

If you'd like to delve into local history, stop by the **Oregon Coast History Center,** 545 SW Ninth St. (© **541/265-7509;** www.oregoncoast.history.museum), which consists of two historic buildings—the Burrows House and the Log Cabin. The Burrows House was built in 1895 as a boardinghouse and now contains exhibits of Victorian household furnishings and fashions. The Log Cabin houses Siletz Indian artifacts from the area, as well as exhibits on logging, farming, and maritime history. June through September, the museum is open Tuesday to Sunday from 10am to 5pm; October through May, it's open Tuesday to Sunday from 11am to 4pm. Admission is free.

Take a drive east from the bayfront along scenic Yaquina Bay Road and you'll come to **Toledo,** a small town that is slowly becoming something of an art community. In downtown Toledo, you'll find several artists' studios and galleries. For more information, contact the **Toledo Chamber of Commerce** (© **541/336-3183;** www.visittoledo oregon.com).

WHERE TO STAY
EXPENSIVE
Starfish Point ★★   Located north of town in a grove of fir trees on the edge of a cliff, the Starfish Point condominiums, although a bit dated in their decor, are among my favorite rooms in the area. Each of the six condos has two bedrooms and two baths spaced over two floors. Between the two floors you'll find a cozy sitting area in an octagonal room that's almost all windows. This little sunroom is in addition to the spacious living room with its fireplace and stereo. The bathrooms here are extravagant, with two-person whirlpool tubs and skylights or big windows. A path leads down to the beach, and to the north is Yaquina Head, one of the coast's most dramatic headlands.

140 NW 48th St., Newport, OR 97365. © **800/870-7795** or 541/265-3751. Fax 541/265-3040. www.starfish point.com. 6 units. $190–$215 double; lower weekday rates in off season. 2-night minimum on weekends. AE, DC, DISC, MC, V. Pets accepted ($17). *In room:* TV/VCR/DVD, kitchen, fridge, coffeemaker, high-speed Internet access.

MODERATE
Anchor Pier ★   Located on the second floor of a bayfront commercial building, these rooms are the prettiest and most up-to-date in town. They are built over the water, and you just can't get any closer to the bay. Stay here and you'll be serenaded by barking sea lions throughout the day, which can get a bit old but is part of the charm of staying here. All the rooms have whirlpool tubs and private decks. The rooms are upstairs from Marine Discovery Tours, which can take you out whale-watching.

345 SW Bay Blvd., Newport, OR 97365. © **541/265-7829.** www.anchorpier.com. 5 units. $175–$199 double. DISC, MC, V. *In room:* TV, fridge, microwave, coffeemaker, hair dryer, Wi-Fi.

Elizabeth Street Inn   Located in the Nye Beach area and within walking distance of Yaquina Bay State Park, this oceanfront hotel, with its stone foundation wall, cedar-shingle facade, and white trim, has a classic beachy feel. There's a nautical theme throughout and all rooms have ocean views, balconies, and fireplaces; some also have whirlpool tubs. The hotel is perched up on a bluff above the beach, and there are several good restaurants within walking distance.

232 SW Elizabeth St. (P.O. Box 1342), Newport, OR 97365. © **877/265-9400** or 541/265-9400. Fax 541/265-9551. www.elizabethstreetinn.com. 74 units. $159–$199 double, $229 suite; lower rates Nov–Mar. Rates include continental breakfast. Children under 12 stay free in parent's room. AE, DC, DISC, MC, V. **Amenities:** Indoor pool; exercise room; Jacuzzi; coin-op laundry. *In room:* TV, dataport, fridge, microwave, coffeemaker, hair dryer, free local calls, high-speed Internet access.

Newport Belle Bed & Breakfast ✦ (Finds)

This 100-foot-long modern stern-wheeler is one of the most unusual B&Bs on the Oregon coast and is docked in the Newport Marina in Yaquina Bay within walking distance of the Oregon Coast Aquarium, Hatfield Marine Science Center, and Rogue Brewery. The guest rooms (staterooms) here are small, as you'd expect on any boat, but they all have big windows, private bathrooms, and wood floors. A salon on the main deck serves as a gathering space and dining room with a wonderful view of the harbor.

P.O. Box 685, South Beach, OR 97366. © **800/348-1922** or 541/867-6290. www.newportbelle.com. 5 units. $145–$165 double. Rates include full breakfast. MC, V. No children accepted. **Amenities:** Concierge. *In room:* Wi-Fi, no phone.

Sylvia Beach Hotel (Finds)

This eclectic four-story cedar-shingled hotel pays homage to literature. The guest rooms are named for different authors, and in each you'll find memorabilia, books, and decor that reflect the authors' lives, times, and works. The Agatha Christie Room seems full of clues, while in the Edgar Allan Poe Room, a pendulum hangs over the bed and a stuffed raven sits by the window. Among the writers represented are Tennessee Williams, Colette, Ernest Hemingway, Mark Twain, Jane Austen, F. Scott Fitzgerald, and Emily Dickinson. Unfortunately, the rooms have not been well maintained in recent years, which, however, doesn't seem to bother most guests, who tend to be obsessed with literature and willing to overlook the hotel's flaws. The Tables of Content restaurant downstairs is a local favorite (p. 206).

267 NW Cliff St., Newport, OR 97365-3707. © **888/795-8422** or 541/265-5428. www.sylviabeachhotel.com. 20 units. $70–$188 double. Rates include full breakfast. 2-night minimum on weekends. AE, MC, V. **Amenities:** Restaurant (Northwest). *In room:* No phone.

Tyee Lodge ✦

Located just south of Yaquina Head, this oceanfront bed-and-breakfast sits atop a high bluff surrounded by tall trees. Guest rooms are large and all have good ocean views, as do the living and dining rooms. There are gas fireplaces in all the rooms, and the house has a modern look with Native American accents. In the breakfast room, you'll find a telescope for whale-watching, and on cooler days, a fireplace warms the living room. A private trail leads down to the beach. This inn also manages the adjacent Ocean House Inn.

4925 NW Woody Way, Newport, OR 97365-1327. © **888/553-8933** or 541/265-8953. www.tyeelodge.com. 5 units. $120–$180 double. Rates include full breakfast. AE, DISC, MC, V. **Amenities:** Concierge; business center. *In room:* Hair dryer, free local calls, Wi-Fi.

CAMPGROUNDS

North of Newport you'll find **Beverly Beach State Park,** which is known for its good surfing and has campsites and yurts. South of town, at the mouth of Yaquina Bay, is **South Beach State Park** (© **541/265-9278**), one of the biggest state-park campgrounds on the coast (it also has yurts). However, I prefer Beverly Beach. To make reservations at either campground, contact **ReserveAmerica** (© **800/452-5687;** www. reserveamerica.com).

WHERE TO DINE

For an espresso, a slice of pizza, or a good panino sandwich, drop by **Panini Bakery,** 232 NW Coast St. (© **541/265-5033**), which is in the Nye Beach neighborhood. For pastries and artisan breads, search out **La Maison Bakery & Cafe,** 315 SW Ninth St. (© **541/265-8812**), which is just off U.S. 101. On a hot summer day, nothing tastes better than a pint of microbrewed ale at **Rogue Ales Public House,** 748 SW Bay Blvd. (© **541/265-3188;** www.rogue.com). There's a second pub over near the Oregon Coast Aquarium at 2320 OSU Dr. (© **541/867-3660**). For coffee, grab a table on the deck at **The Coffee House,** 156 SW Bay Blvd. (© **541/265-6263**), and you'll have front-row seat for watching all the action on the bayfront.

MODERATE

April's at Nye Beach 🎄🎄 MEDITERRANEAN   Located in the historic Nye Beach neighborhood, this restaurant is your best bet for a romantic evening out. Popular both with the hip young crowd that likes to vacation in Nye Beach and patrons of the nearby Newport Center for the Performing Arts, the restaurant dishes up good contemporary Italian fare amid artistic surroundings. The afternoon light here is fabulous, so try to schedule your dinner for sunset (and ask for a table with an ocean view). There's an excellent selection of regional wines at reasonable prices.

749 NW Third St. © 541/265-6855. Reservations recommended. Main courses $16–$23. DISC, MC, V. Wed–Sun 5–8:45pm. Closed in Jan.

Panache 🎄 NORTHWEST   Big and bright, this restaurant brings a highly refined dining experience to the Nye Beach neighborhood, and may be the wave of the future for this once-funky area. Located across the street form the Performing Arts Center, this elegant restaurant is the perfect spot for a pretheater dinner. Start your meal with the "pink martini" shrimp cocktail and then move on to the pan-seared salmon with pomegranate glaze. The menu usually also includes a couple of vegetarian entrees.

614 W. Olive St. © 541/265-2929. www.panachenewport.com. Reservations recommended. Main courses $16–$29. DISC, MC, V. Sun–Thurs 5–9pm; Fri–Sat 5–10pm.

Saffron Salmon 🎄🎄 NORTHWEST   With its walls of glass, bold contemporary styling, and location at the end of a pier on the bayfront, the Saffron Salmon is my favorite restaurant in Newport. As you dine on saffron-scented salmon, you'll watch commercial fishermen unloading their catch just outside the window. Fish just doesn't get any fresher than this. Keep an eye out for sea lions, too. At lunch, go for the saffron salmon sandwich.

859 SW Bay Blvd. © 541/265-8921. Reservations recommended. Main courses $4–$18 lunch, $18–$36 dinner. AE, MC, V. Thurs–Tues 11:30am–2:15pm and 5–8:15pm.

Tables of Content 🎄🎄 *Finds* INTERNATIONAL   Located in the Sylvia Beach Hotel, this restaurant serves delicious and very reasonably priced four-course dinners. Although on any given night you'll have limited choices, if you enjoy creative cookery and eclectic combinations, you'll leave happy. Expect dishes such as mushroom sauté, Greek salad, salmon dijonnaise, and black-bean cakes. Be forewarned, however, that dinners here are designed to foster interactions between guests. You'll be seated at a table for eight, and after dinner, guests participate in a game called "two truths and a lie." If you're outgoing and thrive on fiction, dinner here is unforgettable. On the other hand, if you're looking for a quiet, romantic evening out, this is definitely not the place.

Sylvia Beach Hotel, 267 NW Cliff St. ✆ **541/265-5428.** www.sylviabeachhotel.com. Reservations required. Fixed-price 4-course dinner $22. AE, MC, V. Seatings Sun–Thurs 7pm; Fri–Sat 6 and 8:30pm.

INEXPENSIVE

Local Ocean Seafoods ☞ SEAFOOD   If you want fresh, sustainably harvested seafood, this casual fish-market-style eatery is the place. The modern space, with its big windows, is located directly across the street from the water, so you can watch fishing boats coming and going and know that the fish on your plate was caught only hours ago. The fish tacos and the albacore tuna kabobs are excellent, but you can also get a simple whole crab or a crab po' boy. There are also plenty of oyster and shrimp dishes as well.

213 SE Bay Blvd. ✆ **541/574-7959.** www.localocean.net. Main courses $6–$18. MC, V. Daily 11am–9pm.

Mo's SEAFOOD   Established in 1942, Mo's has become such an Oregon coast institution that it has spawned five other restaurants up and down the coast. Clam chowder is what made Mo's famous, and you can get it by the bowl, by the cup, or family style. ***Be forewarned, though:*** Some people think this clam chowder is the best and others think it's awful. (I'd put it somewhere in between the two extremes.) Basic seafood dinners are fresh, large, and inexpensive, and the seafood-salad sandwiches are whoppers. There are also such dishes as cioppino, oyster stew, and slumgullion (clam chowder with shrimp). Expect a line out the door.

657 SW Bay Blvd. ✆ **541/265-2979.** www.moschowder.com. Complete dinner $4.25–$16. AE, DISC, MC, V. Daily 11am–9pm.

South Beach Fish Market DELI   If you're looking for the best fish and chips on the Oregon coast, be sure to sample the offerings at this little roadside stand near the Oregon Coast Aquarium. You can get salmon and chips, halibut and chips, oysters and chips, shrimp and chips, or the basic house fish and chips, which is made with whatever fresh inexpensive fish is available that day. Okay, so the chips aren't the best, but the fish is very lightly battered, which lets its flavor shine through. They also do smoked salmon and tuna.

3640 SW U.S. 101. ✆ **541/867-6800.** www.southbeachfishmarket.com. Main dishes $7.50–$19. AE, DISC, MC, V. Daily 8am–9pm.

8 Yachats

24 miles S of Newport, 26 miles N of Florence, 138 miles SE of Portland

Located on the north side of 800-foot-high Cape Perpetua, the village of Yachats (pronounced "*yah*-hots") is something of an artists' community that also attracts a good number of counterculture types. When you get your first glimpse of the town's setting, you, too, will likely agree that there's more than enough beauty here to inspire anyone to artistic pursuits. Yachats is an Alsi Indian word meaning "dark waters at the foot of the mountains," and that sums up perfectly the setting of this small community, one of the few on the Oregon coast that could really be considered a village. The tiny Yachats River flows into the surf on the south edge of town, and to the east stand steep, forested mountains. The shoreline on which the town stands is rocky, with little coves here and there where you can find agates among the pebbles paving the beach. Tide pools offer hours of exploring, and, in winter, storm waves create a spectacular show. Uncrowded beaches, comfortable motels, and a couple of good restaurants add up to a great spot for a quiet getaway.

ESSENTIALS

GETTING THERE   From the north, take Ore. 34 west from Corvallis to Waldport and then head south on U.S. 101. From the south, take Ore. 126 west from Eugene to Florence and then head north on U.S. 101.

VISITOR INFORMATION   Contact the **Yachats Area Chamber of Commerce,** 241 U.S. 101 (P.O. Box 728), Yachats, OR 97498 (© **800/929-0477** or 541/547-3530; www.yachats.org).

YACHATS AREA ACTIVITIES & ATTRACTIONS

Looming over tiny Yachats is the impressive bulk of 800-foot-high Cape Perpetua, the highest spot on the Oregon coast. Because of the cape's rugged beauty and diversity of natural habitats, it has been designated the **Cape Perpetua Scenic Area** ⭐⭐⭐. The **Cape Perpetua Interpretive Center,** 2400 U.S. 101 (© **541/547-3289;** www.fs. fed.us/r6/siuslaw), is on a steep road off U.S. 101 and houses displays on the natural history of the cape and the Native Americans who for thousands of years harvested its bountiful seafood. The visitor center is open daily from 10am to 5:30pm between Memorial Day and Labor Day (daily 10am–4pm in spring and fall; closed in winter). Admission is $5 per vehicle. Within the scenic area are 26 miles of hiking trails, tide pools, ancient forests, scenic overlooks, and a campground. Guided hikes are offered (weather permitting) when the visitor center is open. If you're here on a clear day, be sure to drive to the top of the cape for one of the finest vistas on the coast. Waves and tides are a year-round source of fascination along these rocky shores, and Cape Perpetua's tide pools are some of the best on the coast. There's good access to the tide pools at the pull-off at the north end of the scenic area. However, it is the more dramatic interactions of waves and rocks that attract most people to walk the short oceanside trail here: At the **Devil's Churn,** a spouting horn caused by waves crashing into a narrow fissure in the basalt shoreline sends geyserlike plumes of water skyward, and waves boil through a narrow opening in the rocks.

Right in Yachats, be sure to visit **Yachats State Recreation Area,** which is at the southern end of a .8-mile trail that leads north along a rocky stretch of coastline to **Smelt Sands State Recreation Site.** Along the route of the trail, there are little pocket beaches (where smelts spawn) and tide pools. At the north end of the trail, a wide, sandy beach stretches northward. Just across the bridge at the south end of town, you'll find the **Yachats Ocean Road State Natural Site,** another good beach access.

Between April and October each year, **fishing** in Yachats takes an unusual twist. It's during these months that thousands of smelts, sardinelike fish, spawn in the waves that crash in the sandy coves just north of Yachats. The fish can be caught using a dip net, and so popular are the little fish that the town holds an annual **Smelt Fry** each year on the second Saturday in July.

Gray whales also come close to shore near Yachats. You can see them in the spring from Cape Perpetua, and throughout the summer several take up residence at the mouth of the Yachats River. South of Cape Perpetua, Neptune State Scenic Viewpoint at the mouth of Cummins Creek, and Strawberry Hill Wayside are other good places to spot whales, as well as sea lions, which can be seen lounging on the rocks offshore at Strawberry Hill.

A couple of historic buildings in the area are also worth a visit. Built in 1927, the **Little Log Church by the Sea,** 328 W. Third St. (© **541/547-3976**), is now a museum housing displays on local history. The museum is open Friday through Wednesday from noon to 3pm.

The Yachats area has several crafts galleries, the most interesting of which is **Earthworks Gallery,** 2222 U.S. 101 N. (© **541/547-4300**), located north of town and focusing on glass and ceramic art.

WHERE TO STAY

In addition to the hotels listed below, plenty of rental homes are available in Yachats. Contact **Ocean Odyssey,** 261 N. U.S. 101 (P.O. Box 491), Yachats, OR 97498 (© **800/800-1915** or 541/547-3637; www.ocean-odyssey.com), or **Yachats Village Rentals,** 230 Aqua Vista Loop (P.O. Box 44), Yachats, OR 97498 (© **888/288-5077** or 541/547-3501; www.97498.com). Rates for most vacation homes range from around $125 to $225 per night.

Overleaf Lodge 🌟🌟   Overlooking the rocky shoreline at the north end of Yachats, this modern hotel offers some of the most luxurious and tastefully decorated rooms on the central coast. Built in a sort of modern interpretation of the traditional Victorian beach cottage, the lodge caters primarily to couples seeking a romantic escape. Guest rooms all have ocean views, and most have patios or balconies. For a truly memorable stay, book one of the Restless Waters rooms, which have whirlpool tubs overlooking the crashing waves below. If you don't want to spring for one of these rooms, you can still curl up in a sunny little window nook beside your balcony and watch the waves in relative comfort. Many rooms also have fireplaces. The lodge also rents out some attractive cottages that are adjacent to the lodge.

280 Overleaf Lodge Lane, Yachats, OR 97498. © 800/338-0507 or 541/547-4880. www.overleaflodge.com. 54 units. Late June to mid-Sept $170–$260 double, $270–$450 suite; mid-Sept to late June $115–$250 double, $240–$450 suite. Rates include continental breakfast. Children 6 and under stay free in parent's room. AE, DISC, MC, V. **Amenities:** Exercise room; full-service spa; Jacuzzi; sauna; business center; massage; guest laundry. *In room:* TV/DVD, dataport, fridge, coffeemaker, hair dryer, free local calls, Wi-Fi.

Shamrock Lodgettes *Finds*   This collection of classic log cabins at the mouth of the Yachats River bewitched my wife and me the first time we saw it. Spacious lawns and old fir trees give the rustic cabins a relaxed old-fashioned appeal that just begs you to kick back and forget your cares. Each log cabin has a tile entry, hardwood floors, a kitchenette, a stone fireplace, and a big picture window that takes in a view of either the beach or the river. Other than that, they're pretty basic. The motel rooms are more up-to-date and have fireplaces and views, and there are two romantic spa cabins. Some rooms have whirlpool tubs.

105 U.S. 101 S. (P.O. Box 346), Yachats, OR 97498. © 800/845-5028 or 541/547-3312. Fax 541/547-3843. www. shamrocklodgettes.com. 21 units (including 9 cabins). $69–$169 double; $99–$189 cabin. AE, MC, V. Pets accepted ($30 fee). **Amenities:** Exercise room; Jacuzzi; sauna. *In room:* TV, kitchen, fridge, microwave, coffeemaker, free local calls.

CAMPGROUNDS

Beachside State Recreation Site (© **541/265-9278**) is just north of Yachats on U.S. 101, but I don't particularly recommend it. To make reservations, contact **ReserveAmerica** (© **800/452-5687;** www.reserveamerica.com). For exploring the rugged Cape Perpetua area, the Forest Service's **Cape Perpetua Campground,** in a wooded setting set a little way back from the water, is your best option.

WHERE TO DINE

For tasty and creative sandwiches, such as albacore tuna with chipotle mayo on focaccia, stop in at **Grand Occasions Café,** 84 Beach St. (© 541/547-4409), which also does good desserts and sells imported European meats and cheeses. For a glass of wine with a view, don't miss **Yachats Wine Trader,** 125 Ocean View Dr. (© 541/547-5100; www.yachatswinetrader.com), a classy little wine bar/wine shop affiliated with the Yachats River House.

The Drift Inn *Finds* AMERICAN/NORTHWEST   This unprepossessing place, right on U.S. 101 in the center of Yachats, may seem at first glance to be little more than a modern tavern (albeit a tavern with big windows, wooden booths, and polished wood floors), but looks can be deceiving. The Drift Inn actually has a split personality. Sure there's the standard beer-and-burgers menu, but at dinner, there are specials such as salmon topped with a sauté of hazelnuts, mushrooms, and blackberries. There's live music here nightly.

124 U.S. 101 N. © 541/547-4477. www.the-drift-inn.com. Main courses $9–$19. MC, V. Daily 8am–9:30pm.

Yachats River House *母母* NORTHWEST   Yachats has long been one of my favorite Oregon coast destinations, and with the opening of this gorgeous restaurant overlooking the mouth of the Yachats River, I've got one more great reason to love this town. Yachats has never been particularly trendy, but this restaurant has a bold style, with black tablecloths and contemporary art on the walls. The menu is eclectic and ambitious. I always start with the smoked squid-and-seaweed salad, which conjures up fond memories of vacations in Hawaii. I happen to love Indian food, and the tandoori salmon here is superb. Give it a try. In summer, try for a seat on the deck. This restaurant also operates the adjacent Yachats Wine Trader (which is why wines here are so reasonably priced).

131 U.S. 101 N. © 541/547-4100. www.yachatsriverhouse.com. Reservations recommended. Main courses $16–$30. AE, DISC, MC, V. Tues–Sun 5–9pm (winter Wed–Sun 5–9pm).

SOUTH TO FLORENCE

More wide sandy beaches can be found south of Yachats at (in order from north to south) Stonefield Beach State Recreation Site, Muriel O. Ponsler Memorial State Scenic Viewpoint, and Carl G. Washburne Memorial State Park (© 541/547-3416). The latter offers 5 miles of beach, hiking trails, and a campground.

The next park to the south, **Heceta Head Lighthouse State Scenic Viewpoint,** offers the most breathtaking setting. Situated on a small sandy cove, the park has a stream flowing across the beach and several haystack rocks just offshore. As the name implies, the park is home to **Heceta Head Lighthouse** (© 541/547-3416), the most photographed lighthouse on the Oregon coast. From May to September daily from 11am to 5pm and March, April, and October daily between 11am and 3pm, volunteers lead guided tours of the lighthouse. Heceta (pronounced "huh-*see*-tuh") Head is a rugged headland that's named for Spanish explorer Capt. Bruno Heceta. The old lighthouse keeper's home is now a bed-and-breakfast (see below), that has an interpretive center. Between Memorial Day weekend and Labor Day weekend, there are free tours of the lighthouse keeper's house Thursday through Monday between noon and 5pm. There is a $3 day-use fee to use the park.

At more than 300 feet long and 120 feet high, **Sea Lion Caves** *母母*, 91560 U.S. 101 N. (© 541/547-3111; www.sealioncaves.com), 1 mile south of Heceta Head Lighthouse, is the largest sea cave in the United States. The cave was discovered in

1880, and since 1932 it has been one of the most popular stops along the Oregon coast. The cave and a nearby rock ledge are the only year-round mainland homes for Steller's sea lions, hundreds of which reside here throughout the year. This is the larger of the two species of sea lion that frequent this coast, and bulls can weigh almost a ton. The sea lions spend the day lounging and barking up a storm, and the bickering of the adults and antics of the pups are always entertaining. Although at any time of year you're likely to find quite a few of the sea lions here, it is during the fall and winter that the majority of the sea lions move into the cave. Today, a combination of stairs, pathways, and an elevator lead down from the bluff-top gift shop to a viewpoint in the cave wall. The best time to visit is late in the afternoon, when the sun shines directly into the cave and the crowds of people are smaller. Admission is $9 adults, $8 seniors, $5 children 6 to 12. The caves are open daily from 8am to 5:30pm.

Another 6 miles south is the **Darlingtonia State Natural Site,** a small botanical preserve protecting a bog full of rare *Darlingtonia californica* plants, insectivorous pitcher plants also known as cobra lilies. You'll find this fascinating preserve on Mercer Lake Road.

WHERE TO STAY

Heceta Head Lightstation 🐾🐾   Thanks to a spectacular setting on a forested headland, the Heceta Head Lighthouse is the most photographed lighthouse on the Oregon coast. And, although you can't spend the night in the lighthouse itself, you can stay in the former lighthouse keeper's home, a white-clapboard Victorian building high atop an oceanfront bluff and set behind a picket fence. The house is a National Historic Site and has been preserved much the way it might have been when it was active. Breakfasts are elaborate seven-course meals. Because this is one of the most popular B&Bs on the coast, you'll need to book your room 2 to 3 months in advance for a weekday stay and 5 to 6 months in advance for a weekend stay. Oh, and by the way, the inn is haunted.

92072 U.S. 101 S., Yachats, OR 97498. ✆ **866/547-3696.** www.hecetalighthouse.com. 6 units (4 with private bathroom). $133–$189 double with shared bathroom; $168–$265 double with private bathroom. Rates include full breakfast. DISC, MC, V. Children over 10 are welcome. *In room:* Wi-Fi, no phone.

Ocean Haven (Value   Rustic and cozy, the Ocean Haven is a great place to hole up with family or friends. Opt for either the North View or the South View room, and you'll find yourself with two walls of glass overlooking the ocean. When the weather's good, you're only a short walk from the beach and some of the best tide pools around; when it's stormy, watch the waves from your room. (Binoculars are provided.) The Shag's Nest cottage, located across the lawn from the main lodge and perched on the edge of the bluff, is my favorite room here. Stay in the cottage and you can lie in bed gazing out to sea with a fire crackling in the fireplace. A minimum stay may apply, and there are a few nature-friendly house rules, but if you're looking for a good value, great views, and rooms that are a little bit unusual, this is the place. This place is very enviro-friendly (no Hummers or smokers allowed on premises).

94770 U.S. 101, Yachats, OR 97498. ✆ **541/547-3583.** www.oceanhaven.com. 5 units. $90–$100 double. AE, DISC, MC, V. **Amenities:** Concierge. *In room:* Kitchen, fridge, microwave, coffeemaker, Wi-Fi, no phone.

Sea Quest Inn Bed and Breakfast 🐾🐾   Set on a low bluff above the beach and the mouth of Ten Mile Creek, this sprawling contemporary inn is as luxurious a place as you'll find on the central Oregon coast. Privacy and romance are high priorities here, and all rooms have private entrances, ocean views, and whirlpool tubs. The convivial great room on the second floor has expansive views. There's also a huge deck. Miles of beach stretch on either side of the inn.

95354 U.S. 101, Yachats, OR 97498. ℂ 800/341-4878 or 541/547-3782. www.seaquestinn.com. 7 units. $170–$190 double; $350 suite. 2-night minimum on summer weekends. Children 12 and older accepted. AE, MC, V. *In room:* Hair dryer, no phone.

The See Vue *(Value* Recommendable economical oceanfront lodgings are just as hard to find on the Oregon coast as they are anywhere else. The See Vue is an exception. The large themed rooms here all have ocean views, and while you can't get down to the beach from right here, there is access nearby. Rooms to choose from include one decorated with Native American murals, one full of memorabilia from the Far East, and a "study" full of books. The building may be old and rather nondescript, as is the roadside location, but the views are fabulous, which makes this a great place to hole up. Several of the rooms have fireplaces. Many of the rooms have kitchens.

95590 U.S. 101 S., Yachats, OR 97498. ℂ 866/547-3237 or 541/547-3227. www.seevue.com. 12 units. $80–$95 double; $150–$170 suite. MC, V. Pets accepted ($10 per night). 2-night minimum on weekends; 3-night minimum on holiday weekends. *In room:* Fridge, Wi-Fi, no phone.

CAMPGROUNDS

Just south of Cape Perpetua, there are a couple of campgrounds within Siuslaw National Forest. **Rock Creek Campground** (ℂ **541/547-3289;** www.fs.fed.us/r6/siuslaw) is tucked back in the woods along a pretty creek and is a good choice for tenters and anyone who dislikes crowds. **Carl G. Washburne Memorial State Park** (ℂ **800/551-6949** or 541/547-3416; www.oregonstateparks.org) is the area's state park option and is one of only a few coastal state parks that do not take reservations (although you can reserve a yurt here). Campsites are across the highway from a pretty beach just north of Heceta Head.

9 Florence & the Oregon Dunes National Recreation Area

50 miles S of Newport, 50 miles N of Coos Bay, 60 miles W of Eugene

Florence and the Oregon Dunes National Recreation Area, which stretches south of town for almost 50 miles, have long been popular summer vacation spots for Oregon families. The national recreation area is the longest unbroken, publicly owned stretch of coastline on the Oregon coast, and within its boundaries are 14,000 acres of dunes, some of which stand more than 500 feet tall.

Within this vast area of shifting sands—the largest area of sand dunes on the West Coast—there are numerous lakes both large and small, living forests, and skeletal forests of trees that were long ago "drowned" beneath drifting sands. Many area lakes are ringed with summer homes and campgrounds, and it is these lakes that are the primary destination of many vacationers. Consequently, water-skiing and fishing are among the most popular activities, followed by riding off-road vehicles (ORVs) through the sand dunes.

The Umpqua River divides the national recreation area roughly at its midway point, and on its banks you'll find the towns of Gardiner, Reedsport, and Winchester Bay, each of which has a very distinct character. Gardiner was founded in 1841 when a Boston merchant's fur-trading ship wrecked near here. An important mill town in the 19th century, Gardiner has several stately Victorian homes. Reedsport is the largest of these three communities and is the site of the Umpqua Discovery Center, a museum focusing on the history and natural history of this region. The town of Winchester Bay is almost at the mouth of the Umpqua River and is known for its large fleet of charter-fishing boats.

Florence is one of the few towns on the Oregon coast with historic character. Set on the banks of the Siuslaw River, it is filled with restored wooden commercial buildings that house restaurants and interesting shops. The charm of the historic downtown is all the more appealing when compared to the unsightly sprawl of U.S. 101.

ESSENTIALS

GETTING THERE Florence is on U.S. 101 at the junction with Ore. 126 from Eugene. Gardiner, Reedsport, and Winchester Bay are all on U.S. 101 at or near the junction with Ore. 38 from Elkton, which in turn is reached from I-5 by taking either Ore. 99 from Drain or Ore. 138 from Sutherlin.

VISITOR INFORMATION For more information on the dunes, contact the **Oregon Dunes National Recreation Area,** 855 U.S. 101, Reedsport, OR 97467 (© **541/ 271-6000;** www.fs.fed.us/r6/siuslaw). From mid-May to mid-September, this visitor center is open in daily from 8am to 4:30pm; other months, it is closed on Saturday and Sunday.

For more information on Florence, contact the **Florence Area Chamber of Commerce,** 290 U.S. 101, Florence, OR 97439 (© **800/524-4864** or 541/997-3128; www. florencechamber.com).

There is a $5-per-car day-use fee within the recreation area.

THE OREGON DUNES NATIONAL RECREATION AREA

The first Oregon dunes were formed between 12 and 26 million years ago by the weathering of inland mountain ranges, but it was not until about 7,000 years ago, after the massive eruption of the Mount Mazama volcano, that they reached their current size and shape. That volcanic eruption emptied out the entire molten-rock contents of Mount Mazama, and in the process created the caldera that would later become Crater Lake.

Due to water currents and winds, the dunes today are in constant flux. Currents move the sand particles north each winter and south each summer, while constant winds off the Pacific Ocean blow the sand eastward, piling it up into dunes that are slowly marching east. Over thousands of years, the dunes have swallowed up forests, leaving some groves of trees as remnant tree islands.

Freshwater trapped behind the dunes has formed numerous **freshwater lakes,** many of which are now ringed by campgrounds and vacation homes. These lakes are popular for fishing, swimming, and boating. The largest of the lakes lie outside the national recreation area and are, from north to south, Woahink Lake, Siltcoos Lake, Tahkenitch Lake, Clear Lake, Eel Lake, North Tenmile Lake, and Tenmile Lake. Smaller lakes that are within the recreation area include Cleawox Lake, Carter Lake, Beale Lake, and Horsfall Lake. Traditionally, these lakes have been in a constant state of flux; with the construction of homes around their shores, though, the lakes are now maintained at their current shape and size.

European beach grass is playing an even greater role in changing the natural dynamics of this region. Introduced to anchor sand dunes and prevent them from inundating roads and river channels, this plant has been much more effective than anyone ever imagined. Able to survive even when buried under several feet of sand, European beach grass has covered many acres of land and formed dunes in back of the beach. These dunes effectively block sand from blowing inland off the beach, and as winds blow sand off the dunes into wet, low-lying areas, vegetation takes hold, thus eliminating areas of former dunes. Aerial photos have shown that where once 80% of the dunes here were open sand, today only 20% are. It is predicted that within 50 years, these dunes will all have been completely covered with vegetation and will no longer be the barren, windswept expanses of sand seen today.

There are numerous options for exploring the dunes. **Jessie M. Honeyman Memorial State Park** 🐾🐾 (© **541/997-3641;** www.oregonstateparks.org), 3 miles south of Florence, is a unique spot with a beautiful forest-bordered lake and towering sand dunes. The park offers camping, picnicking, hiking trails, and access to Cleawox and Woahink lakes. On Cleawox Lake, there is a swimming area and a boat-rental facility. The dunes adjacent to Cleawox Lake are used by off-road vehicles.

The easiest place to get an overview of the dunes is at the **Oregon Dunes Overlook,** 10 miles south of Florence. Here you'll find viewing platforms high atop a forested sand dune that overlooks a vast expanse of bare sand. Another easy place from which to view the dunes is the viewing platform on the Taylor Dunes Trail, which begins at the **Carter Lake Campground,** 7½ miles south of Florence. It is an easy ½-mile walk to the viewing platform.

There are several places to wander among these sand dunes. If you have time only for a quick walk, head to **Carter Lake Campground,** where you can continue on from the Taylor Dunes viewing platform. The beach is less than a mile beyond the viewing platform, and roughly half this distance is through dunes. From this same campground, you can hike the **Carter Dunes Trail.** The beach is 1½ miles away through dunes, forest, and meadows known as a *deflation plain.* A 3.5-mile loop trail leads from the **Oregon Dunes Overlook** (see above) out to the beach by way of Tahkenitch Creek, a meandering stream that flows through the dunes and out to the ocean. Another mile south of the Oregon Dunes Overlook, you'll find the **Tahkenitch Trail Head,** which accesses an 8-mile network of little-used trails that wander through dunes, forest, marshes, and meadows. However, for truly impressive dunes, the best route is the **John Dellenback Dunes Trail** 🐾🐾, which has its trail head a half-mile south of **Eel Creek Campground** (11 miles south of Reedsport). This 3-mile round-trip trail leads through an area of dunes 2 miles wide by 4 miles long. Don't get lost!

About 30% of the sand dunes are open to **off-road vehicles (ORVs),** and throngs of people flock to this area to roar up and down the dunes. If you'd like to do a little off-roading, you can rent a miniature dune buggy or ATV from **Sand Dunes Frontier,** 83960 U.S. 101 S. (© **541/997-3544;** www.sanddunesfrontier.com), 4 miles south of Florence. Guided tours of the dunes are offered by Sand Dunes Frontier and **Sandland Adventures,** 85366 U.S. 101 S. (© **541/997-8087;** www.sandland.com), 1 mile south of Florence (this company has a little amusement park as well). The tours cost about $12 to $40. One-person dune buggies and ATVs rent for about $45 per hour. Down at the southern end of the recreation area, you can rent vehicles from **Spinreel Dune Buggy Rentals,** 67045 Spinreel Rd. (© **541/759-3313;** www.ridetheoregondunes.com), located just off U.S. 101, about 9 miles south of Reedsport.

Ever heard of sand boarding? It's basically snowboarding in the sand, and at **Sand Master Park,** 87542 U.S. 101 (© **541/997-6006;** www.sandmasterpark.com), you (or your teenage kids) will find 40 acres of sculpted sand dunes designed to mimic a wintertime snowboard park (lots of jumps and rails). June through August, the park is open daily from 9am to 7pm; other months, it's open Thursday through Tuesday from 10am to 5pm. Sand boards rent for $16 to $25.

> ### *Fun Fact* Iditarod in the Sand?
>
> The area's most unusual annual event is the **Dune Musher's Mail Run** (www. oregondunemushers.com), which takes place each year in March and attracts dogsled teams from all over the United States and Canada. Teams race from Horsfall Beach near Coos Bay all the way to Florence, with teams of 5 to 12 dogs covering 70 miles in 2 days. For this race, dogsleds with fat tires (instead of skids) are used. Racers carry special commemorative envelopes that are canceled at both Horsfall Beach and Florence.

If you'd rather avoid the dune buggies and ORVs, stay away from the dunes between the South Jetty area (just south of Florence) and Siltcoos Lake; the area adjacent to Umpqua Lighthouse State Park just south of Winchester Bay; and the area from Spinreel Campground south to the Horsfall Dune & Beach Access Road, which is just north of the town of North Bend.

OTHER ACTIVITIES & ATTRACTIONS
IN THE FLORENCE AREA

Florence's **Old Town,** on the north bank of the Siuslaw River, is one of the most charming historic districts on the Oregon coast. The restored wood and brick buildings, many of which house interesting shops, galleries, and restaurants, capture the flavor of a 19th-century fishing village.

If you'd like to ride a horse along the beach, head north to **C&M Stables,** 90241 U.S. 101 N. (© **541/997-7540;** www.oregonhorsebackriding.com), which is located 8 miles north of Florence and offers rides on the beach and through the dunes. A 2-hour ride on the beach will cost you $45 to $55.

If golf is your sport, try the 18-hole **Sandpines Golf Course,** 1201 35th St. (© **800/ 917-4653;** www.sandpines.com), which plays through dunes and pine forest and is one of Oregon's most popular courses. During the summer, you'll pay $70 to $110 for 18 holes. Alternatively, try the 18-hole **Ocean Dunes Golf Links,** 3345 Munsel Lake Rd. (© **800/468-4833** or 541/997-3232; www.oceandunesgolf.com), which also plays through the dunes and charges $20 to $42 for 18 holes during the summer.

If you'd like to rent a kayak and paddle around on the Siuslaw River or rent a surfboard and catch some waves, contact **Central Coast Watersports,** U.S. 101 at 19th Street (© **800/789-3483** or 541/997-1812). Kayaks rent for $30 to $40 per day and surfboards rent for $18 (wetsuits are $15).

IN THE REEDSPORT AREA

In downtown Reedsport on the Umpqua River waterfront, you can visit the **Umpqua Discovery Center,** 409 Riverfront Way (© **541/271-4816;** www.umpquadiscovery center.com). This museum contains displays on the history and ecology of the area. One of the better exhibits focuses on the natural history of the tidewater region. June through September, it's open daily from 9am to 5pm; other months, daily from 10am to 4pm. Admission is $8 for adults, $7 for seniors, and $4 for children 6 to 15. Outside the discovery center, you'll find an observation tower that is sometimes a good place to do a little bird-watching.

At the **Dean Creek Elk Viewing Area** ⭐, 1 mile east of town on Ore. 38, you can spot 120 or more elk grazing on 1,000 acres of meadows that have been set aside as a preserve. In summer, the elk tend to stay in the forest, where it's cooler.

In Winchester Bay, you can visit the historic **Umpqua River Lighthouse.** The original lighthouse was at the mouth of the Umpqua River and was the first lighthouse on the Oregon coast. It fell into the Umpqua River in 1861 and was replaced in 1894 by the current lighthouse. Adjacent to the lighthouse is the **Visitors Center & Museum,** 1020 Lighthouse Rd. (© **541/271-4631**), which is housed in a former coast-guard station and contains historical exhibits and an information center. Here at the museum, you can arrange to join a tour of the lighthouse. Tours are offered May through September daily between 10am and 4pm and cost $3.

Across the street from the lighthouse is a **whale-viewing platform.** (The best viewing months are Nov–June.) Also nearby is the very pretty **Umpqua Lighthouse State Park** (© **541/271-4118;** www.oregonstateparks.com), the site of the 500-foot-tall sand dunes that are the tallest in the United States. The park offers picnicking, hiking, and camping amid forests and sand dunes.

If you want to do some fishing on the Umpqua and need a guide to lead you to the best fishing holes, contact Todd Hannah at **The Oregon Angler** (© **800/428-8585;** www.theoregonangler.com); rates are $175 to $225 for a day of fishing.

WHERE TO STAY
IN FLORENCE
Driftwood Shores Resort & Conference Center ⭐ *(Kids)*   Located several miles north of Florence's Old Town district, this is the only oceanfront lodging in the area. It's popular year-round, so book early. The rooms vary in size and amenities, but all have ocean views and balconies. Most also have kitchens, and the three-bedroom suites are as large as many vacation homes. The hotel's restaurant has ocean views from every table.

88416 First Ave., Florence, OR 97439. © **800/422-5091** or 541/997-8263. Fax 541/997-3253. www.driftwood shores.com. 136 units. Mid-June to Sept $104–$159 double, $241–$317 suite; Oct to mid-June $90–$132 double, $205–$275 suite. AE, DC, DISC, MC, V. **Amenities:** Restaurant (American); lounge; indoor pool; Jacuzzi; coin-op laundry. *In room:* TV, fridge, coffeemaker, hair dryer, iron, Wi-Fi.

The Edwin K Bed & Breakfast ⭐   Located in Old Town Florence only 2 blocks from shops and restaurants, this 1914 Sears Craftsman home is one of the most luxurious B&Bs on the coast. The four upstairs rooms are the most spacious, and two overlook the Siuslaw River, which is just across the street and has a huge sand dune rising up on its far bank (although a new condominium development may have blocked the view by the time you read this). One of these two front rooms has a clawfoot tub, while the other has a double whirlpool tub and a separate double shower. Other rooms, although not as plush, are still comfortable. Breakfasts are lavish five-course affairs, and in the afternoon, tea, cookies, and sherry are served.

1155 Bay St. (P.O. Box 2687), Florence, OR 97439. © **800/833-9465** or 541/997-8360. Fax 541/997-2423. www. edwink.com. 7 units. May–Oct 15 $150–$175 double, $175–$200 apt/suite; lower rates other months. Rates include full breakfast (except in apt). Children over 14 welcome in main house. DISC, MC, V. *In room:* Fridge, hair dryer, Wi-Fi, no phone.

River House Inn   Overlooking the Siuslaw River drawbridge and sand dunes on the far side of the river, the River House is only 1 block from the heart of Florence's Old Town district. This motel offers comfortable and attractive rooms, most of which have views and balconies. The largest and most expensive have double whirlpool tubs. Riverfront rooms are worth requesting.

1202 Bay St., Florence, OR 97439. C 888/824-2750 or 541/997-3933. Fax 541/997-6263. www.riverhouseflorence. com. 40 units. Late May to mid-Oct $99–$160 double; mid-Oct to late May $75–$150 double. Children 12 and under stay free in parent's room. AE, DISC, MC, V. **Amenities:** Coin-op laundry. *In room:* TV, coffeemaker, hair dryer, free local calls, high-speed Internet access.

CAMPGROUNDS

North of Florence are the first of this region's many campgrounds, **Sutton** and **Alder Dune,** both of which are operated by the Forest Service. Just outside Florence at the Siuslaw River's north jetty is the relatively quiet **Harbor Vista County Park** (C 541/ 682-2000; www.co.lane.or.us/parks/harbor.htm); with nice campsites and day-use areas, it's an alternative to crowded Honeyman State Park. South of Florence, you'll find more than a dozen Forest Service campgrounds and three state-park campgrounds within the Oregon Dunes National Recreation Area. With two lakes, swimming areas, sand dunes, and shady forests, **Jessie M. Honeyman Memorial State Park,** just a few miles south of Florence, is one of the most popular state parks in Oregon and stays full throughout the summer. Just south of here you'll find the Siltcoos Recreation Area, where **Lagoon Campground** and **Waxmyrtle Campground** are the best choices. **Carter Lake Campground,** on a popular swimming and boating lake, is another quiet choice in this area. The **Tahkenitch Campground,** however, is probably the best in the area. It's set in the forest on the edge of the dunes. South of Reedsport and Winchester Bay, you'll find **William M. Tugman State Park** (C 541/888-4902; www.oregonstateparks.org), at the south end of Eel Lake. **Eel Creek Campground,** adjacent to the Umpqua Dunes, is a quiet choice down at the southern end of the national recreation area. For reservations at the state park campgrounds, contact **ReserveAmerica** (C 800/452-5687; www.reserveamerica.com). Several of the national-forest campgrounds in the area accept reservations. Contact **Recreation.gov** (C 877/444-6777 or 518/885-3639; www.reserveusa.com).

WHERE TO DINE
IN FLORENCE

When you need a good cup of espresso, stop in at **Siuslaw River Coffee Roasters,** 1240 Bay St. (C 541/997-3443; www.coffeeoregon.com). If you're looking for some gourmet foods or wine, drop by **Grape Leaf,** 1269 Bay St. (C 541/997-1646), which has a small wine bar and also serves light meals.

Crave's Wine & Tapas Bar ⋆ INTERNATIONAL   Although this old town wine bar, in a former car dealership from 1928, is only a few blocks from the riverfront, it seems less touristy than most of the other restaurants in town. Light meals make up most of the menu here, but there are three or four more substantial daily specials, perhaps duck confit or halibut. For light meals or just an accompaniment to a glass of wine, try the French onion soup or the Alsatian tart, made with Gruyere, caramelized onions, ham, and crème fraiche. There's occasional live jazz, and on cool evenings, nothing beats sitting by the fireplace here sipping a pinot noir.

294 Laurel St. C 541/997-3154. Reservations recommended. Main courses $13–$19. MC, V. Mon and Thurs–Sat 4–11pm; Sun 4–9pm.

International C-Food Market SEAFOOD   Located on a dock on the old waterfront, this restaurant also happens to be a fish-processing facility, which means the seafood served here is as fresh as you'll find anywhere on the coast. The warehouse-like space has loads of windows providing views of the river, and the light at sunset can be gorgeous. While the menu is a bit heavy with fried seafood, there are good steamed Manila clams, and the crab cakes are another good bet. Put these two together for a tasty, light meal. Or, how about a seafood pizza or all-you-can-eat Dungeness crab?

1498 Bay St. ⓒ 541/997-7978. www.internationalcfoodmarket.com. Reservations recommended. Main courses $9–$35. AE, DISC, MC, V. Daily 11am–9pm.

Waterfront Depot Restaurant & Bar 🌟🌟 *Finds* NEW AMERICAN   This dark, cozy waterfront bar/restaurant is my favorite place to dine in Florence. It's housed in the 1913 Mapleton railroad depot, which was moved here from farther up the Siuslaw River and is one of the many white historic buildings that line Bay Street. Inside, the restaurant is a well-balanced blend of hip bar and old-country-inn dining room. There are battered wooden floors and a beautiful little bar. The menu is on blackboards attached to the depot's old sliding doors, and though the menu is not very long, there's plenty of variety and some of the best values on the coast. Among the appetizers, keep an eye out for the oyster stew, which is a great deal. Among the entrees, the grilled salmon is an equally good deal, as are the lamb shanks. For dessert, get a fat slice of cake.

1252 Bay St. ⓒ 541/902-9100. Reservations recommended. Main courses $9–$18. MC, V. Daily 4–10pm.

IN WINCHESTER BAY

If you're craving some smoked salmon or other fish, drop by **Sportsmen's Cannery & Smokehouse,** 182 Bayfront Loop, Winchester Bay (ⓒ **541/271-3293;** www. sportsmenscannery.com).

10 The Coos Bay Area

85 miles NW of Roseburg, 50 miles S of Florence, 24 miles N of Bandon

With a population of around 35,000, the Coos Bay area, consisting of the towns of Coos Bay, North Bend, and Charleston, is the largest urban center on the Oregon coast. Coos Bay and North Bend are the bay's commercial center and have merged into a single large town, while nearby Charleston maintains its distinct character as a small fishing port.

As the largest natural harbor between San Francisco and Puget Sound, Coos Bay has long been an important port. Logs, wood chips, and wood products are the main export. However, shipments of wood products have been down for more than a decade, and in response to the economic downturn of the port, the bay area has been working hard to attract both more tourists and more industry. In downtown Coos Bay, there is an attractive waterfront boardwalk, complete with historical displays, and what was once a huge lumber mill is now the site of the equally large Mill Resort & Casino.

Even if it isn't the most beautiful town on the Oregon coast, Coos Bay has a lot of character and quite a few tourist amenities, including a few decent restaurants, moderately priced motels, and even a few B&Bs. But what makes Coos Bay a town not to be missed is its proximity to a trio of picturesque state parks.

ESSENTIALS
GETTING THERE   From the north, take Ore. 99 from just south of Cottage Grove. This road becomes Ore. 38. At Reedsport, head south on U.S. 101. From the south, take Ore. 42 from just south of Roseburg.

The Southern Oregon Coast

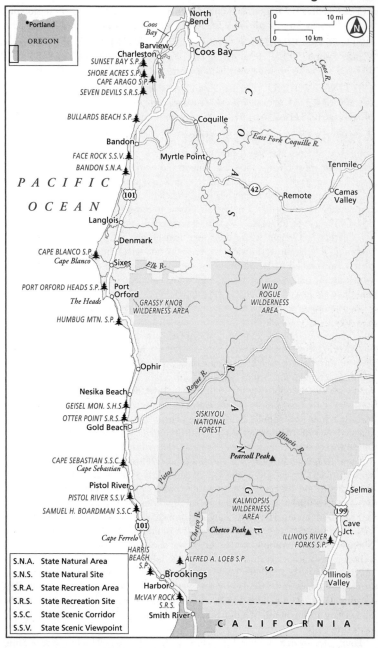

Portland
OREGON

Coos Bay
North Bend
Barview
Charleston
SUNSET BAY S.P.
SHORE ACRES S.P.
CAPE ARAGO S.P.
SEVEN DEVILS S.R.S.

Coos Bay

Coos R.

C O O S

BULLARDS BEACH S.P.

Coquille

East Fork Coquille R.

Bandon
FACE ROCK S.S.V.
BANDON S.N.A.

Myrtle Point

Tenmile

C O A S T

PACIFIC

101

42

Remote

Camas Valley

OCEAN

Langlois

Denmark

CAPE BLANCO S.P.
Cape Blanco
Sixes

Elk R.

PORT ORFORD HEADS S.P.
The Heads

Port Orford

GRASSY KNOB WILDERNESS AREA

WILD ROGUE WILDERNESS AREA

HUMBUG MTN. S.P.

R

Ophir

Rogue R.

A

Nesika Beach
GEISEL MON. S.H.S.
OTTER POINT S.R.S.
Gold Beach

SISKIYOU NATIONAL FOREST

Illinois R.

N

Pearsoll Peak

CAPE SEBASTIAN S.S.C.
Cape Sebastian

Pistol R.

Pistol River
PISTOL RIVER S.S.V.
SAMUEL H. BOARDMAN S.S.C.

G

Selma

KALMIOPSIS WILDERNESS AREA

199

Cape Ferrelo

101

Chetco R.

Chetco Peak

E

Cave Jct.

ILLINOIS RIVER FORKS S.P.

HARRIS BEACH S.P.

ALFRED A. LOEB S.P.

S

Illinois Valley

S.N.A.	State Natural Area
S.N.S.	State Natural Site
S.R.A.	State Recreation Area
S.R.S.	State Recreation Site
S.S.C.	State Scenic Corridor
S.S.V.	State Scenic Viewpoint

Brookings
Harbor
McVAY ROCK S.R.S.
Smith River

C A L I F O R N I A

0   10 mi
0   10 km

N

The **Southwest Oregon Regional Airport,** 2348 Colorado St. (www.cooscounty airportdistrict.com), North Bend, is served by **Horizon Air.**

VISITOR INFORMATION   Contact the **Bay Area Chamber of Commerce & Visitor Center,** 50 E. Central Ave., Coos Bay, OR 97420 (© **800/824-8486** or 541/ 269-0215; www.oregonsbayareachamber.com).

GETTING AROUND   Car rentals are available in the Coos Bay area from **Hertz** (© **800/654-3131** or 541/756-4416; www.hertz.com) and **Enterprise Rent-a-Car** (© **800/261-7331** or 541/751-0298; www.enterprise.com).

A TRIO OF STATE PARKS & MORE
Southwest of Coos Bay you'll find three state parks and a county park that preserve some of the most breathtaking shoreline in the Northwest. The three parks are connected by an excellent trail that is perfect for a rewarding day hike.

Start your exploration of this beautiful stretch of coast by heading southwest on the Cape Arago Highway. In 12 miles you'll come to **Sunset Bay State Park** (© **800/ 551-6949** or 541/888-4902; www.oregonstateparks.org). This park has one of the few beaches in Oregon where the water actually gets warm enough for swimming (although folks from warm-water regions may not agree). Sunset Bay is almost completely surrounded by sandstone cliffs, and the entrance to the bay is quite narrow, which means the waters here stay fairly calm. Picnicking and camping are available, and there are lots of tide pools to explore.

Continuing on another 3 miles brings you to **Shore Acres State Park** (© **800/ 551-6949** or 541/888-4902; www.oregonstateparks.org), once the estate of local shipping tycoon Louis J. Simpson, who spent years developing his gardens. His ships would bring him unusual plants from all over the world, and eventually the gardens grew to include a formal English garden and a Japanese garden with a 100-foot lily pond. His home, which long ago was torn down, and the gardens were built atop sandstone cliffs overlooking the Pacific and a tiny cove. Rock walls rise up from the water and have been sculpted by the waves into unusual shapes. During winter storms, wave-watching is a popular pastime here. The water off the park is often a striking shade of blue, and **Simpson Beach,** in the little cove, just might be the prettiest beach in Oregon. A trail leads down to this beach. There is a $3 day-use fee here.

Cape Arago State Park (© **800/551-6949** or 541/888-4902; www.oregon stateparks.org) is the third of this trio of parks. Just offshore from the rugged cape lie the rocks and small islands of Simpson Reef, which provide sunbathing spots for hundreds of seals (including elephant seals) and sea lions. The barking of the sea lions can be heard from hundreds of yards away, and though you can't get very close, with a pair of binoculars you can see the seals and sea lions quite well. The best viewing point is at **Simpson Reef Viewpoint.** On either side of the cape are coves with quiet beaches, although the beaches are closed from March 1 to June 30 to protect young seal pups. Tide pools along these beaches offer hours of fascinating exploration during other months.

Also in the vicinity of these three state parks, you'll find **Bastendorff Beach County Park** (© **541/888-5353;** www.co.coos.or.us/ccpark/bastendorff), north of Sunset Bay at the mouth of Coos Bay, which offers a long, wide beach that's popular with surfers.

Four miles down Seven Devils Road from Charleston, you'll find the **South Slough National Estuarine Research Reserve** (© **541/888-5558;** www.southsloughestuary. org). An interpretive center (daily 10am–4:30pm Memorial Day to Labor Day; closed

---

Fun Fact **Oregon Myrtlewood**

At Coos Bay you enter **myrtlewood** country. The myrtle tree grows only along a short section of coast in southern Oregon and northern California and is prized by woodworkers for its fine grain and durability. A very hard wood, it lends itself to all manner of platters, bowls, goblets, sculptures, and whatever. All along the south coast, you'll see myrtlewood factories and shops where you can see how the raw wood is turned into finished pieces. At the south end of the town of Coos Bay, watch for **The Oregon Connection**, 1125 S. First St. (© **800/255-5318** or 541/267-7804; www.oregonconnection.com), which is just off U.S. 101. This is one of the bigger myrtlewood factories. **Myrtlewood Factory Showroom**, 68794 Hauser Depot Rd. at U.S. 101 (© **541/756-2220;** www.realoregongift.com), 5 miles north of North Bend, is another large factory and showroom. Six miles south of Bandon on U.S. 101, watch for **Zumwalt's Myrtlewood Factory,** 47422 U.S. 101 (© **541/347-3654;** www.zumwaltsmyrtlewood.com), which has a good selection and prices.

Sun other months) set high above the slough provides background on the importance of estuaries. South Slough is in the process of being restored after many years of damming, diking, and reclamation of marshlands by farmers. A hiking trail leads down to the marshes, and there is good canoeing and sea kayaking.

OTHER AREA ACTIVITIES & ATTRACTIONS

Charleston is the bay area's charter-fishing marina. If you'd like to do some sportfishing, contact **Bob's Sport Fishing** (© **800/628-9633** or 541/888-4241) or **Betty Kay Charters** (© **800/752-6303** or 541/888-9021; www.bettykaycharters.com). Expect to pay around $65 for a 5-hour bottom-fishing trip and $165 to $170 for a 12-hour halibut-fishing trip.

In addition to all the outdoor recreational activities around the bay area, there is also a museum well worth visiting. The **Coos Art Museum**, 235 Anderson Ave., Coos Bay (© **541/267-3901;** www.coosart.org), is a highly regarded little museum that hosts changing exhibits in a wide variety of styles and media. Runners will also be interested to know that up on the second floor of the museum, there is a small exhibit dedicated to long-distance runner Steve Prefontaine, who was from Coos Bay and who died in 1975. The museum is open Tuesday through Friday from 10am to 4pm and Saturday from 1 to 4pm; admission is $5 for adults and $2 for seniors and students.

Part of the renovation of the Coos Bay waterfront has been the construction of **The Mill Casino & Hotel,** 3201 Tremont Ave., North Bend (© **800/953-4800** or 541/756-8800; www.themillcasino.com). Here you can play slot machines, blackjack, poker, and bingo. There are several restaurants and a lounge. Also, you should be sure to check the calendar at the **Egyptian Theatre,** 229 S. Broadway (© **541/260-1033;** www.egyptian-theatre.com), a restored historic movie palace that was built in 1925 and now shows both new and vintage movies.

WHERE TO STAY

Coos Bay Manor B&B   This B&B, in a historic colonial-style home built in 1912, is unusual for a B&B in that it takes both children and pets. However, with its Victorian decor, it does seem more like the sort of place you'd choose for a vacation away from your kids. Rooms are full of antiques, and there are quilts on the beds. Most rooms have TVs and some also have VCRs. The Barron's Room with its four-poster bed is my personal favorite here, though the Victorian Room, which also has a four-poster bed, is the inn's largest room. The suites are created by connecting a couple of the rooms.

955 S. Fifth St., Coos Bay, OR 97420. ℂ **800/269-1224** or 541/269-1224. www.coosbaymanor.com. 5 units. $135 double; $150–$220 suite. Rates include full breakfast. AE, MC, V. Children and pets accepted. *In room:* TV, Wi-Fi, no phone.

Edgewater Inn   This is Coos Bay's only waterfront hotel, and though the water it faces is only a narrow stretch of the back bay, you can sometimes watch ships in the harbor. Guest rooms are large, and deluxe rooms are particularly well designed and spacious, with a breakfast bar and an extra-large TV. Other deluxe rooms have in-room spas. Most rooms also have balconies overlooking the water (and industrial areas).

275 E. Johnson Ave., Coos Bay, OR 97420. ℂ **800/233-0423** or 541/267-0423. www.theedgewaterinn.com. 82 units. $90–$135 double. Rates include continental breakfast. AE, DC, DISC, MC, V. Pets accepted ($8 per night). **Amenities:** Indoor pool; exercise room; Jacuzzi; courtesy van; business center. *In room:* A/C, TV/VCR, dataport, fridge, microwave, coffeemaker, hair dryer, free local calls.

CAMPGROUNDS

About 12 miles outside Coos Bay, you'll find **Sunset Bay State Park** (p. 220). To make a reservation, contact **ReserveAmerica** (ℂ **800/452-5687;** www.reserveamerica.com). **Bastendorff Beach County Park** (ℂ **541/888-5353;** www.co.coos.or.us/ccpark/ bastendorff), north of Sunset Bay at the mouth of Coos Bay, is an alternative to the frequently full Sunset Bay State Park campground. This latter park does not take reservations for campsites but does have a few rustic cabins that can be reserved.

WHERE TO DINE

Benetti's Italian Restaurant ⊛ SOUTHERN ITALIAN   For a city of its size, Coos Bay is surprisingly short of good places to eat, but Benetti's, right in downtown Coos Bay, has long been a local favorite. Large servings of classic southern Italian dishes keep people coming back for more. This is a good choice if you're here with the whole family.

260 S. Broadway, Coos Bay. ℂ **541/267-6066.** www.benettis.com. Reservations recommended. Main courses $9–$21. AE, DISC, MC, V. Sun–Thurs 5–9pm; Fri–Sat 5–10pm.

Blue Heron Bistro INTERNATIONAL   This odd little spot in the heart of downtown Coos Bay is an eclectic international restaurant that specializes in seafood and both Italian and German fare. The Blue Heron also has one of the largest assortments of imported beers on the coast, and is the sort of place that's perfect for lunch, dinner, or just a quick bite to eat. Items range from German bratwurst to blackened salmon salad to pizzas and pastas.

100 Commercial Ave., Coos Bay. ℂ **541/267-3933.** www.blueheronbistro.com. Main courses $8–$13. MC, V. Mon–Sat 11am–10pm; Sun 6–10pm (closed Sun in winter).

The Portside Restaurant ⊛ *Kids* SEAFOOD   Charleston is home to Coos Bay's charter and commercial fishing fleets, so it's no surprise that it's also home to the area's best seafood restaurant. Check the daily fresh sheet to see what just came in on the boat. This place has been around for decades, and preparations tend toward traditional continental dishes, of which the house specialty is a bouillabaisse Marseillaise that's just swimming with shrimp, red snapper, lobster, crab legs, butter clams, prawns, and scallops. The restaurant overlooks the boat basin and is popular with families.

63383 Kingfisher Dr., Charleston. © **541/888-5544.** www.portsidebythebay.com. Reservations recommended. Main courses $9–$34. AE, DC, MC, V. Daily 11:30am–11pm.

11 Bandon

24 miles S of Coos Bay, 85 miles W of Roseburg, 54 miles north of Gold Beach

Once known primarily as the cranberry capital of Oregon (you can see the cranberry bogs south of town along U.S. 101), Bandon is now better known for its world-class Bandon Dunes Golf Resort. It's also set on one of the most spectacular pieces of coastline in the state. Just south of town, the beach is littered with boulders, monoliths, and haystack rocks that seem to have been strewn by some giant hand. Sunsets are stunning.

Just north of town the Coquille River empties into the Pacific, and at the river's mouth stands a picturesque lighthouse. The lighthouse is one of only a handful of Bandon buildings to survive a fire in 1936. Even though most buildings downtown date only from the 1930s, Bandon still has the quaint feel of a historic seaside village, and a waterfront boardwalk connects Bandon with the Coquille River. Be sure to take a stroll along the boardwalk while you're in town.

ESSENTIALS

GETTING THERE   From Roseburg, head west on Ore. 42 to Coquille, where you take Ore. 42S to Bandon, which is on U.S. 101.

VISITOR INFORMATION   For more information, contact the **Bandon Chamber of Commerce,** 300 Second St. (P.O. Box 1515), Bandon, OR 97411 (© **541/347-9616;** www.bandon.com).

FESTIVALS   Bandon is the cranberry capital of Oregon, and each year in September the harvest is celebrated with the **Bandon Cranberry Festival.**

OUTDOOR ACTIVITIES

Head out of Bandon on Beach Loop Road, and you'll soon see why the rocks are a big draw. Wind and waves have sculpted shoreline monoliths into contorted spires and twisted shapes. The first good place to view the rocks and get down to the beach is at **Coquille Point,** at the end of 11th Street. Here you'll find a short, paved interpretive trail atop a bluff overlooking the beach, rock monoliths, and the river mouth. There's also a long staircase leading down to the beach. From here you can see Table Rock and the Sisters. From the **Face Rock Viewpoint** you can see the area's most famous rock, which resembles a face gazing skyward. Nearby stand rocks that resemble a dog, a cat, and kittens. A trail leads down to the beach from the viewpoint, so you can go out and explore some of the rocks that are left high and dry by low tide. South of the rocks, along a flat stretch of beach backed by dunes, there are several beach access areas, all of which are within **Bandon State Natural Area.**

Across the river from downtown Bandon, you'll find **Bullards Beach State Park** (© **541/347-3501;** www.oregonstateparks.org). Within the park are beaches, a marsh overlook, hiking and horseback-riding trails, a picnic area, a campground, and a boat ramp. Fishing, crabbing, and clamming are all very popular. In the park you'll also find the 1896 **Coquille River Lighthouse.** This lighthouse is one of the only lighthouses to ever be hit by a ship—in 1903 an abandoned schooner plowed into the light. May through October, tours of the lighthouse are offered; call for hours and days.

At Bandon, as elsewhere on the Oregon coast, **gray whales** migrating between the Arctic and Baja California, Mexico, pass close to the shore and can often be spotted from land. The whales pass Bandon between December and February on their way south and between March and May on their way north. Gray days and early mornings before the wind picks up are the best times to spot whales. Coquille Point, at the end of 11th Street, and the bluffs along Beach Loop Road are the best vantage points.

More than 300 species of birds have been spotted in the Bandon vicinity, making this one of the best sites in Oregon for **bird-watching.** The **Oregon Islands National Wildlife Refuge,** which includes 1,853 rocks, reefs, and islands off the state's coast, contains the famous monoliths of Bandon. Among the birds that nest on these rocks are rhinoceros auklets, storm petrels, gulls, and tufted puffins. The latter, with their large colorful beaks, are the most beloved of local birds, and their images show up on all manner of local souvenirs. The **Bandon Marsh National Wildlife Refuge (© 541/ 347-1470;** www.fws.gov/oregoncoast/bandonmarsh/index.htm), at the mouth of the Coquille River, is another good spot for bird-watching. In this area you can expect to see grebes, mergansers, buffleheads, plovers, and several species of raptors.

If you'd like to ride a horse down the beach, contact **Bandon Beach Riding Stables,** 54629 Beach Loop Rd. (© **541/347-3423**), south of Face Rock. A 1-hour ride is $40 and a 2-hour sunset ride is $50.

The world-class **Bandon Dunes Golf Course,** 57744 Round Lake Dr. (© **888/ 742-0172** or 541/347-4380; www.bandondunesgolf.com), a classic Scottish-style links course, is Oregon's only oceanfront golf course and has made Bandon a major golfing destination. The course, notorious for its blustery winds, has been compared to Pebble Beach and St. Andrews. The summer green fees are $210 for resort guests and $265 for nonguests ($105 for your second 18 holes). November to April, you can play here for $75 to $220. This is a walking course, and no golf carts are allowed; but caddies are available for an additional $55.

Bandon Crossings Golf Course (© 541/347-3232; www.bandoncrossings.com), an 18-hole course 5 miles south of town on U.S. 101, is the area's newest golf course and is an economical alternative to Bandon Dunes. Green fees are between $45 and $75 in the summer.

If that's out of your price range, there's always the **Bandon Face Rock Golf Course,** 3235 Beach Loop Dr. (© **541/347-3818**), which offers a scenic 9 holes not far from the famous Face Rock. Green fees are $15 to $17 for 9 holes.

If, after you've had enough golf, you decide you'd like to do some fishing, contact **Prowler Charters** (© **800/347-1901** or 541/347-1901; www.prowlercharters.com), which goes out for salmon, halibut, tuna, and bottom fish and charges $70 to $175 for a day of fishing.

OTHER AREA ACTIVITIES & ATTRACTIONS

The **West Coast Game Park Safari** ⊛, 46914 U.S. 101 S. (© **541/347-3106;** www. gameparksafari.com), 7 miles south of Bandon, bills itself as America's largest wild-animal petting park and is a must for families. Depending on what young animals they have at the time of your visit, you might be able to play with a leopard, tiger, or bear cub. The park is open daily from 9am to 6pm in summer, 9am to 5pm in spring and fall (call for hours in other months). Admission is $14 for adults, $13 for seniors, $8.50 for children 7 to 12, and $5.50 for children 2 to 6.

Shopping is one of Bandon's main attractions, and in **Old Town Bandon,** just off U.S. 101, you'll find some interesting shops and galleries. A couple of galleries sell artworks by regional artists. One of the better ones is the **Bandon Glass Art Studio** at 240 U.S. 101 (© **541/347-4723;** www.dutchschulze.com), which is just across the highway from Old Town. Here you can watch glass directly from the furnace being made into the paperweights or fluted glass bowls the gallery sells.

WHERE TO STAY

Bandon Dunes Golf Resort ⚐⚐⚐ Although this is one of the most tasteful and luxurious accommodations on the Oregon coast, the emphasis is so entirely on the golf course that anyone not interested in the game will feel like an interloper. However, if golf is your game then you'll love this place. The lodge sits up on the dunes and looks out over the fairways to the Pacific. Accommodations are also available in a variety of rooms that are here called cottages, but which are not really cottages but rather multi-unit buildings arranged around a pretty little pond. These rooms don't have the golf-course views, but they are very comfortable.

57744 Round Lake Dr., Bandon, OR 97411. © 888/345-6008 or 541/347-4380. www.bandondunesgolf.com. 147 units. $130–$320 double; $200–$1,500 suite. Children under 12 stay free in parent's room. AE, DC, DISC, MC, V. **Amenities:** 5 restaurants (Northwest, American); 3 lounges; 3 18-hole golf courses; exercise room; Jacuzzi; sauna; concierge; business center; room service; massage. In room: TV, coffeemaker, hair dryer, iron, free local calls.

Bandon Inn ⚐ Set atop a hill overlooking old town Bandon and the Coquille River, this older hotel has been transformed into a reasonable facsimile of a Cape Cod inn, complete with cedar-shingle siding and white-trimmed windows. With tastefully traditional decor, this is a good in-town alternative to the Best Western or the Sunset Oceanfront Lodging. Stairs lead down the hill from the inn to old town, so you can walk to some of Bandon's best restaurants.

355 U.S. 101 (P.O. Box 1409), Bandon, OR 97411. © 800/526-0209 or 541/347-4417. Fax 541/347-3616. www.bandoninn.com. 57 units. Late June to early Oct $119–$150 double; mid-May to late June and early Oct to early Nov $94–$130 double; Jan to mid-May and early Nov to Dec $74–$115 double. Children 6 and under stay free in parent's room. AE, DISC, MC, V. Pets accepted ($15 per night). **Amenities:** Access to nearby health club. In room: TV, fridge, microwave, coffeemaker, free local calls, Wi-Fi.

Best Western Inn at Face Rock Resort ⚐⚐ Located about a mile south of Face Rock, this modern hotel is Bandon's original golf resort, and is adjacent to the 9-hole Bandon Face Rock Golf Course. Guest rooms here are the best on Beach Loop Drive, and there are plenty of recreational facilities. Although the hotel is across the street from the beach, many of the rooms have ocean views. The views from the hotel restaurant, however, aren't nearly as good as those at the nearby Lord Bennett's Restaurant. A short path leads down to the beach.

3225 Beach Loop Dr., Bandon, OR 97411. © 800/638-3092 or 541/347-9441. Fax 541/347-2532. www.innatface rock.com. 74 units. Mid-May to mid-Oct $105–$274 double; mid-Oct to mid-May $79–$224 double. Children under 17 stay free in parent's room. AE, DC, DISC, MC, V. Pets accepted ($15 per night). **Amenities:** Restaurant (American); lounge; indoor pool; exercise room; Jacuzzi; sauna; coin-op laundry. In room: TV, dataport, coffeemaker, hair dryer, iron, free local calls.

Lighthouse Bed and Breakfast ⚐ Located on the road that leads to the mouth of the Coquille River, this riverfront B&B has a view of the historic Bandon Lighthouse, and, with its weathered cedar siding, large decks, and small sunroom, it's the quintessential Oregon beach house. Guest rooms range from a small room with the private bathroom across the hall to a spacious room with views of the ocean and lighthouse, a wood-burning stove, and a double whirlpool tub overlooking the river. Both the beach and Old Town Bandon are within a very short walk.

650 Jetty Rd. SW (P.O Box 24), Bandon, OR 97411. (C) **541/347-9316**. www.lighthouselodging.com. 5 units. $140–$245 double; lower rates Nov–Apr. Rates include full breakfast. MC, V. Children over 12 accepted. *In room:* A/C, hair dryer, Wi-Fi.

Sunset Oceanfront Lodging *(Value)*   Dozens of Bandon's famous monoliths rise from the sand and waves in front of this motel, making sunsets from the Sunset truly memorable. The rooms, however, with their the dated furnishings and paneled walls, aren't nearly as nice as the views. On the other hand, since there's everything here from economy motel rooms to condos, rustic cabins, and classic cottages, you should be able to find accommodations to your liking. If you want something rustic and private, try to get one of the cottages. The adjacent Lord Bennett's Restaurant has *the* view in Bandon.

1865 Beach Loop Rd. (P.O. Box 373), Bandon, OR 97411. (C) **800/842-2407** or 541/347-2453. Fax 541/347-3636. www.sunsetmotel.com. 71 units. May 16–Oct 15 $60–$275 double; Oct 16–May 15 $50–$260 double. Rates include continental breakfast. Children under 5 stay free in parent's room. AE, DISC, MC, V. Pets accepted ($10 per day). **Amenities:** Restaurant (seafood); lounge; indoor pool; Jacuzzi; concierge; business center; coin-op laundry; laundry service. *In room:* TV, dataport, coffeemaker, free local calls.

CAMPGROUNDS

Bullards Beach State Park ((C) **541/347-3501**), across the Coquille River from downtown Bandon, has 185 campsites and 13 yurts for rent. To make reservations, call **ReserveAmerica** ((C) **800/452-5687;** www.reserveamerica.com).

Stormy Weather

Throughout the winter, Oregon's rocky shores and haystack rocks feel the effects of storms that originate far to the north in cold polar waters. As these storms slam ashore, sometimes with winds topping 100 mph, their huge waves smash against the rocks with breathtaking force, sending spray flying. The perfect storm-watching days come right after a big storm, when the waves are still big but the sky is clear. This is also the best time to go beachcombing—it's your best chance to find the rare handblown Japanese glass fishing floats that sometimes wash ashore on the Oregon coast.

Among the **best storm-watching spots** on the coast are the South Jetty at the mouth of the Columbia River in Fort Stevens State Park, Cannon Beach, Cape Meares, Depoe Bay, Cape Foulweather, Devil's Punchbowl on the Otter Crest Scenic Loop, Seal Rock, Cape Perpetua, Shore Acres State Park, Cape Arago State Park, Face Rock Viewpoint outside Bandon, and Cape Sebastian.

Some of the **best lodgings** for storm-watching are the Inn at Otter Crest north of Depoe Bay, the Channel House in Depoe Bay, the Overleaf Lodge Resort in Yachats, and the Sunset Motel in Bandon. The coast's **best restaurants** for storm-watching include the Pelican Pub & Brewery in Pacific City, Tidal Raves in Depoe Bay, and Lord Bennett's Restaurant in Bandon.

WHERE TO DINE

When it's time for espresso, stop in at **Bandon Coffee Café,** 365 Second St. SE (© 541/347-1144), in a cottage on the edge of Old Town. The **Bandon Baking Co. and Deli,** 160 Second St. (© 541/347-9440; www.bandonbakingco.com) and **2 Loons Cafe,** 120 Second St. (© 541/347-3750), are good places for pastries and sandwiches. For a quick meal of incredibly fresh fish and chips, you can't beat **Bandon Fish Market,** 249 First St. SE (© 541/347-4282; www.bandonfishmarket.com), which is right on the waterfront and has a few picnic tables. Also here on the waterfront, you can get cooked Dungeness crab at **Tony's Crab Shack,** 155 First St. (© 541/347-2875).

Alloro Wine Bar ☆☆ ITALIAN   This wine bar, inspired by a modern Italian *enoteca,* is a sure sign of things to come in the once-sleepy town of Bandon. Stylish and sophisticated, Alloro fills up nightly with golfers in town to play the fabled Bandon Dunes golf course. With customers from all over the country, Alloro works hard to present creative Italian fare the likes of which you'll find nowhere else on the south coast. You can start your meal with figs and prosciutto or perhaps zucchini blossoms stuffed with shrimp and Dungeness crab. The soup might have house-made halibut tortellini, and the pasta might be pappardelle with rabbit ragu. I tend to go with the fish of the day, but if you're feeling flush go for the Florentine steak. The wine list has lots from both Oregon and Italy, and there are also good desserts.

375 Second St. SE. © **541/347-1850.** www.allorowinebar.com. Reservations recommended. Main courses $17–$21. AE, DISC, MC, V. Summer Tues–Sun 4–10pm; other months Wed–Sat 4–8:30pm.

Lord Bennett's Restaurant and Lounge ☆ AMERICAN   Lord Bennett's is the only restaurant in Bandon that overlooks this town's bizarre beachscape of contorted rock spires and sea stacks, and this alone makes it a must for a meal. The sunsets are unforgettable. Since sunsets come late in the day in the summer, you might want to eat a late lunch the day you plan to come here. I suggest starting dinner with some crab cakes before moving on to such main courses as oysters baked with spinach, bacon, and Pernod or lamb chops with a hazelnut crust. There's a decent wine list, and the desserts are both beautiful and delicious.

1695 Beach Loop Dr., next to the Sunset Motel. © **541/347-3663.** www.bandonbythesea.com/lord_ben.htm. Reservations recommended. Main courses $5–$11 lunch, $15–$26 dinner. AE, DISC, MC, V. Mon–Fri 11am–2:30pm and 5–9pm; Sat–Sun 10am–2:30pm and 5–9pm.

Wild Rose ☆☆ MEDITERRANEAN/ASIAN   This tiny cottage in downtown Bandon houses the most romantic little restaurant in town. The lace curtains and roses in the garden all say English country cottage, though the building itself looks more like an old Northwest fisherman's cabin. The menu here wanders all over the world, though it emphasizes Mediterranean and Asian flavors. However, highlights include a pistachio-crusted halibut and a pancetta-wrapped sturgeon.

130 Chicago St. © **541/347-4428.** Reservations recommended. Main courses $18–$33. MC, V. Daily 5–10pm.

12 The Southern Oregon Coast

Port Orford: 27 miles S of Bandon; 79 miles N of Crescent City, CA; 95 miles W of Grants Pass. Gold Beach: 54 miles N of Crescent City, CA; 32 miles S of Port Orford. Brookings/Harbor: 26 miles N of Crescent City, CA; 35 miles S of Gold Beach

The 60-mile stretch of coast between Port Orford and the California state line is perhaps the most beautiful stretch of the entire Oregon coast, yet because of its distance from major metropolitan areas, it attracts surprisingly few visitors.

Anchoring the northern end of this stretch of coast is Port Orford, which is today little more than a wide spot in the road, yet it is the oldest town on the coast other than Astoria. Named by Captain George Vancouver on April 5, 1792, this natural harbor in the lee of Port Orford Heads became the first settlement right on the Oregon coast when, in 1851, settlers and soldiers together constructed Fort Orford. A fort was necessary because of hostilities with the area's native population. Eventually the settlers fled inland, crossing the Siskiyou Mountains.

Although the first settlers made camp here because there was something of a natural harbor, these days the area's fishing fleet is hauled out of the water nightly by a large crane. Working out of this tiny port is a small commercial fishing fleet.

Cape Blanco, located just north of Port Orford and discovered and named by Spanish explorer Martín de Aguilar in 1603, once made an even grander claim than Port Orford when it was heralded as the westernmost point of land in the lower 48. Today, that claim has been laid to rest by Cape Flattery, Washington, and Cape Blanco now only claims to be the westernmost point in Oregon.

In 19th-century California, gold prospectors had to struggle through rugged mountains in search of pay dirt, but here in Oregon they could just scoop it up off the beach. The black sands at the mouth of the Rogue River were high in gold, and it was this gold that gave Gold Beach its name. The white settlers attracted by the gold soon came in conflict with the local Rogue River (or TuTuNi) Indians. Violence erupted in 1856, but within the year the Rogue River Indian Wars had come to an end and the TuTuNis were moved to a reservation.

The TuTuNis had for centuries found the river to be a plentiful source of salmon, and when the gold played out, commercial fishermen moved in to take advantage of the large salmon runs. The efficiency of their nets and traps quickly decimated the local salmon population, and a hatchery was constructed to replenish the runs.

Brookings and Harbor together comprise the southernmost community on the Oregon coast. Because of the warm year-round temperatures, this region is known as the Oregon Banana Belt, and you'll see palm trees and other cold-sensitive plants thriving in gardens around town. Farms south of town grow nearly all of the Easter lilies sold in the United States. Other plants that thrive in this climate include coast redwoods, Oregon myrtles, and wild azaleas. Dividing the sister towns of Brookings and Harbor is the Chetco River, one of the purest and most beautiful rivers in the state.

ESSENTIALS

GETTING THERE   There is no convenient way to get to this stretch of coast. Coming from the north, the nearest highway connection to I-5 is Ore. 42 from Roseburg to Bandon. Coming from the south, you must either follow U.S. 101 north through California or take U.S. 199 southwest from Grants Pass and then continue north on U.S. 101. There is also a narrow, winding road over the mountains to Gold Beach from Galice (near Grants Pass), but I don't recommend this road, and in winter it is usually closed.

VISITOR INFORMATION   For more information on Port Orford, contact the **Chamber of Commerce Port Orford and North Curry County,** Battle Rock Park, U.S. 101 S. (P.O. Box 637), Port Orford, OR 97465 (© **541/332-8055;** www. discoverportorford.com). For information on the Gold Beach area, contact the **Gold Beach Promotion Committee,** 94080 Shirley Lane (P.O. Box 375), Gold Beach, OR

97444 (© **800/525-2334** or 541/247-7526; www.goldbeach.org), which has its visitor center in South Beach Park at the south end of town. For more information on the Brookings area, contact the **Brookings-Harbor Chamber of Commerce,** 16330 Lower Harbor Rd. (P.O. Box 940), Brookings, OR 97415 (© **800/535-9469** or 541/469-3181; www.brookingsor.com).

THE PORT ORFORD AREA

Cape Blanco is now preserved as **Cape Blanco State Park** (© **541/332-6774;** www.oregonstateparks.org), where you'll find miles of beaches, hiking trails through windswept meadows, picnic areas, and a campground. This high headland is also the site of the **Cape Blanco Lighthouse,** which is the most westerly lighthouse in Oregon. Not far from the lighthouse is the **Hughes House Museum** (© **541/332-0248;** www.hugheshouse.org), a restored Eastlake Victorian home that was built in 1898 and is furnished with period antiques. Both the lighthouse and the Hughes House are open to the public April through October Tuesday through Sunday from 10am to 3:30pm. Lighthouse admission is $2 for adults and $1 for children under 12.

For a good view of Port Orford and this entire section of coast, drive up to the **Port Orford Heads State Park,** which is located on the northern edge of town and has a short trail out to an overlook. The route to the wayside is well marked. Also here you can visit the **Port Orford Lifeboat Station** (© **541/332-0521;** www.portorford lifeboatstation.org), a small museum preserving the history of the coast guard on the southern Oregon coast. The museum is open April through October Thursday through Monday from 10am to 3:30pm; admission is free. Right in town, you can visit **Battle Rock Park** and learn the history of the rock refuge that rises out of Port Orford's beach. This is a good beach on which to walk, as is the beach at **Paradise Point State Recreation Site,** just north of town.

Right in town you'll find several art galleries. One of my favorites is the **Cook Gallery,** 705 Oregon St. (© **541/332-0045**), which features beautiful handcrafted wood furniture and sculptures, as well as prints and ceramics. North of town, check out the wood carvings at **A&T Myrtlewood,** 45683 U.S. 101, Sixes (© **541/348-2586;** www.aandtmyrtlewood.com).

Six miles south of Port Orford, you'll find **Humbug Mountain State Park** (© **541/332-6774;** www.oregonstateparks.org), where Humbug Mountain rises 1,756 feet from the ocean. A pretty campground is tucked into the forest at the base of the mountain, and a trail leads to the summit.

About 12 miles south of Port Orford is a place the kids aren't going to let you pass by. The **Prehistoric Gardens & Rainforest,** 36848 U.S. 101 S. (© **541/332-4463**), is a lost world of life-size dinosaur replicas. Though they aren't as realistic as those in *Jurassic Park,* they'll make the kids squeal with delight. The gardens are open in the summer daily from 8am to dusk; other months, call for hours. Admission is $8 for adults, $7 for seniors and youths 11 to 17, $6 for children 3 to 10.

WHERE TO STAY

Castaway by the Sea *(Value)*   Situated on a hill high above Port Orford harbor and commanding a sweeping panorama of the southern Oregon coast, this modest motel is far more comfortable than it appears from the outside. All the rooms take in the extraordinary view, and most have comfy little sunrooms from which to gaze off to sea. The rooms are quite large and well maintained, and some have kitchenettes. Out back there is a lawn with a few benches overlooking the harbor. The motel also rents out an adjacent historic house.

545 W. Fifth St. (P.O. Box 844), Port Orford, OR 97465. ✆ **541/332-4502.** Fax 541/332-9303. www.castawaybythesea. com. 13 units. $65–$95 double; $85–$145 suite; $200 house (lower rates in winter). AE, MC, V. Pets accepted ($10 per night). *In room:* TV, kitchen/kitchenette, fridge, coffeemaker.

Home by the Sea ✿ Set high atop a bluff overlooking the beach and Battle Rock, this contemporary B&B has large guest rooms (and a downstairs living room) with some of the best views on the coast. The inn is a block off U.S. 101 and within walking distance of several restaurants and art galleries.

444 Jackson St. (P.O. Box 606), Port Orford, OR 97465. ✆ **877/332-2855.** www.homebythesea.com. 2 units. $110–$120 double. Rates include full breakfast. Children under 12 stay free in parent's room. MC, V. **Amenities:** Courtesy beach shuttle; guest laundry. *In room:* TV, fridge, hair dryer, iron, free local calls, Wi-Fi.

WildSpring Guest Habitat ✿✿ With enough tranquillity to restore the most frazzled soul, this woodland retreat overlooking the ocean is a blissful hideaway on the outskirts of Port Orford. Accommodations are in beautifully appointed cabins in the woods. With hardwood floors, living and dining areas, and slate-walled showers, these cabins are so comfortably and attractively furnished that you just might forget to go out and explore the beach. A central guest hall has a kitchen you can use, and on Saturday nights there's a hot-fudge sundae bar. The slate hot tub, with its ocean view, is reason enough to visit Port Orford and stay at this delightful little eco-friendly resort.

92978 Cemetery Loop (P.O. Box R), Port Orford, OR 97465. ✆ **866/333-WILD.** Fax 775/542-1447. www.wildspring. com. 5 units. June–Sept $245–$275 double; Apr–May and Oct $226–$266 double; Nov–Mar $198–$248 double. Rates include continental breakfast. Children 13 and older welcome. AE, MC, V. **Amenities:** Jacuzzi; bikes; concierge; massage. *In room:* TV/VCR, fridge, hair dryer, high-speed Internet access, Wi-Fi, no phone.

CAMPGROUNDS

Cape Blanco State Park is the most popular camping spot in this area, and reservations aren't accepted for campsites. However, there are some basic cabins here that can be reserved through **ReserveAmerica** (✆ **800/452-5687;** www.reserveamerica.com).

WHERE TO DINE

Crazy Norwegian's Fish and Chips SEAFOOD This casual little roadside diner at the south end of Port Orford serves some of the best fish and chips on the Oregon coast. Best of all, it comes in three sizes, so whether you're starving or just want a snack, you should be sure to stop here. If you're not a fish-and-chips person, you can get a burger or crab cakes.

259 Sixth St. ✆ **541/332-8601.** Main courses $4.25–$12. AE, DISC, MC, V. Wed–Mon 11:30am–8pm.

Paula's Bistro ✿ NORTHWEST This eclectic little eatery is an unexpected treat in an area not noted for its good restaurants. Although the menu changes almost daily, you can expect such dishes as roast quail stuffed with hazelnut-cherry rice, rib-eye steak with shiitake mushroom ravioli, or fresh albacore tuna with a Dijon mustard sauce.

236 U.S. 101. ✆ **541/332-9378.** Reservations recommended. Main courses $15–$25. AE, DISC, MC, V. Tues–Sat 5–9pm.

THE GOLD BEACH AREA

There is, of course, a beach at Gold Beach, though it's not really the area's main attraction. That distinction goes to the **Rogue River,** which empties into the Pacific here at the town of Gold Beach and is the most famous fishing and rafting river in the state. You can tour the river in powerful hydrojet boats, which have a very shallow draft and use water jets instead of propellers. These features allow these boats to cross rapids and riffles only a few inches deep. Along the way you may see deer, black bear, river otters, and bald eagles. A running narration covers the river's colorful history. Three different trips are available, ranging in length from 64 to 104 miles. Two companies operate these trips. **Rogue River Mail Boats** (© 800/458-3511 or 541/247-7033; www.mailboat. com) leaves from a dock 200 yards upriver from the north end of the Rogue River Bridge. **Jerry's Rogue Jets** (© 800/451-3645 or 541/247-4571; www.roguejets.com) leaves from the Port of Gold Beach on the south side of the Rogue River Bridge. Fares range from $42 to $84 for adults and $16 to $37 for children.

Fighting salmon and steelhead are what have made the Rogue River famous, and if you'd like to hire a guide to take you to the best **fishing** holes, you have plenty of options. If you're looking to hire a guide, contact Steve and Eva Beyerlin of **Fish Oregon** (© 800/348-4138 or 541/247-4138; www.fishoregon.com). A full day will cost around $175 to $250 per person. If you'd rather do your fishing offshore, contact **Five Star Charters,** Port of Gold Beach (© 888/301-6480 or 541/247-0217; www.gold beachadventures.com), which offers charter fishing trips ranging from $100 to $225 per person. Clamming and crabbing can also be quite productive around Gold Beach.

When you want to get out on the beach at Gold Beach, head north of town across the Rogue River to Nesika Beach. To reach the best stretch of this beach, take the North Nesika Beach turnoff and then continue north to the end of the road. Alternatively, continue a little farther north to Old Coast Road, where you'll find a steep trail down to the beach.

Jerry's Rogue River Museum, 29880 Harbor Way (© **541/247-4571;** www.rogue jets.com), at the Port of Gold Beach and affiliated with Jerry's Jet Boat Tours, is the more modern and informative of the town's two museums. It focuses on the geology and cultural and natural history of the Rogue River. It's open daily in summer from 9am to 7pm and daily in the off season from 9am to 6pm; admission is free. At the diminutive **Curry County Historical Museum,** 29419 Ellensburg Ave. (© **541/247-6396;** www.curryhistory.com), you can learn more about the history of the area and see plenty of Native American and pioneer artifacts. The museum is open Tuesday through Saturday from 10am to 4pm. Admission is $2 for adults and 50¢ for children under 16. The museum is closed in January.

Golfers can play a round at the 9-hole **Cedar Bend Golf Course,** 34391 Cedar Valley Rd. (© **541/247-6911**), 12 miles north of Gold Beach off U.S. 101. If you'd like to go horseback riding, contact **Hawk's Rest Ranch,** 94667 North Bank Pistol River Rd. (© **541/247-6423;** www.siskiyouwest.com) in Pistol River, 10 miles south of Gold Beach. Expect to pay between $35 and $60 for a 90-minute ride.

Hikers have an abundance of options in the area. At the **Frances Schrader Old Growth Trail,** 10 miles up Jerry's Flat Road/South Bank Rogue Road near the Lobster Creek Campground, you can hike through an ancient forest of huge, majestic trees. In this same area, you'll also find the **Myrtle Tree Trail.** Along this ¼-mile trail, you'll find the world's largest myrtle tree, which is 88 feet tall and 42 feet in circumference. For more information on hiking in the Gold Beach area, contact the **Siskiyou National Forest,** Gold Beach Ranger District, 29279 Ellensburg Ave., Gold Beach, OR 97444 (© **541/247-3600;** www.fs.fed.us/r6/rogue-siskiyou).

SOUTH TO BROOKINGS

Gold Beach itself is a wide sandy beach, but just a few miles to the south, the mountains once again march into the sea, creating what in my opinion is Oregon's single most spectacular section of coastline. Though it's only 30 miles from Gold Beach to **Brookings,** you can easily spend the whole day making the trip. Along the way are numerous viewpoints, picnic areas, hiking trails, and beaches.

The **Oregon Coast Trail,** which extends (in short sections) from California to Washington, has several segments both north and south of Gold Beach. The most spectacular sections of this trail are south of town at Cape Sebastian and in Samuel H. Boardman State Scenic Corridor.

The first place you'll come to as you drive south from Gold Beach is **Turtle Rock Wayside,** just south of town. Although this is little more than a roadside pull-off, it does have a nice view. The next place to stop is at **Cape Sebastian** 𝒢𝒢, which is 5 miles south of Gold Beach. This headland, which towers 700 feet above the ocean, is a good vantage point for whale-watching between December and March. A 2-mile trail leads from the parking area out to the end of the cape, and continues down to the beach at Hunter's Cove. This little-visited spot is one of the best places on the south coast for a hike.

Another 2 miles south on U.S. 101, you come to **Meyers Creek** 𝒢𝒢, which is at the **Pistol River State Scenic Viewpoint.** Here, scattered on the beach, you'll find some of the rugged monolithic rock formations that make this coastline so breathtaking. This is the most popular windsurfing and surfing beach on the south coast and is also a good clamming beach. About 2 miles farther south, you'll come to the sand dunes at the mouth of the Pistol River.

South of the Pistol River you enter the **Samuel H. Boardman State Scenic Corridor,** which has numerous viewpoints, **beaches** 𝒢, picnic areas, and stretches of hiking trail. About 6 miles south of the Pistol River, you come to **Arch Rock Viewpoint** 𝒢, a picnic area with a beautiful view of an offshore monolith that has been carved into an arch by the action of the waves. Two miles beyond this, you come to the **Natural Bridge Viewpoint.** These two arches were formed when a sea cave collapsed. In 2 more miles you cross the **Thomas Creek Bridge,** which at 345 feet high is the highest bridge in Oregon. In a little more than a mile, you come to **Whalehead Beach Viewpoint,** where a pyramidal rock just offshore bears a striking resemblance to a spy-hopping whale. There's a better view of Whalehead Rock a half mile south.

In another 1½ miles you'll come to **House Rock Viewpoint,** which offers sweeping vistas to the north and south. At **Cape Ferrelo Viewpoint** and **Lone Ranch Viewpoint** just to the south, you'll find a grassy headland. Just south of here, watch for the **Rainbow Rock Viewpoint,** which has a panorama of a stretch of beach strewn with large boulders. Go another 3 miles, to **Harris Beach State Park** (✆ 541/469-2021), the last stop along this coast. Here you'll find picnicking and camping and a good view of **Goat Island,** which is the Oregon coast's largest island.

WHERE TO STAY

Ireland's Rustic Lodges *Finds*   The name sums it all up—rustic cabins set amid shady grounds that are as green as Ireland (and beautifully landscaped, too). Although there are some modern motel rooms here, they just can't compare to the quaint old cabins, which have stone fireplaces, paneled walls, and unusual door handles made from twisted branches. Built in 1922, the cabins are indeed rustic and are not for those who need modern comforts. The mature gardens surrounding the cabins are beautiful any time of year, but particularly in late spring. Ireland's is managed by the adjacent Gold Beach Inn hotel, which has lots of very predictable modern rooms, if that's what you're looking for.

29346 Ellensburg Ave. (U.S. 101), Gold Beach, OR 97444. © 877/447-3526 or 541/247-7718. www.irelandsrustic lodges.com. 40 units. Mid-June to mid-Sept $99–$104 double, $110–$159 cabin; mid-Sept to mid-June $58–$99 double, $70–$115 cabin. Children under 12 stay free in parent's room. AE, DISC, MC, V. Pets accepted ($10). *In room:* TV.

Jot's Resort 🌟 *(Kids)*   Stretching along the north bank of the Rogue River, Jot's has a definite fishing orientation and is very popular with families. The resort offers a wide variety of room sizes and rates, but every room has a view of the water and the Rogue River Bridge. The deluxe rooms are the most attractively furnished, while the condos are the most spacious (some have spiral staircases that lead up to loft sleeping areas). The dining room and lounge offer reasonably priced meals. Fishing guides and deep-sea charters can be arranged.

94360 Wedderburn Loop (P.O. Box 1200), Gold Beach, OR 97444. © 800/367-5687 or 541/247-6676. Fax 541/247-6716. www.jotsresort.com. 140 units. Summer $120–$135 double, $155–$375 suite/condo; off-season rates $50–$60 double, $100–$250 suite/condo. AE, DC, DISC, MC, V. Pets accepted ($10–$15 per night). **Amenities:** Restaurant (American); lounge; indoor and outdoor pools; exercise room; 3 Jacuzzis; sauna; fishing-boat rentals; activities desk; business center; coin-op laundry. *In room:* TV, dataport, fridge, microwave, coffeemaker, hair dryer, iron, Wi-Fi.

Tu Tu Tun Lodge 🌟🌟🌟   Tu Tu Tun Lodge, located 7 miles up the Rogue River from Gold Beach, provides the most deluxe lodging on the south coast and has a sophisticated styling and an idyllic setting. The main lodge building, with its immense fireplace, incorporates enough rock and natural wood to give it a rustic feel without sacrificing any modern comforts. On warm days, the patio overlooking the river is a great spot for relaxing, and on cold nights logs crackle in a fire pit. The guest rooms are large and beautifully furnished, some with Stickley furniture. Each room has a private patio or balcony, and should you get an upstairs room, you'll have a high ceiling and an excellent river view. Some rooms have maple floors and Tibetan rugs, and some have fireplaces or outdoor soaking tubs. The dining room overlooks the river and serves four-course dinners ($46). Fishing guides and boat rentals can be arranged.

96550 N. Bank Rogue Rd., Gold Beach, OR 97444. © 800/864-6357 or 541/247-6664. Fax 541/247-0672. www.tututun.com. 20 units. $165–$305 double, $260–$300 suite, $325–$425 house; lower rates in winter (dining room closed Nov–Apr). DISC, MC, V. May–Oct children 10 and older welcome; Nov–Apr all ages welcome. **Amenities:** Restaurant (Northwest); lounge; outdoor lap pool; 4-hole pitch-and-putt golf course; access to nearby health club; sea kayaks; lawn games; concierge; room service; massage; guest laundry; laundry service. *In room:* TV, dataport, fridge, hair dryer, iron, high-speed Internet access.

CAMPGROUNDS

Up the Rogue River between Gold Beach and Agness, you'll find two campgrounds: **Lobster Creek** and **Quosatana** (for both: © 541/247-3600; www.fs.fed.us/r6/rogue-siskiyou).

WHERE TO DINE

The best meals in Gold Beach are served in the dining room at **Tu Tu Tun Lodge** (see review above). For delicious, filling breakfasts, head up the Rogue River a mile or so to **Indian Creek Café,** 94682 Jerry's Flat Rd. (© 541/247-0680). If you want to take home some local seafood, head to the Port of Gold Beach and **Fishermen Direct Seafood** (© 888/523-9494 or 541/247-9494; www.fishermendirect.com), which is in the Cannery Building. They sell canned and smoked salmon and albacore tuna.

Nor'wester Seafood 🌟 SEAFOOD/STEAK   Simply prepared fresh seafood and large portions are the mainstays of the menu at this dockside restaurant, which has long been a local favorite. Fish and chips are good, and the steak-and-seafood combinations are popular choices for big appetites; but I prefer such dishes as pasta and prawns with a tapenade sauce or salmon with a glaze made from sake, cayenne, ginger, and soy sauce. From the second-floor dining room, you can watch fishing boats on the Rogue River. You'll find the Nor'wester at the north end of town in the port.

10 Harbor Way, Port of Gold Beach. (℃ 541/247-2333. Reservations for 5 or more people only. Main courses $20–$49. AE, MC, V. Daily 5–9pm.

Riverview Restaurant AMERICAN   At this restaurant just a mile or so up the Rogue River from Gold Beach, you can sit and watch fishermen battle huge salmon and unload their catch at the adjacent marina. You might also spot sea lions going after those very same salmon. So, what should you eat? How about salmon? Try it on a Caesar salad, grilled, or with a whiskey sauce. Alternatively, the fish tacos, which can be ordered two, three, or four at a time, are a good choice. The menu here is pretty simple—pastas, pizzas, burgers, salads, and a few basic entrees, but the view of the river is unsurpassed.

94794 Jerry's Flat Rd. (℃ 541/247-7321. Reservations recommended. Main courses $7–$23. AE, MC, V. Mon–Sat 4:30–9pm; Sun 4–9pm. Closed Oct–Dec.

THE BROOKINGS AREA

The Chetco River is known throughout Oregon as one of the best salmon and steelhead rivers in the state. It is also one of the prettiest rivers and offers opportunities for swimming, rafting, and kayaking. If you want to go out fishing for salmon or steelhead with a guide, contact **Fishawk River Company** (℃ 541/469-2422; www.fishawk.net).

If you want to head out to sea to do your fishing, contact **Tidewind Sportfishing** (℃ 541/469-0337; www.tidewindsportfishing.com), which operates out of Harbor and offers both salmon- and bottom-fishing trips for $80 to $135 per person, as well as whale-watching excursions ($45 per person).

For information on hiking in the area, which includes the high country of the Kalmiopsis Wilderness, contact the **Chetco Ranger District,** 539 Chetco Ave., Brookings, OR 97415 (℃ 541/412-6000; www.fs.fed.us/r6/rogue-siskiyou).

If golf is your game, don't pass up an opportunity to play the very scenic and challenging **Salmon Run Golf Course,** 99040 South Bank Chetco River Rd. (℃ 877/423-1234 or 541/469-4888; www.salmonrun.net), which charges $61 for 18 holes of golf. The clear waters of Jack Creek, which has spawning runs of salmon and steelhead, run through this course.

The area's botanical attractions are one of the most interesting reasons to pay a visit to the Brookings area. Not far from town, at **Alfred A. Loeb State Park** (℃ 541/469-2021; www.oregonstateparks.org), which is 8 miles up the Chetco River from Brookings on North Bank Road, you can see old-growth myrtle trees (from which the ubiquitous myrtlewood souvenirs of the south coast are made). Myrtle *(Umbellularia californica)* grows naturally only along the southern Oregon and northern California coasts. The Brookings area is also the northernmost range of the giant coast redwoods *(Sequoia sempervirens),* and just beyond Loeb State Park, you'll come to one of the largest stands of coast redwoods in Oregon. Here, the 1.3-mile **Redwood Nature Trail** loops past numerous big trees. This nature trail is connected to Loeb State Park via the .8-mile Riverview Trail. The region's wild azaleas, celebrated each year over Memorial Day weekend, come into bloom in May. The best place to see them is at **Azalea Park,** which is a couple of blocks east of U.S. 101 just before the bridge over the Chetco River at the south end of Brookings.

One of the more unusual places to visit in the area is the **Brandy Peak Distillery,** 18526 Tetley Rd. (℃ 541/469-0194; www.brandypeak.com), which is located north of Brookings off U.S. 101. (Take Carpenterville Rd. for 4 miles up into the hills and then go right on Tetley Rd. and immediately right into the distillery.) This microdistillery produces varietal marc brandies (unaged brandies), as well as barrel-aged brandies, grappas, and pear brandy. The distillery is open for tours and tastings Tuesday through Saturday from 1 to 5pm between March and early January, and by appointment the rest of the year. If you want to be absolutely sure, call beforehand. Three miles south of Brookings on U.S. 101, be sure to stop at the **Chetco Valley Museum,** 15461 Museum Rd. (© **541/469-6651**), if for no other reason than to see the largest Monterrey cypress in the state (perhaps the country), in front of the museum. The museum is open Wednesday through Sunday from noon to 5pm (open only on Sun in winter).

WHERE TO STAY

Best Western Beachfront Inn   Located on the edge of the marina in Brookings' sister town of Harbor (on the south side of the Chetco River), the Beachfront Inn has the only oceanfront accommodations in this area. Most rooms are fairly large and all have ocean views, balconies, microwaves, and refrigerators. The more expensive rooms have whirlpool tubs with picture windows. There's also an outdoor pool and whirlpool.

16008 Boat Basin Rd., Harbor, OR 97415. © **800/468-4081** or 541/469-7779. Fax 541/469-0283. 102 units. $119–$295 double. AE, DC, DISC, MC, V. Pets accepted ($10). **Amenities:** Outdoor pool; Jacuzzi. *In room:* TV, fridge, microwave, coffeemaker.

Brookings South Coast Inn ★   This 1917 Craftsman bungalow was designed by the famous San Francisco architect Bernard Maybeck and is filled with the sort of beautiful architectural details that characterized the Arts and Crafts movement. The inn's most spacious guest room is dedicated to Maybeck. Two of the guest rooms have good views, and the cottage, across the garden from the main house, offers a more private setting. Guests have use of a large living room full of antiques, where a fire often crackles in the stone fireplace, although the weather never gets very cold.

516 Redwood St., Brookings, OR 97415. © **800/525-9273** or 541/469-5557. Fax 541/469-6615. www.south coastinn.com. 6 units. $119–$159 double. Rates include full breakfast. AE, DISC, MC, V. Children over 12 welcome. **Amenities:** Sauna. *In room:* A/C, TV/VCR, hair dryer, Wi-Fi.

Chetco River Inn & Lavender Farm ★★ *Finds*   Set on 35 very secluded acres on the banks of the Chetco River, this contemporary B&B caters to nature lovers and anglers and makes a great weekend retreat. However, you'll first have to find the lodge, which is 17 miles from town up North Bank Road (the last bit on gravel). The lodge makes use of alternative energy. The Siskiyou National Forest surrounds the property, and hiking, swimming (there are lots of great swimming holes), and stargazing are popular pastimes. If you don't feel like leaving the woods, you can arrange to have meals at the lodge.

21202 High Prairie Rd., Brookings, OR 97415. © **541/251-0087.** www.chetcoriverinn.com. 6 units. $155–$250 double. Rates include full breakfast. MC, V. **Amenities:** Guest laundry. *In room:* No phone.

CAMPGROUNDS

The best base for exploring the scenic wonders of Samuel H. Boardman State Scenic Corridor is **Harris Beach State Park** (© **800/551-6949** or 541/469-2021; www. oregonstateparks.org), on the beach just north of Brookings. Up the North Bank Chetco River Road out of Brookings, you'll find **Alfred A. Loeb State Park** (© **800/ 551-6949** or 541/469-2021 for information, or 800/452-5687 for reservations;

www.oregonstateparks.org), which is set amid redwood and myrtle trees along the banks of the beautiful Chetco River.

WHERE TO DINE

If it's pizza you're craving, **Wild River Pizza Company,** 16279 U.S. 101 S., just south of Brookings ((C) **541/469-7454;** www.wildriverbrewing.com), turns out a crispy one, accompanied by their own microbrews. Locals swear by **The Hungry Clam,** at the Port of Brookings-Harbor ((C) **541/469-2526**), for fish and chips. For smoked salmon, head south of town to **The Great American Smokehouse,** 15657 U.S. 101 S. ((C) **800/828-3474** or 541/469-6903; www.smokehouse-salmon.com), which sells a wide variety of smoked and canned seafood.

Bella Italia Ristorante ⚓ SOUTHERN ITALIAN   This restaurant is surprisingly sophisticated for Brookings, where there have never been too many options for good food. While the menu doesn't break any new ground and is basically a selection of southern Italian classics, the ambience is more upscale than anywhere else in the region. The big room, attracting diners from up and down the coast, always seems to be lively, and there's a great bar area. The menu emphasizes veal, which can be had prepared in any of a variety of styles—piccata, marsala, scaloppini, or parmesan. There's also a variety of pasta dishes and pizzas.

1025 Chetco Ave., Brookings. (C) **866/40-BELLA** or 541/469-6647. Reservations recommended. Main courses $13–$35. AE, DISC, MC, V. Sun–Thurs 4–9pm; Fri–Sat 4–10pm.

7

The Columbia Gorge

The Columbia Gorge, which begins just a few miles east of Portland and stretches for nearly 70 miles along the shores of the Columbia River, is a dramatic landscape of mountains, cliffs, and waterfalls created by massive Ice Age floods. Flanked by national forests and snow-covered peaks on both the Oregon and Washington sides of the Columbia River, the Gorge is as breathtaking a landscape as you will find anywhere in the West, and the fascinating geology, dramatic vistas, and abundance of recreational opportunities make it a premier vacation destination almost any month of the year. Not only are there waterfalls, trails, and some of the world's best windsurfing, but there are also fascinating museums, resort hotels, hot springs, historic B&Bs, and even wineries. Between 1913 and 1922, a scenic highway (one of the first paved roads in the Northwest) was built through the Gorge, and, in 1986, much of the area was designated the Columbia Gorge National Scenic Area in an attempt to preserve the Gorge's spectacular and unique natural beauty.

The Columbia River is older than the hills. It's older than the mountains, too, which explains why this river flows not from the mountains but through them. The river was already flowing into the Pacific Ocean when the Cascade Range began rising millions of years ago. However, it was a series of recent events, geologically speaking, that gave the Columbia Gorge its very distinctive appearance. About 15,000 years ago, toward the end of the last Ice Age, huge dams of ice far upstream collapsed and sent floodwaters racing down the Columbia. As the floodwaters swept through the Columbia Gorge, they were as much as 1,200 feet high. Ice and rock carried by the floodwaters helped the river to scour out the sides of the once gently sloping valley, leaving behind the steep-walled gorge that we know today. The waterfalls that elicit so many oohs and aahs are the most dramatic evidence of these great floods.

The vast gorge that the Columbia River has formed as it slices through the mountains is effectively a giant bridge between the rain-soaked forests west of the Cascades and the desert-dry sagebrush scrublands of central Oregon. This change in climate is caused by moist air condensing into snow and rain as it passes over the crest of the Cascades. Most of the air's moisture falls on the western slopes, so the eastern slopes and the land stretching for hundreds of miles beyond lie in a rain shadow. Perhaps nowhere else on earth can you witness this rain-shadow effect so easily and in such a short distance. It's so pronounced that as you come around a bend on I-84 just east of Hood River, you can see dry grasslands to the east and dense forests of Douglas fir over your shoulder to the west. In between the two extremes lies a community of plants that's unique to the Columbia Gorge, and consequently, springtime here brings colorful displays of wildflowers.

In North America, the Columbia River is second only to the Mississippi in the volume of water it carries to the sea—but more than just water flows through the Columbia Gorge. As the only break over the entire length of the Cascade Range, the Gorge acts as a massive natural wind tunnel. During the summer, the sun bakes the lands east of the Cascades, causing the air to rise. Cool air from the west side then rushes up the river, at times whipping through Hood River with near gale force. These winds, blowing against the downriver flow of water, set up ideal conditions for windsurfing and kiteboarding on the Columbia. The reliability of the winds, and the waves they kick up, has turned Hood River into something of an Aspen of windsurfing.

For centuries the Columbia River has been an important route between the maritime Northwest and the dry interior. Lewis and Clark canoed down the river in 1805, and pioneers followed the Oregon Trail to its shores at The Dalles. It was here at The Dalles that many pioneers transferred their wagons to boats for the dangerous journey downriver to Oregon City. The set of rapids known as The Dalles and the waterfalls of the Cascades were the two most dangerous sections of the Columbia Gorge, so towns arose at these two points to transport goods and people around the treacherous waters. For a while, locks and a canal helped circumvent some of the treacherous white water, but now the rapids of the Columbia lie flooded beneath the waters behind the Bonneville and The Dalles dams. The ease of navigating the river today has dimmed the importance of the towns of Cascade Locks and The Dalles, both of which are steeped in the history of the Gorge.

1 The Columbia Gorge National Scenic Area ★★★

Columbia Gorge: Begins 18 miles E of Portland

Stretching from the Sandy River in the west to the Deschutes River in the east, the Columbia Gorge National Scenic Area is one of the most breathtakingly dramatic places in the United States. Carved by floods of unimaginable power, this miles-wide canyon is flanked on the north by Mount Adams and on the south by Mount Hood, both of which rise more than 11,000 feet high. With its diaphanous waterfalls, basalt cliffs painted with colorful lichens, and dark forests of Douglas firs rising up from the banks of the Columbia River, the Gorge is a year-round recreational area where hiking trails lead to hidden waterfalls and mountain-top panoramas, mountain-bike trails meander through the forest, and windsurfers race across wind-whipped waters.

The Columbia Gorge National Scenic Area is also as controversial as it is beautiful. Over the years since this area received this federal designation, the fights over the use of private land within the Gorge have been constant. The pressure to develop this scenic marvel of the Northwest has been unrelenting, as landowners throughout the Gorge have fought against restrictions on development. To find out more about protecting the Gorge, contact the **Friends of the Columbia Gorge** (© **503/241-3762;** www.gorgefriends.org), which, each spring, offers numerous guided wildflower hikes.

ESSENTIALS

GETTING THERE   I-84 and the Historic Columbia River Highway both pass through the Gorge on the Oregon side of the Columbia.

VISITOR INFORMATION   Contact the **Columbia River Gorge National Scenic Area,** 902 Wasco Ave., Suite 200, Hood River, OR 97031 (© **541/308-1700;** www. fs.fed.us/r6/columbia). There's also the **Forest Service Visitor Center** (© **503/695-2372**) at Multnomah Falls Lodge (take the Historic Columbia River Hwy. or the

Multnomah Falls exit off I-84) and another in the lobby of **Skamania Lodge,** 1131 SW Skamania Lodge Dr. (© **509/427-2528**), in Stevenson, Washington.

LEARNING ABOUT THE GORGE & ITS HISTORY

Columbia Gorge Interpretive Center Museum ★★   Focusing on the Gorge's early Native American inhabitants and the development of the area by white settlers, this museum is your single best introduction to the Columbia Gorge. Exhibits contain historical photographs by Edward Curtis and others that illustrate the story of portage companies and paddle-wheelers that once operated along this stretch of the Columbia River. A 37-foot-high replica of a 19th-century fish wheel gives an understanding of how salmon runs have been threatened in the past and the present. Displays also frankly discuss other problems that the coming of settlers brought to this area. A slide program tells the history of the formation of the Gorge. When it's not cloudy, the center has an awesome view of the south side of the Gorge.

990 SW Rock Creek Dr., Stevenson. © 800/991-2338. www.columbiagorge.org. Admission $7 adults, $6 seniors and students, $5 children 6–12, free for children 5 and under. Daily 10am–5pm. Closed New Year's Day, Thanksgiving, Christmas.

A DRIVING TOUR

Though I-84 is the fastest road through the Columbia Gorge, it is not the most scenic route. The Gorge is well worth a full day's exploration and is best appreciated at a more leisurely pace on the **Historic Columbia River Highway** ★★, which begins 16 miles east of downtown Portland at the second Troutdale exit off I-84. Opened in 1915, this highway was a marvel of engineering at the time and, by providing access to automobiles, opened the Gorge to casual visits.

At the western end of the historic highway, you'll find **Lewis & Clark State Park,** which is near the mouth of the Sandy River. This park is popular with anglers and Portlanders looking to cool off in the Sandy River during the hot summer months. There is also a rock-climbing area within the park.

The first unforgettable view of the Gorge comes at the **Portland Women's Forum State Scenic Viewpoint,** which may also be your first encounter with the legendary Columbia Gorge winds. To learn more about the historic highway and how it was built, stop at the **Vista House,** 40700 E. Historic Columbia River Hwy. (© **503/695-2230;** www.vistahouse.com), 733 feet above the river on **Crown Point.** Although there are displays of historical photos here at Vista House, most visitors can't concentrate on the exhibits, preferring to gaze at the breathtaking 30-mile view. Vista House is open daily from 9am to 6pm.

From Crown Point, the historic highway drops down into the Gorge and passes several picturesque **waterfalls.** The first of these is 249-foot **Latourell Falls** ★, a diaphanous wisp of a waterfall cascading over basalt cliffs stained lime-green by lichen. A 2.3-mile loop trail leads from this waterfall up to the smaller Upper Latourell Falls. East of these falls, you'll come to Shepherd's Dell Falls, Bridal Veil Falls, Mist Falls, and Wahkeena Falls, all of which are either right beside the road or a short walk away. If you're interested in a longer hike, there are trails linking several of the falls. However, for spectacular views, you can't beat the steep 4.4-mile round-trip hike to Angels Rest. The well-signposted trail head for this hike is on the historic highway near the community of Bridal Veil.

Multnomah Falls ★★★ is the largest and the most famous waterfall along this highway and the state's most visited natural attraction. At 620 feet from the lip to the

The Columbia Gorge & Hood River

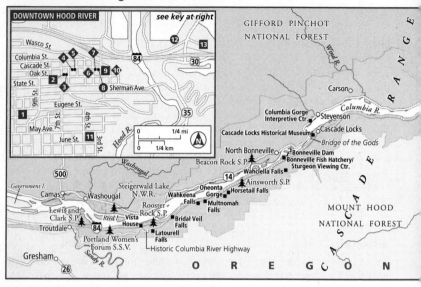

lower pool, it's the tallest waterfall in Oregon and the fourth tallest in the United States. An arched bridge stands directly in front of the falls part way up. This bridge is part of a steep paved trail that leads from the foot of the falls up to the top; from there, other trails lead off into the **Mount Hood National Forest.** The historic Multnomah Falls Lodge (see below) has a restaurant, snack bar, and gift shop, as well as a **National Forest Visitor Center** (© **503/695-2372**) with information on the geology, history, and natural history of the Gorge.

East of Multnomah Falls, the scenic highway passes by **Oneonta Gorge** ✦✦, a narrow rift in the cliffs. Through this tiny gorge flows a stream that serves as a watery pathway for anyone interested in exploring upstream to **Oneonta Falls;** just bear in mind that you'll be walking in the creek if you explore this gorgeous little gorge. Less than a half-mile east of Oneonta Gorge, you'll come to **Horsetail Falls.** From these roadside falls, a trail leads uphill to Upper Horsetail Falls. The trail then passes behind the upper falls and continues another 2 miles to Triple Falls, passing above Oneonta Gorge along the way.

If you'd like to escape the crowds and see a little-visited waterfall, watch for Frontage Road on your right just before the historic highway merges with I-84. Drive east for 2 miles to a gravel parking area at the trail head for **Elowah Falls** ✦✦. These 289-foot-tall falls are set in a beautiful natural amphitheater less than a mile from the road. Just be aware that this parking area is subject to car break-ins; don't leave any valuables in your vehicle.

Just after the two highways merge, you come to the exit for **Bonneville Lock and Dam** (© **541/374-8820;** www.nwp.usace.army.mil/op/b/home.asp). The visitor center here has exhibits on the history of this dam, which was built in 1927. One of the most important features of the dam is its fish ladder, which allows adult salmon to return upriver to spawn. Underwater windows let visitors see fish as they pass through the ladder. Visit the adjacent **Bonneville Fish Hatchery** (© **541/374-8393**) to see

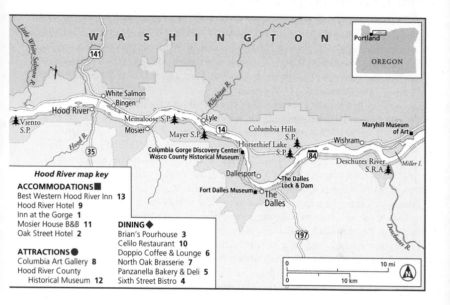

Hood River map key

ACCOMMODATIONS ■
Best Western Hood River Inn **13**
Hood River Hotel **9**
Inn at the Gorge **1**
Mosier House B&B **11**
Oak Street Hotel **2**

ATTRACTIONS ●
Columbia Art Gallery **8**
Hood River County
    Historical Museum **12**

DINING ◆
Brian's Pourhouse **3**
Celilo Restaurant **10**
Doppio Coffee & Lounge **6**
North Oak Brasserie **7**
Panzanella Bakery & Deli **5**
Sixth Street Bistro **4**

how trout, salmon, and steelhead are raised before being released into the river. A **Sturgeon Viewing Center** ⊛⊛ allows you to marvel at several immense sturgeons through an underwater viewing window. At this same exit off I-84 (and at Eagle Creek), you'll find access to a section of the **Historic Columbia River Highway State Trail,** a paved multiuse trail that connects the town of Cascade Locks with Bonneville Dam. This trail incorporates abandoned sections of the Historic Columbia River Highway and is open to hikers and bikers. Near the western trail head for this trail you'll also find the trail to **Wahclella Falls** ⊛, a little-visited yet very picturesque waterfall tucked back in a side canyon. The trail is less than a mile long and relatively flat.

Beyond the dam is Eagle Creek, the single best spot in the Gorge for a hike. The **Eagle Creek Trail** ⊛⊛ leads past several waterfalls, and if you have time for only one hike in the Gorge, it should be this one. You'll also find a campground and picnic area here.

Not far beyond Eagle Creek is the **Bridge of the Gods,** which connects Oregon and Washington at the site where, according to a Native American legend, once stood a natural bridge used by the gods. Geologists now believe that the legend is based in fact; there is evidence that a massive rock slide may have once blocked the river at this point.

Just beyond the Bridge of the Gods is **Cascade Locks.** It was at this site that cascades once turned the otherwise placid Columbia River into a raging torrent that required boats to be portaged a short distance downriver. The Cascade Locks were built in 1896 and allowed steamships to pass unhindered. The locks made traveling between The Dalles and Portland much easier, but the completion of the Columbia River Scenic Highway, in 1915, made the trip even easier by land. With the construction of the Bonneville Lock and Dam, the cascades were flooded, and the locks became superfluous.

There are two small museums here at the locks. The **Cascade Locks Historical Museum,** Port Marina Park (© 541/374-8535), which is housed in the old lock tender's house, includes displays of Native American artifacts and pioneer memorabilia, as well as the Northwest's first steam engine. The museum is open May through October, Sunday through Thursday from noon to 5pm and Friday and Saturday from 10am to 5pm. Admission is by donation.

The **Port of Cascade Locks Visitors Center,** which has displays on river travel in the past, is also the ticket office for the **Sternwheeler *Columbia Gorge*** 🎣🎣 (© 800/224-3901 or 503/224-3900; www.sternwheeler.com), which makes regular trips on the river. These cruises provide a great perspective on the Gorge. Fares for the 2-hour scenic cruises are $25 for adults and $15 for children; dinner and brunch cruises run $42 to $64 for adults and $21 to $59 for children. There are also 6-hour cruises once a week in the summer ($80 for adults, $60 for seniors, and $40 for children). These cruises should not be missed on a visit to the Columbia Gorge.

Should you decide not to take the historic highway and stay on I-84, you may want to stop at **Rooster Rock State Park,** especially if it's a hot summer day. This park has a long sandy beach, and in a remote section of the park there's even a clothing-optional beach. From I-84 there's also easy access to Multnomah Falls, the main attraction of the Historic Columbia River Highway.

Another option is to cross to the Washington side of the Columbia River and take Wash. 14 east from Vancouver. This latter highway actually provides the most spectacular views of both the Columbia Gorge and Mount Hood. If you should decide to take this route, be sure to stop at **Beacon Rock State Park** 🎣🎣 (© 360/902-8844), which has as its centerpiece an 800-foot-tall monolith that has a trail (mostly stairways and catwalks) leading to its summit. In the early 20th century, there was talk of blasting the rock apart to build jetties at the mouth of the river. Luckily, another source of rock was used, and this amazing landmark continues to guard the Columbia. If you want to make better time, you can cross back to Oregon on the Bridge of the Gods. Continuing east on the Washington side of the river, you'll come to Stevenson, site of the above-mentioned Columbia Gorge Interpretive Center.

In the town of North Bonneville, a few miles west of Stevenson, you can swim in the mineral-water pool and soak in the hot tubs at **Bonneville Hot Springs Resort,** 1252 E. Cascade Dr. (© 866/459-1678 or 509/427-7767; www.bonnevilleresort.com), which charges $15 per day for the use of its pool and soaking tubs and is open to nonguests Sunday through Thursday from 8am to 9pm. Massages and other spa services are also available. East of Stevenson, in the town of Carson, you can also avail yourself of the therapeutic waters of the **Carson Hot Springs Resort** (© 800/607-3678 or 509/427-8292; www.carsonhotspringresort.com). This rustic "resort" has been in business since 1897 and has one building that looks every bit its age. However, it's just this old-fashioned appeal that keeps people coming back year after year. Spring through fall, it's open Monday through Thursday from 8am to 7pm and Friday through Sunday from 8am to 8pm; other months it's open Monday through Thursday from 9am to 6pm and Friday through Sunday from 8am to 7pm. A soak and post-soak wrap costs $20, while an hour's massage is $60.

WINDSURFING & OTHER ACTIVITIES

If you want to launch your sailboard along this stretch of the Gorge, try **Rooster Rock State Park,** near the west end of the Gorge, or **Viento State Park,** just west of Hood River. Both parks are right off I-84 and are well marked.

If you're interested in hiring a fishing guide, contact **Page's Northwest Guide Service** (© **866/760-3370** or 503/760-3373; www.fishingoregon.net), which will take you out for salmon, steelhead, walleye, and sturgeon on the Columbia or Willamette Rivers or on other area waters ($150–$160 per person, per day). **Reel Adventures** (© **877/544-7335** or 503/622-5372; www.donsreeladventures.com) offers a similar fishing-guide service ($150 per person, per day).

WHERE TO STAY

Best Western Columbia River Inn ⭐   Located at the foot of the Bridge of the Gods and well situated for exploring the Gorge, this modern motel has splendid views from its riverview rooms. Many of the rooms also have small balconies, although nearby railroad tracks can make them very noisy. Luckily, rooms are well insulated against train noises. For a splurge, try a spa room.

735 Wanapa St., Cascade Locks, OR 97014. © **800/595-7108** or 541/374-8777. Fax 541/374-2279. www.bestwestern. com. 62 units. $79–$159 double. Rates include continental breakfast. Children under 12 stay free in parent's room. AE, DC, DISC, MC, V. Pets accepted ($10 fee). **Amenities:** Indoor pool; exercise room; Jacuzzi; coin-op laundry. *In room:* A/C, TV, dataport, fridge, microwave, coffeemaker, hair dryer, iron.

Bonneville Hot Springs Resort ⭐   Although this hot-springs resort doesn't have any views to speak of and is not nearly as impressive as the nearby Skamania Lodge, it is still one of the more interesting places to stay in the Columbia Gorge. Unfortunately, the decor has felt dated and uninspired from the moment the resort opened, so don't come expecting gorgeous spaces. There is, however, an 80-foot-long, mineral-water indoor pool, a full-service spa, and a big outdoor hot tub in a courtyard with an unusual stone-wall waterfall. Guest rooms have balconies (ask for one overlooking the courtyard), and some have their own mineral-water soaking tubs.

1252 E. Cascade Dr. (P.O. Box 356), North Bonneville, WA 98639. © **866/459-1678** or 509/427-7767. Fax 509/427-7733. www.bonnevilleresort.com. 78 units. $149–$279 double; $399 suite. Children under 4 stay free in parent's room. AE, DC, DISC, MC, V. **Amenities:** Restaurant (Continental); lounge; indoor pool; exercise room; full-service spa; 3 Jacuzzis; room service; massage. *In room:* A/C, TV, dataport, fridge, coffeemaker, hair dryer, iron, Wi-Fi.

McMenamins Edgefield ⭐ *Finds*   Ideally situated for exploring the Columbia Gorge and Mount Hood, this flagship of the McMenamins microbrewery empire is the former Multnomah County poor farm. Today, the property includes not only tastefully decorated guest rooms with antique furnishings, but a brewery, a pub, a beer garden, a restaurant, a movie theater, a winery, a wine-tasting room, a distillery, a golf course, a cigar bar in an old shed, and extensive gardens. With so much in one spot, this makes a great base for exploring the area. The beautiful grounds give this inn the feel of a remote retreat, though you are still within 30 minutes of Portland.

2126 SW Halsey St., Troutdale, OR 97060. © **800/669-8610** or 503/669-8610. www.mcmenamins.com. 114 units (100 with shared bathroom). $50–$139 double with shared bathroom; $116–$147 double with private bathroom; $30 hostel bed per person. Children under 7 stay free in parent's room. AE, DC, DISC, MC, V. **Amenities:** 3 restaurants (Northwest, American); 6 lounges; soaking pool; par-3 golf course; spa; massage. *In room:* Wi-Fi, no phone.

Skamania Lodge ⭐⭐⭐   Boasting the most spectacular vistas of any hotel in the gorge, Skamania Lodge is also the only golf resort around. But it's also well-situated for other activities, whether you brought your sailboard, hiking boots, or mountain bike. The decor is classically rustic, with lots of rock and natural wood, and throughout the hotel, Northwest Indian artworks and artifacts are displayed. Huge windows in the lobby have superb views of the gorge. Of course, the river-view guest rooms are more expensive than the forest-view rooms (which overlook more parking lot than forest), but these rooms are well worth the extra cost. There are also rooms with fireplaces.

1131 Skamania Lodge Way, Stevenson, WA 98648. ⓒ 800/221-7117 or 509/427-7700. Fax 509/427-2547. www.skamania.com. 254 units. $119–$279 double; $229–$279 suite. Children under 17 stay free in parent's room. AE, DC, DISC, MC, V. Pest accepted ($50 per night). **Amenities:** Restaurant (Northwest); lounge; indoor pool; 18-hole golf course; 2 tennis courts; exercise room; full-service spa; Jacuzzi; sauna; bike rentals; activities desk; business center; room service; massage; dry cleaning. *In room:* A/C, TV, dataport, minibar, coffeemaker, hair dryer, iron, free local calls, high-speed Internet access, Wi-Fi.

CAMPGROUNDS

Camping in the Gorge isn't quite the wonderful experience you might think. With an interstate highway and a very active railway line paralleling the river on the Oregon side and another railroad and a secondary highway on the Washington side, the Gorge tends to be quite noisy. However, there are a few camping options between Portland and Hood River, and these campgrounds do what they can to minimize the traffic noises. **Ainsworth State Park,** 3½ miles east of Multnomah Falls, has showers, and the RV sites are quite nice. At exit 41 off I-84, there is **Eagle Creek Campground,** the oldest campground in the National Forest system and popular for its access to the Eagle Creek Trail. At exit 51 off of I-84, there is **Wyeth Campground,** a U.S. Forest Service campground on the bank of Gordon Creek. Over on the Washington side of the Columbia River, there is also first-come, first-served camping at **Beacon Rock State Park,** which is located 7 miles west of the Bridge of the Gods. Because it is tucked back away from the highway and railroad tracks, this is just about the quietest campground in the Gorge.

WHERE TO DINE

The area's best place to eat is the dining room of the Skamania Lodge (see above).

Black Rabbit Restaurant ⓡⓡ NORTHWEST/REGIONAL AMERICAN This casual-yet-upscale restaurant is located on the grounds of McMenamins Edgefield (reviewed above), and is the ideal place to stop for dinner on the way back to Portland after a day of exploring the Gorge. Start with the calamari (perhaps accompanied by a glass of Edgefield wine) and then move on to the halibut in filo with basil or lamb saltimbocca. If you aren't in the mood for a formal dinner, there is also a less expensive and less formal brewpub here.

McMenamins Edgefield, 2126 SW Halsey St., Troutdale. ⓒ 503/669-8610. Main courses $15–$26. AE, DC, DISC, MC, V. Daily 7–10pm.

Multnomah Falls Lodge ⓡ AMERICAN Built in 1925 at the foot of Multnomah Falls, the historic Multnomah Falls Lodge may be the most touristy place to eat in the entire Gorge, but the setting is wonderful and the food isn't half bad. Breakfast, when the crowds haven't yet arrived, is one of the best times to eat here. Try the grilled salmon or trout and eggs. At dinner, stick with the prime rib or lemon-and-herb–roasted salmon. For a peek at the falls, try to get a table in the conservatory room or, in summer, out on the patio.

Historic Columbia River Hwy. (or I-84, exit 31). ⓒ 503/695-2376. www.multnomahfallslodge.com. Reservations recommended. Main courses $10–$16 lunch, $16–$23 dinner. AE, DISC, MC, V. Daily 8am–9pm.

Tad's Chicken 'n Dumplins ⓡ *Finds* AMERICAN Located on the banks of the Sandy River at the western end of the Historic Columbia River Highway, this rustic restaurant has been in business more than 50 years and, as its name implies, specializes in all-American chicken and dumplings. Sure, you can get a steak, pan-fried oysters, or salmon, but you'd be remiss if you passed up this opportunity to fill up on this restaurant's namesake dish. Try to get a seat on the enclosed back porch, which overlooks the river. If you're coming here after dark, just watch for the classic neon sign out front.

1325 E. Historic Columbia River Hwy., Troutdale. (📞) **503/666-5337.** www.tadschicdump.com. Call-ahead wait list. Main courses $12–$28. AE, DISC, MC, V. Mon–Fri 5–10pm; Sat 4–10pm; Sun 2–10pm.

2 Hood River: The Windsurfing Capital of the Northwest

62 miles E of Portland, 20 miles W of The Dalles, 32 miles N of Government Camp

Each summer, hot air rising over the desert to the east of the Cascade Range sucks cool air up the Columbia River Gorge from the Pacific, and the winds howl through what is basically a natural wind tunnel. The winds are incessant and gusts can whip the river into a tumult of whitecaps. They used to curse these winds in Hood River. Not anymore.

Ever since the first person pulled into town with a sailboard, Hood River has taken to praying for wind. Hood River is now the windsurfing capital of America, which has given this former lumber town a new lease on life. People come from all over the world to ride the winds that howl up the Gorge. In early summer the boardheads roll into town in their "Gorge-mobiles," which are equivalent to surfers' woodies, and start listening to the wind reports. They flock to riverside parks on both the Oregon and Washington sides of the Columbia, unfurl their sails, zip up their wet suits, and launch themselves into the melee of hundreds of other like-minded souls shooting back and forth across a mile of windswept water. High waves whipped up by near-gale-force winds provide perfect launching pads for rocketing skyward. Aerial acrobatics such as flips and 360-degree turns are common sights. Now, even boardsailors have had to make way for the newest sport—kiteboarding. This sport replaces the sail with a kite, shortens the board, and enables even more radical maneuvers, and higher speeds, than windsurfing, and lots more time in the air instead of in the water. Even if you're not into this fast-paced sport, you'll get a vicarious thrill from watching the boardheads going for major airtime.

Windsurfing and kiteboarding may be the main events here in Hood River, but this is certainly not a one-trick town. Sometimes the winds just aren't accommodating and even boardheads can get bored sitting on shore waiting for conditions to improve. For this reason, Hood River has become something of an outdoor sports mecca, with a rapidly developing reputation for excellent mountain biking, white-water kayaking and rafting, paragliding, rock climbing, hiking, skiing, and snowboarding. In other words, Hood River is full of active people.

Hood River does not exist on sports alone, however; outside town, in the Hood River Valley, are apple and pear orchards, wineries, and vineyards. Hood River also claims a famous historic hotel and several good restaurants. Most of the town's old Victorian and Craftsman houses have now been restored, giving Hood River a historic atmosphere to complement its lively windsurfing scene. All in all, this town makes a great base whether you're here for the sports, to explore the Gorge, or to visit nearby Mount Hood.

ESSENTIALS

GETTING THERE   Hood River is on I-84 at the junction with Ore. 35, which leads south to connect with U.S. 26 near the community of Government Camp.

Amtrak offers passenger-rail service to the town of Bingen, Washington, just across the Columbia River from Hood River. The station is at the foot of Walnut Street.

VISITOR INFORMATION Contact the **Hood River County Chamber of Commerce,** 405 Portway Ave., Hood River, OR 97031 (℃ **800/366-3530** or 541/386-2000; www.hoodriver.org), near the river at exit 63 off I-84.

FESTIVALS The Hood River Valley Blossom Festival is held in mid-April and celebrates the flowering of the valley's pear and apple trees. In mid-October the Hood River Valley Harvest Fest takes place at the Hood River Expo Center and the Parkdale Fine Arts and Music Festival is held in Parkdale.

WINDSURFING & OTHER OUTDOOR ACTIVITIES ☆☆☆

If you're here to ride the wind or just want to watch, head to the Columbia Gorge Sailpark at Hood River Marina, the nearby Event Site, or The Hook, all of which are accessible via exit 63 off I-84. Across the river in Washington, try the fish hatchery (The Hatchery), west of the mouth of the White Salmon River, or Swell City, a park about 4 miles west of the bridge. If you're a windsurfer or kiteboarder, you'll find all kinds of windsurfing- and kiteboarding-related shops in downtown Hood River. Classes are available through **Hood River WaterPlay** (℃ **800/WND-SURF** or 541/386-WIND; www.hoodriverwaterplay.com) and **Gorge Kiteboard School** (℃ **541/490-4401;** www.windguide.com), which teaches only kite boarding.

When there isn't enough wind for sailing, there's still the option to go **rafting** on the White Salmon River. Companies offering raft trips on this river include **Zoller's Outdoor Odysseys** (℃ **800/366-2004** or 509/493-2641; www.zooraft.com), **Wet Planet Rafting** (℃ **800/306-1673;** www.wetplanetrafting.com), and **All Adventures Rafting** (℃ **877/641-RAFT** or 800/74-FLOAT; www.alladventures.net). Although the White Salmon can be rafted anytime of year, the most popular season runs from April through September. A half-day trip will cost around $60 or $65 per person.

Mountain biking is also very popular, and Hood River bike shops can direct you to some fun area rides. Check at **Discover Bicycles,** 116 Oak St. (℃ **541/386-4820;** www.discoverbicycles.com), or **Mountain View Cycles,** 205 Oak St. (℃ **541/386-2453;** www.mtviewcycles.com), both of which rent bikes. Expect to pay between $25 and $60 per day.

If fly-fishing is your passion, drop by the **Gorge Fly Shop,** 201 Oak St. (℃ **541/386-6977;** www.gorgeflyshop.com), which can fill all your angling needs and point you to where the fish are biting; they can also connect you with a local fly-fishing guide.

Hikers have their choice of trails in Mount Hood National Forest (see "Mount Hood: Skiing, Hiking & Scenic Drives," in chapter 9), the Columbia Gorge (p. 238), or across the river (head up Wash. 141 to Mount Adams). At 12,276 feet in elevation, Mount Adams is the second-highest peak in Washington. For more information about hiking on Mount Adams, contact the **Gifford Pinchot National Forest,** Mount Adams Ranger District, 2455 Wash. 141, Trout Lake, WA 98650 (℃ **509/395-3400;** www.fs.fed.us/gpnf).

THE FRUIT LOOP (EXPLORING THE HOOD RIVER VALLEY)

Before windsurfing took center stage, the Hood River Valley was known as one of Oregon's top fruit-growing regions, and today the valley is still full of apple and pear orchards. From blossom time (Apr) to harvest season (Sept–Oct), the valley offers quiet country roads to explore. Along the way you'll find numerous farm stands, wineries, museums, and interesting shops that reflect the valley's rural heritage. Pick up a brochure called *Hood River County Fruit Loop Guide to Local Farm Stands* at the Hood River County Chamber of Commerce visitor center (see "Visitor Information," above).

Be sure to start your tour of the Hood River Valley by stopping at **Panorama Point,** off of Ore. 35 just south of town (follow the signs). This hilltop park provides a splendid view of the valley's orchards with Mount Hood looming in the distance.

In the fall, fruit stands pop up along the roads around the valley. **Rasmussen Farms,** 3020 Thomsen Rd. (© **800/548-2243** or 541/386-4622; www.rasmussen farms.com), is one of the biggest and best farm stands in the valley and is off Ore. 35 about 6 miles south of Hood River. Also not to be missed is the nearby **Apple Valley Country Store,** 2363 Tucker Rd. (© **541/386-1971;** www.applevalleystore.com), where you can stock up on homemade jams and jellies and maybe buy one of the store's legendary 4-pound apple pies. You'll find the store west of Rasmussen's on the opposite side of the valley. Also in the valley are numerous orchards and farms where you can pick your own fruit. Keep an eye out for U-PICK signs. Between June and August, you can also cut lavender at a couple of area farms. **Lavender Valley,** 3925 Portland Dr. (© **541/386-1906;** www.lavendervalley.com), has 3 acres of lavender and is just north of the Apple Valley Country Store. **Hood River Lavender,** 3801 Straight Hill Rd. (© **888/528-3276** or 541/354-9917; www.lavenderfarms.net), with views of Mounts Hood and Adams, is toward the middle of the valley just south of the community of Odell.

The little hamlet of Parkdale, at the south end of the Fruit Loop, is home to the fascinating little **Hutson Museum,** 4967 Baseline Rd. (© **541/352-6808**), which houses lapidary, archaeology, and anthropology collections, of which the rock collection and exhibits of Native American artifacts are a highlight. Museum days and hours vary with the seasons, so call ahead. Also in Parkdale you'll find the **Elliot Glacier Public House,** 4945 Baseline Rd. (© **541/352-1022**), a brewpub with a great view of Mount Hood from the picnic tables out back.

Any time between late March and late December, but especially during fruit-blossom time, the **Mount Hood Railroad** (© **800/872-4661** or 541/386-3556; www.mthoodrr.com) offers a great way to see the Hood River Valley. The diesel and steam locomotives operated by this scenic railroad company depart from the historic 1911 Hood River depot, pulling restored Pullman coaches on 2- and 4-hour excursions. The 2-hour excursions go to Odell, and the 4-hour excursions wind their way up the valley to Parkdale, where you can get a snack at a cafe or visit the Hutson Museum. Currently, however, damage to the tracks is preventing trains from going all the way to Parkdale. For the 2-hour excursion, fares are $25 for adults, $23 for seniors, and $15 for children 2 to 12. The schedule varies with the season (in July–Aug it's Tues–Sun), so call ahead to make a reservation. There are also regularly scheduled dinner and brunch trains and other specialty excursion trains. Reservations are recommended.

WINE TOURING

In recent years, the Hood River Valley has become one of the fastest-growing new wine regions in the state. Because this region is much hotter than the Willamette Valley in the summer, different varieties of grapes are grown. Stop in at a Hood River winery and you'll be tasting not just pinot noir and pinot gris but also merlot, Syrah, zinfandel, viognier, and other Bordeaux and Rhone varietals.

Cathedral Ridge Winery   This winery produces a good Riesling, as well as pinot gris, chardonnay, a cabernet-merlot blend, and several other varietals. There are great views of both Mount Hood and Mount Adams from here.

4200 Post Canyon Dr. ✆ **800/516-8710** or 541/386-2882. www.cathedralridgewinery.com. Daily 11am–5pm. From downtown, take Oak St./Cascade St. west to Country Club Road.

Hood River Vineyards and Winery   This winery is best known for its many excellent fruit wines, some of which are sweet and some of which are dry. They also produce a variety of port-style dessert wines.

4693 Westwood Dr. ✆ **541/386-3772.** www.hoodrivervineyards.us. Apr–Oct daily 11–5pm; Nov–Mar Wed–Sun 11am–5pm. From downtown, take Oak St./Cascade St. west to Country Club Road.

Mt. Hood Winery   This little winery has its tasting room in an old fruit stand on Ore. 35. The winery produces pinot noir, pinot gris, chardonnay, merlot, and a port-style wine.

3189 Ore. 35. ✆ **541/386-8333.** www.mthoodwinery.com. Apr–Thanksgiving daily 11am–5pm. Drive Ore. 35 south from Hood River for 5½ miles.

Pheasant Valley Vineyard & Winery ✿   At this winery in the middle of the Hood River Valley, you can sample the wines of both Pheasant Valley and **Viento Wines** (✆ **503/434-9587;** www.vientowines.com), which together produce some of my favorite area wines. There are usually some good values to be had here.

3890 Acree Dr. ✆ **866/357-9463** or 541/387-3040. www.pheasantvalleywinery.com. Tasting fee $5. Apr–Oct daily 11am–6pm; Nov–Mar daily 11am–5pm. Closed Jan. From downtown, take 13th Street south to Tucker Road and follow this road through several twists and turns to a right turn onto Acree Drive.

Phelps Creek Vineyards   With a tasting room right on the Hood River Golf Course, this is one of the prettiest places in the valley to sit outside with a glass of wine. Phelps Creek does several pinot noirs and a couple of chardonnays each year.

1850 Country Club Rd. ✆ **541/386-2607.** www.phelpscreekvineyards.com. Mar–Apr and Nov Sat–Sun 11am–5pm; May–Oct Thurs–Mon 11am–5pm. From downtown, take Oak St./Cascade St. west to Country Club Road.

The Pines 1852 ✿✿   Although this winery is actually in The Dalles, it has a tasting room in downtown Hood River. Because the wines here are produced by Peter Rosback, one of the best Oregon winemakers, they are some of my favorite area wines. Don't miss an opportunity to sample these lush wines, particularly the old-vine zinfandel.

202 State St. ✆ **541/993-8301.** www.thepinesvineyard.com. Wed–Fri 1–7pm; Sat–Mon noon–6pm.

Quenett Winery   If you have only a passing interest in wine, this is the best place in the area to sample a bit of local vino. The conveniently located downtown tasting room is a pretty little wine bar. The winery specializes in zinfandel, sangiovese, and barbera.

111 Oak St. ✆ **541/386-2229.** www.quenett.com. Sun–Thurs noon–6pm; Fri–Sat noon–8pm. Closed Tues–Wed in winter.

Wind River Cellars   This winery is located across the Columbia River, near the town of Husum, Washington, and produces a wide range of reds and whites that are mostly in the $20 to $25 range.

196 Spring Creek Rd., Husum. ✆ **509/493-2324.** www.windrivercellars.com. Daily 10am–6pm. Closed Dec 15–Jan 1. Take Wash. 141 north from White Salmon to Husum and turn left on Spring Creek Rd.

OTHER ATTRACTIONS IN HOOD RIVER

Hood River County Historical Museum   Down by the river at Port Marina Park (take exit 63 off I-84), you'll find this small museum, with exhibits of Native American artifacts from this area. There are also displays on pioneer life, but many visitors find the museum's windsurfing exhibit most compelling.

300 E. Port Marina Dr. ✆ 541/386-6772. Admission by donation. Apr daily 1–5pm; May–Sept daily 10am–5pm; Oct Sat–Sun 1–5pm. Closed Nov–Mar.

SHOPPING

In downtown Hood River, drop in at the community-sponsored, not-for-profit **Columbia Art Gallery,** 215 Cascade St. (✆ 541/387-8877; www.columbiaartgallery. org). If you're an avid cook, you'll want to stop in at **Annz Panz,** 315 Oak St. (✆ 541/ 387-2654), a large and well-stocked cookware store with a cafe and espresso counter. The first Friday of each month (May–Oct), downtown galleries and shops are open from 5 to 8pm with local artists on hand to sell their work and demonstrate their skills. Between April and December, you can sample local produce at the **Hood River Saturday Market** at the corner of Fifth and Cascade streets in downtown Hood River. The market is open on Saturday from 9am to 3pm.

WHERE TO STAY

If you're looking for a bed-and-breakfast and those below are full, call **Roomfinder** (✆ 541/386-6767; www.hoodriverroomfinder.com), a free service provided by the Columbia River Gorge–Hood River Bed & Breakfast Association.

Best Western Hood River Inn 🐸🐸   As the only area hotel located right on the water (there's a dock and private beach), the Best Western is popular with windsurfers. The convention hotel atmosphere (crowds of corporate types busily networking) is somewhat constraining, but if you like comfort and predictability, this is a good bet. The Riverside Grill serves dependable meals with a bit of Northwest imagination and a great view across the river.

1108 E. Marina Way, Hood River, OR 97031. ✆ 800/828-7873 or 541/386-2200. Fax 541/386-8905. www.hood riverinn.com. 149 units. Mid-May to Sept $89–$209 double, $179–$269 suite; Oct to mid-May $79–$149 double, $159–$189 suite. AE, DC, DISC, MC, V. Pets accepted ($12). **Amenities:** Restaurant (international); lounge; outdoor pool; exercise room; Jacuzzi; business center; room service; coin-op laundry; dry cleaning. *In room:* A/C, TV, dataport, fridge, microwave, coffeemaker, hair dryer, iron, free local calls, high-speed Internet access, Wi-Fi.

Columbia Gorge Hotel 🐸🐸   Just west of Hood River off I-84, and in business since shortly after 1921, this little oasis of luxury offers a genteel atmosphere that was once enjoyed by Rudolph Valentino and Clark Gable. With its yellow-stucco walls and red-tile roofs, this hotel would be at home in Beverly Hills, and the hotel gardens could hold their own amid the many public gardens of Victoria, British Columbia. The hotel is perched more than 200 feet above the river on a steep cliff, and it is difficult to take your eyes off the view. Be forewarned, though, that the rooms are rather cramped, as are the bathrooms. On Sunday, the hotel's dining room serves a huge multi-course breakfast that has long been legendary in the region. There's also a nightly hosted social hour.

4000 Westcliff Dr., Hood River, OR 97031. ✆ 800/345-1921 or 541/386-5566. Fax 541/386-9141. www.columbia gorgehotel.com. 40 units. $169–$259 double; $279–$379 suite. Children under 5 stay free in parent's room. AE, DC, DISC, MC, V. Closed for 1 week each Jan. Pets accepted ($35). **Amenities:** Restaurant (Northwest/Continental); lounge; full-service spa; concierge; business center; massage; babysitting. *In room:* A/C, TV, dataport, fridge, minibar, hair dryer, iron, free local calls, high-speed Internet access, Wi-Fi.

Hood River Hotel Built in 1913 and located in downtown Hood River, this hotel has a casual elegance and is an economical alternative to the pricey Columbia Gorge Hotel. Now don't expect much; this is sort of a historic hotel for young travelers. Canopy beds, ceiling fans, wood floors, and area rugs give the rooms a classic feel, but bathrooms in some rooms are little larger than closets. Most third-floor rooms have skylit bathrooms—my favorite. The riverview rooms are the most expensive, and there are suites with full kitchens as well. The hotel's casual dining room serves decent Northwest meals. Light sleepers should be aware of the railroad tracks behind the hotel.

102 Oak Ave., Hood River, OR 97031. © 800/386-1859 or 541/386-1900. Fax 541/386-6090. www.hoodriverhotel. com. 41 units. $79–$129 double; $109–$169 suite. Children 12 and under stay free in parent's room. AE, DC, DISC, MC, V. Pets accepted ($15 per day). **Amenities:** Restaurant (new American); lounge; exercise room; Jacuzzi; sauna; laundry service; dry cleaning. *In room:* TV, Wi-Fi.

Inn at the Gorge Though this bed-and-breakfast is housed in a 1908 Victorian home, it's still a casual sort of place popular with windsurfing enthusiasts, in part because each of the three suites has a kitchenette. The sunny Garden Suite, with its claw-foot tub, is my personal favorite. There's also a storage area for windsurfing and skiing gear. The innkeepers can steer you to the best spots for your skill level. The inn also offers discounted lift tickets to Mount Hood Meadows ski area.

1113 Eugene St., Hood River, OR 97031. © 877/852-2385 or 541/386-4429. www.innatthegorge.com. 5 units. $99–$149 double. Rates include full breakfast. MC, V. *In room:* A/C, TV/DVD, fridge, Wi-Fi.

The Mosier House Bed & Breakfast *(Finds)* This beautifully restored Victorian home is in the small town of Mosier, 5 miles east of Hood River, and the views of the Columbia Gorge from the inn's front porch are unforgettable. Inside, you'll find wood floors and period antiques, and although the four rooms with shared baths are all fairly small, they have the feel of an authentic vintage travelers' hotel. One of the shared bathrooms has a claw-foot tub, as does the room with the private bath. All in all, this inn manages to capture a bygone era without being overly frilly or self-consciously romantic, and it makes an excellent base for exploring the eastern end of the Columbia Gorge.

704 Third Ave. (P.O. Box 476), Mosier, OR 97040. © 877/328-0351 or 541/478-3640. www.mosierhouse.com. 5 units (1 with private bathroom). $85–$100 double with shared bathroom; $125 double with private bathroom. Rates include full breakfast. Children under 10 stay free in parent's room. MC, V. Children over 5 accepted. *In room:* A/C, Wi-Fi, no phone.

Oak Street Hotel *(Finds)* This little hotel is in a restored older home in downtown Hood River and shares space with a real-estate office. As sort of a cross between a B&B and a small inn, the Oak Street Hotel may not offer a lot of amenities but it does have loads of contemporary charm. Guest rooms are small but very attractively furnished. Room no. 5, with its views of the Columbia River, is my favorite. One of the best reasons to stay here is for the delicious baked goodies that are served at breakfast. Plus you'll be within a few blocks of several good restaurants.

610 Oak St., Hood River, OR 97031. © 866/386-3845 or 541/386-3845. Fax 541/387-8696. www.oakstreethotel. com. 9 units. Apr–Oct $129 double, $149 suite; Nov–Mar $119 double, $129 suite. Rates include continental breakfast. AE, DC, DISC, MC, V. *In room:* A/C, Wi-Fi.

Vagabond Lodge *(Kids)* If you've got a banker's tastes but a teller's vacation budget, you can take advantage of the Vagabond Lodge's proximity to the Columbia Gorge Hotel and enjoy the latter's gardens and restaurant without breaking the bank. Actually, the back rooms at the Vagabond are some of the best in Hood River simply for their views (some have balconies). In addition, this motel's grounds are also quite attractive. There are lots of big old oaks and evergreens, and natural rock outcroppings have been incorporated into the motel's landscaping. If you're in the mood for a splurge, ask for one of the suites. (Some have fireplaces; others whirlpool tubs.) A playground and lots of grass make this a good choice for families.

4070 Westcliff Dr., Hood River, OR 97031. © 877/386-2992 or 541/386-2992. Fax 541/386-3317. www.vagabond lodge.com. 42 units. $52–$89 double; $89–$112 suite. Children under 11 stay free in parent's room. AE, DC, MC, V. Pets accepted ($5). In room: A/C, TV, fridge, Wi-Fi.

CAMPGROUNDS
Area campgrounds include **Toll Bridge Park,** on Ore. 35, 17 miles south of town, and **Tucker Park,** on Tucker Road (Ore. 281) just a few miles south of town. Both of these county parks are on the banks of the Hood River. Farther south, you'll find the **Sherwood Campground,** a national-forest campground also on the banks of the Hood River. (This campground is favored by mountain bikers.) Eight miles west of Hood River off I-84 is **Viento State Park,** which gets quite a bit of traffic noise both from the interstate and from the adjacent railroad tracks. Eleven miles east of town, you'll find **Memaloose State Park,** which has the same noise problems. These two state parks are popular with windsurfers.

WHERE TO DINE
For fresh-baked rustic breads and great sandwiches made with imported meats and cheeses, go to **Panzanella Bakery & Deli,** 102 Fifth St. (© **541/386-2048**). For creamy gelato and good espresso, stop in at **Doppio Coffee + Lounge,** 310 Oak St. (© **541/386-3000;** www.doppiocoffeelounge.com).

Brian's Pourhouse ★★ ECLECTIC   Located in an old house a few blocks up the hill from downtown Hood River, this restaurant is a casual, fun place with very creative food. In summer, the big deck is the place to eat, and any time of year, the stylish little bar area is a cozy spot for a cocktail or a local microbrew. The menu is highly eclectic and ranges from fish tacos to sesame-crusted ahi tuna served with a wasabi–mashed potato egg roll. Sure, you can get a good grilled rib-eye, but this is someplace to try some bold new flavors.

606 Oak St. © **541/387-4344.** www.brianspourhouse.com. Reservations recommended. Main courses $11–$25. AE, MC, V. Summer, daily 5–11pm; shorter hours other months.

Celilo Restaurant ★★ NORTHWEST   This sister restaurant to the ever-popular Sixth Street Bistro is utterly hip in concept and is a sophisticated alternative to the homey restaurants that have long been popular in Hood River. Think timber-town natural-wood decor meets modern urban design aesthetic, and you'll have a good idea of what this place is like. The concept of fresh and local drives the kitchen here, so you can count on the menu sticking to whatever is in season—luckily, that can cover a lot of territory in this fertile region. Dishes with house-made pasta are always a good bet, and, in the fall, you might get your noodles sauced with fresh chanterelle mushrooms. Lots of fresh herbs flavor many of the dishes here.

16 Oak St. © **541/386-5710.** www.celilorestaurant.com. Reservations recommended. Main courses $16–$25. AE, MC, V. Daily 11:30am–3pm and 5–9:30 or 10pm.

North Oak Brasserie ★★ ITALIAN   Located below street level, this dark, romantic place is one of the most formal fine-dining restaurants in town. The emphasis here is on traditional and creative Italian food and good wine. If you don't have to worry about your cholesterol, be sure to opt for the roasted garlic and brie soup. Keep an eye out for seasonal pasta dishes, including good ravioli dishes.

113 Third St. ℭ 541/387-2310. Reservations recommended. Main courses $8–$22. AE, DISC, MC, V. Tues–Thurs 11am–2pm and 5–9pm; Fri 11am–2pm and 5–10pm; Sat 5–10pm.

Sixth Street Bistro ☞☞ AMERICAN/INTERNATIONAL   Just a block off Oak Street toward the river, the Sixth Street Bistro has an intimate little dining room and patio on the lower floor and a lounge with a balcony on the second floor. Each has its own entrance, but they share a menu. There are numerous international touches, such as green curry with mussels and clams, coconut red curry, and pad thai, and also juicy burgers. You'll find seasonal specials and vegetarian dishes as well.

509 Cascade Ave. ℭ 541/386-5737. www.sixthstreetbistro.com. Reservations recommended. Main courses $5–$10 lunch, $8–$20 dinner. AE, MC, V. Daily 11:30am–10pm.

HOOD RIVER AFTER DARK

Double Mountain Brewery   This little brewpub is Hood River's newest purveyor of hand-crafted ales, and it produces some of the most distinctive brews in town. If you're a fan of microbrews, be sure you pay a visit. 8 Fourth St. ℭ **541/387-0042**. www. doublemountainbrewery.com.

Full Sail Tasting Room & Pub   Full Sail brews some of the most consistently flavorful and well-rounded beers in the Northwest and has developed a loyal following. You have to walk right past the brewery to get to the pub, which is at the back of an old industrial building a block off Hood River's main drag. Big windows look out over the river. 506 Columbia St. ℭ **541/387-2247**. www.fullsailbrewing.com.

EAST OF HOOD RIVER: WILDFLOWERS & VIEWS

East of Hood River, you'll find two more sections of the Historic Columbia River Highway (Ore. 30), one of which is open only to hikers and bikers. The other is open to automobiles. The former section, located between Hood River and Mosier and known as the **Historic Columbia River Highway State Trail** (ℭ **800/551-6949**; www.oregonstateparks.org/park_155.php), was abandoned when I-84 was built and two tunnels on this section of the old highway were filled in. After the tunnels were re-excavated in order to open up this stretch as a 4.5-mile paved trail, a rock catchment had to be built along part of the route leading up to the tunnels from the west. Although the trail receives some traffic noise from I-84, it is a fascinating and easy hike or bike ride. To reach the western trail head, head east out of downtown Hood River and continue east on Old Columbia River Drive. For the eastern trail head, take exit 69 off I-84 and then take the first left. Starting from this latter trail head makes for a much shorter hike. However, the main visitor center for the trail is at the western trail head. There is a $3 fee to use the trail.

The second part of the old highway, beginning at exit 69 off I-84 and stretching from Mosier to The Dalles, climbs up onto the Rowena Plateau, where sweeping vistas take in the Columbia River, Mount Hood, and Mount Adams. Between March and May the wildflowers are some of the finest in the state. The best place to see them is at the Nature Conservancy's **Tom McCall Preserve at Rowena** (ℭ **503/802-8100**; www.nature.org/wherewework/northamerica/states/oregon). On spring weekends there are usually volunteers on hand guiding wildflower walks through the preserve.

3 The Dalles

128 miles W of Pendleton, 85 miles E of Portland, 133 miles N of Bend

The Dalles (rhymes with "the pals"), a French word meaning "flagstone," was the name given to this area by early-19th-century French trappers. These explorers may have been reminded of stepping stones or flagstone-lined gutters when they first gazed upon the flat basalt rocks that forced the Columbia River through a long stretch of rapids and cascades here. These rapids, which were a barrier to river navigation, formed a natural gateway to western Oregon.

For more than 10,000 years, Native Americans inhabited this site because of the ease with which salmon could be taken from the river as it flowed through the tumultuous rapids. The annual fishing season at nearby Celilo Falls was a meeting point for tribes from all over the West. Tribes would come to fish, trade, and stockpile supplies for the coming winter.

Although the Lewis and Clark expedition stopped here when they passed through the region in 1805 and 1806, white settlers, the first of whom came to The Dalles as missionaries in 1838, were latecomers to this area. However, by the 1840s, a steady flow of pioneers was passing through the region, which was effectively the end of the overland segment of the Oregon Trail. Pioneers who were headed for the mild climate and fertile soils of the Willamette Valley would load their wagons onto rafts at this point and float downriver to the mouth of the Willamette and then up that river to Oregon City.

By the 1850s, The Dalles was the site of an important military fort and had become a busy river port. Steamships shuttled from here to Cascade Locks on the run to Portland. However, the coming of the railroad in 1880, and later the flooding of the river's rapids, reduced the importance of The Dalles as a port town. Today, the city serves as the eastern gateway to the Columbia Gorge and, as such, is the site of the Columbia Gorge Discovery Center.

ESSENTIALS

GETTING THERE   The Dalles is on I-84 at the junction of U.S. 197, which leads south to Antelope, where it connects with U.S. 97.

Amtrak passenger trains stop across the Columbia River from The Dalles in Wishram, Washington. The station is at the west end of Railroad Avenue.

VISITOR INFORMATION   Contact **The Dalles Area Chamber of Commerce,** 404 W. Second St., The Dalles, OR 97058 (② **800/255-3385** or 541/296-2231; www.thedalleschamber.com).

LEARNING ABOUT THE GORGE

Columbia Gorge Discovery Center/Wasco County Historical Museum ⟨⚑⟩

These two museums, housed in one building on the outskirts of The Dalles, serve as the eastern gateway to the Columbia Gorge. In the museum building, constructed to resemble a Northwest Native American longhouse, you'll find exhibits on the geology and history of the Gorge. Among the most fascinating exhibits is a film of Native Americans fishing at Celilo Falls before the rising waters behind The Dalles Dam flooded the falls. There is also a short nature trail that leads past a small pond and links to a trail that stretches several miles to Lewis & Clark's Rock Fort campsite (see below). In spring, the trail is lined with beautiful wildflowers.

5000 Discovery Dr. ℂ 541/296-8600. www.gorgediscovery.org. $8 adults, $7 seniors, $4 children 6–16. Daily 9am–5pm. Closed New Year's Day, Thanksgiving, Christmas.

EXPLORING THE DALLES

Long before settlers arrived in The Dalles, Lewis and Clark's expedition stopped here. The site of their camp is called **Rock Fort** and it is one of their only documented campsites. The historic site is on First Street west of downtown, near the Port of The Dalles' industrial area northeast of Webber and Second streets.

Some of The Dalles's most important historic buildings can be seen at the **Fort Dalles Museum,** 500 W. 15th St. (ℂ **541/296-4547;** www.historicthedalles.org/fort_dalles/home.htm), at the corner of Garrison Street. Established in 1850, Fort Dalles was the only military post between Fort Laramie and Fort Vancouver. By 1867, the fort had become unnecessary, and after several buildings were destroyed in a fire, it was abandoned. Today, several of the original buildings, including a Carpenter-Gothic officers' home, are still standing. Though small, this is the oldest history museum in Oregon. Memorial Day through Labor Day, the museum is open daily from 10am to 5pm; call for hours in other months. Admission is $5 for adults, $4 for seniors, and $1 for children 7 to 17.

Not far from the Fort Dalles Museum, at **Sorosis Park,** there's a good view of The Dalles, the Columbia River, and Mount Adams. To reach this park, drive 1 block west from the museum and turn left on Trevitt Street, which becomes Scenic Drive. Continue on this latter street to the park.

Within a decade of the establishment of Fort Dalles, this community became the county seat of what was the largest county ever created in the United States. Wasco County covered 130,000 square miles between the Rocky Mountains and the Cascade Range. The old **Wasco County Courthouse,** 420 W. Second St. (ℂ **541/296-4798**), a two-story wooden structure built in 1859, has been preserved, and the inside looks much as it did when it was a functioning courthouse. June through August it's open Wednesday through Saturday from 11am to 3pm. Admission is free.

The Dalles's other historic landmark is a much more impressive structure. **Old St. Peter's Landmark church** (ℂ 541/296-5686; www.oldstpeterslandmark.org), at the corner of West Third and Lincoln streets, is no longer an active church, but its 176-foot-tall steeple is a local landmark. The church was built in the Gothic Revival style in 1897, and a 6-foot-tall rooster symbolizing The Dalles tops its spire. The church is open Tuesday through Friday from 11am to 3pm and Saturday and Sunday from 1 to 3pm.

If you're interested in learning more about the history and the historic buildings of The Dalles, pick up a copy of the historic walking tours brochure at the chamber of commerce. As you explore The Dalles, also keep an eye out for the city's many **historical murals.**

At the east of town rises **The Dalles Lock and Dam** (ℂ **541/298-7650** or 541/296-1181), which provides both irrigation water and electricity. The dam, which was completed in 1957, stretches for 1½ miles from the Oregon shore to the Washington shore. One of the main reasons this dam was built was to flood the rapids that made this section of the Columbia River impossible to navigate. Among the numerous rapids flooded by the dam were Celilo Falls, which, for thousands of years, was the most important salmon-fishing area in the Northwest. Each year thousands of Native Americans would gather here to catch and smoke salmon, putting the dried fish away for the coming winter. The traditional method of catching the salmon was to use a spear or a net on the end of a long pole. Men would build precarious wooden plat-forms out over the river and catch the salmon as they tried to leap up the falls. You can still see traditional Native American fishing platforms near the Shilo Inn here in The Dalles. The dam's **visitor center** has displays on both the history of the river and the construction of the dam. To reach the visitor center, take exit 87 off I-84 and turn right on Bret Clodfelter Way.

EAST OF THE DALLES

In addition to the two attractions listed here, you'll also find several wineries. **Maryhill Winery,** 9774 Wash. 14, Maryhill (© 877/627-9445; www.maryhillwinery.com), has the best view of any winery in the Northwest and also produces some very good wines. The tasting room is open daily from 10am to 6pm. **Cascade Cliffs Vineyard & Winery,** milepost 88.6, Wash. 14, Wishram (© 509/767-1100; www.cascadecliffs.com), is set at the foot of 400-foot-tall basalt cliffs and produces, among other wines, one of the state's only barberas. The tasting room is open daily from 10am to 6pm. **Marshal's Winery,** 150 Oak Creek Rd., Dallesport (© 509/767-4633; www.marshals vineyard.com), just 2 miles up a gravel road, is a tiny, family-run winery that has pro-duced some very quaffable cabernet sauvignons and merlots, as well as some unusual sweet wines. The tasting room is open daily from 9am to 6pm. A couple of miles west of Lyle, you can stop by **Syncline,** 111 Balch Rd. (© 509/365-4361; www.syncline wine.com), a small winery that produces some outstanding wines. Between Memorial Day and late September, it's open Thursday through Sunday from 11am to 6pm.

Columbia Hills State Park *(Finds)* Between The Dalles Dam and Wishram on Wash. 14, Columbia Hills is the site of Horsethief Lake, a popular fishing area and campground. However, long before the area was designated a state park, this was a gathering ground for Native Americans, who fished for salmon at nearby Celilo Falls. The park isn't far from the famous Celilo Falls, which were, before being inundated by the waters behind The Dalles Dam, the most prolific salmon-fishing spot in the Northwest. Each year for thousands of years, Native Americans would gather here from all over the Northwest. These Native Americans created petroglyphs on rocks that are now protected within this park. The most famous of these is Tsagaglalal ("she who watches"), a large face that gazes down on the Columbia River. The only way to see the park's petroglyphs is on ranger-led walks on Friday and Saturday mornings at 10am between April and October. Reservations for these walks should be made at least 2 to 3 weeks in advance.

Wash. 14. © 509/767-1159. Free admission. Apr–Oct daily 6:30am–dusk. Closed Nov–Mar.

Maryhill Museum of Art/Stonehenge Monument *(Finds)* Between 1914 and 1926, atop a remote, windswept bluff overlooking the Columbia River, eccentric entrepreneur Sam Hill built a grand mansion he called Maryhill. Though he never lived in the mansion, he did turn it into a museum that today is one of the finest, most eclectic, and least visited of the state's major museums. There is an acclaimed collec-tion of sculptures and drawings by Auguste Rodin, an extensive collection of Native American artifacts that includes the finest display of baskets in the state. Furniture, jewelry, and other items that once belonged to Hill's friend, Queen Marie of Roma-nia, are also on display, as is a collection of miniature French fashion mannequins from just after World War II. Note that the Rodins and fashion mannequins are some-times loaned out to other museums. The lush grounds surrounding the museum have sculptures, picnic tables, and plenty of shade trees, making this an ideal spot for a picnic (there's also a cafe inside the museum). A few miles east of Maryhill stands Hill's concrete reproduction of Stonehenge, which he built as a memorial to local men who died in World War I.

35 Maryhill Museum Dr. (Wash. 14). ℭ 509/773-3733. www.maryhillmuseum.org. Admission $7 adults, $6 seniors, $2 children 6–12. Mar 15–Nov 15 daily 9am–5pm. Closed Nov 16–Mar 14.

OUTDOOR ACTIVITIES

East of town 17 miles, you'll find the **Deschutes River State Recreation Area** (ℭ 541/739-2322), which is at the mouth of the Deschutes River and is the eastern boundary of the Columbia Gorge National Scenic Area. The park has several miles of hiking trails, and an old railway right-of-way that parallels the Deschutes River for 17 miles has been turned into a gravel mountain-biking and horseback-riding trail.

WHERE TO STAY

Although there are a few hotels in The Dalles, you should stay in Hood River, which is only 20 miles away and has a better selection of accommodations plus lots of great restaurants.

CAMPGROUNDS

If you want to pitch a tent or park an RV, try **Deschutes River State Recreation Area,** 17 miles east of The Dalles off I-84. For reservations, contact **ReserveAmerica** (ℭ 800/452-5687; www.reserveamerica.com). On the Washington side of the Gorge, there is camping at **Columbia Hills State Park** (no reservations), near the community of Dallesport (take U.S. 197 north to Wash. 14 east).

WHERE TO DINE

For delicious breakfasts, pastries, and good sandwiches, don't miss **Petite Provence Boulangerie & Patisserie,** 408 E. Second St. (ℭ 541/506-0037), a wonderful little French pastry shop. If you'd like to taste some local wines or sit with a glass of wine in a pretty winery tasting room, stop by **Erin Glenn Wines at The Mint,** 710 E. Second St. (ℭ 877/299-ERIN or 541/296-4707; www.eringlenn.com), which is open Friday from noon to 9pm and Saturday through Monday from noon to 5pm.

Baldwin Saloon Historic Restaurant & Bar ☆ AMERICAN/CONTINENTAL Built in 1876, the Baldwin Saloon has one of the few remaining cast-iron facades in town and is one of the only restaurants in The Dalles with much historic character. Brick walls, wooden booths, and a high ceiling add to the old-time feel, as does the collection of late-19th-century landscape paintings and large bar nudes. The menu is pretty straightforward and simple.

205 Court St. ℭ 541/296-5666. www.baldwinsaloon.com. Reservations accepted only for parties of 5 or more. Main courses $9–$20. DISC, MC, V. Mon–Thurs 11am–9pm; Fri–Sat 11am–10pm.

8

The Cascades

From the schussing of January and the kayaking of April to the wildflowers of August and the splashes of fall foliage in October, Oregon's Cascade Range is a year-round recreational magnet. Stretching from the Columbia Gorge in the north to California in the south, the Cascades are a relatively young volcanic mountain range with picture-perfect, snowcapped volcanic peaks rising above lush green forests of evergreens. The Cascades' volcanic heritage sets this mountain range apart from others in the West, and throughout these mountains, signs of past volcanic activity are evident. Crater Lake, formed after a massive volcanic eruption, is the most dramatic evidence of the Cascades' fiery past. But you can also see evidence of volcanic activity in the cones of Mount Hood and Mount Jefferson, and in the lava fields of McKenzie Pass.

As spectacular as this volcanic geology is, however, it is not what draws most people to these mountains. The main attraction is the wide variety of outdoor sports activities available. Crystal-clear rivers, churned into white water as they cascade down from high in the mountains, provide numerous opportunities for rafting, kayaking, canoeing, and fishing. High mountain lakes hold hungry trout, and throughout the summer, lakeside campgrounds stay filled with anglers. The Pacific Crest Trail winds the entire length of the Cascades, but it is the many wilderness areas scattered throughout these mountains that are the biggest draw for day hikers and backpackers. Mountain bikers also find miles of national-forest trails to enjoy. In winter, skiers and snowboarders flock to more than half a dozen ski areas and countless miles of cross-country ski trails—and because winter lingers late in the high Cascades, the ski season here is one of the longest in the country. Skiing often begins in mid-November and continues on into April and even May and June at Mount Bachelor. In fact, on Mount Hood, high-elevation snowfields allow a year-round ski season.

The Cascades also serve as a dividing line between the lush evergreen forests of western Oregon and the dry, high desert landscapes of eastern Oregon. On the western slopes, Douglas firs and western red cedars dominate, while on the east side, the cinnamon-barked ponderosa pine is most common. These trees were the lifeblood of the Oregon economy for much of the 20th century, but with few virgin forests left in the state, a litigious battle to protect the last old-growth forests has been raging here for decades. Today, visitors to the Cascades will be confronted at nearly every turn by the sight of clear-cuts scarring the mountainsides, yet it is still possible to find groves of ancient trees beneath which to hike and camp.

1 Mount Hood: Skiing, Hiking & Scenic Drives ★★★

60 miles E of Portland, 46 miles S of Hood River

At 11,235 feet, Mount Hood, a dormant volcano, is the tallest mountain in Oregon. Located fewer than 60 miles east of downtown Portland, it is also the busiest mountain in the state. Summer and winter, people flock here in search of cool mountain air filled with the scent of firs and pines. Campgrounds, hiking and mountain-biking trails, trout streams and lakes, downhill ski areas, and cross-country ski trails all provide ample opportunities for outdoor recreational activities on Mount Hood.

With five downhill areas and many miles of cross-country trails, the mountain is a ski bum's dream come true. One of the country's largest night-skiing areas is here, and at Timberline you can ski right through the summer. Because even those with a moderate amount of mountain-climbing experience can reach the summit fairly easily, Mount Hood is also the most climbed major peak in the United States.

One of the first settlers to visit Mount Hood was Samuel Barlow, who, in 1845, had traveled the Oregon Trail and was searching for an alternative to taking his wagon train down the treacherous waters of the Columbia River. Barlow blazed a trail across the south flank of Mount Hood, and the following year opened his trail as a toll road. The **Barlow Trail,** though difficult, was cheaper and safer than rafting down the river. The trail is now used for hiking and mountain biking.

During the Great Depression, the Works Progress Administration employed skilled craftsmen to build the rustic **Timberline Lodge** at the tree line on the mountain's south slope. Today, the lodge is a National Historic Landmark and is the main destination for visitors to the mountain. The lodge's vista of Mount Hood's peak and of the Oregon Cascades to the south gets my vote for the state's most unforgettable view.

Don't expect to have this mountain all to yourself, though. Because of its proximity to Portland, Mount Hood sees a lot of visitors throughout the year, and on snowy days the road back down the mountain from the ski areas can be bumper to bumper and backed up for hours. Also keep in mind that you'll need to have a Sno-Park permit in the winter (available at ski shops around the area) and a Northwest Forest Pass to park at trail heads in the summer (available at ranger stations, visitor centers, and a few outdoors-oriented shops).

ESSENTIALS

GETTING THERE   From Portland, Mount Hood is reached by taking I-84 east to exit 16 (Wood Village) and then following U.S. 26 east. From Hood River, take Ore. 35 south. These two highways meet just east of the town of Government Camp, which is the main tourist town on the mountain. The Lolo Pass Road is a gravel road that skirts the north and west sides of the mountain connecting these two highways.

VISITOR INFORMATION   For more information on Mount Hood, contact the **Mount Hood Information Center,** 24403 E. Welches Rd., Welches, OR 97067 (© 888/622-4822 or 503/622-4822; www.mthood.info), or the **Mount Hood Ranger District,** 6780 Ore. 35 S., Parkdale, OR 97041 (© 541/352-6002; www.fs. fed.us/r6/mthood).

SUMMER ON THE MOUNTAIN

In snow-free months, most visitors are heading to historic **Timberline Lodge** (see "Where to Stay," below). Besides having a fabulous view of Mount Hood, the lodge is surrounded by meadows that burst into bloom in July and August. Here you can access the 41-mile-long **Timberline Trail,** which circles the mountain. If you just have time for a short hike, head west from the lodge on this trail rather than east. The route east passes through dusty ash fields and then drops down into the hot, barren White River Valley. You'll find snow here year-round, and there's even summer skiing at the **Timberline ski area.** The lift-accessed ski slopes are high above the lodge on the Palmer Glacier and are open only in the morning. In summer, you can ride the lift even if you aren't skiing. The Magic Mile Skyride, which operates on Saturday and Sunday from 11am to 3pm, costs $15 for adults and $9 for seniors and children 7 to 14.

In summer, you can also ride the lift at **Mt. Hood Skibowl Action Park,** U.S. 26, Government Camp (© **503/222-2695;** www.skibowl.com), where there are mountain-biking trails, hiking trails, an alpine slide (sort of a summertime bobsled run), and numerous other rides and activities.

One of the most popular and most enjoyable hikes on Mount Hood is the trail to **Mirror Lake** ⚐, which, as its name implies, reflects the summit of Mount Hood in its mirrorlike waters. The trail is fairly easy and is good for families with young children. If you want to add a bit more challenge, you can continue to the summit of Tom, Dick & Harry Mountain, the back side of which in winter is part of the Mt. Hood Skibowl ski area. The view from the summit is superb, and in late summer there are huckleberries along the trail. You'll find the trail head on U.S. 26 just before you reach Government Camp.

The east side of the mountain, accessed by Ore. 35 from Hood River, is much drier and less visited than the south side. Here on the east side, you'll find good hiking trails in the vicinity of **Mount Hood Meadows,** where the wildflower displays in late July and August are some of the best on the mountain. The loop trail past Umbrella and Sahalie falls is particularly enjoyable. Also on this side of the mountain, you'll find the highest segment of the Timberline Trail. This section of trail climbs up Cooper Spur ridge from historic Cloud Cap Inn (no longer open to the public). The close-up views of the mountain and the distant views of eastern Oregon's dry landscape make this one of my favorite hiking destinations on Mount Hood. To reach the trail head, follow signs off Ore. 35 for Cooper Spur and Cloud Cap. On the east side of Ore. 35, off Forest Service Road 44, you'll also find the best **mountain-biking trails** in the area. Among these are the Surveyor's Ridge Trail and the Dog Mountain Trail.

If you're interested in a little adventure and an alternative route from the west side of the mountain to the Hood River area, try exploring the gravel **Lolo Pass Road,** which is usually in good enough condition for standard passenger cars. Be sure to have a Forest Service map (available from the **Mount Hood Information Center,** 24403 E. Welches Rd., Welches, OR 97067 (© **888/622-4822** or 503/622-4822; www.mt hood.info), since roads out here are not well marked and it's easy to get lost. Branching off from the Lolo Pass Road are several smaller roads that lead to some of the best hiking trails on Mount Hood. Also off the Lolo Pass Road, you'll find **Lost Lake,** one of the most beautiful (and most photographed) lakes in the Oregon Cascades. When the water is still, the view of Mount Hood and its reflection in the lake is positively sublime. Here you'll find campgrounds, cabins, picnic areas, good fishing, and hiking trails that lead both around the lake and up a nearby butte.

Down at the base of the mountain, just west of the community of Welches, you can learn about the forests, rivers, and fish of the Northwest at the Bureau of Land Management's **Wildwood Recreation Site.** Within this 560-acre natural area there are 2.5 miles of trails, including a boardwalk that crosses a wetland area. The highlight of the trail is an underwater fish-viewing window on the Cascade Streamwatch Trail. There's also a playground here, which makes this a good stop for families with small children. Fishing and swimming in the Salmon River are popular. There's also access to the steep and strenuous Boulder Ridge Trail and the much easier Old Salmon River Trail. There's a day-use fee of $5.

It's also possible to do some paddling while you're in the area. **Blue Sky Whitewater Rafting** (© 800/898-6398 or 503/630-3163; www.blueskyrafting.com), operates white-water-rafting trips on the Clackamas River, which has its source on the flanks of Mount Hood. A half-day trip costs $45 and a full-day trip costs $73 per person. **River Drifters** (© 800/972-0430 or 800/226-1001; www.riverdrifters.net) offers similar Clackamas River trips, and also trips on the Sandy River, which is more convenient if you're short on time. Sandy River trips, which are only offered in April and May, cost $85 per person.

If you're interested in a more strenuous mountain experience, the Mount Hood area offers plenty of mountain- and rock-climbing opportunities. **Timberline Mountain Guides,** P.O. Box 1167, Bend, OR 97709 (© **541/312-9242;** www.timberlinemtguides.com), leads summit climbs on Mount Hood. They also offer ski mountaineering and rock-climbing courses. A 2-day Mount Hood mountaineering course with summit climb costs $425.

WINTER ON THE MOUNTAIN

Although snowpacks that can be slow to reach skiable depths and frequent mid-winter rains make the ski season on Mount Hood unpredictable, in an ordinary year the regular ski season runs from around Thanksgiving right through March or April. Add to this the summer skiing on the Palmer Glacier at Timberline Ski Area, and you have the longest ski season in the United States. There are five ski areas on Mount Hood, though two of these are tiny operations that attract primarily beginners and families looking for an economical way to all go schussing together. For cross-country skiers, there are many miles of marked ski trails, some of which are groomed.

The single most important thing to know about skiing anywhere in Oregon is that you'll have to have a **Sno-Park permit.** These permits, which sell for $3 a day, $7 for 3 days, or $20 for the season, allow you to park in plowed parking areas on the mountain. You can get permits at ski shops in Sandy and Hood River and at a few convenience stores. Expect to pay a service fee wherever you buy your pass.

Mt. Hood Skibowl (© 503/272-3206; 800/754-2695 or 503/222-2695 for snow report; www.skibowl.com) is located in Government Camp on U.S. 26 and is the closest ski area to Portland. Skibowl offers 1,500 vertical feet of skiing and has more expert slopes than any other ski area on the mountain. This is also one of the largest lighted ski areas in the country. Adult lift-ticket prices range from $33 to $39 for an all-day pass ($25 for night skiing). Call for hours of operation.

Timberline Ski Area (© 503/622-0717 or 503/222-2211 for snow report; www.timberlinelodge.com) is the highest ski area on Mount Hood and has one slope that is open throughout the summer. This is the site of the historic **Timberline Lodge.** Adult lift-ticket prices range from $23 for night skiing to between $49 and $54 for an all-day pass. Call for hours of operation.

Mount Hood Meadows 𝞹𝞹 (© 800/SKI-HOOD; 503/227-7669 for snow report; www.skihood.com), 12 miles northeast of Government Camp on Ore. 35, is the largest ski resort on Mount Hood, with more than 2,000 skiable acres, 2,777 vertical feet of slopes, five high-speed quad lifts, and a wide variety of terrain. This is the closest Mount Hood comes to having a destination ski resort, and consequently, it is here that you'll find the most out-of-state skiers. Lift-ticket prices range from $25 for night skiing to between $54 and $64 for an all-day pass. Call for hours of operation.

If you're interested in **cross-country skiing,** there are plenty of trails. For views, head to the **White River Sno-Park,** east of Government Camp. The trails at **Glacier View Sno-Park,** across U.S. 26 from Mount Hood Skibowl, are good for beginner and intermediate skiers. The mountain's best-groomed trails are at the **Mount Hood Meadows Nordic Center** ($10 all-day trail pass) on Ore. 35 and at **Teacup Lake** ($5 donation requested), which is across the highway from the turnoff for Mount Hood Meadows. Teacup Lake is maintained by a local ski club (www.teacupnordic.org) and has the best system of groomed trails on the mountain. In the town of Sandy and at Government Camp, there are numerous ski shops that rent cross-country skis.

EN ROUTE TO THE MOUNTAIN

If you like sweet wines, watch for the **Wasson Brothers wine tasting room,** 17020 Ruben Lane at U.S. 26 (*©* **503/668-3124;** www.wassonbrotherswinery.com), as you drive through Sandy. This winery produces a wide range of fruit wines, and also does quite a few dry varietals. The tasting room is open daily from 9am to 5pm. Also, if you or anyone in your car has a sweet tooth, keep an eye out for the **Oregon Candy Farm,** 48620 SE U.S. 26, Sandy (*©* **503/668-5066**), which is 5½ miles east of Sandy and has a huge assortment of homemade candies. The Candy Farm is open Monday through Friday from 9am to 5pm and Saturday and Sunday from noon to 5pm.

WHERE TO STAY
ON THE MOUNTAIN

Collins Lake Resort *★★*   This town house–condominium resort development in the heart of Government Camp is the biggest thing to hit Mount Hood since Timberline Lodge was built. Collins Lake offers by far the most luxurious and spacious accommodations on the mountain. These are condos, so interior decor is up to owners, but don't worry too much. These three-story, two- and three-bedroom town houses are beautiful, and most have hardwood floors and gorgeous kitchens with granite counters. Be sure to ask about free midweek skiing at Skibowl if you stay here on a weeknight in winter.

88149 E. Creek Ridge Rd., Government Camp, OR 97028. *©* **888/422-4776.** www.collinslakeresortvacations.com. 55 units. $169–$369 double. Children under 13 stay free in parent's room. AE, DISC, MC, V. Pets accepted ($50 fee). **Amenities:** 2 outdoor pools; Jacuzzi; sauna; bike rental; children's programs; concierge; ski shuttle; massage. *In room:* TV, kitchen, fridge, coffeemaker, hair dryer.

Mt. Hood Inn *★*   Located at the west end of Government Camp right on the highway, this modern budget hotel doesn't have a lot of character, but the adjacent Ice Axe Grill, home of the Mt. Hood Brewing Company, makes this a great place to stay if you enjoy craft beers. Pine furnishings give the guest rooms here a contemporary rustic feel. The king spa rooms, with two-person whirlpool tubs beside the king-size beds, are definitely the best rooms, but they're somewhat overpriced.

87450 E. Government Camp Loop, Government Camp, OR 97028. *©* **800/443-7777** or 503/272-3205. Fax 503/272-3307. www.mthoodinn.com. 55 units. Summer and winter $159–$179 double; spring and fall $99–$109 double. Rates include continental breakfast. Children 18 and under stay free in parent's room. AE, DC, DISC, MC, V. Pets accepted ($10 per night). **Amenities:** Jacuzzi; coin-op laundry. *In room:* TV, fridge, microwave, coffeemaker, free local calls, Wi-Fi.

Timberline Lodge ☆☆ Constructed during the Great Depression of the 1930s as a WPA project, this classic alpine ski lodge overflows with craftsmanship. The grand stone fireplace, huge exposed beams, and wide-plank floors of the lobby impress every first-time visitor. Woodcarvings, imaginative wrought-iron fixtures, hand-hooked rugs, and handmade furniture complete the rustic picture. Unfortunately, guest rooms, which vary considerably in size, are not as impressive as the public areas of the lodge. The smallest rooms lack private bathrooms, and windows in most rooms fail to take advantage of the phenomenal views that could be had here. However, you can always visit the Ram's Head lounge for a better view of Mount Hood.

Timberline, OR 97028. © 800/547-1406 or 503/622-7979. Fax 503/622-0710. www.timberlinelodge.com. 70 units (10 with shared bathroom). $99–$115 double with shared bathroom; $150–$275 double with private bathroom. Children under 12 stay free in parent's room. AE, DC, DISC, MC, V. **Amenities:** 2 restaurants (Northwest, American); 2 lounges; year-round outdoor pool; exercise room; Jacuzzi; sauna; children's ski programs; coin-op laundry. *In room (except those w/shared bath):* Dataport, hair dryer, iron, Wi-Fi.

AT THE BASE OF THE MOUNTAIN
The Resort at the Mountain ☆☆ It's a bit of a drive to Timberline or Government Camp and the area's hiking trails and ski areas, but if a round of golf in a gorgeous setting sounds tempting, this golf resort, set in a large clearing in the dense woods at the base of Mount Hood, is one of your best choices in the Mount Hood area. Beautifully landscaped grounds incorporating concepts from Japanese garden design hide the resort's many low-rise buildings and make this a tranquil woodsy retreat. The guest rooms are large and have either a balcony or a patio. The main lodge has a formal dining room, while a more casual dining room overlooks the golf course. In addition to the amenities listed below, there are horseshoe pits, croquet and lawn bowling courts, volleyball and badminton courts, nature trails, and a pro shop.

68010 E. Fairway Ave., Welches, OR 97067. © 800/669-7666 or 503/622-3101. www.theresort.com. 160 units. May–Oct $139–$199 double, $219–$289 suite; Nov–Apr $99–$149 double, $159–$199 suite. Children under 18 stay free in parent's room. AE, DISC, MC, V. Pets accepted ($25). **Amenities:** 2 restaurants (Northwest, American); 2 lounges; outdoor pool; 27-hole golf course; 4 tennis courts; exercise room; spa; Jacuzzi; bike rentals; business center; room service; massage; coin-op laundry; laundry service; dry cleaning. *In room:* A/C, TV/DVD, dataport, coffeemaker, hair dryer, iron, high-speed Internet access, Wi-Fi.

NORTHEAST OF THE MOUNTAIN
Cooper Spur Mountain Resort ☆ *Value* If you want to get away from it all, try this surprisingly remote lodge in the off season. (During ski season it can be difficult to get a reservation.) The inn consists of a main building and a handful of modern log cabins. These latter accommodations should be your first choice here. The cabins have two bedrooms and a loft area reached by a spiral staircase. There are also rooms with full kitchens. The inn's restaurant serves decent, reasonably priced steaks. At the end of the day you can soak yourself in one of the inn's whirlpool spas.

10755 Cooper Spur Rd., Mount Hood, OR 97041. © 541/352-6692. www.cooperspur.com. 16 units. $99–$125 double; $159–$285 cabin or suite; $375–$425 log house. AE, DC, DISC, MC, V. **Amenities:** Restaurant (American); lounge; tennis court; 5 Jacuzzis. *In room:* TV, fridge, microwave, coffeemaker.

WHERE TO DINE
ON THE MOUNTAIN
Cascade Dining Room ☆☆ NORTHWEST It may seem a bit casual from the lobby and there are no stunning views of Mount Hood even though it's right outside the window, but the Cascade Dining Room is by far the best restaurant on Mount Hood. The menu changes regularly, but might include smoked-chicken rigatoni with

crimini mushrooms and cranberries, morel-stuffed pheasant breast, or buffalo loin with a molasses demi-glace. There are also always several interesting vegetarian offerings. There's a good wine selection, and desserts showcase a variety of local seasonal ingredients such as raspberries, pears, and apples. Although the food here is good and the wine list is superb, the service rarely rises to the occasion.

In Timberline Lodge, Timberline. (©) 503/622-7979. Reservations highly recommended. Main courses $14–$17 lunch, $20–$30 dinner, 4-course prix-fixe dinner $33. AE, DC, DISC, MC, V. Daily 7:30–10am, noon–2pm, and 6–8pm.

Ice Axe Grill ⊛ PUB FOOD This casual restaurant brewpub on the edge of Government Camp is home to the Mt. Hood Brewing Company and offers good microbrews and pub food (sandwiches, burgers, salads, pizzas), as well as interesting daily specials. There are also some good seafood dishes, including fish tacos and a daily seafood special. There are usually at least six beers on tap (including cask-conditioned ales and a couple of daily choices on the nitro taps).

87304 E. Government Camp Loop. (©) 503/272-3724. www.iceaxegrill.com. Main courses $9.25–$21. AE, DISC, MC, V. Sun–Thurs 11:30am–9pm; Fri–Sat 11:30am–10pm.

AT THE BASE OF THE MOUNTAIN

Calamity Jane's ⊛ (Finds) BURGERS What, you ask, is a $14 hamburger? Well, at Calamity Jane's, it's a 1-pound pastrami-and-mushroom burger. If you think that's outrageous, wait until you see the other burgers listed on the menu. There's the peanut-butter burger, the George Washington burger (with sour cream and sweet pie cherries), the hot-fudge-and-marshmallow burger—even an unbelievably priced inflation burger. Not all the burgers at this entertaining and rustic eatery are calculated to turn your stomach—some are just plain delicious. There are even pizza burgers. This place is just east of Sandy on U.S. 26.

42015 U.S. 26, Sandy. (©) 503/668-7817. Burgers $5–$16. AE, DISC, MC, V. Sun–Thurs 11am–9pm; Fri–Sat 11am–10pm.

The Rendezvous Grill & Tap Room ⊛⊛ MEDITERRANEAN Located right on U.S. 26 in Welches, this casual, upscale restaurant is a great choice for dinner on your way back to Portland. Although the emphasis is on Mediterranean dishes, other flavors also show up. Don't miss the rigatoni with alder-smoked chicken with toasted hazelnuts and dried cranberries. The pan-fried oysters and the ever-popular crab-and-shrimp cakes, both of which are available at lunch and dinner, are also good bets.

67149 E. U.S. 26, Welches. (©) 503/622-6837. www.rendezvousgrill.net. Reservations recommended. Main courses $8–$13 lunch, $17–$25 dinner. AE, DISC, MC, V. Daily 11:30am–9pm.

2 The Santiam Pass, McKenzie Pass & McKenzie River

Santiam Pass: 82 miles SE of Salem, 40 miles NW of Bend. McKenzie Pass: 77 miles NE of Eugene, 36 miles NW of Bend

As the nearest mountain recreational areas to both Salem and Eugene, the Santiam Pass, McKenzie Pass, and McKenzie River routes are some of the most popular in the state. Ore. 22, which leads over Santiam Pass, is also one of the busiest routes to the Sisters and Bend areas in central Oregon. Along these highways are some of the state's best white-water-rafting and fishing rivers, some of the most popular and most beautiful backpacking areas, and good downhill and cross-country skiing. In the summer, the Detroit Lake recreation area is the main attraction along Ore. 22 and is a favorite of water-skiers and lake anglers. In winter, it's downhill and cross-country skiing at Santiam Pass that brings most people up this way.

Ore. 126, on the other hand, follows the scenic McKenzie River and is favored by white-water rafters and drift-boat anglers fishing for salmon and steelhead. Several state parks provide access to the river. During the summer, Ore. 126 connects to Ore. 242, a narrow road that climbs up and over McKenzie Pass, the most breathtaking pass in the Oregon Cascades.

ESSENTIALS

GETTING THERE   Santiam Pass is open year-round and is reached by Ore. 22 from Salem, U.S. 20 from Albany, and Ore. 126 from Eugene. McKenzie Pass, which is closed in winter, is on Ore. 242 and lies to the south of Santiam Pass. It can be reached by all the same roads that lead to Santiam Pass.

VISITOR INFORMATION   For more information on outdoor recreation in this area, contact the **Detroit Ranger District,** HC73, Box 320, Mill City, OR 97360 (© **503/854-3366**); or the **McKenzie Ranger District,** 57600 McKenzie Hwy., McKenzie Bridge, OR 97413 (© **541/822-3381**). Also check the website of the Willamette National Forest (www.fs.fed.us/r6/willamette). For more general information, contact the **McKenzie River Chamber of Commerce,** 44643 McKenzie Hwy., Leaburg, OR 97489 (© **541/896-3330;** www.members.aol.com/mcrvcofc/chamber. htm), which operates a visitor center at the old Leaburg fish hatchery on Leaburg Lake east of Springfield on the McKenzie Highway.

ALONG THE SANTIAM PASS HIGHWAY

Detroit Lake is the summertime center of activity on this route—fishing and water-skiing are the most popular activities. North of the lake, you'll find **Breitenbush Hot Springs Retreat and Conference Center** (© **503/854-3320;** www.breitenbush.com), a New Age community/retreat center that has rustic cabins, dorms, and campsites and allows day use of its hot springs by advance reservation. The fee is between $12 and $25 per person, and inexpensive vegetarian meals are available. Breitenbush offers massage, yoga, meditation classes, and a wide range of other programs focusing on holistic health and spiritual growth.

At Santiam Pass, you'll find the **Hoodoo Ski Area** (© **541/822-3337** for snow report, or 541/822-3799; www.hoodoo.com), which is the best little ski area in Oregon. The ski area has five chair lifts and 30 runs for all levels of experience. Lift tickets are $39 to $42 for adults and $29 to $31 for children. Night skiing is available. Here you'll also find an awesome tubing run for the kids and the **Hoodoo Nordic Center,** which has almost 10 miles of groomed cross-country ski trails and charges $12 to $14 for a trail pass. Also in the Santiam Pass area, you'll find several Sno-Parks. The Maxwell, Big Springs, and Lava Lake East Sno-Parks access the best trails in the area. In recent years, however, these trails have become very popular with snowshoers. Consequently, you might want to leave the skinny skis at home and bring snowshoes instead.

UP THE MCKENZIE RIVER

The McKenzie River is one of Oregon's most popular white-water-rafting rivers, and the cold blue waters challenge a wide range of experience levels. **Oregon Whitewater Adventures** (© **800/820-RAFT** or 541/746-5422; www.oregonwhitewater.com) and **A Helfrich's McKenzie River Rafting and Fishing Trips** (© **800/328-7688** or 541/726-5039; www.raft2fish.com) both offer half- and full-day trips. Expect to pay $60 for a half-day of rafting and $75 to $85 for a full day.

If you're interested in seeing this area by bike, contact **Oregon Adventures** (© **541/782-2388;** www.oregon-adventures.com), which offers a variety of bike rides, both road and trail, for $30 to $75 per person per day. This company can also arrange car shuttles for one-way bike rides.

The McKenzie River town of Blue River is home to one of the best golf courses in Oregon. **Tokatee Golf Club,** 54947 McKenzie Hwy., McKenzie Bridge (© **888/865-2833** or 541/822-3220; www.tokatee.com), gets consistently high ratings and has a spectacular setting with views of snowcapped Cascade Peaks and lush forests. The green fee is $42 ($30 for electric cart) for 18 holes.

Off Ore. 126, between the towns of Blue River and McKenzie Bridge, you'll find the turnoff for the **Aufderheide National Scenic Byway** (Forest Service Rd. 19). This road meanders for 54 miles through the foothills of the Cascades, first following the South Fork McKenzie River (and Cougar Reservoir) and then following the North Fork of the Middle Fork Willamette River, which offers excellent fly-fishing and numerous swimming holes. Along the route, you'll find several hiking trails, and, at the south end of Cougar Reservoir, a trail that leads to the very popular **Terwilliger Hot Springs.** The southernmost stretch of Forest Service Road 19 is the most scenic portion and passes through a deep, narrow gorge formed by the North Fork of the Middle Fork Willamette River. At the southern end of the scenic byway is the community of Westfir, which is the site of the longest covered bridge in Oregon.

Between the turnoff for McKenzie Pass and the junction of Ore. 126 and U.S. 20, you'll find some of the Cascades' most enchanting water features. Southernmost of these is **Belknap Resort and Hot Springs** (© 541/822-3512; www.belknaphot springs.com), where, for $6.50 for 1 hour or $11 for the day, you can soak in a hot mineral swimming pool. Just north of Trail Bridge Reservoir, on a side road off the highway, a 4-mile round-trip hike on a section of the McKenzie River Trail leads to the startlingly blue waters of the **Tamolitch Pool** ✹✹. This pool is formed by the McKenzie River welling up out of the ground after flowing underground for 3 miles. Five miles south of the junction with Ore. 20, you'll come to two picturesque water-falls, **Sahalie Falls** and **Koosah Falls.** Across the highway from these falls is **Clear Lake,** the source of the McKenzie River. This spring-fed lake truly lives up to its name, and a rustic lakeside resort rents rowboats so you can get out on the water and see for yourself. Be sure to hike the trail on the east side of the lake; it leads to the turquoise waters of **Great Springs,** which is connected to the lake by a 100-yard stream.

One of the most breathtaking sections of road in the state begins just east of **Belk-nap Hot Springs.** Ore. 242, which is open only in the summer, is a narrow, winding road that climbs up through forests and lava fields to **McKenzie Pass** ✹✹, from which there's a sweeping panorama of the Cascades and some of the youngest lava fields in Oregon. An observation building made of lava rock provides sighting tubes so that you can identify all the visible peaks, and a couple of trails will lead you out into this otherworldly landscape. In autumn, this road has some of the best fall color in the state. On the west side of the pass, the short **Proxy Falls** trail leads through old lava flows to a waterfall that in late summer has no outlet stream. The water simply disappears into the porous lava.

WHERE TO STAY

Belknap Lodge & Hot Springs ✹ *(Finds)*   Set on the banks of the McKenzie River, this lodge is one of the most enjoyable mountain retreats in the state. Extensive lawns and perennial gardens have been planted, turning this clearing in the forest into a burst of color in the summer. Guest rooms vary in size, but all have comfortable modern furnishings. Some also have whirlpool tubs or decks overlooking the roaring river. The cabins are much more rustic than the lodge rooms, and linens are not included. Water from the hot springs, which are on the far side of the river and reached by a footbridge, is pumped into two small pools. The lodge also has sites for tents and RVs ($25–$30).

59296 N. Belknap Springs Rd. (P.O. Box 2001), McKenzie Bridge, OR 97413. (℃ **541/822-3512.** Fax 541/822-3327. www.belknaphotsprings.com. 25 units. $95–$120 double; $55–$400 cabin; $155–$185 suite. Rates for lodge include continental breakfast. DISC, MC, V. Pets accepted in some cabins. **Amenities:** 2 hot springs–fed outdoor pools. *In room:* No phone.

Eagle Rock Lodge ᴋ   This bed-and-breakfast on the banks of the McKenzie River has the best rooms in the area and should be your first choice for a luxurious outdoors-oriented escape. Several of the rooms have gas fireplaces and two-person whirlpool tubs, both of which can be very welcome after a long day of hiking.

49198 McKenzie Hwy, Vida, OR 97488. (℃ **541/822-3630.** www.eaglerocklodge.com. 8 units. May–Oct $130–$185 double, $185–$225 suite; Nov–Apr $115–$155 double, $155–$185 suite. Rates include full breakfast. MC, V. *In room:* Fridge, microwave, no phone.

Holiday Farm Resort ᴋ ⒻⒾⁿᵈˢ   This beautifully situated getaway is a collection of renovated white cottages perched on the edge of the McKenzie River, and the setting under the big trees is as idyllic as you'll find in Oregon. Grab a book and a seat on your private riverside deck and you may never give a thought to pulling on your hiking boots. Holiday Farm started out as a stagecoach stop and has been around long enough to have hosted U.S. President Herbert Hoover. A formal dining room and a more casual lounge serve meals. Guests have 800 feet of riverfront to enjoy and two private lakes for fishing and swimming.

54455 McKenzie River Dr., Blue River, OR 97413. (℃ **541/822-3725.** www.holidayfarmresort.com. 8 units. Apr–Oct $150–$275 cottage for 2 people; Nov–Mar $135–$250 cottage for 2 people. AE, MC, V. **Amenities:** Restaurant (international); lounge. *In room:* Kitchen.

Inn at the Bridge ᴋ   The privately owned cabins here are set right on the banks of the McKenzie River and were all recently built, so they are as clean and comfortable as any accommodations you'll find in the area. Although the cabins are close to the highway, the sound of the river is all you'll hear most of the time. Summer or winter, these cedar-shingled two-bedroom cabins are a great choice.

56393 McKenzie Hwy., McKenzie Bridge, OR 97413. (℃ **877/822-6006** or 541/822-6006. Fax 541/822-1080. 10 units. $175 double. MC, V. *In room:* A/C, kitchen, fridge, microwave, coffeemaker.

CAMPGROUNDS

There are several campgrounds along the McKenzie River on Ore. 126. Of these, the **Delta Campground,** set under huge old-growth trees between Blue River and McKenzie Bridge, is one of the finest. If you are up this way to hike, mountain bike, or do some flat-water canoeing, there is no better choice than Clear Lake's **Coldwater Cove Campground** on Ore. 126 just south of Santiam Pass junction. For reservations at this campground, contact Recreation.gov (℃ **877/444-6777;** www. recreation.gov). South of here on Ore. 126, the **Trail Bridge Campground** makes a good alternative to Coldwater Cove. Along the popular McKenzie Pass Highway (Ore. 242), you'll find **Scott Lake Campground, Alder Springs Campground,** and **Lava Camp Lake Campground.**

Along the Aufderheide National Scenic Byway, you'll find several campgrounds. **Cougar Crossing,** toward the north end of the scenic byway, is the closest campground to Terwilliger Hot Springs. South of here you'll find **Frissell Crossing, Homestead,** and **French Pete,** all of which are on the banks of the South Fork of the McKenzie River. Toward the south end of this road is **Kiahanie Campground,** which is on the North Fork of the Middle Fork of the Willamette River and is popular with fly anglers.

WHERE TO DINE
For burgers, try the **Vida Cafe,** 45641 McKenzie Hwy. (© **541/896-3289**), near milepost 26, or, at milepost 38, the **Finn Rock Grill,** 50660 McKenzie Hwy. (© **541/ 822-6080**), which has a deck beside the river.

3 The Willamette Pass Route

Oakridge: 41 miles SE of Eugene; Willamette Pass: 68 miles SE of Eugene

Ore. 58, which connects Eugene with U.S. 97 north of Crater Lake, is the state's fastest and straightest route over the Cascades. This is not to imply, however, that there isn't anything along this highway worth slowing down for. Flanked by two wilderness areas, Waldo Lake and Diamond Peak, and three major lakes, Waldo, Odell, and Crescent, Ore. 58 provides access to a wide range of recreational activities, chief among which are mountain biking, fishing, and boating in summer and both downhill and cross-country skiing in winter.

The sister towns of Oakridge and Westfir are the only real towns on this entire route and are the only places where you'll find much in the way of services. Westfir is also the southern terminus of the Aufderheide National Scenic Byway, which winds through the Cascade foothills to just outside the town of McKenzie Bridge on Ore. 126. For information on this scenic drive, see above.

ESSENTIALS
GETTING THERE   Ore. 58 begins just south of Eugene off I-5 and stretches for 92 miles to U.S. 97.

VISITOR INFORMATION   For more information on recreational activities in this area, contact the **Middle Fork Ranger Station,** 46375 Ore. 58, Westfir, OR 97492 (© **541/782-2283;** www.fs.fed.us/r6/willamette). Another source of information is the **Oakridge-Westfir Area Chamber of Commerce,** P.O. Box 217, Oakridge, OR 97463 (© **541/782-4146;** www.oakridgechamber.com).

WHAT TO SEE & DO: HOT SPRINGS TO SNOW SKIING
In the Willamette National Forest outside the logging town of Oakridge are miles and miles of great **mountain-biking trails** that have turned the Oakridge area into one of Oregon's top mountain-biking regions. Stop by the ranger station in Westfir to get maps and information on riding these trails. One of the most scenic rides is the 22-mile trail around Waldo Lake. You'll also find trails at Willamette Pass Ski Area, where, in summer, the cross-country ski trails are great for biking. This ski area also operates a summertime sightseeing gondola that carries your bike up to the top of the mountain for you. An all-day pass costs $12 for adults, $8 for youths, and $1 for children under 5. Mountain-bike trail passes cost $15 for adults, $11 for youths, and $5 for children.

If you're keen to soak in some natural hot springs, you'll find some right beside Ore. 58 about 10 miles east of Oakridge. **McCredie Hot Springs** are neither the hottest nor the most picturesque springs in the state, and with traffic noise and crowds, they aren't the most pleasant either. But if you want a quick soak without having to go wandering down gravel roads, they do the trick.

Just before reaching Willamette Pass, you'll see signs for **Salt Creek Falls,** which are well worth a stroll down the short trail to the falls overlook. At 286 feet high, these are the second-highest falls in the state. Longer hiking trails also lead out from the falls parking area.

Also just before Willamette Pass is the turnoff for Forest Service Road 5897, which leads 10 miles north to **Waldo Lake,** one of the purest lakes in the world. The lake, which is just over a mile high, covers 10 square miles and is 420 feet deep. When the waters are still, it is possible to see more than 100 feet down into the lake. Because this is such a large lake, and because there are reliable afternoon winds, it is popular for sailboating and windsurfing. Powerboaters, canoeists, and sea kayakers also frequent the lake. There are several campgrounds along the east shore of the lake, while the west shore abuts the Waldo Lake Wilderness Area. The 22-mile loop trail around the lake is popular with mountain bikers and backpackers, but shorter day hikes, particularly at the south end, are rewarding. The mosquitoes here are some of the worst in the state, so before planning a trip, be sure to get a bug report from the Middle Fork Ranger Station.

Just over Willamette Pass lie two more large lakes. **Odell Lake** is best known by anglers who come to troll for kokanee salmon and Mackinaw trout. However, it's also a good windsurfing lake. Though the waters never exactly get warm, **Crescent Lake** is the area's best for swimming, notably at Symax Beach, on the lake's northeast corner.

At **Willamette Pass Ski Area** (© 541/345-SNOW; www.willamettepass.com), 69 miles southeast of Eugene on Ore. 58, you'll find 29 downhill runs and 12 miles of groomed cross-country trails. The ski area is open daily from around Thanksgiving to mid-April. Night skiing is available on Friday and Saturday nights from December to March. Adult lift tickets are $38 per day.

CAMPGROUNDS

On Waldo Lake, the **North Waldo Campground,** with its swimming area and boat launch, should be your first choice. Second choice on the lake should be **Islet Campground** or, at the south end of the lake, **Shadow Bay Campground.** If you have a boat, you can camp at primitive campsites along the west shore of the lake. **Gold Lake Campground,** just west of Willamette Pass on Forest Service Road 500, is a quiet spot on a pretty fly-fishing-only lake that allows no motorboats. Just over Willamette Pass, there are several campgrounds on Odell Lake. **Odell Creek Campground** at the east end of the lake is the quietest campground on this lake.

WHERE TO DINE

Most people heading up this way plan to be self-sufficient when mealtime rolls around, whether they're camping or staying in a cabin. If you don't happen to have a full ice chest, you'll find a few basic restaurants in Oakridge. Although none are particularly memorable, they're the only places to get a meal other than in the dining room of the Odell Lake Lodge or at the Willamette Pass Ski Area.

4 The North Umpqua–Upper Rogue River Scenic Byway

Diamond Lake: 76 miles E of Roseburg, 80 miles NE of Medford

Ore. 138, which heads east out of Roseburg and leads to Diamond Lake and the north entrance to Crater Lake National Park, is one of the state's most scenic highways. Along much of its length, the highway follows the North Umpqua River, which is famed among fly anglers for its fighting steelhead and salmon. As far as I'm concerned, this deep aquamarine stream is the most beautiful river in Oregon and is well worth a visit even if you don't know a Worley Bugger from a muddler minnow (that's fly talk, for the uninitiated). Between Idleyld Park and Toketee Reservoir, you'll find numerous picnic areas, boat launches, swimming holes, and campgrounds.

As Ore. 138 approaches the crest of the Cascades, it skirts the shores of Diamond Lake, which is a major recreational destination (though it's certainly not as beautiful as nearby Crater Lake). Almost a mile in elevation, Diamond Lake is set at the foot of jagged Mount Thielsen, a spire-topped pinnacle known as the "lightning rod of the Cascades." The lake offers swimming, boating, fishing, camping, hiking, biking, and, in winter, snowmobiling and cross-country skiing. Just beyond Diamond Lake is the north entrance to Crater Lake National Park.

The 24-mile-long Ore. 230 connects the Diamond Lake area with the valley of the upper Rogue River at the community of Union Creek. Although this stretch of the Rogue is not as dramatic as the North Umpqua or the lower Rogue River, it has its charms, including a natural bridge, a narrow gorge, and some grand old trees.

ESSENTIALS

GETTING THERE   The North Umpqua River is paralleled by Ore. 138, which connects Roseburg, on I-5, with U.S. 97, which parallels the Cascades on the east side of the mountains. This highway leads to the north entrance of Crater Lake National Park.

VISITOR INFORMATION   For information on recreational activities in this area, contact the **North Umpqua Ranger District,** 18782 N. Umpqua Hwy., Glide, OR 97443 (✆ **541/496-3532**); or the **Diamond Lake Ranger District,** 2020 Toketee Ranger Station Rd., Idleyld Park, OR 97447 (✆ **541/498-2531**). Also check the websites of the **Rogue River-Siskiyou National Forest** (www.fs.fed.us/r6/rogue-siskiyou) and the **Umpqua National Forest** (www.fs.fed.us/r6/umpqua).

WHAT TO SEE & DO: FLY-FISHING, RAFTING & A WATERFALL

Oregon abounds in waterfalls and white-water rivers, but in the town of Glide, 12 miles east of Roseburg, you'll find the only place in the state where rivers collide. At the interesting **Colliding Rivers Viewpoint,** the North Umpqua River, rushing in from the north, slams into the white water of the Little River, which flows from the south, and the two rivers create a churning stew. However, this phenomenon is really only impressive during times of winter rains or during spring snowmelt season.

The most celebrated portion of the North Umpqua is the 31-mile stretch from Deadline Falls, in Swiftwater Park, to Soda Springs Dam. This stretch of river is open to fly-fishing only. Between June and October, you can often see salmon and steelhead leaping up Deadline Falls, which has a designated salmon-viewing area down a short trail on the south bank of the river. For fly-fishing needs and advice, stop in at the **Blue Heron Fly Shop,** 109 Hargis Lane, Idleyld Park (✆ **541/496-0448**), which is just off Ore. 138, or **Steamboat Inn,** 42705 North Umpqua Hwy. (© **541/498-2230;** www.thesteamboatinn.com), in Steamboat. If you want to hire a guide to take you out fishing on the North Umpqua River, try **Jerry Q. Phelps** (© **541/672-8324;** www.jerryphelpsguideservice.com). Expect to pay around $350 per day.

If you'd rather just paddle the river in a kayak or raft, contact **North Umpqua Outfitters** (© **888/454-9696;** www.nuorafting.com), which charges $105 to $120 for its rafting trips.

At the turnoff for Toketee Reservoir, you'll find the trail head for the .5-mile hike to **Toketee Falls** ✮. This double cascade plummets 120 feet over a wall of columnar basalt and is one of the most picturesque waterfalls in the state. The viewing area is on a deck perched out on the edge of a cliff. Also in this same area, past the Toketee Lake Campground, you'll find **Umpqua Hot Springs,** which are down a short trail. These natural hot springs perch high above the North Umpqua River, on a hillside covered with mineral deposits. For longer hikes, consider the many segments of the 79-mile **North Umpqua Trail,** which parallels the river from just east of Glide all the way to the Pacific Crest Trail. The lower segments of this trail are also popular mountain-biking routes.

At **Diamond Lake,** just a few miles north of Crater Lake National Park, you'll find one of the most popular mountain recreation spots in the state. In summer, the popular and somewhat run-down **Diamond Lake Resort** (© **800/733-7593** or 541/793-3333; www.diamondlake.net) is the center of area activities. Here you can rent boats, swim at a small beach, and access the 10.5-mile paved hiking/biking trail that circles Diamond Lake.

Near the community of Union Creek, west of Crater Lake National Park on Ore. 62, are the Rogue River Gorge and a small natural bridge formed by a lava tube. The gorge, though only a few feet wide in places, is quite dramatic and has an easy trail running alongside.

In winter, Diamond Lake Resort serves as the region's main snowmobiling destination, but it's also a decent area for cross-country skiers, who will find rentals and groomed trails at Diamond Lake Resort. There are also many more miles of marked, but not groomed, cross-country ski trails in the area; the more interesting trails are found at the south end of the lake. Snowmobile rentals and tours are also available. You can also do some downhill skiing on untracked nearby slopes through Diamond Lake Resort's **Cat Ski Mt. Bailey** (www.catskimtbailey.com), which charges $250 for a day of skiing and also offers multiday packages. For more information on these activities, contact **Diamond Lake Resort** (© **800/733-7593** or 541/793-3333; www. diamondlake.net).

WHERE TO STAY & DINE

Prospect Historical Hotel ✮ *Finds*   This combination historic hotel and adjoining modern motel is in the tiny hamlet of Prospect, 30 miles from Crater Lake's Rim Village. The hotel, built in the 1880s, is a big white building with a wraparound porch, and although the small rooms are rather spartan, their country styling lends them a bit of charm. If you stay in one of these rooms, you'll get air-conditioning and a full breakfast. The motel rooms are much larger and have TVs, telephones, and coffeemakers; some also have kitchenettes. The elegant dining room, which is open May through October, serves good food.

391 Mill Creek Dr. (P.O. Box 50), Prospect, OR 97536. © **800/944-6490** or 541/560-3664. Fax 541/560-3825. www. prospecthotel.com. 24 units. May–Sept $70–$100 double, $150 suite; Oct–Apr $55–$85 double, $130 suite. DC, DISC,

MC, V. Pets accepted. **Amenities:** Restaurant (American). *In hotel room:* A/C. *In motel room:* A/C, TV, fridge, microwave, coffeemaker.

Steamboat Inn 🏕 Located roughly midway between Roseburg and Crater Lake, this inn on the banks of the North Umpqua River is by far the finest lodging on the river. Although the lodge appeals primarily to anglers, the beautiful gardens, luxurious guest rooms, and gourmet meals also attract a fair number of people looking for a quiet getaway in the forest and a base for hiking and biking. If you aren't springing for one of the suites, which have their own soaking tubs overlooking the river, your best bets will be the streamside rooms, misleadingly referred to as cabins. These have gas fireplaces and open onto a long deck that overlooks the river. The hideaway cottages are more spacious but don't have river views and are half a mile from the lodge (and the cozy dining room). Dinners ($50) are multicourse affairs and are open to the public by reservation. There's a fly-fishing shop on the premises. Some units here have telephones and some have air-conditioning.

42705 N. Umpqua Hwy., Steamboat, OR 97447-9703. 🕾 800/840-8825 or 541/498-2230. Fax 541/498-2411. www. thesteamboatinn.com. 20 units (including 5 cottages and 5 houses). $165 cabin; $200–$235 cottages and houses; $280 suites. Children under 4 stay free in parent's room. MC, V. Closed Jan–Feb. Pets accepted. **Amenities:** Restaurant (Northwest); bike rentals; massage (seasonal); babysitting. *In room:* Coffeemaker, hair dryer, iron.

CAMPGROUNDS

Along the North Umpqua River, between Idleyld Park and Diamond Lake, you'll find the Bureau of Land Management's **Susan Creek Campground,** the most upscale public campground along the North Umpqua. (It even has hot showers.) The large **Horseshoe Bend Campground,** near Steamboat, is popular with rafters and kayakers on weekends and has well-separated campsites, big views of surrounding cliffs, and access to the North Umpqua Trail. **Toketee Lake Campground,** at Toketee Reservoir, is situated back from the lake, but there are a few sites on the river.

Diamond Lake has three U.S. Forest Service campgrounds—Diamond Lake, Broken Arrow, and Thielsen View—with a total of more than 450 campsites. Here you'll also find the **Diamond Lake RV Park,** 3500 Diamond Lake Loop (🕾 541/793-3318; www.diamondlakervpark.com).

Southwest of the Crater Lake National Park, on Ore. 62, you'll find **Farewell Bend Campground,** which is set amid big trees on the Rogue River. The next campgrounds are **Union Creek** and **Natural Bridge,** both of which are also along the Rogue River near the town of Prospect. North of Ore. 62, on Ore. 230, you'll find the **Hamaker Campground,** on a pretty bend in the Rogue River with big trees and meadows across the river.

5 Crater Lake National Park ✦✦✦

71 miles NE of Medford, 83 miles E of Roseburg, 60 miles N of Klamath Falls

Nothing in the forests of the southern Oregon Cascades prepares you for Crater Lake. There are no preliminaries, no teasing glimpses through the trees. You drive through a rather unremarkable mountain forest, wondering why this place was ever made into a national park, and then, with little warning, you arrive at the edge of a cliff and gaze down 1,000 feet to a circular bowl of water a mesmerizing shade of sapphire blue. The view takes your breath away (or is it the elevation?), and you quickly understand why this lake became a national park way back in 1902.

At 1,932 feet deep, Crater Lake is the deepest lake in the United States (and the seventh deepest in the world). The crater (or, more accurately, the caldera) that holds the serene lake was born in an explosive volcanic eruption 7,700 years ago. When the volcano, now known as Mount Mazama, erupted, its summit (thought to have been around 12,000 ft. high) collapsed, leaving a crater 4,000 feet deep. Thousands of years of rain and melting snow turned the empty heart of this volcano into today's cold, clear lake, which today is surrounded by crater walls that in places are nearly 2,000 feet tall. The cone of Wizard Island rises at one end of the lake. This island is the tip of a new volcanic peak that has been building slowly since Mount Mazama's last eruption.

ESSENTIALS

GETTING THERE   If you're coming from the south on I-5, take exit 62 in Medford and follow Ore. 62 for 75 miles. If you're coming from the north, take exit 124 in Roseburg and follow Ore. 138. From Klamath Falls, take U.S. 97 north to Ore. 62. In winter, only the south entrance is open. Due to deep snowpack, the north entrance usually doesn't open until sometime in late July.

VISITOR INFORMATION   For more information, contact **Crater Lake National Park,** P.O. Box 7, Crater Lake, OR 97604 (✆ **541/594-3000;** www.nps.gov/crla).

ADMISSION   Park admission is $10 per vehicle.

SEEING THE HIGHLIGHTS

After your first breathtaking view of the lake, you may want to stop by one of the park's two visitor centers. The **Steel Information Center** is between the south park entrance and the Rim Village, which is where you'll find the smaller and less thorough **Rim Village Visitor Center.** Although the park is open year-round, in winter, when deep snows blanket the region, only the road to Rim Village is kept clear. During the summer (roughly beginning in late June), the **Rim Drive** 🎯🎯 provides many viewing points along its 39-mile length.

Narrated boat trips 🎯🎯 around the lake are the park's most popular activity. These tours last 2 hours and begin at Cleetwood Cove, at the bottom of a very steep 1-mile trail that descends 700 feet from the rim to the lakeshore. Before deciding to take a boat tour, be sure you're in good enough physical condition to make the steep climb back up to the rim. Bring warm clothes because it can be quite a bit cooler on the lake than it is on the rim. A naturalist on each boat provides a narrative on the ecology and history of the lake, and all tours include a stop on Wizard Island. Tours are offered from early July to mid-September and cost $26 to $31 for adults and $15 to $18 for children ages 2 to 11.

Of the many miles of **hiking trails** within the park, the mile-long Cleetwood Trail is the only trail that leads down to the lakeshore, and it's a steep and tiring hike back up from the lake. The trail to the top of Mount Scott, although it's a rigorous 2.5 miles, is the park's most rewarding hike. Shorter trails with good views include the 0.8-mile trail to the top of the Watchman, which overlooks Wizard Island, and the 1.7-mile trail up Garfield Peak. The short Castle Crest Wildflower Trail is best hiked in late July or early August. Backpackers can hike the length of the park on the Pacific Crest Trail (PCT) or head out on a few other trails that lead into more remote, though less scenic, corners of the park.

Other summertime park activities include children's programs, campfire ranger talks, history lectures, and guided walks. To find out about these, check in *Reflections,* a free park newspaper given to all visitors when they enter the park.

In winter, **cross-country skiing** is popular on the park's snow-covered Rim Drive and in the backcountry. At Rim Village, you'll find several miles of well-marked ski trails, affording some of the best views in the state, weather permitting. Skiers in good condition can usually make the entire circuit of the lake in 2 days but must be prepared to camp in the snow. Spring, when the weather is warmer and there are fewer severe storms, is actually the best time to ski around the lake.

WHERE TO STAY & DINE

The Cabins at Mazama Village 𝄐   Though the Mazama Village Motor Inn isn't on the rim of the crater, it's just a short drive away and should be your second choice of lodgings on a Crater Lake vacation. The modern motel-style guest rooms are housed in 10 steep-roofed buildings that look much like traditional mountain cabins. A laundry, gas station, and general store make Mazama Village a busy spot in the summer.

Mailing address: 1211 Ave. C, White City, OR 97503. 𝄐 **888/774-2728.** Fax 303/297-3175. www.craterlakelodges. com. 40 units. $118 double. Children under 12 stay free in parent's room. AE, DC, DISC, MC, V. Closed mid-Oct to late May. *In room:* Coffeemaker, no phone.

Crater Lake Lodge 𝄐𝄐   Perched on the edge of the rim overlooking Crater Lake, this lodge is the finest national-park lodge in the Northwest. The views are breathtaking, and the amenities are modern without sacrificing the rustic atmosphere (a stone fireplace and ponderosa-pine-bark walls in the lobby). Slightly more than half of the guest rooms overlook the lake, and although most rooms have modern bathrooms, eight have claw-foot bathtubs. The very best accommodations are the corner rooms on the lake side of the lodge. The lodge's dining room provides a view of both Crater Lake and the Klamath River basin. Reservations are hard to come by, so plan as far in advance as possible.

Mailing address: 1211 Ave. C, White City, OR 97503. 𝄐 **888/774-2728.** Fax 303/297-3175. www.craterlakelodges. com. 71 units. $138–$191 double; $260 suite. Children under 12 stay free in parent's room. AE, DC, DISC, MC, V. Closed mid-Oct to late May. **Amenities:** Restaurant (Northwest); lounge. *In room:* No phone.

CAMPGROUNDS

Tent camping and RV spaces are available on the south side of the park at the **Mazama Campground,** where there are more than 200 sites ($18–$23 per night). This campground is open mid-June through early October. There are also 16 tent sites available at **Lost Creek Campground** ($10 per night) on the park's east side. This campground is open early July through early October. For reservations at Mazama Campground, contact **Crater Lake National Park Lodges** (𝄐 **888/774-2728;** www.craterlake lodges.com). For information on campgrounds outside the park, see "Campgrounds" in "The North Umpqua–Upper Rogue River Scenic Byway" section above.

---

6 The Klamath Falls Area: Bird-Watching & Native American Artifacts

65 miles E of Ashland, 60 miles S of Crater Lake

Unless you are an avid bird-watcher or are looking for a cheap place to stay close to Crater Lake National Park, you won't find too much to attract you to the Klamath Falls area. However, this region, a wide, windswept expanse of lakes, high desert, and mountain forests just north of the California line, has a history of human presence that stretches back more than 14,000 years. The large lakes in this dry region have long attracted a wide variety of wildlife (especially waterfowl), which once provided a food source for the area's Native American population. The prehistoric residents of the region lived on the shores of the Klamath Basin's lakes and harvested fish, birds, and various marsh plants. Today, two local museums exhibit extensive collections of Native American artifacts that have been found in this area.

Upper Klamath Lake and adjacent Agency Lake have shrunk considerably over the years as shallow, marshy areas have been drained to create pastures and farmland. Today, however, as the lake's native fish populations have become threatened and migratory bird populations in the region have plummeted, there is a growing movement to restore some of the region's drained marshes to more natural conditions. Although large portions of the area are now designated as national wildlife areas that offer some of the best bird-watching in the Northwest, farming and ranching are still considered the primary use of these wildlife lands. Conflicts between local farmers and environmentalists over how best to manage this region's limited water supply often occur during the summer dry season.

The region's shallow lakes warm quickly in the hot summers here, and, partly because of the excess nutrients in the waters from agricultural runoff, they support large blooms of blue-green algae. Although the algae blooms deprive the lake's fish of oxygen, they provide the area with its most unusual agricultural activity. The harvesting and marketing of Upper Klamath Lake's blue-green algae as a dietary supplement has become big business throughout the country as people have claimed all manner of health benefits from this chlorophyll-rich dried algae.

ESSENTIALS

GETTING THERE   Klamath Falls is on U.S. 97, which leads north to Bend and south to I-5 near Mount Shasta in California. The city is also connected to Ashland by the winding Ore. 66 and to Medford by Ore. 140, which continues east to Lakeview in eastern Oregon. The **Klamath Falls Airport,** 6775 Arnold Ave. (© **541/883-5372;** www.klamathfallsairport.com), is served by Horizon Air from Portland. Amtrak's *Coast Starlight* trains stop here en route between San Francisco and Portland.

VISITOR INFORMATION   For more information on the region, contact the **Great Basin Visitor Association,** 205 Riverside Dr., Klamath Falls, OR 97601 (© **800/445-6728** or 541/882-1501; www.travelklamath.com).

GETTING AROUND   Rental cars are available at Klamath Falls Airport from Budget, Enterprise, and Hertz.

DELVING INTO LOCAL HISTORY

In addition to the two museums listed here, you might want to drive by the historic **Ross Ragland Theater & Cultural Center,** 218 N. Seventh St. (© **541/884-0651;** www.rrtheater.org), an impressive Art Deco theater in downtown Klamath Falls. The theater stages a wide variety of performances throughout the year. If you'd like to learn more about the area's logging history, drive 30 miles north of Klamath Falls to **Collier Memorial State Park** 46000 U.S. 97 N., Chiloquin (© **541/783-2471;** www. oregonstateparks.org), where you'll find an outdoor logging museum filled with antique logging equipment. Behind this museum, there's a pretty picnic area on the banks of Spring Creek, one of the clearest and most beautiful little streams in the state.

Favell Museum of Western Art and Indian Artifacts ★★ *Finds*   Anyone with an interest in Native American artifacts or Western art will be fascinated by a visit to this unusual museum, considered one of the best Western museums in the country.

On display are thousands of arrowheads (including one made from fire opal), obsidian knives, spear points, stone tools of every description, baskets, pottery, and even ancient shoes and pieces of matting and fabric. Though the main focus is on the Native Americans of the Klamath Basin and Columbia River, there are artifacts from Alaska, Canada, other regions of the US, and Mexico. Few museums anywhere in the country have such an extensive collection on display, and the cases of artifacts can be overwhelming, so take your time. There's also a collection of Western art by more than 300 artists, including members of the famous Cowboy Artists of America Association. You'll also find the world's largest publicly displayed collection of miniature guns.

125 W. Main St. © 541/882-9996. www.favellmuseum.org. Admission $7 adults, $6 seniors, $4 children 6–16. Mon–Sat 9:30am–5:30pm.

Klamath County Museum ⟨ʀ̂⟩   More Native American artifacts, this time exclusively from the Klamath Lakes area, are on display in this museum, while a history of the Modoc Indian Wars chronicles the most expensive campaign of the American West. Also of particular interest are the early-20th-century photos by local photographer Maud Baldwin. In addition, there's a large collection of stuffed birds.

1451 Main St. © 541/883-4208. www.co.klamath.or.us/museum/index.htm. Admission $3 adults, $2 seniors and students, $1 children 5–12. Mon–Sat 9am–5pm.

BIRD-WATCHING & OTHER OUTDOOR ACTIVITIES
In this dry region between the Cascades and the Rocky Mountains, there are few large bodies of water, so the lakes and marshes of the Klamath Basin are a magnet for birds. White pelicans, great blue herons, sandhill cranes, egrets, grebes, bitterns, and osprey can all be seen here. However, the main attraction for many human visitors is the annual winter gathering of bald eagles. In the winter the region is home to as many as 500 bald eagles, making this the largest concentration of bald eagles in the Lower 48. Each winter morning, starting about 30 minutes before sunrise, as many as 100 eagles can be seen heading out from their roosting areas in the **Bear Valley National Wildlife Refuge** near the town of Worden, 11 miles south of Klamath Falls. To find the eagle-viewing area, drive south out of Klamath Falls on U.S. 97 through the community of Worden and almost to the California state line. Turn west onto the Keno-Worden Road, and, just after the railroad tracks, turn left onto a dirt road. Follow this road for a half-mile or so and pull off on the shoulder. Now start scanning the skies for eagles heading east to the marshlands. For more information on bird-watching in the area, contact the **Klamath Basin National Wildlife Refuges Complex,** 4009 Hill Rd., Tulelake, CA 96134 (© **530/667-2231;** www.fws.gov/klamathbasinrefuges).

The easiest way to get out on Klamath Lake is on an excursion aboard the *Klamath Belle* (© **541/883-4622;** www.klamathbelle.com), a replica paddle wheeler. There are sunset cruises ($11 adults, $5.50 children 4–12), family "Ice Cream Social" cruises ($13 adults, $4.50 children 4–10), and dinner and brunch cruises ($33–$44 adults, $29–$41 seniors, $15–$19 children 4–12). Cruises run early spring to late fall.

If, on the other hand, you want to paddle yourself around one of the local lakes, check out the **Upper Klamath Canoe Trail,** which begins near the junction of Ore. 140 and West Side Road northwest of Klamath Falls. The canoe trail wanders through marshlands on the edge of Upper Klamath Lake. For more information, contact the **Fremont-Winema National Forests,** Klamath Falls Ranger District, 2819 Dahlia St., Klamath Falls, OR 97601 (© **541/883-6714;** www.fs.fed.us/r6/frewin). Canoes and kayaks can be rented at the adjacent **Rocky Point Resort,** 28121 Rocky Point Rd. (② **541/356-2287**), for $30 for half a day or $40 for a full day.

Two area rivers, the Williamson and the Wood, are both well known for their trophy trout fishing. If you want to hire a fishing guide, contact **Roe Outfitters/FlyWay Shop,** 9349 U.S. 97, Klamath Falls (② **877/943-5700** or 541/884-3825; www.roe outfitters.com). Expect to pay $295 to $375 for two people for a half-day and $395 to $495 for a full day.

About 35 miles northwest of Klamath Falls on Ore. 140, you'll find the region's main mountain recreation area. Here, in the vicinity of **Lake of the Woods** and **Fish Lake,** you'll find the fun High Lakes mountain-bike trail, which leads through a rugged lava field. Also in the area is the hiking trail to the summit of Mount McLoughlin. In winter, this same area has cross-country ski trails. There are rustic cabin resorts and campgrounds on both Lake of the Woods and Fish Lake.

WHERE TO STAY

Lake of the Woods 🌟 *Kids*   Lake of the Woods is one of the prettiest lakes in southern Oregon, and is a great spot for families. The log cabins, with their red doors and green trim, look as though they belong in a national park, and the Saturday night barbecues, outdoor movie nights, and wildlife shows give this place the feel of an old-fashioned summer camp for the whole family. Most cabins, although rustic, have full kitchens or kitchenettes, as well as an old-time mountain-cabin decor. You can rent motorboats and canoes for exploring the lake and mountain bikes for area trails (one of which leads through an ancient lava flow). Or you can just swim in the lake.

950 Harriman Rte., Klamath Falls, OR 97601-8518. ② 866/201-4194 or 541/949-8300. www.lakeofthewoods resort.com. 26 units. Memorial Day weekend to Sept $115–$269 cabin. 2-night minimum. AE, DISC, MC, V. Closed Oct to Memorial Day weekend. Pets accepted. **Amenities:** Restaurant (American); lounge; watersports rentals. *In room:* No phone.

Rocky Point Resort 🌟 *Finds*   This rustic fishing resort on the west shore of Upper Klamath Lake may conjure up childhood memories of summer vacations by the lake. Neither the rooms nor the cabins are anything special, but the setting is bewitching. Shaded by huge old ponderosa pine trees and partly built atop the rocks for which this point is named, the resort has a great view across the waters and marshes of the Upper Klamath National Wildlife Refuge. Green lawns set with Adirondack chairs go right down to the water, where there is a small boat-rental dock. The rustic restaurant and lounge have the best views on the property. The Upper Klamath Lake canoe trails originate here, and the bird-watching is excellent, but fishing is still the most popular pastime. The resort also has tent and RV sites.

28121 Rocky Point Rd., Klamath Falls, OR 97601. ② 541/356-2287. Fax 541/356-2222. www.rockypointoregon. com. 9 units. $75 double; $120–$160 cabin. Children under 6 stay free in parent's room. MC, V. Closed Nov–Mar. Pets accepted in cabins ($5 per night). 2-night minimum in cabins weekends and holidays. **Amenities:** Restaurant (American); lounge; boat rentals; coin-op laundry. *In room:* Coffeemaker, no phone.

Running Y Ranch Resort 🌟🌟 *Kids*   With an Arnold Palmer–designed golf course and lots of houses for sale, this remote resort is clearly geared toward golfers buying second homes. Yet with horseback riding, canoe rentals, bike trails, a game room, a winter ice-skating rink, and other kid-oriented activities, golfers should definitely bring the family along as well. The Running Y is located northwest of Klamath Falls off Ore. 140 close to the shore of Upper Klamath Lake and set amid ponderosa pines.

The hotel has a mountain-lodge feel, but rooms feel a bit like a chain motel, though some have balconies. Dining options are limited and not too reliable.

5500 Running Y Rd., Klamath Falls, OR 97601. © **888/850-0275** or 541/850-5500. www.runningy.com. 83 units. May–Sept $169–$209 double, $239 suite, $235–$525 town house or house; Oct–Apr $129–$169 double, $219 suite, $150–$390 town house or house. AE, DC, DISC, MC, V. Pets accepted ($25 fee). **Amenities:** 2 restaurants (Northwest, American); lounge; indoor pool; 18-hole golf course; 2 tennis courts; health club; full-service spa; Jacuzzi; sauna; boat rentals; bike rentals; horseback riding; children's programs; concierge; massage. *In room:* A/C, TV, dataport, coffeemaker, hair dryer, iron.

CAMPGROUNDS

Along Ore. 140 between Klamath Falls and Medford are several national forest campgrounds. On Fish Lake, **Fish Lake Campground** and **Doe Point Campground** have nice locations, but they both get a lot of traffic noise. Just west of Fish Lake on Forest Service Road 37, the **North Fork Campground** provides a quieter setting on a trout stream and a scenic mountain-bike trail. **Sunset Campground** and **Aspen Point Campground** on Lake of the Woods are popular in summer with the boating, fishing, and water-skiing crowd. The latter campground is near Great Meadow Recreation Area, has a swimming beach, and is right on the High Lakes mountain-bike trail.

WHERE TO DINE

For dinner with the best view in the area, head to **Rocky Point Resort** (see above), 30 minutes outside Klamath Falls and open Tuesday to Sunday in summer and on weekends in spring and fall.

Southern Oregon

Roughly defined as the area from the California state line in the south to a little way north of Roseburg, southern Oregon is a mountainous region that has far more in common with Northern California than it has with the rest of Oregon. The landscape is much drier than in northwestern Oregon, and dominating the region are the Siskiyou Mountains, a jumble of rugged peaks and rare plants that link the Cascades and the Coast Range.

It was gold that first brought European settlers to this area, and it was timber that kept them here. The gold is all played out now, but the legacy of the gold-rush days, when stagecoaches traveled the rough road between Sacramento and Portland, can be seen in picturesque towns such as Jacksonville and Oakland.

Although southern Oregon is a long drive from the nearest metropolitan areas, it is relatively easy to plan a multiday trip from San Francisco or Portland. From Ashland, the southernmost city in the region, it's roughly a 6-hour drive to either Portland or San Francisco.

Ashland is the region's most popular destination and is renowned for its **Oregon Shakespeare Festival,** which attracts tens of thousands of theatergoers annually. The festival, which now stretches through most of the year, has turned what was once a sleepy mill town into a facsimile of Tudor England. Not to be outdone, the **Britt Festivals** in the nearby historic town of **Jacksonville** offer summer performances by internationally recognized musicians and dance companies.

However, it isn't just the Bard that attracts visitors to this region. The rugged beauty of the Siskiyous and the wild waters of the Rogue and Umpqua rivers are big draws as well, with rafting and jet boat tours providing options for getting out on the water. In recent years, this region has also seen a proliferation of wineries in both the Umpqua Valley west of Roseburg and the Applegate Valley west of Jacksonville. Because this region is so much warmer than the Willamette Valley wine country, it grows a wide variety of Bordeaux, Rhone, Italian, and Spanish varieties of grapes. So, even if you've got a trunk full of pinot noir, you might want to do a little more wine touring in this region so you can pick up some cabernet sauvignon or tempranillo.

1 Ashland & the Oregon Shakespeare Festival

285 miles S of Portland, 50 miles W of Klamath Falls, 350 miles N of San Francisco

With classy cocktail bars and upscale restaurants, live jazz in the clubs and cafes, lots of art galleries, and day spas that take advantage of Ashland's famed Lithia Springs mineral waters, Ashland has become the most cosmopolitan community in southern Oregon. Sure, this is still a small town 5 to 6 hours by car from San Francisco or Portland, but more than half a century of staging Shakespeare plays has turned Ashland into Oregon's preeminent arts community, which in turn has attracted the city's

Ashland

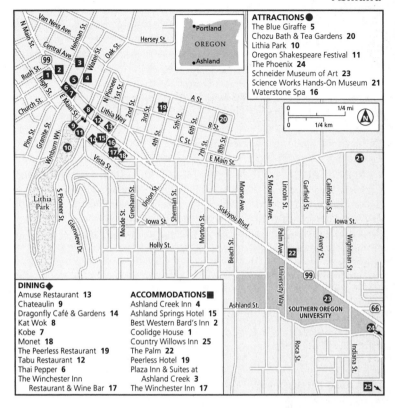

diverse population. Because this is one of the best little arts towns in America, come prepared to fall in love.

Ashland's rise to stardom began on a midsummer's night back in 1935. In a small Ashland theater built as part of the Chautauqua movement, Angus Bowmer, an English professor at Southern Oregon University, staged a performance of Shakespeare's *As You Like It.* Despite the hard times that the Great Depression had brought to this quiet mill town in the rugged Siskiyou Mountains, the show was a success. Although the Depression had dashed any hopes local businessman Jesse Winburne had of turning Ashland into a mineral-springs resort, the hard times did not hit until after he had built beautiful **Lithia Park.** Luckily, each man's love's labor was not lost, and today their legacies have turned the town into one of Oregon's most popular destinations.

The **Oregon Shakespeare Festival,** born of Bowmer's admiration for the Bard, has become a world-class repertory festival that stretches across 9 months, and although Ashland never became a mineral-springs resort, Lithia Park, through which still flow the clear waters of Winburne's dreams, has become the town's centerpiece. When not wandering the park's pathways, you can go wine tasting or check out one of the state's best shopping districts. Head farther afield, and you can hike and bike in the mountains and forests that surround Ashland. In other words, there's plenty to do when the curtains go down and the stages are dark.

ESSENTIALS

GETTING THERE Ashland is located on I-5. From the east, Ore. 66 connects Ashland with Klamath Falls.

The nearest airport is Medford's **Rogue Valley International–Medford Airport,** 3650 Biddle Rd. (© **541/776-7222**), which is served by America West Airlines, Horizon Air, and Skywest Airlines (United Express). A taxi from the airport to Ashland will cost around $30 to $35. Call **Yellow Cab** (© **541/482-3065**).

VISITOR INFORMATION Contact the **Ashland Chamber of Commerce,** 110 E. Main St. (P.O. Box 1360), Ashland, OR 97520 (© **541/482-3486;** www.ashland chamber.com). You can also check the website of the **Southern Oregon Visitors Association** (www.sova.org).

GETTING AROUND If you need a taxi, call **Yellow Cab** (© **541/482-3065**). Car-rental companies with offices at the Rogue Valley International Airport are Avis, Budget, Hertz, and National. **Rogue Valley Transportation District** (© **541/608-2400;** www.rvtd.org) provides public bus service in the Ashland area.

FESTIVALS The month-long Yuletide **Holiday Festival of Light** held each year in December is Ashland's other big annual festival.

THE OREGON SHAKESPEARE FESTIVAL

The raison d'être of Ashland, the Oregon Shakespeare Festival is an internationally acclaimed theater festival with a season that runs from February to October. The season typically includes three or four works by Shakespeare plus eight other classic or contemporary plays. These plays are performed in repertory, with as many as four staged on any given day.

The festival complex, often referred to as "the bricks" because of its brick courtyard, is in the center of town and contains three theaters. The visually impressive outdoor **Elizabethan Theatre,** modeled after England's 17th-century Fortune Theatre, is used only in the summer and early fall. The **Angus Bowmer Theatre** is the festival's largest indoor theater. The **New Theatre** is a small state-of-the-art venue used primarily for contemporary and experimental plays.

In addition to the plays, there are **backstage tours** (tickets are $11 for adults and $8.25 for children). Throughout the festival season there are also talks and special performances. The opening of the Elizabethan Theatre is celebrated each June in Lithia Park with the elaborate Feast of Will. Between June and early October, the Green Show provides 35 minutes of free pre-performance entertainment outside the doors of the Elizabethan Theatre.

For more information and upcoming schedules, contact the **Oregon Shakespeare Festival,** 15 S. Pioneer St., Ashland, OR 97520 (© **541/482-4331;** www.osfashland. org). Ticket prices range from $30 to $75; children's and preview tickets are less expensive. In spring and fall, tickets are discounted 25%.

EXPLORING ASHLAND & ITS SURROUNDINGS

The **Schneider Museum of Art,** 1250 Siskiyou Blvd. (© **541/552-6245;** www.sou. edu/sma), on the campus of Southern Oregon University, mounts art exhibits of a quality you'd expect in a museum in a major city. The museum is open Tuesday through Saturday from 10am to 4pm (until 7pm on first Fri of each month). Admission is by $3 suggested donation.

Ashland's first claim to fame was its healing mineral waters, and today you can still relax and be pampered at one of the city's day spas. **The Phoenix,** 2425 Siskiyou Blvd. (© **541/488-1281;** www.thephoenixspa.com); **The Blue Giraffe,** 51 Water St. (© **541/488-3335;** www.bluegiraffespa.com); and **Waterstone Spa,** 236 E. Main St. (© **541/488-0325;** www.waterstonespa.com), all offer various body treatments, skin care, and massages. However, for the most unusual spa experience in town, plan a visit to the **Chozu Bath and Tea Gardens,** 832 A St. (© **541/552-0202;** www. chozugardens.com), where you can experience the Japanese tea ceremony, soak in a hot salt-water pool in the bath gardens, or get a massage.

If you happen to have the kids along, you may want to schedule time for a visit to the **Science Works Hands-On Museum,** 1500 E. Main St. (© **541/482-6767;** www. scienceworksmuseum.org), which is filled with fun interactive science exhibits. The museum is open Wednesday through Saturday from 10am to 5pm and Sunday from noon to 5pm. Admission is $7.50 for adults and $5 for seniors and children ages 2 to 12.

WINE TOURING

EdenVale Wines ⚶ This winery tasting room, beside a historic mansion on the outskirts of Medford, sells not only wines under its own EdenVale Winery label but also wines from other small wineries in southern Oregon. Between mid-June and mid-September, there's live jazz in the gardens here on Thursday evenings.

2310 Voorhies Rd., Medford. © 541/512-2955. www.edenvalleyorchards.com. Summer Mon–Sat 10am–6pm, Sun noon–4pm; other months Tues–Sat 10am–5pm, Sun noon–4pm. From Ore. 99 north of Phoenix, turn west on S. Stage Rd. and left again on Voorhies Rd.

Paschal ⚶ This winery produces a wide variety of wines that are made by Joe Dobbes, one of the state's best winemakers. The wines here tend to be some of the most reliable in the area, with big reds being a specialty. If you're lucky, they'll be pouring their Italian-style blend of tempranillo, sangiovese, Dolcetto, and Syrah.

1122 Suncrest Rd., Talent. © 541/535-7957. www.paschalwinery.com. Summer daily 11am–6pm; other months Tues–Sun 11am–5pm. From Ore. 99 north of Ashland, take W. Valley View Rd. and turn left onto Suncrest Rd.

Rising Sun Farms Although this little tasting room is first and foremost the retail outlet for a local company that produces a wide variety of gourmet foods, the owners also produce some good wines. Stop in to try pinot noir and take home some fruit-flavored balsamic sauce, a marionberry cheese torta, or some caramelized onion cheese dip. The shop also sells a number of other regional wines.

5126 S. Pacific Hwy., Phoenix. © 800/888-0795 or 541/535-8331, ext. 201. www.risingsunfarms.com. Daily 10am–5pm.

RoxyAnn Winery ⚶⚶ RoxyAnn started out as the Hillcrest Orchard, which has been producing fruit for 100 years. Today, this winery is producing some of the best (and definitely my favorite) southern Oregon wines. A wide variety of wines are produced here under several different labels. Although this winery is actually on the east side of Medford, it is close enough to Ashland to make it an appropriate stop on an afternoon's wine tasting in the area.

3285 Hillcrest Rd., Medford. © 541/776-2315. www.roxyann.com. Daily 11am–6pm. From exit 27 off I-5, drive east on Barnett Rd., turn left on Phoenix Rd., and right on Hillcrest Rd.

Weisinger's ⚶ Just south of town, this family-owned winery has a great view over the hills and valleys. Dry whites are a strong point, though if you're looking for age-worthy wines with a lot of tannin, you may like Weisinger's merlot and Petite Pompadour, a Bordeaux-style blend of cabernet Franc, merlot, Malbec, and cabernet sauvignon.

3150 Siskiyou Blvd. (©) **800/551-9463** or 541/488-5989. www.weisingers.com. May–Sept daily 11am–5pm; Oct–Apr Wed–Sun 11am–5pm. Take Ore. 99 (Siskiyou Blvd.) south from downtown Ashland.

ENJOYING THE GREAT OUTDOORS

No visit to Ashland is complete without taking a long, leisurely stroll through beautiful **Lithia Park.** This 100-acre park follows the banks of Ashland Creek starting at the plaza. Shade trees, lawns, flowers, ponds, fountains, and, of course, the babbling brook are reminiscent of an English garden.

Summertime thrill seekers shouldn't pass up the chance to do some **white-water rafting** on the Rogue or Klamath River while in southern Oregon. Several companies offer trips between April and October. Try **Noah's River Adventures,** 53 N. Main St. ((©) **800/858-2811** or 541/488-2811; www.noahsrafting.com), or **The Adventure Center,** 40 N. Main St. ((©) **800/444-2819** or 541/488-2819; www.raftingtours. com), both of which have trips lasting from half a day to 5 days. Prices range from $69 to $89 for a half-day trip to between $119 and $139 for a full day, depending on the length and type of the trip. The former company also offers salmon- and steelhead-fishing trips, and the latter offers fishing trips as well as downhill bike rides ($69) from the top of Mount Ashland.

Bikes ($10 per hr. or $35 per day) can be rented at **Bear Creek Bicycles,** 1988 Ore. 99N ((©) **541/488-4270;** www.bearcreekbicycle.com), which is just around the corner from the Bear Creek path. This paved path is a great, easy route to ride.

If you'd rather go horseback riding before the play, get in touch with **City Slickers Trail Rides** ((©) **541/951-4611;** www.oregontrailrides.com), which charges $40 for a 1-hour ride and $70 for a 2-hour ride.

Miles of **hiking trails,** including the Pacific Crest Trail, can be found up on Mount Ashland in the Rogue River-Siskiyou National Forest. Another stretch of the Pacific Crest Trail lies within the **Cascade-Siskiyou National Monument,** which is located south and east of Ashland. This monument was created to preserve an area of outstanding botanical diversity, but is limited in its recreational opportunities. For more information, contact the Medford office of the **Bureau of Land Management,** 3040 Biddle Rd., Medford ((©) **541/618-2200**).

In the winter, there's good downhill and cross-country **skiing** at **Mt. Ashland** ((©) **541/482-2897** for information or **541/482-2754** for snow report; www.mt ashland.com), a small downhill ski area 15 miles south of Ashland. All-day lift tickets for adults are $39. You can rent cross-country skis and pick up ski-trail maps at **Ashland Outdoor Store,** 37 Third St. ((©) **541/488-1202;** www.outdoorstore.com).

SHOPPING

Ashland has the best shopping in southern Oregon. Interesting and unusual shops line East Main Street, so when the curtains are down on the stages, check the windows of downtown.

Art galleries abound in Ashland, and on the first Friday of the month, many are open late. My all-around favorite place to check out works by local artists is at **Ashland Art Works,** 291 Oak St. ((©) **541/488-4735;** www.ashlandartworks.com), an artists' cooperative of four separate galleries all housed in a collection of cottages on the banks of Ashland Creek. For contemporary art, check out the **Hanson Howard Gallery,** 82 N. Main St. ((©) **541/488-2562;** www.hhgallery.com). Right on the plaza, be sure to check out the **Ashland Hardwood Gallery,** 17 N. Main St. ((©) **541/488-6200;** www.hardwoodgallery.com), which is filled with fascinating works of art in wood. **Davis & Cline,** 525 A St., Ste. 1 (✆ **541/482-2069;** www.davisandcline.com), which is located in the historic Railroad District about 8 blocks from the plaza, is another of my favorite contemporary art galleries here in town. This gallery even sells Dale Chihuly art glass. And for wearable art, stop by **The Web-sters,** 11 N. Main St. (✆ **541/482-9801;** www.yarnatwebsters.com), a knitting and weaving store carrying beautiful sweaters, woven jackets, and accessories. Between the first weekend in May and the last weekend in October, be sure to stop by the **Lithia Artisan's Market of Ashland** (✆ **888/303-2826;** www.lithiaartisansmarket.com) on Calle Guanajuato. The location is on the banks of Ashland Creek behind the stores on the north side of the plaza. Market hours are Saturday from 10am to 6pm and Sunday from 11am to 5pm. For a well-rounded selection of wines and other gourmet treats, you can't beat the **Chateaulin Wine Shoppe,** 52 E. Main St. (✆ **541/488-9463;** www.chateaulin. com), which is located next door to Chateaulin restaurant.

WHERE TO STAY

It seems Shakespeare and B&Bs go hand in hand. At last count, there were more than 25 bed-and-breakfasts in town. If your reason for coming to Ashland is to attend the Shakespeare Festival and you plan to stay at a B&B, you'll find it most convenient to choose an inn within walking distance of the theaters. By doing so, you'll also be within walking distance of the town's best restaurants and shopping and won't have to deal with finding a parking space before the show. For a comprehensive list of Ashland inns, contact **Ashland's Bed & Breakfast Network** (✆ **800/944-0329;** www. abbnet.com).

EXPENSIVE

Ashland Creek Inn ✹✹　As the name implies, this luxurious B&B is located on the shady banks of Ashland Creek, and the decks here are wonderful places to spend a hot summer afternoon or for a glass of wine before heading off to the theater. The rooms, mostly large suites, have fun themes, including the Caribbean, Morocco, Denmark, and Taos. All are very tastefully decorated with antiques and art, and all but one have a kitchen or kitchenette. Although this inn is only two blocks from the heart of downtown, it feels like a remote forest retreat. Breakfasts are multi-course affairs that you can enjoy on a deck or in the garden when the weather is good.

70 Water St., Ashland, OR 97520. ✆ 541/482-3315. www.ashlandcreekinn.com. 10 units. May–Oct $210–$325 suite; Nov to mid-Feb $110–$200 suite; $120–$250 suite. Rates include full breakfast. MC, V. 3-night minimum May–Oct. Children over 12 are welcome. **Amenities:** Concierge. *In room:* A/C, TV, fridge, coffeemaker, Wi-Fi.

Ashland Mountain House ✹✹　This is, quite simply, Oregon's most beautiful historic inn. The impeccable restoration job and attention to detail by owners Kathy and John Loram have turned what was little more than a run-down heap of a house into a gorgeous B&B. Built in 1852, the Ashland Mountain House served as a stagecoach stop for 25 years. Today, this old yellow farmhouse 5 miles from town is once again welcoming weary travelers with its gracious hospitality and beautiful setting on 6 acres overlooking hills and valleys. Inside the inn, you'll find a library with an antique Steinway piano and floor-to-ceiling shelves of books. Gorgeous wood floors and original woodwork give the interior a classic feel, while hand-silk-screened wallpapers do a great job of conjuring up this old house's early years. My favorite room here is the two-story Brick Building, a little cottage next door to the main house.

1148 Old Highway 99 South, Ashland, OR 97520. © **866/899-2744** or 541/482-2744. www.ashlandmountain house.com. 4 units. May–Oct $150–$180 double; Nov–Jan $115–$145 double; Feb–Apr $135–$165 double. MC, V. Rates include full breakfast. **Amenities:** Concierge. *In room:* A/C, TV, Wi-Fi.

Ashland Springs Hotel *(Finds)*

First opened in 1925, this nine-story historic hotel is one of the finest hotels between Portland and San Francisco. In the light-filled lobby there are cases full of Victorian-era natural-history displays, and, on the mezzanine overlooking the lobby, a continental breakfast is served each morning. Guest rooms are luxuriously appointed and beds sport crisp white linens, feather pillows, and down comforters. Although all the rooms have large windows, the corner rooms are worth requesting, as are rooms facing east over the city and the valley. Be sure to notice the fascinating collection of pressed plants that is on display behind the reception desk, in the elevator, and in guest rooms.

212 E. Main St., Ashland, OR 97520. © **888/795-4545** or 541/488-1700. Fax 541/488-1701. www.ashlandsprings hotel.com. 70 units. Mid-May to early Oct $139–$259 double; early Oct to mid-May $89–$199 double. Rates include continental breakfast. Children under 12 stay free in parent's room. AE, DC, DISC, MC, V. Pets accepted ($30 per night). **Amenities:** Restaurant (American); lounge; access to nearby health club; affiliated adjacent full-service spa; concierge; business center; laundry service; dry cleaning. *In room:* A/C, TV, dataport, fridge, hair dryer, iron, free local calls, high-speed Internet access, Wi-Fi.

Mt. Ashland Inn

Located on 160 acres on the side of Mount Ashland, this massive log home commands distant panoramas from its forest setting, and though the inn is only 20 minutes from downtown Ashland, you're in a different world up here. The Pacific Crest Trail, which stretches from Canada to Mexico, passes through the front yard, and just a few miles up the road is the Mt. Ashland Ski Area. Whether you're in the area for an active vacation or a few nights of theater, this lodge makes a very special base of operations. The decor is straight out of an Eddie Bauer catalog, and every room has a Jacuzzi and a gas fireplace. One guest bathroom even has a stone wall with a built-in waterfall. The Sky Lakes Wilderness Suite has views of Mount Shasta and is the best room in the house.

550 Mt. Ashland Rd., Ashland, OR 97520. © **800/830-8707** or 541/482-8707. www.mtashlandinn.com. 5 units. $175–$230 suite. Rates include full breakfast. 2-night minimum on weekends. DC, DISC, MC, V. Children 10 and older are welcome. **Amenities:** Jacuzzi; sauna; concierge. *In room:* Fridge, microwave, hair dryer, iron, free local calls, Wi-Fi.

Peerless Hotel

Located in the historic Railroad District 7 blocks from the festival theaters, this restored 1900 brick boarding house is one of Ashland's most interesting lodgings. With the feel of a small historic hotel rather than a B&B, the Peerless is filled with antiques and an eclectic array of individually decorated guest rooms. Of these, the West Indies Suite, with its balcony, double whirlpool tub, and view of Ashland, is by far the most luxurious. However, all other rooms feature lush fabrics, unusual murals, stenciling, and tile work that add up to unexpected luxury. Most rooms have either a whirlpool tub or a claw-foot tub. (One even has two side-by-side claw-foot tubs.) The hotel's restaurant (p. 287) is one of the finest in Ashland.

243 Fourth St., Ashland, OR 97520. © **800/460-8758** or 541/488-1082. www.peerlesshotel.com. 6 units. June–Oct $157–$212 double, $244–$263 suite; Nov to mid-Feb $78–$108 double, $145–$165 suite; mid-Feb to May $116–$157 double, $192–$215 suite. Rates include full breakfast (continental breakfast in winter). DISC, MC, V. Children over 14 welcome. **Amenities:** Restaurant (Northwest); lounge; access to nearby health club; room service. *In room:* A/C, TV, fridge, iron, free local calls, Wi-Fi.

Plaza Inn & Suites at Ashland Creek

A bold and colorful decor imbues this luxurious hotel with a distinctly theatrical character, making this one of the most enjoyable lodgings in Ashland. In the guest rooms, the triple-sheeted beds have bed-spreads printed with excerpts from Shakespeare's poems, and carpets have a bold black-and-blue diamond pattern. It all inspires you to make a grand entrance. In summer, you can breakfast on the patio beside a small pond. There are also evening appetizers and late-night snacks. The Plaza Suites are only 2 blocks from the plaza itself, and there's a day spa right next door.

98 Central Ave., Ashland, OR 97520. ✆ **888/488-0358** or 541/488-8900. Fax 541/488-8906. www.plazainnashland. com. 91 units. Mid-June to mid-Oct $169–$239 double, $279 suite; mid-Oct to Mar $89–$129 double, $129 suite; Apr to mid-June $109–$139 double, $139 suite. Rates include continental breakfast. AE, DC, DISC, MC, V. Pets accepted ($25). **Amenities:** Exercise room; Jacuzzi; concierge; coin-op laundry; laundry service; dry cleaning. *In room:* A/C, TV, dataport, fridge, coffeemaker, hair dryer, iron.

MODERATE

Best Western Bard's Inn ✿   If you prefer motels to B&Bs and want to be within walking distance of downtown, the Bard's Inn should be your first choice in Ashland. This motel's best feature is that it's only 2 blocks from the festival theaters. The rooms are large and comfortable, and those in the annex have patios or balconies, though they get a bit of traffic noise.

132 N. Main St., Ashland, OR 97520. ✆ **800/533-9627** or 541/482-0049. Fax 541/488-3259. www.bestwestern. com. 91 units. Mid-May to mid-Oct $150–$226 double; mid-Oct to mid-May $90–$160 double. Rates include continental breakfast. AE, DC, DISC, MC, V. Pets accepted. **Amenities:** Small outdoor pool; Jacuzzi. *In room:* A/C, TV, fridge, coffeemaker, hair dryer, iron.

Coolidge House ✿✿   Located right on busy North Main Street only 3 blocks from the theaters, this 1875 Victorian sits high above the street on a hill with commanding views across the valley. Although this is one of the oldest homes in Ashland, inside you'll find not only interesting antiques but also some decidedly modern amenities. Guest suites have sitting rooms and large luxurious bathrooms, most of which come with either a whirlpool tub or a claw-foot tub. The Parlor Suite, with its draped window seat, is the inn's most romantic room. However, if views and space are what you seek, opt for the Sun Suite or the Grape Arbor. There is a pleasant patio in the back garden.

137 N. Main St., Ashland, OR 97520. ✆ **800/655-5522** or 541/482-4721. www.coolidgehouse.com. 6 units. June–Oct $145–$195 double; Nov–Mar $95–$130 double; Apr–May $120–$160. Rates include full breakfast. 2-night minimum on weekends Apr–Oct. Children over 12 are welcome. MC, V. **Amenities:** Access to nearby health club (June–Sept). *In room:* A/C, no phone.

Country Willows Inn ✿✿   Located just outside town and surrounded by 5 acres of rolling hills and pastures, the Country Willows B&B offers the tranquillity of a farm only minutes by car from Ashland's theaters and excellent restaurants. If you're looking for a very special room, consider the Sunrise Suite, which is in a renovated barn behind the main house: It has pine paneling, a high ceiling, a king-size bed, a gas fireplace, and, best of all, an old-fashioned tub for two with its very own picture window and skylight. Rooms in the restored farmhouse are smaller, but some offer excellent views across the valley. Ducks, geese, and goats call the farm home, and there's a 2-mile hiking trail that starts at the back door. You'll also find a pool and whirlpool on the grounds.

1313 Clay St., Ashland, OR 97520. ✆ **800/WILLOWS** or 541/488-1590. Fax 541/488-1611. www.countrywillows inn.com. 9 units. May–Oct $130–$180 double, $215–$255 suite; Nov–Feb $105–$140 double, $160–$195 suite; Feb–Mar $115–$165 double, $185–$235 suite. Rates include full breakfast. AE, DISC, MC, V. Children over 12 are welcome. **Amenities:** Outdoor pool; access to nearby health club; Jacuzzi; bikes; concierge. *In room:* A/C, dataport, hair dryer, iron, free local calls, Wi-Fi.

Lithia Springs Resort & Gardens ⭐ With its white fences and collection of cottages surrounded by colorful perennial gardens and wide lawns, this little resort on the edge of town has the feel of an English country estate. However, the hillsides that rise up from the edge of the property are purely southern Oregon. Guest accommodations include large suites with double whirlpool tubs, cottages, and even a converted water tower. Fans of mineral springs will definitely want to stay here; the water that flows from the taps here is super-soft mineral water that smells awful but feels great on your skin.

2165 W. Jackson Rd., Ashland, OR 97520. (🎧 800/482-7128. www.ashlandinn.com. 23 units. $135 double; $179–$249 suite; $179–$199 cottage. Rates include full breakfast and afternoon wine and snacks. AE, DISC, MC, V. 3-night minimum June–Sept and holiday weekends. **Amenities:** Full-service spa; concierge; massage. *In room:* A/C, TV, coffeemaker, hair dryer, iron, no phone, Wi-Fi.

The Winchester Inn ⭐⭐ With its massive old shade trees, English tea gardens, and elegant, international restaurant (p. 288), the Winchester is Ashland's premier historic inn. Though it styles itself as a country inn, it's actually right in town within a few blocks of the theaters. The rooms are very comfortably furnished with antiques and modern bath fixtures, including sinks built into old bureaus in some rooms. I prefer the upstairs rooms, which get quite a bit more light than those on the ground floor. There are also rooms in the building next door. If you want a bit more space, stay in one of the eight suites, two of which are in the old carriage house. The suites also come with TVs and DVDs. Throughout the year, special events are held here, including winemaker dinners, nine-course tasting dinners, and Christmas Dickens feasts.

35 S. Second St., Ashland, OR 97520. (🎧 800/972-4991 or 541/488-1113. Fax 541/488-4604. www.winchester inn.com. 19 units. Mid-Feb to Oct $150–$189 double, $225–$295 suite; Nov to mid-Feb $135 double, $185 suite. Rates include full breakfast. Children under 8 stay free in parent's room. AE, DISC, MC, V. **Amenities:** Restaurant (Mediterranean/international); lounge; access to nearby health club; dry cleaning. *In room:* A/C, hair dryer, iron, Wi-Fi.

INEXPENSIVE

The Palm ⭐ *Value* Located about a mile from the theaters of the Shakespeare Festival, this older but upgraded motor court is an excellent value. The collection of little Cape Cod cottages is surrounded by colorful perennial gardens, and there's even a tiny swimming pool on the grounds. All the old cottages have been completely redone and have a classic cottage feel. Some rooms have kitchens.

1065 Siskiyou Blvd., Ashland, OR 97520. (🎧 877/482-2635 or 541/482-2636. www.palmcottages.com. 13 units. Summer $95–$169 double; fall and spring $69–$115 double; winter $64–$98 double. MC, V. **Amenities:** Outdoor pool. *In room:* A/C, TV, dataport, Wi-Fi.

WHERE TO DINE

If you're headed to the theater after dinner, let your waitstaff know. They will usually do whatever they can to make sure you aren't late! For a light post-theater meal, try Chateaulin (see below).

EXPENSIVE

Amuse Restaurant ⭐⭐ NORTHWEST/FRENCH Ashland may be a long way from Seattle or Portland, but that doesn't mean you can't have an extremely urban dining experience. Amuse is by far the most contemporary restaurant in town and is thoroughly stylish. The food here comes to your table looking almost too good to eat. The menu changes regularly, but you might start with the crispy veal sweet breads or some grilled prawns. From there, it might be black truffle roasted game hen or slow-roasted king salmon. In summer, request a table on the patio.

Tips Food, Glorious Food!

As you meander around southern Oregon, keep your eyes out for local gourmet foods. Some of my favorites include the chocolate bars produced by Ashland's **Dagoba Organic Chocolate** (www.dagobachocolate.com), the cocoa-covered cracked cocoa beans produced by Jacksonville's **Lillie Belle Farms** (www.lilliebellefarms.com) in Jacksonville, the savory and sweet tortas made by **Rising Sun Farms** (www.risingsunfarms.com) in Phoenix, and the buffalo sausage and jerky made by **Full Circle Bison Ranch** (www.fullcirclebisonranch. com) in Williams.

---

15 N. First St. ⓒ **541/488-9000.** www.amuserestaurant.com. Reservations recommended. Main courses $19–$32. AE, DC, DISC, MC, V. Wed–Sun 5:30–9pm.

Chateaulin 愛愛 FRENCH   Located just around the corner from the festival theaters, this has long been one of the finest restaurants in town. Exposed brick walls and old champagne bottles give Chateaulin a casually elegant appearance that's accented by Art Nouveau touches and dark-wood furnishings. The menu is almost as traditional as the decor; you can start your meal with escargots or house pâté and then move on to rack of lamb. A separate bar menu (items are $9–$13) caters to smaller or après-theater appetites. The restaurant's award-winning wine list features French wines, as well as lots of hard-to-find wines from Oregon, Washington, and California. For visitors on a budget, there is a more affordable and contemporary prix-fixe menu ($38) that changes weekly. There's also an attached wine and gourmet-food store for classy picnic fare.

50 E. Main St. ⓒ **541/482-2264.** www.chateaulin.com. Reservations recommended. Main courses $16–$41. AE, DISC, MC, V. June–Oct Mon 5:30–9:30pm, Tues–Sun 5–9:30pm; Nov–May Wed–Sun 5:30–9pm.

Monet 愛愛 FRENCH   For fine French cuisine with an emphasis on lighter, more contemporary preparations, it's hard to beat Monet. Owned and operated by chef Pierre Verger, Monet has been in business for more than a decade, a testament to the popularity and quality of the restaurant's Gallic cuisine. Be sure to start with the smoked salmon wrapped around avocado mousse and served with a lemon-lime vinaigrette. From there, you've got plenty of good choices, including a filet mignon with the chef's sauce of the day. For lighter appetites, there are always several interesting salads and an excellent French onion soup. Though the big white house looks rather plain from the outside, inside you'll find a somewhat formal and impeccably set dining room. On warm days, you may want to dine in the garden surrounded by many of the same flowers that grow in Monet's famous garden in France.

36 S. Second St. ⓒ **541/482-1339.** www.restaurantmonet.com. Reservations recommended. Main courses $17–$30. MC, V. Tues–Sun 5:30–8:30pm. Closed Jan.

The Peerless Restaurant 愛愛 NORTHWEST   With its theatrical warehouse-tropical decor, this upscale restaurant a few blocks from the plaza seems decidedly out of place in the southern Oregon hills, but good food is good food no matter where it's served. And the cuisine served here is some of the best in Oregon. Flavor combinations are often complex and can seem at first to be a bit contrived (duck confit and corn crepes), but one bite will convince you that this is great food. Because The Peerless is out of Ashland's restaurant mainstream, it tends to work just a little bit harder to satisfy its customers, so although prices are high, dinners here are the best in town. In summer, there's a garden patio for summertime alfresco dining.

265 Fourth St. ℂ **541/488-6067**. www.peerlessrestaurant.com. Reservations recommended. Main courses $13–$43. AE, DISC, MC, V. Apr to late May and Oct Tues–Sun 5:30–9pm; late May to Sept daily 5:30–9pm; Nov–Mar Tues–Sat 5:30–9pm.

The Winchester Inn Restaurant & Wine Bar ☆☆ MEDITERRANEAN Located on the ground floor of Ashland's premier inn, this restaurant and wine bar melds a historic Victorian setting with an ambitious menu that is primarily Mediterranean but that sometimes wanders into other corners of the culinary world. Starters here tend toward such delectable preparations as seared buffalo and bleu cheese empanadas with smoked tomato aioli and risotto-stuffed portobello mushroom with amaretto-rosemary smoked salmon. For an entree, you might find such dishes as coriander-crusted halibut with lavender jasmine rice or pork loin rubbed with achiote and accompanied by spaetzle and mango-chocolate sauce. Sunday brunch is the perfect way to finish a weekend of theater before heading home. The dining rooms overlook the inn's English gardens, and in summer there is dining on the porch and deck as well. During the Christmas season, there are special Dickens feasts here.

35 S. Second St. ℂ **541/488-1115**. www.winchesterinn.com. Reservations highly recommended. Main courses $22–$34, Sun brunch $10–$16. AE, DISC, MC, V. Mon–Sat 5:30–8:30pm; Sun 9:30am–12:30pm (brunch) and 5:30–8:30pm. Closed early to mid-Jan.

MODERATE
Dragonfly Café and Gardens ☆ LATIN-ASIAN FUSION   With good prices and great food three meals a day, this restaurant is an all-around winner. Start the day with the coconut French toast or the banana-blackberry pancakes. At lunch, try the carne asada sandwich or an Asian-influenced bonsai burrito. At dinner, be sure to start with the crispy shoestring plantains or the plantains with caviar. Follow up with one of the big bowls of soup or the grilled salmon with papaya-mango-mint salsa. Vegetarians have lots of choices here.

241 Hargadine St. ℂ **541/488-4855**. www.dragonflyashland.com. Reservations accepted for parties of 6 or more. Main courses $9–$20. AE, DC, DISC, MC, V. Daily 8am–3pm and 5–9pm.

Kat Wok ☆ PACIFIC RIM   With the sort of clever ambience you'd find in a hip restaurant in Portland or Seattle, Kat Wok is a prime example of Ashland's cosmopolitan atmosphere. If you happen to enter from "the bricks," you'll think you've stumbled onto a theater's backstage. Each table is dramatically lit, and there are tables on a catwalklike mezzanine (hence the name). Kat Wok is popular with people of all ages who come here for light Asian-style cuisine, including an excellent Asian pear salad with roasted chicken, sesame-crusted pork medallions, or Szechwan green beans. Later in the evening, Kat Wok becomes a nightclub with live music.

62 E. Main St. ℂ **541/482-0787**. www.katwok.com. Reservations recommended. Main courses $13–$20. AE, MC, V. Mon–Tues 5–9pm; Wed–Sun 11:30am–2:30pm and 5–9pm.

Kobe ☆ JAPANESE   Affiliated with Thai Pepper (see below), this stylish little sushi bar is also set on the banks of Ashland Creek and has a pleasant deck for summer dining. While you'll find all your favorite traditional Japanese dishes on the menu, Kobe bills itself as serving modern Japanese food, which means you'll find a bit of food fusion going on here. I like the various ceviches and carpaccios they serve here, which, because they're made with raw fish, are in keeping with the sushi theme. However, you can also get the likes of grilled rack of lamb, roasted duck breast with orange-miso glaze, and steamed sea bass. Be sure to try one of the sake cocktails.

96 N. Main St. ℭ **541/488-8058.** Reservations recommended. Main courses $15–$24. AE, DISC, MC, V. Mon–Thurs 5:30–9pm; Fri 5:30–9:30pm; Sat 5–9:30pm; Sun 5:30–8:30pm.

Tabu Restaurant ℱ NUEVO LATINO   Casual and not too expensive, Tabu may seem like the absolute antithesis of a pretheater restaurant, but there's only so much French food you can eat. The fish tacos, which come three to a plate, each with its own distinctive sauce, are my favorite dish here. For a side dish, try the unusual fried plantains with black beans and jalapeño cream sauce. Tabu is also one of Ashland's most popular night spots, and several nights a week there's live music or salsa dancing.

16 N. Pioneer St. ℭ **541/482-3900.** www.taburestaurant.com. Main courses $13–$27. AE, MC, V. Daily 11:30am–9pm.

INEXPENSIVE

For great breakfasts, head to the **Ashland Bistro Café,** 38 E. Main St. (ℭ **541/482-2117;** www.ashlandbistrocafe.com), for polenta pancakes or a smoked-salmon scramble. If you're late for the theater or forgot to make dinner reservations, you can still get a slice or two of organic pizza at **Cozmic Pizza,** 143 A St. (ℭ **541/482-0844;** www.cozmicpizza.com), in the A Street Marketplace in the Railroad District. For simple, inexpensive Mexican food, stop by **Agave,** 92 N. Main St. (ℭ **541/488-1770;** www.agavetaco.com). For delicious wraps with international influences, head to **Pangea,** 272 E. Main St. (ℭ **541/552-1630;** www.pangeaashland.com). If you're in need of a latte and a pastry, stop by **Mix Sweet Shop,** 57 N. Main St. (ℭ **541/488-9885**). If you want to sip a latte with some left-leaning SOU students, stop by **Evo's Coffee Lounge,** 376 E. Main St. (ℭ **541/482-2261**). If you just need a good loaf of artisan bread, perhaps for a picnic in the park, try the **Village Baker of Ashland,** 372 E. Main St. (ℭ **541/488-9130**).

Thai Pepper ℱ THAI   If menu prices around Ashland have left you wondering how you're going be able to afford dinner *and* a show, search out this elegant little Thai restaurant. Thai Pepper has long been a local favorite for its spicy, fragrant food, and its great location on the banks of Ashland Creek. I like to start with the lime-beef salad with mango chutney, but the rather nontraditional tiger rolls, made with cream cheese and crab, are a perennial favorite here. The menu includes lots of vegetarian dishes. You'll find the restaurant down a flight of stairs from the street. In summer, try to get a seat on the deck.

84 N. Main St. ℭ **541/482-8058.** Reservations recommended. Main courses $12–$16. AE, MC, V. Mon–Thurs 5:30–9pm; Fri 11:30am–2pm and 5:30–9:30pm; Sat 5:30–9:30pm; Sun 5:30–8:30pm.

ASHLAND AFTER DARK

The Oregon Shakespeare Festival may be the main draw, but Ashland is overflowing with talent. From experimental theater to Broadway musicals, the town sees an amazing range of theater productions. To find out what's going on while you're in town, pick up a free copy of *Sneak Preview.* If you've had enough Shakespeare or happen to be in town when the Oregon Shakespeare Festival is not staging performances, check out the performance calendars of the **Oregon Cabaret Theatre,** First and Hargadine streets (ℭ **541/488-2902;** www.oregoncabaret.com), a professional dinner theater; **Oregon Stage Works,** 191 A St. (ℭ **541/482-2334;** www.oregonstageworks. org), a small theater staging everything from classics to world premiers; or the town of

Talent's little **Camelot Theatre Company,** 101 Talent Ave. (© **541/535-5250;** www.camelottheatre.org), which specializes in making live theater affordable. The university also has its **One World Concert Series** (© **541/552-6461;** www.oneworldseries.org), which brings in touring musical acts and other performers.

For a glass of wine before or after a show, **Liquid Assets Wine Bar,** 96 N. Main St. (© **541/482-WINE;** www.liquidassetswinebar.com), is the place to go. They serve some tasty, light meals here, too. If you're just looking for someplace to heft a pint of local microbrew, stop by **Standing Stone Brewing,** 101 Oak St. (© **541/482-2448;** www.standingstonebrewing.com). Or, to keep with the merrie olde England theme of Ashland, head to **The Black Sheep,** 51 N. Main St. (© **541/482-6414;** www.theblacksheep.com), an English pub on the plaza. Thursday through Saturday nights, you can do a little salsa dancing at the Nuevo Latino restaurant **Tabu,** 16 N. Pioneer St. (© **541/482-3900;** www.taburestaurant.com).

2 Jacksonville & Medford: After the Gold Rush

16 miles N of Ashland, 24 miles E of Grants Pass

Jacksonville is a snapshot from southern Oregon's past. After the Great Depression it became a forgotten backwater, and more than 80 buildings from its glory years as a gold-mining boom town in the mid-1800s were left untouched. The entire town has been restored to much the way it looked in the late 19th century, thanks in large part to the photos of pioneer photographer Peter Britt, who moved to Jacksonville in 1852 and operated the first photographic studio west of the Rockies. His photos of 19th-century Jacksonville have provided preservationists with invaluable 150-year-old glimpses of many of the town's historic buildings. Where Britt's home once stood, visitors now attend the performances of the **Britt Festivals,** another southern Oregon cultural binge that rivals the Oregon Shakespeare Festival in its ability to stage first-rate entertainment.

Though thousands of eager gold-seekers were lured into California's Sierra Nevada by the **gold rush** of 1849, few struck it rich. Many of those who were smitten with gold fever and were unwilling to give up the search for the mother lode headed out across the West in search of golder pastures. In 1851, at least two prospectors hit pay dirt in the Siskiyou Mountains of southern Oregon at a spot that would soon be known as Rich Gulch. Within a year Rich Gulch had become the site of booming Jacksonville, and within another year the town had become the county seat and commercial heart of southern Oregon. Over the next 30 years, Jacksonville developed into a wealthy town with brick commercial buildings and elegant Victorian homes. However, in the 1880s, the railroad running between Portland and San Francisco bypassed Jacksonville in favor of an easier route 5 miles to the east. It was at this spot that the trading town of **Medford** developed.

Despite a short-rail line into Jacksonville, more and more businesses migrated to the main railway in Medford. Jacksonville's fortunes began to decline, and by the time of the Depression, residents were reduced to digging up the streets of town for the gold that lay there. In 1927, the county seat was moved to Medford, and Jacksonville was left with its faded grandeur and memories of better times.

Off the beaten path, forgotten by developers and modernization, Jacksonville inadvertently preserved its past in its buildings. In 1966, the entire town was listed on the National Register of Historic Places, and Jacksonville, with the aid of Britt's photos, underwent a renaissance that has left it a historical showcase. Together the Britt Festivals and Jacksonville's history combine to make this one of the most fascinating towns anywhere in the Northwest.

ESSENTIALS

GETTING THERE   Medford is right on I-5, 30 miles north of the California state line, and Jacksonville is 5 miles west on Ore. 238.

America West Airlines, Horizon Air, and SkyWest Airlines (United Express) serve **Rogue Valley International–Medford Airport,** 3650 Biddle Rd., Medford (© **541/ 776-7222**).

VISITOR INFORMATION   Contact the **Jacksonville Chamber of Commerce,** 185 N. Oregon St. (P.O. Box 33), Jacksonville, OR 97530 (© **541/899-8118;** www. jacksonvilleoregon.org), or the **Medford Visitor & Convention Bureau,** 101 E. Eighth St., Medford, OR 97501 (© **800/469-6307** or 541/779-4847; www.visitmedford.org).

THE BRITT FESTIVALS & OTHER AREA PERFORMANCES

The Britt Festivals are a celebration of music and the performing arts featuring internationally renowned performers, and each summer between early June and mid-September, people gather in Jacksonville several nights a week for concerts and theater and modern dance performances. The setting for most of the performances is an amphitheater on the grounds of Peter Britt's estate. Located only a block from historic California Street, the ponderosa pine–shaded amphitheater provides not only a great setting for the performances but a view that takes in distant hills and the valley far below. When planning to attend a show, be sure that it will be held here on the festival grounds; some concerts are now held at the Lithia Motors Amphitheater in nearby Central Point. This latter amphitheater lacks the character of the original Britt Pavilion amphitheater.

Both reserved and general-admission tickets are available for most shows. If you opt for a general-admission ticket, arrive early to claim a prime spot on the lawns behind the reserved seats—and be sure to bring a picnic. For information, contact the festival at 216 W. Main St., Medford (© **800/882-7488** or 541/773-6077; www.britt fest.org). Tickets range from $22 to $91, with most performances in the $40 to $50.

Not wanting to lose out to its better-known neighbors, Medford has a renovated old downtown theater now known as the **Craterian Ginger Rogers Theater,** 23 S. Central Ave. (© **541/779-3000;** www.craterian.org), in honor of the famous dancer who lived in the area after her retirement. The theater stages everything from performances by the Rogue Opera (© **541/608-6400;** www.rogueopera.com) to touring Broadway shows and classical music performances.

When the Britt Festivals have closed up shop for the year, you can still catch Dixieland jazz at the annual **Medford Jazz Jubilee** (© **800/599-0039** or 541/770-6972; www.medfordjazz.org), which is held in mid-October.

MUSEUMS & HISTORIC HOMES

With more than 80 buildings listed on the National Register of Historic Places, Jacksonville boasts that it's the most completely preserved historic town in the nation. Whether or not this claim is true, there are certainly enough restored old buildings to make the town a genuine step back in time. Along California Street you'll find restored brick commercial buildings that now house dozens of interesting shops, art galleries, and boutiques. On the side streets you'll see the town's many Victorian homes.

Butte Creek Mill   In nearby Eagle Point, you can visit Oregon's only operating water-powered flour mill. The Butte Creek Mill was built in 1873, and its millstones are still grinding out flour. After looking around at the workings of the mill, you can stop in at the mill store and buy a bag of flour or cornmeal. Also on this same block is the **Eagle Point Museum,** 301 N. Royal Ave. (℃ **541/826-4166**), which unfortunately has very limited hours. The Antelope covered bridge is also here in Eagle Point.

402 N. Royal Ave., Eagle Point. ℃ 541/826-3531. www.buttecreekmill.com. Free admission. Mon–Sat 9am–5pm; Sun 11am–5pm.

Jacksonville Museum of Southern Oregon History   In order to get some background on Jacksonville, make this museum your first stop in town. Housed in the 1883 county courthouse, the museum has displays on the history of Jacksonville, including 19th-century photos by Peter Britt. The price of admission also includes admission to the adjacent Children's Museum, housed in the former jail.

206 N. Fifth St. ℃ 541/773-6536. Admission $5 adults, $3 seniors and children 3–12. Wed–Sat 1–4pm.

MORE TO SEE & DO

Pears and roses both grow well in the Jacksonville and Medford area, and these crops have given rise to two of the country's best-known mail-order businesses. **Harry and David's Country Village,** 1314 Center Dr. (℃ **877/322-8000** or 541/864-2278; www.harryanddavid.com), is the retail outlet of a fruit company specializing in mail-order gift baskets. You'll find the store just 1 mile south of Medford at exit 27 off I-5. You can tour the Harry and David's packinghouse and then wander through the store in search of bargains. In summer, the store is open Monday through Saturday from 9am to 8pm and on Sunday from 10am to 8pm; other months the store closes 1 to 2 hours earlier. Associated with this store is the **Jackson and Perkins rose test garden** and mail-order rose nursery. Not far away, in the town of Central Point, you can see how cheese is made at the **Rogue Creamery,** 311 N. Front St. (℃ **866/665-1155** or 541/665-1155; www.roguecreamery.com), which is known for its blue cheeses, including the delicious Oregonzola. The creamery is open Monday through Saturday from 9am to 5pm and Sunday from 11am to 5pm. Both Harry and David's and the Rogue Creamery are part of the **Southern Oregon Wine and Farm Tour** (www.oregonwineandfarmtour.com).

There are lots of great stores in Jacksonville, and one of our favorites is the **GeBzz Gallery,** 150 S. Oregon St. (℃ **541/899-7535**), which carries a diverse selection of contemporary art works.

OUTDOOR ACTIVITIES

Rafting and **fishing** on the numerous fast-flowing, clear-water rivers of southern Oregon are two of the most popular sports in this region, and Medford makes a good base for doing a bit of either, or both. **Arrowhead River Adventures** (℃ **800/227-7741** or 541/830-3388; www.arrowheadadventures.com), **River Trips Unlimited** (℃ **800/ 460-3865** or 541/779-3798; www.roguefishing.com), and **Rogue Excursions** (℃ **800/797-4293** or 541/549-1336; www.fishandraft.com) all offer both rafting and fishing trips. A day of rafting will cost $95 to $125, and fishing trips cost about $165 to $175 per person per day (with a minimum of two people).

If you're here in the spring, you can catch the colorful **wildflower displays** at Table Rocks. These mesas are just a few miles northeast of Medford, and because of their great age and unique structure, they create a variety of habitats that allow the area to support an unusual diversity of plants. For more information, contact the **Bureau of Land Management,** Medford District Office, 3040 Biddle Rd., Medford, OR 97504 (© **541/618-2200;** www.blm.gov/or/districts/medford/index.php).

Information on **hiking** and **backpacking** is available from the **Rogue River-Siskiyou National Forest,** 333 W. Eighth St. (P.O. Box 520), Medford, OR 97501 (© **541/858-2200;** www.fs.fed.us/r6/rogue).

WINE TOURING

The Applegate Valley has recently become one of the best places in southern Oregon to spend a day wine touring. There are more than half a dozen wineries in the area that you can now visit on a regular basis. For more information on area wineries, contact **Applegate Valley Wineries Information** (www.applegatewinetrail.com).

Wine connoisseurs also won't want to miss perusing the wine racks at the **Jacksonville Inn Wine Shop,** 175 E. California St., Jacksonville (© **541/899-1900**), where you might find a bottle of 1811 Tokay Essencia or a bottle of Chateau Lafite-Rothschild. Oregon wines (and beef jerky) can also be tasted at the **Gary R. West Tasting Room,** 690 N. Fifth St., Jacksonville (© **800/833-1820;** www.garywest.com).

Applegate Red Winery   This is one of the most unusual wineries in the state in that the owner not only produces red wines (and only red wines) but also raises miniature Sicilian donkeys and Australian rosellas (birds that are as colorful as parrots). Wines are made from organic, estate-grown grapes. I've had some excellent Syrah here.

222 Missouri Flat Rd. © 541/846-9557. Sat–Sun 11am–5pm. From Jacksonville, drive west on Ore. 238, turn right onto N. Applegate Road and then right again on Kubli Road.

Bridgeview Applegate Tasting Room ⊛   Bridgeview has its main facility near Cave Junction, but this tasting room is a bit more convenient if you are staying in Ashland or Jacksonville and are out for a day of wine tasting. Bridgeview is best known for its inexpensive white wines, at least two of which come in distinctive blue bottles.

16995 N. Applegate Rd. © 541/846-1039. www.bridgeviewwine.com. Memorial Day to Labor Day daily 11am–5pm; mid-Mar to May and Labor Day to Nov Sat–Sun 11am–5pm. Closed Dec to mid-Mar. From Jacksonville, drive west on Ore. 238 and turn right onto N. Applegate Rd.

Devitt Winery & Vineyards ⊛⊛ *Finds*   This tiny family-run winery is the retirement occupation of James Devitt and his wife, Susan. Devitt had a winery in the Napa Valley area more than 20 years ago, and has now brought to his Applegate Valley operation the winemaking skills he developed years ago. Look for good cabernet sauvignon and cabernet Franc in the $25 to $30 range. There are also plenty of less expensive wines.

11412 Ore. 238. © 541/899-7511. www.devittwinery.com. Daily noon–5pm. From Jacksonville, drive west on Ore. 238 past the community of Ruch.

Jacksonville Vineyards/Fiasco Winery ⊛   This small, family winery produces some outstanding red wines, with the 2004 cabernet sauvignon and 2004 claret being particularly noteworthy. They also produce a couple of different rosés and a chardonnay.

9730 Ore. 238. © 541/899-6923. www.jacksonvillevineyards.com. Mar to New Year's weekend Thurs–Mon 11am–5pm. Closed Jan–Feb. From Jacksonville, drive west on Ore. 238 past the community of Ruch.

Longsword Vineyard   While the tasting room here is little more than a little roadside shed with a little deck, the wines are quite good. Chardonnay, produced from vines that are more than 25 years old, is the specialty here, but winemaker Maria

Largaespada likes to experiment, so you might run across a dolcetto rosé or a sweet sparkling wine.

8555 Ore. 238. ℂ **541/899-1746**. www.longswordvineyard.com. Memorial Day weekend to Halloween Sat–Sun noon–5pm. From Jacksonville, drive west on Ore. 238 past the community of Ruch.

Schmidt Family Vineyards   This is one of the newer wineries in the valley, and it has one of the prettiest settings and tasting rooms. Wines are produced from estate-grown grapes, and although the winery has not been around very long, its red wines have been garnering some acclaim.

330 Kubli Rd. ℂ **541/846-9985**. www.sfvineyards.com. Daily noon–5pm. From Jacksonville, drive west on Ore. 238, turn right onto N. Applegate Road and then right again on Kubli Road.

Troon Vineyard   This winery has the prettiest facility in the Applegate Valley, with a Mediterranean look to the winery and tasting room. However, Troon's wines seem to be made for people who don't normally drink wine. The winery made its name with its unusual Druid's Fluid sweet red wine (zinfandel, Syrah, cabernet sauvignon blend) that has up to 3% residual sugar. You might encounter several rosé or blush wines.

1475 Kubli Rd. ℂ **541/846-9900**. www.troonvineyard.com. Feb to Memorial Day and Oct–Dec daily 11am–5pm; Memorial Day to Sept daily 11am–6pm. Closed Jan. From Jacksonville, take Ore. 238 west to N. Applegate Rd.

Valley View Vineyard   This is the oldest winery in the area and is the first you'll come to as you head out into the Applegate Valley from Jacksonville. Valley View is known for its big red wines but also produces good dry whites.

1000 Upper Applegate Rd. ℂ **800/781-WINE** or 541/899-8468. www.valleyviewwinery.com. Daily 11am–5pm. From Jacksonville, drive west on Ore. 238 to Ruch, and turn left onto Upper Applegate Rd.

WHERE TO STAY
IN JACKSONVILLE

Historic Orth House ⋒⋒   This 1880 Italianate brick house stands behind majestic old shade trees 1 block from busy California Street. The picket fence and inviting front porch bring back small-town America and slower times. Inside, the glowing woodwork, pressed-tin ceilings, and antique furnishings conjure up the 19th century. Don't miss the inn's extensive collection of teddy bears and antique toys. One of our favorite rooms is romantic Josie's Room with its in-room claw-foot tub. Keep an eye out for deer in the yard. The inn also operates a limousine service that does wine tours to local wineries.

105 W. Main St. (P.O. Box 1437), Jacksonville, OR 97530. ℂ **800/700-7301** or 541/899-8665. www.orthbnb.com. 3 units. May–Oct $145–$165 double, $225 suite; Nov–Apr $110–$135 double, $175 suite. Rates include full breakfast. DISC, MC, V. *In room:* A/C, Wi-Fi.

Jacksonville Inn ⋒⋒   Located in the heart of the town's historic business district in a two-story brick building, the Jacksonville Inn is best known for its gourmet restaurant (p. 296). Upstairs, however, there are eight antiques-filled rooms that offer traditional elegance mixed with modern amenities. Rooms are elegantly furnished and several have exposed brick walls that conjure up the inn's past. (Part of the inn was built in 1861.) Room 1, with its queen-size canopy bed and whirlpool tub for two, is the most popular. If you're looking for more privacy and greater luxury, consider the cottages, which are a couple of blocks away and have whirlpool tubs, steam showers, and entertainment centers.

175 E. California St. (P.O. Box 359), Jacksonville, OR 97530. ℂ **800/321-9344** or 541/899-1900. Fax 541/899-1373. www.jacksonvilleinn.com. 12 units (including 4 cottages). $145–$189 double; $250–$395 cottage. Rates include full

breakfast. AE, DISC, MC, V. Pets accepted. **Amenities:** Restaurant (Northwest/Continental); lounge; bike rentals; laundry service. *In room:* A/C, TV, fridge, high-speed Internet access, Wi-Fi.

McCully Country House Inn 🐾🐾
Built in 1861, the McCully House is one of the oldest buildings in Oregon being used as an inn, and with its classic, symmetrical lines and simple pre-Victorian styling, it looks as if it could easily be an 18th-century New England inn. If you like being steeped in local history, this is Jacksonville's best choice. In the McCully Room, you'll even find the original black-walnut master bedroom furnishings. Surrounding the inn, and enclosed by a white picket fence, is a formal rose garden with an amazing variety of roses. This inn also rents out rooms in the nearby Reames Country House Inn.

240 E. California St. (P.O. Box 13), Jacksonville, OR 97530. (© 800/367-1942 or 541/899-1942. www.countryhouse inns.com. 11 units. $135 double; $150 cottage; $175 suite. Rates include continental breakfast. AE, MC, V. *In room:* A/C, no phone.

The Stage Lodge 🐾
Jacksonville has several bed-and-breakfast inns, but it's short on moderately priced motels. Filling the bill in the latter category is this motel designed to resemble a 19th-century stage stop, with gables, clapboard siding, and turned-wood railings along two floors of verandas. These details allow the lodge to fit right in with all the original buildings in town. The rooms are spacious and comfortable and have a few nice touches such as ceiling fans, TV armoires, and country decor.

830 N. Fifth St. (P.O. Box 1316), Jacksonville, OR 97530. (© 800/253-8254 or 541/899-3953. www.stagelodge.com. 27 units. $92–$102 double; $175 suite. AE, DISC, MC, V. Pets accepted ($10 per day). *In room:* A/C, TV.

Touvelle House 🐾
This luxurious B&B is located just a few blocks from downtown and the Britt Festival grounds and is the town's prettiest inn. Built in 1916, the three-story Craftsman bungalow sits a bit above and well back from the street and is surrounded by over an acre of attractive gardens. The grand feel of this old house never fails to impress first-time guests. The inn's great room is furnished with Stickley and other Arts-and-Crafts furniture, while the guest rooms are a mix of sophisticated Victorian and rustic lodge styling. If you have trouble with stairs, be sure to ask for the Judge's Chambers room.

455 N. Oregon St. (P.O. Box 1891), Jacksonville, OR 97530. (© 800/846-8422 or 541/899-8938. www.touvelle house.com. 6 units. $149–$170 double. Rates include full breakfast. DISC, MC, V. Children over 12 welcome. **Amenities:** Outdoor pool; sauna; concierge. *In room:* A/C, Wi-Fi, no phone.

IN MEDFORD
In addition to the B&B listed below, you'll find dozens of inexpensive chain motels clustered along I-5.

Under the Greenwood Tree 🐾🐾
Located just west of Medford and taking its name from the 300-year-old oaks that shade the front yard, this B&B offers a step back in time to the days of iced tea on the veranda, croquet on the lawn, and stolen kisses behind the barn. Romance is the name of the game here, with beds piled with plump pillows and lace curtains swaying in the summer breezes. The guest rooms are furnished with antiques, and two have separate sitting rooms. Throughout the house you'll find antique quilts and Tibetan carpets, which give the inn a touch of country class, and in summer, fresh-cut flower arrangements fill the house. Out back there is a huge deck that overlooks the inn's 10 acres of land and its gazebo, garden, and barns.

3045 Bellinger Lane, Medford, OR 97501. (© 541/776-0000. www.greenwoodtree.com. 4 units. $120–$140 double. Rates include full breakfast. Children under 18 stay free in parent's room. AE, DC, DISC, MC, V. **Amenities:** Bikes; massage. *In room:* A/C, dataport, hair dryer, free local calls, Wi-Fi.

IN THE APPLEGATE VALLEY

Applegate Lodge 🌟🌟 *(Finds)*   Situated on the bank of the Applegate River 16 miles outside Jacksonville, this lodge has one of the prettiest settings in southern Oregon and is a masterpiece of woodworking, with burnished woods (including rare fiddle-back redwood paneling) and unique wooden details throughout. The high-ceilinged great room with a river-rock fireplace features a wall of glass looking out on the river, and across the length of the lodge is a deck where you can sit and listen to the river. The guest rooms are all very large, and several of them have loft sleeping areas. Lots of peeled log furniture gives the inn a solidly western feel. Right next door is the Applegate River Ranch House (p. 297). The river here is great for swimming.

15100 Ore. 238 (P.O. Box 3282), Applegate, OR 97530. ☎ **541/846-6690** or 541/846-6408. www.applegateriver lodge.com. 7 units. $140–$155 double; lower rates in winter. Rates include continental breakfast. DISC, MC, V. Pets accepted. **Amenities:** Restaurant (steak/seafood); lounge; massage. *In room:* A/C.

WHERE TO DINE
IN JACKSONVILLE

In addition to the establishments mentioned below, **Good Bean Coffee,** 165 S. Oregon St. (☎ **541/899-8740;** www.goodbean.com), is *the* place for a cup of espresso. **MacLevin's Whole Foods Saloon,** 150 W. California St. (☎ **541/899-1251**), will pack up a deli-style picnic for a Britt performance (or any other occasion).

Bella Union Restaurant & Saloon 🌟 ITALIAN/AMERICAN   For casual dining or someplace to just toss back a cold beer or sip an Italian soda, the Bella Union is Jacksonville's top choice. The lounge evokes the days when the Bella Union was one of Jacksonville's busiest saloons, but in the back of the building is a pretty little garden patio. However, it's the main dining room up front that's most popular. Old wood floors, storefront windows, and exposed brick walls bring to mind images of gold miners out on the town. Meals range from pizzas and pastas to a delicious chicken marinated in Gorgonzola and walnut pesto.

170 W. California St. ☎ **541/899-1770.** www.bellau.com. At dinner, call ahead to be placed on wait list. Main courses $7–$27. AE, DC, DISC, MC, V. Mon–Sat 11:30am–10pm; Sun 10am–10pm.

Gogi's Restaurant 🌟🌟 REGIONAL AMERICAN   With an ambience somewhere between the casual atmosphere of Bella Union and the formality of the Jacksonville Inn Dinner House, this restaurant is a gleaming and comfortable little bistro. The small plates, such as crispy calamari with wasabi aioli or fresh mozzarella with basil pesto, heirloom tomatoes, and olive oil, make good choices for sharing around the table. Other tasty standouts include rum-glazed sea scallops and rack of lamb in an almond-honey crust with a red-wine reduction sauce. Gogi's also packs box lunches for people attending Britt Festivals events.

235 W. Main St. ☎ **541/899-8699.** www.gogis.net. Reservations recommended. Main courses $19–$28. DISC, MC, V. Wed–Sun 5–9pm.

Jacksonville Inn Dinner House 🌟🌟 *(Value)* CONTINENTAL/MEDITER-RANEAN   Old-world atmosphere, either in the cozy and cellarlike downstairs or in the airier upstairs dining room, sets the mood for reliable continental fare. Together the cuisine and the decor attract well-heeled families and retirees that favor well-prepared, though familiar, dishes such as rack of lamb, veal scaloppini, and prime rib. The bistro menu is lighter and leans toward Mediterranean influences, with such dishes as goat-cheese ravioli and roasted garlic pasta. Pears are a mainstay of the local economy and show up frequently in both entrees and desserts. The inn's wine shop gives diners access to a cellar boasting more than 2,000 wines. In summer, ask for a table on the patio.

175 E. California St. ℂ **541/899-1900.** www.jacksonvilleinn.com. Reservations recommended. Main courses lunch $9–$16, dinner $10–$33. DISC, MC, V. Mon 7:30–10:30am and 5–9 or 10pm; Tues–Sat 7:30–10:30am, 11:30am–2pm, and 5–9 or 10pm; Sun 7:30am–2pm and 5–9pm. Bistro menu served daily 4pm–closing.

IN THE APPLEGATE VALLEY

Applegate River Ranch House 𝒦 *Finds* STEAK/SEAFOOD   With a deck overlooking the beautiful Applegate River, the location here just can't be beat. I like to enjoy the view with a plate of succulent oak-wood-broiled mushrooms and a glass of chardonnay followed by the "angels on horseback" (large prawns wrapped in bacon and then broiled with mushrooms, apples, and water chestnuts). From the chicken to various cuts of beef, anything broiled over the local red-oak wood is delicious. For dessert, top it all off with a piece of the "hula" pie, a mocha-almond-fudge ice cream cake.

15100 Ore. 238, Applegate. ℂ **541/846-6082.** www.applegateriverlodge.com. Reservations recommended. Main courses $12–$27. DISC, MC, V. Wed–Sun 5–9pm.

3 Grants Pass & the Rogue River Valley

63 miles S of Roseburg, 40 miles NW of Ashland, 82 miles NE of Crescent City

"It's the climate," proclaims a sign at the entrance to Grants Pass, and with weather almost as reliably pleasant as California's, the town has become a popular base for outdoor activities of all kinds. The Rogue River runs through the center of town, so it's not surprising that most local recreational activities revolve around the waters of this famous river. Grants Pass is located at the junction of I-5 and U.S. 199 and is the last large town in Oregon if you're heading over to the redwoods, which are about 90 miles southwest on the northern California coast. About the same distance to the northeast, you'll find Crater Lake National Park, so Grants Pass makes a good base if you're trying to see a lot of this region in a short time.

The city is slowly reviving its few blocks of historic commercial buildings, and it's worth wandering down SW G Street to see what's new along the historic blocks.

ESSENTIALS

GETTING THERE   Grants Pass is at the junction of I-5 and U.S. 199. The **Rogue Valley International–Medford Airport,** 3650 Biddle Rd. (ℂ **541/776-7222**), Medford, is served by America West Airlines, Horizon Air, and SkyWest (United Express).

VISITOR INFORMATION   Contact the **Grants Pass Visitors & Convention Bureau,** 1995 NW Vine St., Grants Pass, OR 97526 (ℂ **800/547-5927** or 541/476-7717; www.visitgrantspass.org).

FESTIVALS   **Boatnik,** held Memorial Day weekend, is Grants Pass's biggest annual festival and includes jet-boat and hydroplane races on the Rogue River, as well as lots of festivities at Riverside Park.

OUTDOOR ACTIVITIES

Grants Pass is midway between the source of the Rogue River and the river's mouth, and is an ideal base for river-oriented activities. The Rogue, first made famous by Western novelist and avid fly-fisherman Zane Grey, is now preserved for much of its length as a National Wild and Scenic River. Originating in Crater Lake National Park, the river twists and tumbles through narrow gorges and steep mountains as it winds its way to the coast at Gold Beach. The most famous section of the river is 250-foot-deep **Hellgate Canyon,** where the river narrows and rushes through a cleft in the rock. The canyon can be seen from an overlook on Merlin-Galice Road, which begins at exit 61 off I-5. From I-5, it's about 10 miles to the canyon overlook.

Several area companies offer **river trips** of varying length and in a variety of watercraft. You can spend the afternoon paddling the Rogue in an inflatable kayak or several days rafting the river with stops each night at riverside lodges. If you have only enough time for a short trip on the river, I'd recommend a jet-boat trip down to Hellgate Canyon, which, as mentioned above, is the most scenic spot on this section of the river. **Hellgate Jetboat Excursions,** 966 SW Sixth St., Grants Pass (© **800/648-4874;** www.hellgate.com), operates five different jet-boat trips (three of which include a meal at a riverside ranch). Adult ticket prices range from $31 to $56.

Local **white-water-rafting** companies offer half-day, full-day, and multiday trips, with the latter stopping either at rustic river lodges or at campsites along the riverbanks. Area rafting companies include **Rogue Wilderness** (© **800/336-1647** or 541/479-9554; www.wildrogue.com); **Galice Resort,** 11744 Galice Rd., Merlin (© **541/476-3818;** www.galice.com); **Orange Torpedo Trips,** 210 Merlin Rd., Merlin (© **866/479-5061** or 541/479-5061; www.orangetorpedo.com); and **Rogue River Raft Trips,** Morrison's Lodge, 8500 Galice Rd., Merlin (© **800/826-1963;** www.rogueriverraft.com). Expect to pay around $60 to $75 for a half-day and $70 to $100 for a full day. Three-day lodge or camping trips are in the $650 to $800 range.

At several places near Merlin, you can rent rafts and kayaks of different types and paddle yourself downriver. Try **White Water Cowboys,** 210 Merlin Rd., Merlin (© **800/635-2925** or 541/479-0132; www.whitewatercowboys.com); **Galice Resort Store,** 11744 Galice Rd., Merlin (© **541/476-3818;** www.galice.com); or **Ferron's Fun Trips** (© **800/404-2201** or 541/474-2201; www.roguefuntrips.com). Rental rates range from $25 to $40 for inflatable kayaks and from $55 to $95 for rafts.

If **fishing** is your passion, the steelhead and salmon of the Rogue River probably already haunt your dreams. To make those dreams a reality, you'll want to hire a guide to take you where the fish are sure to bite. Good local guide services include Rogue Wilderness (mentioned above), and **Rogue Excursions** (© **800/797-4293** or 541/549-8005; www.fishandraft.com), which charges $390 per boat with two clients.

OTHER THINGS TO SEE & DO

Though most people visiting Grants Pass are here to enjoy the mountains and rivers surrounding the town, history buffs can pick up a free map of the town's historic buildings at the Tourist Information Center. Two small art museums—the **Grants Pass Museum of Art,** 229 SW G St. (© **541/479-3290;** www.gpmuseum.com), and Rogue Community College's **Wiseman Gallery,** 3345 Redwood Hwy. (© **541/956-7339;** www.roguecc.edu/galleries/wiseman.asp)—offer changing exhibits of classical and contemporary art by local and national artists. Rogue Community College also operates the **Fire House Gallery,** 214 SW Fourth St. (© **541/956-7489;** www.rogue cc.edu/galleries/firehouse.asp), in downtown Grants Pass. On the first Friday of each month, art galleries and other stores in downtown stay open late. During this roving gallery party, there's always live entertainment of some sort.

Wildlife Images Rehabilitation & Education Center ⊕, 11845 Lower River Rd. (© **541/476-0222;** www.wildlifeimages.org), is dedicated to nurturing injured birds

---

Moments **To Market, To Market!**

Grants Pass is home to one of the biggest and best farmers' markets in Oregon, and should you be in town on a Saturday any time between March and November, you should be sure to stop by. The open-air **Growers' Market**, Fourth and F streets (© **541/476-5375**; www.growersmarket.org), has not only lots of fresh produce, but jams and jellies, meats and seafoods, pies and cookies, and a wide variety of crafts. The market is open from 9am to 1pm.

---

of prey and other wild animals back to health and then releasing them back into the wild, if possible. The center is 14 miles south of Grants Pass and is open for tours daily by reservation only. Admission is by donation. One of the best things about this place is that you can get closer to the animals than you can at a zoo.

Riverside Park, in the center of town, is a popular place to play, especially in the warmer months when people come to cool off in the river.

About midway between Medford and Grants Pass and about 6 miles off I-5 (take exit 40), you'll find one of Oregon's most curious attractions: the **Oregon Vortex,** 4303 Sardine Creek Rd., Gold Hill (© **541/855-1543**; www.oregonvortex.com). Straight out of *Ripley's Believe It or Not!*, this classic tourist trap is guaranteed to have the kids, and many adults, oohing and aahing in bug-eyed amazement at the numerous strange phenomena that defy the laws of physics. People grow taller as they recede. You, and the trees surrounding the House of Mystery, lean toward magnetic north rather than stand upright. Seeing is believing—or is it? It's open March through May and September through October, daily from 9am to 4pm; June through August, daily from 9am to 5pm (closed Nov–Feb). Admission is $8.75 for adults, $7.75 for seniors, and $6.75 for children 6 to 11.

Also in Gold Hill, you'll find the large **Del Rio Vineyards & Winery,** 52 N. River Rd. (© **541/855-2062**; www.delriovineyards.com), which is just off I-5 at exit 43. With nearly 200 acres of vineyards, Del Rio is one of Oregon's biggest vineyards and sells grapes to wineries across the state. In the winery's tasting room, housed in a historic stagecoach stop built in 1864, you can sample both Del Rio wines and wines produced at other wineries from Del Rio grapes. The tasting room is open daily 11am to 5pm (11am–6pm June–Aug.). You can also taste local wines in downtown Grants Pass at the **Oregon Outpost,** 137 SW G St. (© **541/474-2918**), which also sells a wide variety of gourmet foods from Oregon.

Fourteen miles north of Grants Pass in Sunny Valley, you'll find the **Applegate Trail Interpretive Center,** 500 Sunny Valley Loop, Sunny Valley (© **888/411-1846** or 541/472-8545; www.rogueweb.com/interpretive). This small museum documents the little-known Applegate Trail, which was an alternative to the Oregon Trail. To find the museum, take exit 71 off I-5 and go 2 blocks east. March through May, the museum is open Thursday through Sunday from 10am to 5pm; June through October, it's open daily from 10am to 5pm; and November through February, it's open Friday and Saturday from 10am to 5pm. Admission is $5.95 for adults, $4.95 for seniors and children 13 to 18. The historic Grave Creek covered bridge is adjacent to this museum.

WHERE TO STAY

IN TOWN

The Lodge at Riverside 🏨🏨 You'll likely do a double take when you see the log-cabin lodge fronting this recently renovated and upgraded riverside hotel. Although the original building is built of cinder blocks, it is now painted brown with green trim and looks as if it belongs in a national park. The log-walled lobby is decorated with mounted trophy animals, including a black bear and an elk head. Guest rooms are large and quite plush, with a sort of modern cabin decor. There are overstuffed wicker easy chairs, plus more wicker chairs on the balconies. All the rooms have river views, and most have patios or balconies facing the Rogue. If you can ignore the traffic noise from the adjacent bridge, you can almost imagine you're out in the wilderness. Be aware that there are plans to add a third floor to the lodge in late 2008.

955 SE Seventh St., Grants Pass, OR 97526. ☎ 877/955-0600 or 541/955-0600. Fax 541/955-0611. www.thelodgeat riverside.com. 33 units. $135–$195 double; $325 suite. Children under 12 stay free in parent's room. AE, DISC, MC, V. Rates include continental breakfast. **Amenities:** Outdoor pool; Jacuzzi; laundry service; dry cleaning. *In room:* A/C, TV/VCR, coffeemaker, hair dryer, iron, free local calls, Wi-Fi.

OUTSIDE OF TOWN

Morrison's Rogue River Lodge 🏨🏨 If you're in the area to do a bit of fishing or rafting, I can think of no better place to stay than at Morrison's. Perched on the banks of the Rogue, this fishing lodge epitomizes the Rogue River experience. The main lodge is a massive log building that's rustic yet comfortable, with a wall of glass that looks across wide lawns to the river. Although there are B&B–style accommodations in the main lodge, the cabins seem more appropriate in this setting. The spacious cabins stand beneath grand old trees, and all have good views of the river. Fireplaces will keep you warm and cozy in the cooler months. The dining room serves surprisingly creative four-course dinners ($32–$42). Fishing and rafting trips are the specialty here, but, in addition to amenities listed below, there is also a private beach.

8500 Galice Rd., Merlin, OR 97532. ☎ 800/826-1963 or 541/476-3825. Fax 541/476-4953. www.morrisonslodge.com. 17 units. $240–$410 double. Rates include 2–3 meals per day. Children under 3 stay free in parent's room. AE, DISC, MC, V. Closed mid-Nov to Apr. **Amenities:** Restaurant (Northwest); lounge; outdoor pool; putting green; tennis court; concierge; room service (breakfast only); coin-op laundry. *In room:* A/C, TV/VCR/DVD, dataport, fridge, coffeemaker, hair dryer, free local calls.

Rogue Forest Bed & Breakfast and River Company 🏨 While most of the accommodations along the Rogue River are rustic lodges aimed primarily at anglers, this small B&B is more about romantic retreats in the woods. The two guest suites, one of which is in a separate cabin, have king beds and down comforters, and there are decks for enjoying the forest-shaded views. The owners of this inn can also help you arrange a full-day or half-day rafting trip on the Rogue River while you're here.

12035 Galice Rd., Merlin, OR 97532. ☎ 541/472-1052. www.rogueforest.com. 2 units. May–Oct $210–$230 double; Nov–Apr $175–$195 double. Rates include full breakfast. MC, V. **Amenities:** Jacuzzi. *In room:* Fridge.

Weasku Inn 🏨🏨 *Finds* Located a few miles out of Grants Pass and set beneath towering trees on the banks of the Rogue River, this inn is one of the most memorable lodgings in the state, the quintessential mountain/fishing lodge. The log lodge was built in 1924 and was once *the* area fishing lodge. That was back in the days when Clark Gable, Carole Lombard, Walt Disney, Zane Grey, Bing Crosby, and Herbert Hoover used to stay here. Today, the renovated lodge is once again the sort of place where such luminaries would feel comfortable. Guest rooms, on the second floor of the old log lodge, are spacious and modern and have interesting details such as bent-willow furnishings. The riverside cabins are in a modern lodge style with whirlpool tubs, fireplaces, and private decks.

5560 Rogue River Hwy., Grants Pass, OR 97527. © 800/493-2758 or 541/471-8000. www.weaskuinn.com. 18 units. $195 double; $220–$325 suite/cabin; $395 3-bedroom house. Rates include continental breakfast. Children under 12 stay free in parent's room. AE, DISC, MC, V. 3-night minimum in house. **Amenities:** Laundry service; dry cleaning. *In room:* A/C, TV/VCR, dataport, fridge, coffeemaker, hair dryer, iron, free local calls, Wi-Fi.

Wolf Creek Inn ✦ *(Finds)*   Originally opened in 1883 on the old stagecoach road between Sacramento and Portland, the Wolf Creek Inn is a two-story clapboard building with wide front verandas along both floors. Today the inn, which is 25 miles north of Grants Pass and just off I-5, is the oldest hotel in Oregon and is owned and managed by the Oregon State Parks and Recreation Division. The interior is furnished in period antiques dating from the 1870s to the 1930s. On a winter's night there's no cozier spot than by the fireplace in the downstairs "ladies parlor." The guest rooms are small and comfortably furnished, much as they might have been in the early 1900s. Meals are available in the inn's dining room. All in all, this inn has a genuinely timeless feel. Nearby are hiking trails and a small ghost town.

100 Front St. (P.O. Box 6), Wolf Creek, OR 97497. © 541/866-2474. Fax 541/866-2692. www.thewolfcreekinn.com. 9 units. $80–$107 double; lower rates in winter. Rates include full breakfast. Children under 5 stay free in parent's room. MC, V. **Amenities:** Restaurant (American); lounge. *In room:* A/C, no phone.

CAMPGROUNDS

Along the Rogue River east of Grants Pass, you'll find the very busy **Valley of the Rogue State Park** (© 541/582-1118; www.oregonstateparks.org) just off I-5 near the town of Rogue River. West of Grants Pass, there are several county-operated campgrounds, of which **Indian Mary Park,** near Galice on Merlin-Galice Road in the Hellgate Canyon area, is the nicest. Near Indian Mary Park, you'll also find **Almeda Park,** which is close to the Grave Creek trail head of the Rogue River Trail.

WHERE TO DINE

For tasty sandwiches and panini, don't miss **Trattoria Rosso's,** 225 SE Sixth St. (© 541/476-8708), in downtown Grants Pass. If all you need is a pizza and a microbrew, try **Wild River Brewing & Pizza Co.,** 595 NE F St. (© 541/471-7487; www.wildriverbrewing.com). Alternatively, check out the same company's **Wild River Pub,** 533 NE E St. (© 541/474-4456). For espresso drinks and light meals, visit the **Bluestone Bakery,** 412 NW Sixth St. (© 541/471-1922). **Morrison's Rogue River Lodge,** 8500 Galice Rd., Merlin (© 800/826-1963; www.morrisonslodge.com), serves the best meals on the river. For nonguests, dinners are $32 to $42. Reservations are required. See "Outside of Town," above, for details.

River's Edge ✦ INTERNATIONAL   If you're eager to soak up as much Rogue River atmosphere as you can while you're in Grants Pass, be sure to have a meal at this elegant restaurant on the banks of the river. Three levels of decks outside provide plenty of seating in pleasant weather, and even if you have to eat inside, there are big windows that let you gaze out at the water. The menu is pretty eclectic and includes everything from fish tacos to Asian chicken salad to king crab and lamb chops, but be sure to start with the great calamari. Come for lunch and you'll get good views of the river and save considerably on your bill.

1936 Rogue River Hwy. ℂ 888/511-3343 or 541/479-3938. www.riversedgerestaurant.net. Reservations recommended. Main courses $7–$13 lunch, $9–$33 dinner. AE, DC, MC, V. Sun–Thurs 11am–10pm; Fri–Sat 11am–11pm (closed 1 hour earlier in winter).

Summer Jo's Farm, Garden & Restaurant ★★ *Finds* STEAK/SEAFOOD
Located out in the country on an organic farm growing flowers, herbs, and vegetables, this casual restaurant provides a glimpse of the good life, Grants Pass style. If you like gardens, you'll especially enjoy a meal here in high summer when the gardens are bursting with life and color. The cafe also uses organically grown herbs and produce from the surrounding farm. Dishes here are among the most creative in Grants Pass, and there is even a weekly "epicurean adventure" multi-course dinner to highlight fresh produce from the farm here. Brunch is served inside or outside on the lawn.

2315 Upper River Rd. Loop. ℂ 541/476-6882. www.summerjo.com. Reservations recommended. Main courses $9–$17 brunch, $15–$29 dinner. AE, DISC, MC, V. Wed–Sat 9:30am–2pm and 5–8:30pm; Sun 9:30am–2pm. Closed Jan to mid-Feb. Drive west on G St. and look for the sign; it's 1½ miles from downtown Grants Pass.

4 Oregon Caves National Monument & the Illinois Valley

Cave Junction: 30 miles SW of Grants Pass, 56 miles NE of Crescent City

For many people, U.S. 199 is simply the road to the redwoods from southern Oregon. However, this remote stretch of highway passes through the Illinois Valley and skirts the Siskiyou Mountains, two areas that offer quite a few recreational activities. The Illinois River, which flows into the Rogue River, is an even wilder river than the Rogue, and experienced paddlers looking for real white-water adventures often run its Class V waters. Because the Siskiyou Mountains are among the oldest in Oregon, they support a unique plant community. These mountains are also known for their rugged, rocky peaks, which, though not very high, can be very impressive.

In 2002, a huge forest fire ravaged much of the forest in this area. However, in some areas, the fire only cleared out the underbrush and left the mature trees undamaged. If you are planning on doing hiking around here, be sure to check the status of the area in which you plan to hike.

ESSENTIALS
GETTING THERE   Cave Junction is on U.S. 199 between Grants Pass and the California state line. Oregon Caves National Monument is 20 miles outside Cave Junction on Ore. 46.

VISITOR INFORMATION   For more information on this area, contact the **Illinois River Valley Visitor Center**, 201 Caves Hwy., Cave Junction, OR 97523 (ℂ **541/592-4076**).

EXPLORING THE CAVES
Great Cats World Park   With tigers, leopards, cougars, and other exotic wild cats, this 10-acre wildlife park is one of the most interesting family attractions in southern Oregon. Interactive programs allow visitors to watch as big cats demonstrate their hunting skills. Species here include lions, tigers (including a white tiger), leopards, and other smaller wild cats.

27919 Redwood Hwy., Cave Junction. ℂ 541/592-2957. www.greatcatsworldpark.com. Admission $12 adults, $10 seniors, $8 children ages 4–12. June–Oct daily 10am–6pm; mid-Mar to May and Nov and Feb Sat–Sun 11am–4pm. Park closed Dec to mid-Mar. Located 1¼ miles south of Cave Junction on U.S. 199.

Oregon Caves National Monument ⋔   High in the rugged Siskiyou Mountains, a clear mountain stream cascades through a narrow canyon, and here stands one of southern Oregon's oldest attractions. Known as the marble halls of Oregon and first discovered in 1874, the caves, which stretch for 3 miles under the mountain, were formed by water seeping through marble bedrock. The slight acidity of the water dissolves the marble, which is later redeposited as beautiful stalactites, stalagmites, draperies, soda straws, columns, and flowstone. Guided tours of the caves take about 1½ hours, and up above ground there are several miles of hiking trails that start near the cave entrance. Bear in mind that children under 42 inches tall are not allowed on tours. In summer, there are also candlelight tours and "off-trail" tours that are essentially introductions to spelunking. To reach the monument, take Ore. 46 out of Cave Junction and follow the signs.

19000 Caves Hwy. ℰ **541/592-2100.** www.nps.gov/orca. Admission $8.50 adults, $6 children under 17. Cave tours late Mar to late May and early Oct to late Nov daily 10am–4pm; late May to mid-June and Labor Day to early Oct daily 9am–5pm; mid-June to early Sept daily 9am–6pm. Closed late Nov to mid-Mar.

OTHER THINGS TO SEE & DO IN THE ILLINOIS VALLEY

The Illinois River, when it isn't raging through rock-choked canyons, creates some of the best **swimming holes** in the state. Try the waters at Illinois River Forks State Park, just outside Cave Junction, or ask at the **Wild Rivers Ranger District,** 26568 Redwood Hwy., Cave Junction, OR 97523 (ℰ **541/592-4000;** www.fs.fed.us/r6/rogue-siskiyou), for directions to other good swimming holes in the area. At this ranger station, you can also pick up information and directions for **hiking trails** in the Siskiyous, where the 180,000-acre Kalmiopsis Wilderness is a destination for backpackers. Unfortunately, this wilderness was the site of the huge Biscuit Fire in 2002. This massive blaze burned the entire wilderness and other adjacent forests. Because some areas survived the fire better than others, it is important to check with the ranger station about conditions of trails before heading out hiking.

WINE TOURING

The Cave Junction area is one of the warmest regions of Oregon and consequently produces some of the best cabernet sauvignon and merlot in the state. This is about as far south as you can get and still claim to be producing Oregon wines—just a few more miles and you're in California (though it's still a long way to Napa Valley).

Bear Creek Winery   This winery is affiliated with the nearby Bridgeview Winery and is home to one of the oldest vineyards in Oregon. Open to the public during the summer, the winery produces a wide range of reds and whites and can sometimes have some very good deals.

6220 Caves Hwy., Cave Junction. ℰ **541/592-3977.** www.sv-wine.com. Memorial Day to Labor Day daily noon–5pm. From Cave Junction, drive east on Ore. 46 to just past the 2nd turnoff for Holland Loop Rd.

Bridgeview ⋔   Best known for its distinctive blue bottles, Bridgeview is one of the largest wineries in the state and produces primarily inexpensive white wines. This place is not for wine snobs, but for those who enjoy a pleasant glass of wine with dinner. The tasting room boasts an idyllic setting beside a large pond that is stocked with trout. (Don't forget to feed them.) Whites are usually under $10, while most reds tend to be around $20.

4210 Holland Loop Rd. ℰ **877/273-4843** or 541/592-4688. www.bridgeviewwine.com. Daily 11am–5pm. From Cave Junction, go east on Ore. 46 and turn right on Holland Loop Rd.

Foris Vineyards Winery ⊛ Full-bodied and complex red wines are the hallmark of Foris Vineyards Winery. The pinot noir and cabernet sauvignon/merlot/cabernet Franc blend can be outstanding. They also do very good chardonnay, a popular and inexpensive pinot gris, and even a port. Lots of good values here.

654 Kendall Rd., Cave Junction. ℭ **800/843-6747**. www.foriswine.com. Daily 11am–5pm. Closed major holidays.

WHERE TO STAY

Chateau at the Oregon Caves ⊛ A narrow road winds for 20 miles south from Cave Junction into the Rogue River–Siskiyou National Forest, climbing through deep forests before finally coming to an end in a narrow, steep-walled canyon. At the very head of this canyon stands the Oregon Caves Chateau, a rustic six-story lodge built in 1934. The lodge has thick bark siding, and inside the lobby there is a two-sided marble fireplace and huge fir beams supporting the ceiling. Because the lodge is in a wooded canyon, there are no sweeping vistas. Guest rooms aren't nearly as grand as the lobby, but do have the original Monterey-style furnishings and a rustic mountain-lodge character. A 1930s-style soda fountain (an absolute classic) serves burgers, shakes, and other simple meals, while in the main dining room steak and seafood dinners are available.

P.O. Box 1824, Cave Junction, OR 97523. ℭ **541/592-3400**. Fax 541/592-4106. www.oregoncavesoutfitters.com. 23 units. $80–$115 double; $130–$140 suite. Children under 12 stay free in parent's room. MC, V. Closed late Oct to early May. **Amenities:** 2 restaurants (steak/seafood, American). *In room:* No phone.

Out 'n' About Treehouse Treesort ⊛ *(Finds)* These are by far the most unusual accommodations in southern Oregon: a complex of treehouses. Choices include a Tree Room Schoolhouse, the Swiss Family Complex (complete with swinging bridge to the kids' room), the Peacock Perch, the Cabintree (actually a landlocked cabin), a saloon-style treehouse, and a "Cavaltree" fort (big hit with kids). The Tree Room Schoolhouse has a bathroom and the Treezebo and Forestree have a toilet and sink. Despite the address, Out 'n' About is actually located in the community of Takilma.

300 Page Creek Rd., Cave Junction, OR 97523. ℭ **541/592-2208**. www.treehouses.com. 13 units. $110–$240 double. 2- to 3-night minimum. Rates include full breakfast. MC, V. **Amenities:** Outdoor pool; horseback riding; massage. *In room:* No phone.

CAMPGROUNDS

Although there are no campgrounds in Oregon Caves National Monument, there are a couple of national-forest campgrounds nearby. On the road to the national monument, you'll find **Grayback Campground** and **Cave Creek Campground,** both of which are in forest settings on creek banks.

WHERE TO DINE

Wild River Brewing & Pizza Company ⊛ *(Finds)* PIZZA/DELI If you're a fan of microbrewery ales, a pleasant surprise awaits you in the crossroads community of Cave Junction. This very casual combination pizza parlor and deli also happens to be a respectable little brewery specializing in British ales. The rich and flavorful ales go great with the pizzas. For fans of the unusual, there's a pizza with smoked sausage and sauerkraut and another with avocado and sprouts.

249 N. Redwood Hwy. ℭ **541/592-3556**. www.wildriverbrewing.com. Sandwiches $4.50–$5.50; pizzas $4–$20. DISC, MC, V. Mon–Thurs 11am–9pm; Fri–Sat 11am–10pm; Sun noon–9pm.

5 The Roseburg Area: Lions & Tigers & Wineries

68 miles N of Grants Pass, 68 miles S of Eugene, 83 miles W of Crater Lake National Park

Although primarily a logging mill town, Roseburg is set at the mouth of the North Umpqua River and, consequently, is well situated for exploring one of the prettiest valleys in Oregon. The surrounding countryside bears a striking resemblance to parts of northern California, so it should come as no surprise that there are a half-dozen wineries in the area. The hills south of town also look a bit like an Africa savanna, which may be why the Wildlife Safari park is located here. Today this drive-through wildlife park is one of the biggest attractions in southern Oregon. In downtown Roseburg, you'll find numerous old Victorian homes, and a drive through these old neighborhoods will be interesting for fans of late-19th-century architecture.

ESSENTIALS

GETTING THERE   Roseburg is right on I-5 at the junction with Ore. 138, which leads east up the North Umpqua River to Crater Lake National Park.

VISITOR INFORMATION   For more information on this area, contact the **Roseburg Visitors & Convention Bureau,** 410 SE Spruce St. (P.O. Box 1262), Roseburg, OR 97470 (℮ **800/444-9584** or 541/672-9731; www.visitroseburg.com).

WHAT TO SEE & DO: LOCAL HISTORY & A WILDLIFE PARK

Douglas County Museum of History & Natural History 👁   South of town at the Douglas County Fairgrounds, you'll find this surprisingly well-designed museum. It is housed in an unusual, large building that resembles an old mining structure or mill. Inside are displays on the history and natural history of the region. Pioneer farming and mining displays interpret the settlement of the region, but it's the very large elk that really grabs people's attention. Interesting traveling exhibits often show up here, so it's worth checking to see what is scheduled.

123 Museum Dr. (exit 123 off I-5). ℮ **541/957-7007.** www.co.douglas.or.us/museum. $4 adults, $3 seniors, $2 children 4–17. Mon–Fri 9am–5pm; Sat 10am–5pm; Sun noon–5pm. Closed New Year's Day, Easter, Thanksgiving, and Christmas.

Wildlife Safari 👁👁 (Kids)   This 600-acre drive-through nature park is home to wild animals from around the world. You'll come face-to-face with curious bears, grazing gazelles and zebras, ostriches, and even lumbering elephants and rhinos. You can also visit the educational center or attend an animal show. Convertibles are not allowed in the lion, cheetah, or bear enclosures.

1790 Safari Rd. (off Ore. 42, just outside Winston, which is south of Roseburg). ℮ **541/679-6761.** www.wildlife safari.org. Admission summer $18 adults, $15 seniors, $12 children 4–12, free for children under 4; other months admission discounted $3. Apr–Aug daily 9am–5pm; Sept–Mar daily 10am–4pm. Closed Christmas.

THE NEARBY HISTORIC TOWN OF OAKLAND

About 15 miles north of Roseburg is the historic town of Oakland, which is listed on the National Register of Historic Places. The town was founded in the 1850s, and most of the buildings date from the 1890s. Soaking up the atmosphere on a stroll through town is a pleasant way to spend a morning or an afternoon. You can pick up a self-guided walking-tour map at the **Oakland Museum,** 130 Locust St. (℮ **541/459-3087**), which is housed in an 1893 brick building and contains collections of historic photos, old farm tools, household furnishings, and clothing from Oakland's past. The museum is open daily from 12:30 to 3:30pm, and admission is by donation.

WINE TOURING

The Roseburg area is home to more than half a dozen wineries, all of which are located within a few miles of I-5.

Abacela Winery ★★ This winery produces some of the best red wines in Oregon and has become so popular in the past few years that they have begun releasing their wines when they are still quite young. Tempranillo is the specialty, but they also do an excellent Syrah, and their Dolcetto always sells out quickly. Don't miss this one.

12500 Lookingglass Rd., Roseburg. ① 541/679-6642. www.abacela.com. Daily 11am–5pm. Take exit 119 off I-5, drive west 2 miles, turn right on Lookingglass Rd., and continue 2 miles.

Girardet Wine Cellars & Vineyard ★ This winery is known for its big, bold red wines, and is unique in Oregon for producing Baco Noir. This red wine is made from a hybrid grape that produces wines of deep, inky color. Soft and silky and with low tannins, these wines are very easy drinkers even when they're young. Personally, I love this wine and wish more wineries would make it.

895 Reston Rd., Roseburg. ① 541/679-7252. www.girardetwine.com. Daily 11am–5pm. Closed major holidays. Take Ore. 42 (exit 119) west from I-5 south of Roseburg, go 9 miles, and turn right on Reston Rd. (before Tenmile).

Henry Estate Winery This winery on the bank of the Umpqua River produces a wide range of wines, which are generally not very remarkable. However, they do on occasion produce decent pinot noir. Grapes are grown on a special trellising system known as a Scott Henry trellis, named for the winery's founder and now used all over the world.

687 Hubbard Creek Rd., Umpqua. ① 800/782-2686 or 541/459-5120. www.henryestate.com. Daily 11am–5pm. Closed major holidays. From exit 136 off I-5 at Sutherlin, go west on through Umpqua and cross the Umpqua River.

Hillcrest Vineyard ★★ This winery is worth seeking out if for no other reason than that it's Oregon's oldest continuously operating winery producing wines from vinifera (European) grapes. Vineyards here were first planted in 1961. The current owners of the winery, Dyson and Susan DeMara, are producing the best wines in southern Oregon.

240 Vineyard Lane. ① 541/673-3709. Mar–Dec daily 11am–5pm. From Roseburg, go west on Garden Valley Rd., and turn left on Melrose Rd., right on Doerner Rd., right onto Elgarose Rd., and left onto Vineyard Lane.

MarshAnne Landing Winery Located outside the historic town of Oakland on the site of a former stagecoach stop, this winery specializes in Bordeaux and Rhone varietals. Despite the flying saucers on the labels, the winery's name is a reference to owners Gregory Marsh and Frances Anne Cramer.

381 Hogan Rd., Oakland. ① 541/459-8497. www.marshannelanding.com. Memorial Day weekend to Labor Day weekend Sat–Sun 11am–5pm; other times by appointment. Take exit 142 (Metz Hill) off I-5, drive east on Goodrich Hwy. to a right onto Hogan Rd.

Melrose Vineyards With its tasting room in a converted 100-year-old barn, this vineyard has for many years sold grapes to other Oregon wineries. Today they also produce decent wines from their own grapes. Prices are reasonable for most of their wines. Their merlot can be quite good.

885 Melqua Rd., Roseburg. ① 541/672-6080. www.melrosevineyards.com. Daily 11am–5pm. From Roseburg, go west on Garden Valley Rd., turn left on Melrose Rd., continue almost to the community of Melrose, and turn right on Melqua Rd.

Misty Oaks Vineyard   This is one of the Umpqua Valley's newer wineries, but its wines are already wining awards. The 2005 Gobbler's Knob red blend was particularly good (as was the 2004), but this little winery also does good pinot blanc, pinot gris, and Gewürztraminer. The setting is beautiful.

2955 Cole Rd., Oakland. ✆ **541/459-3558.** www.mistyoaksvineyard.com. Memorial Day weekend to Nov Fri–Sun 11am–5pm. Take exit 136 off I-5 and drive west on Fort McKay Road to a right turn on Cole Road.

Palotai Vineyard and Winery   Here at this little family-run winery you can sample the wines of Hungarian-born Gabor Palotai, who learned winemaking in the Old World. There's a wide range of wines available here, including Palotai's version of Hungary's popular "Bull's Blood" red wine.

272 Capital Lane, Roseburg. ✆ **541/464-8127.** www.palotaiwines.com. Apr–Dec daily 11am–5pm. From Roseburg, go west several miles on Garden Valley Rd., and turn left on Old Garden Valley Rd.

Spangler Vineyards   This small winery just off I-5 is very convenient if you just want to make a quick foray into the world of Oregon wines. They produce a wide range of reds and whites, and their reserve cabernet (around $30) can be excellent.

491 Winery Lane, Roseburg. ✆ **541/679-9654.** www.spanglervineyards.com. Daily 11am–5pm. 5 miles south of Roseburg, take exit 119 off I-5 and go west a half mile.

WHERE TO STAY
IN ROSEBURG
Holiday Inn Express ✦   Although it's located just off I-5, this modern economy hotel also happens to sit on the banks of the Umpqua River, and every room has a balcony and a view of the river. The Jacuzzi is set in a gazebo amid green lawns between the hotel building and the river. Downtown Roseburg and a couple of good restaurants are a short walk away.

375 W. Harvard Blvd., Roseburg, OR 97470. ✆ **800/898-7666** or 541/673-7517. Fax 541/673-8331. www.hiexpress. com. 100 units. $109–$139 double. Rates include continental breakfast. AE, DC, DISC, MC, V. Pets accepted ($10 fee). **Amenities:** Indoor pool; exercise room; Jacuzzi; business center; guest laundry. *In room:* A/C, TV, dataport, coffeemaker, hair dryer, iron, Wi-Fi.

WHERE TO DINE
IN ROSEBURG
Dino's Ristorante Italiano ✦ ITALIAN   Ask anyone in Roseburg where to get the best meal in town, and they'll invariably send you to Dino's, a little Italian restaurant in downtown Roseburg. This is a good place for a romantic dinner or simply to satisfy your Italian-food cravings with the likes of portobello-and-ricotta ravioli or lasagna Bolognese.

404 SE Jackson St. ✆ **541/673-0848.** Main courses $12–$20. AE, DISC, MC, V. Tues–Sat 5–9pm.

Roseburg Station Pub & Brewery ✦ PUB   Another jewel in the McMenamins brewpub crown, the Roseburg Station Pub is a good example of the way McMenamins breathes new life into historic buildings. This restored train station celebrates Roseburg's rail culture and is a casual place for dinner and a microbrew. An eclectic collection of chandeliers decorates the 16-foot ceiling, and street signs from around the world punctuate the room. A straightforward menu features burgers, sandwiches, and a handful of more creative entrees. Be sure to accompany your meal with one of the craft ales for which the McMenamins pubs are famous.

700 SE Sheridan St. ✆ **541/672-1934.** www.mcmenamins.com. Main courses $5.75–$19. AE, DISC, MC, V. Mon–Thurs 11am–11pm; Fri–Sat 11am–midnight; Sun 11am–10pm.

IN OAKLAND

Tolly's *Ⓡ* *(Kids* SODA FOUNTAIN/REGIONAL AMERICAN Since 1964, folks from all over the region have been stopping at Tolly's in downtown Oakland to have dinner or sometimes just a root-beer float or sundae. Housed in a storefront on Locust Street, Tolly's is both an elegant restaurant and an old-fashioned soda fountain. You can hop onto a stool at the counter and sip a cold malted milk shake in a tall glass, or linger over a dinner of steak or salmon.

115 Locust St., Oakland. Ⓒ 541/459-3796. www.tollys-restaurant.com. Reservations recommended for dinner. Main courses $9–$16 lunch, $28–$38 dinner. AE, MC, V. Daily 7am–8:30pm.

NORTH OF ROSEBURG: A SERIOUS ICE-CREAM STOP

Consider yourself very lucky if you happen to be driving north from Roseburg on I-5 on a hot summer day. Respite from the heat lies just off the interstate at the Rice Hill exit ramp, at legendary **K&R Drive Inn** (Ⓒ **541/849-2570**), where every scoop of ice cream you order is actually a double scoop! Remember this before you order two scoops of Rocky Road. The K&R is open daily from 10am to 8 or 9pm in summer, daily from 10:30am to 7 or 8pm in winter.

10

Central Oregon

On the west side of the Cascade Range, rain is as certain as death and taxes. But cross the dividing line formed by the mountains and you leave the deluge behind and enter the region known as central Oregon. The term "central Oregon" is a bit of a misnomer. It does not so much refer to a geographical area as to a recreational region, and it doesn't actually lie in the central part of the state. It does, however, bask under blue skies nearly 300 days of the year—in fact, central Oregon gets so little rain that parts of the region are considered high desert. Such a natural attraction is a constant enticement for Oregonians living west of the Cascades. In summer, people head to central Oregon for golfing, hiking, fishing, rafting, and camping, and in winter they descend on the ski slopes of Mount Bachelor, Oregon's best ski resort.

All this popularity is due to the Cascade Range, which causes a climatological rain-shadow effect that creates a distinct and visible dividing line between the wet west side and the dry east side. Ponderosa pines, rather than Douglas firs and western red cedars, dominate the eastern foothill forests of this region. Farther east, where there is even less annual rainfall, juniper and sagebrush country takes over. It is this classically Western environment that has in part led to the adoption of a Wild West theme in the town of Sisters, which has covered wooden sidewalks and false-fronted buildings (albeit in modern pastel colors).

On closer inspection, however, it becomes evident that it is more than just a lack of rainfall that sets this region apart. Central Oregon's unique volcanic geography provides the scenic backdrop to the region's many recreational activities. Obsidian flows, lava caves, cinder cones, pumice deserts—these are the sorts of features that make the central Oregon landscape unique.

Despite the region's volcanic legacy, the greens and fairways of the region's many golf courses are what come to mind when many people think of central Oregon. The abundant sunshine here has made this area home to most of the state's golf resorts. Between Kah-Nee-Ta in the north and Sunriver in the south, there are half a dozen major golf resorts and dozens of golf courses.

Despite the dryness of the landscape here, water is one of the region's primary recreational draws. The Deschutes River is the state's most popular rafting river, and is fabled among fly anglers for its steelhead runs and its wild red-side rainbow trout. West of Bend, a scenic highway loops past a dozen or so lakes, each with its own unique character and appeal. Closer to Bend, the Deschutes River cascades over ancient lava flows, forming impressive waterfalls that are favorite destinations of area hikers.

However, for solitude and scenic grandeur, most hikers and backpackers head out from Sisters and Bend into the Three Sisters Wilderness, which encompasses its snow-clad namesake peaks. Outside the wilderness, there are also many miles of mountain-biking trails that have made the Bend and Sisters areas the best mountain-biking destinations in the state.

Although the open slopes of Mount Bachelor ski area attract the most visitors in the winter, the area also has many miles of cross-country ski trails, including the state's finest Nordic center (at Mount Bachelor, of course). Snowmobiling is also very popular.

1 North Central Oregon & the Lower Deschutes River

Maupin: 95 miles N of Bend, 100 miles E of Portland, 40 miles S of The Dalles

Dominated by two rivers—the Deschutes and the John Day—north central Oregon is the driest, most desertlike part of this region. It is also the closest sunny-side destination for rain-soaked Portlanders, which has long made it a popular spot for weekend getaways.

Hot springs, canyon lands, and some of the best rafting and fishing in the state are the main draws in this part of central Oregon. For many visitors, the high-desert landscape is a fascinating change from the lushness of the west side of the Cascades. For others it is just too bleak and barren. But there is no denying that the Deschutes River, which flows through this high desert, is one of the busiest rivers in the state. Rafters and anglers descend en masse throughout the year—especially in summer—to challenge the rapids and the red-side trout.

Even if the Deschutes is not your primary destination, this region has several unusual attractions that make it worthwhile for a weekend's exploration. First and foremost of these is the Kah-Nee-Ta Resort, which, with its warm-spring swimming pool and its proximity to Portland, is a powerful enticement after several months of gray skies and constant drizzle west of the Cascades.

Not far from the resort, in the town of Warm Springs, is a fascinating modern museum dedicated to the cultures of Northwest Native Americans. A forgotten page of pioneer days can be found at nearby Shaniko, a ghost town that once made it big as a wool-shipping town. Much older history, up to 40 million years of it, is laid bare in the three units of the John Day Fossil Beds National Monument. If the stark hills of the national monument don't give you enough sense of being in the desert, be sure to visit The Cove Palisades State Park, where three steep-walled canyons have been flooded by the waters of Lake Billy Chinook.

ESSENTIALS

GETTING THERE   Maupin, which is the staging site for most rafting and fishing trips on the lower Deschutes River, is at the junction of U.S. 197, the main route from The Dalles south to Bend, and Ore. 216, which connects to U.S. 26 east of Mount Hood.

VISITOR INFORMATION   For more information on this area, contact the **Maupin Area Chamber of Commerce,** P.O. Box 220, Maupin, OR 97037 (© **541/ 395-2599;** www.maupinoregon.com).

RAFTING, FISHING & OTHER AQUATIC ACTIVITIES

Flowing through a dry sagebrush canyon lined with basalt cliffs, the lower Deschutes River, from the U.S. 26 bridge outside Warm Springs down to the Columbia River, is one of the most popular stretches of white water in Oregon. This section of the river provides lots of Class III rapids, and 1-day **rafting trips** here are very popular.

However, at almost 100 miles in length, the lower Deschutes also provides several options for multiday rafting trips.

Popular 1-day splash-and-giggle trips, which are offered by dozens of rafting companies, usually start just upstream from Maupin and end just above the impressive Sherar's Falls. Some companies also offer 2- and 3-day trips. Rafting companies operating on the lower Deschutes River include **All Star Rafting** (© 800/909-7238; www.asrk.com), which also rents rafts and offers kayaking lessons; **Imperial River Company** (© 800/395-3903 or 541/395-2404; www.deschutesriver.com), which operates a bed-and-breakfast inn for rafters in Maupin; and **Rapid River Rafters** (© 800/962-3327 or 541/382-1514; www.rapidriverrafters.com). Expect to pay around $70 to $95 for a day trip up to around $395 to $445 for a 3-day trip.

If you're just passing through the region but would like to catch a glimpse of some of the lower Deschutes River's more dramatic sections, you can visit **Sherar's Falls,** which are at the Sherar Bridge on Ore. 216, between Tygh Valley and Grass Valley. Native Americans can sometimes be seen dip-netting salmon from the waters of these falls, which can also be reached by following the river road north from Maupin for 8 miles. Just west of Sherar Bridge, you'll also find **White River Falls State Park** (© 800/551-6949; www.oregonstateparks.org), where there are more waterfalls.

The stretch of the Deschutes River from Pelton Dam to the Columbia River is one of Oregon's most legendary stretches of **fishing** water and is managed primarily for wild steelhead and the famed red-side rainbow trout. Together these two types of fish provide fly anglers with nearly year-round action. From the mouth of the river upstream to several miles above Maupin, there are several good access points. Fly-fishing supplies and equipment rentals are available in Maupin at the **Deschutes Canyon Fly Shop,** 599 S. U.S. 197, Maupin (© 866/647-4721 or 541/395-2565; www.fly fishingdeschutes.com).

Twelve miles south of Madras, you'll find one of the most unexpected and unlikely settings in the state. **Lake Billy Chinook,** a reservoir created by the construction of Round Butte Dam in 1964, fills the canyons of the Metolius, Crooked, and Deschutes rivers, and seems lifted straight out of the canyon lands of Arizona or Utah. Here, nearly vertical basalt cliffs rise several hundred feet above the lake waters, and sagebrush and junipers cling to the rocky hillsides. The lake is most popular with waterskiers and anglers who come to fish for kokanee (landlocked sockeye salmon) and bull trout (also known as dolly vardens). **The Cove Palisades State Park** (© 541/546-3412; www.oregonstateparks.org), which is on the south shore, offers easy 3-hour sea-kayak tours of the lake. These inexpensive tours are offered throughout the summer and on a few weekends at other times of year. Reservations are recommended. At the state park, you'll also find boat ramps, a marina, campgrounds, picnic areas, and swimming beaches. There are even houseboats for rent (see below), and at the marina you'll find a restaurant atop a hill overlooking the lake. The park day-use fee is $3.

A NATIVE AMERICAN HERITAGE MUSEUM

The Museum at Warm Springs *★★ (Finds* For thousands of years the Warm Springs, Wasco, and Paiute tribes have inhabited this region and adapted to its environment. At this fascinating, don't-miss museum, you'll learn the history of these peoples. Designed to resemble a traditional encampment and accented by architectural details drawn from the cultures of the three tribes, the museum houses an outstanding collection of regional Native American artifacts. Various styles of traditional houses have been reconstructed at the museum and serve as backdrops for displays on everything from basketry and beadwork to fishing and root gathering. Temporary exhibits, including exhibitions of Native American artwork, fill out the main collection and focus on specific topics.

2189 U.S. 26, Warm Springs. (C) 541/553-3331. www.warmsprings.biz/museum. Admission $6 adults, $5 seniors, $4.50 students, $3 children 5–12. Apr–Oct daily 9am–5pm; Nov–Mar Wed–Sun 9am–5pm. Closed New Year's Day, Thanksgiving, and Christmas.

A GHOST TOWN & A FOSSIL EXCURSION

Between 1900 and 1911, the central Oregon town of **Shaniko** was the largest wool-shipping center in the country, and it claims to have been the site of the last range war between cattle ranchers and sheepherders. However, when the railroad line from the Columbia River down to Bend bypassed Shaniko, the town fell on hard times. Eventually, when a flood washed out the railroad spur into town, Shaniko nearly ceased to exist. Today the false-fronted buildings and wooden sidewalks make this Oregon's favorite and liveliest ghost town. Antiques shops, a wedding chapel, and a historic hotel make for a fun excursion or overnight getaway.

The **John Day Fossil Beds National Monument,** 32651 Ore. 19, Kimberly, OR 97848 (© **541/987-2333;** www.nps.gov/joda), consisting of three individual units separated by as much as 85 miles, preserves a 40-million-year fossil record indicating that this region was once a tropical or subtropical forest. From tiny seeds to extinct relatives of rhinoceroses and elephants, an amazing array of plants and animals has been preserved in one of the world's most extensive and unbroken fossil records.

To see fossil leaves, twigs, branches, and nuts in their natural state, visit the **Clarno Unit** (© **541/763-2203**), 23 miles southeast of Shaniko and U.S. 97. Here, ancient mudflows inundated a forest, and today these ancient mudflows appear as eroding cliffs. At the base of these cliffs, a quarter-mile trail leads past numerous fossils. Although you can't collect fossils in the national monument, you can dig them up behind the Wheeler High School in the small town of **Fossil,** 20 miles east of the Clarno Unit. From the Clarno Unit, it is an 85-mile drive on Ore. 218 and Ore. 19 to the national monument's **Sheep Rock Unit,** which is the site of the monument's **Thomas Condon Paleontology Center** and the **Cant Ranch Historical Museum.** Here you can get a close-up look at numerous fossils and sometimes watch a paleontologist at work. In the summer, the paleontology center is open daily from 9am to 5:30pm; spring and fall, it's open daily from 9am to 5pm, and in winter, it's open daily from 9am to 4pm (closed holidays Thanksgiving to Presidents' Day). The Cant Ranch Museum is open Monday through Thursday from 9am to 4pm. Just north of the visitor center you'll pass **Blue Basin,** where there's an interpretive trail.

From the Sheep Rock Unit, the monument's **Painted Hills Unit** (© **541/462-3961**), along the John Day River 9 miles northwest of Mitchell, is another 30 miles west on U.S. 26. You won't see any fossils here, but you will see strikingly colored rounded hills that are favorites of photographers. The weathering of volcanic ash under different climatic conditions created the bands of color on these hills.

WHERE TO STAY & DINE

In addition to the accommodations listed below, you'll find three modern log cabins for rent on the shore of Lake Billy Chinook at **The Cove Palisades State Park.** These cabins rent for $70 per night for up to five people ($48 Oct–Apr) and are right beside the water. For reservations, contact **ReserveAmerica** (© **800/452-5687;** www.reserve america.com). Houseboats are also available for rent at Lake Billy Chinook. Contact

> **Tips** **Travelers' Tip**
>
> For reservations at Forest Service campgrounds, contact **Recreation.gov** (© 877/444-6777 or 518/885-3639; www.reserveusa.com).

Cove Palisades Marina (© 541/546-3521; www.covepalisadesmarina.com), for $2,695 to $7,395 per week in summer (lower rates in spring and fall), or **Lake Billy Chinook Houseboats**, P.O. Box 1921, Redmond, OR 97756 (© 866/546-2939 or 541/504-5951; www.lakebillychinook.com), for $1,850 to $2,725 per week.

Hotel Condon   Although the town of Condon is way off the beaten path, it is fairly convenient if you have spent the day visiting different units of the John Day Fossil Beds National Monument. This restored historic hotel in downtown Condon has a classic small-town feel, but guest rooms have modern furnishings and good beds. Within the hotel, you'll find an upscale steakhouse.

202 S. Main St., Condon, OR 97823. © 800/201-6706 or 541/384-4624. www.hotelcondon.com. 18 units. $100 double, $125–$165 suite. Rates include continental breakfast. Children 12 and under stay free in parent's room. AE, MC, V. **Amenities:** Restaurant (American); lounge; room service. *In room:* A/C, TV, hair dryer, iron, free local calls, high-speed Internet access, Wi-Fi.

Imperial River Company *(Finds*   Popular primarily with people heading out rafting on the Deschutes River, this lodge may not be your classic B&B, but it is the most comfortable place for many miles around. Guest rooms, all of which have private entrances, sport Oregon themes and have handmade quilts on the beds. The riverview rooms are the best and have whirlpool tubs. Dinner is available, and meals feature local beef and lamb. Imperial River Company also offers a wide variety of rafting trips.

304 Bakeoven Rd., Maupin, OR 97037. © 800/395-3903 or 541/395-2404. Fax 541/395-2494. www.deschutes river.com. 25 units. Apr–Thanksgiving $75–$125 double, $195 suite; Thanksgiving–Mar $50–$85 double, $145 suite. Rates include continental breakfast. Children under 5 stay free in parent's room. AE, DISC, MC, V. Pets accepted ($10). **Amenities:** Restaurant (American/Northwest); lounge. *In room:* A/C, fridge, high-speed Internet access, Wi-Fi.

Kah-Nee-Ta High Desert Resort & Casino *(Kids*   Located 120 miles from Portland and set in a remote high-desert canyon, Kah-Nee-Ta Resort, operated by the Confederated Tribes of the Warm Springs Reservation, is the closest sunny-side resort to rain-soaked Portland. The main attraction here is the resort's huge warm-springs-fed main swimming pool (fed by the spring for which the Warm Springs Reservation is named). Because Kah-Nee-Ta offers a wide range of activities and accommodations, it is particularly popular with families, who tend to stay in the resort's large and modern mountain-lodge-style "Village" rooms, which are located beside the main pool. Couples tend to opt for rooms in the main lodge, which is set high on a hillside adjacent to the resort's casino. Rooms here are quite a bit nicer than at resorts in the Sisters area. Down by the main pool, you'll also find teepees and RV sites. The main dining room has a great view and serves creative Northwest dishes. Salmon bakes and Native American dance performances are all part of a stay here.

P.O. Box 1240, Warm Springs, OR 97761. © 800/554-4786 or 541/553-1112. www.kahneeta.com. 169 units (plus 20 teepees). $89–$166 double; $182–$306 suite or cottage; $69 teepee (for 4 people). Children under 14 stay free in parent's room. MC, V. **Amenities:** 2 restaurants (American/Northwest, American); lounge; casino; 2 outdoor pools; 18-hole golf course and miniature golf; 2 tennis courts; 2 exercise rooms; full-service spa; 3 Jacuzzis; kayak and white-water-rafting trips; bike rentals; horseback riding; game room; courtesy resort shuttle; massage; coin-op laundry. *In room:* A/C, TV, coffeemaker, hair dryer.

CAMPGROUNDS

Downriver from Sherar's Falls, there are many undeveloped campsites along the Deschutes River. At Lake Billy Chinook, west of U.S. 97 between Madras and Redmond, there are several campgrounds. The most developed are the two at **The Cove Palisades State Park.** Reservations can be made through **ReserveAmerica** (© 800/ 452-5687; www.reserveamerica.com). Farther west, up the Metolius arm of the reservoir on F.S. Road 64, you'll find the Forest Service's primitive **Perry South Campground.** A little bit farther west is the **Monty Campground,** which is the lowermost campground on the Metolius River's free-flowing waters.

2 The Sisters Area

108 miles SE of Salem, 92 miles NE of Eugene, 21 miles NW of Bend

Lying at the eastern foot of the Cascades, the small town of Sisters takes its name from the nearby Three Sisters mountains, which loom majestically over the town. Ponderosa pine forests, aspen groves, and wide meadows and pastures surround Sisters, giving it a classic Western setting that the town has taken to heart. Today, Sisters is designed to resemble an old cow town; modern buildings sport false fronts and covered sidewalks. However, the predominantly pastel color schemes are more 1990s than 1890s and make the town feel as though the school marms took control away from the cowboys.

Once just a place to stop for gas on the way to Bend, Sisters has now become a destination in itself. A few miles outside of town is the Black Butte Ranch resort, one of the state's finest golf resorts, and also nearby is the tiny community of Camp Sherman, which has been a vacation destination for nearly a century. Sisters is also Oregon's llama capital, with numerous large llama ranches around the area.

ESSENTIALS

GETTING THERE   Sisters is at the junction of U.S. 20 (which connects I-5 near Corvallis with Bend), Ore. 126 (which links Redmond with Eugene), and Ore. 242 (the McKenzie Pass scenic highway). From the Portland area, take I-5 south to Salem and then take Ore. 22 east. Allegiant Air, Horizon Air, and SkyWest Airlines (United Express and Delta Airlines) serve **Roberts Field/Redmond Municipal Airport,** 2522 SE Jesse Butler Circle (© 541/548-0646, ext. 3499; www.flyrdm.com), the Redmond airport, 20 miles east of Sisters.

VISITOR INFORMATION   Contact the **Sisters Area Chamber of Commerce,** 291 E. Main St. (P.O. Box 430), Sisters, OR 97759 (© 541/549-0251; www.sisters chamber.com).

FESTIVALS   During the annual **Sisters Outdoor Quilt Show** on the second Saturday in July, buildings all over town are hung with quilts. The **Sisters Rodeo & Parade,** held the second weekend of June, also attracts large crowds. In early September, American music, from blues to bluegrass, is celebrated during the **Sisters Folk Festival** (© 541/549-4979; www.sistersfolkfestival.com). In late September or early October, sisters get together for a weekend in Sisters during the **Sisters in Sisters** festival (© 541/549-0251; www.sistersinsisters.com).

ENJOYING THE OUTDOORS

Although shopping may be the number-one recreational activity right in Sisters, the surrounding lands are the town's real main attraction. Any month of the year, you'll find an amazing variety of possible activities within a few miles of town. Northwest of Sisters, in the community of Camp Sherman, is one of the area's most unusual outdoor attractions—the springs that form the **headwaters of the Metolius River.** Cold, crystal-clear waters bubble up out of the ground and, within only a few hundred yards, produce a full-blown river. Follow signs from the Camp Sherman turnoff on U.S. 20.

FLY-FISHING   If you need some fly-fishing supplies or want to hire a guide to take you out on the local waters, try **The Fly Fisher's Place,** 151 W. Main Ave., Sisters (© **541/549-3474;** www.flyfishersplace.com). The folks here can guide you to the best **fly-fishing** spots on the Metolius, Deschutes, McKenzie, and Crooked rivers.

GOLFING   With its red-cinder sand traps, **Aspen Lakes Golf Course,** 16900 Aspen Lakes Dr. (© **541/549-GOLF;** www.aspenlakes.com), is the area's most distinctive golf course (green fees $45–$70). At **Black Butte Ranch** (© **800/399-2322** or 541/595-1500; www.blackbutteranch.com), west of Sisters, you'll find two courses surrounded by ponderosa pines and aspens (green fees $45–$69). At **Eagle Crest,** 1522 Cline Falls Rd., Redmond (© **877/818-0286;** www.eagle-crest.com), east of Sisters, you get a more desertlike experience with junipers and sagebrush surrounding the fairways (green fees $35–$90). There are great views at both resorts. Another good golf value can be found at the **Crooked River Ranch Golf Course,** 5010 Clubhouse Rd., Crooked River Ranch (© **800/833-3197** or 541/923-6343; www.crookedriver ranch.com), which is northwest of Redmond off U.S. 97 and plays through and alongside a spectacular canyon (green fees $41–$46 in summer).

HIKING   West and south of Sisters, several excellent scenic trails lend themselves to both day hikes and overnight trips. Many of these trails lead into the Mount Washington, Mount Jefferson, and Three Sisters wilderness areas. Near Camp Sherman, you can hike to the summit of Black Butte for 360-degree views or hike along the spring-fed Metolius River (try starting at the beautiful blue section of river beside the Wizard Falls Fish Hatchery). Farther west off U.S. 20, you'll find trails leading up to the base of craggy Three Fingered Jack. South of town there are trails heading into the Three Sisters Wilderness. (The Chambers Lakes area is particularly scenic.) The hike up Tam McArthur Rim is another good one if you're looking for spectacular views. Stop by the **Sisters Ranger Station,** Pine Street and U.S. 20 (© **541/549-7700;** www.fs.fed.us/r6/centraloregon), at the west end of town, for information and trail maps.

    To the east of Sisters outside the town of Terrebonne, there are several miles of very scenic hiking trails within **Smith Rock State Park** (© **800/551-6949** or 541/548-7501; www.oregonstateparks.org), a park known primarily for its superb rock climbing. The park's 400-foot crags and the meandering Crooked River provide the backdrops for hikes through high desert scrublands. Hiking trails lead through the canyon and up to the top of the rocks. The view of the Cascades framed by Smith Rock is superb. There is a $3 day-use fee here.

HORSEBACK RIDING   If Sisters has put you in a cowboy or cowgirl state of mind, you can saddle up a palomino and go for a ride at **Black Butte Stables** (© **541/595-2061;** www.oregoncowboy.com), which has stables at Black Butte Ranch west of Sisters. These stables offer a variety of rides, with an hour ride costing $40.

MOUNTAIN BIKING   Sisters makes an excellent base for mountain bikers, who will find dozens of miles of trails of all skill levels within a few miles of town. In fact, one fun, easy ride, the Peterson Ridge Trail, starts on Elm Street only a few blocks south of downtown's many shops. Other fun rides include the Butte Loops Trail around Black Butte and the strenuous Green Ridge Trail. Stop by the **Sisters Ranger Station,** Pine Street and U.S. 20 (© **541/549-7700**), at the west end of town for information and trail maps. You can rent bikes in town at **Eurosports,** 182 E. Hood Ave. (© **541/549-2471**), for $20 to $35 per day.

ROCK CLIMBING   Located east of Terrebonne, **Smith Rock State Park** is one of central Oregon's many geological wonders. Jagged rock formations tower above the Crooked River here and attract rock climbers from around the world. A couple of shops in the area cater primarily to climbers. If you want to learn how to climb, contact **First Ascent Climbing Services** (© **800/325-5462** or 541/548-5137; www.go climbing.com), which offers classes ($250 for an all-day private class).

OTHER AREA ATTRACTIONS

Rail-travel enthusiasts might consider an excursion on the **Crooked River Dinner Train,** U.S. 97 at O'Neil Road, Redmond (© **541/548-8630;** www.crookedriver railroad.com). The 38-mile, approximately 3-hour rail excursion travels from Redmond to Prineville and back. Restored dining cars are the setting for dinners or brunches that may feature train-robbery or murder-mystery themes. Fares are $69 to $79 for adults and $39 for children 3 through 12. Reservations are required.

Fans of folk art should be sure to stop by the **Petersen Rock Gardens & Museum,** 7930 SW 77th St., Redmond (© **541/382-5574**), 9 miles north of Bend just off U.S. 97. This 4-acre folk-art creation consists of buildings, miniature bridges, terraces, and tiny towers all constructed from rocks. The gardens, built between 1935 and 1952 by a Danish immigrant farmer, are open daily from 9am to dusk (until 7pm in summer). The museum here is open daily from 9am to 5:30pm in summer and from 9am to 4:30pm in winter. Admission is $3 for adults, $1.50 for children 12 to 16, and 50¢ for children 6 to 11.

If, after a hard day of playing in the outdoors, you need a massage (or a facial or a detox wrap), make a reservation at **Shibui,** 720 Buckaroo Trail (© **541/549-6164;** www.shibuispa.com), a beautiful Asian-inspired day spa affiliated with the luxurious FivePine Lodge & Conference Center.

WHERE TO STAY

Black Butte Ranch (★★ (*Kids*)   Located 8 miles west of Sisters, the Black Butte Ranch resort community has the most breathtaking mountain views of any Central Oregon resort and is set amid aspen-ringed meadows. Add a pair of golf courses, 18 miles of paved biking/jogging paths, and lots of recreational activities and you have a great family vacation resort. The biggest drawback is that, because this is a condominium development, rooms and vacation homes here are very hit and miss. The accommodations are set amid open lawns between the forest and the meadows, and most have fireplaces and kitchens. In the majority of rooms, large decks and sliding glass doors let you enjoy the views. In the resort's main dining room, which serves good steaks, large windows provide nearly every table with a view of the mountains or adjacent lake. In winter, you're a long way from Mount Bachelor's ski slopes, though the slopes at Hoodoo Ski Area are nearby.

P.O. Box 8000, Black Butte Ranch, OR 97759. © **866/901-2961** or 541/595-6211. www.blackbutteranch.com. 124 units. May–Oct $110–$235 condo, $200–$250 cabin, $175–$390 home; Nov–Apr $85–$190 condo, $150–$200 cabin, $150–$295 home. 2- to 6-night minimum July–Aug. AE, DC, DISC, MC, V. **Amenities:** 2 restaurants (American); lounge; 4 outdoor pools and 1 indoor pool; 2 18-hole golf courses; 23 tennis courts; exercise room; full-service spa; 2 Jacuzzis; sauna; watersports rentals; bike rentals; horseback riding; children's programs; game room; massage. *In room:* TV, dataport, coffeemaker.

FivePine Lodge & Conference Center ★★

Set beneath shady ponderosa pines on 15 acres on the edge of Sisters, this collection of Craftsman-style cottages was an instant classic when it opened in 2007. The main building, with its stone walls, grand fireplace, and mission-style furnishings, is the quintessential mountain lodge, while the large cottages offer space, luxury and more Arts and Crafts styling. In all the rooms, you'll find fireplaces and huge bathrooms with big soaking tubs and tiled showers. Patios and balconies, with their Adirondack chairs, are the perfect place to linger over a glass of wine at the end of a summer day. On the pretty grounds, through which winds an artificial stream, you'll find a spa, health club, movie theater, restaurant, and, by summer 2008, a brewpub and outdoor pool. A gift shop sells fly-fishing supplies.

1021 Desperado Trail, Sisters, OR 97759. © 866/974-5900 or 541/549-5900. Fax 541/549-5200. www.fivepine lodge.com. 32 units. June–Sept $179–$209 suite or cottage; Oct–May $139–$179 suite or cottage. Rates include continental breakfast and nightly wine reception. AE, DISC, MC, V. Pets accepted ($20 per day). **Amenities:** Restaurant (Northwest); lounge; health club with indoor pool; full-service spa; bikes; room service. *In room:* A/C, TV/DVD, fridge, coffeemaker, hair dryer, iron, high-speed Internet access, Wi-Fi.

The Lodge at Suttle Lake ★

Set on the shores of Suttle Lake, just east of Santiam Pass, this mountain lodge sports a classic Adirondack decor. Throw in an ornately carved front door and some very detailed chainsaw art in the lodge lobby, and you have the quintessential Cascadian mountain lodge. In the main lodge, the large lake-view rooms are the ones to ask for, or, for even more space, go for a cabin with a loft sleeping area and complete kitchen. While some of the cabins go a bit overboard with the cutesy cabin decor, these are still immensely comfortable accommodations, the best you'll find at any lakeside setting in the state.

13300 U.S. 20, Sisters, OR 97759. © 541/595-2628. Fax 541/595-2267. www.thelodgeatsuttlelake.com. 24 units. $135–$240 double; $135–$425 cabin. 2-night minimum in summer; 3- to 4-night minimum on holidays. AE, DISC, MC, V. **Amenities:** Restaurant (American); lounge; boat rentals; bike rentals. *In room:* TV, high-speed Internet access.

Metolius River Resort ★ *Finds*

Despite the name, this hardly ranks as a resort. However, it's perfect for those seeking peace and quiet or a romantic getaway. Set on the banks of the crystal-clear, spring-fed Metolius River 14 miles west of Sisters, the contemporary cedar-shingled two-story cabins are exceptional, offering modern amenities and styling with a bit of a rustic feel. Peeled-log beds, wood paneling, river-stone fireplaces, and green roofs give the cabins a quintessentially Western appeal. The Metolius River is legendary as the most difficult trout-fishing stream in Oregon, and the cabins here are particularly popular with trout anglers. Not far away, you'll find the springs of the Metolius, where the river comes welling up out of the ground.

25551 SW F.S. Rd. 1419, Camp Sherman, OR 97730. © 800/81-TROUT. www.metoliusriverresort.com. 11 cabins. $235 double. 2- to 3-night minimum. MC, V. **Amenities:** Restaurant (Northwest). *In room:* TV/VCR/DVD, dataport, kitchen, fridge, coffeemaker, hair dryer, free local calls.

CAMPGROUNDS

About a dozen Forest Service campgrounds are strung out along F.S. Road 14 north of Camp Sherman. All of these campgrounds are on the banks of the Metolius River and are most popular with anglers. The **Camp Sherman Campground** is only a half-mile north of Camp Sherman. South of Sisters, at the end of F.S. Road 16, there are three campgrounds at or near Three Creek Lake. None of these campgrounds take reservations.

WHERE TO DINE

No visit to Sisters is complete without a stop at the **Sisters Bakery,** 251 E. Cascade St. (© **541/549-0361**), for marionberry pastries and bear claws. For light meals or just a glass of wine, stop by **Cork Cellars,** 161A Elm St. (© **541/549-2675;** www. corkcellars.com), a combination wine bar and wine shop. For meals with a view of the mountain, you can't beat the **Restaurant at Black Butte Ranch** (see "Where to Stay," above).

Bronco Billy's Ranch Grill and Saloon   STEAK/SEAFOOD/MEXICAN Located in the old Hotel Sisters building (no longer a hotel), Bronco Billy's serves up good old-fashioned Wild West grub in the form of belt-loosening platters of barbecued ribs, steaks, and green-chile burgers. Step through the swinging saloon doors leading from the dining room to the bar and you'll find genuine Western decor, including various trophy animal heads on the walls.

190 E. Cascade St. © **541/549-7427.** www.broncobillysranchgrill.com. Reservations recommended. Main courses $9–$27. MC, V. Daily 11:30am–9 or 10pm (winter Mon–Thurs 3–9 or 9:30pm, Fri–Sun 11:30am–9 or 9:30pm).

Jen's Garden 🌟🌟🌟 NORTHWEST   Quite simply, the dinner I had recently at this red cedar-shingled cottage restaurant was the best meal I had all year in Oregon. I opted for the prix fixe menu with wine pairings, and you should, too. Every course had some sort of delightful flavor surprise, and every wine was distinctive. Flavors in such dishes as a caramelized sweet-onion tart with red-wine syrup, roasted duck breast over chopped pineapple with a ginger-port reduction and mixed berry bread pudding, and a frozen terrine of fresh figs and ginger, were both complex and subtle. While the dining room is wonderfully romantic, I love the back patio.

403 E. Hood Ave., Sisters. © **541/549-2699.** www.intimatecottagecuisine.com. Reservations highly recommended. Main courses $25; 5-course prix fixe dinner $49, $69 with wine. MC, V. Summer Tues–Sun 5–8 or 9pm; other months Wed–Sun 5–8 or 9pm.

Kokanee Café 🌟🌟 *Finds* NORTHWEST   This out-of-the-way place, located about 14 miles west of Sisters adjacent to the Metolius River Resort in Camp Sherman, is one of the best restaurants in the region. The interior of the cedar-shingled building is contemporary rustic with an open-beamed ceiling and a wrought-iron chandelier, and out back there's a deck under the ponderosa pines. The menu is short and almost always includes some sort of fresh rainbow trout entree, as well as such interesting dishes as roast duck with lavender-ancho chili glaze. There are also daily specials— often seafood prepared in whatever style is currently the rage. Lots of reasonably priced wines are available by the bottle or glass, with the emphasis on Oregon wines.

25545 SW F.S. Rd. 1419, Camp Sherman. © **541/595-6420.** www.kokaneecafe.com. Reservations highly recommended. Main courses $25–$38. AE, DISC, MC, V. May and Oct–Nov Wed–Sun 5–9pm; June–Sept daily 5–9pm. Closed Dec–Apr.

3 Bend & Sunriver: Skiing, Hiking, Fishing, Mountain Scenery & More

160 miles SE of Portland, 241 miles SW of Pendleton

Situated on the banks of the Deschutes River, Bend is the largest city east of the Oregon Cascades, and the surrounding area has more resorts than any other region in the

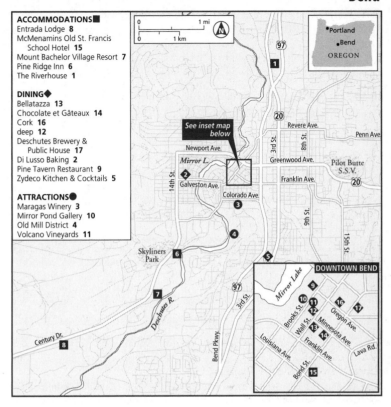

ACCOMMODATIONS■
Entrada Lodge **8**
McMenamins Old St. Francis
   School Hotel **15**
Mount Bachelor Village Resort **7**
Pine Ridge Inn **6**
The Riverhouse **1**

DINING◆
Bellatazza **13**
Chocolate et Gâteaux **14**
Cork **16**
deep **12**
Deschutes Brewery &
   Public House **17**
Di Lusso Baking **2**
Pine Tavern Restaurant **9**
Zydeco Kitchen & Cocktails **5**

ATTRACTIONS●
Maragas Winery **3**
Mirror Pond Gallery **10**
Old Mill District **4**
Volcano Vineyards **11**

state. To understand why a small town on the edge of a vast high desert could attract so many vacationers, just look to the sky. It's blue. And the sun is shining. For the web-foots who spend months under gray skies west of the Cascades, that's a powerful attractant.

However, Bend doesn't end with sunny skies. It is also home to Mount Bachelor, the biggest and best ski area in the Northwest. The pine-covered slopes of several other mountains—the Three Sisters and Broken Top among them—provide a breathtaking backdrop for the city, and out amid the forests on the flanks of those mountains are lakes and trout streams that attract hikers, mountain bikers, anglers, and paddlers. A lively downtown filled with interesting shops, art galleries, excellent restaurants, and attractive Drake Park (which is named for the city's founder, A. M. Drake, and not for the ducks that are the park's major attraction) complements the outdoor offerings of the area.

For several years now, Bend has been one of the fastest-growing cities in Oregon, and it has attracted lots of well-heeled new residents. Many Oregonians complain that Bend now feels more like a California town than an Oregon community, and, what with the pricey restaurants and fancy art galleries, it's hard to argue this point. Still, all the new upscale amenities make this a very pleasant town in which to spend a vacation.

ESSENTIALS

GETTING THERE   Bend is at the junction of U.S. 97, which runs north and south, and U.S. 20, which runs east to west across the state. From the Portland area, the most direct route is by way of U.S. 26 to Madras and then south on U.S. 97.

Allegiant Air, Horizon Air, and SkyWest Airlines (United Express and Delta Airlines) serve **Roberts Field/Redmond Municipal Airport,** 2522 SE Jesse Butler Circle (© **541/548-0646,** ext. 3499; www.flyrdm.com), 16 miles north of Bend. The **Central Oregon Breeze** (© **800/847-0157** or 541/389-7469; www.cobreeze.com) is a shuttle that operates between Portland and Bend, with a stop at the Redmond Airport. Round-trip tickets are $88 for adults, $78 for seniors and students. There are also taxis operating from the Redmond Airport.

VISITOR INFORMATION   Contact the **Bend Visitor & Convention Bureau,** 917 Harriman St., Bend, OR 97701 (© **877/245-8484** or 541/382-8048; www.visit bend.org). You can also contact the **Central Oregon Visitors Association,** 661 SW Powerhouse Dr., Suite 1301, Bend, OR 97702 (© **800/800-8334** or 541/389-8799; www.visitcentraloregon.com).

GETTING AROUND   Car rentals are available at Redmond Municipal Airport from **Avis, Budget, Enterprise,** and **Hertz.** If you need a taxi, call **Owl Taxi** (© **541/ 382-3311**).

FESTIVALS   The **Sunriver Music Festival** (© 541/593-9310; www.sunriver music.org) is a big classical-music binge that takes place in the first half of August. When this festival finishes up, the baton is taken up by the **Cascade Festival of Music** (© **888/545-7435** or 541/382-8381; www.cascademusic.org), which is held the last week in August and the first week in September in Drake Park.

EXPLORING THE BEND AREA

If you'd like to have a guide show you around the area, contact **Wanderlust Tours** (© **800/962-2862** or 541/389-8359; www.wanderlusttours.com), which offers summer canoe trips, winter snowshoe walks, volcano hikes, and even a cave-exploration outing. Rates range from $42 to $105.

The High Desert Museum 🖈🖈🖈 *Kids*   Bend lies on the westernmost edge of the Great Basin, a region that stretches from the Cascade Range to the Rocky Mountains and is often called the high desert. Through the use of historical exhibits, live animal displays, and reconstructions of pioneer buildings, this combination museum and zoo, one of the finest in the Northwest, brings the cultural and natural history of the region into focus. In the main building is a walk-through timeline of Western history, as well as a fascinating exhibit on the region's Plateau Indians. The natural history of the region comes alive in the Desertarium, where live animals of the region can be observed in a very natural setting. Outside, frolicking river otters and slow-moving porcupines are the star attractions, but the birds of prey center is just as interesting. A pioneer homestead and a forestry exhibit with a steam-driven sawmill round out the outdoor exhibits. Informative talks are scheduled throughout the day. The museum's cafe is a good place for lunch.

59800 S. U.S. 97. © 541/382-4754. www.highdesertmuseum.org. Admission $15 adults, $12 seniors, $9 children 5–12. Daily 9am–5pm. Closed New Year's Day, Thanksgiving, and Christmas. Take U.S. 97 3½ miles south of Bend.

Moments **Seeing Stars**

Central Oregon's clear skies not only provide the region with abundant sun-shine but also allow the stars to shine brightly at night. At two area obser-vatories you can get a closer look at those stars. At the small **Pine Mountain Observatory** (© 541/382-8331; http://pmo-sun.uoregon.edu), 26 miles southeast of Bend off U.S. 20, you can gaze at the stars and planets through 15- to 32-inch telescopes. Admission is a $3 suggested donation, and the observatory is open from late May through late September on Friday and Saturday nights with programs starting between 8pm and 9pm, depending on the month.

In the resort community of Sunriver, south of Bend, the **Sunriver Nature Center & Observatory** (© 541/598-4406; www.sunrivernaturecenter.org) has star-gazing programs, with days and hours varying with the seasons. The observatory can be found by following the Nature Center signs through Sunriver. Admission is $6 for adults and $4 for children. There are also day-time solar viewing programs here.

EXPLORING CENTRAL OREGON'S VOLCANIC LANDSCAPE

From snow-covered peaks to lava caves, past volcanic activity and geologic history are visible everywhere around Bend. For a sweeping panoramic view of the Cascade Range, head up to the top of **Pilot Butte** at the east end of Greenwood Avenue. From the top of this cinder cone, you can see all of the Cascades' major peaks—from Mount Hood to Mount Bachelor—every one of which is volcanic in origin.

To the south of Bend lies a region of relatively recent volcanic activity that has been preserved as the **Newberry National Volcanic Monument** (© 541/593-2421; www.fs.fed.us/r6/centraloregon/newberrynvm/index.shtml). The best place to start an exploration of the national monument is at the **Lava Lands Visitor Center,** 58201 S. U.S. 97, 13 miles south of Bend and open from May through mid-October. Here you can learn about the titanic forces that sculpted this region. An interpretive trail out-side the center wanders through a lava flow at the base of 500-foot-tall **Lava Butte** *(¶,* an ominous black cinder cone, and a road leads to the top. From the summit of the cinder cone you have an outstanding view of the Cascades. A $5 Northwest Forest Pass is necessary to visit the Lava Lands Visitor Center. If you don't already have one, you can purchase one here. As you leave the parking lot of the Lava Lands Visitor Center, the side road (F.S. Rd. 9702) to the right leads to the trail head for the impres-sive **Benham Falls** *(¶¶,* which are an easy .8-mile walk from the trail head. Be sure to bring mosquito repellant if you visit the falls during the summer.

A mile to the south, you'll find **Lava River Cave,** which is actually a long tube formed by lava flows. The cave is more than a mile long and takes about an hour to explore. A $5 Northwest Forest Pass is necessary to visit the cave; lanterns rent for $3. The cave is open late June through mid-September daily from 9am to 4:45pm and mid-September to mid-October Wednesday to Sunday from 9am to 4:45pm (no lantern rentals after 4pm). Be sure to bring warm clothes! When lava flowed across this landscape, it often inundated pine forests, leaving in its wake only molds of the trees.

At **Lava Cast Forest,** 9 miles down a very rough road off U.S. 97 south of Lava River Cave, a paved trail leads past such molds. Continuing farther south on U.S. 97 will bring you to the turnoff for the **Newberry Caldera** area, the centerpiece of the monument. Covering 500 square miles, the caldera contains Paulina and East Lakes and numerous volcanic features, including an astounding flow of obsidian. There are rental cabins and campgrounds within the national monument, and 150 miles of hiking trails.

HITTING THE SLOPES & OTHER WINTER SPORTS

If downhill skiing is your passion, you probably already know about the fabulous skiing conditions and myriad runs of **Mount Bachelor** ✮✮✮ (© **800/829-2442,** 541/382-2442, or, for snow reports, 541/382-7888; www.mtbachelor.com), 22 miles west of Bend on the Cascades Lakes Highway. With a 3,365-foot vertical drop, 71 runs, 11 lifts, 6 day-lodges, and 4 terrain parks, it's no wonder this place is so popular. All-day lift tickets are $56 to $66 for adults, $47 to $56 for teenagers 13 to 18, $34 to $42 for children 6 to 12, and free for children 5 and under. There's also a tubing park for families, and for snowboarders, a half pipe with 18-foot walls. The ski area's **Super Shuttle** ($5 each way) operates to and from Bend and leaves from the west side of town at the corner of Colorado Avenue and Simpson Street, where there's a large parking lot.

Cross-country skiers will also find plenty of trails to choose from. Just be sure to stop by a ski shop and buy a **Sno-Park** permit before heading up to the cross-country trails, the best of which are along the Cascades Lakes Highway leading to Mount Bachelor ski area. At the ski area itself, there are 35 miles of groomed trails. Passes to use these trails are $13 to $16 for adults and $8 to $9 for children 6 to 12 years old. Ski shops abound in Bend, and nearly all of them rent both downhill and cross-country equipment. If you're heading to Mount Bachelor, you can rent equipment there, or try the **Powder House,** 311 SW Century Dr. (© **541/389-6234**), on the way out of Bend heading toward Mount Bachelor.

If you've had enough skiing, how about a **dogsled ride?** At **Mount Bachelor** (© **800/829-2442**), you can participate in 1½-hour programs that include a dogsled ride and an orientation session on the care of sled dogs. Rates are $75 for adults, $30 for children under 80 pounds. All-day trips to Elk Lake ($450) are also available.

Easy 1-hour **snowshoe walks** are led by ranger-naturalists on weekends and holidays starting from the **West Village Ski & Sport Building** at Mount Bachelor. For more information, call © **541/383-4771.**

SUMMER ACTIVITIES

If you want to do some mountain hiking without all that uphill slogging, head to **Mount Bachelor** (© **800/829-2442** or 541/382-2442; www.mtbachelor.com), where, from early July to early September, a chair lift operates to the 9,065-foot summit. The fare is $15 for adults, $12 for seniors, and $9 for children ages 6 to 12. From here you may either ride the chair or hike down. The lift also operates on Friday and Saturday evenings in summer for access to Scapolo's, a restaurant high on the slopes of the mountain.

FISHING   If fishing is your passion, you've come to the right place. The Deschutes River flows right through downtown Bend, and good trout waters can be found both upstream and downstream from town. The lakes of the Cascade Lakes Highway west of Bend are, however, the most popular fishing destinations in the area. Of these, Hosmer Lake (a catch-and-release fly-fishing-only lake), and Crane Prairie and Wickiup reservoirs, which are known for their trophy trout, are among the most fabled area fishing spots. If you want to hire a guide to show you where to hook a big one, try contacting **Garrison's Fishing Guide Service** (© **541/593-8394;** www.garrison guide.com). Expect to pay around $175 for a day of fishing. Fly-fishing supplies are available at **The Riffle Fly Shop,** 1255 NE Third St. (© **541/388-3330;** www.the riffleflyshop.com), and in Sunriver at **Sunriver Fly Shop,** 56805 Venture Lane (© **541/593-8814;** www.sunriverflyshop.com).

GOLF   For many of central Oregon's visitors, Bend's abundance of sunshine means only one thing—plenty of rounds of golf at the area's many golf courses. Of the resort courses in the area, the three courses at **Sunriver** (© **541/593-4402;** www.sunriver-resort.com)—Meadows, Woodlands, and Crosswater (open to hotel guests and members only)—are the most highly regarded. Expect to pay anywhere from $55 to $170, depending on which course you play and when.

Right in Bend, you'll find more reasonable prices at the Riverhouse Resort's **River's Edge Golf Course,** 3075 N. Business U.S. 97 (© **541/389-2828;** www.riverhouse.com), where 18 holes will cost you $38 to $80 in the summer. The recently renovated and upgraded **Widgi Creek Golf Club,** 18707 Century Dr. (© **541/382-4449;** www.widgi.com), is another of the area's highly regarded semiprivate clubs. Green fees range from $33 to $100, depending on the season.

HIKING   Hiking is one of the most popular summer activities here, but keep in mind that high-country trails may be closed by snow until late June or early July.

My favorite trail in the Bend area is the **Deschutes River Trail** *𝒜𝒜*, which parallels the Deschutes for nearly 9 miles. Any stretch of this trail is beautiful. To reach the trail, drive the Cascades Lakes Highway 6 miles west from Bend, turn left at a sign for the Meadow Picnic Area, and continue 1⅓ miles to the trail head at the picnic area. Another enjoyable, though strenuous, hike is to the summit of **Pilot Butte,** a cinder cone within the Bend city limits. To find the trail head, drive east from downtown on Greenwood Avenue and watch for signs. For a few more recommended hikes, see "A Scenic Drive Along the Cascade Lakes Highway," below.

The **Three Sisters Wilderness,** which begins just over 20 miles from Bend and Sisters, offers secluded hiking among rugged volcanic peaks. Permits are required for overnight trips in the wilderness area and are available at trail heads. Currently, you'll also need a Northwest Forest Pass (available at the Bend and Sisters ranger stations) to park at area trail heads. Contact the **Bend/Fort Rock Ranger Station,** 1230 NE Third St., Suite A-262, Bend (© **541/383-4000;** www.fs.fed.us/r6/centraloregon), or the **Sisters Ranger Station,** Pine Street and U.S. 20 (© **541/549-7700;** www.fs.fed.us/r6/centraloregon), in Sisters for trail maps and other information.

HORSEBACK RIDING   Down in Sunriver, you can get saddled up and ride the meadows and ponderosa pine forests at **Sunriver Stables** (© **541/593-6995;** www.sunriver-resort.com/stables.php), which offers a variety of rides, with an hour's ride costing $35. Be sure to call for a reservation.

MOUNTAIN BIKING *𝒜𝒜*   Mountain biking is one of the most popular activities in central Oregon, partly because when the snow melts, the cross-country ski trails become mountain-bike trails. Contact the **Bend/Fort Rock Ranger Station,** 1230 NE Third St., Suite A-262 (© **541/383-4000;** www.fs.fed.us/r6/centraloregon), to find out about trails open to mountain bikes. The most scenic trail open to bikes is the Deschutes River Trail mentioned above. Mountain bikes (and touring bikes) can be rented from **Hutch's Bicycles,** 725 NW Columbia St. (© **541/382-9253;** www. hutchsbicycles.com), which charges $25 to $45 per day for mountain bikes. Bikes can also be rented from **Northwest Adventure,** 1346 NW Galveston Ave. (© **541/385-6599;** www.northwestadventure.net).

The **Paulina Plunge** (© **800/296-0562** or 541/389-0562; www.paulinaplunge. com) offers guided mountain-bike rides in Newberry National Volcanic Monument. The outing is an easy downhill ride that includes stops at waterfalls and a natural water slide and costs $60. These tours are outrageously fun, and should not be missed if you're at all athletic. A much wider range of mountain-bike tours is offered by **Cog Wild Bicycle Tours** (© **866/610-4822** or 541/385-7002; www.cogwild.com). Tours vary in length and degree of difficulty, so there's something for every level of rider and a wide range of prices.

KAYAKING & WHITE-WATER RAFTING   The Deschutes River, which passes through Bend, is the most popular river in Oregon for white-water rafting, although the best sections of river are 100 miles north of here (see the earlier "North Central Oregon & the Lower Deschutes River" section for details). However, numerous local companies offer trips both on the lower section of the Deschutes and on the stretch of the upper Deschutes between Sunriver and Bend. This latter stretch of the river is known as the Big Eddy run, and though it is short and really has only one major rapid, it offers a quick introduction to rafting. **Sun Country Tours** (© **800/770-2161** or 541/382-6277; www.suncountrytours.com) does both the Big Eddy run ($44) and the lower Deschutes ($103–$108). **Rapid River Rafters,** 500 SW Bond St., Suite 160 (© **800/962-3327** or 541/382-1514; www.rapidriverrafters.com), also offers full-day trips on the lower Deschutes ($75–$85).

For a much mellower experience, book a kayak tour with **Alder Creek Kayak & Canoe,** 805 SW Industrial Way, Suite 6 (© **877/571-4545** or 541/317-9407; www. aldercreek.com), which leads tours on the gentle waters of the upper Deschutes River ($95). This company also rents canoes and kayaks, with rates starting at $30 for 2 hours, so, if you have a car you can put a boat on top of, you can head out to one of the lakes on the Cascade Lakes Highway. Sparks Lake and Hosmer Lake are my two favorite paddling spots. You can also do an easy flat-water paddle through the community of Sunriver. At **Sunriver Marina** (© **541/593-3492**), which is west of Circle 3 and adjacent to the Trout House restaurant, you can take a two-hour canoe or kayak tour on a beautiful, meandering stretch of the Deschutes River. Tours cost $55 to $90.

A SCENIC DRIVE ALONG THE CASCADE LAKES HIGHWAY 🍁🍁

During the summer, the **Cascade Lakes Highway** is the most popular excursion out of Bend. This National Scenic Byway is an 87-mile loop that packs in some of the finest scenery in the Oregon Cascades. Along the way are a dozen lakes and frequent views of the jagged Three Sisters peaks and the rounded Mount Bachelor. The lakes provide ample opportunities for boating, fishing, swimming, and picnicking. At the **Bend Visitor & Convention Bureau,** 917 Harriman St. (© **877/245-8484** or 541/ 382-8048; www.visitbend.org), you can pick up a guide to the Cascade Lakes National Scenic Byway. Keep in mind that from mid-November to late May, this road is closed west of Mount Bachelor due to snow.

The first area of interest along the highway is **Dutchman Flat,** just west of Mount Bachelor. A thick layer of pumice produces desertlike conditions that support only a few species of hardy plants. A little farther and you come to **Todd Lake,** a pretty little lake a bit off the highway; it's reached by a short trail. Swimming, picnicking, and camping are all popular here.

Sparks Lake, the next lake along this route, is shallow and marshy and has lava fields at its southern end. An easy trail with frequent glimpses of the lake meanders through these forested lava fields. To find this trail, drive to the end of the Sparks Lake access road. The lake is a popular canoeing spot, though you'll need to bring your own boat. At the north end of the lake, closer to the highway, you'll also find the trail head for a popular mountain-biking trail that heads south to Lava Lake. Across the highway from the marshes, at the north end of the lake, is the trail head for **Green Lakes,** a series of small lakes that are in the Three Sisters Wilderness at the foot of Broken Top Mountain. This is one of the most popular backpacking routes in the region and offers spectacular scenery. The hike to Green Lakes can also be done as a day hike. West of the Green Lakes trail head is an area known as **Devils Garden,** where several springs surface on the edge of a lava flow. On a boulder here you can still see a few **Native American pictographs.**

With its wide-open waters and reliable winds, **Elk Lake** is popular for sailing and windsurfing. There are cabins, a lodge, and campsites around the lake. **Hosmer and Lava Lakes** are both known as good fishing lakes, while spring-fed **Little Lava Lake** is the source of the Deschutes River. **Cultus Lake,** with its sandy beaches, is a popular swimming lake. At the **Crane Prairie Reservoir** you can observe osprey between May and October. The **Twin Lakes** are examples of volcanic maars (craters) that have been filled by springs. These lakes have no inlets or outlets.

IN-TOWN EXPLORING

Downtown Bend is full of great shops, women's clothing boutiques, and art galleries, and it's easy to spend an afternoon shopping here. Be sure to check out the works by regional artists at **Mirror Pond Gallery,** 875 NW Brooks St. (© **541/317-9324;** www.mirrorpondgallery.org). On the first Friday of each month, Bend galleries stay open from 5 to 9pm for a gallery walk. Also be sure to check out the shops in the **Old Mill District** (© **541/312-0131;** www.theoldmill.com), a redeveloped area of town that once housed several lumber mills. Today the old mill buildings have been converted into shopping arcades, and new buildings with the look of old mill buildings have been added. You'll find the Old Mill District south of downtown.

It seems you can't go anywhere in Oregon anymore without finding a winery. Bend has two. **Volcano Vineyards,** 930 NW Brooks St. (© **541/617-1102;** www.volcano vineyards.com), which has its tasting room right downtown overlooking Mirror Pond, makes merlot, Syrah, and a red blend from grapes grown in southern Oregon. The tasting room is open Wednesday through Saturday from 11:30am to 6pm and Sunday and Monday from 11:30am to 5pm. At **Maragas Winery,** 643 NW Colorado Ave. (© **541/330-0919;** www.maragaswinery.com), south of downtown, wine labels sport beatnik-theme cartoon art and zinfandel is a specialty. The tasting room is open daily from noon to 5pm.

WHERE TO STAY

EXPENSIVE

Pine Ridge Inn ★★   This small luxury inn on the outskirts of town provides alternative accommodations for anyone who wants first-class surroundings but doesn't need all the facilities (and crowds) of the area's family-oriented resorts. This is an ideal choice for romantic vacations and honeymoons, but it is also a favorite of business travelers who need to be close to town. The inn is set on a bluff high above the Deschutes River, though you'll pay extra for a river view. Whether you get a regular room or a suite, you'll have tons of space that includes features such as sunken living rooms and fireplaces. Lots of antiques and artworks by regional artists add a distinctive style. Although the inn doesn't have a restaurant, there is a complimentary afternoon wine-and-cheese tasting.

1200 SW Century Dr., Bend, OR 97702. ✆ 800/600-4095 or 541/389-6137. Fax 541/385-5669. www.pineridgeinn. com. 20 units. $139–$189 double; $199–$329 suite. Rates include full breakfast. AE, DC, DISC, MC, V. **Amenities:** Access to nearby health club; massage. *In room:* A/C, TV/VCR, dataport, fridge, coffeemaker, hair dryer, iron, free local calls, Wi-Fi.

MODERATE

McMenamins Old St. Francis School Hotel ★ *(Finds*   Attention, lapsed Catholics (and anyone else who ever attended a parochial school): You can finally sleep in class without getting your knuckles smacked by a ruler. McMenamins, the Portland-based brewpub empire, has converted this former Catholic school into the coolest hotel in central Oregon. While guest rooms are simply furnished, they do have wood paneling and feel like cabins. There are also four cute cottages available. What makes this place really special, though, are all the great little bars and garden spaces scattered around the property. There's a pub, of course, plus a cigar bar in an old shed, a billiards room, and a nightclub that features live music. There's also a very comfy movie theater that serves food and beer. After a long day of hiking or skiing, you can soak your muscles in the giant hot tub, which is designed to resemble a classic Turkish bath.

700 NW Bond St., Bend, OR 97701. ✆ 877/661-4228 or 541/382-5174. Fax 541/330-8561. www.mcmenamins.com. 24 units. $119–$164 double; $175–$415 cottage. Children 6 and under stay free in parent's room. AE, DC, DISC, MC, V. **Amenities:** Restaurant (American); 4 lounges; hot soaking pool; movie theater; room service. *In room:* A/C, TV, dataport, coffeemaker, hair dryer, iron, free local calls, high-speed Internet access.

Mount Bachelor Village Resort ★★   Set along the top of a narrow ridge overlooking the Deschutes River, this neatly manicured resort on the road to Mount Bachelor is a somewhat more relaxed version of the family ski-and-summer resorts so common in central Oregon. The resort is close enough to town to make going out for dinner convenient but deep enough in the pine forests to feel away from it all. Keep in mind that this is a condominium resort; most of the accommodations have separate bedrooms, and many have fireplaces and kitchens. For the best views, request a River Ridge condo, right on the edge of the bluff. These rooms are quite simply some of the nicest places to stay in the area, with private outdoor hot tubs on the view decks and whirlpool tubs in the bathrooms. A 2-mile nature trail surrounding the property leads down to the banks of the Deschutes River.

19717 Mount Bachelor Dr., Bend, OR 97702. ✆ 800/583-4923 or 541/389-5900. Fax 541/388-7401. www.mt bachelorvillage.com. 120 units. $139–$189 double; $189–$425 suite/condo. 2-night minimum stay. AE, DC, DISC, MC, V. **Amenities:** Restaurant (Northwest/American); lounge; outdoor pool; 6 tennis courts; access to nearby health club; 2 Jacuzzis; concierge; business center. *In room:* A/C, TV/VCR, dataport, kitchen, fridge, coffeemaker, hair dryer, iron, free local calls, high-speed Internet access, Wi-Fi.

Sunriver Lodge & Resort ★★★ *Kids*   This sprawling resort is less a hotel than a town unto itself, and with a wealth of activities available for active vacationers, it is the first choice of many families vacationing in central Oregon. Most of the lodge accommodations overlook both the golf course and the mountains. My favorite rooms are the loft suites, which have stone fireplaces, high ceilings, and rustic log furniture, although the rooms in the River Lodge building are the most luxurious. Pine trees shade the grounds, and 38 miles of paved bicycle paths connect the resort with the surrounding community. However, no matter how impressive the other facilities are, it is the three golf courses that attract the most business. The resort's main dining room features creative Northwest cuisine and has superb views of the mountains. An adjacent lounge offers a cozy fireplace.

1 Center Dr. (P.O. Box 3609), Sunriver, OR 97707. © 800/801-8765. Fax 541/593-5458. www.sunriver-resort.com. 640 units. $150–$349 double; $169–$339 suite. AE, DC, DISC, MC, V. Pets accepted. **Amenities:** 4 restaurants (Northwest, American); 2 lounges; 2 outdoor pools, 1 indoor pool; 3 18-hole golf courses, 9-hole putting course; 28 tennis courts (3 indoor courts); health club; full-service spa; Jacuzzi; sauna; canoe and kayak rentals; bike rentals; children's programs, concierge; business center; room service; massage; babysitting; laundry service. *In room:* A/C, TV, dataport, minibar, coffeemaker, hair dryer, iron, safe, high-speed Internet access, Wi-Fi.

INEXPENSIVE

Entrada Lodge *Value*   Located a few miles west of Bend on the road to Mount Bachelor ski area, this motel is in a tranquil setting shaded by tall pine trees. Stay here and you'll be just a little bit closer to Mount Bachelor in winter and the region's many lakes and hiking and mountain-biking trails in summer. Although you'll have to drive back into town or to a nearby resort for meals, it's worth that small inconvenience to get such a pleasant setting at economical rates. The Deschutes National Forest borders the property, and a trail leads from the parking lot to the popular Deschutes River Trail, which is only a mile away.

19221 Century Dr., Bend, OR 97702. © 541/382-4080. www.entradalodge.com. 79 units. $79–$99 double; $139 suite. Rates include continental breakfast. AE, DC, DISC, MC, V. Pets accepted ($10 per day). **Amenities:** Outdoor pool; Jacuzzi; coin-op laundry. *In room:* A/C, TV, dataport, coffeemaker, hair dryer.

The Riverhouse ★ *Value*   Located at the north end of town on the banks of a narrow stretch of the Deschutes River, the Riverhouse is one of the best hotel deals in the state; and with its golf course and other resort facilities, it's an economical choice for anyone who wants resort amenities without the high prices. Try to get a ground-floor room; these allow you to step off your patio and almost jump right into the Deschutes. However, the rooms on the upper floor have a better view of this rocky stretch of river. The hotel's main dining room also has a view of the river, and there's a poolside cafe and a lounge that features a variety of live entertainment. Without a doubt, this is the best deal in Bend. Book early.

3075 N. U.S. 97, Bend, OR 97701. © 800/547-3928 or 541/389-3111. www.riverhouse.com. 220 units. $89–$189 double; $135–$265 suite. Rates include continental breakfast. AE, DC, DISC, MC, V. Pets accepted. **Amenities:** 2 restaurants (steak, American); lounge; 2 pools (1 indoor, 1 outdoor); 18-hole golf course; tennis courts; exercise room; Jacuzzi; saunas; business center; room service; coin-op laundry. *In room:* A/C, TV, dataport, refrigerator, microwave, coffeemaker, hair dryer, iron, free local calls, Wi-Fi.

Seventh Mountain Resort ★★ *Kids*   Offering the closest accommodations to Mount Bachelor, this sprawling resort is especially popular with skiers. But summer is still the high season here, and during the warm months, families descend on the property to take advantage of the seemingly endless array of recreational activities. The guest rooms come in a wide range of sizes (most with balconies and/or kitchens). My favorites are the rooms perched on the edge of the wooded Deschutes River canyon. Golfers should note that Widgi Creek Golf Course is adjacent to the resort. In addition to the amenities listed below, the resort also has a roller-skating/ice-skating rink, hiking/jogging trails, a miniature golf course, playgrounds and playing fields, and volleyball and basketball courts. All in all, this is the best place to stay in the immediate Bend vicinity.

18575 SW Century Dr., Bend, OR 97702. ℂ **800/452-6810** or 541/382-8711. Fax 541/382-3517. www.seventh mountain.com. 240 units. $89–$139 double; $129–$209 suite or condo. AE, DC, DISC, MC, V. **Amenities:** 2 restaurants (American); lounge; 3 outdoor pools; 4 tennis courts; exercise room; 3 Jacuzzis; sauna; bike rentals; horseback riding; children's programs; concierge; tour/activities desk; business center; massage; coin-op laundry. *In room:* A/C, TV/DVD, kitchen, fridge, coffeemaker, hair dryer, iron, Wi-Fi.

IN SUNRIVER

The resort community of Sunriver is Oregon's most popular summer destination resort and has hundreds of condos, cabins, and vacation homes at a wide range of prices. **Sunset Realty** (ℂ **877/864-9767** or 541/593-5018; www.sr-sunset.com) is one of the area's biggest rental companies.

CAMPGROUNDS

The closest campground to Bend is **Tumalo State Park,** 5 miles northwest of Bend off U.S. 20. The biggest campground in the area is **La Pine State Park,** which is accessible from U.S. 97 between Sunriver and La Pine. Reservations can be made at these parks through Reserve America (ℂ **800/452-5687;** www.reserveamerica.com).

Of the many campgrounds along the Cascade Lakes Highway, the walk-in **Todd Lake Campground,** 25 miles west of Bend, is my favorite because it is enough of a walk from the parking lot to keep things pretty quiet. **Devil's Lake Campground,** also a walk-in campground, is another favorite of mine. Farther south, there are lots of campgrounds on the many lakes along this road. Two of my favorites are the **Mallard Marsh** and **South** campgrounds, both of which are on beautiful Hosmer Lake. The campgrounds at **Lava Lake** and **Little Lava Lake** are also fairly quiet, and the view from Lava Lake is the finest at any campground on this stretch of road.

WHERE TO DINE
IN BEND

Coffee addicts will want to drop by **Bellatazza,** 869 NW Wall St., #101 (ℂ **541/318-0606**), for good espresso. For rustic bread and sandwiches, drop by **Di Lusso Baking,** 744 NW Bond St. (ℂ **541/312-4036;** www.dilusso.com), or 1135 NW Galveston Ave. (ℂ **541/383-8155**). For pastries and imported Belgian chocolates, don't miss **Chocolate et Gâteaux,** 141 NW Minnesota St. (ℂ **541/318-8457**), in downtown Bend. If it happens to be summer and you're craving a meal with an unforgettable view, head to **Mount Bachelor** (ℂ **541/382-2442;** www.mtbachelor.com) and take the chair lift up to the Pine Marten Lodge, where you can have lunch, dinner, or just drinks at Scapolo's, an Italian restaurant.

Expensive

Cork ⭐⭐ ECLECTIC   Small and romantic, this place is evenly split between its dining room and its wine bar, so whether you're looking to have a romantic dinner or just a glass of wine, this is Bend's top spot for couples. The menu shows a lot of Asian influences but is more fusion than anything else, so expect highly imaginative combinations of flavors and ingredients. You might get something as simple as a braised lamb shank with green-peppercorn demi glace and scallion-feta crushed potatoes or something as unusual as lavender-injected rack of pork with spinach and mission figs on a nest of chive-goat cheese angel hair pasta. Needless to say, there are lots of great wines available by the glass.

150 NW Oregon Ave. © 541/382-6881. www.corkbend.com. Reservations recommended. Main courses $22–$30. MC, V. Tues–Sat 5:30–9 or 9:30pm (wine bar opens at 5pm).

Moderate

deep ✿ PAN-ASIAN   You'll literally be in over your head when you dine at deep. The ceiling of this stylish sushi bar and pan-Asian restaurant is a sheet of glass with water on it. If that doesn't put you in the mood for a Kumamoto oysters with cucumber ice, monkfish pâté with three caviars, or a barbecued eel and crab roll, I don't know what will. Be sure to order the "nine bites," an assortment of nine hot and cold small plates chosen for you by the chef. This dish always packs a lot of great flavors and is a tasty introduction to what this restaurant is all about.

821 NW Wall St. © 541/323-9841. www.deepbend.com. Reservations recommended. Small plates $4–$19. AE, DC, DISC, MC, V. Sun–Thurs 5–9pm; Fri–Sat 5–10pm.

Pine Tavern Restaurant AMERICAN/NORTHWEST   Opened in 1936, the Pine Tavern Restaurant has been a local favorite for generations, and neither the decor nor the view has changed much over the years. Knotty pine and cozy booths give the restaurant an old-fashioned feel, while a 250-year-old ponderosa pine growing up through the center of one dining room provides a bit of grandeur. The menu is designed to appeal to a wide range of tastes and includes such comfort foods as meat loaf and baby back ribs, but the prime rib and the sourdough scones with honey butter are what this place is best known for. Try to get a table in the back room, which overlooks Mirror Pond.

967 NW Brooks St. © 541/382-5581. www.pinetavern.com. Reservations recommended. Main courses $5.50–$13 lunch, $15–$36 dinner. AE, DISC, MC, V. Mon–Sat 11:30am–2:30pm and 5:30–9:30pm; Sun 5:30–9:30pm.

Zydeco Kitchen & Cocktails ✿ NEW AMERICAN   This rather nondescript restaurant on Bend's busy Third Street is one of my favorite restaurants in town. With creative food and good service, Zydeco Kitchen is a far more enjoyable place for dinner than some of the much publicized downtown restaurants. Despite the name, this is not specifically a Cajun or New Orleans–style restaurant, although you can start your meal with wonderful shrimp and grits cakes. After that, I always go for the grilled redfish with Dungeness crab and spicy Zydeco sauce. Be sure to start your meal with a blueberry martini and finish up with the almond wet cake, which is like the classic Latin American *tres leches* cake.

1085 SE Third St. © 541/312-2899. www.zydecokitchen.com. Reservations recommended. Main courses $9–$28. MC, V. Tues–Sat 4:30–9 or 9:30pm.

Inexpensive

Deschutes Brewery & Public House *Value* REGIONAL AMERICAN   For good handcrafted ales (I'm partial to the Mirror Pond Pale Ale and the Obsidian Stout) and a range of pub food more creative and tastier than you'd expect, this bustling pub is the place. The Buffalo wings are some of the best I've ever had and are available in three different renditions. Not only do the cooks do an exemplary job on the normal pub menu, but they also prepare more complex daily specials, and there are daily sausage specials as well. Bring the family—even the ones who don't drink beer.

1044 NW Bond St. ℂ **541/382-9242.** www.deschutesbrewery.com. Main courses $8–$19. AE, DISC, MC, V. Mon–Thurs 11am–11pm; Fri–Sat 11am–midnight; Sun 11am–10pm.

IN SUNRIVER

For the best views and food in Sunriver, make a reservation at the **Meadows at the Lodge** restaurant at Sunriver Lodge (p. 327).

Trout House Restaurant *★ Value* NORTHWEST/AMERICAN   One of the best things about this little restaurant is that it's right on the Deschutes River and is a great place for a waterfront breakfast, lunch, or dinner. It's a popular spot with visitors, so be sure to make reservations during the summer. Seafood predominates, with trout available at all three meals (perhaps hazelnut-crusted with a huckleberry and preserved lemon reduction). Razor clams (in season), smoked seafood pasta, or grilled salmon with pinot noir barbecue sauce can assuage a hunger earned by canoeing on the river or playing a round of golf.

Next to the Marina in Sunriver. ℂ **541/593-8880.** Reservations recommended. Main courses $8–$16 lunch, $16–$34 dinner. DISC, MC, V. Apr–Oct daily 8am–9pm; Nov–Mar Wed–Sun 8am–9pm.

BEND AFTER DARK

For good handcrafted ales and pub food, the **Bend Brewing Co.,** 1019 NW Brooks St. (ℂ **541/383-1599;** www.bendbrewingco.com), is a good alternative to the Deschutes Brewery Public House (see above). In downtown Bend, you'll also find **McMenamins Old St. Francis School Hotel,** 700 NW Bond St. (ℂ **541/382-5174;** www.mcmenamins.com; p. 326), which is home to a pub, several small bars, and a movie theater where you can get McMenamins beers. At **Bendistillery,** 850 NW Brooks St. (ℂ **541/388-6868;** www.bendistillery.com), you can get a martini made with this micro-distillery's own gin or vodka. The gin is made with local juniper berries, and there is a delicious hazelnut-espresso vodka. Hip and retro, the **Astro Lounge,** 147 NW Minnesota Ave. (ℂ **541/388-0116**), is Bend's most popular singles bar.

The **Les Schwab Amphitheater,** 520 SW Powerhouse Dr. (ℂ **541/312-8510;** www.bendconcerts.com), in the Old Mill District, books all kinds of great music each summer. The band shell and big, grassy field have seen the likes of Bob Dylan, James Brown, and Lyle Lovett.

11

Eastern Oregon

So different is eastern Oregon from the wet west side of the Cascades that it is often difficult to remember that it is still the same state. Indeed, the dry eastern ranch lands, deserts, canyons, and mountain ranges of this region have more in common with the landscapes of neighboring Idaho and Nevada. Yet Oregon it is, and though it is remote, the fascinating geography makes it an interesting region to explore.

With huge cattle ranches sprawling across the countryside (cattle greatly outnumber people in these parts), the arts community of Joseph casting western-art bronze statues, and the **Pendleton Round-Up** attracting cowboys and cowgirls from around the country, eastern Oregon is the state's Wild West. This part of the state is also steeped in the history of the Oregon Trail, and although it was to the Willamette Valley that most wagon trains were heading, it is here that signs of their passing 150 years ago still abound. All across this region, **wagon ruts** can still be seen, and the history of the Oregon Trail is chronicled at several regional museums. Although the first pioneers never thought to stop and put down roots in this region, when gold was discovered in the Blue Mountains in the 1860s, fortune seekers flocked to the area. Boom towns flourished and as quickly disappeared, leaving the land to the cattle ranchers and wheat farmers who still call this area home.

Today, however, the region also attracts outdoors enthusiasts. They come to hike and horseback ride in the Eagle Cap Wilderness of the Wallowa Mountains, to bird-watch in the Malheur National Wildlife Refuge, to ski in the Blue Mountains, to explore the deepest canyon in the United States, and to raft and fish the Snake, Owyhee, and Grande Ronde rivers.

Because this region is so far from the state's population centers, it is little visited by west-siders, who rarely venture farther east than the resorts of central Oregon. Eastern Oregon is also so vast, and the road distances so great, that it does not lend itself to quick weekend trips. At the very least, it takes a 3-day weekend to get out to Joseph and the Wallowa Mountains or the Malheur National Wildlife Refuge. Should you travel to this part of the state, leave yourself plenty of time for getting from point A to point B.

1 Pendleton

125 miles E of The Dalles, 52 miles NW of La Grande, 40 miles S of Walla Walla, Washington

If not for its famous woolen mills, few people outside the Northwest would be familiar with the Pendleton name. But because the blankets and clothing long manufactured by the **Pendleton Woolen Mills** (here and at other mills around the region) have gained such a reputation, the name has become as much a part of the West as

Winchester, Colt, and Wells Fargo. Today, Pendleton blankets and clothing are as popular as ever, and this town's mill is one of its biggest attractions.

But what brings even more visitors to town than the mill is a single annual event—the **Pendleton Round-Up.** Located at the western foot of the Blue Mountains in northeastern Oregon, Pendleton prides itself on being a real Western town; and as the site of one of the largest and oldest rodeos in the West, it has a legitimate claim. Each year in mid-September, the round-up fills the town with cowboys and cowgirls, both real and urban. For the rest of the year, Pendleton sinks back into its quiet small-town character and begins preparing for the next round-up.

Once the homeland of the Cayuse, Umatilla, Walla Walla, and Nez Perce Indians, the Pendleton area began attracting settlers in the 1840s, as pioneers who had traveled the Oregon Trail started farming along the Umatilla River. In the 1850s, gold strikes created boomtowns in the nearby mountains, and Pendleton gained greater regional significance. Sheep ranching and wheat farming later became the mainstays of the local economy, and by the turn of the century, Pendleton was a rowdy town boasting dozens of saloons and bordellos. Today Pendleton is a much quieter place, one that few people notice as they rush by on the interstate. But those who do pull off find a quiet town whose downtown historic district is filled with attractive brick buildings and some stately old Victorian homes.

ESSENTIALS

GETTING THERE   I-84 runs east to west through Pendleton. From the south take U.S. 395 and from the north, Ore. 11, which leads to Walla Walla, Washington. **Horizon Airlines** (**℄ 800/547-9308;** www.horizonair.com) has service to the **Eastern Oregon Regional Airport** (www.pendleton.or.us/airport.htm), which is located about 4 miles west of downtown Pendleton.

VISITOR INFORMATION   Contact the **Pendleton Chamber of Commerce,** 501 S. Main St., Pendleton, OR 97801 (**℄ 800/547-8911** or 541/276-7411; www. pendletonchamber.com).

GETTING AROUND   **Hertz** rents cars at the Eastern Oregon Regional Airport.

THE PENDLETON ROUND-UP

The Pendleton Round-Up and Happy Canyon Pageant, held the second week of September each year, is one of the biggest rodeos in the country and has been held since 1910. In addition to daily rodeo events, there's a nightly pageant that presents a history of Native American and pioneer relations in the area. After the pageant, there's live country-and-western music in the **Happy Canyon Dance Hall.** A country-music concert and a parade round out the events. **The Hall of Fame,** 1205 SW Court Ave. (under the south grandstand), holds a collection of cowboy and Indian memorabilia. The city is packed to overflowing during round-up week, so if you plan to attend, reserve early. Tickets sell for $14 to $18, and some types of tickets sell out a year in advance. For more information, contact the **Pendleton Round-Up Association,** 1114 SW Court Ave. (P.O. Box 609), Pendleton, OR 97801 (**℄ 800/457-6336** or 541/276-2553; www.pendletonroundup.com).

EXPLORING PENDLETON

If you happen to be in town any other week of the year, there are still a few things worth doing. This is the hometown of **Pendleton Woolen Mills,** 1307 SE Court

Place (© **800/568-3156** or 541/276-6911), the famed manufacturer of Native American–inspired blankets and classic wool sportswear. At the mill here in Pendleton, the raw wool is turned into yarn and then woven into fabric before being shipped off to other factories to be made into clothing. Tours are offered Monday through Friday at 9 and 11am, and 1:30 and 3pm. Also at the mill is a salesroom that's open Monday through Saturday from 8am to 6pm and Sunday from 9am to 5pm.

At one time there were supposedly 10 miles of underground passages and rooms beneath the streets of Pendleton, where gamblers, drinkers, and Chinese laborers rubbed shoulders. Over the years, these spaces were home to speakeasies and saloons, opium dens, and the living quarters of Chinese laborers who were forbidden to be above ground after dark. On 90-minute walking tours operated by **Pendleton Underground Tours,** 37 SW Emigrant Ave. (© **800/226-6398;** www.pendletonundergroundtours.org), you can learn all about old Pendleton's shady underside. After exploring the underground, you'll visit a former bordello, whose rooms have been decorated much the way they once might have looked. Between March and October, tours are offered Monday through Saturday from 9:30am to 3pm; call for a schedule in other months. Tickets are $10. Reservations are strongly recommended.

At the **Heritage Station/Umatilla County Historical Society Museum,** 108 SW Frazer Ave. (© **541/276-0012;** www.heritagestationmuseum.org), you can learn about the region's more respectable history. The museum is partly housed in the city's 1909 railway depot and contains changing exhibits that focus on regional history, including the Oregon Trail, Pendleton Woolen Mills, and Native American culture. This little museum is well worth a visit, and is open Tuesday through Saturday from 10am to 4pm; admission is $6 for adults and $2 for children.

At the **Pendleton Center for the Arts,** 214 N. Main St. (© **541/278-9201;** www. pendletonarts.org), in a renovated Carnegie Library, there are regularly scheduled art exhibits as well as concerts and other performances.

If you're looking for glimpses of the **Oregon Trail,** head 20 miles west of Pendleton to the town of Echo, where you can see wagon ruts left by early pioneers. There's an interpretive exhibit in town at Fort Henrietta Park on Main Street; and a mile of ruts can also be seen about 5½ miles west of town north of Ore. 320.

EAST OF TOWN: NATIVE AMERICAN HISTORY & A CASINO

East of Pendleton, at exit 216 off I-84, you'll find a complex of attractions operated by the Confederated Tribes of the Umatilla Indian Reservation. Included here is the **Wildhorse Casino Resort,** 72777 Ore. 331 (© **800/654-WILD;** www.wildhorse resort.com), a golf course, a motel, an RV park, and the following museum.

Tamástslikt Cultural Institute ✸✸   This modern museum focuses on the impact the Oregon Trail had on the Native Americans of this region. The exhibits incorporate artifacts, life-size dioramas, and audio and video presentations that document the effect pioneer settlement had on the indigenous Cayuse, Walla Walla, and Umatilla Indians who were living in the region when the first settlers arrived. Exhibits are well done and quite interesting. Worth a stop.

72789 Ore. 331. © 541/966-9748. www.tamastslikt.com. Admission $6 adults; $4 seniors, students, and children; and free for children under 5. Daily 9am–5pm. Closed New Year's Day, Thanksgiving, Christmas.

WHERE TO STAY

Bar M Ranch at Bingham Hot Springs ✸   This historic 3,000-acre dude ranch is about 30 miles northeast of Pendleton in the Blue Mountains. Originally built in

1864, the ranch's buildings were once part of a stagecoach stop. Today the old log building is a rustic lodge for guests. There are also a couple of cabins and the old homestead building. As the name implies, there are hot springs here, which can feel mighty welcome at the end of a long day in the saddle. With its hot-springs-fed swimming pool, horseback riding, petting zoo, recreation barn, and game room, this is the ultimate eastern Oregon family-vacation spot.

58840 Bar M Lane, Adams, OR 97810. ℂ 888/824-3381. www.barmranch.com. 15 units. Mid-May to mid-Sept $476–$504 double, $516–$536 cabin or house; mid-Sept to mid-May $190–$204 double, $210–$220 cabin or house. Lower rates for children under 17. 3-night minimum mid-June to mid-Aug. Rates include all meals, horseback riding twice per day (horseback riding not included in off season). MC, V. **Amenities:** Dining room (American); swimming pool; hot tub; horseback riding; bikes; game room; coin-op laundry. *In room:* No phone.

The Pendleton House Bed and Breakfast 🐾🐾　Built in 1917, this Italianate villa is only 2 blocks from downtown Pendleton and is surrounded by colorful perennial gardens. As befits the villalike surroundings, a formal atmosphere reigns. The Gwendolyn Room, with its fireplace and semiprivate balcony, is the best room in the house; and in the Mandarin Room, you'll find the original Chinese wallpaper and Asian styling. Throughout the inn, there are plenty of antiques. Guest rooms share a bathroom, but what a bathroom it is, with the original multiple-head shower and lots of big old porcelain fixtures.

311 N. Main St., Pendleton, OR 97801. ℂ 800/700-8581 or 541/276-8581. Fax 541/276-2827. www.parkerhouse bnb.com. 6 units (all with shared bathroom). $100–$135 double. Rates include full breakfast. AE, MC, V. *In room:* A/C, no phone.

Wildhorse Casino Resort 🐾　Whether or not you're interested in gambling, the Wildhorse Casino Resort is a good place to stay in the area. Not only are the rooms modern and comfortable, but there are also plenty of recreational amenities, including the casino with its casual restaurant. The Tamástslikt Cultural Institute (p. 333) is also nearby. The hotel is 4 miles east of Pendleton and has nice views of the nearby foothills of the Blue Mountains.

72777 Ore. 331, Pendleton, OR 97801. ℂ 800/654-9453. www.wildhorseresort.com. 100 units. $70–$90 double; $109–$119 suite. AE, DISC, MC, V. **Amenities:** 4 restaurants (American); indoor pool; 18-hole golf course; Jacuzzi; sauna; room service; coin-op laundry. *In room:* A/C, TV, coffeemaker, hair dryer, iron, free local calls.

Working Girls Hotel 🐾 (Finds　Pendleton likes to play up its Wild West heritage, and there was a time when brothels were legal here. The historic building that now houses the Working Girls Hotel was just such an establishment, and although female companionship doesn't come with the rooms anymore, you will get comfortable accommodations. The rooms all have private bathrooms, but only one of these is actually in the room; all others have their bathrooms directly across the hall. The hotel is operated in conjunction with Pendleton Underground Tours.

17 SW Emigrant Ave., Pendleton, OR 97801. ℂ 800/226-6398 or 541/276-0730. 5 units. $50–$70 double. MC, V. No children permitted. *In room:* A/C, no phone.

WHERE TO DINE

If you're looking for someplace to get a sandwich or a bowl of soup, drop by **The Great Pacific Wine and Coffee Company,** 403 S. Main St. (ℂ **541/276-1350;** www. greatpacific.biz). Cookies, muffins, truffles, and other sweets round out the menu.

Raphael's Restaurant 🐾🐾　NORTHWEST　This restaurant has long been Pendleton's best fine-dining establishment and should be your top choice for dinner while you're in town. Housed in a 1904 Queen Anne–style home, the restaurant is

known for its Indian-style salmon (made with huckleberry purée), hickory-smoked prime rib, elk chops, and a variety of fettuccines.

233 SE Fourth St. © **888/944-CHEF** or 541/276-8500. www.raphaelsrestaurant.com. Reservations recommended. Main dishes $17–$34. AE, DISC, MC, V. June 1–Sept 15 Tues–Sat 5–9pm; Sept 16–May 31 Tues–Thurs 5–8pm, Fri–Sat 5–9pm.

2 La Grande, Baker City & the Blue Mountains

La Grande: 260 miles E of Portland, 52 miles SE of Pendleton; Baker City: 41 miles SE of La Grande, 75 miles NW of Ontario

Though pioneers traveling the Oregon Trail in the 1840s found good resting places in the Powder River and Grande Ronde valleys, where Baker City and La Grande now stand, few stayed to put down roots in this remote region. It would not be until the 1860s that pioneers actually looked on these valleys as places to live and make a living. However, even those first pioneers who just passed through left signs of their passage that persist to this day. **Wagon ruts** of the Oregon Trail can still be seen in this region, and outside of Baker City stands the most interesting and evocative of the state's museums dedicated to the Oregon Trail experience.

By 1861, however, the Blue Mountains, which had been a major impediment to wagon trains, were crawling with people—gold prospectors, though, not farmers. A gold strike in these mountains started a small gold rush that year, and soon prospectors were flocking to the area. The gold didn't last long—when mining was no longer financially feasible, the miners left the region. In their wake, they left several ghost towns, but the prosperity of those boom times also gave the region's larger towns an enduring legacy of stately homes and opulent commercial buildings, many built of stone that was quarried in the region. Today, the historic commercial buildings of Baker City, the ornate Victorian homes of Union, and the Elgin Opera House are reminders of past prosperity. Although the gold has played out, signs of those raucous days, from gold nuggets to ghost towns, are now among the region's chief attractions.

One of the most arduous and dangerous sections of the Oregon Trail—the crossing of the Blue Mountains—lies just west of present-day La Grande. These mountains are no longer the formidable obstacles they once were, but they are still among the least visited in Oregon. The Blues, as they are known locally, offer a wide variety of recreational activities, including skiing, hiking, mountain biking, fishing, camping, and even soaking in hot springs. With their numerous hotels and restaurants, both La Grande and Baker City make good bases for exploring this relatively undiscovered region.

ESSENTIALS

GETTING THERE   Both La Grande and Baker City are on I-84. La Grande is at the junction of Ore. 82, which heads northeast to Joseph and Wallowa Lake. Baker City is at the junction of Ore. 7, which runs southwest to John Day, and Ore. 86, which runs east to the Hells Canyon National Recreation Area.

VISITOR INFORMATION   Contact the **Baker County Chamber of Commerce and Visitors Bureau,** 490 Campbell St., Baker City, OR 97814 (© **800/523-1235** or 541/523-5855; www.visitbaker.com), or **Union County Tourism,** 102 Elm St., La Grande, OR 97850 (© **800/848-9969** or 541/963-8588; www.visitlagrande.com).

OREGON TRAIL SITES

Oregon Trail history is on view west of La Grande, in downtown Baker City, and just north of Baker City. At the **Oregon Trail Interpretive Park at Blue Mountain**

Crossing (© 541/963-7186), at exit 248 off I-84, you'll find a .5-mile trail that leads past wagon ruts in the forest. Informational panels explain the difficulties pioneers encountered crossing these rugged mountains. On most weekends between Memorial Day and Labor Day, there are living history programs as well.

National Historic Oregon Trail Interpretive Center Atop sagebrush-covered Flagstaff Hill, just north of Baker City, stands a monument to the largest overland migration in North American history. Between 1842 and 1860, an estimated 300,000 people loaded all their worldly belongings onto wagons and set out to cross the continent to the promised land of western Oregon. Their route took them through rugged landscapes, and many perished along the way. This museum commemorates the journeys of these hardy souls, who endured drought, dysentery, and starvation in the hopes of a better life. Through the use of diary quotes, a life-size wagon-train scene, artifacts, and interactive exhibits, the center takes visitors through every aspect of life on the trail. Outside, a trail leads to ruts left by the wagons on their journey west.

22267 Ore. 86, Baker City. © 541/523-1843. http://oregontrail.blm.gov. $5 adults, $3.50 seniors, free for children 16 and under. Apr–Oct daily 9am–6pm; Nov–Mar daily 9am–4pm. Closed New Year's Day, Thanksgiving, and Christmas.

Oregon Trail Regional Museum In a large building that once housed Baker City's public swimming pool, this museum is filled with pioneer memorabilia, as well as an extensive mineral collection.

2480 Grove St., Baker City. © 541/523-9308. Admission $5 adults, $4.50 seniors. Late Mar to Oct daily 9am–5pm.

EXPLORING LA GRANDE & BAKER CITY

Five miles east of La Grande, you'll find the steaming waters of Hot Lake, on the banks of which local bronze sculptor David Manuel has a bronze foundry, sculpture park, art gallery, and fire-truck and wagon museums. Manuel and his family are also restoring the historic hospital building that stands on the shores of Hot Lake, and there are plans to add a bed-and-breakfast, a restaurant, and spa. Be sure to check on the status of this attraction when you are in the area. For information, contact **Hot Lake Springs,** 66172 Ore. 203, La Grande (© 541/963-HOTL; www.hotlakeresort.com).

Not far from Hot Lake, in the community of Cove, you can sample locally made wines at the **Gilstrap Brothers Vineyard & Winery,** 69789 Antles Lane, Cove (© 866/568-4200 or 541/568-4646; www.gilstrapbrothers.com). This winery makes a wide range of red wines. Call for hours.

At the Baker City Visitors and Convention Bureau, you can pick up a brochure that outlines a **walking tour** of the town's most important historic buildings, including the restored **Geiser Grand Hotel,** which, when it first opened, was one of the finest hotels in the west. (See "Where to Stay," below, for details.)

If you'd like to take a look inside one of Baker City's restored old homes, drop by the **Adler House Museum,** 2305 Main St. (© 541/523-9308), a stately Victorian structure. Everything on the second floor, from the wallpaper to the furniture, is original, dating to the 1890s. The first floor has been refurbished and decorated to look the way it might have more than 100 years ago. The museum is open from May through September, Friday through Monday from 10am to 2pm. Admission is $5 per adult.

Baker City's fortunes were made by gold mines in the Blue Mountains, and if you'd like to see some samples from those golden years, stop in at the **U.S. Bank** on Main

---

Tips **An Almost Grand Old Opera House**

In the town of **Elgin,** 18 miles north of La Grande on Ore. 82, you can take in a play or concert at the restored **Elgin Opera House Theater,** 104 N. Eighth St. (© 541/437-2014), which was built in 1912. The opera house is also home to a small historical museum that's open Tuesday through Friday from 10am to 4pm between mid-May and mid-October. Admission is $2.

Street in Baker City. The gold collection here includes a nugget that weighs in at 80.4 ounces.

OUTDOOR ACTIVITIES
SPRING THROUGH FALL
If you're interested in **bird-watching,** head out to the **Ladd Marsh Wildlife Area,** 59116 Pierce Rd. (© 541/963-4954; www.dfw.state.or.us), 5 miles south of La Grande off I-84 at the Foothill Road exit (exit 268). March through May, the refuge has lots of waterfowl, and in summer, the wetland is home to sandhill cranes, geese, ducks, avocets, black-necked stilts, and numerous raptors. Also keep an eye out for elk. The best way to visit this area is by walking the 1-mile nature trail east of I-84 near exit 268.

The **hot springs** of this region have been attracting people since long before the first white settlers arrived, and you can still soak your sore muscles in thermal waters at **Lehman Hot Springs** (© 541/427-3015; www.lehmanhotsprings.com), which is in a remote forested setting near Ukiah, 38 miles west of La Grande on Ore. 244. Here you'll find a large hot swimming pool, perfect for an afternoon of lounging around. There are also two smaller and hotter soaking pools, as well as an unheated swimming pool. Also on the premises are campsites and some rustic accommodations, and nearby there are hiking, mountain-biking, cross-country-skiing, and snowmobiling trails. In summer, the springs are open Wednesday through Friday from 10am to 8pm and Saturday and Sunday from 9am to 8pm. (Call for hours the rest of the year.) Admission is $7.

In summer, there are plenty of nearby trails for hiking or mountain biking. My favorite trails are those that radiate out from Anthony Lake, high in the Elkhorn Mountains 45 minutes from Baker City. These trails start at an elevation of over 7,000 feet and meander through open forests with views of craggy granite peaks. The 8-mile loop hike from Anthony Lake up the Elkhorn Crest Trail to Dutch Flat Saddle and back to Anthony Lake via Crawfish Basin Trail makes a good day hike. By the way, the campground at Anthony Lake might just be my favorite campground in the state. Contact the Wallowa-Whitman National Forest's, **La Grande Ranger District,** 3502 Ore. 30, La Grande, OR 97850 (© 541/963-7186), or **Baker Ranger District,** 3285 11th St., Baker City, OR 97814 (© 541/523-4476), for more information. On the Internet, visit www.fs.fed.us/r6/w-w.

If you happen to have your golf clubs with you, play a round at Union's **Buffalo Peak Golf Course,** 1224 E. Fulton St. (© 866/202-5950 or 541/562-5527; www. buffalopeakgolf.com), a scenic and challenging 18-hole course on the outskirts of Union. Green fees run $26 to $30 for 18 holes.

WINTER SPORTS & ACTIVITIES

With the highest base elevation and the most powderlike snow in the state, **Ski Anthony Lakes** (☎ 541/856-3277; www.anthonylakes.com), 45 minutes west of Baker City, is a good little ski area—small, but with a nice variety of terrain. Daily lift tickets are $35. You'll also find good, groomed cross-country ski trails here, and the area is very popular with snowmobilers.

Winter is also the best time of year to see some of the region's Rocky Mountain elk. Each year December through February, the Oregon Department of Fish & Wildlife feeds a large herd of elk at the **Elkhorn Wildlife Area,** 61846 Powder River Lane (☎ 541/898-2826), in North Powder, about halfway between La Grande and Baker City. You can usually see between 100 and 150 elk. During the Christmas holidays, **T and T Tours** (☎ 541/856-3356; www.tnthorsemanship.com) takes visitors out to the feeding area by horse-drawn wagon. Tours last about a half-hour and cost $6 for adults and $4 for children. To reach Elkhorn, take exit 285 off I-84 and follow the WILDLIFE VIEWING signs.

THE ELKHORN MOUNTAIN SCENIC LOOP

Rising up on the outskirts of Baker City is the Elkhorn Range of the Blue Mountains. A paved loop road winding up and around the south side of these mountains features scenic vistas, access to the outdoors throughout the year, and even a couple of sparsely inhabited ghost towns. Start this loop by heading south out of Baker City on Ore. 245 and then take Ore. 7 west to **Sumpter,** 30 miles from Baker City.

As you approach Sumpter, you'll notice that the valley floor is covered with large piles of rocks. These are the tailings (the refuse left after the mining operations have worked over the land), from the Sumpter Dredge, preserved as the **Sumpter Valley Dredge State Heritage Area** (☎ 541/894-2486; www.oregonstateparks.org). Between 1935 and 1954, the ominous-looking dredge laid waste to the valley floor as it sat in its own little pond sifting through old streambed gravel for gold. Although you can stop and view the dredge any time of year, between May and October it is possible to board the strange machine (open daily 9am–5pm), which has a few interpretive exhibits on board. Admission is by donation.

In its wake, the dredge left 6 miles of tailings that formed hummocks of rock and gouged-out areas that have now become small ponds. Although such a mining-scarred landscape isn't usually scenic, the Sumpter Valley is surprisingly alive with birds attracted to the ponds.

A favorite way of visiting the Sumpter Dredge is aboard the **Sumpter Valley Railroad** (☎ 866/894-2268 or 541/894-2268; www.svry.com), which operates a classic steam train on a 5-mile run from west of Phillips Reservoir to the Sumpter Valley Dredge. This railway first began operation in 1890 and was known as the stump dodger. Excursions are operated on Saturdays, Sundays, and holidays from Memorial Day weekend through September; round-trip fares are $13 for adults, $12 for seniors, and $8 for children 6 to 16.

Gold kept Sumpter alive for many decades, and a bit of gold-mining history is still on display in this rustic mountain town, which, though it has a few too many people to be called a ghost town, is hardly the town it once was. In the boom days of the late 19th and early 20th century, Sumpter boasted several brick buildings, hotels, saloons, and a main street crowded with large buildings. However, when a fire destroyed the town in 1917, it was never rebuilt. Today, only one brick building and a few original wooden structures remain.

Continuing west on a winding county road for 14 miles will bring you to **Granite** ⟨⟨, another ghost town with a few flesh-and-blood residents. The weather-beaten old buildings on a grassy hillside are the epitome of a Western ghost town, and most buildings are marked. You'll see the old school, general store, saloon, bordello, and other important town buildings.

Beyond Granite, the road winds down to the North Fork of the John Day River and then heads back across the mountains by way of the Anthony Lakes area. Although Anthony Lakes is best known for its small ski area, in summer there are hiking trails (see above) and fishing in the area's small lakes. The vistas in this area are the best on this entire loop drive, with rugged, rocky peaks rising above the forest. Also in this same area, you'll catch glimpses of the irrigated pastures of the Powder River Valley far below.

Coming down onto the valley floor, you reach the tiny farming community of Haines, which is the site of the **Eastern Oregon Museum,** 610 Third St. (⟨⟨ **541/856-3233**), a small museum cluttered with all manner of artifacts of regional historic significance. It's open May 15 to September 15 Thursday through Monday from 9:30am to 4:30pm; admission is by donation. Here in Haines you'll also find the Haines Steakhouse (see below), a favorite of area residents.

WHERE TO STAY
IN LA GRANDE
Stange Manor Bed & Breakfast ⟨⟨   This Georgian colonial mansion, built in the 1920s, looks a bit like the White House and is the best place to stay in La Grande. It's filled with beautiful woodwork and comfortable guest rooms, a couple of which have the original bathroom and lighting fixtures and even original decor and furniture. The best deal here is the three-room suite, which has a fireplace and a sun porch that has been converted into a sleeping room. Breakfasts are elegant affairs served in the formal dining room.

1612 Walnut St., La Grande, OR 97850. ⟨⟨ **888/286-9463** or 541/963-2400. www.stangemanor.com. 4 units. $110 double; $130–$145 suite. Rates include full breakfast. MC, V. Children over 12 are welcome. *In room:* Dataport, hair dryer, iron, Wi-Fi.

IN UNION
The Union Hotel ⟨⟨ *(Value*   Although Union today is a sleepy town, it was once the county seat and a booming little place. This grand little hotel first opened its doors in 1921, and now, after an extensive renovation, it has become one of eastern Oregon's more interesting historic hotels. Surrounded by lawns and shade trees, the three-story brick hotel goes a long way toward conjuring up Union's lively past. The lobby, with its white-tile floor, could be straight out of a movie set, while the upstairs guest rooms are decorated in various themes. To make the most of a visit here, try to stay in the room with the whirlpool tub. Although Union is 14 miles from La Grande, the location is still fairly convenient for exploring this region.

326 N. Main St. (P.O. Box 569), Union, OR 97883. ⟨⟨ **888/441-8928** or 541/562-6135. www.theunionhotel.com. 16 units. $39–$119 double. Children welcome, though over 8 years old preferred. AE, DISC, MC, V. *In room:* No phone.

IN BAKER CITY
Geiser Grand Hotel ⟨⟨⟨ *(Finds*   Built in 1889 at the height of the region's gold rush, the Geiser Grand is by far the grandest hotel in eastern Oregon. With its corner turret and clock tower, the hotel is a classic 19th-century Western luxury hotel. In the center of the hotel is the Geiser Grill dining room, above which is suspended the

largest stained-glass ceiling in the Northwest. Throughout the hotel, including in all the guest rooms, ornate crystal chandeliers add a crowning touch. Guest rooms also feature 10-foot windows, most of which look out to the Blue Mountains. The two cupola suites are the most luxurious and evocative of the past. These two suites also have whirlpool tubs. Meals are served both in the formal dining room and in the much more relaxed 1889 saloon. No trip to eastern Oregon is complete without a stay at this grande dame of the old West.

1996 Main St., Baker City, OR 97814. © 888/434-7374 or 541/523-1889. Fax 541/523-1800. www.geisergrand. com. 30 units. $79–$119 double; $129–$229 suite. Children under 12 stay free in parent's room. AE, DISC, MC, V. Pets accepted ($15 per night). **Amenities:** 2 restaurants (American); lounge; access to nearby health club; room service; massage. *In room:* A/C, TV/VCR/DVD, dataport, hair dryer, iron, free local calls, high-speed Internet access, Wi-Fi.

CAMPGROUNDS

You'll find several national forest campgrounds along the Elkhorn National Scenic Byway, including **Union Creek Campground** (© **541/523-4476;** www.fs.fed.us/r6/ w-w; reservations not taken), which is on the shore of Phillips Reservoir southeast of Baker City. Others can be found near Anthony Lakes.

WHERE TO DINE
IN LA GRANDE

For good pastries and fresh-baked bread, stop in at **Kneads,** 1113 Adams Ave. (© **541/963-5413;** www.kneadsbakery.com).

Foley Station ☆ AMERICAN   Located in a historic building in downtown La Grande, Foley Station is this town's most sophisticated restaurant. While the restaurant has long been known for its breakfasts (especially the Belgian waffles), it's also a good place for lunch and dinner. At lunch, try the reuben or the oyster stew, while at dinner, there are good steaks and pasta dishes. On weekends, you can get prime rib.

1114 Adams Ave. © **541/963-7473.** www.foleystation.com. Reservations recommended for dinner. Main dishes $8.50–$50 dinner. DISC, MC, V. Mon–Sat 10:30am–10pm; Sun 7am–10pm.

Ten Depot Street ☆ *(Value* STEAK/SEAFOOD   Housed in a historic brick commercial building, this restaurant has a classic 19th-century feel, complete with a saloon on one side. Although the steaks and prime rib are what most people order, the salads are large and flavorful, and there are even some vegetarian dishes. There are inexpensive nightly specials. There's live music (usually rock) in the bar on the weekends.

10 Depot St. © **541/963-8766.** Reservations recommended. Main courses $8–$26. AE, MC, V. Mon–Sat 5–10pm.

IN THE BAKER CITY AREA

For pub food and microbrews, there's **Barley Brown's Brew Pub,** 2190 Main St. (© **541/523-4266**). For espresso, try **Mad Matilda's Coffee House,** 1917 Main St. (© **541/523-4588;** www.madmatildas.com). If it's a hot day, stop in at **Charley's Ice Cream Parlor,** 2101 Main St. (© **541/524-9307**).

Baker City Café ☆ SANDWICHES/PIZZA   Locals flock to this casual, downhome spot not only for its good pizzas and but also for its fun country-clutter sort of decor. If you're not in the mood for pizza, there are sandwiches, soups, and a daily pasta dish.

1840 Main St. © **541/523-6099.** Sandwiches $7.50–$8; pizzas $16–$27. MC, V. Mon–Fri 7am–3pm; Sat 11am–2pm.

Geiser Grand ☆ AMERICAN   Located in the central court of the historic Geiser Grand Hotel, this restaurant, with its stained-glass ceiling, conjures a gold rush–era

Chinese History in Eastern Oregon

In the town of John Day, the fascinating little **Kam Wah Chung & Co. Museum** (☆☆ (ⓒ **541/575-2800**), on Northwest Canton Street adjacent to City Park, is well worth a visit. It preserves the home and shop of a Chinese doctor who, for much of the first half of the 20th century, administered to his fellow countrymen laboring here. The building looks much as it might have at the time of the doctor's death and contains an office, a pharmacy, a general store, and living quarters. It's open May through October only, daily from 9am to 5pm. Admission is free.

You'll find more Chinese history in Baker City, where an old Chinese cemetery can be seen on Allen Street, just east of exit 304 off of I-84. This cemetery has a modern Chinese pavilion that was built in Souzhou, China, designed by the same company that built the Portland Classical Chinese Garden. The Pendleton Underground Tours in Pendleton (p. 333) also focus on the region's Chinese history.

elegance. Mesquite-smoked prime rib and the wide variety of steaks are always good bets, but this restaurant is also committed to serving excellent fresh seafood dishes, including line-caught wild salmon. There are also plenty of pasta dishes. Before or after dinner, you'll need to spend a little time in the 1889 saloon just to complete your historical evening. At lunch you can order a buffalo burger.

Geiser Grand Hotel, 1996 Main St. ⓒ **541/523-1889.** www.geisergrand.com. Reservations recommended. Main courses $11–$29. AE, DISC, MC, V. Daily 7am–9pm.

Haines Steakhouse ☆ STEAK   Thick, juicy steaks are the specialty of the house here, but it's the decor as much as the food that attracts people. Log walls and booths, a chuck-wagon salad bar, mounted buffalo and elk heads, a totem pole, and an old buggy keep diners amused as they eat. This is a longtime favorite in the area.

910 Front St., Haines. ⓒ **541/856-3639.** www.hainessteakhouse.com. Reservations recommended. Main courses $7–$23. AE, DISC, MC, V. Mon and Wed–Fri 5–10pm; Sat 4–10pm; Sun 1–9pm.

3 Joseph, Enterprise & the Wallowa Mountains

Joseph: 355 miles E of Portland, 80 miles E of La Grande, 125 miles N of Baker City

The Wallowa Mountains, which stand just south of the town of Joseph, are a glacier-carved range of rugged beauty that has been called both the Alps of Oregon and the Little Switzerland of America. Though the range is small enough in area to drive around in a day, it is big on scenery and contains the largest designated wilderness area in the state: the **Eagle Cap Wilderness.**

In the northeast corner of the mountains lies Wallowa Lake, which was formed when glacial moraines blocked a valley that had been carved by the glaciers. With blue waters reflecting the rocky peaks, the lake has long attracted visitors. In the fall, the lake also attracts bald eagles that come to feed on spawning kokanee salmon, which turn a bright red in the spawning season.

The town of Joseph, just north of Wallowa Lake, is a center for the casting of West-ern-themed **bronze sculptures,** and there are several art galleries and foundries in the area. With its natural beauty, recreational opportunities, and artistic bent, this corner of the state today has more to offer than any other area in eastern Oregon.

ESSENTIALS

GETTING THERE   Ore. 82 connects Joseph to La Grande in the west, and Ore. 3 heads north from nearby Enterprise to Lewiston, Idaho, by way of Wash. 129.

VISITOR INFORMATION   For more information, contact the **Wallowa County Chamber of Commerce,** 115 Tejaka Lane (P.O. Box 427), Enterprise, OR 97828 (© **800/585-4121** or 541/426-4622; www.wallowacountychamber.com).

FESTIVALS   Check out the rowdy **Chief Joseph Days Rodeo** (www.chiefjoseph days.com), over the last full weekend in July. In mid-July, the Nez Perce hold their annual **TamKaLiks Celebration** (www.wallowanezperce.org) and powwow in the nearby town of Wallowa. The **Alpenfest,** on the third weekend after Labor Day, is the other big annual event in the area.

EXPLORING JOSEPH

Though the lake and mountains are the main attractions of this area, the presence of several bronze foundries in Joseph and Enterprise has turned the area into something of a Western art community. Along Main Street in Joseph, you'll find several galleries that specialize in bronze statues and Western art. You'll also find more than half a dozen life-size bronze wildlife and Western art sculptures in sidewalk gardens along Main Street. Joseph's **Valley Bronze of Oregon** has a gallery at 18 S. Main St. (© **541/ 432-7445;** www.valleybronze.com), and is one of the largest bronze foundries in the country. Tours of the foundry ($15 per person) are offered daily and begin at the gallery. **Parks Bronze,** 331 Golf Course Rd., Enterprise (© **541/426-4595**), offers foundry tours Monday through Thursday. Tours are $8 per person, with a $24 mini-mum. For more information on area artists, visit the website of **Joseph Oregon Artists** (www.josephoregonartists.com).

At the **Wallowa County Museum,** 110 S. Main St. (© **541/432-6095;** www.co. wallowa.or.us/museum), you can see pioneer artifacts, displays on the Nez Perce Indi-ans, and other items donated to the museum by local families. This old-fashioned community museum is housed in a former bank building and is open daily from 10am to 5pm between Memorial Day and the third weekend in September.

On Saturdays between June and the end of October, you can go for a train ride on the **Eagle Cap Excursion Train** (© **800/323-7330** or 541/963-9000; www.eaglecap train.com). Trains run between Wallowa and Joseph or between Elgin and Minam, and fares range from $65 to $85 for adults.

OUTDOOR ACTIVITIES

Down at the south end of Wallowa Lake, you'll find **Wallowa Lake State Park** (© **541/432-4185;** www.oregonstateparks.org), where there is a swimming beach, picnic area, and campground. Adjacent to the park is the **Wallowa Lake Marina** (© **541/432-9115;** www.wallowalakemarina.com), where you can rent canoes, row-boats, paddleboats, and motorboats (first weekend in May to mid-Sept). This end of the lake has an old-fashioned mountain resort feel, with pony and kiddy rides, go-cart tracks, miniature golf courses, and the like. It is also the trail head for several trails into the Eagle Cap Wilderness. The park is home to numerous large deer, which have become accustomed to begging for handouts from campers. Although the deer are entertaining, they are still wild animals and can be dangerous.

For a different perspective on the lake, ride the **Wallowa Lake Tramway,** 59919 Wallowa Lake Hwy. (✆ **541/432-5331;** www.wallowalaketramway.com) to the top of 8,200-foot Mount Howard. This is the steepest tramway in America and provides great views both from the gondolas and from the summit of Mount Howard. The views take in Wallowa Lake and the surrounding jagged peaks. The tramway operates between late May and September, daily from 10am to 4pm (July through Labor Day until 5pm); the fare is $20 for adults, $17 for students 12 to 17, and $13 for children 4 to 11. Food is available at the **Summit Grill & Alpine Patio.**

Because most hikes on the north side of the Wallowas start out in valleys and can take up to a dozen miles or so to reach the alpine meadows of the higher elevations, there aren't a lot of great day hikes here. The **backpacking,** however, is excellent. If you're looking for **day hikes,** try taking the tramway to the top of Mount Howard, where there are about 2 miles of easy walking trails with great views. If you'd like to head into the **Eagle Cap Wilderness** to the popular **Lakes Basin** or anywhere else in the Wallowas, you'll find the trail head less than a mile past the south end of the lake. For more information on hiking in the Wallowas, contact the **Wallowa Valley Ranger District,** 88401 Ore. 82, Enterprise, OR 97828 (✆ **541/426-4978;** www.fs.fed.us/ r6/w-w). This ranger station also serves as the Wallowa Mountains Visitor Center and has interesting displays on the flora and fauna of the region.

Horse packing into the Wallowas is a popular activity, and rides of a day or longer can be arranged through **Eagle Cap Wilderness Pack Station,** 59761 Wallowa Lake Hwy., Joseph, OR 97846 (✆ **800/681-6222** or 541/432-4145; www.eaglecapwilderness packstation.com), which offers trips into the Eagle Cap Wilderness during the summer. These stables also offer hourly, half-day, and full-day rides.

This region also offers some of the best **trout fishing** in Oregon, and if you're looking for a guide to take you to the best holes, contact **Eagle Cap Fishing Guides,** P.O. Box 865, Joseph, OR 97846 (✆ **800/940-3688;** www.eaglecapfishing.com), or the **Joseph Fly Shoppe,** 203 N. Main St., Joseph, OR 97846 (✆ **541/432-4343;** www. josephflyshop.com). Expect to pay anywhere from $365 to $375 for a day of fishing for one or two people.

In winter, the Wallowas are popular with cross-country and backcountry skiers. Check at the ranger station in Enterprise for directions to trails. You'll also find a small downhill ski area and groomed cross-country trails at **Ferguson Ridge,** which is 9 miles southeast of Joseph on Tucker Down Road.

Wing Ridge Ski Tours, P.O. Box 714, Joseph, OR 97846 (✆ **800/646-9050;** www.wingski.com), rents backcountry huts for $35 per person, per night. This company also offers four-day avalanche-safety courses for $325 per person.

WHERE TO STAY

Bronze Antler Bed and Breakfast ✿   This beautifully restored Craftsman bungalow is Joseph's finest B&B and has by far the best view of any lodging in the area. Throughout the 1925-vintage home, you'll see lots of beautiful architectural details, and furnishings are in keeping with the style of the period. Guest rooms have fluffy down comforters and European antiques collected by the innkeepers Bill Finney and Heather Tyreman during travels in Europe. Joseph's restaurants and art galleries are within a few blocks of the inn, which makes this a very convenient place to stay if you're in town to soak up Joseph's artistic atmosphere.

"I Will Fight No More, Forever"

The Wallowa Mountains and Hells Canyon areas were once the homeland of the **Nez Perce people.** Sometime in the early 1700s, the Nez Perce acquired horses that were descended from Spanish stock and that had been traded northward from the American Southwest. The Nez Perce land proved to be ideal for raising horses, and the tribe began selectively breeding animals. Their horses became far superior to those used by other tribes and came to be known as **Appaloosas.** Eventually, the hills in southeast Washington where these horses were first bred became known as the **Palouse Hills.**

The Nez Perce had befriended explorers Lewis and Clark in 1805 and remained friendly to white settlers when other Indian tribes were waging wars. This neutrality was "rewarded," however, with treaties that twice cut the size of their reservation in half. When one band refused to sign a new treaty and relinquish its land, it began one of the great tragedies of Northwest history.

En route to a reservation in Idaho, several Nez Perce men ignored orders from the tribal elders and attacked and killed four white settlers to exact revenge for the earlier murder by whites of the father of one of these Nez Perce men. This attack angered settlers, and the cavalry was called to hunt down the Nez Perce. Tribal elders decided to flee to Canada, and, led by Chief Joseph (also known as Young Joseph), 700 Nez Perce, including 400 women and children, began a 2,000-mile march across Idaho and Montana on a retreat that lasted 4 months.

Along the way, several skirmishes were fought, and the Nez Perce were defeated only 40 miles from Canada. At their surrender, Chief Joseph spoke his famous words: "Hear me my Chiefs, I am tired; my heart is sick and sad. From where the sun now stands, I will fight no more, forever."

The town of Joseph is named after Chief Joseph, and on the town's outskirts, you'll find the grave of his father, Old Joseph. Young Joseph is buried on the Colville Indian Reservation in central Washington. In town, you can view historic photos and read quotes from Chief Joseph at the **Nez Perce Wallowa Homeland Exhibit,** 302 N. Main Street (© **541/886-3101**). Not far from Joseph, in Spalding, Idaho (near Lewiston), is the **Nez Perce National Historical Park** (© **208/843-7001;** www.nps.gov/nepe).

309 S. Main St. (P.O. Box 74), Joseph, OR 97846. © **866/520-9769** or 541/432-0230. www.bronzeantler.com. 4 units. $75–$150 double; $150–$250 suite. Rates include full breakfast. AE, DISC, MC, V. Children over 12 are welcome by prior arrangement. **Amenities:** Concierge. *In room:* A/C, hair dryer, Wi-Fi, no phone.

Eagle Cap Chalets *Kids*   Set under tall pines just a short walk from hiking trails and the lake, Eagle Cap Chalets has a wide variety of rooms, as well as an indoor pool and Jacuzzi, and a miniature golf course. Consequently, this place is very popular with families and groups. The rooms here vary from motel style to rustic-though-renovated cabins, and most have phones. Siding on all the buildings makes them appear to be built of logs. Cabins and condos have kitchens. In the early fall, there always seem to be deer hanging out on the lawns.

59879 Wallowa Lake Hwy., Joseph, OR 97846. ⓒ 541/432-4704 or 541/432-8800. www.eaglecapchalets.com. 35 units. $55–$120 double; $75–$170 cabin; $90–$160 1- and 2-bedroom condos. DISC, MC, V. Pets accepted in off season only ($20). **Amenities:** Indoor pool; Jacuzzi. *In room:* TV.

Imnaha River Inn ⓐ   Located 35 miles northeast of Joseph on the edge of Hell's Canyon, this remote log inn is set deep in the Imnaha River Canyon. The sprawling modern inn is filled with animal hides and trophy heads, and the log construction conjures up the wild pioneering spirit of this region. The lofty, high-ceilinged living room, with its big stone fireplace, is the perfect place to relax after a day in the outdoors. However, the deck overlooking the river is equally enticing. Fishing, hunting, rafting, and hiking are the primary pursuits, but if you just want to get away from it all in an awe-inspiring setting, this is the best choice in all of eastern Oregon. Lunches ($8) and dinners ($16) are available.

73946 Rimrock Rd., Imnaha, OR 97842. ⓒ 866/601-9214 or 541/577-6002. www.imnahariverinn.com. 7 units (all with shared bathroom). $120–$130 double. Rates include full breakfast. No credit cards. **Amenities:** Dining room; game room. *In room:* A/C, no phone.

Wallowa Lake Lodge ⓐ   This rustic two-story lodge at the south end of Wallowa Lake was built in 1923 and is surrounded by big pines and a wide expanse of lawn that attracts deer in late summer and early fall. Big comfortable chairs fill the lobby, where folks often sit by the stone fireplace in the evening. The guest rooms are divided between those with carpeting and modern bathrooms and those with hardwood floors, original bathroom fixtures, and antique furnishings (my favorites). All but two of the latter have two bedrooms each, and two rooms have balconies overlooking the lake. The cabins are rustic but comfortable and have full kitchens. The dining room is the best place in the area for dinner.

60060 Wallowa Lake Hwy., Joseph, OR 97846. ⓒ 541/432-9821. Fax 541/432-4885. www.wallowalakelodge.com. 30 units (including 8 cabins). May to mid-Oct $89–$160 double, $135–$215 cabin; mid-Oct to Apr $75–$115 double, $95–$135 cabin. DISC, MC, V. **Amenities:** Restaurant (American); lounge. *In room:* No phone.

CAMPGROUNDS

At the south end of Wallowa Lake, you'll find a campground under the trees at **Wallowa Lake State Park** (ⓒ 541/432-4185; www.oregonstateparks.org). In addition to campsites, the park has yurts and cabins for rent. For campsite reservations, contact **ReserveAmerica** (ⓒ 800/452-5687; www.reserveamerica.com).

WHERE TO DINE

If you're just looking for a good espresso, some baked goodies, or a light lunch, check out the **Calderas,** 300 N. Lake St., Joseph (ⓒ 541/432-0585), which is done up in a beautiful Art Nouveau style.

Terminal Gravity Brewery & Pub ⓐ INTERNATIONAL   Although it's small, this brewery on the east side of Enterprise gets raves across the state for its excellent beers. The beer alone would be worth a stop, but this little place, housed in an old Craftsman bungalow, also serves some of the best food in this corner of the state. There are only a couple of tables and a few barstools in the main dining room, but there are a few more tables upstairs and out on the veranda, plus some picnic tables in the front yard. Expect a couple of dinner specials each night; the menu itself has only a handful of basic dishes on the menu.

803 SE School St., Enterprise. © **541/426-0158.** www.terminalgravitybrewing.com. Main courses $7–$17. MC, V. Wed–Sat 11am–10pm; Sun–Mon 4–9pm.

Vali's Alpine Restaurant and Delicatessen ⊛ EASTERN EUROPEAN Just past the Wallowa Lake Lodge you'll find this little restaurant, which specializes in the hearty fare of Eastern Europe. Only one dish is served each evening, so if you like to have options, you won't want to eat here. Cabbage rolls or Hungarian goulash (Wed), chicken paprikas (Thurs), beef kabobs (Fri), steak (Sat), and schnitzel (Sun) should help you stay warm on cold mountain evenings. Hungarian gypsy music plays on the stereo, and at breakfast on Saturday and Sunday, there are fresh homemade doughnuts.

59811 Wallowa Lake Hwy. © **541/432-5691.** Reservations required. Main courses $10–$14. No credit cards. Memorial Day to Labor Day Wed–Fri 5–8pm, Sat–Sun 9–11am and 5–8pm; Labor Day to Sept and Apr to Memorial Day Sat–Sun 9–11am and 5–8pm. Closed Oct–Mar.

Wallowa Lake Lodge Dining Room ⊛ AMERICAN This historic lodge at the far end of Wallowa Lake from Joseph is the quintessential Wallowa Mountains dining experience. There's sometimes live music in the lobby of the lodge, and in the fall, you'll usually see deer on the lawns surrounding the hotel. Although the prime rib (served Fri and Sat nights only) is probably the most popular item on the menu, the halibut with marionberry glaze is also very good. Hazelnut pancakes with marionberry butter are a breakfast specialty.

60060 Wallowa Lake Hwy. © **541/432-9821.** www.wallowalakelodge.com. Reservations recommended. Main courses $14–$29. DISC, MC, V. Summer Sun–Thurs 8–11am and 5:30–8pm, Fri–Sat 8–11am and 5:30–9pm; other months closed Wed–Thurs.

4 Hells Canyon & the Southern Wallowas

South access: 70 miles NE of Baker City; North access: 20 to 30 miles E of Joseph

Sure, the Grand Canyon is an impressive sight, but few people realize that it isn't the deepest canyon in the United States. That distinction goes to **Hells Canyon,** which forms part of the border between Oregon and Idaho. Carved by the Snake River and bounded on the east by the Seven Devils Mountains and on the west by the Wallowa Mountains, Hells Canyon is as much as 8,000 feet deep. Although it's not quite as spectacular a sight as the Grand Canyon, neither is it as crowded. Because there is so little road access to Hells Canyon, it is one of the least-visited national recreation areas in the West.

The Hells Canyon area boasts a range of outdoor activities, but because of blazing hot temperatures in summer, when this rugged gorge lives up to its name, spring and fall are the best times to visit. Despite the heat, though, boating, swimming, and fishing are all popular in the summer.

ESSENTIALS

GETTING THERE The south access to Hells Canyon National Recreation Area is reached off of Ore. 86 between 9 and 48 miles northeast of the town of Halfway, depending on which route you follow. Northern sections of the national recreation area, including the Hat Point Overlook, are reached from Joseph on Ore. 82, which begins in La Grande.

VISITOR INFORMATION For more information, contact the **Hells Canyon National Recreation Area,** 88401 Ore. 82, Enterprise, OR 97828 (© **541/426-5546;** www.fs.fed.us/hellscanyon).

EXPLORING THE REGION

Much of **Hells Canyon** ✦ is wilderness and is accessible only by boat, on horseback, or on foot. Few roads lead into the canyon, and most of these are recommended only for four-wheel-drive vehicles. If you are driving a car without high clearance, you'll have to limit your exploration of this region to the road to Hells Canyon Dam and the scenic byway that skirts the eastern flanks of the Wallowa Mountains. If you don't mind driving miles on gravel, you can also head out to the **Hat Point Overlook** east of Joseph.

From the south, river-level access begins in the community of Oxbow, but the portion of the Snake River that has been designated a National Wild and Scenic River starts 27 miles farther north, below Hells Canyon Dam. Below the dam, the Snake River is turbulent with white water and provides thrills for jet boaters and rafters. To get this bottom-up view of the canyon, take Ore. 86 to Oxbow, cross the river into Idaho, and continue 22 miles downriver to **Hells Canyon Creek Visitor Center** (© 541/785-3395), which is located 1 mile past the Hells Canyon Dam. This center has informative displays on the natural history of Hells Canyon and is open daily 9am to 5pm from early May to mid-October. The Stud Creek Trail leads 1 mile down the river from the visitor center and is an easy way to get a sense of what it's like to hike in the canyon.

To get a top-down overview of the canyon, drive to the **Hells Canyon Overlook,** 30 miles northeast of Halfway on Forest Road 39. From here you can gaze down into the canyon, but you won't be able to see the river.

You'll find many miles of **hiking trails** within the national recreation area, but summer heat, rattlesnakes, and poison oak keep all but the most dedicated hikers at bay. However, in early June, the wildflowers in Hells Canyon can be spectacular. For information on trails here, contact the information center for the recreation area (see above).

The best way to see Hells Canyon is by **white-water raft** or in a **jet boat.** Both sorts of trips can be arranged through **Hells Canyon Adventures,** 4200 Hells Canyon Dam Rd. (P.O. Box 159), Oxbow, OR 97840 (© 800/422-3568 or 541/785-3352; www. hellscanyonadventures.com). Jet-boat tours range from $35 to $45 per adult for a 2-hour tour to $128 per adult for a 6-hour tour. Children pay half price or less. A day of white-water rafting runs $170.

Multiday horseback trips into the southern Wallowas are offered by **Cornucopia Wilderness Pack Station,** P.O. Box 568, Union, OR 97883 (© 866/562-8075 or 541/562-1181; www.cornucopiapackstation.com), which charges around $145 to $225 per person per day for most of its trips.

You can also opt to explore the southern Wallowas with a llama carrying your gear. Contact **Wallowa Llamas,** 36678 Allstead Lane, Halfway, OR 97834 (© 541/742-2961; www.wallowallamas.com), for more information. Trips range in price from $395 to $1,595.

WHERE TO STAY & DINE

Pine Valley Lodge ✦✦ *Finds* This little lodge, composed of four old buildings in downtown Halfway, is a Wild West fantasy of an inn and is owned by a local cattle ranch. With handmade furniture and Western collectibles scattered about, the main lodge is a fascinating place to wander around. The main house has a large suite on the ground floor and two smaller rooms upstairs. Next door is the Blue Dog, a four-bedroom cottage. Outdoorsy types will like the Main Street Shack and Bunkhouse, which truly is a shack, albeit a charming one.

163 N. Main St. (P.O. Box 609), Halfway, OR 97834. ⓒ **541/742-2027.** Fax 541/742-2028. www.pvlodge.com. 8 units (7 with private bathroom). $80–$160 double. Rates include continental breakfast. MC, V. Pets accepted ($10). **Amenities:** Business center; laundry service. *In room:* A/C, no phone.

5 Ontario & the Owyhee River Region

Ontario: 72 miles SE of Baker City, 63 miles NW of Boise, 130 miles NE of Burns

Ontario, the easternmost town in Oregon, lies in the Four Rivers region, at the confluence of the Owyhee, Snake, Malheur, and Payette rivers. Irrigated by waters from the massive Owyhee Reservoir, these wide, flat valleys are prime agricultural lands that produce onions, sugar beets, and, as in Idaho, plenty of potatoes. This region is also where most of the world's zinnia seeds are grown. During the summer, zinnia fields color the landscape in bold swaths. If you're curious to see the flower fields, head south out of Ontario on Ore. 201.

The biggest attraction in the region is the **Four Rivers Cultural Center,** which focuses on the various cultures that have made the region what it is today. However, there is also some Oregon Trail history to be seen nearby, and south of Ontario lies one of Oregon's most rugged and remote regions. This corner of the state is a vast untracked high desert, and along the banks of the Owyhee River and Succor Creek, you can see canyons and cliffs that seem far more suited to a Southwestern landscape.

ESSENTIALS

GETTING THERE   Ontario is on the Idaho line at the junction of I-84 and U.S. 20/26, all of which link the town to western Oregon.

VISITOR INFORMATION   For more information on the Ontario area, contact the **Ontario Chamber of Commerce,** 676 SW Fifth Ave., Ontario, OR 97914 (ⓒ **866/989-8012** or 541/889-8012; www.ontariochamber.com).

Note: Ontario follows Mountain Time, not Pacific Time.

A CULTURAL MUSEUM

Four Rivers Cultural Center & Museum ⓐ   Although this remote corner of Oregon may seem an unlikely place for a multicultural museum, that is exactly what you'll find here. The museum focuses on four very distinct cultures that have called this region home. The Paiutes were the original inhabitants of the area, and an exploration of their hunting-and-gathering culture is the first exhibit. In the mid–19th century, the first pioneers began arriving in the area and quickly displaced the Paiutes. By the late 19th century, many Mexican cowboys, known as *vaqueros* or *buckaroos,* had come north to the region to work the large cattle ranches. At the same time, Basque shepherds settled in the area and tended large herds of sheep in the more remote corners of the region. The fourth culture is that of the Japanese, who were forced to live in internment camps in the area during World War II. The museum also has a Japanese garden.

676 SW Fifth Ave. ⓒ **541/889-8191.** www.4rcc.com. Admission $4 adults, $3 seniors and children 6–14. Mon–Sat 10am–5pm. Closed all national holidays.

MORE TO SEE & DO: EXPLORING THE REGION

For more Oregon Trail history, head 18 miles west of Ontario to the small farming community of **Vale.** Here you'll find the **Rinehart Stone House Museum,** 255 Main St. S. (© **541/473-2070**), which was built in 1872 and was a stage stop and an important wayside along the route of the Oregon Trail. Today, it houses a small historical museum that is open from March through October Tuesday through Saturday from 12:30 to 4pm; admission is free. Six miles south of Vale, at Keeney Pass, you can see **wagon ruts** left by pioneers traveling the Oregon Trail.

South of Ontario 15 miles, you'll find **Nyssa,** the "Thunderegg Capital of Oregon." **Rockhounding** is the area's most popular pastime, and thundereggs (also known as *geodes*) are the prime find. These round rocks look quite plain until they are cut open to reveal the agate or crystals within. You'll find plenty of cut-and-polished thundereggs in the rock shops around town. If you'd like to do a bit of rockhounding yourself, you can head south to **Succor Creek State Natural Area** ⟨★, a rugged canyon where you'll find a campground, picnic tables, and thundereggs waiting to be unearthed.

If you have a four-wheel-drive or high-clearance vehicle, you can continue another 30 minutes to **Leslie Gulch** ⟨★★, an even more spectacular canyon with walls of naturally sculpted sandstone. If you're lucky, you might even see bighorn sheep here. Few places in Oregon have more of the feel of the desert than these two canyons, and just as in the desert Southwest, here, too, rivers have been dammed to provide irrigation water and aquatic playgrounds. **Lake Owyhee,** 45 miles south of Ontario off Ore. 201, is the longest lake in Oregon and offers boating, fishing, and camping. The Owyhee River above the lake is a designated State Scenic Waterway and is popular for **white-water rafting** ⟨★★. If you're interested in running this remote stretch of river, contact **Destination Wilderness** (© **800/423-8868** or 541/549-1336; www.wilderness trips.com), or **Oregon Whitewater Adventures** (© **800/820-RAFT** or 541/746-5422; www.oregonwhitewater.com), both of which occasionally run this river. Expect to pay $895 to $1,140 for a 5-day trip.

WHERE TO STAY

For the most part, Ontario is a way station for people traveling along I-84, and as such, the city's accommodations are strictly off-ramp budget motels. Motel options include a **Best Western Inn,** 251 NE Goodfellow St., Ontario, OR 97914 (© **800/828-0364** or 541/889-2600), charging $74 to $149 double; a **Super 8 Motel,** NE 266 Goodfellow St., Ontario, OR 97914 (© **800/800-8000** or 541/889-8282), charging $52 to $68 double; and a **Motel 6,** 275 NE 12th St., Ontario, OR 97914 (© **800/466-8356** or 541/889-6617), charging $39 to $62 double.

At nearby **Farewell Bend State Recreation Area** (© **541/869-2365;** www.oregon stateparks.org), 25 miles northwest of Ontario on I-84, you'll find not only campsites but also cabins ($38 per night). For reservations, contact **ReserveAmerica** (© **800/452-5687;** www.reserveamerica.com).

WHERE TO DINE

In downtown Ontario, you'll find a couple of basic Mexican restaurants and some places specializing in steaks, but that's about it.

6 Southeastern Oregon: Land of Marshes, Mountains & Desert

Burns: 130 miles SE of Bend, 130 miles SW of Ontario, 70 miles S of John Day

Southeastern Oregon, the most remote and least populated region of the state, is a region of extremes. Vast marshlands, the most inhospitable desert in the state, and a mountain topped with aspen groves and glacial valleys are among the most prominent features of this landscape. Although cattle outnumber human inhabitants, and the deer and the antelope play, it's birdlife that's the region's number-one attraction. At **Malheur National Wildlife Refuge,** birds abound almost any month of the year, attracting flocks of bird-watchers, binoculars and bird books in hand.

Because this is such an isolated region (Burns and Lakeview are the only towns of consequence), it is not an area to be visited by the unprepared. Always keep your gas tank topped off and carry water for both you and your car. Two of the region's main attractions, **Steens Mountain** and the **Hart Mountain National Antelope Refuge,** are accessible only by way of gravel roads more than 50 miles long. A visit to the Alvord Desert will also require spending 60 or more miles on a gravel road.

ESSENTIALS

GETTING THERE   The town of Burns is midway between Bend and Ontario on U.S. 20. Malheur National Wildlife Refuge, Steens Mountain, and Hart Mountain National Antelope Refuge are all located south of Burns off Ore. 205.

VISITOR INFORMATION   For more information on this area, contact the **Harney County Chamber of Commerce,** 76 E. Washington St., Burns, OR 97720 (© 541/573-2636; www.harneycounty.com).

EXPLORING THE REGION

Because water is scarce here in the high desert, it becomes a magnet for wildlife wherever it appears. Three marshy lakes—Malheur, Harney, and Mud—south of Burns cover such a vast area and provide such an ideal habitat for birdlife that they have been designated the **Malheur National Wildlife Refuge** ⊛. The shallow lakes, surrounded by thousands of acres of marshlands, annually attract more than 300 species of birds, including waterfowl, shorebirds, songbirds, and raptors. Some of the more noteworthy birds that are either resident or migratory at Malheur are trumpeter swans, sandhill cranes, white pelicans, great blue herons, and great horned owls. Of the more than 58 mammals that live in the refuge, the most visible are mule deer, pronghorn antelope, and coyotes, but I once saw a bobcat near the visitor center.

The refuge headquarters is 32 miles south of Burns on Ore. 205, but the refuge stretches for another 30 miles south to the crossroads of Frenchglen. The refuge is open daily from dawn to dusk. The **visitor center,** where you can find out about recent sightings and current birding hot spots, is open weekdays and most weekends during the spring and summer, while a **museum** housing a collection of nearly 200 stuffed-and-mounted birds is open daily. About 6 miles north of the visitor center, you can visit **Historic Sod House Ranch,** which at one time was the northern headquarters for the huge ranch created by 19th-century rancher Peter French (for whom the nearby community of Frenchglen is named). The ranch preserves several historic buildings including a 116-foot-long barn. The ranch, which is part of the wildlife refuge, is open August 15 to October 31 daily from 8am to 4pm, and there are guided interpretive tours when volunteers are available. Camping is available at two campgrounds near Frenchglen. For more information on the refuge, contact Refuge Manager, **Malheur National Wildlife Refuge,** 36391 Sodhouse Lane, Princeton, OR 97721 (© **541/493-2612;** www.fws. gov/malheur).

Steens Mountain, at 9,733 feet high, is a different sort of desert oasis. This mountain rises so high that it creates its own weather, and on the upper slopes the sagebrush of the high desert gives way to juniper and aspen forests. From Frenchglen, there's a 66-mile loop road that leads to the summit and back down by a different route. Due to early snows and lingering snow in the spring, this road is usually open only between July and October. Even then the road is not recommended for cars with low clearance, but if you have the appropriate vehicle, it's well worth a visit.

Steens Mountain is a fault-block mountain that was formed when the land on the west side of a geological fault line rose in relationship to the land on the east side of the fault. This geologic upheaval caused the east slope of Steens Mountain to form a precipitous escarpment that falls away to the Alvord Desert a mile below. From the summit of Steens Mountain, the panorama across southeastern Oregon is spectacular. The road leads almost to the summit, but then you'll have to walk 5 or 10 minutes to the very top of the peak. Stretched out below you when you stand on the summit, or at the nearby East Rim Overlook, are four glacier-carved gorges—Kiger, Little Blitzen, Big Indian, and Wildhorse. From near the summit, a steep and strenuous trail leads down into Wildhorse Gorge to Wildhorse Lake. Although the round-trip hike is only 2.6 miles in length, it involves descending and then ascending 1,100 feet to and from the floor of the gorge. And there are wild horses in the area, known as Kiger mustangs.

For more information on Steens Mountain, contact the **Bureau of Land Management (BLM),** Burns Office, 28910 U.S. 20 W., Hines, OR 97738 (© **541/573-4400;** www.blm.gov/or/districts/burns/index.php).

More wildlife-viewing opportunities are available at the **Hart Mountain National Antelope Refuge** ✪, which is a refuge for both pronghorns, the fastest land mammal in North America, and California bighorn sheep. The most accessible location for viewing pronghorns is the refuge headquarters, 49 miles southwest of Frenchglen on gravel roads. Bighorn sheep are harder to spot and tend to keep to the steep cliffs west of the refuge headquarters. Primitive camping is available near the headquarters at **Hot Springs Campground,** where there is a hot spring. For more information, contact the **Sheldon-Hart Mountain National Wildlife Refuge Complex,** 18 S. G St. (P.O. Box 111), Lakeview, OR 97630 (© **541/947-3315;** www.fws.gov/sheldonhartmtn).

If you're a fan of rustic hot springs, then be sure to visit **Crystal Crane Hot Springs,** 59315 Ore. 78 (© **541/493-2312;** www.cranehotsprings.com), 25 miles southeast of Burns. You'll find not only a hot-springs-fed pond, but also indoor private soaking tubs and a few very basic cabins that are for rent. It costs $3.50 to use the pond for the day and $7.50 per person per hour for a tub (reservations recommended).

If you'd like to learn more about the history of this region, I recommend stopping by the **Round Barn Visitor Center,** 51955 Lava Bed Rd., Diamond (© **541/493-2070;** www.roundbarn.net), which also operates **Jenkins Historical Tours** (© **888/493-2420**). The tour company offers several different tours including a Steens Mountain Tour, a Heritage Tour, and Peter French Barn Tour. The tours cost $110 for adults and $60 for children 12 and under. There's a discount if you do both the Steens Mountain Tour and the Heritage Tour back to back.

WHERE TO STAY & DINE

If bird-watching in Malheur National Wildlife Refuge has left you famished, you can get a simple meal at **The Narrows,** 33468 Sod House Lane, Princeton (© **800/403-3294** or 541/495-2006; www.thenarrowsrvpark.com), a combination restaurant, minimart, and RV park about 5 miles west of the refuge headquarters.

Frenchglen Hotel *(Finds* Frenchglen is in the middle of nowhere, so for decades the Frenchglen Hotel (now owned by Oregon State Parks) has been an important way station for travelers passing through this remote region. The historic two-story hotel is 60 miles south of Burns on the edge of Malheur National Wildlife Refuge. The hotel is most popular for bird-watchers. The guest rooms are on the second floor and are small and simply furnished. This hotel is often booked up months in advance. Three meals a day will cost $25 to $35 per person, and the hearty dinners are quite good.

39184 Ore. 205, Frenchglen, OR 97736. © **800/551-6949** or 541/493-2825. www.oregonstateparks.org/park_3.php. 8 units (all with shared bathroom). $68–$70 double. DISC, MC, V. Closed Nov 1–Mar 15. **Amenities:** Restaurant (American). *In room:* No phone.

Hotel Diamond *(Æ* Located 54 miles south of Burns off Ore. 205, the Hotel Diamond, built in 1898, is on the opposite side of Malheur National Wildlife Refuge from Frenchglen. The historic hotel was completely restored in the late 1980s and now has rooms with hand-stitched quilts and artwork by one of the owners. There's a big screened porch across the front and a green lawn that attracts deer. Family-style dinners are available for around $19 (make reservations at least 24 hr. in advance).

10 Main St., Diamond, OR 97722. © **541/493-1898.** www.central-oregon.com/hoteldiamond. 8 units (3 with private bathroom). $68 double with shared bathroom; $90 double with private bathroom. MC, V. Closed Nov–Mar. **Amenities:** 2 restaurants (American). *In room:* A/C, no phone.

Appendix: Oregon in Depth

1 The Natural Environment

At 97,073 square miles (roughly 1½ times the size of the New England region of the northeastern United States), Oregon is the 10th-largest state in the Union, and it encompasses within its vast area an amazing diversity of natural environments—not only lush forests, but also deserts, glacier-covered peaks, grasslands, alpine meadows, sagebrush-covered hills, sand beaches, and rugged ocean shores. Together, these diverse environments support a wide variety of natural life.

The **Oregon coast** stretches for nearly 300 miles from the redwood country of Northern California north to the mouth of the Columbia River, and for most of this length is only sparsely populated. Consequently, this coastline provides habitat not only for large populations of seabirds—such as cormorants, tufted puffins, and pigeon guillemots—but also for several species of marine mammals, including Pacific gray whales, Steller's sea lions, California sea lions, and harbor seals.

Each year between December and April, more than 20,000 **Pacific gray whales** pass by the Oregon coast as they make their annual migration south to their breeding grounds off Baja California. These whales can often be seen from shore at various points along the coast, and numerous whale-watching tour boats operate out of different ports. Many gray whales also spend the summer in Oregon's offshore waters, and it is possible to spot these leviathans any month of the year. More frequently spotted, however, are **harbor seals** and Steller's and California **sea lions,** which are frequently seen lounging on rocks. The Newport bayfront, Sea Lion Caves, and Cape Arago State Park, all on the central Oregon coast, are the best places to spot sea lions.

The **Coast Range,** which in places rises directly from the waves, gives the coastline its rugged look. However, even more than the mountains, it is **rain** that gives this coastline its definitive character. As moist winds from the Pacific Ocean rise up and over the Coast Range, they drop their moisture as rain and snow. The tremendous amounts of rain that fall on these mountains have produced dense forests that are home to some of the largest trees on earth. Although the south coast is the northern limit for the coast redwood, the **Douglas firs,** which are far more common and grow throughout the region, are almost as impressive in size, sometimes reaching 300 feet tall. Other common trees of these coastal forests include Sitka spruce, Western hemlocks, Port Orford cedars, Western red cedars, and, along the southern Oregon coast, evergreen myrtle trees. The wood of these latter trees is used extensively for carving, and myrtle-wood shops are common along the south coast.

More than a century of intensive **logging** has, however, left the state's forests of centuries-old trees shrunken to remnant groves scattered in largely remote and rugged areas. How much exactly is still left is a matter of hot debate between the timber industry and environmentalists, and the battle to save the remaining old-growth forests continues, with both sides claiming victories and losses with each passing year.

Among this region's most celebrated and controversial wild residents is the **Northern spotted owl,** which, because of its requirements for large tracts of undisturbed old-growth forest and its listing as a federally endangered species, brought logging of old-growth forests to a virtual halt in the 1990s. Since that time, barred owls, which compete for the same habitat as spotted owls, have been expanding their range and have a negative impact on spotted owl populations. Concern has also focused on the **marbled murrelet,** a small bird that feeds on the open ocean but nests exclusively in old-growth forests. Destruction of forests has also been partially blamed for the demise of trout, salmon, and steelhead populations throughout the region.

Roosevelt elk, the largest commonly encountered land mammal in the Northwest, can be found throughout the Coast Range, and there are even designated elk-viewing areas along the coast (one off U.S. 26 near Jewell and one off Ore. 38 near Reedsport).

To the east of the northern section of the Coast Range lies the **Willamette Valley,** which, because of its mild climate and fertile soils, was the first region of the state to be settled by pioneers. Today, the Willamette Valley remains the state's most densely populated region and is home to Oregon's largest cities. It also still contains the most productive farmland in the state.

To the east of the Willamette Valley rise the mountains of the 700-mile-long **Cascade Range,** which stretches from Northern California to southern British Columbia. The most prominent features of the Oregon Cascades are their **volcanic peaks:** Hood, Jefferson, Three Fingered Jack, Washington, the Three Sisters, Broken Top, Thielsen, and McLoughlin. The eruption of Washington's Mount St. Helens on May 18, 1980, reminded Northwesterners that this is still a volcanically active region. However, here in Oregon, it is the remains of ancient Mount Mazama, which erupted with unimaginable violence 7,000 years ago, that provide the most dramatic reminder of the potential power of Cascade volcanoes. Today, the waters of **Crater Lake** fill the shell of this long-gone peak. Near the town of Bend, geologically recent volcanic activity is also visible in the form of cinder cones, lava flows, lava caves, and craters. Much of this volcanic landscape near Bend is now preserved as **Newberry National Volcanic Monument.**

The same moisture-laden clouds that produce the near rainforest conditions in the Coast Range frequently leave the Cascades with heavy snows and, on the highest peaks (Mount Hood, Mount Jefferson, the Three Sisters), numerous glaciers. The most readily accessible glaciers are on **Mount Hood,** where ski lifts keep running right through the summer, carrying skiers and snowboarders to slopes atop the Palmer Glacier, high above the historic Timberline Lodge.

East of the Cascades, less than 200 miles from the damp Coast Range forests, the landscape becomes a desert. The **Great Basin,** which reaches its northern limit in central and eastern Oregon, comprises a vast, high-desert region that stretches east to the Rockies. Through this desolate landscape flows the **Columbia River,** which, together with its tributary, the Snake River, forms the second-largest river drainage in the United States. During the last ice age, roughly 13,000 years ago, glaciers repeatedly blocked the flow of the Columbia, forming huge lakes behind dams of ice. These vast prehistoric lakes repeatedly burst the ice dams, sending massive and devastating walls of water flooding down the Columbia. These floodwaters were sometimes 1,000 feet high and carried with them ice and rocks, which scoured out the **Columbia Gorge.** The gorge's many waterfalls are the most evident signs of these prehistoric floods.

Today, it is numerous large, modern **dams,** not ice, that impound the Columbia, and these dams have become the focus of another of the region's environmental battles. The large dams, mostly built during the middle part of the 20th century, present a variety of barriers both to adult salmon heading upstream and to young salmon heading downstream to the Pacific. Though many of the dams have fish ladders to allow **salmon** to return upriver to spawn, salmon must still negotiate an obstacle course of degraded spawning grounds, slower river flows in the reservoirs behind the dams, turbines that kill fish by the thousands, and irrigation canals that often confuse salmon into swimming out of the river and into farm fields. Overfishing for salmon canneries in the late 19th century struck the first major blow to salmon populations, and for more than a century, these fish have continued to struggle against man-made and natural obstacles. Compounding the problems faced by wild salmon has been the use of fish hatcheries to supplement the wild fish populations (hatchery fish tend to be less vigorous than wild salmon).

South-central and southeastern Oregon are the most remote and unpopulated regions of the state. However, this vast desert area does support an abundance of wildlife. The **Hart Mountain National Antelope Refuge** shelters herds of pronghorn antelopes, which are the fastest land mammals in North America. This refuge also protects a small population of California bighorn sheep. At **Malheur National Wildlife Refuge,** more than 300 bird species frequent large shallow lakes and wetlands, and at the **Lower Klamath National Wildlife Refuge,** large numbers of bald eagles gather each winter. Several other of the region's large lakes, including Summer Lake and Lake Abert, also attract large populations of birds.

2 Oregon Today

Oregon is a state dominated by a **love of the outdoors,** and this isn't surprising when you realize just how much nature dominates beyond the city limits. From almost anywhere in Oregon, it's possible to look up and see green forests and snow-capped mountains, and a drive of less than 2 hours from any Willamette Valley city will get you to the mountains or the Pacific Ocean's beaches.

Oregonians don't let the weather stand between them and the outdoors. The temptation is too great to head for the mountains, the river, or the beach—no matter what the forecast. Consequently, life in Oregon's cities tends to revolve less around cultural venues and shopping than around parks, gardens, waterfronts, rivers, mountains, and beaches. Portland has its Forest Park, Rose Garden, Japanese Garden, Classical Chinese Garden, and Waterfront Park. Eugene has its miles of riverside parks, bike paths, and even a park just for rock climbing. In Hood River, the entire Columbia River has become a playground for windsurfers and kiteboarders, and when the wind doesn't blow, there are always the nearby mountain-bike trails and rivers for kayaking. In Bend, mountain biking, downhill skiing, and snowboarding are a way of life. These outdoor areas are where people find tranquillity, where summer festivals are held, where locals take their visiting friends and relatives, and where Oregonians tend to live their lives when they aren't being interrupted by such inconveniences as work and sleep.

This is not to say, however, that the region is a cultural wasteland. Both Portland and Eugene have large, modern, and active **performing arts centers.** During the summer months, numerous **festivals** take music, theater, and dance outdoors. Most impressive of these are the Oregon Shakespeare Festival and the Britt Festivals, both of which are staged in southern Oregon. Many other festivals feature everything from chamber music to alternative rock.

Word of the state's natural beauty and the Oregon good life has been spreading far and wide in recent years, and the state has been experiencing unprecedented growth. As the population in urban areas of the Willamette Valley has expanded, a pronounced urban–rural **political split** has developed in Oregon. Citizens from the eastern part of the state argue that Salem and Portland are dictating to rural regions that have little in common with the cities, while urban dwellers, who far outnumber those living outside the Willamette Valley, argue that majority rule is majority rule. This split has pitted conservative voters (often from rural regions) against liberal voters (usually urban) on a wide variety of issues, and the reality of Oregon politics is now quite a bit different from the popular perception of a state dominated by liberal, forward-thinking environmentalists and former hippies.

Some areas outside of Oregon's urban population centers have also been experiencing rapid growth. Hood River in the Columbia Gorge, Bend in central Oregon, and the Ashland/Medford area of southern Oregon have all been attracting large numbers of wealthy retirees and other transplants. These areas have all seen lots of development in the past few years, and along with this development has come a proliferation of high-end restaurants. So, for anyone visiting the state, Oregon's popularity as a place to live has also made the state a great place to visit.

3 Oregon History 101

EARLY HISTORY   The oldest known inhabitants of what is now the state of Oregon lived along the shores of huge lakes in the Klamath Lakes Basin some 10,000 years ago. Here they fished and hunted ducks and left records of their passing in several caves. These peoples would have witnessed the massive eruption of Mount Mazama, which left a vast caldera that eventually filled with water and was named Crater Lake. Along the coast, numerous small tribes subsisted on salmon and shellfish. In the northeast corner of the state, the Nez Perce tribe became expert at horse breeding even before Lewis and Clark passed through the region at the start of the 19th century. In fact, the appaloosa horse derives its name from the nearby Palouse Hills of Washington.

However, it was the **Columbia River tribes** that became the richest of the Oregon tribes through their control of Celilo Falls, which was historically the richest salmon-fishing area in the Northwest. These massive falls on the Columbia River, east of present-day The Dalles, witnessed the annual passage of millions of salmon, which were speared and dipnetted by Native Americans, who then smoked the fish to preserve it for the winter. Today, Native Americans sometimes still fish for salmon as they once did, perched on precarious wooden platforms with dip nets in hand. However, Celilo Falls are gone, inundated by the water impounded behind The Dalles Dam, which was completed in 1957. Today, little remains of what was once the Northwest's most important Native American gathering ground, a place where tribes from hundreds of miles away congregated each year to fish and trade.

Even before this amazing fishing ground was lost, a far greater tragedy had been visited upon Northwest tribes. Between the 1780s, when white explorers and traders began frequenting the Northwest coast, and the 1830s, when the first settlers began arriving, the Native American population of the Northwest was reduced to perhaps a tenth of its historic numbers. These people were not wiped out by war but by European diseases—smallpox, measles, malaria, and influenza. The Native Americans had no resistance to these diseases, and entire tribes were soon wiped out by fast-spreading epidemics.

THE AGE OF EXPLORATION

Though a Spanish ship reached what is now southern Oregon in 1542, the Spanish had no interest in the gray and rainy coast. Nor did famed British buccaneer Sir Francis Drake, who in 1579 sailed his ship the *Golden Hind* as far north as the mouth of the Rogue River. Drake called off his explorations in the face of what he described as "thicke and stinking fogges."

However, when the Spanish found out that Russian fur traders were establishing themselves in Alaska and along the North Pacific coast, Spain took a new interest in the Northwest. Several **Spanish expeditions** sailed north from Mexico to reassert the Spanish claim to the region. In 1775, Spanish explorers Bruno de Heceta and Francisco de la Bodega y Quadra charted much of the Northwest coast, and though they found the mouth of the Columbia River, they did not enter it. To this day, four of the coast's most scenic headlands—Cape Perpetua, Heceta Head, Cape Arago, and Cape Blanco—bear names from these early Spanish explorations.

It was not until 1792 that an explorer, American trader Robert Gray, risked a passage through treacherous sandbars that guarded the mouth of the long-speculated-upon Great River of the West. Gray named this newfound river Columbia's River, in honor of his ship, the *Columbia Rediviva*. This discovery established the first American claim to the region. When news of the *Columbia's* discovery reached the United States and England, both countries began speculating on a northern water route across North America. Such a route, if it existed, would facilitate trade with the Northwest.

In 1793, Scotsman Alexander MacKenzie made the first overland trip across North America north of New Spain.

Dateline

- **13,000 B.C.** Massive floods, as much as 1,200 feet deep, rage down Columbia River and carve the Columbia Gorge.
- **10,000 B.C.** Earliest known human inhabitation of Oregon.
- **5,000 B.C.** Mount Mazama erupts violently, creating a caldera that will later fill with water and become known as Crater Lake.
- **A.D. 1542** Spanish exploratory ship reaches what is now the southern Oregon coast.
- **1579** Englishman Sir Francis Drake reaches the mouth of the Rogue River.
- **1602** Spain's Martín de Aguilar explores the coast of Oregon, probably as far as Coos Bay.
- **1792** Robert Gray becomes the first explorer to sail a ship into a great river he names the Columbia, in honor of his ship the *Columbia Rediviva*.
- **1805–06** Expedition led by Meriwether Lewis and William Clark crosses the continent and spends the winter at the mouth of the Columbia River.

continues

Crossing British Canada on foot, MacKenzie arrived somewhere north of Vancouver Island. After reading MacKenzie's account of his journey, Thomas Jefferson decided that the United States needed to find a better route overland to the Northwest. To this end, he commissioned Meriwether Lewis and William Clark to lead an expedition up the Missouri River in hopes of finding a single easy portage that would lead to the Columbia River.

Beginning in 1804, the members of the **Lewis and Clark expedition** paddled up the Missouri, crossed the Rocky Mountains on foot, and then paddled down the Columbia River to its mouth. A French Canadian trapper and his Native American wife, Sacagawea, were enlisted as interpreters, and it was probably the presence of Sacagawea that helped the expedition gain acceptance among Western tribes. After spending the wet and dismal winter of 1805 to 1806 at the mouth of the Columbia at a spot they named **Fort Clatsop,** the expedition headed back east. Discoveries made by the expedition added greatly to the scientific and geographical knowledge of the continent. A replica of Fort Clatsop in the Lewis and Clark National Historical Park burned down in late 2005, just prior to the park's bicentennial celebrations, but the fort has since been rebuilt and is one of the most interesting historical sites in the state. Outside of The Dalles, a campsite used by Lewis and Clark has also been preserved.

In 1819, the Spanish relinquished all claims north of the present California-Oregon state line, and the Russians gave up their claims to all lands south of Alaska. This left only the British and Americans dickering for control of the Northwest.

SETTLEMENT Fur Traders, Missionaries & the Oregon Trail Only 6 years after Lewis and Clark spent the winter at the mouth of the Columbia, employees of John Jacob Astor's Pacific Fur Company managed to establish themselves at a nearby spot they called **Fort Astoria.** This was the first permanent settlement in the Northwest, but with the War of 1812 being fought on the far side of the continent, the fur traders at Fort Astoria, with little protection against the British, chose to relinquish control of their fort. In the wake of the war, the fort returned to American control, though the United States and Britain produced no firm decision about possession of the Northwest. The British still dominated the region, but American trade was tolerated.

With the decline of the sea-otter population, British fur traders turned to

- **1811** Americans attempt first settlement at the Columbia River's mouth.
- **1819** Spain cedes all lands above 42 degrees north latitude to the U.S.
- **1824–25** Russia gives up claims to land south of Alaska; Fort Vancouver founded by Hudson's Bay Company on Columbia River near present-day Portland.
- **1834** Methodist missionary Jason Lee founds Salem, which later becomes the state capital.
- **1842** Jason Lee founds first school of higher learning west of the Mississippi.
- **1843** First wagons cross the continent on the Oregon Trail; Asa Lovejoy and William Overton stake claim on land that will soon become Portland.
- **1844** Oregon City becomes the first incorporated town west of the Mississippi.
- **1846** The 49th parallel is established as the boundary between American and British territories in the Northwest.
- **1848** Oregon becomes first U.S. territory west of the Rockies.
- **1851** Portland is incorporated; gold is discovered in southern Oregon.
- **1915** Columbia Gorge scenic highway is constructed.

Did You Know?

- Oregon was home to America's first policewoman, Lola Greene Baldwin, who joined the Portland force in 1908.
- Portland is home to the world's smallest dedicated park—Mill Ends Park—measuring only 24 inches in diameter.
- Oregon is one of the few states with no sales tax.
- Astoria, in the very northwest corner of the state, is the oldest American community west of the Mississippi.
- Oregon's Crater Lake is the deepest lake in the U.S.
- Hells Canyon is the deepest gorge in North America.

beaver and headed inland up the Columbia River. For the next 30 years or so, fur-trading companies would be the sole authority in the region. Fur-trading posts were established throughout the Northwest, though most were on the eastern edge of the territory in the foothills of the Rocky Mountains. The powerful Hudson's Bay Company (HBC) eventually became the single fur-trading company in the Northwest.

In 1824, the HBC established its Northwest headquarters at **Fort Vancouver,** 100 miles up the Columbia near the mouth of the Willamette River; and in 1829, the HBC founded **Oregon City** at the falls of the Willamette River. Between 1824 and 1846, when the 49th parallel was established as the boundary between British and American northwestern lands, Fort Vancouver was the most important settlement in the region. A replica of the fort now stands in the city of Vancouver, Washington, across the Columbia River from Portland. In Oregon City, several homes from this period are still standing, including that of John McLoughlin, who was chief factor at Fort Vancouver and aided many of the early pioneers who arrived in the area after traveling the Oregon Trail.

By the 1830s, the future of the Northwest had arrived in the form of **American missionaries.** The first was Jason Lee,

- **1935** Angus Bowmer stages *As You Like It* in Ashland and plants the seed of the Oregon Shakespeare Festival.
- **1940s** Kaiser shipyards in the Portland area become the world's foremost shipbuilders.
- **1945** Oregon becomes the only state with mainland civilian war casualties when a Japanese balloon bomb kills six children.

- **1957** The Dalles Dam is completed; backwaters inundate Celilo Falls, the region's most productive Native American salmon-fishing grounds.
- **1974** In a bold step toward making Portland a more livable city, a freeway along the city's downtown waterfront is removed.
- **2005** The replica of Lewis and Clark's Fort Clatsop near Astoria burns down only

months prior to planned bicentennial celebrations. Fort is later reconstructed.

who established his mission in the Willamette Valley near present-day Salem. (Today, the site is Willamette Mission State Park.) Two years later, in 1836, Marcus and Narcissa Whitman, along with Henry and Eliza Spaulding, made the overland trek to Fort Vancouver, then backtracked into what is now eastern Washington and Idaho, to establish two missions. This journey soon inspired other settlers to make the difficult overland crossing.

In 1840, a slow trickle of American settlers began crossing the continent, a 2,000-mile journey. Their destination was the Oregon country, which had been promoted as a veritable Eden where land was waiting to be claimed. In 1843, Marcus Whitman, after traveling east to plead with his superiors not to shut down his mission, headed back west, leading 900 settlers on the **Oregon Trail.** Before these settlers ever arrived, the small population of retired trappers, missionaries, and HBC employees who were living at Fort Vancouver and in nearby Oregon City had formed a provisional government in anticipation of the land-claim problems that would arise with the influx of settlers to the region. Today, the best places to learn about the experiences of the Oregon Trail emigrants are at the Oregon Trail Interpretive Center outside Baker City and the End of the Oregon Trail Interpretive Center in Oregon City. In many places in the eastern part of the state, **Oregon Trail wagon ruts** can still be seen.

In 1844, Oregon City became the first incorporated town west of the Rocky Mountains. This outpost in the wilderness, a gateway to the fertile lands of the Willamette Valley, was the destination of the wagon trains that began traveling the Oregon Trail, each year bringing more and more settlers to the region. As the land in the Willamette Valley was claimed, settlers began fanning out to different regions of the Northwest so that during the late 1840s and early 1850s many new towns, including Portland, were founded.

Though the line between American and British land in the Northwest had been established in 1846 at the 49th parallel (the current U.S.–Canada border), Oregon was not given U.S. territorial status until 1848. It was the massacre of the missionaries at the Whitman mission in Walla Walla (now in Washington state) and the subsequent demand for territorial status and U.S. military protection that brought about the establishment of the first U.S. territory west of the Rockies.

The discovery of **gold** in eastern Oregon in 1860 set the stage for one of the saddest chapters in Northwest history. With miners pouring into eastern Oregon and Washington, conflicts with Native Americans over land were inevitable. Since 1805, when Lewis and Clark had first passed this way, the **Nez Perce tribe** (the name means "pierced nose" in French) had been friendly to the white settlers. However, in 1877 a disputed treaty caused friction. Led by Chief Joseph, 700 Nez Perce, including 400 women and children, began a march from their homeland to their new reservation. Along the way, several angry young men, in revenge for the murder of an older member of the tribe, attacked a white settlement and killed several people. The U.S. Army took up pursuit of the Nez Perce, who fled across Idaho and Montana, only to be caught 40 miles from the Canadian border and sanctuary.

INDUSTRIALIZATION & THE 20TH CENTURY From the very beginning of white settlement in the Northwest, the region based its growth on an extractive economy. **Lumber** and **salmon** were exploited ruthlessly. The history of the timber and salmon-fishing industries ran parallel for more than a century and led to similar results in the 1990s.

The trees in Oregon grew to gigantic proportions. Nurtured on steady rains, such trees as Douglas fir, Sitka spruce, Western red cedar, Port Orford cedar, and hemlock grew tall and straight, sometimes as tall as 300 feet. The first sawmill in the Northwest began operation near present-day Vancouver, Washington, in 1828, and between the 1850s and the 1870s, Northwest sawmills supplied the growing California market as well as a limited foreign market. When the transcontinental railroads arrived in the 1880s, a whole new market opened up, and mills began shipping to the eastern states.

Lumber companies developed a cut-and-run policy that leveled the forests. By the turn of the century, the government had gained more control over public forests in an attempt to slow the decimation of forestlands, and sawmill owners began buying up huge tracts of land. At the outbreak of World War I, more than 20% of the forestland in the Northwest was owned by three companies—Weyerhaeuser, the Northern Pacific Railroad, and the Southern Pacific Railroad—and more than 50% of the workforce labored in the timber industry.

The timber industry, which has always been extremely susceptible to fluctuations in the economy, experienced a roller-coaster ride of boom and bust throughout the 20th century. Boom times in the 1970s brought on record-breaking production that came to a screeching halt in the 1980s, first with a nationwide recession and then with the listing of the **Northern spotted owl** as a threatened species. When the timber industry was born in the Northwest, there was a belief that the forests of the region were endless. However, by the latter half of this century, big lumber companies had realized that the forests were dwindling. Tree farms were planted with increasing frequency, but the large old trees continued to be cut faster than younger trees could replenish them. By the 1970s, environmentalists, shocked by the vast clear-cuts, began trying to save the last **old-growth trees.** The battle between the timber industry and environmentalists is today still one of the state's most heated debates, and tree-sitters continue to attract media attention as they attempt to stop the cutting of old-growth forests.

In the Northwest, salmon was the mainstay of the Native American diet for thousands of years before the first whites arrived in the Oregon country, but within 10 years of the opening of the first salmon cannery in the Northwest, the fish population was decimated. In 1877, the first fish hatchery was developed to replenish dwindling runs of salmon, and by 1895, salmon canning had reached its peak on the Columbia River. Later, in the 20th century, salmon runs would be further decimated by the construction of numerous dams on the Columbia and Snake rivers. Though fish ladders help adult salmon make their journeys upstream, the young salmon heading downstream have no such help, and the turbines of hydroelectric dams kill a large percentage of fish. One solution to this problem has been the barging and trucking of young salmon downriver. Today the **salmon populations** of the Northwest have been so diminished that entire runs of salmon have been listed as threatened or endangered under the Endangered Species Act. Talk in recent years has focused on the removal of certain dams that pose insurmountable barriers to salmon. However, there has been great resistance to this.

The dams that have proved such a detriment to salmon populations have, however, provided irrigation water and cheap electricity that have fueled both industry and farming. Using irrigation water, potato and wheat farms flourished in northeastern Oregon after the middle of the 20th century. The reservoirs behind the Columbia and Snake River dams have also turned these rivers into waterways that can be navigated by huge barges, which often carry wheat downriver from ports in Idaho. Today, the **regional salmon recovery plan** is attempting to strike a balance between saving salmon runs and meeting all the other needs that have been created since the construction of these dams.

Manufacturing began gaining importance during and after World War II. In the Portland area, the Kaiser Shipyards employed tens of thousands of people in the construction of warships, but the postwar years saw the demise of the Kaiser facilities. In the 1980s and 1990s, there was a diversification into **high-tech industries,** with such major manufacturers as Intel, Epson, and Hewlett-Packard operating manufacturing facilities in the Willamette Valley.

However, it is in the area of **sportswear manufacturing** that Oregon businesses have gained the greatest visibility. With outdoor recreation a way of life in this state, it comes as no surprise that a few regional companies have grown into international giants. Chief among these is Nike, which is headquartered in the Portland suburb of Beaverton. Other familiar names include Jantzen, one of the nation's oldest swimwear manufacturers; Pendleton Woolen Mills, maker of classic wool shirts, Indian-design blankets, and other classic wool fashions; and Columbia Sportswear, which in recent years has become one of the country's biggest sports-related outerwear manufacturers. If you like to play outside, you probably own some article of clothing that originated in Oregon.

4 Eat, Drink & Be Merry

Although there is no cuisine that can be specifically identified as Oregon cuisine, there is a regional Northwest cooking style that can be distinguished by its pairings of meats and seafood with local fruits and nuts. This cuisine features such regional produce as salmon, oysters, halibut, raspberries, blackberries, apples, pears, and hazelnuts. A classic Northwest dish might be raspberry chicken or halibut with a hazelnut crust.

Salmon is king of Oregon fish and has been for thousands of years, so it isn't surprising that in one shape or another, it shows up on plenty of menus throughout the state. It's prepared in seemingly endless ways, but the most traditional method is what's known as **alder-planked salmon.** Traditionally, this Native American cooking style entailed preparing a salmon as a single filet, splaying it on readily available alder wood, and slow-cooking it over hot coals. The result is a cross between grilling and smoking. Today, however, it's hard to

find salmon prepared this traditional way. Much more readily available, especially along the Oregon coast, is traditional **smoked salmon.** Smoked oysters are usually also available at smokehouses and are a treat worth trying.

With plenty of clean cold waters in many of its bays and estuaries, Oregon raises large numbers of **oysters,** especially in Tillamook and Coos bays. If you see an oyster burger listed on a menu, give it a try; there's no beef, just oysters. Plenty of mussels and clams also come from these waters. Of particular note are **razor clams,** which can be tough and chewy if not prepared properly, but which are eagerly sought after along north-coast beaches when the clamming season is open. After salmon, though, **Dungeness crab** is the region's other top seafood offering. Though not as large as a king crab, the Dungeness is usually big enough to make a meal for one or two people. Crab cakes are also ubiquitous on Oregon restaurant menus, and along the coast, you can find old-fashioned crab shacks that boil up crabs on a daily basis.

The Northwest's combination of climate and abundant irrigation waters has also helped make this one of the nation's major fruit-growing regions. The Hood River Valley and the Medford area are two of the nation's top **pear-growing regions,** and just a few miles east of Hood River, around The Dalles, cherries reign supreme, with the blushing **Rainier cherry** a regional treat rarely seen outside the Northwest. The Willamette Valley, south of Portland, has become the nation's center for the production of **berries,** including strawberries, raspberries, and numerous varieties of blackberries. All these fruits show up in the summer months at farm stands, making a drive through the Willamette Valley at that time of year a real treat. Pick-your-own farms are also fairly common throughout the Northwest. So famed are Oregon's fruits that the Harry and David's company ships regional produce all over the country.

When hunger strikes on the road, Oregon offers what seems to be a regional potato preparation known as **jo-jos.** Consisting of potato wedges dipped in batter and fried, jo-jos are traditionally served with ranch dressing. These belly bombs are usually purchased as an accompaniment to fried or baked chicken.

Wild mushrooms are one last Northwest staple not to be overlooked. As you'd expect in such a rainy climate, mushrooms abound here. The most common wild mushrooms are morels, which are harvested in spring, and chanterelles, which are harvested in autumn. You'll find wild mushrooms on menus of better restaurants throughout the state, so by all means try to have some while you're here.

Oregon's thriving wine industry has for several decades now been producing **award-winning varietal wines.** Oregon is on the same latitude as the French wine regions of Burgundy and Bordeaux and produces similar wines. Oregon pinot noirs rank up there with those from France, and local pinot gris and other varietals are getting good press as well. Wineries throughout the state are open to the public for tastings, with the greatest concentrations to be found southwest of Portland in Yamhill County, just west of Salem, northwest of Roseburg, and west of Jacksonville.

Oregon is at the center of the national obsession with **craft beers,** and new brewpubs continue to open across the state. Such Oregon breweries as Bridgeport, Full Sail, and Widmer, which have long been at the forefront of the state's craft brewing industry, have grown so large that the term "microbrewery" no longer applies to them. Although Portland is still the state's (and the nation's) microbrewery mecca, brewpubs can now be found throughout the state.

Local wines may be the state's preferred accompaniment to dinner, and microbrews the favorite social drink, but it's **coffee** that keeps Oregonians going through long gray winters—and even through hot sunny summers, for that matter. Although Seattle gets all the press for its espresso obsession, this dark and flavorful style of coffee is just as popular in Oregon. There may still be a few small towns in the state where you can't get an espresso, but you certainly don't have to worry about falling asleep at the wheel for want of a decent cup of java. In parking lots throughout the state, tiny espresso stands dispense all manner of coffee concoctions to the state's caffeine addicts.

Index

— I don't speak sign language.

A hotel can close for all kinds of reasons.

Our Guarantee ensures that if your hotel's undergoing construction, we'll let you know in advance. In fact, we cover your entire travel experience. See www.travelocity.com/guarantee for details.

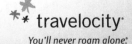

You'll never roam alone.